Contract Changes, Disputes and Terminations—Mastering the Fundamentals

Contract Changes, Disputes and Terminations—Mastering the Fundamentals

John Cibinic, Jr.
Stephen D. Knight
James F. Nagle
Ralph C. Nash, Jr.

Printed in the United States of America.

Media ID No. 10038226-0001

ISBN No. 978-1-4548-6964-1

SUSTAINABLE FORESTRY INITIATIVE Certified Sourcing www.sfiprogram.org SFI-00756

INTRODUCTION

Contract Changes, Disputes and Terminations—Mastering the Fundamentals, is an essential desktop reference for contract professionals irrespective of education or experience. The book succinctly addresses the issues of contract changes, both express and constructive; guides us through the disputes process; and clearly identifies contract terminations procedures—both for default and for the convenience of the government.

I have been honored by the National Contract Management Association (NCMA) to prepare and teach a National Education Seminar based on this text—a task made easier by its content and organization.

As a bonus, this text includes a very helpful appendix addressing many day-to-day contract administration issues ranging from funds management (i.e., limitation of funds or limitation of cost) to some not-so-routine issues such as delays and breach of contract. This is truly one of the most useful books I have seen on the subject and one that I can highly recommend.

Donald E. Shannon, PMP, CFCM, CPCM, Fellow

ABOUT THE AUTHORS

John Cibinic, Jr. was Professor Emeritus at The George Washington University Law School where he taught from 1963 to 1993. From 1966 to 1974, he was Director of the Government Contracts Program. A respected spokesman in the field of government contracts, Professor Cibinic conducted seminars and conferences on government contracts for professionals in government and corporations, and for lawyers. He also served as a consultant to government agencies, private corporations, and law firms. He was vice-chairman of the Cost and Pricing Committee of the Public Contract Section of the American Bar Association. Professor Cibinic coauthored several books, including *Formation of Government Contracts*, *Administration of Government Contracts*, *Competitive Negotiation: The Source Selection Process*, and *Construction Contracting*. Together, with Professor Ralph Nash he coauthored the *Nash & Cibinic Report*, a monthly newsletter. He received an A.B. from the University of Pittsburgh and a J.D. from George Washington University.

Stephen D. Knight is a member of Smith Pachter McWhorter PLC and has practiced law in Government Contracts since 1978. He counsels and represents clients in litigation on all aspects of government contracts. Mr. Knight places special emphasis on claims and disputes, government contract cost accounting, cost allowability, Cost Accounting Standards, defective pricing, government audits, and contract compliance. He has substantial expertise in performance issues, including defective specifications, delay and disruption, changes, and terminations. Mr. Knight also has significant experience in procurement fraud matters, representing clients during grand jury and Inspector General criminal investigations, as well as civil investigations and litigation pursuant to the Civil False Claims Act. Mr. Knight is the Sy Herman Professorial Lecturer in Government Contract Law in the Masters in Procurement Law Program at The George Washington University Law School. He has taught in that program since 1993 as an adjunct professor. Mr. Knight is a frequent author and speaker on government contract issues.

James F. Nagle, a Partner in Seattle's Oles Morrison Rinker & Baker LLP, received his Bachelor's degree from Georgetown University School of Foreign Service, his J.D. from Rutgers, and his LL.M. and S.J.D. in government contracts from the National Law Center, George Washington University. Mr. Nagle has written five books on federal contracting, Federal Procurement Regulations: Policy, Practice and Procedures (American Bar Association Press, 1987); How to Review a Federal Contract and Research Federal Contract Law, Second Edition (ABA Press, 2000); Federal Construction Contracting (Wiley Law Publications, 1992); The History of Government Contracting, Second Edition (CCH Incorporated, 1999), and Whelan and Nagle, Cases and Materials on Federal Government Contracts (Foundation Press). He has also co-authored and co-edited Washington Building Contracts and Construction Law (Aspen Publishers, 1994). Besides being a contributing author to eight other books, his over 80 articles, on subjects as diverse as protests, changes, terminations, claims, and the Federal Acquisition Regulation, have appeared in such publications as The Public Contract Law Journal, Military Law Review, NCMA Journal, and Contract Management.

Ralph C. Nash, Jr. is a widely recognized author and lecturer in the Government contracts field. He taught at the George Washington University Law School from 1960 to 1993, retiring to become Professor Emeritus. In 1960, he founded the University's Government Contracts Program and served as its Director from 1960 to 1966 and from 1979 to 1984. In addition to teaching, he does consulting work for government agencies, private corporations, and law firms. He is a member of the Public Contract Section of the American Bar Association, is a member of the Procurement Round Table, and is a Fellow and serves on the Board of Advisors of the National Contract Management Association. He was a member of the DOD Advisory Panel on Streamlining and Codifying Acquisition Laws (Section 800 Panel). Professor Nash is the author of Government Contract Changes and the coauthor of several texts, including *Formation of Government Contracts*, *Administration of Government Contracts*, *Competitive Negotiation: The Source Selection Process*, *Construction Contracting*, *Intellectual Property in Government Contracts*, and *The Government Contracts Reference Book*. He is also the coauthor of the *Nash & Cibinic Report*, a monthly newsletter. He received an A.B. from Princeton University and a J.D. from George Washington University.

Table of Contents

Chapter 4

Appendix A

CHAPTER 1

CHANGES

Most government contracts include a Changes clause, which gives the government the unilateral right to order changes in contract work during the course of performance. The contractor has no right to receive such change orders because the clause vests the ordering power solely in the government. See *Hunkin Conkey Constr. Co. v. United States*, 198 Ct. Cl. 638, 461 F.2d 1270 (1972), in which a contracting officer was permitted to buy changed work from another contractor after finding that the contractor's price for changed work was unacceptably high, and *Bridgewater Constr. Corp.*, VABCA 2936, 91-3 BCA ¶24,273, *recons. denied*, 92-1 BCA ¶24,446, where a contracting officer was allowed to buy items inadvertently omitted from the specifications from a vendor after obtaining an engineering change proposal from the contractor.

The FAR contains two basic Changes clauses for fixed-price contracts. The fixed-price supply contract clause is contained in FAR 52.243-1. Alternatives, with minor modifications, are provided for service contracts. A separate clause for fixed-price construction contracts is contained in FAR 52.243-4. The clauses contain procedures for the ordering of changes and describe the types of changes that may be made. They provide for an "equitable adjustment" if the change increases or decreases the cost or time of performance. They are also used to process claims where the cost of the work has been changed as a result of government actions or orders not identified as changes, under a theory of "constructive changes." Contracts for commercial items contain a unique changes provision greatly limiting the operation of the clause. See ¶(c) of the Contract Terms and Conditions—Commercial Items clause, FAR 52.212-4, stating:

> *Changes*. Changes in the terms and conditions of this contract my be made only by written agreement of the parties.

The first section of this chapter considers the purposes served by the clauses and the types of changes which they cover. The second section discusses the procedures used by the government in ordering changes. The third section deals with the special problems related to value engineering where the contractor is encouraged to submit proposals for price reduction changes. The next section is a detailed analysis of the use of the Changes clause in processing claims under the constructive changes doctrine. The chapter concludes with a discussion of the notice provisions. The pricing of equitable adjustments is discussed in Chapter 8.

I. PURPOSE AND COVERAGE OF THE CHANGES CLAUSE

There are many reasons why the government may wish to order changes. However, although the Changes clause confers broad powers on the government to alter or adjust the work performed by the contractor, there are definite limits to such powers. This section considers the purposes served by and the limitations on the Changes clauses.

A. Purposes Served

The Changes clause serves four major purposes:

1. To provide operating flexibility by giving the government the unilateral right to order changes in the work to accommodate advances in technology and changes in the government's needs and requirements.

This flexibility is particularly advantageous to the government in a procurement environment where rapid advances in "state-of-the-art" and applicable technologies might make agreed-upon methods of performance unduly costly, time-consuming, or burdensome to the government. In addition, since government needs are very often defined well before a contract is issued or has been substantially performed, this flexibility helps ensure that the government's actual requirements are met.

The flexibility afforded by the clause can also operate to the benefit of the contractor, who will usually have an interest in keeping abreast of technological changes and utilizing them during contract performance. Furthermore, changes in the government's requirements will, in most instances, result in additional sales through increases in the contract price. Such sales may be particularly desirable price-wise since they are obtained outside the competitive procurement environment.

The government is deprived of this flexibility when procuring commercial items.

2. To provide the contractor a means of proposing changes to the work, thereby facilitating more efficient performance and improving the quality of contract end products.

This function of the clause is important to the government. In many instances the contractor is much more abreast of the technical aspects of the work than are the employees of the contracting agency. If the contractor knows that the change procedure will be used to order changes that it suggests, the contractor will be much more willing to suggest improvements than if it is unsure of the use the government will make of the suggestions. Here the clause serves to open communications between the parties.

The fact that the Changes clause provides for an equitable adjustment serves to encourage contractors to propose suggestions of changed methods of performance when the result will be an increase in costs. However, cost-saving suggestions are not encouraged because their adoption would result in a price reduction for the costs saved plus overhead and profit on those costs. To encourage such suggestions, Value Engineering clauses are used in most contracts.

3. To furnish procurement authority to the contracting officer to order additional work within the "general scope" of the contract without using the procedures required for "new procurement" or utilizing new funds.

The purchase of work under an existing contract permits the government to avoid the additional time and expense associated with a new procurement. This is permitted as long as such work meets the test of being within the general scope of the contract. Thus, the Changes clause serves as the basis for the authority to make such sole source purchases. Since such changes are within the scope of the original work on the contract, they may also be funded with the same funds that were used on that contract, 23 Comp. Gen. 943 (1944).

4. To provide the legal means by which the contractor may process claims against the government.

Prior to the Contract Disputes Act of 1978, 41 U.S.C. § 601 et seq., the boards of contract appeals devised the doctrine of "constructive changes" in order to take jurisdiction of contractor claims for a variety of communications and actions of the government that had increased their costs of performance. While this jurisdictional basis is no longer necessary, the boards as well as the Court of Federal Claims have continued to place this class of claims under the Changes clause in order to determine the amount due the contractor in accordance with the rules governing the computation of equitable adjustments.

B. Coverage

The Changes clauses describe the limits on their use in two ways. First, changes are permitted only "within the general scope of the contract." Second, the clauses contain descriptive words setting forth the types of changes that may be made. For a change to be obligatory on the contractor, it must meet both tests, that is, it must be within the general scope and be one of the types of changes described by the clause.

This section addresses the coverage of the Changes clause in defining the limits of the power it grants the government. It should be noted that this issue is not vigorously contested by the contractor receiving the change order because, in most cases, the contractor is completely willing to perform changed work for the extra compensation provided by the clause. Hence, the litigated cases tend to derive from two sources: (1) those rare instances in which the contractor is displeased with the equitable adjustment it receives and therefore seeks to obtain a new trial by persuading a court to rule that the change was not under the clause, and (2) the more common situation in which a competitor of the contractor protests the issuance of a change order as depriving it of the opportunity to compete for the work.

1. Meaning of "Within the General Scope"

Most decisions defining the coverage of the Changes clause are resolved on the basis of the interpretation of the contract limitation that changes must be "within the general scope of the contract." This phrase is somewhat vague and has been subject to considerable judicial and administrative interpretation. Because of the slightly different focus of the analysis, the following discussion of these cases separates the cases dealing with disputes between the contractor and the government from those cases dealing with protests of competitors. In the former type of litigation, the Court of Claims coined the term "cardinal change" to describe those changes that are beyond the scope of the contract.

a. Disputes Between Contractor and Government

Whether changes are beyond the general scope of the contract is usually determined by comparing the total work performed by the contractor to the work called for by the original contract. The tests used in making this comparison are stated in different ways. One test focuses on changes in the nature of the work to be performed. The other focuses on the amount of effort the contractor is required to perform. The distinction between these tests, however, is not always clear. In *Air-A-Plane Corp. v. United States*, 187 Ct. Cl. 269, 408 F.2d 1030 (1969), the court held that a contractor that has failed in its attempts to obtain satisfactory equitable adjustments under the Change clause may pursue a claim for damages based on the fact that the changes were outside of the scope of the contract. In that case the government had issued approximately a thousand changes, which had led to disruption of the work and had added a significant development element to a manufacturing contract.

The time of issuance of change orders has not been considered a factor in determining whether they were beyond the general scope of the contract. For example, in *J.D. Hedin Constr. Co. v. United States*, 171 Ct. Cl. 70, 347 F.2d 235 (1965), the contracting officer issued six changes after completion of the work and granted a time extension of 102 days plus an equitable adjustment for the extra work. The court held that these changes were within the general scope.

(1) Nature of Work

In *Freund v. United States*, 260 U.S. 60 (1922), the Court stated that the work performed falls within the general scope if it "should be regarded as having been fairly and reasonably within the contemplation of the parties when the contract was entered into." The Court of Claims usually stated the test as being whether the work performed was "essentially the same work as the parties bargained for when the contract was awarded," *Aragona Constr. Co. v. United States*, 165 Ct. Cl. 382 (1964). In *Air-A-Plane Corp. v. United States*, 187 Ct. Cl. 269, 408 F.2d 1030 (1969), the court stated that a cardinal change occurs if the ordered deviations alter the nature of the thing to be constructed. In *Allied Materials & Equip. Co. v. United States*, 215 Ct. Cl. 406, 569 F.2d 562 (1978), the court stated that the test was whether the government made alterations so drastic that the contractor was required to perform duties materially different from those originally called for. See *Airprep Tech., Inc. v. United States*, 30 Fed. Cl. 488 (1994), in which the court found that the government's order to a contractor was a cardinal change. The contract was for design and installation of a "bag house" (a structure to hold filter bags intended to extract pollutants from an air stream). The court held that the government's order would have required a cylindrical structure of much thicker steel requiring fabrication at the site rather than the sheet metal box that would have met contract requirements. See also *Information Sys. & Networks Corp.*, ASBCA 46119, 02-2 BCA ¶31,952, in which the government's order to provide a worldwide telecommunications system was found to be a cardinal change because the original contract was for a system in the Washington, D.C. area, and *Hughes-Groesch Constr. Corp.*, VABCA 5448, 00-1 BCA ¶30,912, in which requiring a construction contractor to redesign a part of a building was found to be a cardinal change because such design work was not within the scope of a construction contract.

It appears that, if the function or nature of the work as changed is generally the same as the work originally called for, the changes will be held to fall within the general scope. For example, in *Aragona*, no changes beyond the scope were found where there were numerous changes in the materials used to build a hospital but the size and layout of the building remained the same. See also *Keco Indus., Inc. v. United States*, 176 Ct. Cl. 983, 364 F.2d 838 (1966), *cert. denied*, 386 U.S. 958 (1967) (change from gas to electric refrigeration units within the scope because the units were basically the same with the exception of the power system), and *Wunderlich Contracting Co. v. United States*, 173 Ct. Cl. 180, 351 F.2d 956 (1965) (extensive changes to the details of a hospital requiring over 50 percent additional performance time within the scope because the resulting hospital was not substantially different from that contracted for). The same result was reached in *Contact Int'l, Inc. v. Widnall*, 106 F.3d 426 (Fed. Cir. 1997), in which the court rejected the argument that protests regarding the award of a contract amounted to a cardinal change because, although they altered the time of performance, they did not affect the work that was performed. See also *PCL Constr. Servs., Inc. v. United States*, 47 Fed. Cl. 745 (2000), *aff'd*, 96 Fed. Appx. 672 (Fed. Cir. 2004), holding that analyzing numerous problems encountered during performance was within the general scope of the contract, and *Contel Advanced Sys., Inc.*, ASBCA 49072, 02-1 BCA ¶31,808, holding that construction of a building at a different site was not a cardinal change.

(2) Cost and Disruption

The other test for determining whether a change is outside the general scope deals with the degree of work disruption and cost increases experienced by the contractor. Contractors have rarely been successful on these grounds. However, there are a few cases holding that the work was so much greater that it amounted to a cardinal change. In *Peter Kiewit Sons' Co. v. Summit Constr. Co.*, 422 F.2d 242 (8th Cir. 1969), a change requiring the subcontractor to place backfill simultaneously with the work of other subcontractors was held to be so disruptive as to be a change beyond the scope because it added over 200 percent to the cost of the backfill work. In *Atlantic Dry Dock Corp. v. United States*, 773 F. Supp. 335 (M.D. Fla. 1991), the court decided to hold a trial on the cardinal change issue where there had been 130 changes, the time of performance had been doubled, and costs of $4.6 million had been incurred above the contract price of $5.8 million. Compare *Axel Elecs., Inc.*, ASBCA 18990, 74-1 BCA ¶10,471, in which the board found no changes beyond the scope in a situation where the contractor was claiming equitable adjustments of 170 percent of the contract price because of alleged overinterpretation of the specifications. See also *Akcon, Inc.*, ENGBCA 5593, 90-3 BCA ¶23,250, stating that changes would not be outside the scope unless they made the work "wholly different" from the originally contracted work. In *Rumsfeld v. Freedom N.Y., Inc.*, 329 F.3d 1320, *reh'g denied*, 346 F.3d 1359 (Fed. Cir. 2003), *cert. denied*, 541 U.S. 987 (2004), no cardinal change was found even though the government (1) improperly denied, suspended, and delayed making progress payments; (2) improperly interfered with the contractor's ability to obtain financing; (3) diverted government-furnished material, (4) delayed delivery of government-furnished material it was contractually obligated to deliver; (5) imposed improper inspections; and (6) imposed improper testing requirements.

Changes have also been found to be outside the general scope of the contract when they resulted from defective government specifications and had a significant impact on the performance of the work. For example, in *Edward R. Marden Corp. v. United States*, 194 Ct. Cl. 799, 442 F.2d 364 (1971), the airplane hangar under construction collapsed because of defective specifications. The accident exposed the contractor to a number of claims by workers and led to significant costs to rebuild the project. The court concluded that the additional effort expended by the contractor was outside the general scope. Similarly, in *Luria Bros. & Co. v. United States*, 177 Ct. Cl. 676, 369 F.2d 701 (1966), the court found a change requiring extensive redesign of the work to be beyond the scope because it resulted from defective specifications. However, most defective specification claims have been treated as changes within the scope of the contract, and it has been stated that the impact of the defects would have to be "profound" in order to justify ruling that the changes were outside the scope of the contract, *Cannon Structures, Inc.*, AGBCA 90-207-1, 93-3 BCA ¶26,059. Compare *Big Chief Drilling Co. v. United States*, 26 Cl. Ct. 1276 (1992), with *American Line Builders, Inc. v. United States*, 26 Cl. Ct. 1155 (1992). In the former case, the court found changes resulting from defective specifications to be outside the scope of the contract, while in the latter case, a similar number of changes was found to be within the scope. In neither case did the defective specifications cause a severe impact on the contractor.

The number of changes issued has not been considered to be a major factor in evaluating whether changes are beyond the scope of the contract. In *Coley Props. Corp.*, PSBCA 291, 75-2 BCA ¶11,514, *recons. denied*, 76-1 BCA ¶11,701, *rev'd on other grounds*, 219 Ct. Cl. 227, 593 F.2d 380 (1979), the board found that approximately 100 change orders were not beyond the general scope. Other cases finding a large number of changes to be within the scope include *Action Support Servs. Corp.*, ASBCA 46524, 00-1 BCA ¶30,701 (797 specification revisions); *Combined Arms Training Sys., Inc.*, ASBCA 44822, 96-2 BCA ¶28,617 (277 engineering change proposals); *Reliance Ins. Co. v. United States*, 20 Cl. Ct. 715 (1990), *aff'd*, 931 F.2d 863 (Fed. Cir. 1991) (200 changes); *Magoba Constr. Co. v. United States*, 99 Ct. Cl. 662 (1943) (62 change orders); and *In re Boston Shipyard Corp.*, 886 F.2d 451 (1st Cir. 1989) (86 changes). It seems apparent that an excessive number of changes might so alter the work that it would be beyond the scope, but the closest that a court or board has come to such a determination is in *Air-A-Plane*, in which a case involving 1,000 changes was sent back for trial.

In looking at the issue of the work contemplated by both parties at the time the contract was signed, the court has reasoned that contractors taking contracts for technologically sophisticated products should expect more changes than those taking contracts for relatively simple products, *General Dynamics Corp. v. United States*, 218 Ct. Cl. 40, 585 F.2d 457 (1978). In that case, a major series of changes that increased the price of the shipbuilding contract by approximately 165 percent and extended the time of performance by three years was held to be within the general scope of the contract, since the court believed that the contractor should have anticipated such changes in a contract for nuclear submarines. In this regard, the rule is similar to that discussed below for third-party protests—the broader the language of the contract, the greater the scope of the contract for purposes of ordering changes.

b. Third-Party Protests

When competitors protest the government's issuance of changes in lieu of using new procurement procedures, the test is whether the proposed change is within the scope of the competition. This is slightly different from the test used when the contractor questions a change. See *AT&T Communications, Inc. v. WilTel, Inc.*, 1 F.3d 1201 (Fed. Cir. 1993), stating at 1205:

> This case does not ask whether Government modifications breached a contract, but asks instead whether Government modifications changed the contract enough to circumvent the statutory requirement of competition. The cardinal change doctrine asks whether a modification exceeds the scope of the contract's changes clause; this case asks whether the modification is within the scope of the competition conducted to achieve the original contract. In application these questions overlap. . . . A modification generally falls within the scope of the original procurement if potential bidders would have expected it to fall within the contract's changes clause.

The court appears to be saying that the "scope of the competition" test is essentially the same as the "scope of the contract" test (used in the breach cases) but that the focus is different. In the breach litigation, the focus is on what the contractor should have anticipated to be within the scope of the contract. In the protest litigation, the focus is on what the competitors should have anticipated to be within the scope of the competition. This requires analysis of the entire solicitation to determine what contract alterations might be called for. Thus, the court stated at 1205:

> This analysis . . . focuses on the scope of the entire original procurement in comparison to the scope of the contract as modified. Thus a broad original competition may validate a broader range of later modifications without further bid procedures.

The GAO gave a more precise description of the analysis used in making this determination in *Neil R. Gross & Co.*, 69 Comp. Gen. 247 (B-237434), 90-1 CPD ¶212:

> In weighing [whether a modification is beyond the scope of the competition], we look to whether there is a material difference between the modified contract and the prime contract that was originally competed. . . . In determining the materiality of a modification, we consider factors such as the extent of any changes in the type of work, performance period and costs between the contract as awarded and as modified. . . . We also consider whether the solicitation for the original contract adequately advised offerors of the potential for the type of changes during the course of the contract that in fact occurred . . . or whether the modification is of a nature which potential offerors would reasonably have anticipated under the changes clause.

The General Services Board of Contract Appeals used this same analysis when it had protest jurisdiction, *MCI Telecommunications Corp. v. General Servs. Admin.*, GSBCA 11963-P, 93-1 BCA ¶25,541.

The primary focus appears to be on whether the change could have been anticipated by the offerors. In this regard, the language of the solicitation is of great importance. For example, substantial changes have been permitted in data processing and telecommunications equipment contracts where the solicitation provided that equipment upgrades were anticipated during performance, *AT&T Communications, Inc. v. WilTel, Inc.*, 1 F.3d 1201 (Fed. Cir. 1993); *MCI Telecommunications Corp.*, GSBCA 10450-P, 90-2 BCA ¶22,735; *Engineering & Prof'l Servs., Inc.*, Comp. Gen. Dec. B-289331, 2002 CPD ¶24; *Hewlett Packard Co.*, Comp. Gen. Dec. B-245293, 91-2 CPD ¶576. See also *National Data Corp.*, Comp. Gen. Dec. B-207340, 82-2 CPD ¶222, where one of two corporations sharing a teleprocessing contract was dropped and its share of the work was added to the other's contract. The GAO found that the substantial increase to the remaining contract was not a change beyond the scope of the competition because the bidders had been warned that such changes might occur. Similarly, in *Phoenix Air Group, Inc. v. United States*, 46 Fed. Cl. 90 (2000), a modification ordering additional work was held to be within the scope because the statement of work was broadly worded; in *Paragon Sys., Inc.*, Comp. Gen. Dec. B-284694.2, 2000 CPD ¶114, a modification adding higher-level engineers to a task order contract was held to be within the scope because the work they were assigned was contemplated by the original contract; and in *Astronautics Corp. of Am.*, 70 Comp. Gen. 554 (B-242782), 91-1 CPD ¶531, a major task order was held to be within the scope of an indefinite-quantity contract that described the work in very general terms. In contrast, in *Avtron Mfg., Inc.*, 67 Comp. Gen. 404 (B-229972), 88-1 CPD ¶458, a change expressly disallowed in the original solicitation was found to be outside the scope, and in *Sprint Communications Co.*, Comp. Gen. Dec. B-278407.2, 98-1 CPD ¶60, added services were found to be outside the scope because the contract stated that such services were not included in the contract effort. See also *MCI Communications Corp.*, Comp. Gen. Dec. B-276659.2, 97-2 CPD ¶90, in which a service that was intrinsically different from that covered by the contract was held to be beyond its scope.

If the change alters the type of work called for by the contract, it is very likely to be held to be outside the scope of the competition. See *American Air Filter Co.*, 57 Comp. Gen. 567 (B-188408), 78-1 CPD ¶443, in which a change substituting diesel for gasoline engines in heating units was held to be a change beyond the scope of an advertised manufacturing contract because it required significant development work, doubled the performance time, and increased the price by 29 percent. The GAO stated that "any modification is in our view to be determined by examining whether the alteration is within the scope of the competition which was originally conducted," and that this standard is based on "what potential offerors would have reasonably expected." Similarly, in *Makro Janitorial Servs., Inc.*, Comp. Gen. Dec. B-282690, 99-2 CPD ¶39, a task order for housekeeping work was found to be outside the scope of a contract for equipment maintenance, and in *Stoehner Sec. Servs., Inc.*, Comp. Gen. Dec. B-248077.3, 92-2 CPD ¶285, a change adding work calling for higher-skilled personnel was found to be outside the scope. Compare *Everpure, Inc.*, Comp. Gen. Dec. B-226395.4, 90-2 CPD ¶275, in which the change of the technical approach in a research and development contract was found to be within the scope, and *CESC Plaza Ltd. P'ship v. United States*, 52 Fed. Cl. 91 (2002), in which changes to the terms of a lease were held to be within the scope. See also *Northrop Grumman Corp. v. United States*, 50 Fed. Cl. 443 (2001), holding that major changes in technology during performance of a development contract did not constitute changes outside the scope requiring a recompetition of the follow-on production of the system.

Changes reducing the quality of the work have also been held to be outside the scope of the competition when such changes are seen as potentially enlarging the field of competition. See, for example, *Poly-Pac. Techs., Inc.*, Comp. Gen. Dec. B-296029, 2005 CPD ¶288, holding that a change deleting the requirement for the most difficult element of the work was outside the scope. See also *Marvin J. Perry & Assocs.*, Comp. Gen. Dec. B-277684, 97-2 CPD ¶128 (change allowing use of more available wood in furniture contract outside the scope), and *Avtron Mfg., Inc.*, 67 Comp. Gen. 404 (B-229972), 88-1 CPD ¶458, *recons. denied*, 67 Comp. Gen. 614 (B-229972.2), 88-2 CPD ¶273 (relaxed specification permitting method of performance prohibited by original contract outside the scope).

Major changes in the quantity of the work have been held to be outside the scope of the competition. Hence, large reductions in quantity are outside the scope, *PAI Corp.*, Comp. Gen. Dec. B-244287.7, 91-2 CPD ¶508; *Source AV, Inc.*, Comp. Gen. Dec. B-241155, 91-1 CPD ¶75. Similarly, a change adding quantities above the contractual maximums was found to be outside the scope, *Liebert Corp.*, 70 Comp. Gen. 448 (B-232234.5), 91-1 CPD ¶413.

Changes granting additional time to perform the work are generally within the scope of the competition. See, for example, *Saratoga Indus., Inc.*, Comp. Gen. Dec. B-247141, 92-1 CPD ¶397 (additional time to correct errors in the design), and *Ion Track Instruments, Inc.*, Comp. Gen. Dec. B-238893, 90-2 CPD ¶31. See, however, *CPT Corp.*, Comp. Gen. Dec. B-211464, 84-1 CPD ¶606, in which a significant modification to a contract adding requirements and extending the performance time was held to be outside the scope of the competition.

The focus on the competitive process can lead to a different result than would a focus on the work alone. For example, in *Webcraft Packaging, Div. of Beatrice Foods Co.*, Comp. Gen. Dec. B-194087, 79-2 CPD ¶120, a minor change permitting the use of a slightly different grade of paper in a printing contract was ruled beyond the scope of the original competition because the new grade of paper was readily available on the market, whereas the prior specified grade was very difficult to obtain. The GAO found that many potential competitors who were not able to bid because of the specified paper would have been able to bid if the new grade of paper had been specified. Similarly, in *Dynamac Corp.*, Comp. Gen. Dec. B-252800, 93-2 CPD ¶37, a task order adding slightly different engineering services was held to be outside the scope of the competition because the offerors would not have contemplated such services. See also *CCL, Inc. v. United States*, 39 Fed. Cl. 780 (1997), in which a small amount of services at more locations and for additional agencies was held to be outside the scope, and *Techplan Corp.*, Comp. Gen. Dec. B-232187, 88-2 CPD ¶580, in which services for a different component of the agency were held to be outside the scope. In *Memorex Corp.*, 61 Comp. Gen. 42 (B-200722), 81-2 CPD ¶334, *recons. denied*, 82-1 CPD ¶349, a change beyond the scope was found where an option to purchase disk drives was converted into a five-year lease-to-ownership plan that added an obligation to ensure continuous satisfactory performance of the disks. Although the end product remained unchanged, the burden and risk of nonperformance shifted from the government to the contractor, thus changing the obligations for which it originally competed. In an unusual case, a major change in the work, conceded to be beyond the scope, was allowed since compliance with statutory program deadlines required restricted competition, *Die Mesh Corp.*, Comp. Gen. Dec. B-190421, 78-2 CPD ¶36.

Concern about the use of the Changes clause to circumvent the statutory requirements for competition has led to a rule that a contracting officer may not award a contract when it is clear that changes would have to be made in the specifications and such changes were contemplated at the time of award, *A & J Mfg. Co.*, 53 Comp. Gen. 838 (B-178163), 74-1 CPD ¶240; *Midland Maint., Inc.*, Comp. Gen. Dec. B-184247, 76-2 CPD ¶127. See *NV Servs.*, Comp. Gen. Dec. B-284119.2, 2000 CPD ¶64, stating:

> The appropriate standard in reviewing these pre-contract actions is not whether the subsequent modification is within the scope of the original contract but whether the changed work could significantly affect the competitive positions of offerors such that the RFP should have been amended. *United Tel. Co. of Northwest*, [B-246977, Apr. 20, 1992, 92-1 CPD ¶374] at 10. Here it should have been apparent . . . that increasing the scope of the contract work by approximately 6 percent could affect the offerors' respective proposals.

Compare *RS Info. Sys., Inc.*, Comp. Gen. Dec. B-287185.2, 2001 CPD ¶98, in which the GAO stated that this rule would not be applied unless the change materially altered the work.

The GAO has also ordered the termination of a contract where the government improperly added another year's work to the contract and then attempted to comply with the law by writing a sole source justification for a new procurement after a protest had been lodged, *Kent Watkins & Assocs.*, Inc., Comp. Gen. Dec. B-191078, 78-1 CPD ¶377.

2. Descriptive Words

The clauses contain somewhat different statements of the types of changes that can be made. The supply clause at FAR 52.243-1 permits changes "in any one or more of the following":

> (1) Drawings, designs, or specifications when the supplies to be furnished are to be specially manufactured for the Government in accordance with the drawings, designs, or specifications.
> (2) Method of shipping or packing.
> (3) Place of delivery.

When the contract is for services, the changes may be made "in any one or more of the following":

(1) Description of services to be performed.
(2) Time of performance (i.e., hours of the day, days of the week, etc.).
(3) Place of performance of the services.

The construction contract clause at FAR 52.243-4(a) permits changes in the work within the general scope of the contract, "including" changes:

(1) In the specifications (including drawings and designs);
(2) In the method or manner of performance of the work;
(3) In the government-furnished facilities, equipment, materials, services, or site; or
(4) Directing acceleration in the performance of the work.

In considering whether the government is entitled to make a change not specifically listed in these clauses, the language of the clauses should be considered. By the use of the term "including," the construction clause would permit the government to order unlisted changes if they are of the kind and character of those specified. By contrast, the supply and services contract clauses do not indicate that unlisted changes are authorized since they use the term "in any one or more of the following." The following discussion deals with litigation over the types of changes permitted by the clauses.

a. The Contract Work

Every Changes clause provides for changes in the work called for by the contract, since this is the area where the government is primarily interested in having the right to direct changes. Generally, this is accomplished by providing for changes to the drawings or specifications. The clear intent of this term is to allow changes in the technical details of the end product or services called for by the contract. An exception to this rule is contained in supply contracts, which preclude such changes when the supplies are not specially manufactured.

The terms "drawings" and "specifications" may be given a broader meaning than the actual contractual documents, if necessary, to permit the government to keep control of the contract work. For example, prior to the issuance of the FAR, the civilian agencies of the government were using the supply contract Changes clause for service contracts. Although the language was imprecise when applied to such contracts, the boards attempted to give it meaning when possible, *JCM Corp.*, DOTCAB 70-6, 70-2 BCA ¶8586; *D&D Aero Spraying, Inc.*, AGBCA 259, 70-1 BCA ¶8356; *Basys, Inc.*, GSBCA TD-7, 73-1 BCA ¶9798, *rev'd in part*, 74-1 BCA ¶10,565. Thus, in *Basys* the board reasoned that the government, having included the clause in a service contract, intended it to have a meaningful effect. The board broadly construed the term "specifications" as used in the clause to encompass changes in the amount of work to be done where that was described in the contract. Such interpretation will no longer be necessary under the FAR changes clauses for service contracts that contain a more precise description of the types of changes that can be made. However, these cases illustrate the breadth of interpretation that can be anticipated in this area.

b. Terms and Conditions

A literal reading of the Changes clause would not permit the government to change the terms and conditions of the contract. See *BMY Div. of Harsco Corp.*, ASBCA 36926, 91-1 BCA ¶23,565, in which the board ruled that a change could not be made to a warranty included in one of the standard contract clauses. The board reasoned that the warranty was not part of the drawings and specifications. Similar reasoning was followed in *E.L. Hamm & Assocs., Inc.*, ASBCA 43972, 94-2 BCA ¶26,724, holding that the government could not change the lease of a building to ownership of the building, and *B.F. Carvin Constr. Co.*, VABCA 3224, 92-1 BCA ¶24,481, holding that the government could not use the Changes clause to alter the payment terms of the contract. See also *TEM Assocs., Inc.*, DOTCAB 2556, 93-2 BCA ¶25,759, holding that the Changes clause did not permit the reduction of funding on a terminated cost-reimbursement contract; and *Cessna Aircraft Co.*, ASBCA 37726, 95-1 BCA ¶27,373, holding that the Changes clause did not permit deletion of contract line items (with commensurate deobligation of funds) when the contractor had begun work on the items. Similarly, in *Welbilt*

Constr., Inc., GSBCA 2530, 68-1 BCA ¶7031, the board held that the government had no right to unilaterally change one of the clauses in Standard Form 23-A. However, using a liberal definition of drawings and specifications, some boards have allowed the terms and conditions to be subject to the Changes clause. For example, in *Space Age Eng'g Inc.*, ASBCA 16588, 72-2 BCA ¶9636, the board apparently considered a minimum wage determination in a service contract to be part of the specifications and found a change when the government insisted on a different wage. Similarly, in *CompuDyne Corp.*, ASBCA 14556, 72-1 BCA ¶9218, the board apparently considered a technical data clause to be part of the specifications in its ruling on whether the government had violated the Changes clause. In *Melrose Waterproofing Co.*, ASBCA 9058, 1964 BCA ¶4119, the board held that the government could change the special conditions of the contract under the Changes clause because such provisions were listed as part of the contract specifications. See Spector, *An Analysis of the Standard "Changes" Clause,* 25 Fed. B. J. 177, 188 (1965), 2 YPA 1273. It therefore appears that the government may be able to greatly broaden the coverage of the Changes clause by arbitrarily calling all contract documents "specifications."

c. Changes in Quantity

Increases in the quantity of the major items to be furnished are generally thought not to be authorized by the Changes clause. For example, on a construction project separate buildings may not be added, 15 Comp. Gen. 573 (A-66501) (1935); 30 Comp. Gen. 34 (B-95069) (1950). A similar rule is applied to the addition of materials on a unit-price contract, *P.L. Saddler v. United States*, 152 Ct. Cl. 557, 287 F.2d 411 (1961). In that case, a change order almost doubling the amount of material required for an embankment was found to be beyond the scope of a contract to build a levee. Similar reasoning was used to hold that a major increase in the quantity of flags ordered under a requirements contract was outside of the scope of the Changes clause, *Valley Forge Flag Co.*, VABCA 4667, 97-2 BCA ¶29,246. Increases in the quantity of subsidiary items are generally authorized by the clause unless a variation is so large that it alters the entire bargain. See, for example, *Symbolic Displays, Inc.*, Comp. Gen. Dec. B-182847, 75-1 CPD ¶278, in which the addition of a quantity of new lights was held to be within the general scope of a contract for the manufacture of aircraft.

Deletions of major items or portions of the work are not authorized by the Changes clause. Buildings may not be deleted from construction contracts, *General Contracting & Constr. Co. v. United States*, 84 Ct. Cl. 570 (1937); *Nolan Bros., Inc.*, ASBCA 4378, 58-2 BCA ¶1910. The same rule is appropriate for application to supply contracts. For example, where a contract for radios was modified so that a reduced number of components was required, the board treated the modification as a partial termination for convenience rather than a change. The board considered the components to be the major contract item since the contractor was originally to deliver components, not assembled radios, *Doughboy Indus., Inc.*, FAACAP 67-3, 66-2 BCA ¶5712. One court stated that deletion of a portion of the work can be accomplished by change order unless it becomes so large as to alter the original bargain, *J.W. Bateson Co. v. United States*, 308 F.2d 510 (5th Cir. 1962). The court in *Bateson* suggested that "thinking in terms of major and minor variations in the plans" would help in determining how large a variation in quantity is permitted under the Changes clause. However, significant decreases in quantities have been held to be outside the Changes clause in a contract for drilling services, *Manis Drilling*, IBCA 2658, 93-3 BCA ¶25,931 (major deletions to two line items); construction work, *Kahaluu Constr. Co.*, ASBCA 33248, 90-2 BCA ¶22,663 (deletion of approximately one-half of work); cleaning services, *Toke Cleaners*, IBCA 1008-10-73, 74-1 BCA ¶10,633; and use of a computer facility, *Burroughs Corp.*, GSBCA 5019, 79-2 BCA ¶14,083, *recons. denied*, 80-2 BCA ¶14,487. In *Capital Elec. Co.*, GSBCA 5300, 81-2 BCA ¶15,281, deletion of more than 73 percent of unit-priced electrical and telephone outlets was outside the scope of the Changes clause and treated as partial termination for convenience. See *P.J. Dick, Inc. v. General Servs. Admin*, GSBCA 12215, 95-1 BCA ¶27,574, *modified on recons.*, 96-1 BCA ¶26,017 (deletion of part of building renovation treated as a change); *John N. Brophy Co.*, GSBCA 5122, 78-2 BCA ¶13,506 (deletion of instructional services permitted under Changes clause); and *Bromley Contracting Co.*, HUDBCA 75-8, 77-1 BCA ¶12,232 (minor change in amount of work considered a constructive change). If the parties negotiate an equitable adjustment for deleted work (in lieu of termination for convenience compensation), they may be bound by their bargain even though a major portion of the work is deleted, *Robinson Contracting Co. v. United States*, 16 Cl. Ct. 676 (1989), *aff'd*, 895 F.2d 1420 (Fed. Cir. 1990).

d. Changes in Time of Performance

Changes in the scheduled completion date of the work were traditionally thought to be outside the Changes clause because they were not enumerated as permissible types of changes. However, the boards altered this view with regard to constructive accelerations of performance, originally reasoning that such orders were changes to the specifications because the contract schedule was part of the specifications, Spector, *An Analysis of the Standard "Changes" Clause,* 25 Fed. B. J. 177 (1965), 2 YPA 1273. The construction contract Changes clause now lists accelerations as one of the permissible types of changes. In contracts not containing such specific language, one board has held that accelerations may not be ordered, *Coastal States Petroleum Co.*, ASBCA 31059, 88-1 BCA ¶20,468.

When the government delays the contractor, boards and courts focus primarily on whether the work has been changed or whether there has merely been an increase in the contractor's costs. Thus, decelerations of the schedule or delays have been held to be outside the coverage of the clause, *Simmel–Industrie Meccaniche Societa per Azioni*, ASBCA 6141, 61-1 BCA ¶2917; *Broome Constr., Inc.*, AGBCA 232, 71-2 BCA ¶9100, *aff'd*, 203 Ct. Cl. 521, 492 F.2d 829 (1974); *Cosmos Eng'rs, Inc.*, IBCA 979-12-72, 73-1 BCA ¶9972; *Freedom N.Y., Inc.*, ASBCA 43965, 02-1 BCA ¶31,676, *rev'd on other grounds*, 329 F.3d 1320, *reh'g denied*, 346 F.3d 1359 (Fed. Cir. 2003), *cert. denied*, 541 U.S. 987 (2004). See *Gunther & Shirley Co.*, ENGBCA 3691, 78-2 BCA ¶13,454, in which extra costs incurred as a result of a constructive deceleration order were treated under both the Suspension of Work clause and the Changes clause depending on whether the costs were in the nature of delay costs or costs of extra and changed work. When the construction contract Changes clause was issued, it was stated that this was the legal principle incorporated in the clause, 32 Fed. Reg. 16269 (1967). The logic of this principle is that such delays are in the nature of suspensions of work, which are covered by separate contract clauses. However, some decisions have refused to follow this rule on the theory that delays resulting in a change of sequence of the work are changes in the method or manner of performance of the work, *Commercial Contractors, Inc.*, ASBCA 30675, 88-3 BCA ¶20,877 (direction to work one building at a time is a change in sequence); *Pan Arctic Corp.*, ASBCA 20133, 77-1 BCA ¶12,514 (delay in issuance of notice to proceed added costs by depriving contractor of opportunity to perform two contracts simultaneously as had been understood by the parties before award); *Fred A. Arnold, Inc.*, ASBCA 18915, 75-2 BCA ¶11,496 (government delay in furnishing information forced contractor to do part of work out of sequence). Since these cases involve delays to only part of the work, making it possible to argue a change in sequence of performance, it is arguable that there have been no departures from the rule that "pure delay"—delay to the entire job under contract—is not a change. However, this theory will not be followed if the government action is a "pure delay," *McGaughan Co.*, PSBCA 2074, 90-1 BCA ¶22,411. For another theory making a delay a change, see *Kenyon Magnetics, Inc.*, GSBCA 4769, 77-2 BCA ¶12,786, in which the board held that government delay in testing a sample product was a constructive change in the nature of a defective specification because the contract did not contain a clause informing the contractor of the test requirement. See also *QES, Inc.*, ASBCA 22178, 78-2 BCA ¶13,512, *recons. denied*, 79-1 BCA ¶13,592, in which the board held delay in specifying whether renovation of office space was included in an Architect-Engineer contract to be compensable under the Changes clause, since it was in the nature of a defective specification.

The GAO has held that extensions of time to permit the contractor to complete the work called for by the original contract are within the scope of the competition, *Saratoga Indus., Inc.*, Comp. Gen. Dec. B-247141, 92-1 CPD ¶397 (additional time needed to overcome defective specifications); *Ion Track Instruments, Inc.*, Comp. Gen. Dec. B-238893, 90-2 CPD ¶31 (extension of research and development contract to a period more than five years in length). This more liberal interpretation merely holds that a contractor is not gaining an advantage over competitors by being permitted to complete the work. There is no implication in these decisions that the contractor was granted an equitable adjustment for the time extension.

If specific language is included in the Changes clause permitting changes to the schedule, it will be held that the clause has been broadened to include this category of change, *Spencer-Safford Loadcraft, Inc.*, ASBCA 6592, 1962 BCA ¶3315; *Ardell Marine Corp.*, ASBCA 7682, 1963 BCA ¶3991.

e. Method or Manner of Performance

Changes in the method or manner of performance were considered to be permissible changes at an early date, *Farnsworth & Chambers Co.*, ASBCA 5408, 59-2 BCA ¶2329; *Carpenter Constr. Co.*, NASABCA 18, 1964 BCA ¶4452. The logic was that such changes were changes to the work itself because they deprived the contractor of the opportunity of performing the contract in a way not prohibited by the specifications. The construction contract clause now lists such changes as an enumerated type of permissible change, and the cases have included a wide variety of types of changes in this category, *Melrose Waterproofing Co.*, ASBCA 9058, 1964 BCA ¶4119 (change in location of field office); *John McShain, Inc.*, GSBCA

3541, 73-1 BCA ¶9981 (change in storage area for materials to be used on job); *Liles Constr. Co. v. United States*, 197 Ct. Cl. 164, 455 F.2d 527 (1972) (improper disapproval of use of subcontractor); *Nichols Dynamics, Inc.*, ASBCA 17949, 75-2 BCA ¶11,556 (excessive noise adjacent to construction site); *M & H Constr. Co.*, ASBCA 21528, 79-1 BCA ¶13,688 (government entitled to deductive change where same individual performed function of quality control representative and superintendent); *Atlantic Dry Dock Corp.*, ASBCA 42609, 98-2 BCA ¶30,025, *recons. denied*, 99-1 BCA ¶30,208 (change to approved schedule for performing work). It is not necessary that there be specific contract language specifying a method of performance in order to find such a change if, in fact, the contractor has been ordered to use a method other than one that could properly have been used, *H.E. Johnson Co.*, ASBCA 48248, 97-1 BCA ¶28,921 (change in sequence of work contractor had planned to use); *Eagle Contracting, Inc.*, AGBCA 88-225-1, 92-3 BCA ¶25,018 (refusal to stake entire project to permit work as planned by contractor); *Thomas Elec., Inc.*, ASBCA 30832, 89-1 BCA ¶21,516 (refusal to permit performance method desired by contractor). But see *Continental Serv. Co.*, DOTCAB 73-27, 74-1 BCA ¶10,538, *recons. denied*, 74-1 BCA ¶10,631, in which the board found no change in the method of performance when the contracting officer revised the position descriptions of the contractor's employees but did not alter the statement of work to be performed.

f. Government-Furnished Property

Under the construction contract Changes clause, the government may make changes in "the Government-furnished facilities, equipment, materials, services, or site." This broad language makes it clear that this class of changes is within the coverage of the clause. The Court of Claims has indicated, however, that the government's failure to provide government-furnished property (GFP) might still be outside the coverage of the clause if it was beyond the scope of the contract, *Allied Materials & Equip. Co. v. United States*, 215 Ct. Cl. 406, 569 F.2d 562 (1978).

Other Changes clauses, such as the supply and service contract clauses and the pre-1968 construction contract clause, do not refer to GFP, raising a question as to whether it is covered by the clause. A few cases have held that it is covered on the theory that defective GFP is the equivalent of a defective specification, *Forest Dev., Inc.*, AGBCA 77-144, 79-1 BCA ¶13,626 (claim denied for failure to prove defects); *General Instrument Corp.*, NASABCA 268-3, 70-2 BCA ¶8460; *Wayne Constr., Inc.*, AGBCA 242, 70-2 BCA ¶8443. The opposite result was reached in *Computer Real Time Sys., Computer Usage Dev. Corp.*, NASABCA 570-8, 72-1 BCA ¶9250. In *Wayne*, the board distinguished between defective GFP, which it held was under the Changes clause, and late-delivered GFP, which it held was a delay that could only be administratively adjusted under the Suspension of Work clause. See also *Koppers/Clough, A Joint Venture v. United States*, 201 Ct. Cl. 344 (1973), in which the court commented that, had there been no separate Government-furnished Property clause in the contract, furnishing GFP late might have been a change in the manner of performance.

g. Place of Delivery

In the supply contract Changes clause, changes are permitted in the place of delivery. It has been held that this language permits the government to change the f.o.b. point from destination to origin, with the result that the supplies are shipped on commercial bills of lading, *L.B. Foster Co.*, ASBCA 12425, 69-1 BCA ¶7549.

C. Contractor's Acceptance of Change

If a contractor accepts a change and performs the changed work without reservation, it cannot subsequently claim that the change was beyond the scope of the contract for the purpose of claiming breach of contract, *Silberblatt & Lasker, Inc. v. United States*, 101 Ct. Cl. 54 (1944). Similarly, in *Amertex Enters., Ltd. v. United States*, 41 CCF ¶77,047 (Fed. Cl. 1995), *aff'd*, 108 F.3d 1392 (Fed. Cir. 1997), *cert. denied*, 522 U.S. 1075 (1998), the court rejected the contractor's argument that a cardinal change had occurred because it had entered into bilateral contract modifications revising the contract price to reflect the impact of over 100 changes. See also *International Tel. & Tel. v. United States*, 197 Ct. Cl. 11, 453 F.2d 1283 (1972), in which the court found a change where the contractor agreed to perform work on a multiyear contract but reserved the right to argue that the required notice of additional work had not been timely. The appeals boards have followed the principle that acquiescence by the contractor deprives it of the right to argue later that the change was beyond the scope of the contract, *Ashton-Mardian Co.*, ASBCA 7912, 1963 BCA ¶3836, *reh'g denied*, 1963 BCA ¶3928; *Edward E.*

Harwell, ASBCA 9624, 66-1 BCA ¶5329. It has also been held that this reasoning requires the government to compensate the contractor for work ordered under the Changes clause, even though such work is beyond the scope of the contract, *Texas Trunk Co.*, ASBCA 3681, 57-2 BCA ¶1528. The board in *Texas Trunk* found that the government is bound once the contractor waives its right to object to a cardinal change. Accord, *Mac-Well Co.*, ASBCA 23097, 79-2 BCA ¶13,895. In these latter cases, the board did not address the issue of whether the contracting officer had authority to order such work without following the procedures required for new procurements.

II. FORMAL CHANGE ORDERS

The idea underlying a change can originate with either the government or the contractor, depending on the circumstances involved. In either case, the changes procedure will generally call for an interchange of documentation. Only in rare cases will the government issue a change without first coordinating with the contractor to obtain at least preliminary information as to the technical aspects of the change and its impact on the price and schedule of the contract. In some cases, formal procedures are provided to facilitate contractor-proposed changes in the work.

A. Contractor-Originated Changes

Under all government contracts, the contractor is free to suggest changes. In fact, it is widely believed that contractors propose changes as a means of increasing profits on their contracts. Those contractors with design cognizance and sizeable engineering staffs are best able to take advantage of this situation. Since the government is interested in improving the quality and performance of the supplies and services that it buys, it often encourages such suggestions.

The Department of Defense used an Engineering Change Proposals clause for many years to permit the contractor to propose changes. This clause was found in DFARS 252.243-7000 and called for such proposals to be submitted with a proposed "not to exceed" price. It was removed from the DFARS on October 1, 2001, 66 Fed. Reg. 49865, and the following guidance was added to DFARS 243.204-71:

> Engineering changes can originate with either the contractor or the Government. In either case, the Government will need detailed information from the contractor for evaluation of the technical, cost, and schedule effects of implementing the change.

The National Aeronautics and Space Administration still uses a clause of this type. See NFS 1852.243-70:

> **ENGINEERING CHANGE PROPOSALS (OCT 2001)**
>
> (a) Definitions.
>
> "ECP" means an Engineering Change Proposal (ECP) which is a proposed engineering change and the documentation by which the change is described, justified, and submitted to the procuring activity for approval or disapproval.
>
> (b) Either party to the contract may originate ECPs. Implementation of an approved ECP may occur by either a supplemental agreement or, if appropriate, as a written change order to the contract.
>
> (c) Any ECP submitted to the Contracting Officer shall include a "not-to-exceed"—[price or estimated cost] increase or decrease adjustment amount, if any, and the required [time of delivery or period of performance] adjustment, if any, acceptable to the originator of the ECP. If the change is originated within the Government, the Contracting Officer shall obtain a written agreement with the Contractor regarding the "not-to-exceed"—[price or estimated cost] and [delivery or period of performance] adjustments, if any, prior to issuing an order for implementation of the change.
>
> (d) After submission of a Contractor initiated ECP, the Contracting Officer may require the Contractor to submit the following information:

(1) Cost or pricing data in accordance with FAR 15.403-5 if the proposed change meets the criteria for its submission under FAR 15.403-4; or

(2) Information other than cost or pricing data adequate for Contracting Officer determination of price reasonableness or cost realism. The Contracting Officer reserves the right to request additional information if that provided by the Contractor is considered inadequate for that purpose. If the Contractor claims applicability of one of the exceptions to submission of cost or pricing data, it shall cite the exception and provide rationale for its applicability.

(e) If the ECP is initiated by NASA, the Contracting Officer shall specify the cost information requirements, if any.

Prior to October 2001 these clauses required the submission of information in accordance with MIL-STD-973, which provided an elaborate system of configuration management and change control for all contractors. Under that standard, the contractor was expected to "fully document" the impact of any proposed change to engineering specifications. This standard was canceled by 66 Fed. Reg. 49865, October 1, 2001. However, contractors should still accompany ECPs with a complete submission in order to provide the government with full information upon which to make a sound decision as to whether the change should be adopted.

Contractor-suggested changes may be phrased in terms of offers that can be immediately accepted by the government, but more often they are invitations for the government to issue a change order that will then be priced under the Changes clause. See, however, *Bruce-Andersen Co.*, ASBCA 28125, 83-2 BCA ¶16,892, in which the board held that the government had accepted a contractor's proposal for a change and further held that the parties had impliedly agreed that the change would be at no increase in price. See also *L.J.C. Mech. Contractors, Inc.*, VABCA 3507, 94-1 BCA ¶26,266, in which the government was found to have accepted a proposed change when it issued a change order containing the language "per your proposal," and *General Ry. Signal Co.*, ENGBCA 6168, 96-1 BCA ¶27,981, finding no acceptance of a proposed change because the offer had been withdrawn prior to the government's acceptance. In view of these cases, contractors proposing changes for additional work should make it clear whether they are making offers to which they can be bound and, if so, how long the offer will remain open.

Contractors should also make it clear when suggesting a change when an equitable adjustment is expected if the change is approved. This will preclude the possibility that the government will claim that the change was being made voluntarily. See *S-TRON*, ASBCA 45893, 96-2 BCA ¶28,319, holding that a change improving a product was found to be voluntarily performed even though the contracting officer approved the change; *Jack Swedberg*, PSBCA 3876, 96-2 BCA ¶28,337, holding that a change improving the services rendered was voluntary even though the agency knew of the change; and *Lane Constr. Corp.*, ENGBCA 5834, 94-1 BCA ¶26,358, finding a "tacit agreement" that a change would be at no increase in price. See also *Nagy Enters.*, ASBCA 48815, 98-1 BCA ¶29,695, finding voluntary additional work where a contractor made changes to the material in order to obtain better compaction without obtaining the approval of the agency.

When a contractor proposes a change, it has no right to have the change adopted, and it must proceed with the work while the government is considering the change, *Exide Corp.*, ASBCA 43624, 92-3 BCA ¶25,154. However, if the changes are proposed as a means of correcting defective specifications, the government has an obligation to consider them in a reasonable time. If it does not, the contractor may be entitled to an excusable delay, *Umpqua Marine Ways, Inc. v. United States*, Civ. No. 91-282-FR (D. Ore. 1992) (holding that such delay could be a material breach overcoming a default termination); *DCX, Inc.*, ASBCA 37669, 92-3 BCA ¶25,125 (overturning a default termination because of the government's failure to act on proposed changes to correct defective specifications); or to compensation for the delay, *Perma-Cal Corp.*, ASBCA 42155, 91-2 BCA ¶24,034, *recons. denied*, 91-3 BCA ¶24,294.

B. Government Originated Changes

A significant number of changes originate because of changed government requirements or the identification of a problem by agency personnel. Engineering Change Proposals clauses permit the government to originate such changes in contracts for development or production of products. The clauses require contractors to prepare ECPs when the agency identifies the need for a change. However, the clauses are silent on the means of compensation to the contractor for the work of preparing such ECPs.

Most construction agencies originate changes with their own forces or through independent design agents. In such cases, the agency usually desires a pricing proposal from the contractor before issuance of a change order. This practice is used, for instance, by the Army Corps of Engineers and the Veterans Administration. For example, the Veterans Administration has used the following supplemental clause in construction contracts:

> When requested by the Contracting Officer, the Contractor shall submit proposals for changes in work to the Resident Engineer. Proposals, to be submitted within 30 calendar days after receipt of request, shall be in legible form, original and five copies, with an itemized breakdown that will include material, quantities, and unit prices, labor costs (separated into trades), construction equipment, etc. (Labor costs are to be identified with specific material placed or operation performed.) The Contractor must obtain and furnish with his proposal an itemized breakdown, as described above, signed by each subcontractor participating in the change regardless of tier.

This clause also is silent on the issue of compensation for the cost of preparing the change proposal.

When the government requests the contractor to prepare change proposals but later decides not to order the change, the contractor will not normally be entitled to compensation for the preparation costs, *Greenhut Constr. Co.*, ASBCA 14354, 70-1 BCA ¶8209; *Energy Eng'g Corp.*, PSBCA 319, 77-1 BCA ¶12,422, *recons. denied*, 77-2 BCA ¶12,578; *Fireman's Fund Ins. Co.*, ASBCA 35284, 89-1 BCA ¶21,343; *B.F. Carvin Constr. Co. v. General Servs. Admin.*, GSBCA 12770, 95-1 BCA ¶27,445; *BMT Servs.*, IBCA 3794A-97, 98-2 BCA ¶29,893; *Program & Constr. Mgmt. Group, Inc. v. General Servs. Admin.*, GSBCA 14178, 00-1 BCA ¶30,641. In some cases the reasoning is that these costs are considered to be included in the contractor's overhead, *Blake Constr. Co.*, VABCA 1725, 83-1 BCA ¶16,431. The rule has also been explained by the theory that the legal relationship between the contracting officer and the contractor is the same whether the contracting officer requests a change proposal or an original bid, *George E. Jensen Contractor, Inc.*, GSBCA 3260, 71-1 BCA ¶8850. This rule appears to be the same regardless of whether the contractor is compelled to submit the estimate or has submitted it voluntarily, *Bridgewater Constr. Corp.*, VABCA 2936, 91-3 BCA ¶24,273, *recons. denied*, 92-1 BCA ¶24,446 (estimate submitted under Veterans Administration contract clause set forth above). See also *Delco Indus. Textile Corp.*, ASBCA 21379, 78-1 BCA ¶12,912, applying the same rule to the costs of preparing a value engineering proposal.

A request for the preparation of an ECP has been considered a compensable change order where significant technical effort is required to prepare the ECP, *Cocoa Elec. Co.*, ASBCA 33921, 91-1 BCA ¶23,442, *recons. denied*, 91-2 BCA ¶23,780; *Bechtel Nat'l, Inc.*, NASABCA 1186-7, 90-1 BCA ¶22,549; *Discon Corp.*, ASBCA 15981, 71-2 BCA ¶9069; *Harman–B.J. Gladd Constr. Co.*, VACAB 1093, 75-1 BCA ¶11,262; where the work is done to correct errors in government specifications, *Acme Missiles & Constr. Corp.*, ASBCA 11786, 69-2 BCA ¶8057; where the government retains and uses the information in the ECP, *Campos Constr. Co.*, VABCA 3019, 90-3 BCA ¶23,108; and where the contracting officer was found to have ordered the preparation of the ECP, *Century Eng'g Corp.*, ASBCA 2932, 57-2 BCA ¶1419, *recons. denied*, 58-1 BCA ¶1625; *Mac-Well Co.*, ASBCA 23097, 79-2 BCA ¶13,895. See also *Bechtel Nat'l, Inc.*, ASBCA 51589, 02-1 BCA ¶31,673, *aff'd*, 65 Fed. Appx. 277 (Fed. Cir. 2002), and *Raytheon Co.*, ASBCA 50166, 01-1 BCA ¶31,245, *aff'd in part and remanded on other grounds*, 305 F.3d 1354 (Fed. Cir. 2002), awarding the cost of preparing ECPs documenting defects in the technical data package when that work was called for by the contract. In *Fire Sec. Sys., Inc. v. General Servs. Admin.*, GSBCA 12120, 97-1 BCA ¶28,994, *recons. denied*, 97-2 BCA ¶29,186, the board awarded the contractor the cost of travel to prepare the proposal, because it was a "substantial cost beyond that which would normally be contemplated for a change order," but denied the balance of the costs of preparing the proposal. The same result was reached in *Fire Sec. Sys., Inc. v. General Servs. Admin.*, GSBCA 12267, 97-2 BCA ¶28,992.

C. Unilateral versus Bilateral Change Orders

Although the major Changes clauses only discuss the possibility of unilateral orders from the contracting officer changing the work, most agencies favor the ordering of changes in the form of a bilateral modification to the contract. Thus, the general government policy is not covered by the language of the Changes clauses other than the clause used for commercial items.

1. Policy

The general government policy is set forth in FAR 43.102(b) as follows:

> Contract modifications, including changes that could be issued unilaterally, shall be priced before their execution if this can be done without adversely affecting the interest of the Government. If a significant cost increase could result from a contract modification and time does not permit negotiation of a price, at least a maximum price shall be negotiated unless impractical.

This policy is based on experience demonstrating that contractors' original estimates of the cost of changes are frequently low, causing the equitable adjustment following a unilateral change order to be higher than anticipated by the contracting officer. When that occurs, the agency has not set aside sufficient funds to cover the changed work and may find it difficult to obtain the funds at the time the work is finally priced. This result is precluded if the parties are able to negotiate the price of a proposed change at the time it is being considered and then to issue the change as a bilateral modification to the contract. The contractor is also benefited by the issuance of fully priced changes through bilateral modifications because payments for the costs of the changed work can then be obtained as soon as permitted by the normal payment procedures in the contract.

There are two major impediments to the use of bilateral changes. First, the parties may not know the point at which the change will become effective. They may need to do additional work, such as design or prototype manufacture and testing, to determine the specific nature of the change, and the time required for this work may be of indeterminate length. Second, the parties may not agree on the price of the change. In many cases, there is very little time available for the government to issue the change, and hence little time to estimate its cost and negotiate its price. For example, on construction projects, the need for changes is frequently perceived shortly before the contractor arrives at the point in the work where the change is required.

As a general proposition, forward pricing of changes is to the advantage of both parties. However, there are definite risks for both parties when the bilateral change order is used. The contractor runs the risk that it has not fully evaluated the impact of the change and has not included a sufficient amount in its price. This can be an especially troublesome problem when there are numerous changes because the impact costs may accumulate as the work progresses, and such costs probably are not adequately covered in early estimates of the cost of proposed changes. To avoid this risk, the contractor may include a contingency in its estimate. Therein lies the risk for the government. If the contingency is too large or the feared events do not occur, the government will have paid too much.

2. Modifying Language in Unilateral Change Orders

FAR 43.102(b) directs contracting officers to "negotiate" a "maximum price" when a firm price cannot be negotiated for change orders that could have a significant cost impact. To fully implement this regulation, the contracting officer would have to obtain the contractor's agreement to limiting language by issuing such changes as bilateral modifications to the contract. However, some agencies have attempted to obtain such maximum prices by including them in unilateral change orders. This practice has raised the question of whether such maximums are binding on the contractor—since it has not agreed to the amount in writing.

Agencies have also varied in the form of modifying language used to obtain maximum prices. The most common language is the "not to exceed" language called for by the Engineering Change Proposals clauses discussed above. Other agencies use language establishing a "ceiling price"—frequently based on the contractor's proposal. Whenever such language is used, a contractor should assume that it will be bound by it if it signs the contract modification. See *Contel Advanced Sys., Inc.*, ASBCA 49072, 02-1 BCA ¶31,808, and *City of Oxnard*, ASBCA 30344, 87-2 BCA ¶19,901, *aff'd*, 851 F.2d 344 (Fed. Cir. 1988), in which contractors were held bound to the "not to exceed" language in an original contract. In one case, a contractor was held to be bound by a ceiling price in a bilateral modification even though it did not sign the modification, *Samuel S. Barnett Co.*, GSBCA 4855, 80-1 BCA ¶14,355. Compare *General Ry. Signal Co.*, ENGBCA 6168, 96-1 BCA ¶27,981, holding that the contractor was not bound by the "not to exceed" price because its subsequent proposals for a higher price indicated that it had not agreed to be bound by the unilateral change order. See also *Decker & Co., GmbH*, ASBCA 33285, 88-3 BCA ¶20,925, *revised*, 89-1 BCA ¶21,399, in which the board held that the contractor was not bound by a "ceiling price" because it had not signed the change order. The change order was somewhat ambiguous in that it stated that the contractor should not exceed the ceiling "without prior approval of the contracting officer."

If a contractor wants to question a maximum price in a contract modification, it should do so when the change order is issued, not when the equitable adjustment is being negotiated. If the contractor has any reason to believe that the maximum amount may be insufficient, the contracting officer should be informed immediately and told that the contractor is reserving its right to request a greater amount. See *Accurtron Tool & Instrument Co.*, NASABCA 684-7, 85-3 BCA ¶18,340, in which the contractor was not bound to the ceiling because it objected to it at the time it signed the modification; *Delco Elec. Corp. v. United States*, 12 Cl. Ct. 367 (1987), *aff'd*, 909 F.2d 1595 (Fed. Cir. 1990), in which the contractor was not bound to a "not to exceed" price because it promptly objected; *Hemphill Contracting, Inc.*, ENGBCA 5698, 91-2 BCA ¶23,761, in which the contractor was not bound by the modification because it refused to sign it and immediately reserved its right to additional compensation; and *Hardrives, Inc.*, IBCA 2319, 94-1 BCA ¶26,267, where the contractor immediately objected to the "not to exceed" language only to be faced with another modification containing a ceiling price and a statement that commencement of work would constitute agreement with the ceiling. In the latter case, the board commented that these procedures were "atypical and unacceptable."

The most troublesome technique used to modify the change order when agreement cannot be reached on the price is the issuance of a unilateral change order with the notation that the price of the change is "not to exceed" a stated dollar amount. While the contractor might obtain some protection from the fact that it did not sign the change order, there is still a risk that it will be bound to the ceiling price by proceeding with the work. Some contractors have dealt with this type of form by adding clarifying language reserving their rights and returning the form to the contracting officer. Such a statement might read:

> The contractor's signature signifies only that receipt of this change order is acknowledged—not that the contractor is bound by the ceiling price. The contractor will proceed with the work as changed with the understanding that an equitable adjustment will be negotiated pursuant to the Changes clause of the contract.

The contractor should be protected by such a reservation of rights. See *Utley-James, Inc.*, GSBCA 5370, 85-1 BCA ¶17,816, *aff'd*,14 Cl. Ct. 804 (1988), in which such a reservation was enforced even though the contracting officer crossed it out before signing the contract modification ordering the change.

After returning the change order with the reservation, the contractor should proceed with the work. See *Discount Co. v. United States*, 213 Ct. Cl. 567, 554 F.2d 435, *cert. denied*, 434 U.S. 938 (1977), in which a contractor was held to have been properly default terminated for failing to proceed with work called for under a unilateral change order that provided for no increase in price. The court rejected the contractor's contention that the order constituted only a proposal upon which the contractor was not bound to proceed. The court stated at 574:

> In the circumstances here, it is immaterial whether the designation of the new borrow place was merely a government proposal or a fully operative and effective change order. Plaintiff knew that the designation of the alternate borrow site came to it in June 1969 on a form labeled "Contract Change Order or Data Sheet Covering Amendments" as "Change Order Number 3"; it also knew that the new site was available, that the Government was willing to have it used and wanted it used if it became the only suitable borrow open to the contractor. Moreover, plaintiff was aware, or should have known, that it could have protected its right to an equitable adjustment by simply saying so—that it would comply with Change Order Number 3 but would still pursue its alleged right to an increase in the contract price.

See also *Swiss Prods., Inc.*, ASBCA 40031, 93-3 BCA ¶26,163, in which a contractor was held to have been properly default terminated when it did not proceed with changed work ordered with a limitation of funds that was considerably less than the contractor believed was due for the work. The board commented that the contractor was protected by being able to assert its rights to a larger equitable adjustment under the disputes procedure in the contract. Compare *Wilner v. United States*, 26 Cl. Ct. 260 (1992), *rev'd on other grounds*, 24 F.3d 1397 (Fed. Cir. 1994), in which the court found that the contractor had acted properly in refusing to proceed with a change order that stated: "[Y]ou are hereby authorized to proceed with the following proposed change order. Cost of the work shall not exceed $90,000." Although the court did not discuss its reasoning, it may have read the change order language as not requiring the contractor to implement the change.

Another situation that occurs with some frequency is one in which the contractor is willing to agree to the direct costs of a change but requires that any delay or impact costs be reserved for future negotiation. Such a provision will be enforced if it is clearly written, *Bechtel Nat'l, Inc.*, NASABCA 1186-7, 90-1 BCA ¶22,549, *recons. denied*, 90-3 BCA ¶23,105 (reservation of costs of "cumulative effect of changes"). A reservation of such costs has also been found where the contracting officer specifically deleted such proposed costs when issuing the changes, *Freeman-Darling, Inc.*, GSBCA 7112, 89-2 BCA ¶21,882.

The parties can also reserve other types of costs when negotiating an equitable adjustment. See *CTA, Inc.*, ASBCA 47062, 00-2 BCA ¶30,946, where the parties negotiated the cost of altering the quantities of a production option but reserved the impact of changing subcontractors for a portion of the work.

3. Clause Permitting Only Bilateral Change Orders

Clauses stating that changes can be implemented only by bilateral agreement have rarely been used in government contracts. However, as discussed above, ¶(c), of the commercial items clause, Contract Terms and Conditions—Commercial Items, in FAR 52.212-4 contains such a provision. Under such a clause, the government does not have the power to issue unilateral change orders. However, the boards have taken jurisdiction of claims that the government changed the work by its actions in *SAWADI Corp.*, ASBCA 53073, 01-1 BCA ¶31,357, and *Bradford E. Englander, Liquidating Tr. for Dulles Networking Assocs., Inc.*, VABCA 6473, 01-2 BCA ¶31,466. Prior to the Contract Disputes Act of 1978, it had been held that the boards and courts could not find communications or actions of the government to be constructive change orders under a bilateral changes clause, *Len Co. & Assocs. v. United States*, 181 Ct. Cl. 29, 385 F.2d 438 (1967); *Boise Cascade Corp.*, AGBCA 76-166, 78-1 BCA ¶12,957. See also *Zip-O-Log Mills*, Comp. Gen. Dec. B-188304, 78-2 CPD ¶178, suggesting that the agency use a standard unilateral Changes clause in order to facilitate the agency's ability to settle claims during performance.

D. Procedure for Ordering Changes

There has been considerable controversy over two issues regarding the ordering of changes: (1) whether such orders are effective only if in writing, and (2) whether they are effective only if ordered on Standard Form 30.

1. Requirement for Written Change Order

All Changes clauses require that change orders be in writing. The clauses, however, do not prevent a contractor from getting an equitable adjustment when the contracting officer orally orders a change and promises an equitable adjustment as soon as a fair amount can be determined, *W.H. Armstrong & Co. v. United States*, 98 Ct. Cl. 519 (1943). The appeals boards generally follow *Armstrong* in situations where the only government defense is the lack of a written change order, *C.A. Logeman Co.*, ASBCA 5692, 61-2 BCA ¶3232; *A.L. Harding, Inc.*, DCAB PR-44, 65-2 BCA ¶5261, *recons. denied*, 66-1 BCA ¶5463; *Lincoln Constr. Co.*, IBCA 438-5-64, 65-2 BCA ¶5234, *recons. denied*, 66-1 BCA ¶5343. See also *Len Co. & Assocs. v. United States*, 181 Ct. Cl. 29, 385 F.2d 438 (1967), in which the court stated at 38:

> The court has considered it to "be idle for the contractor to demand a written order from the contracting officer for an extra when the contracting officer was insisting that the work required was not additional . . ." and, therefore, has often dispensed, on these occasions, with the formality of issuing a written change order under the standard clause. *Fleisher Eng'r & Constr. Co. v. United States*, 98 Ct. Cl. 139, 158 (1942); *Fox Valley Eng'r, Inc. v. United States*, 151 Ct. Cl. 228, 238 (1960).

The construction contract Changes clause in FAR 52.243-4 recognized this rule by providing that constructive changes may occur through oral orders. This had been the rule prior to the adoption of the clause, *Holt Hauling & Warehousing Sys., Inc.*, ASBCA 19136, 76-2 BCA ¶12,185. Note that this clause continues to require that ordered changes be in writing, *Oren Childers Paint Contracting Co.*, ASBCA 13987, 70-2 BCA ¶8388. In *R/W Contracting*, ASBCA 17239, 73-2 BCA

¶10,130, the board found that a direct oral order to accelerate was not binding on the government because the parties had contemplated a written order in their negotiations.

The Court of Claims also held that the lack of a written change order does not bar recovery when the contracting officer and the appeals board consider the contractor's claim on the merits, *Centre Mfg. Co. v. United States*, 183 Ct. Cl. 115, 392 F.2d 229 (1968); *Kings Elecs. Co. v. United States*, 169 Ct. Cl. 433, 341 F.2d 632 (1965). See also *Del-Rio Drilling Programs, Inc. v. United States*, 46 Fed. Cl. 683 (2000), rejecting a government defense that there was no written order when the contract required the agency to issue a written confirmation of oral orders.

Another line of cases cites the lack of a written change order as a reason for denying a claim for price adjustment, *General Bronze Corp. v. United States*, 168 Ct. Cl. 176, 338 F.2d 117 (1964); *Instruments for Indus., Inc.*, DCAB NBS-16, 69-2 BCA ¶8025, *recons. denied*, 70-1 BCA ¶8169. These cases deny recovery on several grounds, and it can be argued that the lack of a written order is not dispositive. For example, in *Comspace Corp.*, GSBCA 3550, 72-2 BCA ¶9674, the board noted that, where a contractor's failure to get written approval had proven fatal, "the Contractor performed without the express or implied approval of the Contracting Officer or his authorized representative." The board also noted that the requirement for a written order "is an attempt to insure that there is evidence . . . of the change," and that while a written order is the best evidence, it is "not the only" evidence of a change order. There is a Supreme Court case denying recovery because of a lack of a written change order, *Plumley v. United States*, 226 U.S. 545 (1913).

In contrast to the rule regarding change orders, *Mil-Spec Contractors v. United States*, 835 F.2d 865 (Fed. Cir. 1987), appears to require bilateral contract modifications to be in writing. In that case, the contractor had orally agreed with a government contract negotiator to a modification subject to the approval of the contracting officer. The contracting officer prepared the modification, signed it, and sent it to the contractor. After the contractor refused to sign the modification, the government argued that the parties had a binding agreement. The court rejected this argument, stating at 867-69:

> Unless and until there was a binding modification to which both Mil-Spec and the contracting officer had agreed in writing, there could not be a binding modification of the contract. The oral agreement [between the contractor and the negotiator] could not and did not constitute a valid accord and satisfaction. The contracting officer's subsequent approval of the oral agreement, reflected in his signature of the written contract modification form he prepared, did not *nunc pro tunc turn the prior oral agreement into a valid contractual commitment that bound the government.*
>
> * * *
>
> *In SCM Corp. v. United States*, 219 Ct. Cl. 459, 595 F.2d 595, 598 (1979), the Court of Claims held that where the pertinent regulations required that contract modifications be written, an oral modification that had not been reduced to writing and signed by both parties was ineffective. The situation in *SCM* was analogous to that in the present case. . . . The court stated:
>
>> Oral understandings which contemplate the finalization of the legal obligations in a written form are not contracts in themselves. When legal obligations between the parties will be deferred until the time when a written document is executed, there will not be a contract until that time. Under the regulations, Government funds were not obligated until the execution of standard form 30. The parties were well aware of the fact that only the written contract modification could finalize their agreement. . . . We thus conclude that neither party was bound by its negotiations until standard form 30 was executed.

These cases have been interpreted as establishing a strict rule that alleged oral agreements to modify the terms of a contract are not valid, *Marshall Assoc. Contractors, Inc. & Columbia Excavating, Inc. (J.V.)*, IBCA 1901, 98-1 BCA ¶29,565 (alleged agreement converting default to convenience termination and settling claims); *Cooper Realty Co. v. United States*, 36 Fed. Cl. 284 (1996) (alleged agreement by contracting officer that government would vacate premises earlier than term of lease); *Merrimac Mgmt. Inst., Inc.*, ASBCA 45291, 94-3 BCA ¶27,251 (alleged agreement that task order would fulfill government's minimum quantity ordering requirement on indefinite-delivery, indefinite-quantity contract); *Centennial Leasing v. General*

Servs. Admin., GSBCA 11451, 93-1 BCA ¶25,350, *aff'd*, 11 F.3d 1072 (Fed. Cir. 1993) (alleged agreement to extend term of contract); *Daly Constr., Inc.*, ASBCA 34322, 92-1 BCA ¶24,469, *aff'd*, 5 F.3d 520 (Fed. Cir. 1993) (alleged settlement agreement); *Edwards v. United States*, 22 Cl. Ct. 411 (1991) (alleged agreement to modify terms of lease); *Woodington Corp.*, ASBCA 37885, 91-1 BCA ¶23,579 (alleged bilateral changes); *C.M.P. Corp.*, ASBCA 36664, 89-1 BCA ¶21,317 (alleged option exercise). This rule has also precluded the government from enforcing oral modifications, *Staff, Inc.*, AGBCA 96-112-1, 97-2 BCA ¶29,285; *Knights' Piping, Inc.*, ASBCA 46986, 95-2 BCA ¶27,700. However, in *J.S. Alberici Constr. Co. v. General Servs. Admin.*, GSBCA 12386, 94-2 BCA ¶26,776, the board found the government liable on an oral agreement that was followed by a written contract modification that had been signed by the contractor but not signed by the government. The board cited *Essex Electro Eng'rs, Inc.*, ASBCA 30118, 88-1 BCA ¶20,440, holding the government liable in similar circumstances because, after reaching complete agreement on the modification, both parties "viewed the formal writing as a mere formality and not as a contingency." See *Johnson Mgmt. Group CFC, Inc.*, HUDBCA 96-C-132-C15, 00-2 BCA ¶31,116, *aff'd*, 308 F.3d 1245 (Fed. Cir. 2002), refusing to follow this reasoning in a case where a contract modification was prepared by the contracting officer but not signed by the contractor. In affirming, the Federal Circuit did not apply the *Mil-Spec* rule strictly but held that the *Alberici* exception did not apply because "there was not a sufficient meeting of the minds on the terms of the agreement to definitize it orally." See also *TRW, Inc.*, ASBCA 51003, 00-2 BCA ¶30,992, stating that the *Mil-Spec* rule is that, "The absence of a formal settlement agreement suggests the absence of a binding agreement."

Oral agreements have been held binding when they are not "contract modifications." See *Texas Instruments, Inc. v. United States*, 922 F.2d 810 (Fed. Cir. 1990), enforcing an oral agreement establishing the prices of unpriced contract line items, and *Montgomery Ross Fisher, Inc. & H.A. Lewis, Inc., A Joint Venture*, VABCA 3696, 94-1 BCA ¶26,527, enforcing an oral agreement settling a dispute. In the latter case, the board relied on *United States v. Bissett-Berman Corp.*, 481 F.2d 764 (9th Cir. 1973). Similarly, in *Tiburzi v. Department of Justice*, 269 F.3d 1346 (Fed. Cir. 2001), the court cited *Sargent v. Department of Health & Human Servs.*, 229 F.3d 1088 (Fed. Cir. 2000), for the proposition that "it is well-established that an oral settlement agreement is binding on the parties, particularly when the terms are memorialized into the record." See also *Adams Constr. Co.*, VABCA 4669, 97-1 BCA ¶28,801, in which the board concluded there were sufficient indications in writing to enforce an oral agreement that a contract completion date would be extended.

2. Standard Form 30

FAR 43.301 requires Standard Form 30 to be used in issuing either unilateral or bilateral change orders. Prior to the issuance of the FAR, the Federal Procurement Regulations were silent on whether use of the form was mandatory, whereas DAR 16-203 and DAR 16-405.4 required its use. In *SCM Corp. v. United States*, 219 Ct. Cl. 459, 595 F.2d 595 (1979), the court held that the contractor was responsible for knowing this regulatory requirement, with the result that the government was not bound by an oral agreement on the amount the government would add to the contract for changed work. The court found that the parties intended their agreement to be finalized by means of a supplemental agreement using Standard Form 30. Subsequently, *Mil-Spec Contractors, Inc. v. United States*, 835 F.2d 865 (Fed. Cir. 1987), and *Texas Instruments, Inc. v. United States*, 922 F.2d 810 (Fed. Cir. 1990), contained language that could be interpreted to impose the same requirement with regard to bilateral modifications.

Several cases have found the parties bound by written bilateral modifications not using Standard Form 30 by following the theory that neither party should be able to avoid a written contractual agreement because of a mechanical defect in the form of the agreement. See *Robinson Contracting Co. v. United States*, 16 Cl. Ct. 676 (1989), *aff'd*, 895 F.2d 1420 (Fed. Cir. 1990), and *Folk Constr. Co.*, ENGBCA 5839, 93-3 BCA ¶26,094. On the other hand, the lack of a Standard Form 30 was one element in a decision precluding the effectiveness of a written modification that had been signed by a government employee who was not a contracting officer, *Solar Turbines, Inc. v. United States*, 23 Cl. Ct. 142 (1991).

A contractor's insistence on the use of Standard Form 30 was held to be an unacceptable reason for a compensable delay, *P&M Indus., Inc.*, ASBCA 36625, 90-2 BCA ¶22,839. In the decision, the board did not discuss the FAR 43.301 requirement that this form be used to issue contract modifications.

Standard Form 30 is used for a number of purposes not related to the issuance of changes. Hence, the form does not necessarily signify that a change is being made, *Southwest Marine, Inc.*, DOTCAB 1497, 93-3 BCA ¶26,170.

3. Obtaining Proposal for Downward Adjustment

When the contracting officer has issued a unilateral change order that reduces the amount of work to be done, the contractor has little incentive to submit a proposal for a downward equitable adjustment. If such a proposal is not forthcoming, it has been held proper for the contracting officer to issue a unilateral modification reducing the price, *Metric Constructors, Inc.*, ASBCA 49343, 97-2 BCA ¶29,076; *Bruce-Andersen Co.*, ASBCA 29412, 89-2 BCA ¶21,872; or issue a final decision under the Disputes clause reducing the price, *Dawson Constr. Co.*, VABCA 3558, 94-1 BCA ¶26,362. When the parties cannot agree on the price reduction, after the contractor has submitted a proposal, the contracting officer has little choice but to issue a contract modification establishing the amount of the reduction. See, for example, *Connor Bros. Constr. Co.*, VABCA 2519, 95-1 BCA ¶27,409, *aff'd*, 113 F.3d 1256 (Fed. Cir. 1997). See also *Cottman Mech. Contractors, Inc.*, ASBCA 48882, 00-1 BCA ¶30,777, in which the board affirmed the propriety of the issuance of a unilateral modification, without asking for a contractor proposal, decreasing the price in an amount determined by using the Means estimating guide, and *Litton Sys., Inc.*, ASBCA 36976, 93-2 BCA ¶25,705, in which the board approved the issuance of a unilateral modification to the contract after the contractor refused to agree to the conversion of a letter contract into a firm contract. In *Blount, Inc.*, VABCA 3236, 93-1 BCA ¶25,474, the board commented that this was not a desirable manner for determining a downward equitable adjustment, indicating that it would have preferred to base the adjustment on a proposal from the contractor. However, some contractors may refuse to submit such a proposal in order to place the burden of proof of the amount of the adjustment on the government. See *State Mech. Corp.*, VABCA 2797, 91-2 BCA ¶23,830.

III. VALUE ENGINEERING

Contractors often can perform work in ways that are less expensive than the methods called for in the contract documents. However, since normal contract changes that reduce the cost of performance also reduce the contractor's profit, there is little incentive to propose such changes, even though the government could benefit from them. Value engineering is the procurement technique developed to encourage submission of cost-reducing change proposals by promising the contractor a share of the savings and no reduction in profit.

Value engineering regulations have undergone frequent revision since their first adoption by the Department of Defense in the early 1960s. The DoD regulations and clauses were periodically revised from 1964 to 1979, and in 1977 uniform regulations and clauses were adopted by the Department of Defense and the General Services Administration for use by all federal agencies. In 1984 these regulations and clauses were consolidated in Part 48 of the FAR. In 1988, after considerable congressional criticism of agencies that were not using value engineering, OMB Circular A-131 was promulgated to ensure that agencies were making full use of these procedures. The circular was reissued on May 21, 1993, and currently requires that senior management of agencies endeavor to make greater use of value engineering techniques.

One result of the constant revision of the standard Value Engineering clauses is that legal interpretation of one clause may not apply to another. Thus, it is essential to identify precisely the language relevant to a dispute in this area. In the following discussion references are to the FAR, unless otherwise indicated.

A. Standard Clauses

There are three Value Engineering clauses, FAR 48.201. The first has various provisions for supply and service contracts. The basic clause of this type, Value Engineering, in FAR 52.248-1, encourages contractors to voluntarily develop, prepare, and submit Value Engineering Change Proposals (VECPs) in return for a relatively large share of the savings and recovery of development and implementation costs if the VECP is accepted. This "incentive" clause is used primarily in contracts where the contractor is working to detailed specifications and is likely to recognize cost-saving measures. Alternate I to this Value Engineering clause requires a specific value engineering program effort as a part of the contract work. Under this type of clause, the contractor's share of the savings is smaller since its value engineering activities are priced into the contract. This "program requirement" clause is used primarily in contracts where contract specifications are less detailed and the government anticipates that considerable cost savings will be possible during performance. Alternate II to this Value Engineering clause can be used when the incentive will be placed on some contract line items and the program requirements on others.

The second clause, Value Engineering—Architect Engineer, in FAR 52.248-2, is a program requirements clause calling for specific value engineering efforts during the design of a project and precluding any share of the savings of such efforts.

The third clause, Value Engineering—Construction, FAR 52.248-3, is an incentive clause giving the contractor a share of the savings for adopted VECPs.

1. Types of Savings

Government savings that can be generated by a VECP are identified by FAR 48.001 as either "acquisition savings" or "collateral savings." Acquisition savings are those generated by contractors, while collateral savings are those of the government.

a. Acquisition Savings

Acquisition savings are defined differently in the clause for supply and service contracts and the clause for construction contracts. In the supply and service contract clause, these savings result from the application of a VECP to "contracts awarded by the same contracting office or its successor for essentially the same unit." Thus, there are no acquisition savings when the idea in the VECP is used by the government on in-house manufacturing work, *M. Bianchi of Cal.*, ASBCA 37029, 97-1 BCA ¶28,767, *aff'd but vacated on other grounds*, 178 F.3d 1310 (Fed. Cir. 1998). Neither are there acquisition savings if the contract is awarded by a different military service, *Ordnance Devices, Inc.*, ASBCA 42709, 93-2 BCA ¶25,794. There, the board ruled that the term "or its successor" required that there be a reorganization or a change of cognizance for the item being procured. See *Ordnance Devices, Inc.*, ASBCA 42709, 96-2 BCA ¶28,437, finding that, under the applicable regulations, the contractor was entitled to the savings if the head of the contracting activity had extended the coverage to the other service, but that no such extension had occurred. Similarly, the term "essentially the same unit" has been interpreted narrowly. See *M. Bianchi of Cal.*, ASBCA 36518, 93-2 BCA ¶25,801, *aff'd*, 19 F.3d 40 (Fed. Cir. 1994), in which the board rejected the contractor's contention that its VECP for a better way of stitching the clothing called for by the contract had been used in a large number of contracts for other types of clothing. The same result was reached in *M. Bianchi of Cal.*, ASBCA 37395, 94-1 BCA ¶26,417, *aff'd*, 61 F.3d 920 (Fed. Cir. 1995), *cert. denied*, 516 U.S. 1094 (1996), and *M. Bianchi of Cal.*, ASBCA 37029, 93-1 BCA ¶25,309, *aff'd but vacated on other grounds*, 31 F.3d 1163 (Fed. Cir. 1994). See also *Cosmos Eng'rs, Inc.*, ASBCA 24270, 88-2 BCA ¶20,795, holding that an item that did not meet the similarity test for the recovery of the costs of reprocurement after default termination did not meet the "essentially the same unit" test. Similarly, in *Johnny F. Smith Truck & Dragline Serv., Inc.*, ENGBCA 6261, 98-2 BCA ¶30,006, *aff'd*, 232 F.3d 915 (Fed. Cir. 2000), the board determined that no collateral savings had been justified because other service contracts awarded by the same contracting office were not for "essentially the same work" as the service contract on which the VECP had been submitted.

In supply and service contracts, acquisition savings are calculated on the basis of the cost reduction in the "unit cost" on the contract. As a result, there are no acquisition savings on such contracts if the contractor's VECP increases the life of an item with the result that the government buys fewer items, *Hayes Targets, PEMCO Aeroplex, Inc.*, ASBCA 44137, 93-3 BCA ¶25,999.

In contrast, the construction contract clause calls for the sharing of any cost reductions on the contract created by VECPs. Thus, acquisition savings occurred on such contracts when the VECPs suggested reducing the number of motors used on a hangar door, *W.R. Johnson, Inc.*, ASBCA 40251, 91-3 BCA ¶24,172, and reusing materials on the contract, *King Constr. Co.*, ASBCA 38303, 94-1 BCA ¶26,434, *recons. denied*, 94-2 BCA ¶26,630. However, no savings were generated on a contract where the element of the project to which the VECP pertained was deleted from the project by the government, *Dunn Constr. Co.*, ASBCA 48145, 97-2 BCA ¶29,103, *recons. denied*, 98-1 BCA ¶28,485.

The three types of savings that comprise acquisition savings are instant contract savings, concurrent contract savings, and future contract savings. See FAR 48.104-1. When all three types of savings are included in a contract, the normal procedure is to calculate each type of savings separately and to pay the total savings on the instant contract, as discussed below. However, FAR 48.104-3 permits the contracting officer to bypass this detailed calculation and to negotiate a "no cost settlement" where the parties agree to adopt the VECP without amending the contract price. This technique is appropriate when the government's share of savings on the instant contract is roughly commensurate with the contractor's share of savings on concurrent and future contracts.

(1) Instant Contract Savings

Instant contract savings are the net reductions generated by the application of a VECP to the instant contract. These savings are calculated by determining the cost reduction resulting from the VECP under the instant contract and subtracting allowable contractor costs of development and implementation. Any government costs (excluding the costs of processing the VECP) are then deducted, and sharing is based on the net result. In supply and service contracts, this calculation may result in negative instant contract savings—in which case concurrent and future contract savings are offset before the contractor is entitled to any sharing. If the end result is negative contract savings, the contract price is increased by that amount. See *Rig Masters, Inc.*, ASBCA 52891, 03-1 BCA ¶32,294, *aff'd*, 96 Fed. Appx. 683 (Fed. Cir. 2004), denying a claim for all development costs because the clause only called for payment of negative savings, comprising development costs minus instant savings.

In supply and service contracts, the term "instant contract" is defined narrowly to exclude "increases in quantities after acceptance of the VECP that are due to contract modifications, exercise of options, or additional orders." In multiyear contracts, the term does not include any quantities "funded after VECP acceptance." These limitations are omitted from the construction contract clause.

Instant contract savings must be savings incurred by the contractor, *Vemo Co.*, ASBCA 31911, 88-3 BCA ¶20,977, *aff'd*, 878 F.2d 1446 (Fed. Cir. 1989). Hence, government savings cannot be classified as instant contract savings.

(2) Concurrent Contract Savings

Concurrent contract savings are the "net reductions in the prices of other contracts that are definitized and ongoing at the time the VECP is accepted," FAR 48.001. Generally, these are the savings on supply or service contracts with other contractors for the same or similar units. Concurrent contract savings are calculated and shared in the same manner as instant contract savings, except that government costs are deducted only to the extent that they have not been fully recouped in the calculation of other savings.

(3) Future Contract Savings

Future contract savings are the net unit cost reduction multiplied by the number of units scheduled for delivery under a future contract during the "sharing period." The normal sharing period begins with acceptance of the first unit incorporating the VECP and ends at a date determined by the contracting officer, FAR 48.001. This date can be from 36 to 60 months after acceptance of the first unit in the discretion of the contracting officer and can be different for each VECP, FAR 48.104-1. Under the pre-2000 clauses the sharing period ended "the later of (a) three years after the first unit affected by the VECP is accepted or (b) the last scheduled delivery date of an item affected by the VECP under the instant contract delivery schedule in effect at the time the VECP is accepted." Under that prior regulation, the sharing period could be extended on contracts for items requiring an extended period of production, such as ships, to include any item that was essentially the same as the one for which the VECP was accepted and was produced under a contract awarded during what would otherwise be a normal sharing period.

Future contract savings are shared in the same proportions as concurrent contract savings and can be calculated in two ways. One way is to estimate purchases of items affected by the VECP under future contracts during the sharing period, in which case the contractor's share is paid in a lump sum. The second way is to calculate the savings as future contracts are awarded during the sharing period and to make royalty payments under the instant contract. In deciding between these two methods, the contracting officer should consider the accuracy of the estimate of future purchases, the availability of funds for making lump sum payments, and the expense of modifying the instant contract each time a royalty payment is made, FAR 48.104-1(a) and (b). When the lump sum method is used, the Value Engineering clause states that the payment "shall not be subject to subsequent adjustment." However, an appeals board agreed to review whether the lump sum amount was too low because the contracting officer materially misrepresented the anticipated future purchases of the item, *Sayco, Ltd.*, ASBCA 36534, 89-1 BCA ¶21,319.

It has been held that acceptance of a VECP (entitling a contractor to future contract savings resulting from future utilization of the VECP) did not obligate the government to utilize the VECP in future acquisitions, *Turco Prods.*, ASBCA 20290, 75-2 BCA ¶11,442.

Future contract savings provisions have generated a number of unique controversies. In *Applied Cos.*, ASBCA 50593, 99-2 BCA ¶30,554, the board denied a motion for summary judgment by the government contending that a modification disclaiming any "future contract sharing provisions" was an agreement to forego all future contract savings. In *Northeastern Mfg. & Sales, Inc.*, ASBCA 38307, 90-1 BCA ¶22,562, the cost of transportation was included in future contract savings because the later contracts called for delivery f.o.b. destination. The board rejected the argument that this was improper because the instant contract called for delivery f.o.b. origin, with the result that in that contract the savings in transportation cost were collateral savings. In *East-West Research, Inc.*, ASBCA 32367, 86-3 BCA ¶19,219, the government was held bound to a contract modification making royalty payments for future contract savings even though the government subsequently determined that the savings were not the result of the VECP. In *Honeywell, Inc.*, ASBCA 25553, 83-1 BCA ¶16,180, where a VECP changed a gasket from lead to cork and rubber, a second VECP changing the cork and rubber to fiber earned the contractor royalties in addition to those for the first VECP, notwithstanding the government's argument that the first VECP was no longer being "used." The precedential value of *Honeywell* is uncertain since the second VECP included a reservation providing that savings generated from the first VECP would be unaffected by the second. In *Antaya Bros.*, ASBCA 19390, 75-2 BCA ¶11,403, a contractor was not entitled to future savings awards on items originally scheduled for delivery within its future savings period where actual delivery occurred after expiration of the savings period. This decision dealt with a special clause basing future savings on the time of actual delivery rather than on the time of scheduled delivery under the standard clauses. It is therefore of little effect with regard to the proper interpretation of the standard clause. Under the standard clause it has been held that a contractor is not entitled to calculate the beginning of the future savings period based on options exercised under the instant contract since such orders are not within the definition of "originally scheduled," *Fermont Div., Dynamics Corp. of Am.*, ASBCA 22250, 79-2 BCA ¶14,086. In another case involving a special clause, it was held that a defaulted contractor's savings period began from the last scheduled delivery by that contractor, rather than the last scheduled delivery of the successor contractor after the default, *Guenther Sys., Inc.*, ASBCA 20363, 77-1 BCA ¶12,501. In *Raytheon Co. v. United States*, 2 Cl. Ct. 763 (1983), *aff'd*, 730 F.2d 1470 (Fed. Cir. 1984), the court held that there was no abuse of discretion in not including a longer future savings period in the clause. The court also literally interpreted the pre-1974 clause, which used different times for calculating future savings from the current clause. In *RCS Enters. v. United States*, 57 Fed. Cl. 590 (2003), the court denied future savings because they were to be paid from contract options that were held to be invalid because they violated the Anti-Deficiency Act, 31 U.S.C. § 1341(a).

b. Collateral Savings

Collateral savings are the net reductions in collateral costs incurred by the government (costs of operation, maintenance, logistic support, and government-furnished property) resulting from a VECP. The contractor's share of collateral savings is "20 to 100 percent of the estimated savings to be realized during a typical year of use but must not exceed the greater of—(1) the contract's firm fixed-price, target price, target cost, or estimated cost, at the time the VECP is accepted; or (2) $100,000," FAR 48.104-3. If the head of the contracting activity finds that the cost of measuring and tracking collateral savings exceeds the savings themselves, the collateral savings provisions can be excluded from the contract, FAR 48.201(e). However, collateral savings cannot be excluded from an individual VECP if the clause is in the contract, *Overstreet Elec. Co.*, ASBCA 52401, 00-2 BCA ¶30,981. In contrast, when a sharing provision is properly excluded from the Value Engineering clause of a contract, no award for the excluded type of savings is due the contractor, *Pathman Constr. Co.*, ASBCA 22002, 78-2 BCA ¶13,318 (deletion of future contract savings and collateral savings provisions); *Al Johnson Constr. Co.*, ENGBCA 3279, 73-2 BCA ¶10,295 (deletion of collateral savings provision); Comp. Gen. Dec. B-167932, Jan. 15, 1970, *Unpub.* (deletion of future contracts savings provision).

The limitation on collateral savings to the amount of the contract price "at the time the VECP is accepted" is interpreted to be the price *before* the contract is amended to reflect the impact of the VECP, *Sayco, Ltd.*, ASBCA 39366, 94-3 BCA ¶27,284, *aff'd*, 86 F.3d 1173 (Fed. Cir.), *cert. denied*, 519 U.S. 865 (1996).

Paragraph (j) of the Value Engineering clause in FAR 52.248-1 states that the amount of collateral savings generated by a VECP is determined solely by the contracting officer. However, if the contracting officer has incorrectly calculated the contractor's share of those savings, an appeal may be taken, *Banner Fabricators, Inc.*, ASBCA 25088, 81-2 BCA ¶15,215.

Collateral savings can be related to the work on the contract even though they are not part of the work directly. See, for example, *ICSD Corp.*, ASBCA 28028, 90-3 BCA ¶23,027, *aff'd*, 934 F.2d 313 (Fed. Cir. 1991), where collateral savings were found in a VECP suggesting a different type of battery for the equipment called for by the contract even though the contractor was not furnishing it.

2. Uses of the Value Engineering Clause

FAR 48.201 requires the use of Value Engineering clauses in all contracts of $100,000 or more except contracts for (1) research and development, (2) engineering services by nonprofit or not-for-profit organizations, (3) personal services, (4) product improvement, or (5) commercial products.

If a Value Engineering clause is erroneously included in a contract where it is prohibited, it will have no effect. See, for example, *Charles Beseler Co.*, ASBCA 22669, 78-2 BCA ¶13,483, where a military contract for commercial items included a Value Engineering clause without the necessary invocation of special military requirements and specifications required by DAR 1-1702.1(b) (July 1976). The board reasoned, following the *Christian* doctrine (*G.L. Christian & Assocs. v. United States*, 160 Ct. Cl. 1, 312 F.2d 418, *reh'g denied*, 160 Ct. Cl. 58, 320 F.2d 345, *cert. denied*, 375 U.S. 954 (1963)), that the regulations precluding the use of such clauses on contracts for commercial items were binding on the parties.

a. *Supply and Service Contracts*

The Value Engineering clause used for supply and service contracts, FAR 52.248-1, may be written as an incentive or program requirement clause, or both. This is the only clause that provides for all four types of savings. The shares for instant, concurrent, and future savings are set at the rates called for by the following table in FAR 48.104-2(a)(1):

Government/Contractor Shares of Net Acquisition Savings

(Figures in percent)

	Incentive (voluntary)		Program requirement (mandatory)	
Contract Type	Instant contract rate	Concurrent and future contract rate	Instant contract rate	Concurrent and future contract rate
Fixed-price (other than incentive)	50/50*	50/50*	75/25	75/25
Incentive (fixed-price or cost)	**	50/50*	**	75/25
Cost-reimbursement (other than incentive)	75/25***	75/25***	85/15	85/15

* The contracting officer may increase the contractor's sharing rate to as high as 75 percent for each VECP. (See 48.102(g)(1) through (7).)

** Same sharing arrangement as the contract's profit or fee adjustment formula.

*** The contracting officer may increase the contractor's sharing rate to as high as 50 percent for each VECP. (See 48.102(g)(1) through (7).)

b. *Construction Contracts*

The Value Engineering clause used for construction contracts, FAR 52.248-3, is the incentive-type clause, but it cannot be used on incentive-type construction contracts. It provides for sharing instant savings, with the contractor getting 55 percent on fixed-price contracts and 25 percent on cost-reimbursement contracts. It also provides for collateral contract savings. The previous construction clause, DAR 7-602.50, did not allow sharing of collateral savings.

c. *Architect/Engineer Contracts*

The Value Engineering clause used for architect/engineer contracts, FAR 52.248-2, is used at the discretion of the agency. See FAR 48.201(f), stating that the clause will be used whenever such a contract "pays for a specific value engineering effort." The clause does not allow sharing of savings but compensates the contractor for its value engineering effort as a separately priced line item in the contract schedule. FAR 48.201(f) prohibits the use of the Value Engineering clause for supply and service contracts in architect/engineer contracts.

B. Interpretation

The length and complexity of the Value Engineering clauses has led to a large number of disputes regarding their application to specific situations encountered in processing and adopting VECPs. The major areas in which disputes have arisen are addressed below.

1. Liberal versus Literal Interpretation

In the early cases, the Court of Claims and the appeals boards frequently enunciated the policy that the provisions of the Value Engineering Incentive clause should be liberally interpreted in the contractor's favor, *Airmotive Eng'g Corp. v. United States*, 210 Ct. Cl. 7, 535 F.2d 8 (1976); *Dravo Corp. v. United States*, 202 Ct. Cl. 500, 480 F.2d 1331 (1973); *Mishara Constr. Co.*, ASBCA 17957, 75-1 BCA ¶11,206, *aff'd*, 230 Ct. Cl. 1008 (1982). In *Airmotive Eng'g Corp.*, ASBCA 17139, 74-1 BCA ¶10,517, *recons. denied*, 74-2 BCA ¶10,696, the board explained that, if the clause was not interpreted liberally, contractors would lose the incentive to propose money-saving devices and procedures. One board determined, however, that the normal rules of contract interpretation govern in construing value engineering clauses, *Umpqua River Navigation Co.*, ENGBCA 3881, 78-1 BCA ¶13,051. In addition, in *Raytheon Co.*, ASBCA 22711, 82-1 BCA ¶15,663, *aff'd*, 2 Cl. Ct. 763 (1983), *aff'd*, 730 F.2d 1470 (Fed. Cir. 1984), the board pointed out that a liberal interpretation still must be reasonable. The board denied Raytheon's claim for an extended royalty period, finding unreasonable the argument that acceptance of a VECP is not complete until the equitable adjustment is made.

More recent cases appear to apply a more literal interpretation to the Value Engineering clauses. See, for example, *Hayes Targets, PEMCO Aeroplex, Inc.*, ASBCA 44137, 93-3 BCA ¶25,999, holding that the clause did not apply to a change reducing the number of units because it did not reduce the unit price of the item being acquired on a supply contract; *M. Bianchi of Cal.*, ASBCA 37029, 93-1 BCA ¶25,309, *aff'd but vacated on other grounds*, 31 F.3d 1163 (Fed. Cir. 1994), holding that no collateral or future contract savings were earned when a packaging technique in a VECP was used for articles other than those bought on the instant contract; and *M. Bianchi of Cal.*, ASBCA 37395, 94-1 BCA ¶26,417, *aff'd*, 61 F.3d 920 (Fed. Cir. 1995), *cert. denied*, 516 U.S. 1094 (1996), holding that no future savings were earned when a sewing process in a VECP was used on articles other than those bought under the instant contract.

The liberal interpretation of the Value Engineering clause is illustrated by the decision in *Norair Eng'g Corp.*, ENGBCA 3730, 78-1 BCA ¶13,190. There, the contractor orally suggested that the government eliminate a part of a pending change order covering additional work that had been designed by the contractor. Although the change calling for the additional work was never formally issued, the board found that the contractor had been told to proceed with the work and, therefore, the later direction not to perform the work was an adoption of the VECP. Similarly, a contractor was found entitled to savings resulting from a VECP that was submitted to reduce the cost of a change order that has not yet been finalized, *Sentara Health Sys.*, ASBCA 51540, 00-2 BCA ¶31,122, *recons. denied*, 01-1 BCA ¶31,198. The board reasoned that the proposed change was an "implied contractual requirement." See also *McDonnell Douglas Corp.*, ASBCA No. 14314, 71-1 BCA ¶8859, finding a valid VECP to reduce the price of a change that had not yet been issued. Similarly, in *Morse Diesel Int'l., Inc. v. General Servs. Admin.*, GSBCA 13419, 97-1 BCA ¶28,634, the value engineering clause was applied when the contractor suggested a more efficient way of dealing with hazardous material after the government had selected the technique to be used when the material was discovered. Compare *J.S. Alberici Constr. Co. & Martin K. Eby Constr. Co. (A Joint Venture)*, ENGBCA 6178, 98-2 BCA ¶29,875, finding that no VECP had been submitted when the contractor suggested a different method but did not follow any of the procedures required for the submission of a VECP. Similarly, in *C.A. Rasmussen, Inc. v. United States*, 52 Fed. Cl. 345 (2002), the court held that no VECP had been submitted when the government adopted a contractor's oral cost-saving suggestion because the informational requirements in the clause had not been completely followed.

2. Applicability of the Value Engineering Clause

The Value Engineering clause generally applies to any contractor suggestion that reduces the cost of work called for by the contract. But the contractor is not entitled to compensation for VECPs affecting work outside the contract scope. See *John J. Kirlin, Inc. v. United States*, 11 Cl. Ct. 199 (1986), *aff'd on other grounds*, 827 F.2d 1538 (Fed. Cir. 1987), rejecting a contractor's claim on a VECP that affected adjacent work on a construction project; *Commonwealth Elec. Co.*, EBCA 108-12-79, 84-1 BCA ¶16,961, holding that a VECP correcting government information was not compensable because it did not affect contract work; and *Electra-Mech. of Am.*, GSBCA 6201, 83-2 BCA ¶16,806, holding that a VECP suggesting the use of different categories of government workers using the equipment was not within the scope of the contract. See also *Robin Indus., Inc. v. United States*, 29 Fed. Cl. 122 (1993), holding that a request for a deviation from the specifications was not a proper VECP because it did not result in the costs of performance being less than the contract price.

Other cases are more liberal in ruling that VECPs affect work within the scope of the contract. Thus, in *ICSD Corp.*, ASBCA 28028, 90-3 BCA ¶23,027, *aff'd*, 934 F.2d 313 (Fed. Cir. 1991), the board found that a VECP suggesting the use of a different type of battery to power the equipment being manufactured under the contract was within the scope of the contract even though the contractor was not responsible for furnishing the battery. Similarly, in *McDonnell Douglas Corp.*, ASBCA 14314, 71-1 BCA ¶8859, the board ruled that a VECP reducing the cost of maintenance work on a part of a building not covered by the maintenance contract was within the scope. The board reasoned that the maintenance could have been added to the contract by change order and hence was subject to the Value Engineering clause. See also *Sentara Health Sys.*, ASBCA 51540, 00-2 BCA ¶31,122, *recons. denied*, 01-1 BCA ¶28,767, finding valid a VECP that affected work that was not required by the contract but was later added to the contract by change order.

VECPs need not be related to major aspects of the work. They can be changes to minor contract items and corrections of errors in specifications. See *Cardan Co.*, ASBCA 25765, 82-1 BCA ¶15,628, where, under a contract for the construction of a rocket motor facility, the contractor corrected an error in the specified quantity of grass seed required for the grounds. The board stated at 77,199:

> While it may be true that it was contemplated by the Government that the greatest savings would result from proposals relating to complicated engineering problems, we know of nothing . . . which states that proposals must relate to such problems. As a matter of fact, the imposition of such a requirement would run counter to the entire value engineering incentive program.
>
> * * *
>
> [It] doesn't make any difference how the contractor discovers the problem. The entire concept is to save the Government money in its procurement activities. If a contractor through a "routine estimating exercise" achieves that goal it should not be denied participation in the savings just because it did not engage in some difficult engineering analysis.
>
> Likewise, we do not see any prohibition against paying a contractor if its suggestion results in the correction of an error as opposed to suggesting a new engineering concept.

3. Origination of the Proposed Change

To obtain compensation for a VECP, the contractor must demonstrate that it originated the change. This is so even though the current Value Engineering clauses merely require that contractors "develop, prepare, and submit" a VECP. Thus, if the government can demonstrate that its employees actually originated the change before receipt of the VECP, the contractor will obtain no compensation. See *Metric Constructors, Inc.*, NASABCA 76-0692, 93-2 BCA ¶25,780, *aff'd*, 14 F.3d 613 (Fed. Cir. 1993), where the government was processing the change internally at the time the VECP was submitted, and *Tennier Indus., Inc.*, ASBCA 29464, 86-3 BCA ¶19,046, where the government proved that its laboratory had completed work on the change before receipt of the VECP. In *Traylor Bros., Inc.*, ENGBCA 5305, 89-2 BCA ¶21,679, the contractor discussed a prospective change with the government but was told not to submit a VECP because the change was being processed. The board held that the contractor did not originate the idea because it was being processed within the agency. See also *Holloway Constr. Co.*, ENGBCA 3859, 79-1 BCA ¶13,551, where the government conceived an additional cost-savings measure based on a contractor's VECP. The contracting officer adopted the contractor's suggestion, giving the contractor a 50 percent share of the savings, and subsequently issued a separate change order covering the additional savings. The board ruled that the government was entitled to all of the savings on the second change because it was not a part of the contractor's original VECP.

The clauses require VECPs to contain detailed information on the saving technique proposed and the impact of its use. The lack of such information in a suggested method to improve performance has been held to indicate that no VECP was proposed, *C.A. Rasmussen, Inc. v. United States*, 52 Fed. Cl. 345 (2002); *J.S. Alberici Constr. Co. & Martin K. Eby Constr. Co. (A Joint Venture)*, ENGBCA 6178, 98-2 BCA ¶29,875.

Earlier clauses applied only to proposals "initiated and developed" by the contractor, yet the government's arguments that proposals were not "initiated" were almost uniformly rejected by the Court of Claims and the appeals boards, *B.F. Goodrich Co. v. United States*, 185 Ct. Cl. 14, 398 F.2d 843 (1968); *Airmotive Eng'g Corp.*, ASBCA 17139, 74-1 BCA ¶10,517, *recons. denied*, 74-2 BCA ¶10,696; *Xerox Corp.*, ASBCA 16374, 73-1 BCA ¶9784, *recons. denied*, 73-1 BCA ¶9881; *North Am. Rockwell Corp.*, ASBCA 14485, 71-1 BCA ¶8773; *Covington Indus., Inc.*, ASBCA 12426, 68-2 BCA ¶7286. In *Syro Steel Co.*, ASBCA 12530, 69-2 BCA ¶8046, the board explained that it "would serve neither justice nor the policy intended by the clause" to allow the Government to "escape sharing the resultant savings on the basis that it thought of the idea first, although not enough to use it until induced to do so by contractor action."

4. Origination by Two Contractors

Although the Value Engineering clauses used for supply and service contracts require that a contractor be given the specified share of savings on concurrent and future contracts with other contractors, the Federal Circuit has ruled that such savings must be shared when the VECP is submitted by two contractors working on concurrent contracts for the same item, *NI Indus., Inc. v. United States*, 841 F.2d 1104 (Fed. Cir. 1988). In subsequent litigation on the case, the Armed Services Board refused to give instructions on the precise method of sharing that should be used, *Chamberlain Mfg. Corp.*, ASBCA 33203, 88-2 BCA ¶20,724. However, in a later case, *Gulf Apparel Corp.*, ASBCA 27784, 89-2 BCA ¶21,735, the board held that the contractor that submitted the first VECP should be given "priority." Then in *ICSD Corp.*, ASBCA 28028, 90-3 BCA ¶23,027, *aff'd*, 934 F.2d 313 (Fed. Cir. 1991), the board agreed with the contracting officer's decision to give the first submitter 75 percent of the savings and the second submitter 25 percent on the grounds that one part of the second submitter's VECP was superior to that of the first proposer. These cases do not contain clear guidance on how the government should deal with VECPs that are submitted by two parallel contractors, but they do indicate that the government should not comply with the literal provisions of the clause in these circumstances. Compare *M. Bianchi of Cal.*, ASBCA 37029, 96-2 BCA ¶28,410, *recons. denied*, 97-1 BCA ¶28,767, and 01-1 BCA ¶31,237, *aff'd*, 26 Fed. Appx. 978 (Fed. Cir. 2002), in which the board awarded the contractor a 50 percent share of savings after another contractor had been awarded a 50 percent share on the same VECP.

5. Finality of Contracting Officer Decisions

The current Value Engineering clauses, which became effective on February 25, 2000 (see Federal Acquisition Circular 97-15, 64 Fed. Reg. 72414) provide that the decision to accept or reject a VECP "is a unilateral decision made solely at the discretion of the Contracting Officer." The prior clauses provided that "the Contracting Officer's decision to accept or reject all or part of any VECP and the decision as to which of the sharing rates applies shall be final and not subject to the Disputes clause or otherwise subject to litigation under the Contract Disputes Act." This language was given binding effect in *NI Indus., Inc. v. United States*, 841 F.2d 1104 (Fed. Cir. 1988), but similar language in an Award Fee clause was held to be void to divest the courts of jurisdiction because of the broad language in the Contract Disputes Act, *Burnside-Ott Aviation Training Ctr. v. Dalton*, 107 F.3d 854 (Fed. Cir. 1997). In *RCS Enters., Inc. v. United States*, 46 Fed. Cl. 509 (2000), the court refused to take jurisdiction of a decision to reject a VECP, holding that *Burnside-Ott* did not overrule *NI Industries*. Under the current clauses, this will no longer be an issue, and boards or courts will be able to review such decisions to determine whether rejection of a VECP by a contracting officer is arbitrary or capricious.

Substantially similar language in previous clauses has been held not to bar the board's jurisdiction over cases where government "constructive acceptance" of a proposal is alleged, *North Am. Rockwell Corp.*, ASBCA 14485, 71-1 BCA ¶8773. If the government rejected a proposal and did not use the contractor's idea, this decision was not appealable to a board, *Charles Beseler Co.*, ASBCA 22669, 78-2 BCA ¶13,483. In *McClain Int'l, Inc.*, ASBCA 23132, 80-1 BCA ¶14,365, the board found that no constructive acceptance of a contractor's VECP had occurred where the proposal was rejected on the merits and the government subsequently accepted a competitor's VECP making the same suggestion. The board found that the competitor had independently conceived the idea and the government had adopted the process as a result of that proposal rather than the first contractor's proposal.

Contractors have been unsuccessful in using VECPs as a means of curing defective specifications because, in such cases, the contracting officer can merely reject the proposal, *Dewey Elecs. Corp.*, ASBCA 33869, 91-1 BCA ¶23,443, *recons. denied*, 91-1 BCA ¶23,656; *DK's Precision Mach. & Mfg.*, ASBCA 39616, 90-2 BCA ¶22,830. See also *Rowe Indus., Inc.*, ASBCA 31875, 89-3 BCA ¶22,155, *aff'd*, 918 F.2d 186 (Fed. Cir. 1990), *cert denied*, 500 U.S. 952 (1991), in which the board held that the contractor could not avoid a default termination because it had delayed the work while awaiting a response to a VECP suggesting the correction of defective specifications. The board held that the contractor should have proceeded with the work pending action on the VECP.

Prior Value Engineering clauses stated that "the Contracting Officer shall be the sole determiner of the amount of collateral savings, and that amount shall not be subject to the Disputes clause or otherwise subject to litigation under 41 U.S.C. §§ 601-13 [Contract Disputes Act]." In *ICSD Corp.*, ASBCA 28028, 90-3 BCA ¶23,027, *aff'd* 934 F.2d 313 (Fed. Cir. 1991), the board held that this language did not preclude it from reviewing such a determination to find if it was arbitrary or capricious. See also *Whittaker Corp.*, ASBCA 18422, 81-1 BCA ¶15,055, in which a substantially similar provision was held to have no effect with respect to a particular VECP because the contracting officer had written a "right to appeal the Government's decision on collateral savings" into one of the modifications awarding royalty payments for the VECP. See also *Banner Fabricators, Inc.*, ASBCA 25088, 81-2 BCA ¶15,215, in which the board deferred to the contracting officer's decision on the amount of collateral savings generated by a VECP, but recalculated the contractor's share of those savings because the government had incorrectly calculated the share as zero. Under the current clauses boards or courts will be able to review determinations of the amount of collateral savings under an arbitrary or capricious standard.

6. Identification of Proposals Not Required

The current Value Engineering clauses do not require the identification of a VECP as a prerequisite to entitlement to an award. Prior to 1974, the clause did specifically require such identification, but failure to properly identify proposals was consistently held not to bar recovery, *B.F. Goodrich Co. v. United States*, 185 Ct. Cl. 14, 398 F.2d 843 (1968); *Covington Indus., Inc.*, ASBCA 12426, 68-2 BCA ¶7286 (equitable estoppel); *McDonnell Douglas Astronautics Co.*, ASBCA 19971, 76-2 BCA ¶12,117 (government not misled and board and court refused to undermine the enlightened objectives of value engineering by technicalities over the form of the value engineering submission).

If both parties change the contract without recognizing any VECP, they will not be permitted to later claim that a value engineering suggestion has been adopted. See *M.C. & D. Capital Corp.*, ASBCA 38181, 91-1 BCA ¶23,563, *aff'd*, 948 F.2d 1251 (Fed. Cir. 1991), where the parties discussed a value engineering idea but the contractor subsequently signed a contract modification containing a price adjustment deducting the full amount of the savings. The board held that the parties were bound by the modification. See also *Erickson Air Crane Co.*, EBCA 50-6-79, 83-1 BCA ¶16,145, *aff'd*, 731 F.2d 810 (Fed. Cir. 1984), in which the board denied a value engineering claim because the parties treated a modification of concrete footings as a normal change and neither party considered it to be value engineering until six months after the government accepted the change in writing. Although the Value Engineering clause in the contract did not require specific identification of a proposal as value engineering, the board focused on the lack of notice to the government and on the fact that the contractor did not originally intend to pursue a value engineering claim. In *U.S. Eng'g Co.*, ASBCA 28835, 83-2 BCA ¶16,902, *recons. denied*, 84-2 BCA ¶17,305, the government was foreclosed from claiming a credit under the Value Engineering clause where it had authorized a specification deviation without reference to that clause. See also *Fire Sec. Sys., Inc.*, ASBCA 53498, 02-1 BCA ¶31,806, *recons. denied*, 02-2 BCA ¶31,939, holding that the government was entitled to an equitable adjustment for all of the savings suggested by the contractor. Apparently, the contractor did not know it could treat its proposal as a VECP.

7. Acceptance of Proposals

A VECP is accepted when the contracting officer issues a contract modification incorporating the VECP, FAR 48.103(b). It is the order incorporating the VECP that controls when acceptance takes place, not the pricing of the VECP, which may take place much later, *Raytheon Co.*, ASBCA 22711, 82-1 BCA ¶15,663, *aff'd*, 2 Cl. Ct. 763 (1983), *aff'd*, 730 F.2d 1470 (Fed. Cir. 1984). If the government accepts the proposal contingent on test results, it will be bound by its acceptance if the test results prove that the VECP is successful, *Arden Eng'g Co.*, ASBCA 24829, 83-2 BCA ¶16,603.

The Value Engineering clauses permit acceptance of proposals either before or within a reasonable time after performance has been completed on the contract. In *Delco Indus. Textile Corp.*, ASBCA 21379, 78-1 BCA ¶12,912, the board permitted acceptance of a VECP 19 months after contract completion at a time when no compensation was due the contractor under the sharing provisions of the clause. The board rejected the contractor's arguments that it was entitled to compensation for this long delay in acceptance and that it was entitled to separate compensation for the costs of developing the VECP in these circumstances. The board commented that the protection against the late acceptance given the contractor by the Value Engineering clause is the right to withdraw the VECP if it is not accepted within a time specified in the proposal. In *Delco*, the contractor did not take advantage of this right, which has been preserved in all the FAR Value Engineering clauses for supply and service contracts and construction contracts. In *Tranco Indus., Inc.*, ASBCA 22379, 78-2 BCA ¶13,307, *recons. denied*, 78-2 BCA ¶13,522, the contractor orally withdrew a VECP and the government later issued a change using the ideas embodied in the proposal. The board held that this was permissible but that the government assumed the risk that the new performance method was practicable. In *Baltimore Contractors, Inc.*, ASBCA 17049, 74-1 BCA ¶10,442, the board commented that the contractor could have declined to proceed with the government's partial adoption of a VECP since it was not a full acceptance. This view seems questionable since the clauses provide for partial acceptance of proposals.

In an effort to assure contractors that the government will not delay in accepting value engineering proposals, the regulations provide that acceptance be made within 45 days of submission or that the contractor be notified of the estimated decision date and given the reasons for the delay, FAR 48.103(b). In *O.R. Ramstad*, ENGBCA 3722, 80-1 BCA ¶14,234, the board denied compensation for delay costs incurred while awaiting government action on a VECP for two months. The board noted that the clause provides that the government will not be liable for such delays and that the contractor remains liable for performance as originally specified until a VECP is adopted.

If the government rejects a VECP but subsequently uses the idea, it will be found to have "constructively accepted" the proposal. See *North Am. Rockwell Corp.*, ASBCA 14485, 71-1 BCA ¶8773, in which the contracting officer's decision that there was no acceptance of a VECP was reversed when it was found that the contract had been changed to include a requirement for the performance of a test "virtually identical" to that previously submitted as a VECP by the contractor. Similarly, in *Gulf Apparel Corp.*, ASBCA 27784, 89-2 BCA ¶21,735, the board found constructive acceptance when the contracting officer rejected a part of a contractor's VECP but later accepted the same idea from another contractor. Accord, *Thompson Aircraft Tire Corp.*, ASBCA 14432, 71-2 BCA ¶8981; *American Standard, Inc.*, DOTCAB 71-1, 72-1 BCA ¶9433; *McDonnell Douglas Astronautics Co.*, ASBCA 19971, 76-2 BCA ¶12,117.

In *John J. Kirlin Inc. v. United States*, 827 F.2d 1538 (Fed. Cir. 1987), the Federal Circuit ruled that no constructive acceptance could be found after the final completion of the contract. The court reached this conclusion on the questionable reasoning that the Value Engineering clause expired when the contract was closed out. This rule has been followed in *Amplitronics, Inc.*, ASBCA 44119, 94-1 BCA ¶26,520, and *M. Bianchi of Cal.*, ASBCA 37029, 93-1 BCA ¶25,309, *aff'd but vacated on other grounds*, 31 F.3d 1163 (Fed. Cir. 1994). This rule can be avoided by keeping the contract open by not submitting an invoice for the final work on the contract, *M. Bianchi of Cal.*, ASBCA 37029, 96-2 BCA ¶28,410, *recons. denied*, 97-1 BCA ¶23,7678. In *Vantage Assocs., Inc.*, ASBCA 51418, 00-2 BCA ¶31,141, the board rejected the contractor's argument that the contract was still open when a VECP was submitted four years after contract completion and only $5 for one spare part remained unbilled on the contract. The ruling was reversed in *Vantage Assocs., Inc. v. Secretary of the Navy*, 25 Fed. Appx. 859 (Fed. Cir. 2001).

8. Finality of Contract Modification

Price adjustments for VECPs are frequently based on estimated savings rather than actual costs. Nonetheless, once the adjustment has been finalized by the signing of a contract modification, neither party can claim a further adjustment to the price if the estimate is incorrect. See *Airmotive Eng'g. Corp.*, ASBCA 15235, 71-2 BCA ¶8988, rejecting the government's claim that the contracting officer that had negotiated the adjustment had participated in a mutual mistake. Contractors have also been denied repricing of the adjustment when the costs of performing the VECP were higher than estimated, *Guy F. Atkinson Const. Co.*, ENGBCA 6145, 98-1 BCA ¶29,582. In that case, the contractor was denied the costs of reinforcing a tunnel liner to ensure that it met the safety requirement called for by the VECP. The same result was reached in *G&P Constr. Co.*, ASBCA 49524, 98-1 BCA ¶29,457, and *H&S Corp.*, ASBCA 29156, 87-2 BCA ¶19,764. Similarly, the savings should not include price escalation on the work deleted from the contract by the VECP, *Dillon Constr., Inc.*, ENGBCA PCC-197, 99-2 BCA ¶30,576. If it is apparent that there will be no instant contract savings before the parties agree to a contract modification adopting the VECP, the contractor will be entitled to be paid the contract price for the work plus any collateral savings, *Johnny F. Smith Truck & Dragline Serv., Inc.*, ENGBCA 6261, 98-2 BCA ¶30,006, *aff'd*, 232 F.3d 915 (Fed. Cir. 2000).

C. Government Use of Data

The Value Engineering clauses for supply and service contracts and construction contracts provide that all data submitted by the contractor may be marked with a restrictive legend precluding the government from disclosing the information outside the government or using it for any purpose other than evaluation. Prior to 1977, the clause also provided that once the VECP was adopted the government was granted full rights to use, disclose, and duplicate the data in any manner and for any purpose whatsoever. Thus, by acceptance of a VECP the government acquired sweeping rights to the data contained in the proposal. See Comp. Gen. Dec. B-167932, Jan. 15, 1970, *Unpub.* The contractor's only protection against such loss of rights was withdrawal of the proposal before acceptance, in accordance with the provisions of the clause. In 1977, the regulations and clauses were modified to permit the contractor to submit technical data subject to continuing limited rights in the government to the extent that it could properly have been submitted as "limited rights technical data" in accordance with the clause of DAR 7-104.9(a). The current clauses state:

> If a VECP is accepted, the Contractor hereby grants the Government unlimited rights in the VECP and supporting data, except that, with respect to data qualifying and submitted as limited rights technical data, the Government shall have the rights specified in the contract modification implementing the VECP and shall appropriately mark the data.

It is not clear whether this provision permits a contracting officer to take unlimited rights in data by so stating in the contract modification, and the FAR contains no guidance on this issue.

D. Unsolicited Value Engineering Proposals

Under the current regulations there is no provision for accepting unsolicited value engineering proposals submitted without a contract containing a Value Engineering clause. The Court of Claims has held that, when a value engineering proposal is submitted without such a contract clause, there is no statutory authority to purchase "suggestions," *Grismac Corp. v. United States*, 214 Ct. Cl. 39, 556 F.2d 494 (1977). In this questionable decision, the court construed 10 U.S.C. § 2386, authorizing acquisition of "designs, processes, and manufacturing data," to be the only authority for acquisition of cost-saving proposals and held that Grismac's mere suggestion to use cheaper wood to make smaller pallets for stacking ammunition crates did not fall within the scope of this statute. In contrast to this reasoning, it would appear that every procuring agency has the authority to take necessary steps to reduce its costs.

The government can adopt regulations allowing the purchase of an unsolicited value engineering proposal that does not rise to the definition in 10 U.S.C. § 2386, *Alan Scott Indus.*, ASBCA 24729, 82-1 BCA ¶15,494. There the board held that the contractor was entitled to compensation for its idea, to heat-treat dental instruments in continuous belt furnaces instead of in batch furnaces, on the basis of a provision in ASPR 1-1708 from July 1974 to August 1977, which encouraged the submission of unsolicited value engineering proposals without a contract. The board reasoned that there was sufficient authority in ASPR 1-1708 to purchase the contractor's idea even it if did not rise to the definition of procurable items in 10 U.S.C. § 2386 since ASPR 1-1708 was based on the "statutory underpinning for the value engineering program long established for Department of Defense procurements." The GAO reached the opposite conclusion in *A Better Way, Inc.*, 58 Comp. Gen. 35 (B-191130), 78-2 CPD ¶298.

IV. CONSTRUCTIVE CHANGES

One of the major uses of the Changes clause has been to serve as the basis for administrative resolution of claims for price adjustment when the work performed during the course of a government contract is different from that called for. This section briefly discusses the basic theory underlying this use of the clause and reviews the different types of constructive changes that have been identified in the hundreds of litigated cases in this area. It concludes with a discussion of the procedures that should be used when constructive changes are encountered.

A. Basic Theory

A constructive change occurs when the contract work is actually changed but the procedures of the Changes clause have not been followed. In such cases, when the early appeals boards perceived that such changed work was informally ordered by the government or caused by government fault, they found that a change had "constructively" occurred. Similarly, if the different work reduced the contractor's costs, the boards held that the government could assert a claim for a constructive change. Under common law contractual analysis, such fact patterns would more likely be placed under theories of implied contract or breach of contract, but the administrative procedures developed for the resolution of disputes in federal contracts prior to the Contract Disputes Act of 1978 prevented the boards of contract appeals from using these theories. Hence, boards developed the alternate theory of constructive changes.

1. Continuing Vitality of the Doctrine

Although appeals boards can now resolve cases under breach of contract theory and thus use common law reasoning in disputes arising under the Contract Disputes Act, they have continued to deal with the type of conduct described in this section under the Changes clause in order to grant relief in the form of an equitable adjustment rather than in the form of contract damages. See *Johnson & Son Erectors*, ASBCA 24564, 81-1 BCA ¶15,082, *aff'd*, 231 Ct. Cl. 753, *cert. denied*, 459 U.S. 971 (1982), in which the board refused to permit a contractor to use breach of contract logic where the facts indicated that a constructive change had occurred. The board stated at 74,599:

> [A]ssuming that the evidence adduced is sufficient to establish entitlement we would find entitlement under the contract and not outside of it. It has long been the policy of this Board to seek a remedy under the contract. The constructive change doctrine is, perhaps, the foremost example of our commitment to providing relief under the contract whenever it is possible to do so.

See *Hardrives, Inc.*, IBCA 2319, 94-1 BCA ¶26,267, reanalyzing this issue and concluding that there are still valid reasons for treating most contract breaches as constructive changes. This reasoning permits the appeals boards to take advantage of the considerable amount of precedent covering the computation of equitable adjustments. The expansive definition of changes exemplified by the constructive changes doctrine is also likely to remain in use by government agencies in order to provide freedom of program implementation through use of the Changes clause rather than through new procurement procedures. Further reasons for continued adherence to the constructive changes doctrine are that the contractor will be held to the notice requirements in the clause and will be required to proceed with work pending resolution of disputes redressable under the contract. Thus, the concept of constructive changes appears to have become a fixture in the field of government contract law.

2. Elements of the Doctrine

Although the scope of constructive changes has become very broad, one board described the elements of such changes as being simple in their nature. See *Industrial Research Assocs., Inc.*, DCAB WB-5, 68-1 BCA ¶7069, at 32,685-86:

> As we see it, the constructive change doctrine is made up of two elements—the "change" element and the "order" element. To find the change element we must examine the actual performance to see whether it went beyond the minimum standards demanded by the terms of the contract. But, this is not the end of the matter.
>
> The "order" element also is a necessary ingredient in the constructive change concept. To be compensable under the changes clause, the change must be one that the government ordered the contractor to make. The government's representative, by his words or his deeds, must require the contractor to perform work that is not a necessary part of his contract. This differs from advice, comments, suggestions, or opinions ,which government engineering or technical personnel frequently offer to a contractor's employees.

Using this analysis, any government action or communication could be characterized as a constructive change order if it was found to have forced or induced the contractor to undertake extra work. However, the *Industrial Research* analysis is too narrow, since it is clear that government fault, either prior to or during contract performance, may meet the "order" requirement. Hence, it is more correct to state that a constructive change requires work beyond the contract requirements plus either an "order" or "fault" on the part of the government.

As the doctrine of constructive changes became established in case law, the government began to revise its contract language to reflect these new principles. The first instance of this was in the revised Changes clause for construction contracts contained in Standard Form 23-A, which became effective in 1968. This clause is now found in FAR 52.243-4. Its pertinent paragraphs state:

> (b) Any other written order or an oral order (which, as used in this paragraph (b), includes direction, instruction, interpretation, or determination) from the Contracting Officer that causes a change shall be treated as a change order under this clause; provided, that the Contractor gives the Contracting Officer written notice stating (1) the date, circumstances, and source of the order and (2) that the Contractor regards the order as a change order.
>
> (c) Except as provided in this clause, no order, statement, or conduct of the Contracting Officer shall be treated as a change under this clause or entitle the Contractor to an equitable adjustment.

Note that these paragraphs set forth a somewhat limited definition of constructive changes—particularly with regard to action or inaction of the government. Apparently, this was an attempt to narrow the scope of the doctrine. The clause also requires in ¶(b) that notice be given of all constructive changes, and in ¶(d) provides a penalty for failure to give notice of certain constructive changes. A detailed analysis of the intent of the drafters of the clause is found in Hiestand, *A New Era in Government Construction Contracts,* 28 Fed. B.J. 165 (1968).

Although the supply and services contract clauses do not contain similar language dealing with constructive changes, the doctrine is applied to such contracts. Constructive changes are recognized in the Notification of Changes clause set forth in FAR 52.243-7 primarily for use in supply and research and development contracts for the acquisition of weapons systems and subsystems. It contains a broader definition of constructive changes than that in the construction clause and does not provide a penalty for failure to give notice. The key language of this clause defining constructive changes states:

> Except for changes identified as such in writing and signed by the Contracting Officer, the Contractor shall notify the Administrative Contracting Officer in writing promptly, within . . . (to be negotiated) calendar days from the date that the Contractor identifies any Government conduct (including actions, inactions, and written or oral communications) that the Contractor regards as a change to the contract terms and conditions.

3. Government Claims for Price Decreases

The constructive changes doctrine can be used by the government to obtain deductive equitable adjustments in the contract price. Although such cases are a small minority of the constructive change cases, the principle was clearly established in *Varo, Inc.*, ASBCA 16087, 73-2 BCA ¶10,206, *rev'd on other grounds*, 212 Ct. Cl. 432, 548 F.2d 953 (1977). In that case the board stated at 48,144:

> Constructive changes are not a one-way street. While parties involved in a constructive change are usually in the posture where a contractor is claiming increased costs, the Board sees no reason why the government cannot also claim a decrease in the contract price where a contractor is permitted to save costs through the authorized or unauthorized actions of its officers and employees.

Accord, *M & H Constr. Co.*, ASBCA 21528, 79-1 BCA ¶13,688. The apparent reasoning is that, since the government has the right to reject nonconforming work, it also has the right to issue an after-the-fact change order reducing the contract price to reflect the cost difference between the item specified and the item delivered. See *Farwell Co. v. United States*, 137 Ct. Cl. 832, 148 F. Supp. 947 (1957) (court upheld contracting officer's change order reducing price after contractor used copper tube instead of specified copper pipe); *Porshia Alexander of Am.*, GSBCA 9604, 91-1 BCA ¶23,657 (board affirmed contracting officer's deduction from final payment to compensate government for work not performed at direction of government inspector); *Plaza Maya Ltd. P'ship*, GSBCA 9086, 91-1 BCA ¶23,425 (government credit for not complying with local building code, even though no amount had been included in price for compliance); *Arnold M. Diamond, Inc.*, ASBCA 38974, 92-2 BCA ¶24,869 (credit for fewer expansion joints than called for by specifications, even though contractor had design responsibility); *Santa Fe Eng'rs, Inc.*, ASBCA 44906, 93-1 BCA ¶25,298, *aff'd*, 19 F.3d 39 (Fed. Cir. 1994) (government credit for use of less expensive doors); *Marine Constr. & Dredging, Inc.*, ASBCA 38412, 95-1 BCA ¶27,286, *recons. denied*, 95-2 BCA ¶27,699 (credit for failure to perform required testing); *Environmental Data Consultants, Inc. v. General Servs. Admin.*, GSBCA 13244, 96-2 BCA ¶28,614 (credit for contractor-suggested redesign of excavation); *Fire Sec. Sys., Inc. v. General Servs. Admin.*, GSBCA 12120, 97-1 BCA ¶28,994 (credit for deleted work); *Jimenez, Inc.*, VABCA 6351, 02-2 BCA ¶32,019 (work not completed at end of contract); and *Taylor Constr. Co. v. General Servs. Admin.*, GSBCA 15421, 03-2 BCA ¶32,320 (credit for deleted work). Compare *Dawson Constr. Co.*, GSBCA 5672, 81-2 BCA ¶15,387, *recons. denied*, 82-2 BCA ¶15,914 (deduction denied since lower cost material was reflected in the bid price and deduction would have given government a windfall). If the government acts as a volunteer in curing a problem encountered by the contractor, there will be no recovery. See *Nationwide Postal Mgmt.*, PSBCA 3988, 98-1 BCA ¶29,364, denying recovery when the Postal Service paid a company to repair the air conditioning in a leased building when the owner of the building was asserting the right to have the work done without payment.

This theory has also been used when the government lost its right to correct defective work under the Inspection clause of the contract because it had not given the contractor the opportunity to correct it, as required by the clause. In that situation, when the government proceeded to correct the defects, the board concluded that the government had reduced the work of the contractor and was entitled to an equitable adjustment measured by the amount of the contractor's cost savings, *Techni Data Labs.*, ASBCA 21054, 77-2 BCA ¶12,667. The same theory was applied in *Worldwide Parts, Inc.*, ASBCA 38896, 91-2 BCA ¶23,717, but the price reduction was computed on the cost of correcting the work rather than the costs saved. Compare *Lionsgate Corp.*, ENGBCA 5809, 92-2 BCA ¶24,983, in which the government was denied relief in this situation—apparently because it asserted its claims under the Default and Inspection clauses, not the Changes clause.

B. Types of Constructive Changes

Constructive changes can be divided into four categories that represent the major uses of the constructive changes doctrine in administratively resolving claims against the government. In general, the substantive merits of these claims (the "change" element) are determined by the same rules that have been developed by the courts in dealing with contract interpretation disputes and breach of contract actions against the government, discussed in prior chapters. Thus, this section focuses on the different types of government actions that have been held to constitute orders or fault under the Changes clause (the "order/fault" element). However, with regard to acceleration claims, the change element is also covered because there has been no independent development of legal rules outside the constructive changes case law. The four categories of constructive changes follow:

Category	Change Element	Order/Fault Element
1. Disagreements between the parties over the contract requirements	Determined by application of rules of contract interpretation in Chapter 2	Part 1, below
2. Defective specifications and government nondisclosure of information	Determined in accordance with implied duties in Chapter 3	Part 2, below
3. Acceleration	Part 3, below	Part 3, below
4. Failure of the government to cooperate during performance	Determined in accordance with implied duties in Chapter 3	Part 4, below

Although categories 1 and 2 both relate to the specifications in the contract, they are very different in nature. In claims involving the interpretation of the specifications, the change results from a disagreement between the parties over the method of performance permitted by the contract (with the contractor arguing for a less expensive method), but there is no disagreement over the technical feasibility of either method. In contrast, in the defective specification and nondisclosure claims, the contractor has usually attempted to perform the work in accordance with the government's requirements but has encountered undue difficulties or has failed. Here there is no disagreement over the interpretation of the specifications—merely a claim that they did not lead to satisfactory results.

1. Disagreements Over Contract Requirements

The earliest type of constructive change found by the appeals boards involved a situation in which a contractor and the government disagreed on the work required to meet the contract specifications. Typically, the contractor proposes to perform the contract in a certain manner, and the contracting officer asserts that a more expensive method of performance is called for. Often, the ultimate result of this type of controversy is insistence by the government that the contractor perform in accordance with the government's interpretation of the contract requirements. As discussed in Chapter 10, the contractor is required to proceed with performance in accordance with directions of the contracting officer or suffer the risk of default termination, and hence it will normally utilize the method of performance that is required by the government. Only later, when the board of contract appeals or court rules on the issue of contract interpretation, will the parties know whether the contractor has been required to do work not called for by the contract.

The basic rule covering this type of constructive change is summarized in *Emerson-Sack-Warner Corp.*, ASBCA 6004, 61-2 BCA ¶3248, at 16,827:

> Where as a result of the Government's misinterpretation of contract provisions a contractor is required to perform more or different work, or to higher standards, not called for under its terms, the contractor is entitled to equitable adjustments pursuant to the Changes Article, including extensions of time. *Inca Metal Products Corp.*, ASBCA Nos. 4239, 4243, 58-1 BCA ¶1719; *James A. Dunbar d.b.a. Dunbar Roofing Co.*, ASBCA No. 3559, 57-2 BCA ¶1487; *White Star Heating & Supply, Inc.*, ASBCA No. 2815; *Taag Designs, Inc.*, ASBCA No. 2371; *Fansteel Metallurgical Corp.*, ASBCA No. 1689, and cases collected.

The rule was recognized by the Court of Claims in *W.H. Edwards Eng'g Corp. v. United States*, 161 Ct. Cl. 322 (1963). Two categories of constructive changes have occurred in these interpretation disputes: (1) those that fall clearly within the bounds of the Changes clause of the contract, and (2) those that could not normally be ordered under that clause.

a. *Work That Could Have Been Ordered as a Change*

Most instances of extra work required by contract interpretation involve work that clearly could have been ordered by the issuance of a change order. Such work is "within the general scope of the contract" and is within the limiting words of the Changes clause, as discussed earlier in this chapter. The government occasionally argues that, because there was no change order, the contractor has voluntarily performed the additional work. However, the usual understanding is that contractors do not, as a general rule, voluntarily perform work not called for by the contract, *Chris Berg, Inc. v. United States*, 197 Ct. Cl. 503, 455 F.2d 1037 (1972); *M.S.I. Corp.*, GSBCA 2428, 68-2 BCA ¶7262; *Brown Constr. Co.*, ASBCA 22648, 79-1 BCA ¶13,745; *Sigma Constr. Co.*, ASBCA 37040, 91-2 BCA ¶23,926; *North Star Alaska Hous. Corp. v. United*

States, 30 Fed. Cl. 259 (1993); *Integrated Clinical Sys., Inc.*, VABCA 3745, 95-2 BCA ¶27,902; *Edsall Constr. Co.*, ASBCA 51787, 01-2 BCA ¶31,425, *aff'd*, 296 F.3d 1081 (Fed. Cir. 2002). Evidence of such voluntary effort has been required to be clear and convincing, *Driftwood of Ala.*, GSBCA 5429, 81-2 BCA ¶15,169, and the government has the burden of proving such voluntary effort, *Carl J. Bonidie, Inc.*, ASBCA 25769, 82-2 BCA ¶15,818. Compare *Quiller Constr. Co.*, ASBCA 14964, 72-1 BCA ¶9322 (voluntary performance found upon the preponderance of the evidence), with *Service Eng'g. Co.*, ASBCA 42126, 96-2 BCA ¶28,376 (no proof of voluntary performance when key government employees failed to testify at trial). However, when there is no indication of government direction to perform extra work, voluntary performance will frequently be found. See *Basic Marine, Inc.*, ASBCA 53256, 02-1 BCA ¶31,677 (services provided on IDIQ contract with no order from government); *NavCom Def. Elec., Inc.*, ASBCA 50767, 01-2 BCA ¶31,546 (minor design changes to product after successful testing without government approval); *Inslaw, Inc. v. United States*, 40 Fed. Cl. 843 (1998) (delivery of enhanced version of software); *Nagy Enters.*, ASBCA 48815, 98-1 BCA ¶29,695 (change in construction method with no prior government approval); *S-TRON*, ASBCA 45893, 96-2 BCA ¶28,319 (contractor, with government permission, recalled product for rework exceeding specification requirement to ensure its safety); *Tempo, Inc.*, ASBCA 37589, 95-2 BCA ¶27,618 (rework voluntarily done to meet contractor's interpretation of specifications even though problem brought to contractor's attention by government personnel); *Knight Architects Eng'rs, Planners, Inc.*, PSBCA 3474, 94-3 BCA ¶27,178 (voluntary work in reviewing shop drawings in more detail than required by contract); *Jowett, Inc.*, ASBCA 47364, 94-3 BCA ¶27,110 (contractor voluntarily performed necessary survey work without telling government employees); *JEM Dev. Corp.*, ASBCA 42872, 92-1 BCA ¶24,709 (contractor voluntarily corrected problem with transformers on which work was to be done); and *Bay Decking Co.*, ASBCA 33868, 89-2 BCA ¶21,834 (contractor voluntarily performed desired work that was inadvertently omitted from specifications). In deciding whether a contractor has performed voluntarily or the government's actions have been sufficiently compelling to be a constructive change order, the courts and boards must balance the extent and directness of government pressure against the voluntary nature of the contractor's performance, taking the totality of circumstances into account.

The most common types of government action and inaction that have been held to be constructive change orders are discussed below.

(1) Direct Government Orders

The classic example of a constructive change occurs when the government directly orders the contractor to perform the work in a specified manner but simultaneously states that such order shall not be construed as a change order. For example, in *R.P. Farnsworth & Co.*, WDBCA 20, 1 CCF 32 (1943), an order to install benches, which the contract clearly did not require, was treated as a change order since the government "had the time, the opportunity, and the power" to issue a change order. Such orders are generally based on the mistaken belief that the work ordered was required by the specifications. See *Johnson Controls, Inc.*, ASBCA 26660, 82-2 BCA ¶15,909 (contractor required to do work not required by specifications); *Tecom, Inc.*, ASBCA 26022, 82-2 BCA ¶16,121, *recons. denied*, 83-1 BCA ¶16,372, *aff'd*, 732 F.2d 935 (Fed. Cir. 1984) (order to add off-base bus routes to a transportation contract not within the scope of other contract clauses permitting changes to routes); *Hudson Contracting, Inc.*, ASBCA 41023, 94-1 BCA ¶26,466 (order to cut trees one at a time when no contract provision so required); *Bay Ship & Yacht Co.*, DOTBCA 2913, 96-1 BCA ¶28,236 (order to remove asbestos not required by specifications); *Mertz Constr., Inc.*, AGBCA 94-165-1, 97-1 BCA ¶28,802, *recons. denied*, 97-2 BCA ¶29,016 (order to paint doors with high-gloss paint not required by specifications); *Agro-Lawn Sys., Inc.*, ASBCA 49648, 98-1 BCA ¶29,635 (order to limit work during burials an unreasonable interpretation of contract language); *J&J Oilfield & Elec. Serv.*, ASBCA 46044, 98-2 BCA ¶29,965 (order to use separate people to manage different contracts not required by clause calling for management personnel); *Steele & Sons, Inc.*, ASBCA 49077, 00-1 BCA ¶30,837 (order to size heating system to provide for future expansion); and *Hensel Phelps Constr. Co. v. General Servs. Admin.*, GSBCA 14744, 01-1 BCA ¶31,249, *aff'd*, 36 Fed. Appx. 649 (Fed. Cir. 2002) (order to provide vibration isolation to plumbing).

In some cases the "order" is the result of a change in the government's operations. See, for example, *T&M Distribs., Inc.*, ASBCA 51405, 00-1 BCA ¶30,677, in which a constructive change was found when the closing of a government supply depot greatly altered the mix of bulk shipments versus single shipments for a contractor supplying parts to the agency. Compare *Cleveland Telecommunications Corp. v. United States*, 39 Fed. Cl. 649 (1997), rejecting a claim for a constructive change based on the contractor's payment of premium wages during the 1995–1996 government shutdown. The court reasoned that the contractor bore the risk that an arbitrator would order the payment of such wages.

(2) Government Suggestions

Suggestions by government personnel that the contractor perform work in a specified manner either can be treated as "orders" or can be seen as mere communications during the performance of the contract. This determination is made by ascertaining whether the suggestion was "coercive" in nature, *Watson, Rice & Co.*, HUDBCA 89-4468-C6, 90-1 BCA ¶22,499; *OFEGRO*, HUDBCA 88-3410-C7, 91-3 BCA ¶24,206; *Donald R. Stewart & Assocs.*, AGBCA 84-226-1, 92-1 BCA ¶24,705; *Valley Asphalt, Inc.*, AGBCA 97-118-1, 97-2 BCA ¶29,275. See also *A.D. & G.D. Fox*, AGBCA 76-139-4, 80-2 BCA ¶14,788, stating that "mere discussion of methods" is not sufficient to constitute a constructive change order "where the contractor is not directed or compelled to use a method other than by choice." Similarly, both *SAE/Americon-Mid-Atl., Inc. v. General Servs. Admin.*, GSBCA 12295, 97-1 BCA ¶28,912, *aff'd*, 178 F.3d 1312 (Fed. Cir. 1998), and *Quality Plus Equip., Inc.*, ASBCA 46932, 96-2 BCA ¶28,595, cite *Industrial Research Assocs., Inc.*, DCAB WB-5, 68-1 BCA ¶7069, for the proposition that there is a significant difference between ordered changes and the "advice, comments, suggestions, or opinions from Government engineering or technical personnel frequently offered to a contractors' employees." Earlier cases seem to have followed similar reasoning. For example, in *Lorentz Bruun Co.*, GSBCA 1023, 1964 BCA ¶4357, where the government gave the contractor a drawing calling for extra work without directly requiring compliance, the board found that it was logical to attribute the contractor's performance of the extra work to a belief that a change was being directed rather than that the government was making a suggestion that the contractor was free to reject. Similarly, a constructive change was found where there was a request for additional hours in *Environment Consultants, Inc.*, IBCA 1192-5-78, 79-2 BCA ¶13,937, and *Urban Pathfinders, Inc.*, ASBCA 23134, 79-1 BCA ¶13,709. In *Space Servs. of Ga., Inc.*, ASBCA 25793, 81-2 BCA ¶15,250, the government was held to have ordered extra labor hours through the issuance of memoranda marked in red ink and discussion with the contractor in which the Chief of Services stated that the alleged understaffing "makes me sick" and that he expected the problem to be corrected immediately. See also *S & M Traylor Bros. (JV)*, ENGBCA 3878, 82-1 BCA ¶15,484, in which the board reasoned that, since the contractor was not permitted to continue tunneling without an approved plan for protecting surface structures and had been informally advised that the government had decided that a grouting program was the best solution, its submission and execution of such a program could not have been voluntary given the alternative of remaining idle indefinitely. In contrast, mere suggestions followed without protest have been held not to constitute constructive change orders, *McElroy Mach. & Mfg. Co.*, ASBCA 46477, 99-1 BCA ¶30,185; *Hudson Contracting, Inc.*, ASBCA 41023, 94-1 BCA ¶24,466; *Lott Constructors, Inc.*, ENGBCA 5852, 93-1 BCA ¶25,449; *Singer Co., Librascope Div. v. United States*, 215 Ct. Cl. 281, 568 F.2d 695 (1977); *Iversen Constr. Co.*, IBCA 981-1-73, 76-1 BCA ¶11,644, *recons. denied*, 76-1 BCA ¶11,844; *Barbour Boat Works*, CGBCA T-4, 68-1 BCA ¶6790, *recons. denied*, 68-1 BCA ¶7009; *Twombly Tree Experts, Inc.*, ASBCA 6456, 61-1 BCA ¶3001. In addition, suggestions specifically identified as such have been held insufficiently compelling to be constructive change orders, *Labarge, Inc.*, ASBCA 19845, 78-2 BCA ¶13,376.

(3) Government Interpretation of Specifications

Government interpretation of the specifications has been held to be a constructive change even though the contractor was not explicitly ordered to follow the interpretation. In *Mifflinburg Body Works, Inc.*, ASBCA 427, 4 CCF ¶60,999 (1950), the board stated at 51,559:

> [S]ince the contractor had been called upon to produce under a more costly method by virtue of the government's interpretation of the ambiguous specifications, . . . such interpretation by the government amounted in reality to a change in the contract for which an equitable adjustment should be made.

Similarly, in *Triangle Elec. Mfg. Co.*, ASBCA 15995, 74-2 BCA ¶10,783, a constructive change was found where a contractor asked the government for assistance in devising a method of performing the work and the government included work beyond the contract requirements in the guidance given. See also *U.S. Fed. Eng'g & Mfg., Inc.*, ASBCA 19909, 75-2 BCA ¶11,578, finding a constructive change where the government responded to the contractor's request for an interpretation of the specifications by calling for work in addition to the minimum necessary to meet the contract. Similarly, a change was found in *Raytheon Serv. Co.*, ASBCA 36139, 92-1 BCA ¶24,696, where the government offered to accept a more expensive alternate mode of performance after the specified mode had failed because the government had not been able to furnish the property called for by the contract. Of course, if pressure is brought on the contractor to follow the government's interpretation, there is little question that a constructive change will be found, *Al Johnson Constr. Co. v. United States*, 20 Cl. Ct. 184 (1990).

Such interpretations can be communicated to the contractor indirectly as well as directly. For example, in *Unidynamics/ St. Louis, Inc.*, ASBCA 17592, 73-2 BCA ¶10,360, the contractor told the government of its interpretation of the specifications, but the government permitted another contractor to perform the work in a way that precluded the contractor from following that interpretation. Finding the contractor's interpretation reasonable, the board held the government's action to be a constructive change. See also *Brown Constr. Co.*, ASBCA 22648, 79-1 BCA ¶13,745, in which a series of ambiguous communications from the government was held to communicate the government's interpretation requiring higher-priced material to the contractor.

Constructive changes may not be found in these interpretation situations if there is doubt whether the government employees knew that the contractor was asserting that a change had occurred. See *Green's Multi-Servs., Inc.*, EBCA C-9611207, 97-1 BCA ¶28,649, *recons. denied*, 97-1 BCA ¶28,811 (no proof of government direction to provide larger buses and no evidence that contractor questioned alleged order); *N & A Builders, Inc.*, VABCA 2610, 89-1 BCA ¶21,382 (no communication informing government that extra work being done was responsibility of government); and *Lloyd Moore Constr.*, AGBCA 87-151-3, 89-2 BCA ¶21,875 (no "persuasive" evidence of order and no notice that change had occurred). Similarly, in *Calfon Constr., Inc. v. United States*, 18 Cl. Ct. 426 (1989), *aff'd*, 923 F.2d 872 (Fed. Cir. 1990), the court found no constructive change where the parties had discussed two methods of performance and the contractor had adopted the more expensive method without making it clear to the government employees that this was considered a change.

Interpretations initially proffered by the contractor may not qualify as constructive changes under this theory. See, for example, *Rohr Indus., Inc.*, ENGBCA 4138, 83-1 BCA ¶16,509, in which the board concluded that government concurrence that certain work was required was not a constructive change because the contractor had decided earlier to include the work.

(4) Government Rejection of a Method Permitted by the Contract

Rejection of a method of performance selected or used by a contractor is clearly a constructive change if that method was permitted by the contract. For example, in *Grumman Aerospace Corp.*, ASBCA 50090, 01-1 BCA ¶31,316, *aff'd*, 34 Fed. Appx. 710 (Fed. Cir. 2002), a constructive change was found when the government imposed more stringent quality assurance procedures than had been used in the past 18 years. Similarly, in *J.B. Williams Co. v. United States*, 196 Ct. Cl. 491, 450 F.2d 1379 (1971), a constructive change was found where the government refused to approve a preproduction sample that performed as well as a government-furnished model, with the result that the contractor performed work beyond that required by the contract. In *Ocean Elec. Corp.*, NASABCA 371-8, 73-2 BCA ¶10,335, a constructive change resulted from the government's refusal to permit use of an item equal to a specified item where the contract contained an "or equal" clause. See also *Adventure Group, Inc.*, ASBCA 50188, 97-2 BCA ¶29,081, *recons. denied*, 98-1 BCA ¶29,362 (rejection of proposed model unit that met the specifications); *Max J. Kuney Co.*, DOTBCA 2759, 94-3 BCA ¶27,245 (prohibiting the use of local trade practice); *Abbott Prods., Inc.*, ASBCA 43054, 93-3 BCA ¶26,006 (rejection of first article); *ITT Gilfillan Div.*, ASBCA 37834, 92-1 BCA ¶24,490 (failure to conditionally accept work as required by contract); *CWC, Inc.*, ASBCA 28847, 84-2 BCA ¶17,282, *recons. denied*, 85-1 BCA ¶17,876 (rejection of alternate equipment permitted by specification); *Vi-Mil, Inc.*, ASBCA 25111, 82-2 BCA ¶15,840 (rejection of contractor's previously approved instruction plans); *Algernon Blair, Inc.*, ASBCA 23585, 81-2 BCA ¶15,375, *recons. denied*, 82-1 BCA ¶15,491 (rejection of contractor's previously approved construction plans); *John Murphy Constr. Co.*, AGBCA 418, 79-1 BCA ¶13,836 (prevention of planned sequence of performance); *John R. Hollingsworth Co.*, DOTCAB 69-15, 71-1 BCA ¶8760 (rejection of equipment); *Tecon-Green*, ENGBCA 2667, 67-1 BCA ¶6147, *aff'd*, 188 Ct. Cl. 15, 411 F.2d 1262 (1969) (rejection of method of performance); and *Gil-Brown Constructors, Inc.*, DOTCAB 67-21, 69-2 BCA ¶7804 (refusal to obtain fill from other borrow areas).

In these cases, the act of rejection is so clearly an adverse interpretation that the requirement of filing a protest is rarely raised or discussed. However, the lack of a clear rejection of the contractor's proposed method of performance has been used to support a holding that no constructive change order has occurred, *Blake Constr. Co.*, ASBCA 3406, 57-1 BCA ¶1281; *Ruscon Constr. Co.*, ASBCA 9371, 65-1 BCA ¶4599; *Avien, Inc.*, AECBCA 14-65, 67-2 BCA ¶6461, *recons. denied*, 67-2 BCA ¶6701.

(5) "Orders" of Authorized Representatives

In many instances the action or order resulting in extra work is made by a government inspector or other representative without formal contracting officer authority. See Chapter 9 for a discussion of the inspector cases. In such cases, the contractor must show not only that its interpretation was correct and that there was a constructive change order, but also that the inspector had the authority to act for the contracting officer or that the inspector's actions were ratified by a contracting officer. The rules used in determining authority of authorized representatives of the contracting officer are discussed in Chapter 1. See also *Urban Pathfinders, Inc.*, ASBCA 23134, 79-1 BCA ¶13,709, and *Randall H. Sharpe*, ASBCA 22800, 79-1 BCA ¶13,869. However, not all of the cases in this area specifically discuss the authority issue—in some instances the boards appear to assume that the government employee making the interpretation is closely enough associated with a contracting officer to circumvent the need for analysis.

b. Work Outside the Changes Clause

In some cases, the appeals boards and courts have stretched the constructive changes doctrine to cover situations that probably would not be held to be within the bounds of the Changes clause if the government attempted to use the clause to directly order such a change. These are cases in which the clause is used administratively to settle a controversy that could not have been resolved at that level because it was a breach of contract. With the advent of the Contract Disputes Act, all such claims can be resolved administratively without the use of this fiction. Hence, this use of the constructive change logic may not be as common in the future.

(1) Unauthorized Government Disclosure of Technical Data

In *Joanell Labs., Inc.*, ASBCA 15798, 72-1 BCA ¶9300, it was held that there was no appeals board jurisdiction over a claim for damages for unauthorized removal of proprietary legends and disclosure of proprietary data. In *CompuDyne Corp.*, ASBCA 14556, 72-1 BCA ¶9218, the same board treated such a claim as a constructive change. It does not appear logical to argue that this holding permits the government to directly order the contractor to give up proprietary rights under the Changes clause. Since such an order is not related to an alteration of the work being performed under the contract, it is not a change to the designs, drawings, or specifications included in the contract, and this relationship is one of the prerequisites to the issuance of a change order under one of the standard Changes clauses. Thus, this type of constructive change should be classified as one where an appeals board has used the doctrine to assume jurisdiction rather than as one based on an interpretation of the scope of the Changes clause.

The *CompuDyne* reasoning was followed in *General Elec. Automated Sys. Div.*, ASBCA 36214, 89-1 BCA ¶21,195. Compare *E.M. Scott & Assocs.*, ASBCA 45869, 94-1 BCA ¶26,258, in which the board took jurisdiction of a claim that the government had misused proprietary data under a breach of contract theory. In that case, the board could not use a constructive changes theory because there was no contract involved. The board took jurisdiction on the theory that there might be an implied contract not to misuse the data.

(2) Improper Exercise of Options

In several cases, constructive changes have been found where the government exercised an option after it had expired and the contractor proceeded to perform under protest. For example, in *International Tel. & Tel. v. United States*, 197 Ct. Cl. 11, 453 F.2d 1283 (1972), the contracting officer's failure to give required notice to the contractor that funds were available to continue the contract led to a constructive change when the contracting officer required the contractor to furnish equipment at option prices after the time for ordering the work had expired. Accord, *Keco Indus., Inc.*, ASBCA 16645, 73-2 BCA ¶10,056, *recons. denied*, 73-2 BCA ¶10,211; *Lear Siegler, Inc.*, ASBCA 12164, 69-1 BCA ¶7563. See also *Dynamics Corp. of Am. v. United States*, 182 Ct. Cl. 62; 389 F.2d 424 (1968), applying the same rule to an indefinite delivery/indefinite quantity contract calling for the issuance of orders before a specified date. It is clear that the Changes clause does not permit the ordering of large numbers of additional items, since such amounts would clearly constitute new procurement. In fact, in *Keco* the contracting officer commenced the purchase by issuing an IFB under the sealed bidding statute but later canceled it and exercised the contract option. In *General Dynamics Corp.*, ASBCA 20882, 77-1 BCA ¶12,504, the deciding judge noted that the Changes clause of the contract "limits itself specifically to modification affecting drawings, designs or specifications, methods of shipments and/or packing and places of delivery." Still, after acknowledging the lack of logic in the reasoning of *International Tel. & Tel.*, *Keco*, and *Lear Siegler*, the judge followed these cases and ruled that a constructive change resulted from the government's order of additional quantities.

The improper exercise of an option under a multiyear contract has also been found to be a constructive change, *Electrospace Corp.*, ASBCA 19742, 78-1 BCA ¶12,949. For another case involving the addition of work, see *Westinghouse Elec. Corp.*, DCAB NOAA-3-74, 78-1 BCA ¶13,133, where retaining a chartered vessel in standby status pending possible additional work was held to be a constructive change because government personnel knew of the situation. For other cases holding that option exercises were constructive changes, see *Holly Corp.*, ASBCA 24975, 83-1 BCA ¶16,327 (exercise of an option without adequate funds where contractor could not reasonably have known of the lack of funds); *New England Tank Indus. of N,H.*, ASBCA 26474, 88-1 BCA ¶20,395, *vacated and remanded*, 861 F.2d 685 (Fed. Cir. 1988), *decision on remand*, 90-2 BCA ¶22,892 (exercise of an option citing funds that could not be used for the work where contractor did not know of the unpublished regulation precluding the use of the funds); *Grumman Technical Servs., Inc.*, ASBCA 46040, 95-2 BCA ¶27,918 (changing terms of contract in option exercise); *Varo, Inc.*, ASBCA 47945, 96-1 BCA ¶28,161 (adding contract clauses to option quantities); and *Lockheed Martin IR Imaging Sys., Inc. v. West*, 108 F.3d 319 (Fed. Cir. 1997) (partial exercise of a "100 percent option"). In *Alliant Techsystems, Inc. v. United States*, 178 F.3d 1260, *reh'g denied*, 186 F.3d 1379 (Fed. Cir. 1999), the court expanded on these cases by holding that a contractor was properly terminated for default because it had a duty to proceed when it received such an improperly issued option.

(3) Improper Withholding of Progress Payments

Several cases have found improper withholdings of progress payments to be constructive changes and have ordered reimbursement to the contractor for interest costs of funds borrowed to finance the work in the interim. In the first such case, *Aerojet-Gen. Corp.*, ASBCA 13548, 70-1 BCA ¶8245, the board held that the government's erroneous interpretation of a Progress Payments clause, which deprived the contractor of substantial amounts of funds, was "an unauthorized and compensable unilateral change in the contract." Accord, *Ingalls Shipbuilding Div., Litton Sys., Inc.*, ASBCA 17717, 76-1 BCA ¶11,851; *Virginia Elecs. Co.*, ASBCA 18778, 77-1 BCA ¶12,393 (compensation granted for two-week delay resulting from improper rejection of progress payment request). See, however, *Lockheed Shipbuilding & Constr. Co.*, ASBCA 18460, 77-1 BCA ¶12,458, in which the board denied the contractor's motion to dismiss a government counterclaim based on the theory that a constructive change had occurred when the government allegedly made overpayments under a Progress Payments clause. In returning the matter for trial, the board commented that it doubted if such a claim was a valid constructive change even though *Aerojet-Gen.* had so held in the converse situation.

Since this type of constructive change is highly unusual and limited in nature, it is doubtful that it will be found in future cases. See *DMJM/Norman Eng'g Co.*, ASBCA 28154, 84-1 BCA ¶17,226, taking jurisdiction of a withholding case without reference to the Changes clause. See also *Systems Consultants, Inc.*, ASBCA 18487, 75-2 BCA ¶11,402, in which the board held that no such constructive change existed in a cost-reimbursement contract where the government had improperly withheld payments. This holding was based on the reasoning that *Aerojet-Gen.* could not be followed because the cost principles in DAR 15-205.17 precluded the payment of interest on cost-type contracts and interest on the withheld payments was the measure of the equitable adjustment under this type of constructive change.

In a similar situation, a constructive change was found where the government failed to make timely payment of Vietnamese currency with the result that the contractor was forced to acquire such currency at a higher exchange rate, *Daniel, Mann, Johnson & Mendenhall*, ASBCA 14360, 71-2 BCA ¶9003.

(4) Government Action Leading the Contractor to Increase Employee Wages

Constructive changes have also been found where government action induced or required the contractor to increase wages paid to employees. For example, in *Geronimo Serv. Co.*, ASBCA 14686, 70-2 BCA ¶8540, a constructive change was found where the government issued a new service contract wage determination containing higher minimum wages with the exercise of an option for additional work, and in *J.R. Cianchette*, ASBCA 4508, 60-2 BCA ¶2814, the board held that a constructive change had occurred when the contracting officer ruled that a labor classification with higher wages applied to the work under a contract subject to the Davis-Bacon Act. In two cases, constructive changes were found where contracts for work in Vietnam contained clauses stating that the contractor was required to pay the same wage rates as the Army and then the Army issued directives raising its wages, *Philco-Ford Corp.*, ASBCA 14623, 72-1 BCA ¶9390; *Pacific Architects & Eng'rs, Inc.*, ASBCA 16083, 74-2 BCA ¶10,755. See also *Thaihuat Eng'g Co.*, ASBCA 21906, 79-1 BCA ¶13,691, in which acquiescence to increases in severance pay required by Thai law was held to be a constructive change. Constructive changes were also found where the government applied pressure to the contractor to hire employees of a predecessor contractor at wage rates higher than required by the Service Contract Act wage determination, *Space Age Eng'g, Inc.*, ASBCA 16588, 72-2 BCA ¶9636, and where a new Service Contract Act wage determination was issued immediately after award, *C&H Reforesters, Inc.*, AGBCA 84-295-1, 88-3 BCA ¶21,067. The logic of these cases—that wage increases can be ordered under the Changes clause—was first enunciated by the Court of Claims in *Sunswick Corp. v. United States*, 109 Ct. Cl. 772, 75 F. Supp. 221, *cert. denied*, 334 U.S. 827 (1948), in which the court stated that a contracting officer should have issued a change order when the government forced the contractor to pay higher wages. However, since the wage rates are not part of the work under the contract, it is questionable if such an order is within the bounds of the Changes clause.

(5) Government-Ordered Change in Accounting System

In *Ford Aerospace & Communications Corp.*, ASBCA 23833, 83-2 BCA ¶16,813, a government order that the contractor use a total cost input base to allocate general and administrative expenses under Cost Accounting Standard 410 was held to be a constructive change. Similarly, in *Aydin Corp. v. Widnall*, 61 F.3d 1571 (Fed. Cir. 1995), an order to use a more precise accounting system not required by the contract was held to be a constructive change. It is unclear how such orders are within the bounds of the Changes clause.

2. Defective Specifications and Misleading Information

A second major category of constructive change occurs when the government misleads the contractor with the information it provides and the contractor incurs additional expense in attempting to perform in accordance with such information. In this situation, the government's breach of an implied duty is claimed to have caused the contractor to perform work beyond that originally contemplated. However, in many cases, there is nothing that can be characterized as a constructive change "order." Rather, to find a constructive change, the board or court focuses on the government fault—in effect satisfying the "order" element of this type of constructive change by finding that the government was at fault in breaching its implied duty. The cases fall within several categories discussed in Chapter 3—the implied warranty of specifications, impracticability of performance, misrepresentation, and nondisclosure.

a. *Defective Specifications*

In one of the first Court of Claims cases dealing with a constructive change for a defective specification, *Hol-Gar Mfg. Corp. v. United States*, 175 Ct. Cl. 518, 360 F.2d 634 (1966), the court accepted the doctrine by ruling that the costs of a change issued to overcome defective specifications should include costs incurred from the inception of the contract, since the contractor had incurred expenditures made useless by the faulty specifications. This logic effectively converts a government breach of its implied warranty of the specifications into a constructive change, thereby substituting the recovery of an equitable adjustment for breach of contract damages. The law evolved even further when constructive changes were found in situations where performance of the work was impossible or impracticable. The impracticability doctrine developed in the common law as a method of relieving contracting parties from liability for nonperformance, but it did not entitle one party to a damages claim against the other party. Yet in the government contracts field there exists a line of cases in which impracticability has been characterized as a constructive change, with the result that the contractor obtains an equitable adjustment compensating for the costs incurred in attempting to perform. In effect, a defense for nonperformance has been converted into an affirmative claim for compensation.

Although there are numerous decisions finding constructive changes based on defective government specifications or impracticability of performance, the "order" element of the change is not generally addressed by the appeals board. The early cases occasionally contained language pertaining to an order of the government, although it is questionable if an actual order had been given. For example, in *F.J. Stokes Corp.*, ASBCA 6532, 1963 BCA ¶3944, the board based its holding on the rule that "[a] direction to proceed under defective specifications imposing an unattainable requirement is itself a basis for price adjustment under the Changes clause." See also *Northeastern Eng'g, Inc.*, ASBCA 5732, 61-1 BCA ¶3026. In *Pastushin Indus., Inc.*, ASBCA 7663, 1963 BCA ¶3757, the order was found in the refusal of the government to recognize the defects and its insistence on performance in accordance with the specifications. However, some of the early cases contain no mention of an order but merely indicate that the use of defective specifications by the government is a constructive change, *Spencer Explosives, Inc.*, ASBCA 4800, 60-2 BCA ¶2795; *Unexcelled Chem. Corp.*, ASBCA 2399, 60-1 BCA ¶2587. In *Consolidated Diesel Elec. Corp.*, ASBCA 10486, 67-2 BCA ¶6669, the board stated at 30,952:

> [W]hen defective or impossible specifications cause frustration and "wheel-spinning" and increase the time and cost of performance until the specifications are corrected or relaxed, this also gives rise to a constructive change.

More recent cases rarely address the need for an order because they apparently accept as well established the rule that the change actually occurs when the contract is issued. Accordingly, these cases also accept the basic principle that the costs of this type of constructive change include all costs incurred in attempting to cope with the defective specification from the inception of the contract. This explains why no order in the form of an act or direction from the government is required, since issuance of the contract is the event that constitutes the constructive change. In effect, the government is liable for a constructive change in these circumstances because it was at fault when it issued a contract containing defective specifications or calling for work that was impracticable to perform.

In some cases, government fault is balanced against contractor responsibility to determine liability. Thus, no constructive change was found when the contractor participated in the drafting of the defective specification, *Bethlehem Corp. v. United States*, 199 Ct. Cl. 247, 462 F.2d 1400 (1972); *Johns-Manville Corp. v. United States*, 13 Cl. Ct. 72 (1987), *vacated for lack of jurisdiction*, 855 F.2d 1571 (Fed. Cir. 1988). Subsequent contractor fault can also determine the outcome of these types of constructive changes. For example, in *S. Head Painting Contractor, Inc.*, ASBCA 26249, 82-2 BCA ¶15,886, the board denied a contractor's claim for repainting necessitated by a defect in the specifications for primer because the contractor knew of the defect and failed to notify the government. Similarly, in *Oconto Elec., Inc.*, ASBCA 40421, 93-3 BCA ¶26,162, the contractor was denied relief for impracticability in part because it failed to give the government the opportunity to alter the specification to overcome the difficulty.

b. Undisclosed or Incorrect Information

Nondisclosure of information by the government is a later evolutionary step from the constructive change of furnishing defective specifications. As with defective specifications, such nondisclosure can result in extra work being done and is the breach of a duty that the government owes the contractor. Here, too, it is the fault of the government, rather than an act or communication, that constitutes the change "order." In recent years, the boards of contract appeals have ruled that constructive changes have occurred in a number of instances of nondisclosure. At the same time, the Court of Federal Claims treats nondisclosure as either breaches of contract or constructive changes, depending on how the case is pleaded by the contractor. Compare *J.F. Shea Co. v. United States*, 4 Cl. Ct. 46 (1983) (breach of contract) with *Granite Constr. Co. v. United States*, 24 Cl. Ct. 735 (1991) (constructive change). It is now accepted that nondisclosure of information is treated as essentially the same claim whether it is stated as a constructive change or a breach of contract, *Petrochem Servs., Inc. v. United States*, 837 F.2d 1076 (Fed. Cir. 1988). See *Ellett Constr. Co. v. United States*, 93 F.3d 1537 (Fed. Cir. 1996), holding that this type of claim was properly submitted as a constructive change claim.

The constructive change cases based on misrepresentation or nondisclosure of information do not contain a clear rationale as to why such action is a change. Most of the cases seem to follow the logic that a specification that contains incorrect information or from which vital information is missing is defective, *Lear Siegler, Inc.*, ASBCA 16079, 73-1 BCA ¶10,004; *F.F. Slocomb Corp.*, ASBCA 16715, 73-2 BCA ¶10,209. Some of the cases, however, use the logic that nondisclosure of information is an indication of assumption of risk by the government, *Ortronix, Inc.*, ASBCA 12745, 72-2 BCA ¶9564. A third line of cases seems to treat nondisclosure as a constructive change of a distinct type, *General Precision, Inc.*, ASBCA 12078, 70-1 BCA ¶8144; *Walden Landscape Co.*, ENGBCA 3534, 75-2 BCA ¶11,538; *Beckman Constr. Co. v. General Servs. Admin.*, GSBCA 11796, 93-3 BCA ¶26,205; *Raytheon Co.*, ASBCA 50166, 01-1 BCA ¶31,245, *aff'd in part, vacated in part*, 305 F.3d 1354 (Fed. Cir. 2002). One case has also held nondisclosure to be a breach of the government's affirmative duty to cooperate with the contractor, *Automated Servs., Inc.*, GSBCA EEOC-2, 81-2 BCA ¶15,303.

Some constructive changes in this category are based on difficulties encountered during performance when the government enforced the specifications in a way that was unforeseen by the contractor at the time of bidding. In these cases, one basis for finding a constructive change is that the government knew of the difficulties inherent in its interpretation but did not disclose them to the contractor, *Koppers Co.*, ENGBCA 3033, 73-2 BCA ¶10,237; *Piracci Constr. Co.*, GSBCA 3715, 74-2 BCA ¶10,719, *recons. denied*, 74-2 BCA ¶10,767. Similarly, in *Elrich Constr. Co.*, GSBCA 3657, 73-2 BCA ¶10,187, a constructive change was found where the government ordered the contractor to comply literally with the specification, which required the contractor to buy a proprietary item at a high price. The board reasoned that a change had occurred because the government should have known, but did not disclose, that the item was proprietary. Cases in which the board would not follow this holding include *Arnold M. Diamond, Inc.*, ASBCA 22733, 78-2 BCA ¶13,447 (contractor had access to knowledge that item was patented because patents are published), and *Southwood Builders, Inc.*, ASBCA 43489, 93-3 BCA ¶26,072 (contractor could have determined that item was proprietary by making inquiry of prospective vendors). See also *Stanwick Corp.*, ASBCA 16113, 72-1 BCA ¶9285, where the government advised the contractor that correcting work of a prior contractor was part of its effort. The board found a constructive change based partially on the government's failure to reveal the state of the prior work in the solicitation. Accord, *NAB-Lord Assocs.*, PSBCA 318, 77-2 BCA ¶12,802; *Boland Mach. & Mfg. Co.*, ASBCA 13664, 70-2 BCA ¶8556.

Allocation of fault can be a key issue in nondisclosure cases. Where there is both government nondisclosure and contractor error in the bid preparation, the trend is to find the nondisclosure as the more egregious act. See *Commercial Mech. Contractors, Inc.*, ASBCA 25695, 83-2 BCA ¶16,768, in which government nondisclosure was held to override contractor negligence in not investigating the conditions prior to bidding. In *Perini Corp.*, ENGBCA 3745, 78-1 BCA ¶13,191, the board stated that a contractor may rely on positive representations by the government about the amount of material to be used and need not make its own inspection to confirm the government's representations. Similarly, in *Logics, Inc.*, ASBCA 46914, 97-2 BCA ¶29,125, *recons. denied*, 98-1 BCA ¶29,483, a government misstatement that an item of needed test equipment was a stock item overcame the contractor's certification that it had determined the availability of all needed materials.

Nondisclosure of vital information by the government can also override a contractor's obligation to inquire about conflicts in the specifications. For example, in *Norair Eng'g Corp.*, ENGBCA 3787, 78-1 BCA ¶13,202, the board found that although the contractor normally must clarify conflicts in specifications or bear the risk of misinterpretation, the drawings indicated that the item in question was not in the contract, so the contractor was under no duty to inquire. Similarly, in *Record Elec., Inc.*, ASBCA 26385, 82-1 BCA ¶15,784, although the contractor was at fault for failing to inquire, the government committed the "more grievous fault" by failing to warn the contractor that it had to make an extraordinary modification to existing equipment (citing *Aerodex, Inc. v. United States*, 417 F.2d 1361 (Ct. Cl. 1969)). Compare *Dewey Elecs. Corp.*, ASBCA 33869, 91-1 BCA ¶23,443, *recons. denied*, 91-1 BCA ¶23,656, in which the government was absolved from liability for misrepresentation because the contractor had hired the designer of the equipment as a consultant and thus was fully capable of resolving problems with the specifications. The knowing inclusion of incorrect information in the specifications has also overcome the contractor's normal obligation to follow a manufacturer's installation instructions, *V&Z Heating Corp.*, DOTBCA 2953, 98-2 BCA ¶29,818. In *Pacific W. Constr., Inc.*, DOTCAB 1084, 82-2 BCA ¶16,045, *recons. denied*, 83-1 BCA ¶16,337, the board apportioned the costs of government nondisclosure coupled with contractor fault.

3. Acceleration

Acceleration of contract performance is another of the early types of constructive change recognized by the boards of contract appeals, *Sanders*, Army BCA 1468, 4 CCF ¶60,526 (1948); *Samuels et al., Exrs.*, Army BCA 1147, 4 CCF ¶60,703 (1949). The concept that accelerations were changes evolved rapidly, and acceleration was included as one of the enumerated changes in the expanded construction contract Changes clause that was issued in 1968.

An acceleration is a speeding up of the work in an attempt to complete performance earlier than otherwise anticipated. In some instances, a contractor may accelerate on its own initiative to ensure completion within the contract schedule or for some other purpose. The costs of such acceleration are, of course, not recoverable from the government. See, for example, *International Maint. Res., Inc.*, ASBCA 48157, 96-2 BCA ¶28,436 (contractor volunteered in meeting with contracting officer to acquire additional workers and equipment); *Atlantic Indus., Inc.*, ASBCA 46710, 95-2 BCA ¶27,610 (no acceleration where contractor accelerated for its own convenience but the government was unable to provide the necessary government-furnished property to permit delivery as early as intended); and *Robert H. O'Hair & O'Hare Constr. Co., a Joint Venture*, AGBCA 82-115-1, 89-1 BCA ¶21,384 (no acceleration where subcontractor worked overtime with extra equipment to finish prior to end of construction season). See also *SAWADI Corp.*, ASBCA 53073, 01-1 BCA ¶31,357, in which no acceleration was found when a contractor had to hire new employees and rent additional equipment because task orders were issued at the end of the contract. The board concluded that such actions were "the normal ongoing costs of doing business."

Compensable acceleration occurs when the government orders the effort. In almost all cases, such an order is found constructively where the government requires the contractor to speed up work to meet the current contract delivery schedule in the face of excusable delays—that is, since excusable delays give the contractor a theoretical entitlement to schedule extensions, an order to meet the unadjusted schedule is equivalent to an order to complete the work in advance of that extended schedule.

a. *Elements of Constructive Acceleration*

While the case law is not dogmatic in application, there appear to be five common elements of a constructive acceleration:

1. Excusable delay,
2. Knowledge by the government of such delay,
3. Some statement or act by the government that can be construed as an acceleration order,
4. Notice by the contractor that the order is a constructive change (required by the construction contract Changes clause), and
5. Incurring additional costs of accelerated effort in response to the order.

A more elaborate set of requirements for a constructive acceleration is set forth in *Fermont Div., Dynamics Corp. of Am.*, ASBCA 15806, 75-1 BCA ¶11,139, *aff'd*, 216 Ct. Cl. 448 (1978), at 52,999-53,000:

(1) existence of a given period of excusable delay; and
(2) contractor notice to the Government of the excusable delay, and request for extension of time together with supporting information sufficient to allow the Government to make a reasonable determination; EXCEPTIONS:
 (a) such notice, request and information are not necessary if the Government's order (see (3) below) directs compliance with a given schedule expressly without regard to the existence of any excusable delay,
 (b) the supporting information is unnecessary if it is already reasonably available to the Government; and
(3) failure or refusal to grant the requested extension within a reasonable time; and
(4) a Government order, either express or implied from the circumstances, to (a) take steps to overcome the excusable delay, or (b) complete the work at the earliest possible date, or (c) complete the work by a given date earlier than that to which the contractor is entitled by reason of the excusable delay. Circumstances from which such an order may be implied include expressions of urgency by the Government, especially if coupled

with (i) a threat of default or liquidated damages for not meeting a given accelerated schedule, or (ii) actual assessment of liquidated damages for not meeting a given accelerated schedule; and

(5) reasonable efforts by the contractor to accelerate the work, resulting in added costs, even if the efforts are not actually successful.

(1) Excusable Delay

The cornerstone of the constructive acceleration theory is an excusable delay. Thus, even under the Default (Fixed-Price Supply and Service) clause in FAR 52.249-8, which is silent as to the contractor's entitlement to a time extension, a constructive acceleration will be found if the contractor is required to accelerate to overcome an excusable delay. See, e.g., *Standard Store Equip. Co.*, ASBCA 4348, 58-2 BCA ¶1902. However, in no situation can there be a constructive acceleration without an excusable delay, *R. J. Lanthier Co.*, ASBCA 51636, 04-1 BCA ¶32,481; *National Radio Co.*, ASBCA 14707, 72-2 BCA ¶9486. See Chapter 6 for a full discussion of the legal rules on excusable delays.

(2) Knowledge of the Contracting Officer

For a constructive acceleration to occur, the contracting officer must have knowledge of the excusable delay at the time the acceleration is ordered. Apparently, it is reasoned that it is not logical to hold a contracting officer responsible for having issued a constructive acceleration order unless he or she knew of the contractor's entitlement to a time extension. In some cases, this element has been stated as a requirement that the contractor have actually submitted a request for a time extension, *Mechanical Utils., Inc.*, ASBCA 7466, 1962 BCA ¶3556; *California Shipbuilding & Dry Dock Co.*, ASBCA 21394, 78-1 BCA ¶13,168; *Commercial Contractors Equip., Inc.*, ASBCA 52930, 03-2 BCA ¶32,381. However, the key factor seems to be knowledge, as indicated in *Corbetta Constr. Co.*, PSBCA 299, 77-2 BCA ¶12,699, in which it was stated that the rule calling for a request for time extension "is flexible enough to be satisfied in the absence of a formal request but only where there is a very clear indication from the contracting officer that no delays in the schedule will be tolerated." See also *Sylvania Elec. Prods., Inc.*, ASBCA 11206, 67-2 BCA ¶6428, *recons. denied*, 67-2 BCA ¶6721. Hence, constructive accelerations were found without any notice of excusable delay or request for time extensions in *William Lagnion*, ENGBCA 3778, 78-2 BCA ¶13,260 (contracting officer closely monitored job and granted some time extensions without contractor request); *Fort Howard Paper Co.*, ASBCA 20284, 78-1 BCA ¶12,873, *recons. denied*, 78-1 BCA ¶13,027 (government-caused disruption was a direct cause of contractor acceleration effort without regard to excusable delay); *E.C. Morris & Son, Inc.*, ASBCA 20697, 77-2 BCA ¶12,622 (direct order to simultaneously perform work scheduled sequentially); *Greulich, Inc.*, ENGBCA 3832, 78-2 BCA ¶13,417 (requesting time extension a futile gesture where the government urged timely completion and maintained data showing the flood conditions that delayed the contractor); and *Hurst Excavating, Inc.*, ASBCA 37351, 93-3 BCA ¶25,935 (direct order to speed up work).

Where the government had neither actual nor constructive knowledge of the contractor's excusable delay, claims for constructive accelerations will be denied unless the contractor has given notice, requested a time extension, and furnished supporting information at the time of the delay, *Carney Gen. Contractors, Inc.*, NASABCA 375-4, 79-1 BCA ¶13,855, *recons. denied*, 80-1 BCA ¶14,243. See also *R. J. Lanthier Co.*, ASBCA 51636, 04-1 BCA ¶32,481 (no contemporaneous request for time extensions); *Gavosto Assocs., Inc.*, PSBCA 4058, 01-1 BCA ¶31,389 (no request for time extension submitted until two days before end of claimed acceleration period); *Hemphill Contracting Co.*, ENGBCA 5698, 94-1 BCA ¶26,491 (no notice of excusable delays or request for time extensions); *Allen L. Bender, Inc.*, PSBCA 2322, 91-2 BCA ¶23,828 (no requests for time extension before the contracting officer at the time of the alleged acceleration order); and *Nello L. Teer Co. v. Washington Metro. Area Transit Auth.*, 695 F. Supp. 583 (D.D.C. 1988) (no response to contracting officer's request for substantiating information to support claim of excusable delays).

(3) Orders to Accelerate

An essential element of a constructive acceleration is an act or a communication that can be reasonably construed as an order to accelerate. Thus, if a contractor accelerates to overcome job conditions without an order from the government, no constructive acceleration will be found. See, for example, *GBQC Architects v. General Servs. Admin.*, GSBCA 15578, 02-1

BCA ¶31,846, in which no government liability for an acceleration was found where the architect was forced to speed up its contract administration work because the construction contractor worked to an earlier schedule than the contract schedule.

The deciding factor is the degree of compulsion to accelerate produced by a particular set of circumstances. A number of fact patterns have been dealt with by the boards and courts.

(A) DIRECT ORDERS

Most of the instances of direct orders to accelerate arose under the construction contract clause entitled Progress Charts and Requirements for Overtime Work, which was set forth in DAR 7-603.48. A slightly revised version of this provision is now contained in FAR 52.236-15, as follows:

SCHEDULES FOR CONSTRUCTION CONTRACTS (APR 1984)

> (a) The Contractor shall, within five days after the work commences on the contract or another period of time determined by the Contracting Officer, prepare and submit to the Contracting Officer for approval three copies of a practicable schedule showing the order in which the Contractor proposes to perform the work, and the dates on which the Contractor contemplates starting and completing the several salient features of the work (including acquiring materials, plant, and equipment). The schedule shall be in the form of a progress chart of suitable scale to indicate appropriately the percentage of work scheduled for completion by any given date during the period. If the Contractor fails to submit a schedule within the time prescribed, the Contracting Officer may withhold approval of progress payments until the Contractor submits the required schedule.
>
> (b) The Contractor shall enter the actual progress on the chart as directed by the Contracting Officer, and upon doing so shall immediately deliver three copies of the annotated schedule to the Contracting Officer. If, in the opinion of the Contracting Officer, the Contractor falls behind the approved schedule, the Contractor shall take steps necessary to improve its progress, including those that may be required by the Contracting Officer, without additional cost to the Government. In this circumstance, the Contracting Officer may require the Contractor to increase the number of shifts, overtime operations, days of work, and/or the amount of construction plant, and to submit for approval any supplementary schedule or schedules in chart form as the Contracting Officer deems necessary to demonstrate how the approved rate of progress will be regained.
>
> (c) Failure of the Contractor to comply with the requirements of the Contracting Officer under this clause shall be grounds for a determination by the Contracting Officer that the Contractor is not prosecuting the work with sufficient diligence to ensure completion within the time specified in the contract. Upon making this determination, the Contracting Officer may terminate the Contractor's right to proceed with the work, or any separable part of it, in accordance with the default terms of this contract.

This clause gives the contracting officer the right to order accelerated efforts at no additional cost to the government if the contractor falls behind the contract schedule. Some of the earliest acceleration cases established the principle that an improper order under such a clause, when the contractor was entitled to excusable delay, was a constructive acceleration, *Farnsworth & Chambers Co.*, ASBCA 4945, 59-2 BCA ¶2433; *Hagstrom Constr. Co.*, ASBCA 5698, 61-1 BCA ¶3090. See also *Norair Eng'g Corp.*, ENGBCA 3804, 90-1 BCA ¶22,327, in which an order under this clause to accelerate work not on the critical path was found to be a constructive acceleration order. An order under this clause to accelerate performance to meet a noncontractual interim completion date was also found to be a constructive acceleration, *Hurst Excavating, Inc.*, ASBCA 37351, 93-3 BCA ¶25,935. Compare *Granite Constr. Co. v. United States*, 24 Cl. Ct. 735 (1991), in which an order under this clause to meet a contractual interim date was found to be a proper order. In *Yukon Constr. Co., Ltd.*, ASBCA 10859, 67-1 BCA ¶6334, the board stated that the substantial rights granted the contracting officer by this clause require that purported acts under the provision be closely scrutinized, and that the contracting officer was not justified in invoking the clause where the contractor's actual progress demonstrated a "close relationship" with the progress schedule under which the contractor was operating at the time of the order. See, however, *Robert Simmons Constr. Co.*, ASBCA 11019, 67-1 BCA ¶6279, for a less stringent view of the government's obligations. In *Carney Gen. Contractors, Inc.*, NASABCA 375-4, 80-1

BCA ¶14,243, the board noted that a notice to accelerate under this clause is "valid" if the contractor is behind schedule at the time of the order.

Other direct orders have been held to be constructive acceleration orders. For example, in *Alley-Cassetty Coal Co.*, ASBCA 33315, 89-3 BCA ¶21,964, *recons. denied*, 89-3 BCA ¶22,204, an order was found when the contracting officer directed the contractor to deliver coal in the face of an excusable delay, and in *Atlantic Dry Dock Corp.*, ASBCA 42609, 98-2 BCA ¶30,025, *recons. denied*, 99-1 BCA ¶30,208, an order was found when the government demanded a compressed schedule of work to make up for a late start that was not the fault of the contractor. Similarly, in *Maintenance Eng'rs*, ASBCA 23131, 81-2 BCA ¶15,168, *modified on recons.*, 83-1 BCA ¶16,411, the government constructively accelerated the contract when it ordered the contractor to continue mowing a field that had become soaked by heavy rains. The board emphasized that the contractor's costs for pulling its equipment out of the mud were compensable because the government refused to allow the time extension it was entitled to. Compare *Sherman R. Smoot Corp.*, ASBCA 52173, 03-1 BCA ¶32,212, finding no acceleration order when the contracting officer informed the contractor that it was required to meet a specified occupancy date but excepted from the direction a specific claim for a time extension. The board reasoned that the order was not "unconditional."

(B) REQUESTS TO ACCELERATE

In *Hyde Constr. Co.*, ASBCA 8393, 1963 BCA ¶3911, the board held that a request to accelerate was tantamount to an acceleration order, noting that in both a request and an order the initiative comes from the government for the government's convenience. In contrast, it has been held that urging a contractor to complete the work in accordance with the original schedule was not an acceleration order, *Kingston Bituminous Prods. Co.*, ASBCA 9964, 67-2 BCA ¶6638; *Guaranty Constr. Co.*, GSBCA 3109, 70-2 BCA ¶8483. In *A. Teichert & Son, Inc.*, ASBCA 10265, 68-2 BCA ¶7175, *recons. denied*, 68-2 BCA ¶7410, a request that the contractor submit a plan showing how lost time could be regained was held not to constitute an acceleration order. Similarly, giving advice to a contractor that more workers were needed was not an acceleration order, *Evergreen Forest Mgmt., Inc.*, AGBCA 84-299-1, 88-3 BCA ¶20,950.

(C) THREATS TO TERMINATE FOR DEFAULT

The consequences of a default termination are so serious that the boards have consistently ruled that a threat to terminate for default will constitute an acceleration order, *Lewis Constr. Co.*, ASBCA 5509, 60-2 BCA ¶2732; *Mechanical Utils., Inc.*, ASBCA 7345, 1962 BCA ¶3556; *William Lagnion*, ENGBCA 3778, 78-2 BCA ¶13,260. However, merely informing a contractor of the government's right to default terminate was held not to be an acceleration order in *Donald R. Stewart & Assocs.*, AGBCA 84-226-1, 92-1 BCA ¶24,705. Furthermore, issuing a cure notice when a contractor is behind schedule, mainly due to its own difficulties, is not the type of threat to default that will be construed as an acceleration order, *Consolidated Constr., Inc.*, ASBCA 46498, 99-1 BCA ¶30,148, *aff'd*, 230 F.3d 1378 (Fed. Cir. 2000). However, a constructive acceleration was found when the contracting officer issued a cure notice after failing to grant sufficient time extensions to cover the excusable delays that had been encountered, *Monterey Mech., Inc.*, ASBCA 51450, 01-1 BCA ¶31,380.

(D) GOVERNMENT PRESSURE TO COMPLETE ON SCHEDULE

Statements by government employees that a program is of high priority and delays cannot be tolerated will be construed as an acceleration order, *Electronic & Missile Facilities, Inc.*, ASBCA 9031, 1964 BCA ¶4338, *motion sustained in part, denied in part*, 1964 BCA ¶4474; *Gibbs Shipyard, Inc.*, ASBCA 9809, 67-2 BCA ¶6499; *Norair Eng'g Corp. v. United States*, 229 Ct. Cl. 160, 666 F.2d 546 (1981). In *Pathman Constr. Co.*, ASBCA 14285, 71-1 BCA ¶8905, a government statement of urgent need for completion coupled with a threat to assess liquidated damages was held to constitute an acceleration order. When the program for which the contract is issued is of lesser priority, it is more difficult to argue that government pressure is properly interpreted as an acceleration order. For example, continued expressions of concern about the progress of the contractor were held to be insufficient to constitute acceleration orders in *Gibson Co.*, ASBCA 13307, 70-1 BCA ¶8289. Other cases finding insufficient pressure to constitute an acceleration order include *Fermont Div., Dynamics Corp. of Am.*, ASBCA 15806, 75-1 BCA ¶11,139, *aff'd*, 216 Ct. Cl. 448 (1978) ("reasonable" pressure to complete on schedule); *Lamb Eng'g. & Constr. Co.*, EBCA C-9304172, 97-2 BCA ¶29,207, *recons. denied*, 98-1 BCA ¶29,359 (agency "continuously pressed" the contractor to complete on time); and *R. J. Lanthier Co.*, ASBCA 51636, 04-1 BCA ¶32,481 (single communication requesting that the project be completed on time).

(E) REFUSAL TO GRANT TIME EXTENSIONS PLUS LIQUIDATED DAMAGES

In one early case, the board ruled that the combination of a refusal to grant time extensions and assessment of heavy liquidated damages was sufficiently coercive to constitute an acceleration order, *Keco Indus., Inc.*, ASBCA 8900, 1963 BCA ¶3891. The Court of Claims in *Norair Eng'g Corp. v. United States*, 229 Ct. Cl. 160, 666 F.2d 546 (1981), stated at 165 that pressure to accelerate "even if it were merely implicit . . . is particularly strong where liquidated damages hover in the background" and that if the "Government refuses . . . to tell the contractor until the end of the project just what delay is excusable and what is not, the contractor [will be] under considerable additional pressure to accede to a request [to accelerate] because it does not know whether it will be found liable for liquidated damages." Similarly, in *Constructors-Pamco*, ENGBCA 3468, 76-2 BCA ¶11,950, an acceleration order was found where the contract contained a liquidated damages provision and the government refused to grant a time extension that was obviously due, refused to give instructions on how to proceed in face of problems, and insisted on maintaining the original schedule. In contrast, in *Robert A. Verrier Co.*, ASBCA 8693, 1964 BCA ¶4062, *recons. denied*, 65-1 BCA ¶4667, the board found that the failure to grant a time extension plus the mere presence of a liquidated damages clause did not result in constructive acceleration. In these cases, the board appeared to weigh the entire factual context in which the contractor found itself at the time the decision to accelerate was made to determine if it was reasonable to interpret the government's actions and communications as an order. Thus, in *Barrett Co.*, ENGBCA 3877, 78-1 BCA ¶13,075, the combination of liquidated damages plus a two-month delay in acting on a request for a time extension was found to be an acceleration order on a contract to be performed in 60 days. See *Larry Azure v. United States*, 129 F.3d 136 (Fed. Cir. 1997), affirming a Court of Federal Claims decision that failure to act on requests for time extensions until after contract completion, plus a reminder that the contractor was liable for liquidated damages, was held to be a government order to accelerate. See also *Unarco Material Handling*, PSBCA 4100, 00-1 BCA ¶30,682, finding an acceleration order when the contracting officer unilaterally imposed a contract completion date, refused to grant a time extension to overcome the improper data, and threatened liquidated damages.

(F) REFUSAL TO GRANT TIME EXTENSION AND INSISTENCE THAT CONTRACTOR MEET ORIGINAL SCHEDULE

If, in the course of refusing to grant time extensions, the contracting officer insists on contract completion as called for by the original schedule, an acceleration order will be found, *Earth Tech Indus., Ltd.*, ASBCA 46450, 99-1 BCA ¶30,341. Apparently, in this case the board concluded that the contracting officer was well aware of the impact of his actions. See also *P.J. Dick, Inc.*, VABCA 5597, 01-2 BCA ¶31,647, *rev'd on other grounds*, 324 F.3d 1364 (Fed. Cir. 2003), in which a constructive acceleration was found where the government continually pressed for completion in accordance with the schedule while it was granting short time extensions that did not reflect the excusable delays that had actually occurred. In this case, the contractor's claim was greatly enhanced because it continually notified the agency that it was being forced to accelerate by the government's inaction in dealing with the delays that were occurring during contract performance. Similarly, in *Hensel Phelps Constr. Co. v. General Servs. Admin.*, GSBCA 14744, 01-1 BCA ¶31,249, a constructive acceleration was found because the contractor made it clear to the contracting officer that it would have to accelerate if time extensions were not granted and the contracting officer continued to refuse to act on the requests for time extensions. In this instance, it appears that the board concluded that the contracting officer had unreasonably demanded more adequate documentation of the time extensions and had rejected some of them because they were not requested in a timely fashion. The Federal Circuit reached a similar result in *Fraser Constr. Co. v. United States*, 215 F.3d 1344 (Fed. Cir. 1999), in which it remanded a case to the Court of Federal Claims to determine if the government had, as alleged, refused to grant time extensions and pressed the contractor to complete the work in accordance with the contract schedule. On remand, 57 Fed. Cl. 56 (2003), *aff'd*, 384 F.3d 1359 (Fed. Cir. 2004), the court denied relief because, although agency personnel frequently expressed concern about the progress of the work, the contracting officer always timely acknowledged and granted the contractor's requests for weather-based time extensions.

(G) FAILURE TO GRANT TIME EXTENSION

A failure to grant a time extension, without more, has been held insufficiently compelling to constitute an order to accelerate, *Carroll Servs., Inc.*, ASBCA 8362, 1964 BCA ¶4365, *recons. denied*, 65-1 BCA ¶4613. While awaiting the contracting officer's response to its request for a time extension, the contractor has two alternatives: (1) continue performing at its current pace, thereby risking late completion, or (2) accelerate performance in order to complete according to the original schedule. In *Peter Kiewit Sons' Co.*, ASBCA 9921, 69-1 BCA ¶7510, the board stated that only if the contracting officer takes away the contractor's option of continuing performance at a normal pace will there be an order to accelerate. See also *Intermax, Ltd.*, ASBCA 41828, 93-2 BCA ¶25,699, *recons. denied*, 93-3 BCA ¶26,207, *aff'd*, 78 F.3d 604 (Fed. Cir. 1996), in which no acceleration order was found when the contracting officer refused to act on requests for time extensions because the contractor did not provide substantiating information with requests.

This can be a harsh rule, because if the contractor elects to continue at its current pace while assuming it will get an extension but then does not, it may find it more difficult to recoup lost time than it would have been had it accelerated earlier. If it assumes that it will not get the extension and accelerates, it will not be able to later prove the order element necessary for a constructive acceleration claim. According to the board in *Carroll*, this is simply the result of the contractor's duty to perform diligently during the resolution of a dispute, and the mere fact that a contractor that has not been granted an extension adjusts its schedule to complete the work on time does not show that the contractor was compelled to adjust its schedule. This situation can leave the contractor with a time extension that it cannot use since it was granted late in contract performance and acceleration costs that it cannot recover. Of course, if the contractor is certain that it has experienced an excusable delay, it should continue working at its current pace and can use the excusable delay as a defense to termination for default or assessment for liquidated damages. It is when the contractor is uncertain that this rule can work a hardship.

(H) DELAYS IN GRANTING EXTENSIONS

The logic of the rule is stronger where the delay in granting the extension is reasonable in relation to the contractor's opportunity to adjust its schedule, *Peter Kiewit Sons' Co.*, ASBCA 9921, 69-1 BCA ¶7510. See, however, *Olin Mathieson Chem. Corp.*, ASBCA 7605, 1963 BCA ¶3983, *aff'd*, 179 Ct. Cl. 368 (1967), in which a three-to-four-month delay was found reasonable on a complex project even though the extensions were ultimately granted after contract completion. One board has commented with disapproval on the government technique of waiting to act on requests for time extensions until completion of the work, *Ashton Co.*, IBCA 1070-6-75, 76-2 BCA ¶11,934, noting that such practice can easily lead to a constructive acceleration. What the board seems to have said is that the compelling force of an unreasonable delay in granting a request for a time extension is greater than that of a reasonable delay, and therefore less additional compulsion will be required to constitute an order to accelerate. See also *Continental Consolidated Corp. v. United States*, 17 CCF ¶81,137 (Trial Judge Dec. 1972), *aff'd by order*, 200 Ct. Cl. 737 (1972), in which the court emphasized the importance of a timely response to requests for time extensions. In *Human Advancement, Inc.*, HUDBCA 77-215-C15, 81-2 BCA ¶15,317, delay in granting a time extension was held to have been a constructive acceleration since, by the time the extension was granted, the contractor had adjusted its work schedule to complete the added work without a time extension. See also *McKenzie Eng'g Co.*, ASBCA 53374, 02-2 BCA ¶31,972, denying a motion to dismiss because the contractor had offered proof that the government's substantial delay in acting on a request for a time extension had compelled it to accelerate the work.

Once the contracting officer knows of the delay and of the contractor's request for a time extension, the request should be acted on promptly, if at all possible. However, contracting officers frequently request contractors to substantiate their claims for time extensions. Such a request is somewhat questionable in construction contracts. The Default clause in FAR 52.249-10 contains the following provision regarding the responsibility of the contracting officer once notice of the causes of an excusable delay has been given:

> (b)(2) . . . The Contracting Officer shall ascertain the facts and the extent of delay. If, in the judgment of the Contracting Officer, the findings of fact warrant such action, the time for completing the work shall be extended. The findings of the Contracting Officer shall be final and conclusive on the parties, but subject to appeal under the Disputes clause.

In *Electronic & Missile Facilities, Inc.*, ASBCA 9031, 1964 BCA ¶4338, *motion sustained in part, denied in part*, 1964 BCA ¶4474, the board analyzed this clause and noted that, "while it is customary and proper for the contracting officer or his representative to request the contractor to submit a specific request for a stated number of days extension substantiated by supporting data, the contracting officer's authority to act under GP-5 is not conditional on any such submission by the contractor." The board went on to find that the government was not justified in delaying the granting of a time extension when information about the cause of the delay—unusually severe weather—was readily available.

In *Iversen Constr. Co.*, IBCA 981-1-73, 76-1 BCA ¶11,644, *aff'd*, 244 Ct. Cl. 692 (1980), the board agreed with the view that the contracting officer has an obligation to act on time extension requests but held that, once a contracting officer had refused to grant a time extension and had asked for more information, a reasonable contractor would furnish information in its possession. Similarly, in *Freeman Elec. Constr. Co.*, DOTCAB 74-23A, 77-1 BCA ¶12,258, *aff'd*, 221 Ct. Cl. 884 (1979), the board stated that the contract language obligated the contractor to submit sufficient information to at least make a prima facie showing that it was entitled to a time extension and to furnish information peculiarly within its knowledge. See also *Fermont Div., Dynamics Corp. of Am.*, ASBCA 15806, 75-1 BCA ¶11,139, *aff'd*, 216 Ct. Cl. 448 (1978), and *Intermax, Ltd.*, ASBCA 41828, 93-2 BCA ¶25,699, *recons. denied*, 93-3 BCA ¶26,207, *aff'd*, 78 F.3d 604 (Fed. Cir. 1996).

The length of the contract performance period may have a significant impact on what will be considered to be a reasonable amount of time to grant a time extension under this provision. For example, in *Barrett Co.*, ENGBCA 3877, 78-1 BCA ¶13,075, an acceleration was found when the contracting officer delayed for two months in acting on a request for a time extension to a contract with a 60-day performance period. Compare *Allen L. Bender, Inc.*, PSBCA 2322, 91-2 BCA ¶23,828, where the contracting officer was slow in acting on time extensions but, over the course of the contract, they were granted fairly. The board concluded that, in these circumstances, there was no reason for the contractor to believe that the government was desirous of acceleration to make up for excusable delays. See also *Riennes Constr. Co.*, IBCA 3572-96, 98-2 BCA ¶29,821, in which a time extension shortly before the end of contract completion was held sufficient to overcome any claim of an acceleration order.

(I) DENIAL OF REQUEST FOR TIME EXTENSION

Denial of a request for a time extension should be sufficiently compelling to constitute an order to accelerate. This had been recognized by the Court of Claims in *Norair Eng'g Corp. v. United States*, 229 Ct. Cl. 160, 666 F.2d 546 (1981), in which the court, in discussing the requirements for finding an acceleration order, noted that a requirement for a request for and a denial of a time extension is "in effect equivalent to the requirement of an order to accelerate." The court also noted that "mere failure to grant an extension at the time will not constitute a constructive order to accelerate." This is in recognition of the fact that, when the government affirmatively denies a time extension, it is in effect insisting on performance of the contract according to the original schedule subject to all the original contract provisions. See also *Fischbach & Moore Int'l Corp.*, ASBCA 18146, 77-1 BCA ¶12,300, *aff'd*, 223 Ct. Cl. 119, 617 F.2d 223 (1980), in which the board held that the contractor had been compelled to accelerate because denials and tardy approvals of time extensions coupled with government intransigence led the contractor to reasonably believe that the requested time extensions would not be granted and that it would be held to the original contract completion date. Applying the reasoning in *Fischbach* to a case of flat denial, it is clear that a denial leaves in force all the original contract provisions, including, for example, the completion date and any liquidated damages, and that a reasonable contractor will consider itself obligated to comply.

(4) CAUSATION

The final element of a constructive acceleration is proof that the acceleration was in response to the "order." In most cases this is clear from the facts but, when there is doubt, the contractor must prove such causation. See, for example, *Solar Foam Insulation*, ASBCA 46278, 94-1 BCA ¶26,288, in which a claim was denied because the evidence showed that the contractor had increased its crew sizes prior to the alleged acceleration order and had taken no further steps to accelerate after the order was received. The board concluded that the accelerated effort had not resulted from the order of the government. Compare *Atlantic Dry Dock Corp.*, ASBCA 42609, 98-2 BCA ¶30,025, *recons. denied*, 99-1 BCA ¶30,208, in which the board found the government liable for acceleration because the contractor regularly informed government officials that it was accelerating to overcome government-caused delays and the officials did not object to this course of action.

b. Acceleration to Mitigate Delay

Acceleration costs are also recoverable against the government if they are incurred in mitigation of the effects of a government-caused delay, *Fischbach & Moore Int'l Corp.*, ASBCA 18146, 77-1 BCA ¶12,300, *aff'd*, 223 Ct. Cl. 119, 617 F.2d 223 (1980); *King Constr. Co.*, ASBCA 38303, 94-1 BCA ¶26,434, *recons. denied*, 94-2 BCA ¶26,630; *Canon Constr. Corp.*, ASBCA 16142, 72-1 BCA ¶9404. This type of acceleration is actually a claim for mitigation of delay costs pursued under the Suspension of Work clause rather than the Changes clause, *Day & Zimmermann-Madway*, ASBCA 13367, 71-1 BCA ¶8622. Thus, the normal elements of a constructive acceleration claim need not be present. In *Weaver Constr. Co.*, ASBCA 12577, 69-1 BCA ¶7455, it was held that such acceleration costs were not recoverable because the contractor was responsible for delays in addition to the government delays, and insufficient time had been recouped to prove that the acceleration costs had been incurred for the benefit of the government, since final performance was late a greater number of days than the amount of the government delay.

c. Post-Constructive Acceleration Time Extensions

A contracting officer can cut off the government's continuing liability for a constructive acceleration order by granting time extensions for excusable delays, *William Lagnion*, ENGBCA 3778, 78-2 BCA ¶13,260. After the granting of such extensions, the contractor is under no further pressure to meet an unenforceable schedule and hence has no claim against the government for subsequent acceleration costs.

d. Acceleration Orders Where There Are Both Excusable and Nonexcusable Delays

When an acceleration order has been given under a special clause granting the government the right to order acceleration without compensation to make up delays for which the contractor is responsible, it has been held that no acceleration costs are recoverable when the contractor did not make up such delays, even though there were also excusable delays, *Pan-Pac. Corp.*, ENGBCA 2479, 65-2 BCA ¶4984; *Joseph E. Bennett Co.*, GSBCA 2362, 72-1 BCA ¶9364. In both of these cases, the decision may have been influenced by the fact that the delay for which the contractor was responsible preceded the excusable delay. However, the theory of the cases seems to be that this special clause gives the government the right to specify which delays will be made up first. In *Electrical Enters., Inc.*, IBCA 971-8-72, 74-1 BCA ¶10,528, the board ruled that no compensable acceleration had occurred where there were both excusable and nonexcusable delays at the time of the acceleration order but no clause giving the government the right to order acceleration without compensation to make up nonexcusable delays. The board reasoned that the contractor would not have completed on time even if a time extension for excusable delays had been granted. This reasoning appears to be questionable since without the special clause, the contracting officer had no right to order acceleration without compensation. See also *Yukon Constr. Co.*, ASBCA 10859, 67-1 BCA ¶6334, in which the board found that costs should be apportioned when the government had the right to order acceleration for nonexcusable delays, both excusable delays and nonexcusable delays were present at the time of the acceleration order, and it was clear from the facts that all of the costs were not attributable to making up time lost through the excusable delays.

When there are both excusable delays and delays of the contractor, the contracting officer can ensure that the government is not liable for acceleration costs by granting time extensions for the excusable delays. This occurred in *Michael-Mark Ltd.*, IBCA 2697, 94-1 BCA ¶26,453, and *Donald R. Stewart & Assocs.*, AGBCA 84-226-1, 92-1 BCA ¶24,705. In *Lake Union Drydock Co. v. Department of Commerce*, GSBCA 10394-COM, 93-1 BCA ¶25,285, *recons. denied*, 93-2 BCA ¶25,838, the contracting officer avoided an acceleration claim by reducing the work and granting a time extension to overcome the entire excusable delay. The board ruled that there was no acceleration because all of the remaining delay was the fault of the contractor.

e. Recovery Not Dependent on Contractor's Recoupment of Lost Time

When the contractor accelerates the work at the direction of the government but cannot demonstrate that time lost through excusable delays was recouped, it is generally held that acceleration costs may be recovered since their reimbursement is not dependent on making up lost time. For example, in *Varo, Inc.*, ASBCA 15000, 72-2 BCA ¶9717, where the contracting officer had ordered completion ahead of the original contract schedule, the board permitted recovery of acceleration costs since the contractor had used its "best effort" to complete the work ahead of schedule. Accord, *M.S.I. Corp.*, GSBCA 2429, 68-2 BCA ¶7377. See also *Continental Consolidated Corp. v. United States*, 17 CCF ¶81,137 (Trial Judge Dec. 1972), *aff'd by order*, 200 Ct. Cl. 737 (1972), in which the trial judge found the contractor entitled to all of the acceleration costs incurred even though very little time had been made up in comparison with the amount of acceleration effort expended. The judge reasoned that, since the contractor was on schedule at the time the acceleration order was issued, the government had the burden of proving that the contractor was responsible for the failure to recoup much time.

4. Hindrance or Failure to Cooperate

The final major category of constructive change is the failure of the government to perform its obligation to cooperate with the contractor or not to hinder, interfere with, or delay its performance of the work. As discussed in Chapter 3, this duty is a part of the duty of good faith and fair dealing, which is imposed on both parties to the contract. The most common result of a breach of this duty is the performance of work beyond that called for by the contract—a result easily analyzed as a constructive change. However, because this was not a well-defined area of constructive change in 1978 when the Contract Disputes Act was enacted, contractors may be able to seek recovery either under the contract, on a constructive change theory, or under a breach of contract theory. Normally, the same legal standards are applied to ascertain government liability in noncooperation or hindrance of performance cases whether the claim is characterized as a breach of contract or constructive change. However, several older cases indicate that a contractor may recover from a board of contract appeals with a less egregious act of government interference than that necessary for a breach of contract claim. Compare *Banks Constr. Co. v. United States*, 176 Ct. Cl. 1302, 364 F.2d 357 (1966), with *A. Geris, Inc.*, ENGBCA 2869, 68-2 BCA ¶7320, and *John M. Bragg*, ASBCA 9515, 65-2 BCA ¶5050. Compare also *Bruno Law v. United States*, 195 Ct. Cl. 370 (1971), with *Carpenter Constr. Co.*, NASABCA 18, 1964 BCA ¶4452. Thus, it can be expected that such claims will be filed primarily as constructive change claims.

Whether the government has breached an implied duty to cooperate is determined by the reasonableness of its actions under the circumstances. Thus, in *Ben C. Gerwick, Inc. v. United States*, 152 Ct. Cl. 69, 285 F.2d 432 (1961), the contractor was denied relief where availability of the work site was delayed by another government contractor, not by an act or omission of the government. The officer in charge did all he could reasonably do to hasten the performance of the preceding contractor. See also *Asheville Contracting Co.*, DOTCAB 74-6, 76-2 BCA ¶12,027 (government "reasonably executed its duty to get timely completion" of other contract); *Tolis Cain Corp.*, DOTCAB 72-2, 76-2 BCA ¶11,954 (no government fault or negligence where government had no notice of any problems prior to shutdown and promptly had services restored upon receipt of notice); *Sun Oil Co. v. United States*, 215 Ct. Cl. 716, 572 F.2d 786 (1978) (contractor failed to establish that government acted unreasonably); *Zinco Gen. Contractor, Inc.*, GSBCA 6182, 82-2 BCA ¶15,917 (government acted with reasonable promptness in first rejecting contractor's proposal and then in negotiating a modification after reviving the proposal); *GLR Constructors, Inc.*, ENGBCA 6128, 96-1 BCA ¶28,218, *aff'd*, 114 F.3d 1206 (Fed. Cir. 1997) (government reasonably refused to revise specification to permit contractor to work more efficiently); *Commercial Prods. & Eng'g Co.*, ASBCA 40392, 96-2 BCA ¶28,411, *aff'd*, 155 F.3d 566 (Fed. Cir. 1998) (government action reasonable, although not completely responsive, in dealing with government-furnished material, first article approval and numerous changes); *Reflectone, Inc.*, ASBCA 42363, 98-2 BCA ¶29,869 (government administered contract strictly but responded to contractor with diligence); *Consolidated Constr., Inc.*, ASBCA 46498, 99-1 BCA ¶30,148, *aff'd*, 230 F.3d 1378 (Fed. Cir. 2000) (government direction to continue work in cold weather not interference because contractor was well behind schedule at time); *Tri Indus., Inc.*, ASBCA 47880, 99-2 BCA ¶30,529 (government failure to loan part or approve deviations not failure to cooperate because neither was necessary for performance); and *Centurion Elecs. Serv.*, ASBCA 48750, 00-1 BCA ¶30,642 (failure to make advance payments or accept partial deliveries not failure to cooperate because neither required by contract).

When courts and boards apply the logic of constructive change to breaches of this duty, they frequently grant relief without analyzing whether there has been an order to perform extra work. Rather, they look to whether the government's fault has compelled the contractor to perform extra work. Fault may arise from the mere fact that the government has breached its duty. More frequently, government fault results in a finding of constructive change where there has been a breach of duty, the contractor has put the government on notice that its failure to cooperate is costing the contractor money, and the government does not then move to correct the problem. Chapter 3 sets forth fully the nature of the government duty to cooperate or not hinder performance of the work and what constitutes a breach of that duty. A finding of breach will demonstrate that there has been a change to the contract. The additional element—an order or government fault required to prove constructive change—is discussed in the following subsections.

a. *Direct Order*

Where the government affirmatively insists that the contractor perform in a more expensive manner, a constructive change order is easily found. For example, in *Carpenter Constr. Co.*, NASABCA 18, 1964 BCA ¶4452, the government was informed that the contractor's pouring of concrete was being obstructed by other contractors on the project who were behind schedule. The government nevertheless directed the contractor to continue pouring rather than wait until the other work was completed. The board found the directive to be an order for additional work within the scope of the Changes clause. Similarly, in *Richerson Constr., Inc. v. General Servs. Admin.*, GSBCA 11161, 93-1 BCA ¶25,239, a direct order was found when the contracting officer ordered the contractor to obtain a different subcontractor.

b. *Actions and Inactions*

Direct or indirect actions or inactions that amount to a breach of the government's duty to cooperate or not hinder may also be held to be constructive changes. In these cases the key findings are that the government was at fault and had adequate notice, either actual or constructive, that its action or inaction was causing increased costs of performance to the contractor. In *Yarno & Assocs.*, ASBCA 10257, 67-1 BCA ¶6312, the government was informed in writing that it was allowing a second contractor to perform in such a way as to obstruct and ruin an on-site source of topsoil promised to Yarno. The board found "a change effected by the contracting officer in permitting the on-site contractor . . . [to prevent] . . . appellant from proceeding in the most efficient manner." Thus, government action, in the form of tacit permission to another contractor working on the same job, can constitute a constructive change order. Compare *Skip Kirchdorfer, Inc.*, ASBCA 40516, 00-1 BCA ¶30,625, in which no constructive change was found because the contractor did not request needed assistance in obtaining material from a supplier.

(1) Overzealous Inspection

Overzealous inspection is another type of government action that frequently results in a breach of implied duty to cooperate or not hinder. Although the government has the right to inspect work to ensure that it strictly complies with the specifications, *George Ledford Constr., Inc.*, ENGBCA 6218, 97-2 BCA ¶29,172, *recons. denied*, 98-2 BCA ¶29,335, *aff'd*, 178 F.3d 1308 (Fed. Cir. 1998); *Engineering Tech. Consultants, S.A.*, ASBCA 45065, 95-2 BCA ¶27,804, it may not exercise this right in a manner that unduly interferes with the contractor's performance. Such interference was recognized by the Court of Claims as a constructive change in *Adams v. United States*, 175 Ct. Cl. 288, 358 F.2d 986 (1966). Similarly, in *Murdock Constr. Co.*, IBCA 1050-12-74, 77-2 BCA ¶12,728, the project supervisor directed the contractor to perform in a specific way. This interference was immediately protested to the contracting officer, who refused to replace the supervisor. The contractor recovered the cost of redoing the work correctly under a constructive change theory. The same result occurs when the inspector completely takes over supervision of the work, instead of just inspecting, and requests additional work, *Stanley W. Wasco*, ASBCA 12288, 68-1 BCA ¶6986 (takeover of one part of the job requiring all-night work is a constructive change although no protest to higher authority). Overzealous inspection may also impact performance by changing the contractor's inspection system or significantly slowing progress, *Karnavas Painting Co.*, NASABCA 28, 1963 BCA ¶3633 (constructive change by directing contractor's employees on details of work—mild but ineffective protests by contractor sufficient to alert government to situation); *G.W. Galloway Co.*, ASBCA 16656, 73-2 BCA ¶10,270, *recons. denied*, 74-1 BCA ¶10,521 (constructive change by multiple inspections having disruptive effect that was known to contracting officer); *H.G. Reynolds Co.*, ASBCA 42351, 93-2 BCA ¶25,797 (constructive change when agency sent in project users and compiled a second punchlist containing a large number of minor items); *Centric/Jones Constructors*, IBCA 3139, 94-1 BCA ¶26,404 (constructive change when government rejected work without giving reason, demanded "novel test," and refused to pay for extra effort after the work passed the test); *Neal & Co. v. United States*, 36 Fed. Cl. 600 (1996), *aff'd*, 121 F.3d 683 (Fed. Cir. 1997) (a "nit-picking" punchlist); and *Grumman Aerospace Corp.*, ASBCA 50090, 01-1 BCA ¶31,316, *aff'd*, 34 Fed. Appx. 710 (Fed. Cir. 2002) (significantly more stringent inspection standards after 18-year use of more lenient procedures).

(2) Failure to Provide Assistance

Constructive changes through failure to cooperate with the contractor have been found when the government fails to provide assistance after a contractor has encountered problems during performance and has asked for assistance. For example, in *Hardrives, Inc.*, IBCA 2319, 94-1 BCA ¶26,267, the agency failed to respond to calls for assistance in resolving numerous problems encountered with the specifications and the site of the work. In lieu of obtaining resolution of the problems by the designing architect, the agency told the contractor to prepare change proposals containing solutions to the problems and refused to act without such proposals. The board held that this "misadministration" of the contract was a constructive change. Other cases of failure to provide assistance include *Environmental Safety Consultants, Inc.*, ASBCA 47498, 00-1 BCA ¶30,826 (failure to provide timely analysis of waste to be removed by contractor); *R.W. Jones Constr., Inc.*, IBCA 3656-96, 99-1 BCA ¶30,268 (continually refusing to help the contractor work with a utility that was operating the dam where the required work was being performed); *Turbine Aviation*, ASBCA 51323, 98-2 BCA ¶29,945 (failure to provide technical information in timely fashion); *Century Concrete Servs., Inc.*, ASBCA 48137, 97-1 BCA ¶28,889 (refusal to allow contractor's on-site batch plant to be added to government's environmental permit); *Celeron Gathering Corp. v. United States*, 34 Fed. Cl. 745 (1996) (failure to provide accurate information regarding ongoing problems with source of oil needed for contractor performance); *Midland Maint., Inc.*, ENGBCA 6085, 96-2 BCA ¶28,539 (failure to enforce rule that public could not build "fire rings" on camp site); *Keno & Sons Constr. Co.*, ENGBCA 5837, 95-2 BCA ¶27,687 (failure to provide reasons for refusing to permit contractor to use preferred method of performance); *Engineering Tech. Consultants, S.A.*, ASBCA 44912, 93-1 BCA ¶25,556, *recons. denied*, 93-2 BCA ¶25,732 (refusal to allow the contractor to use the existing utilities); *Eagle Contracting, Inc.*, AGBCA 88-225-1, 92-3 BCA ¶25,018 (failure to stake all culverts at beginning of road reconditioning contract so as to facilitate the contractor's efficiency); *James Lowe, Inc.*, ASBCA 42026, 92-2 BCA ¶24,835, *recons. denied*, 93-1 BCA ¶25,516 (failure to promptly reduce water pressure after break in water line); *Robert R. Marquis, Inc.*, ASBCA 38438, 92-1 BCA ¶24,692 (failure to resolve problems with another contractor on the site); *Old Dominion Sec.*, ASBCA 40062, 91-3 BCA ¶24,173, *recons. denied*, 92-1 BCA ¶24,374 (failure to issue a sufficient number of security clearances to permit contractor to perform guard service contract); *Harvey C. Jones, Inc.*, IBCA 2070, 90-2 BCA ¶22,762, *recons. denied*, 91-1 BCA ¶23,388 (failure to replace its inspection crew that was minimally competent and was rejecting work that had been correctly performed); and *Kahaluu Constr. Co.*, ASBCA 31187, 89-1 BCA ¶21,308, *recons. denied*, 89-1 BCA ¶21,525 (failure to tell contractor how to proceed after encountering differing site condition).

(3) Inaction or Silence

Government inaction or silence can also compel a contractor to perform work that goes beyond that called for in the contract. In *Altman Carpentry, Inc.*, HUDBCA 77-217-C16, 81-2 BCA ¶15,414, the board stated at 76,378:

> Earlier case law required that the Contracting Officer take some affirmative step to require performance in the face of a delay caused by another contractor in order to entitle the affected contractor to an equitable adjustment under the Changes clause rather than a pure cost adjustment under the Suspension of Work clause. See, Carpenter *Construction Company*, NASA BCA 18, 1964 BCA ¶4452. However, the Boards now recognize that inaction of a Contracting Officer to take steps to correct a delay by another contractor, after due notice and protest by the affected contractor, can constitute a constructive change.

In *Altman*, the board found a constructive change where the contractor notified the government that the site contained substantial amounts of pre-construction debris that was supposed to have been removed. The contractor received no response to its notification and then removed the debris itself in order to proceed with the work. The board remarked at 76,379:

> Corrective work that is done, as the only practical response to Government silence and inaction on a request for removal of a delay factor over which the Government has control, constitutes a change in the quantity of work under the contract.

See also *Midland Maint., Inc.*, ENGBCA 6085, 96-2 BCA ¶28,539, finding a constructive change where the government failed to enforce a rule that the public could not build "fire rings" on the campsite being maintained. Similarly, in *Hensel Phelps Constr. Co.*, ENGBCA 3368, 74-2 BCA ¶10,728, the board, though not directly addressing whether there was an order, found a constructive change where the contractor first notified the government that an access road had been damaged by a prior contractor, and then after an adverse response from the contracting officer, repaired the road. The board apparently reasoned that, because the road was essential to performance of the contract and the government was on notice of the damage, the government's failure to require the prior contractor to repair the damage or to otherwise have it fixed forced the contractor to do the repair work. Inaction also led to a constructive change in *Steele & Sons, Inc.*, ASBCA 49077, 00-1 BCA ¶30,837, where the government returned as-built drawings for correction without noting the precise information that was missing.

A constructive change has been found when the government observes the contractor performing extra work and intentionally does not inform the contractor of that fact. See *Chris Berg, Inc. v. United States*, 197 Ct. Cl. 503, 455 F.2d 1037 (1972), where a government project engineer who knew that certain areas were not to be painted by the contractor reprimanded the contractor's crew for not cleaning those areas as they were about to be painted. See also *Hydrospace Elecs. & Instrument Corp.*, ASBCA 17922, 74-2 BCA ¶10,682, in which the board found that a constructive change had occurred in these circumstances, stating at 50,806:

> [T]he Government was aware that [the contractor] was deviating from the contract requirement for stainless steel in a manner that was determined to be patently unacceptable. In our opinion the Government, under these circumstances, had a duty to inform [the contractor] of its erroneous course of action in a timely manner and the [contractor] is entitled to recovery for the consequences of the Government's failure to do so.

To recover on these grounds, the contractor must prove that government personnel "had actual knowledge of the nonconforming work and deliberately refrained from informing [the contractor] of its erroneous course of action," *G&C Enters., Inc.*, DOTBCA 1736, 89-1 BCA ¶21,556; *Hunter Ditch Lining*, AGBCA 87-391-1, 91-2 BCA ¶23,673. In spite of the difficult standard of proof, the appeals boards have found constructive changes in situations where the government employees watched the defective work being performed, *W. Southard Jones, Inc.*, ASBCA 6321, 61-2 BCA ¶3182, or where they did not inform the contractor that work was defective and thereby permitted the performance of a substantial amount of defective work after they knew of the defects, *Bromley Contracting Co.*, HUDBCA 75-8, 77-1 BCA ¶12,232, *aff'd*, 229 Ct. Cl. 750 (1982). See also *Maxwell Dynamometer Co. v. United States*, 181 Ct. Cl. 607, 386 F.2d 855 (1967), in which the court held that watching the contractor perform a test to more stringent standards than required by the specifications would bind the government to compensate for the extra work. Similarly, in *Altman Carpentry, Inc.*, HUDBCA 77-217-C16, 81-2 BCA ¶15,415, a constructive change was found where the government knew that the contractor was forced by government inaction to remove pre-construction debris that was not the contractor's responsibility, and in *BH Servs., Inc.*, ASBCA 39460, 93-3 BCA ¶26,082, the board found a constructive change where the authorized representative of the contracting officer observed the contractor performing extra work but did not inquire as to why it was being performed. See also *William F. Klingensmith, Inc.*, GSBCA 5451, 83-1 BCA ¶16,201, in which the board held the government liable when it did not reject defective work in a timely manner. There are some cases reaching the conclusion that government employees have no obligation to inform the contractors of defective performance, *Rosendin Elec., Inc.*, ASBCA 22996, 81-1 BCA ¶14,827; *Gene Fuller, Inc.*, ASBCA 21682, 79-2 BCA ¶14,039. In view of this disagreement in the decisions, the best course of action would be for government employees to inform the contractor when the work is clearly defective.

(4) Unreasonable Conduct

Failure to cooperate through unreasonable conduct can occur in a number of ways, including very late issuance of the notice to proceed and continual failure to respond when problems were raised, *Piedmont Painting Contractors*, IBCA 3772, 98-1 BCA ¶29,618; inducing an adjacent landowner not to enter into agreement to provide materials, *HK Contractors, Inc.*, DOTBCA 2766, 96-1 BCA ¶28,175; the failure to respond to a contractor's requests for information, *Hardie-Tynes Mfg. Co.*, ASBCA 20582, 76-2 BCA ¶11,972; approving contractor's proposed schedule of progress and billings knowing that "funds of this magnitude would not be appropriated because not requested," *S.A. Healy Co. v. United States*, 216 Ct. Cl. 172, 576 F.2d 299 (1978); failing to issue timely orders, *Raytheon Serv. Co.*, GSBCA 5695, 81-1 BCA ¶15,002; untimely furnishing of delivery orders needed for performance, *George A. Fuller Co. v. United States.*, 108 Ct. Cl. 70, 69 F. Supp. 409 (1947); late deliveries of materials and delayed acceptance of contractor's products, *Kehm Corp. v. United States*, 119 Ct. Cl. 454, 93 F. Supp. 620 (1950); untimely delivery of information on government-furnished property, *Ballenger Corp.*, DOTCAB 74-32, 84-1 BCA ¶16,973, *modified on other grounds*, 84-2 BCA ¶17,277; failing to provide plans and drawings when necessary, *Cedar Lumber, Inc. v. United States*, 5 Cl. Ct. 539 (1984); failing to provide access to work site, *Blinderman Constr. Co. v. United States*, 695 F.2d 552 (Fed. Cir. 1982); and failing to issue a notice to proceed at time specifically required by contract, *Abbett Elec. Corp. v. United States*, 142 Ct. Cl. 609, 162 F. Supp. 772 (1958).

There are a few cases finding a failure to cooperate because a government employee or agent has administered the contract in a manner intended to harm the contractor, *Libertatia Assocs., Inc. v. United States*, 46 Fed. Cl. 702 (2000) (personal animosity toward contractor); *Donohoe Constr. Co.*, ASBCA 47310, 98-2 BCA 30,076, *recons. denied*, 99-1 BCA ¶30,387 (withholding payments, delaying approvals, overinterpreting specifications, and rejecting satisfactory work).

(5) Other Actions

Other government actions that have been held to constitute constructive change by interference with a contractor's performance include incompetent management of shop drawing approval process, *Sterling Millwrights, Inc. v. United States*, 26 Cl. Ct. 49 (1992); failure to ensure that another contractor on the site performed in accordance with its contract, *Toombs & Co.*, ASBCA 34590, 91-1 BCA ¶23,403; refusal of permission to conduct preliminary test to determine whether work could be successfully accomplished, *Alonso & Carus Iron Works, Inc.*, ASBCA 38312, 90-3 BCA ¶23,147, *recons. denied*, 91-1 BCA ¶23,650; use of excessively high standard for approving welders, *Tom Shaw, Inc.*, DOTBCA 2108, 90-1 BCA ¶22,579; excessive noise from jet engines, *Nichols Dynamics Inc.*, ASBCA 17949, 75-2 BCA ¶11,556; diverting water into the construction site, *John M. Bragg*, ASBCA 9515, 65-2 BCA ¶5050; and preventing drainage from a site, *A. Geris, Inc.*, ENGBCA 2869, 68-2 BCA ¶7320, *recons. denied*, 71-1 BCA ¶8764. In each instance the government ordered continued performance despite the interference or failed to act to alleviate the problem.

c. *Abuse of Discretion*

The breach of the government's duty not to hinder, delay, or increase the costs of performance has frequently been found to be a constructive change when the government has been unreasonable in exercising its discretion. Discretion is granted to the government in a number of different areas of contract performance, including situations where the contract makes the precise manner of performance subject to the approval of the contracting officer and where the contracting officer may approve proposed subcontractors or make determinations of whether certain components meet the specifications. See Chapter 3 for a full discussion of abuse of discretion as a breach of the duty to cooperate. In almost all of these cases, a constructive change order is found in an overt act or communication that knowingly forces or induces the contractor to perform in a manner desired by the government, *Chris Berg, Inc. & Assocs.*, ASBCA 3466, 58-1 BCA ¶1792, *recons. denied*, 58-2 BCA ¶1894 (government rejection of plan for thawing permafrost and requirement that more expensive method be used); *S. Rosenthal & Son, Inc.*, ASBCA 6684, 1963 BCA ¶3791, *recons. denied*, 1964 BCA ¶4467 (contracting officer forced performance of the work in certain sequence by using his right to approve progress schedule); *Hensel Phelps Constr. Co.*, ENGBCA 3674, 77-1 BCA ¶12,475 (government order to cut off tops and leave bottoms of cofferdam pilings in place served no government purpose and contract reasonably gave right to contractor to salvage entire piling); *John C. Grimberg Co. v. United States*, 869 F.2d 1475 (Fed. Cir. 1989) (government rejection of request for waiver of Buy American Act when price differential was substantial); *Manning Elec. & Repair Co. v. United States*, 22 Cl. Ct. 240 (1991) (contracting officer disapproved an "equal" item); *Blount, Inc.*, VABCA 3719, 95-2 BCA ¶27,874 (refusal to approve an "equal" material handling system); *Environmental Safety Consultants, Inc.*, ASBCA 47498, 00-1 BCA ¶30,826 (refusal to approve competent subcontractors).

In the area of variable quantity contracts, the Armed Services Board has recognized constructive changes where the Court of Claims might not have found a breach of contract. In *Raby Hillside Drilling, Inc.*, ASBCA 20178, 76-2 BCA ¶11,982, *recons. denied*, 77-1 BCA ¶12,245, the government directed the contractor to drill a well deeper despite serious difficulties and in face of a vigorous protest from the contractor. The well collapsed, destroying the drilling equipment and requiring the contractor to start over. This request to drill deeper was held to be a constructive change order because of an unreasonable exercise of discretion. In an analogous case, *Brighton Sand & Gravel Co.*, ASBCA 11277, 66-2 BCA ¶5905, a constructive change was found when the contracting officer refused to order more excavation in a variable quantity contract, causing the contractor to expend extra sums in correcting the effects of an unstable subgrade. In both cases, decisions about quantity resulted in a constructive change.

C. Procedures for Resolving Constructive Changes

Almost all constructive changes result from problems that are encountered during the performance of a contract. Successful resolution of these problems requires prompt, cooperative effort by both parties to the contract. Initially, this calls for identification of the problem by the contractor and prompt communication with the government. The government then must investigate the situation, take prompt steps to resolve the problem, and communicate the solution to the contractor.

1. The Contractor's Obligations

In many constructive change situations, the government is at a significant disadvantage if it does not receive prompt notice of the problems being encountered by the contractor. Its main difficulty is that it cannot devise a solution to the problem if it does not know that it exists. This deprives the government of control of the work and of the amount of financial resources needed to complete it. The second difficulty is that the contracting officer—the government official charged with contract administration—is left out of the decision-making process. The contractual notice requirements, as discussed in the next section, have not proved to be effective in overcoming these difficulties, but the courts and boards have recognized them and have frequently denied constructive changes claims when they have concluded that the contractor has not been diligent in bringing problems to the government's attention.

a. *Loss of Control of Work*

In 1965 the Court of Claims recognized that the government is prejudiced by lack of notice of defective specifications and announced a rule denying a contractor compensation for costs that might have been avoided if the contractor had given timely notice, *Kings Elecs. Co. v. United States*, 169 Ct. Cl. 433, 341 F.2d 632 (1965). This rule was followed in other constructive changes cases where a contractor failed to give notice of a failure to cooperate, *Cameo Bronze, Inc.*, GSBCA 3646, 73-2 BCA ¶10,135, *recons. denied*, 73-2 BCA ¶10,365; of alleged impossibility of performance, *SMC Info. Sys., Inc. v. General Servs. Admin.*, GSBCA 9371, 93-1 BCA ¶25,485, *aff'd*, 16 F.3d 420 (Fed. Cir. 1993); *Sanders Assocs., Inc.*, ASBCA 17550, 74-1 BCA ¶10,536, *recons. denied*, 76-1 BCA ¶11,632; and of furnishing defective government-furnished special tooling, *Ferguson Propeller, Inc. v. United States*, 59 Fed. Cl. 51 (2003). See *Power Regulator Co.*, GSBCA 4668, 80-2 BCA ¶14,463, stating that this is basically a mitigation of damages rule—reasoning that failure to give notice is a failure to allow the government to reduce the financial impact of the problem.

The rule has been applied most widely in cases of defective specifications, *Dynalectron Corp. v. United States*, 207 Ct. Cl. 349, 518 F.2d 594 (1975) (failure to give notice of defective specifications prevents recovery of full costs of performance when improper default termination is converted to termination for convenience); *Canadian Commercial Corp.*, ASBCA 17187, 76-2 BCA ¶12,145, *recons. denied*, 77-2 BCA ¶12,758 (no recovery of costs because of failure to notify government of defective specifications); *Reese Mfg., Inc.*, ASBCA 35144, 88-1 BCA ¶20,358 (delay prior to notice of defective specification not chargeable to government); *Argo Tech., Inc.*, ASBCA 30522, 88-1 BCA ¶20,381, *recons. denied*, 89-1 BCA ¶21,395, *aff'd*, 889 F.2d 1099 (Fed. Cir. 1989) (defective specification claim denied because of lack of notice); *Signal Contracting, Inc.*, ASBCA 44963, 93-2 BCA ¶25,877, *recons. denied*, 93-3 BCA ¶26,058, *aff'd*, 17 F.3d 1442 (Fed. Cir. 1994) (failure to give notice of defective specifications precludes recovery of delay costs prior to notice); *Environmental Devices, Inc.*, ASBCA 37430, 93-3 BCA ¶26,138 (failure to give notice of defective specification precludes recovery for delay); *AIW - Alton, Inc.*, ASBCA 47921, 95-2 BCA ¶27,881 (contractor responsible for delays prior to notifying government that a key drawing was missing); *Precision Specialities, Inc.*, ASBCA 48717, 96-1 BCA ¶28,054; *McElroy Mach. & Mfg. Co.*, ASBCA 46477, 99-1 BCA ¶30,185 (alteration of design without notice deprives contractor of claim for defective specification).

The contractor will be given a reasonable time to determine the cause of problems being encountered before this notice requirement will be enforced. See *Tyger Constr. Co. v. United States*, 31 Fed. Cl. 177 (1994), concluding that the long time it took the contractor to identify the cause of its problems was understandable because of the complexity of the situation.

If the government is aware of defective specifications, the contractor will be relieved of its obligation to bring them to the government's attention. See *Metal Trades, Inc.*, ASBCA 41583, 94-2 BCA ¶26,611 (contractor promptly complained that the work conditions were different than represented); *Hoffman Constr Co.*, DOTBCA 2150, 93-2 BCA ¶25,803 (notice not required because government not prejudiced by lack of notice); and *Lloyd Kessler, Inc.*, AGBCA 88-170-3, 89-3 BCA ¶22,055 (notice defenses rejected, without discussing special rule for defective specifications, on basis that government was aware that contractor was performing extra work). The contractor can meet its obligation to inform the government of problems during performance by oral notice without the submission of any documented claim, *Pittsburgh-Des Moines Corp.*, EBCA 314-3-84, 89-2 BCA ¶21,739. See also *Casson Constr. Co.*, GSBCA 4884, 83-1 BCA ¶16,523, in which the rule was not applied because the contractor had told an employee of the government's construction manager about the defective specification.

If a problem makes it impossible for the contractor to proceed with some element of the work, with the result that delay costs will be incurred, the contractor should also notify the government of that fact. Otherwise, these delay costs will not be compensable as part of the equitable adjustment for the constructive changes, *Signal Contracting, Inc.*, ASBCA 44963, 93-2 BCA ¶25,877, *recons. denied*, 93-3 BCA ¶26,058, *aff'd*, 17 F.3d 1442 (Fed. Cir. 1994).

b. Informing the Contracting Officer

In situations where contractors have been directed or induced to perform extra work by a person without contracting officer authority, they have been held to have a "duty to protest" to the contracting officer in order to ensure that a person with authority knows that the contractor believes a constructive change has occurred. The Court of Claims enunciated this rule in the case of *J.A. Ross & Co. v. United States*, 126 Ct. Cl. 323, 115 F. Supp. 187 (1953), at 329:

> Whenever the [government] orders work done which the [contractor] thinks is in violation of the contract, or in addition to its requirements, [the contractor] is required to protest against doing it, or to secure an order in writing before doing it. It is basic in all Government contracts that the [contractor] cannot do work which it is not required to do by the contract, without registering a protest against being required to do it, or securing an order for extra work, and then later make a claim against the Government for additional compensation.
>
> If the [contractor] thought that an unforeseen condition had been encountered which necessitated revision of the contract, it was its duty to call that situation to the attention of the contracting officer, so that he could investigate the condition and make an equitable adjustment in the contract, in case the conditions warranted it. Or, if [the contractor] claimed that the contract had been changed in a way which increased the cost of doing the work, it was necessary for it to make claim therefor in order that the contracting officer might make an equitable adjustment.

This rule has been less strictly followed in recent years—probably because some government employee was aware of the problem and was expected to bring it to the attention of the contracting officer. See, for example, *A.R. Mack Constr. Co.*, ASBCA 50035, 01-2 BCA ¶31,593 (oral notice to project engineer and resident engineer sufficient to permit the agency to deal with the problem); *CEMS, Inc. v. United States*, 59 Fed. Cl. 168 (2003) (on-site project engineer knew of constructive changes); and *SIPCO Servs. & Marine, Inc. v. United States*, 41 Fed. Cl. 196 (1998) (contracting officer's technical representative was delegated broad responsibility to oversee the contract). However, it is still an important factor in deciding constructive change cases when it appears that a protest to the contracting officer could have altered the situation. For example, in *Singer Co., Librascope Div. v. United States*, 215 Ct. Cl. 281, 568 F.2d 695 (1977), the court held against a contractor who had failed to protest. The court explained that, although such failure was no longer an outright bar to a claim, it is "an evidentiary consideration" that can take on controlling significance when circumstances indicate that the government would not have known that the contractor considered the work to be "extra-contractual" absent a protest. Accord, *Kurz & Root Co.*, ASBCA 11436, 68-1 BCA ¶6916; *Astro Dynamics, Inc.*, NASABCA 1067-38, 74-1 BCA ¶10,634, reconsideration denied, 75-2 BCA ¶11,479; *Flinchbaugh Prods. Corp.*, ASBCA 19851, 78-2 BCA ¶13,375; *Wayne L. Grist, Inc.*, ENGBCA 5503, 90-2

BCA ¶22,915. Most of the recent cases have discussed this obligation in terms of "prejudice" to the government, and it is not always clear whether the courts and boards are enforcing a contractual notice requirement (as discussed in the next section) or this general obligation to protest. See, for example, *Northrop Grumman Corp. v. United States*, 47 Fed. Cl. 20 (2000) (constructive changes claims not presented to contracting officer after warnings that other employees had no authority); *Lamar Constr. Co.*, ASBCA 39593, 92-2 BCA ¶24,813, *aff'd*, 985 F.2d 583 (Fed. Cir. 1992) (claim for excessive preparation work on painting contract submitted after final painting—depriving the government of the opportunity to investigate claim); *Sol Flores Constr.*, ASBCA 32278, 89-3 BCA ¶22,154 (lack of notice to contracting officer of directions received from technical representative); *Calfon Constr., Inc. v. United States*, 18 Cl. Ct. 426 (1989), *aff'd*, 923 F.2d 872 (Fed. Cir. 1990) (no notice to contracting officer that direction of representative was causing extra work); *Southland Constr. Co.*, VABCA 2217, 89-1 BCA ¶21,548 (lack of notice impeded government's ability to defend against claim); *E.W. Jerdon, Inc.*, ASBCA 32957, 88-2 BCA ¶20,729 (lack of notice prevented government from correcting problem); and *Tompkins & Co.*, ENGBCA 4484, 85-1 BCA ¶17,853 (claim submitted after work had been completed deprived contracting officer of opportunity to countermand order of COR). Similarly, when a contractor asserts that a constructive change has occurred through failure of the government to approve substitute performance, the claim will fail if there has been no clear request for such approval. See *C. Sanchez & Son, Inc. v. United States*, 6 F.3d 1539 (Fed. Cir. 1993) (claim of abuse of discretion in granting a Buy American Act waiver denied because no clear request for the waiver). In *WRB Corp. v. United States*, 183 Ct. Cl. 409 (1968), the Court of Claims stated that overzealous inspection violating the duty not to impede, hinder, or interfere with the contractor's work imposes a lesser duty to protest to the contracting officer than a case of a "mere misinterpretation" of a specification by an inspector.

When a disagreement over contract requirements is clearly apparent and an order to proceed in a certain manner is given, a constructive change will almost always be found in spite of a lack of protest if the government's interpretation is later determined to call for work beyond the contract requirements, *Dunbar Roofing Co.*, ASBCA 3559, 57-2 BCA ¶1487; *George A. Fuller Co.*, ENGBCA 2875, 71-2 BCA ¶8973. The same result will occur if the government gives a direct order to proceed in a specified manner, the contractor protests that the order is a change, and the government permits performance to proceed in accordance with the order, *M.S.I. Corp.*, GSBCA 2428, 68-2 BCA ¶7262; *Eagle Paving*, AGBCA 75-156, 78-1 BCA ¶13,107; *Urban Pathfinders, Inc.*, ASBCA 23134, 79-1 BCA ¶13,709; *Granite Constr. Co.*, ENGBCA 4172, 89-2 BCA ¶21,683. In some cases the board finds a constructive change as a result of a direct order of the government without any indication that there was disagreement about the contract requirements at the time of the order, *Master Mfg. Co.*, ASBCA 12132, 68-1 BCA ¶6953; *COMPEC*, IBCA 573-6-66, 68-1 BCA ¶6776; *Goslin-Birmingham, Inc.*, ENGBCA 2800, 67-2 BCA ¶6402. The explanation for these decisions may be that they involve requirements that are rather obviously beyond the original contract specifications and that agency personnel, including the contracting officer, should have known that such requirements were constructive changes.

The requirement for identification of constructive changes has been incorporated into the construction contract Changes clause in FAR 52.243-4. See the discussion in the next section.

2. Government Resolution of Problem

Once the government is aware of a problem, it has the responsibility to arrive at a solution, *Hardrives, Inc.*, IBCA 2319, 94-1 BCA ¶26,267. Thus, it is improper to request that the contractor devise a solution and to defer action until the solution is proposed. See *Pilcher, Livingston & Wallace*, ASBCA 13391, 70-1 BCA ¶8331, *recons. denied*, 70-2 BCA ¶8488, stating at 38,764:

> Much of the delay and expense experienced by the contractor as a result of inadequate and defective specifications could have been avoided if the [government] representatives had recognized their responsibility for providing the contractor with correct and adequate specifications and taken prompt corrective action to correct deficiencies in the specifications promptly after they had been reported by [the contractor]. Instead, when [the contractor] reported a problem the general practice of the COR and his inspection staff was to impose on [the contractor] the burden of working out a proposed solution to the problem, submitting a shop drawing showing the proposed solution, and getting it approved by the COR, which was time consuming and was not the contractual responsibility of the contractor.

See also *Hughes-Groesch Constr. Corp.*, VABCA 5448, 00-1 BCA ¶30,912, holding that the government acted improperly in requiring a construction contractor to perform redesign work rather than obtaining the redesign from the cognizant architect/engineer.

The result of this rule is that the government is responsible for any costs of delay that occurred because the government ordered the contractor to solve the problem. See, for example, *Atlas Grinding & Mach. Corp.*, ASBCA 33011, 87-1 BCA ¶19,612, in which the government was held liable for the contractor's costs of wasted effort when it delayed dealing with a problem for 20 months after it learned that the contractor was interpreting a drawing in a way that made it impossible to complete the contract performance.

Once a solution has been devised, the government should issue a change order, priced or unpriced, directing the contractor to implement it. The contractor is not obligated to proceed until such a change order is issued, and any delay costs incurred while awaiting such a change order are compensable as a part of the change, *Wilner v. United States*, 26 Cl. Ct. 260 (1992), *aff'd*, 994 F.2d 783 (Fed. Cir. 1993). See also *Sterling Millwrights, Inc. v. United States*, 26 Cl. Ct. 49 (1992), holding that a default termination was improper because of government delays in responding to a contractor's requests for changes to correct defective drawings.

V. CONTRACTUAL NOTICE REQUIREMENTS

All of the standard Changes clauses contain notice requirements, but with the exception of the construction contract clause, these requirements are not well attuned to the needs of the government. As a result, the courts and boards have been reluctant to enforce the literal requirements of the clauses to deny claims in their entirety—understanding that this would amount to forfeiture of claims for which contractors should be paid. Thus, at the present time the notice requirements of the Changes clauses are enforced sporadically while the noncontractual obligation to give notice, which has been created by the courts and boards, as discussed above, is enforced when fairness demands. This has created the anomalous situation in which the notice requirements currently being imposed on contractors are those found in the decisional law rather than those found in the contract language.

A. Assertion of Right to Equitable Adjustment on Ordered Changes

When the contracting officer unilaterally orders a change, the contractor or the government is entitled to an equitable adjustment depending on the cost impact of the change. The supply contract clause requires the contractor to "assert its right" to an equitable adjustment as follows:

> (c) The Contractor must assert its right to an adjustment under this clause within 30 days from the date of receipt of the written order. However, if the Contracting Officer decides that the facts justify it, the Contracting Officer may receive and act upon a proposal submitted before final payment of the contract.

The construction contract clause contains more specific guidance on the nature of the required assertion, providing:

> (e) The Contractor must assert its right to an adjustment under this clause within 30 days after (1) receipt of a written change order under paragraph (a) of this clause . . . by submitting to the Contracting Officer a written statement describing the general nature and amount of proposal, unless this period is extended by the Government.

1. Contractor Claims

The requirement that the contractor give a form of notice within 30 days of the receipt of a change order is clearly intended to expedite the process of negotiation of equitable adjustments. A meaningful notice must include the contractor's estimate of the cost impact of the change, but this cannot always be done within a 30-day period. Furthermore, there is no significant harm to the government if this notice is late. As a result, this notice requirement has not been strictly enforced.

A technical reading of this notice provision also leads to the conclusion that it should not be strictly enforced. The current clauses in FAR 52.243 state that the contractor "must assert its right to an adjustment" within this time period. Prior to 1987 the clauses called for the submission of a "proposal for adjustment," and prior to 1980 they called for the assertion of a "claim for equitable adjustment." None of these formulations appears to have called for a fully documented proposal but, rather, for notice that the contractor believes that an equitable adjustment is called for by the change order. Thus, the notice does not appear to be a critical part of the contract administration process. It has been interpreted liberally in numerous holdings that failure to submit this notice will not bar a contractor's claim unless the government can show that the lack of notice was prejudicial in some way, *Golden W. Envtl. Servs.*, DOTBCA 2895, 00-2 BCA ¶30,990; *Valley Asphalt, Inc.*, AGBCA 97-118-1, 97-2 BCA ¶28,997; *Chimera Corp.*, ASBCA 18690, 76-1 BCA ¶11,901; *Weaver Constr. Co.*, ASBCA 12577, 69-1 BCA ¶7455; *Precision Tool & Eng'g Corp.*, ASBCA 14148, 71-1 BCA ¶8738. As noted in *Chimera*, an alternate way of dealing with this issue is to increase the contractor's burden of persuasion to compensate for the prejudice to the government when significant delay has occurred in the submission of the claim. See *Onsrud Mach. Works, Inc.*, ASBCA 14800, 71-2 BCA ¶9013; *Gardner Constr. Co.*, DOTCAB 70-18, 73-2 BCA ¶10,342. In *Progressive Enters., Inc.*, ASBCA 17360, 73-2 BCA ¶10,065, the board explained this version of the rule to mean that "[f]ailure to file such claims as soon as they have matured merely increases the burden of persuasion which rests upon the claimant." Some boards have also discussed the rule as involving the equitable doctrine of laches, drawing on court decisions in that area of the law to decide the case, *L. Rosenman Corp.*, GSBCA 4265, 77-2 BCA ¶12,843.

The Court of Claims affirmed a board finding of prejudice and barred a claim that was submitted five years after the date required by the contract in *Eggers & Higgins v. United States*, 185 Ct. Cl. 765, 403 F.2d 225 (1968). Board cases that have barred claims because of prejudice to the government include *Hawaiian Airmotive*, ASBCA 7892, 65-2 BCA ¶4946 (nearly three-year delay in submitting claim and government records lost in aircraft accident); *Industrial Research Assocs., Inc.*, DCAB WB-5, 67-1 BCA ¶6309 (claim submitted after completion of hearing before appeals board); and *L. Rosenman Corp.*, GSBCA 4265, 77-2 BCA ¶12,843 (12-year delay in submitting claim). See also *J.S. Alberici Constr. Co. & Martin K. Eby Constr. Co., A Joint Venture*, ENGBCA 6178, 98-2 BCA ¶29,875, barring a claim for defective government-furnished materials because the government was prejudiced when it did not receive timely notice, which would have permitted it to correct the materials.

In *B.L.I. Constr. Co.*, ASBCA 45560, 94-1 BCA ¶26,308, the government attempted to persuade the board to reverse the long line of cases that refused to strictly enforce the notice requirements, arguing that these cases were incorrectly decided because the government had never waived its sovereign immunity from suit when notice requirements were not complied with. The board rejected this argument, stating that it was "reluctant to depart from the well-established applications of the contract's notice requirements."

Claims asserted after final payment are specifically barred by the Changes clauses. Final payment is defined and discussed fully in Chapter 12. For this purpose the "assertion" requirement is quite liberal. In *Machinery Assocs., Inc.*, ASBCA 14510, 72-2 BCA ¶9476, the board gave guidance on the assertion of claims at 44,141:

> In asserting a claim a contractor need not cite a particular contract provision on which it relies or describe the substance or the claim of the amount, *Discon Corporation*, ASBCA No. 15981, 71-2 BCA ¶9069. It must, however, reasonably manifest to the Government its present intention to seek recovery of money based on a claim of legal right under the contract.

A casual statement expressing an indefinite intent to seek "additional compensation" made to a government employee authorized only to provide the contractor with technical assistance is not an assertion of a claim for purposes of the Changes clause, *Jo-Bar Mfg. Corp. v. United States*, 210 Ct. Cl. 149, 535 F.2d 62 (1976). However, if the contracting officer knows or is chargeable with knowledge that a claim either has been made or is outstanding prior to final payment, the fact of final payment will not bar consideration of that claim, *Missouri Research Labs., Inc.*, ASBCA 12355, 69-1 BCA ¶7762. Late assertion of a claim prior to final payment will not bar it from consideration by a board of contract appeals if the contracting officer has addressed the claim on its merits, *A.L. Harding, Inc.*, DCAB PR-44, 65-2 BCA ¶5261, *recons. denied*, 66-1 BCA ¶5463; *Proper Mfg. Co.*, GSBCA 3579, 73-2 BCA ¶10,029; *Monaco Builders, Inc.*, PSBCA 323, 78-1 BCA ¶12,924; *Human Advancement, Inc.*, HUDBCA 77-215-C15, 81-2 BCA ¶15,317; *West Land Builders*, VABCA 1664, 83-1 BCA

¶16,235, *recons. denied*, 83-1 BCA ¶16,430. The Court of Claims followed a similar rule, holding that late claims were not barred if they had been considered by the contracting officer and the appeals board on their merits, *Fox Valley Eng'g, Inc. v. United States*, 151 Ct. Cl. 228 (1960); *Dittmore-Freimuth Corp. v. United States*, 182 Ct. Cl. 507, 390 F.2d 664 (1968). However, if the claim is only addressed in a final decision of the contracting officer under the Disputes clause, final payment will still bar the claim, *Navales Enters., Inc.*, ASBCA 52202, 99-2 BCA ¶30,528.

2. Government Claims

Although the Changes clauses are silent as to notice by the government, claims by the government for a downward equitable adjustment will also be barred if not submitted to the contractor in a reasonable time. In *Joseph H. Roberts v. United States*, 174 Ct. Cl. 940, 357 F.2d 938 (1966), the court barred a government counterclaim asserting claims a number of years after completion of the contract. The court reasoned that the Changes clause "imposes upon the contracting officer the duty to make such an adjustment within a reasonable time, so as to afford the contractor an opportunity to appeal from an unreasonable or arbitrary decision while the facts supporting the claim are readily available and before the contractor's position is prejudiced by final settlement with his subcontractors, suppliers, and other creditors." After the *Roberts* decision a six-year statute of limitations on government claims was enacted, 28 U.S.C. § 2415. This statute, of course, applies only to assertion of claims in court and does not deal directly with claims asserted by the contracting officer under the Changes clause. Hence, the *Roberts* rule has been followed by the appeals boards in *Southwestern Eng'g Co.*, NASABCA 425-15, 68-1 BCA ¶6977, *recons. denied*, 68-2 BCA ¶7317 (more than two-year delay in asserting claim); *Futuronics, Inc.*, DOTCAB 67-15, 68-2 BCA ¶7079, *recons. denied*, 68-2 BCA ¶7235 (claim asserted more than one year after appeal process had commenced); and *Lindwall Constr. Co.*, ASBCA 23148, 79-1 BCA ¶13,822 (claim asserted as a counterclaim in a contract appeal proceeding 13 months after government knew of claim). In *Norcoast-Beck Aleutian*, ASBCA 26389, 83-1 BCA ¶16,152, the board stated that government claims for deductive changes under the Changes clause "must be made within a reasonable time after it becomes apparent that a change will cause a cost savings, and no later than final payment." See also *M&C Cumberland*, DOTBCA 3014, 00-1 BCA ¶30,700, in which the board rejected the government's claims for price reductions for reduced work because they were not asserted until after contract completion. The board concluded that the contractor had been prejudiced by the late notice because it had not taken steps to reduce its costs when it found that the government was not asking for the price reductions on a quarterly basis as called for by the contract. Compare *Olympia-reinigung, GmbH*, ASBCA 53643, 04-1 BCA ¶32,458, permitting the government to assert a claim for a deductive change after payment for the work.

Oral notice to the contractor may meet the government's obligation. See *Porshia Alexander of Am.*, GSBCA 9604, 91-1 BCA ¶23,657, in which the contractor's defense that it had not been informed of a government claim was denied because it had been informally told during performance that the work should be reduced.

B. Constructive Changes Claims

Most government contracts contain no notice requirements that explicitly pertain to constructive changes. Thus, it is far more likely that the special requirements imposed by the courts and boards, as discussed earlier, will apply. This section discusses those instances when the government has alleged that a contractual provision applies to constructive changes.

1. Applicability of 30-Day Notice Requirement

The notice requirement that is common to all standard Changes clauses is the provision calling for assertion of a right to an adjustment within 30 days of the receipt of a change order. The appeals boards originally held that this requirement was not applicable to constructive changes since there was no written order that started the notice period running, *Burton-Rodgers, Inc.*, ASBCA 5438, 60-1 BCA ¶2558; *MECO, Inc.*, ASBCA 9849, 65-2 BCA ¶5132; *Carlin-Atlas*, GSBCA 2061, 66-2 BCA ¶5872; *ITT Commercial Servs., Inc.*, GSBCA 4210, 75-1 BCA ¶11,218; *Honeywell, Inc.*, VABCA 1166, 76-1 BCA ¶11,745. More recently, courts and boards have held that this type of notice requirement applies to constructive changes at least to the extent that the claim will be denied if the government is prejudiced by lack of notice, *R.R. Tyler*, AGBCA 381, 77-1 BCA ¶12,227; *JEMCO, Inc.*, ENGBCA 3879, 77-2 BCA ¶12,749; *Mingus Constructors, Inc. v. United*

States, 812 F.2d 1387 (Fed. Cir. 1987); *Togaroli Corp.*, ASBCA 32995, 89-2 BCA ¶21,864, *recons. denied*, 89-3 BCA ¶22,102; *Watson, Rice & Co.*, HUDBCA 89-4468-C6, 90-1 BCA ¶22,499; *Max Blau & Sons, Inc.*, GSBCA 9827, 91-1 BCA ¶23,626; *Integrated Clinical Sys., Inc.*, VABCA 3745, 95-2 BCA ¶27,902; *SIPCO Servs. & Marine, Inc., v. United States*, 41 Fed. Cl. 196 (1998); *A.R. Mack Constr. Co.*, ASBCA 50035, 01-2 BCA ¶31,593. However, these cases hardly ever find that the government has been prejudiced. See, however, *Jo-Bar Mfg. Corp. v. United States*, 210 Ct. Cl. 149, 535 F.2d 62 (1976) (complaint dismissed because contractor's vague complaints to a technician were not sufficient to put government on notice); *John Murphy Constr. Co.*, AGBCA 418, 79-1 BCA ¶13,836 (claim denied because government had neither actual nor constructive notice under either ¶ (d) or (e) of the construction contract Changes clause and was prejudiced thereby); *Schouten Constr. Co.*, DOTCAB 78-14, 79-1 BCA ¶13,553 (board considered motion to dismiss for failure to give 30-day notice of constructive change but found waiver of notice requirement by government consideration of claim); and *T. Brown Constructors, Inc. v. Peña*, 132 F. 3d 724 (Fed. Cir. 1997) (claim denied because change in conditions of site kept government from investigating claim). In addition, some boards have adopted the position that, when prejudice is found, the result will be a higher burden of persuasion on the contractor rather than outright rejection of the claim, *Onsrud Mach. Works, Inc.*, ASBCA 14800, 71-2 BCA ¶9013; *M.M. Sundt Constr. Co.*, ASBCA 17475, 74-1 BCA ¶10,627. This result is based on the reasoning of the Court of Claims that was first stated in *B-W Constr. Co. v. United States*, 100 Ct. Cl. 227 (1943).

2. Construction Contract Notice Requirement

The construction contract Changes clause issued in 1968 and now contained in FAR 52.243-4 contains special notice provisions in paragraphs (b) and (d) pertaining to constructive change orders. Paragraph (b) requires that notice be given of all constructive changes but contains no time limitations on when the notice must be given. Paragraph (d) limits recovery for constructive changes to costs incurred no more than 20 days prior to the notice but excludes constructive changes based on defective specifications. Although the results of this 20-day notice provision are harsh, it was applied strictly by the appeals boards in most of the early cases interpreting the clause, *Preferred Contractors, Inc.*, ASBCA 15569, 72-1 BCA ¶9283 (letter giving notice dated 20 days after costs were incurred not timely absent proof that letter was mailed or received on twentieth day). The boards continue to apply the provision when there are no extenuating circumstances, such as actual knowledge of the government, *Northeastern Constr. Co.*, ENGBCA 3820, 78-1 BCA ¶13,052; *G.C. Indus., Inc.*, ASBCA 22890, 79-1 BCA ¶13,721; *Joseph Morton Co.*, GSBCA 4815, 81-1 BCA ¶14,980; *Hunt Bldg. Corp.*, ASBCA 31775, 89-1 BCA ¶21,196; *Pittsburgh-Des Moines Corp.*, EBCA 314-3-84, 89-2 BCA ¶21,739; *Lloyd Moore Constr.*, AGBCA 87-151-3, 89-2 BCA ¶21,875; *LaDuke Constr. & Krumdieck, Inc., J.V.*, AGBCA 83-177-1, 90-1 BCA ¶22,302; *Potomac Marine & Aviation, Inc.*, ASBCA 42417, 93-2 BCA ¶25,865. See also *Jimenez, Inc.*, LBCA 2001-BCA-2, 02-2 BCA ¶31981, in which the board denied claims where no notice was given, without citing the paragraph of the clause that was applicable.

In 1972 the Court of Claims refused to apply a 20-day notice provision when the government actually knew of a situation that constituted a constructive suspension of work, *Hoel-Steffen Constr. Co. v. United States*, 197 Ct. Cl. 561, 456 F.2d 760 (1972). Thereafter, boards have generally followed a more liberal interpretation of this notice provision, finding that the requirement is met when the government has actual knowledge of the facts constituting the constructive change, *R.C. Hedreen Co.*, ASBCA 19439, 76-1 BCA ¶11,816 (request for clarification of specification by government field representative); *United Baeton Int'l*, VACAB 1209, 76-2 BCA ¶12,133 (discussion with resident government engineer and observation of extra work); *Hartford Accident & Indem. Co.*, IBCA 1139-1-77, 77-2 BCA ¶12,604 (discussion with government field inspector); *Corbell Constr. Co.*, AGBCA 77-129, 78-1 BCA ¶13,080 (government representatives directed performance of the work); *Building Maint. Corp.*, DOTCAB 76-42, 79-1 BCA ¶13,560 (oral and written notice that problems were being encountered); *J.W. Bateson Co.*, VACAB 1148, 79-1 BCA ¶13,573 (government aware of difficulties but left solution to contractor); *J.D. Abrams*, ENGBCA 4332, 89-1 BCA ¶21,379 (contractor told Resident Officer in Charge of Construction that it disagreed with interpretation); *Niko Contracting Co.*, IBCA 2368, 91-1 BCA ¶23,321 (problem raised with government representative on site); *Toland & Sons*, IBCA 2716, 91-3 BCA ¶24,263 (government showed no prejudice from lack of notice); *Dan Rice Constr. Co.*, ASBCA 52160, 04-1 BCA ¶32,595 (COTR had full knowledge of changes). For a case not following this type of reasoning, see *Piracci Constr. Co.*, GSBCA 3477, 74-1 BCA ¶10,647, *recons. denied*, 74-2 BCA ¶10,799 (notice to the government under the Suspension of Work clause insufficient to put the government on notice of problems under the Changes clause). In these cases, the boards frequently justify a liberal interpretation on the grounds that the government has not been prejudiced, but the critical factor appears to be the actual knowledge of a responsible government employee. However, a considerably broader view is expressed in *Mil-Pak Co.*, ASBCA 19733, 76-1 BCA ¶11,725, *recons. denied*, 76-1 BCA ¶11,836, in which the standard was whether the government would have acted differently had notice been given. Accord, *Imbus Roofing Co.*, GSBCA 10430, 91-2 BCA ¶23,820; *Atlantic Constr. Co.*, ASBCA 22647, 79-1 BCA ¶13,612. See also *Andy Int'l, Inc.*, ASBCA 20397, 76-2 BCA ¶12,046, in which the board noted at 57,815 that there is a "trend toward making the rule the same for both 'mandatory' and 'discretionary' notice provisions notwithstanding the contractual language and the published regulatory intent of the different clauses." Compare *R.R. Tyler*, AGBCA 381, 77-1 BCA ¶12,227, reaching the opposite conclusion.

Another basis for not enforcing the notice requirement is a finding by the board that the failure to give notice has been induced by actions or statements of the government, *Ionics, Inc.*, ASBCA 16094, 71-2 BCA ¶9030; *J.A. LaPorte, Inc.*, IBCA 1014-12-73, 75-2 BCA ¶11,486. See also *Universal Painting Corp.*, ASBCA 20536, 77-1 BCA ¶12,355. In *LaPorte*, the board also explained its nonenforcement of the 20-day notice provision on the grounds that there was no single, identifiable event upon which the claim was grounded that could be used to start the notice period running.

In *Powers Regulator Co.*, GSBCA 4668, 80-2 BCA ¶14,463, the board reviewed the decisions of all the boards of contract appeals and, at 71,320, stated the following instances in which the government's invocation of the 20-day notice provision will fail:

- Written notice is in fact given the contracting officer.
- The contracting officer has actual or imputed knowledge of the facts giving rise to the claim.
- Notice to the contracting officer would have been useless.
- The contracting officer frustrated the giving of the notice.
- The contracting officer considered the claim on the merits.

The 20-day notice requirement in the construction contract Changes clause specifically excludes claims for defective specifications. It can thus be argued that this contract language removes any requirement for notice of defective specifications, *H.M. Byars Constr. Co.*, IBCA 1098-2-76, 77-2 BCA ¶12,568. However, one board has reasoned that the same prejudice rule should apply under this clause because of the notice requirement in ¶(b), *H.A. Anderson Co.*, ENGBCA 3724, 77-2 BCA ¶12,712. In that case, the board referred to the contractor's withholding of information about the defective specifications, to the government's prejudice, as a "failure to mitigate." A defective specification claim was denied on this basis in *Time Contractors, Joint Venture*, DOTBCA 1747, 1986 DOT BCA LEXIS 74.

3. Notification of Changes Clause

FAR 43.107 provides for the optional use of a Notification of Changes clause, FAR 52.243-7, in contracts for major weapon systems or subsystems. This clause contains the following notice requirement:

> (b) *Notice*. The primary purpose of this clause is to obtain prompt reporting of Government conduct that the Contractor considers to constitute a change to this contract. Except for changes identified as such in writing and signed by the Contracting Officer, the Contractor shall notify the Administrative Contracting Officer in writing promptly, within (to be negotiated) calendar days from the date that the Contractor identifies any Government conduct (including actions, inactions, and written or oral communications) that the Contractor regards as a change to the contract terms and conditions. On the basis of the most accurate information available to the Contractor, the notice shall state—
>
> (1) The date, nature, and circumstances of the conduct regarded as a change;
> (2) The name, function, and activity of each Government individual and Contractor official or employee involved in or knowledgeable about such conduct;
> (3) The identification of any documents and the substance of any oral communication involved in such conduct;

(4) In the instance of alleged acceleration of scheduled performance or delivery, the basis upon which it arose;

(5) The particular elements of contract performance for which the Contractor may seek an equitable adjustment under this clause, including—

  (i) What contract line items have been or may be affected by the alleged change;

  (ii) What labor or materials or both have been or may be added, deleted, or wasted by the alleged change;

  (iii) To the extent practicable, what delay and disruption in the manner and sequence of performance and effect on continued performance have been or may be caused by the alleged change;

  (iv) What adjustments to contract price, delivery schedule, and other provisions affected by the alleged change are estimated; and

(6) The Contractor's estimate of the time by which the Government must respond to the Contractor's notice to minimize cost, delay or disruption of performance.

In *Grumman Aerospace Corp.*, ASBCA 46834, 03-1 BCA ¶32,203, *recons. denied*, 03-2 BCA ¶32,289, the board held that this notice requirement should be enforced in the same way that the 30-day notice requirements had been enforced—not "hypertechnically" but only if the government was prejudiced. It found no prejudice because the government officials administering the contract were well aware of the problems being encountered by the contractor. Compare *Ervin & Assocs., Inc. v. United States*, 59 Fed. Cl. 267 (2004), in which the court strictly enforced the 15-day notice requirement in the clause in denying a constructive changes claim. The court stated that the contracting officer should have been notified "directly." See also *MC II Generator & Elec.*, ASBCA 53389, 04-1 BCA ¶32,569, where the contracting officer denied a claim based on lack of notification as required by this clause but the board denied the claim because the government project manager did not direct a change and had no authority to do so.

4. Accelerations

The construction contract Changes clause requires written notice of constructive acceleration orders in ¶(b) and denies recovery of costs incurred prior to 20 days before such notice is given in ¶(d). In one case in which the government argued lack of notice as a defense to an acceleration claim, the board ruled that the requirement would not be enforced because the government had not been prejudiced by lack of notice, *E.C. Morris & Son, Inc.*, ASBCA 20697, 77-2 BCA ¶12,622. The facts indicated that the government knew of the acceleration order since it had directed the contractor to speed up. In addition, the board found that the government would not have been able to avoid the costs had it received notice. In contrast, acceleration claims have been barred for lack of notice, *Nello L. Teer Co. v. Washington Metro. Area Transit Auth.*, 695 F. Supp. 583 (D.D.C. 1988) (no notice for one year after excusable delay had occurred); *Girardeau Contractors, Inc.*, ENGBCA 5034, 88-1 BCA ¶20,391 (no proof of notice of acceleration). Compare *P.J. Dick, Inc.*, VABCA 5597, 01-2 BCA ¶31,647, where timely notice was given.

In a case involving an acceleration claim under the pre-1968 Standard Form 23-A Changes clause not containing the 20-day notice provision, the Court of Claims ruled that failure to give notice of an acceleration barred recovery because the government was prejudiced by lack of notice, *Eggers & Higgins v. United States*, 185 Ct. Cl. 765, 403 F.2d 225 (1968). The court concluded that the government could have altered the performance to avoid the acceleration costs if it had known that the contractor was construing the refusal to grant a time extension as an acceleration order.

5. Military Shipbuilding Contracts

In 1984 Congress enacted a special statute requiring timely notice of constructive changes claims on military shipbuilding contracts. 10 U.S.C. § 2405 read:

(a) The Secretary of a military department may not adjust any price under a shipbuilding contract entered into after December 7, 1983, for an amount set forth in a claim, request for equitable adjustment, or demand for payment under the contract (or incurred due to the preparation, submission, or adjudication of any such claim, request, or demand) arising out of events occurring more than 18 months before the submission of the claim, request, or demand.

> (b) For the purposes of subsection (a), a claim, request, or demand shall be considered to have been submitted only when the contractor has provided the certification required by section 6(c)(1) of the Contract Disputes Act of 1978 (41 U.S.C. 605(c)(1)) and the supporting data for the claim, request, or demand.

This statute was repealed by § 810(a)(1) of Pub. L. No. 105-85, 111 Stat. 1839, Nov. 18, 1997. This repeal was "effective with respect to claims, requests for equitable adjustment, and demands for payment under shipbuilding contracts that have been or are submitted before, on, or after the date of the enactment of this Act." However, it was not effective with regard to claims that had been resolved with finality in the government's favor prior to the enactment of the statute.

The statute was interpreted to be in the nature of a notice requirement, not a statute of limitations, *Bath Iron Works Corp. v. United States*, 27 Fed. Cl. 114 (1992), *aff'd*, 20 F.3d 1567 (Fed. Cir. 1994). Thus, while it was binding on the military departments, it did not preclude the Court of Federal Claims from taking jurisdiction of cases where contractors were asserting constructive changes claims that had not been submitted to the government within the 18-month period. However, the court never stated what standard it would use in reviewing such claims—a strict rule or a prejudice rule. The Armed Services Board ruled that the statute should be interpreted strictly to bar untimely claims, *Bath Iron Works Corp.*, ASBCA 43303, 93-2 BCA ¶25,792, *recons. denied*, 93-3 BCA ¶25,992.

The "event" that began the running of this 18-month period was the beginning of work that is not called for by the contract, *Peterson Builders, Inc. v. United States*, 26 Cl. Ct. 1227 (1992), *aff'd*, 155 F.3d 566 (Fed. Cir. 1998). In that case, the court rejected the contractor's argument that the date should be the time when the contractor could fully quantify the claim. Thus, the contractor had 18 months to assemble all of the data necessary to submit a fully documented claim meeting the terms of ¶(b) of the statute.

CHAPTER 2

DEFAULT TERMINATION, DAMAGES AND LIQUIDATED DAMAGES

Default termination is the ultimate method of dealing with a contractor's unexcused present or prospective failure to perform in accordance with the contract specifications and schedule. By exercising its right to terminate for default, the government effectively notifies the contractor that its performance failure discharges government duties under the contract while exposing the contractor to potential liability for the consequences of its breach.

The FAR contains two basic clauses covering default termination. The default clause in FAR 52.249-8 is used for both fixed-price supply and service contracts. The clause for fixed-price construction contracts is contained in FAR 52.249-10. The government's policies with respect to termination for default are contained in FAR Subpart 49.4. The termination for cause of contracts for commercial items is covered in FAR 12.403 and the applicable clause is ¶(m) of FAR 52.212-4.

With the exception of the relatively new FAR 52 212-4, the government's rights and obligations under these clauses have been litigated extensively. (For one case dealing with terminations under FAR 52.212-4, see *Southeast Tech. Servs.*, ASBCA 52319, 02-1 BCA ¶31,727.) This litigation has developed a number of legal rules, which are the subject of this chapter. The first section examines the consequences of a default termination. The second section reviews the types of performance failures that entitle the government to terminate for default and the circumstances under which it can waive these rights. The third section discusses the termination decision. The fourth section covers procedures for termination. The fifth section discusses excess costs of reprocurement. The chapter concludes with a discussion of liquidated damages. Much of the litigation that arises regarding default terminations focuses on whether the failure to perform on time is "excused" as being attributable to causes beyond the control or without the fault or negligence of the contractor. These issues are discussed in detail in Chapter 6.

I. CONSEQUENCES OF DEFAULT TERMINATION

A default termination is a traumatic event for both parties. The contractor and the government are both likely to suffer severe economic and time consequences.

A. Impact on Contractor

The impact of a default termination under a fixed-price supply contract is usually quite severe. A default termination may have the following effects on the relationship between the parties:

- The government is not liable for the costs of unaccepted work—the contractor is entitled to receive payment only for work accepted by the government;
- The government is entitled to the return of progress, partial, or advance payments;
- The government has the right but not the duty to appropriate the contractor's material, inventory, construction plant and equipment at the site, and, under supply contracts, drawings and plans—with the price for the appropriated items to be negotiated;

- The contractor is liable for excess costs of reprocurement or completion;
- The contractor is liable for actual or liquidated damages; and
- The contractor may be subject to debarment.

See FAR 9.406-2(b)(1)

A default termination may also adversely affect the contractor's eligibility for award of other government contracts since past performance is considered in determining responsibility and is evaluated in negotiated contracts. Because of these consequences and since a default termination not infrequently leads to the contractor's financial ruin, the Court of Claims has branded default termination a species of forfeiture, *De Vito v. United States*, 188 Ct. Cl. 979, 413 F.2d 1147 (1969). Although some of these consequences are also applicable to construction and service contracts, a contractor who has been properly terminated for default under those contracts is nevertheless entitled to payment for work that was properly performed prior to the default termination, *J.G. Enters., Inc.*, ASBCA 27150, 83-2 BCA ¶16,808; *Ventilation Cleaning Eng'rs, Inc.*, ASBCA 18580, 74-2 BCA ¶10,873; *Mercury Co.*, ASBCA 14926, 70-2 BCA ¶8419. However, it is not entitled to recover the contract amount minus the cost of completion of the work, *Century Marine, Inc. v. United States*, 153 F.3d 225 (5th Cir. 1998) (reasoning that such recovery would permit the recovery of anticipatory profit). In contrast, under supply contracts, the contractor generally has no right following proper default termination to recover costs incurred in producing supplies not accepted by the government, *Valley Sand & Gravel*, AGBCA 385, 75-1 BCA ¶10,986. The logic underlying this different treatment is that in the case of service and construction contracts the government has benefited from the contractor's partial performance in the form of services rendered or permanent improvement of government-owned property. In the case of supply contracts, however, the government is not benefited by the contractor's performance efforts unless it has accepted the supplies.

Even if the contractor is successful in overturning the termination, the relief obtainable may well be limited. The default clauses provide that if the termination is improper the "rights and obligations" of the parties will be "the same as if the termination had been issued for the convenience of the Government." The Termination for the Convenience of the Government clause permits recovery of costs incurred but does not permit the recovery of anticipated profit (see Chapter 11). Furthermore, it contains a provision reducing the recovery by the rate of anticipated loss. Thus, recovery of anticipatory profits will occur only in those rare cases where the contractor can prove that the government terminated in bad faith. See *Apex Int'l Mgmt. Servs. Inc.*, ASBCA 38087, 94-2 BCA ¶26,842; *Carter Indus.*, DOTBCA 4108, 02-1 BCA ¶31,738.

In addition, the contractor may not recover more than it would have been entitled to if the government had exercised all of the rights available to it. Thus, in *A/S Dampshibssetshabet Torm v. United States*, 64 F. Supp. 2d 298 (S.D.N.Y. 1999), even though the court found that the agency improperly terminated for default, the court denied the contractor's request to convert the termination into one for convenience when the agency proved that it could have canceled the contract under the "Inspection" clause.

Even extra costs resulting from government-directed changes in the work may not be recoverable following a valid default termination of a fixed-price supply contract where the product of the extra effort has not been accepted by, or has not resulted in a benefit to, the government. In *A.C. Hoyle Co.*, ASBCA 15363, 71-2 BCA ¶9137, the board stated that a "valid termination for default negates the Government's liability for . . . any equitable increase for extra work performed in producing rejected winches." See also *Jules Teitelbaum, Tr. in Bank. for Victory Elecs., Inc.*, ASBCA 12885, 70-1 BCA ¶8210, in which the board rejected the contention that the contractor was entitled to recover costs of performing "additional testing." The board reasoned that, since the testing was incomplete at the time of the default and no test data had ever been delivered, "no benefit accrued to the Government." See, however, *Laka Tool & Stamping Co. v. United States*, 226 Ct. Cl. 83, 639 F.2d 738 (1980), *reh'g denied*, 227 Ct. Cl. 468, 650 F.2d 270, *cert. denied*, 454 U.S. 1086 (1981), in which the Court of Claims held that a fixed-price contractor was entitled to recover the "excess costs" it incurred in trying to comply with defective government specifications despite its eventual default for reasons unrelated to the defective specifications. In concluding that the government's proper default termination action did not serve as an absolute bar to recovery of the contractor's "out-of-pocket loss in the form of expenditures for efforts wasted because of the impossible specifications," the court emphasized that the costs resulted from acts that the government "had no right to do under the contract," stating at 472:

> This last factor distinguishes the case where a contractor terminated for default would seek to recover for a mere change. The Government does have the right under the contract to issue change orders. If, instead of supplying impossible specifications, the Government had simply increased the amount of magazines required under the contract by change order and [the contractor] had completed the contract, it would have been entitled to the contract price for the originally required work plus an equitable adjustment for the additional work. However, should [the contractor] be properly terminated for default without making any acceptable deliveries in such a case, it would get nothing for the original work. Furthermore, our opinion today should not be read as allowing a recovery for work covered by a change order, even though the change order might have caused a [contractor] to do extra work just as the impossible specifications did here. A crucial distinction is that the Government does have the right to issue change orders.

See *Harent, Inc.*, ASBCA 16206, 73-2 BCA ¶10,074, in which the board held that a ship repair contractor could recover for extras following a valid default termination where the government had "received the benefit" of the extra work. See also *Robert B. Joy*, PSBCA 938, Sept. 30, 1981, *Unpub.*, allowing the contractor to rely on an "adjustment in compensation" provision despite a valid default termination.

B. Impact on Government

Even if the government is successful in litigating the propriety of a default termination, it will also most likely suffer severe consequences. The impact of a default termination on the government was discussed in *Clay Bernard Sys. Int'l, Ltd v. United States*, 22 Cl. Ct. 804 (1991), as follows at 810:

> Termination for default, however, is a drastic adjustment of the contractual relationship and the Government is held to strict accountability in using this sanction. *J.D. Hedin Constr. Co. v. United States*, 408 F.2d 424, 431, 187 Ct. Cl. 45 (1969); *Schlesinger v. United States*, 390 F.2d 702, 709, 182 Ct. Cl. 571 (1968). A termination for default generally results in lost time to the Government in obtaining the services or goods it sought; it always penalizes the contractor, and frequently the Government is exposed to substantial additional costs, particularly if the action subsequently is found to be one for convenience of the Government. Further, a default termination is an acknowledgment that previous procedural safeguards—i.e., bidding and negotiation procedures to select a contractor, examinations to determine contractor competence and qualifications, and review and approval of contractor competence and qualifications, and review and approval of subcontract and subcontractors—have failed to realize their purposes.

For these reasons, if the government still needs the work, it will usually not terminate the contract unless it is convinced that the contractor is incapable of performing the work or another contractor will be able to satisfy its needs in a significantly shorter period of time than the defaulting contractor.

C. Fixed-Price Supply Termination Inventory

Paragraph (e) of the FAR default clause for supply and service contracts provides that, following default termination, the government may direct the contractor to "transfer title and deliver to the Government . . . any (1) completed supplies, and (2) partially completed supplies and materials, parts, tools, dies, jigs, fixtures, plans, drawings, information, and contract rights (collectively referred to as `manufacturing materials' in this clause)." Paragraph (f) states that payment for "completed supplies delivered and accepted" will be at the "contract price." In contrast, payment for "manufacturing materials" delivered to and accepted by the government will be in an amount agreed to by the parties. In *Metadure Corp.*, ASBCA 24533, 83-1 BCA ¶16,325, the board upheld the government's use of a "percentage of completion" method for valuing termination inventory. This technique was described by the board at 81,136:

> Using the inventory obtained by the Government through its replevin suit, the team determined the material and component parts that were not included in the inventory delivered and had yet to be procured by [the contractor] to complete the contract. These missing items were priced and that amount subtracted from the total contract price to arrive at a cost basis for determining the percentage of contract completion.

> Based upon a Defense Contract Audit Agency (DCAA) audit report and the contract, the team determined the value of the missing material and component parts using [the contractor's] available purchase orders for those items. The team used this process throughout their evaluation. Based upon the available purchase orders the team applied a value to each item. The team concerned itself only with the high cost items. It did not include peripheral parts to complete the contract. Based upon its evaluation, the team made its determination as to the percentage of contract completion. Based upon an evaluation of material and component part costs, the percentage of contract completion was determined to be 78 percent. This percentage figure did not include the labor necessary to complete the contract. The team determined that the requisite labor constituted 9 percent of the estimate to complete the contract. The 9 percent for labor was deducted from the 78 percent, resulting in a percentage of 69.

Note that this approach, by using the original contract price as the basis for determining the percentage of completion, will for the most part preserve the contractor's profit or loss position relative to the partially completed items.

In *Jules Teitelbaum, Tr. in Bankr. for Victory Elecs., Inc.*, ASBCA 12885, 70-1 BCA ¶8210, the board rejected the proposition that the total cost incurred by the contractor in producing "manufacturing materials" was conclusive of the true value of such termination inventory, essentially objecting to this approach as a form of total cost valuation long disfavored by the boards and courts. In addition, the board recognized that costs incurred in producing termination inventory that were attributable to causes for which an equitable adjustment was available under the contract would be recoverable, but it found no proof supporting such entitlement in that case. The board also acknowledged that the costs the contractor incurred in "converting components into assemblies" should be considered in arriving at a "fair and reasonable value" for this termination inventory. As to valuation of termination inventory taken from subcontractors, the board did accept as conclusive the costs set forth in the purchase orders under which the materials had been furnished by the contractor to the subcontractors. See also *Munck Sys., Inc.*, ASBCA 25600, 83-1 BCA ¶16,210, *aff'd*, 727 F.2d 1118 (Fed. Cir. 1983), holding that the contractor was entitled to recover additional amounts for components taken by the government following default where the government had directed changes in the contractor's previously approved quality control procedures and had directed the contractor to use a particular control device not specifically required by the contract.

In *Meyer Labs, Inc.*, ASBCA 18989, 83-2 BCA ¶16,598, the board held that in computing excess costs the government could not charge the contractor for expenses it incurred in removing termination inventory. The board also concluded that there was no need to determine the value of the inventory since the government had turned it over to the reprocurement contractor, thus making its value a "cost of reprocurement" and resulting in a "wash" transaction. For cases relating to a contractor's post-termination costs relating to the inventory, compare *Dennis Berlin d/b/a Spectro Sort & as Spectro Sort Mfg. Co.*, ASBCA 51919, 02-1 BCA ¶31,675 (contractor not entitled to the costs of performing an inventory of material after the termination for default because the contract obligated the contractor to do so), with *C.T. Genvis Indus., Inc.*, ENGBCA 6255, 99-1 BCA ¶30,334 (contractor's claimed costs relating to the government's efforts to take delivery of partially completed work after the default termination "could constitute a separate claim under the changes provision of the contract").

II. RIGHT TO TERMINATE

The common law right to follow a course of action equivalent to default termination is said to arise when there is an "uncured material failure" to perform, *Restatement, Second, Contracts* § 237. In describing these material failures, the courts have used terms such as "material breach" or "failure of consideration." These terms have been invoked when the failure to perform on time involves a very significant portion of the contract work. They may also be used when it appears that completion of performance will be delayed long beyond the specified completion date. When termination is considered to be justified for relatively short delays, the courts often state that "time is of the essence." Thus, when such a termination is considered improper, the judicial response is usually that the parties did not make time of the essence in their contract.

The presence of the default clauses in government contracts has raised the question of whether these common law concepts are applicable to federal contracts. Consequently, this section first deals with the types of performance failures or contractor conduct that will justify default termination by the government. It then considers the matter of when a failure to perform a portion of the stated contract work justifies termination of the entire contract. The section concludes with a discussion of the concept of waiver through which the government, by conduct inconsistent with the exercise of its default rights, loses the right to terminate. This discussion includes an examination of the rights of the parties once a waiver has occurred.

A. Grounds for Termination

The standard default clauses identify three different grounds for termination: (1) failure to deliver the product or complete the work or service within the stated time, (2) failure to make progress in prosecuting the work and thereby endangering timely completion, and (3) breach of "other provisions" of the contract.

In addition to these specifically enumerated grounds for default termination, two additional types of contractor conduct have frequently served as the basis for default termination. The first—failure to proceed—arises when the contractor fails or refuses to go forward with the work according to the contracting officer's directions. The second—anticipatory repudiation—occurs when the contractor clearly expresses through words or conduct an intention not to complete the contract work on time. This subsection discusses in detail each of these bases for default termination.

1. Failure to Perform or Deliver

The supply and service contracts default clause provides that the government may terminate for default if the contractor "fails to deliver the supplies or to perform the services within the time specified." The construction contract default provision states that the government may terminate for default when the contractor "fails to complete" the work within the "time specified in this contract." Similar language is set forth in the other FAR default clauses.

Although these clauses explicitly make untimely performance the basis for the default action, it is important to recognize that nearly every government contract spells out the contractor's required performance in terms of the nature of the product or service that is to be delivered or performed as well as the time by which this performance is to be completed. Thus, in order for the contractor to render "timely performance," two basic requirements must be satisfied: (1) the product, service, or construction work must conform to the required contract design/performance specifications, and (2) the product must be delivered or the work completed by the specified due date. See *Radiation Tech., Inc. v. United States*, 177 Ct. Cl. 227, 366 F.2d 1003 (1966); *Air, Inc.*, GSBCA 8847, 91-1 BCA ¶23,352; and *Nash Metalware Co.*, GSBCA 11951, 94-2 BCA ¶26,780.

a. *Slight Delays in Performance*

The government rarely terminates contracts for slight delays. Thus, there are relatively few decisions in which the issue to be decided is whether "time is of the essence." It has been argued that the presence of default clauses gives the contractor sufficient notice that time is of the essence in all government contracts, Coons & Whelan, *Default Termination of Defense Department Fixed Price Supply Contracts,* 32 Notre Dame L. Rev. 189, 191 (1957). For the contrary view, see Risik, *Defaults in Federal Government Contracts,* 14 Fed. B.J. 339, 348 (1954).

The Court of Claims never squarely decided the question of whether a termination for a slight delay is appropriate, and neither has the Court of Appeals for the Federal Circuit. However, there is language in Court of Claims decisions supporting both views. One view is expressed in *De Vito v. United States*, 188 Ct. Cl. 979, 413 F.2d 1147 (1969), in which the court stated that "[t]ime is of the essence in any contract containing fixed dates for performance." This view was taken in *National Farm Equip. Co.*, GSBCA 4921, 78-1 BCA ¶13,195 (contract's default clause grants the government the right to terminate the contract when delivery is not made on the contractually specified date and does not require the government to wait one day more); and *Thomas C. Wilson, Inc.*, ASBCA 26035, 83-1 BCA ¶16,149 (time became of the essence where the contract specified the delivery date and included the default clause; time remained an essence of the contract even though the government did not need the supplies at the time of the delivery date).

De Vito was apparently followed by the Armed Services Board of Contract Appeals in *Nuclear Research Assocs., Inc.*, ASBCA 13563, 70-1 BCA ¶8237, where a contractor tendered specially manufactured supplies on the first working day after the due date, but the government issued a default termination notice 30 minutes after delivery. In upholding the termination, the ASBCA Senior Deciding Group stated that, once a contractor "has failed to deliver on time, the Government, absent excusable cause of delay, has an indefeasible right to terminate the contract, unless its own conduct deprives it of that right." The board also noted that it did not matter that the late delivery was made before the sending of the default termination telegram. However, in a dissenting opinion, three judges stated that the substantial performance doctrine was applicable because time was not of the essence in the contract. (Much of *Nuclear Research* was later overruled by *Darwin Constr. Co. v. United States*, 811 F.2d 593 (Fed. Cir. 1987), but the requirement that "time is of the essence" remained intact.)

For other cases, involving both standard and specially manufactured goods, expressing the view that the default clause in supply contracts gives the government the immediate right to terminate once the due date has arrived, see *M.H. Colvin & Co.*, GSBCA 5209, 79-2 BCA ¶13,981 (screw driver bits and adapters not delivered on scheduled inspection dates); *National Farm Equip. Co.*, GSBCA 4921, 78-1 BCA ¶13,195 (pruning shears and garden spades available for delivery one day after scheduled date); *Fairfield Scientific Corp.*, ASBCA 21152, 78-1 BCA ¶12,869, *aff'd*, 228 Ct. Cl. 264, 655 F.2d 1062 (1981) (termination five days after contractor failed to deliver impulse cartridges on scheduled date); *H.N. Bailey & Assocs.*, ASBCA 21300, 77-2 BCA ¶12,681 (link assemblies for RC-135 C/M aircraft not timely delivered for first article testing despite two time extensions); and *R & O Indus., Inc.*, GSBCA 4804, 80-1 BCA ¶14,196 (cooking knives not delivered despite five time extensions). See also *Riggs Eng'g Co.*, ASBCA 26509, 82-2 BCA ¶15,955, in which the board recognized a right to immediately terminate because the contractor failed to deliver a first article on the specified date.

Time has also been held to be of the essence in construction contracts. For example, in *Ajax Co.*, ENGBCA 3377, 76-1 BCA ¶11,645, the board noted that, despite the absence of monetary damages, the contractor's delays could interfere with the discharge of governmental functions. Note that in *Ajax* the original contract contained a provision requiring the contractor to work as many shifts as were necessary to ensure completion within the specified time period. Further, a contract amendment extending the delivery date contained a specific provision reserving the government's right to terminate for untimely performance. The government terminated the day following the extended delivery date.

The contrary view that time may not necessarily be of the essence is supported by the trial judge's opinion as adopted by the court in *Franklin E. Penny Co. v. United States*, 207 Ct. Cl. 842, 524 F.2d 668 (1975). There, the issue of whether time is of the essence was said to depend on the nature of the contract and the particular circumstances of the case. See also *Clay Bernard Sys. Int'l, Ltd. v. United States*, 22 Cl. Ct. 804 (1991), which involved the design, development, and delivery of a material handling system. The court observed that this was not the "normal" supply contract. *Franklin E. Penny* was cited with approval in *West Coast Research Corp.*, ASBCA 21087, 77-1 BCA ¶12,510, stating that failure to deliver goods strictly "on time" was not, under the circumstances, sufficient of itself to authorize termination for default. The board observed that time was certainly not of the essence in a contract where delivery due on Friday was actually made on Sunday, although the goods remained unopened for 16 or 17 days after delivery. Nevertheless, the default was upheld because the delivered items did not substantially comply with contract requirements.

Service contracts are covered by the FAR 52.249-8 clause, which permits termination for failure "to perform the services within the time specified." A predecessor clause with this language for use only on service contracts was included in DAR 7-1902.8. Since service contracts often contemplate performance according to detailed work schedules, it has been stated that time is of the essence, *Riteway Sanitation Serv.*, ASBCA 14304, 70-2 BCA ¶8553 (contractor failed to comply with collection schedules of a sanitation services contract). In *Michigan Bldg. Maint., Inc.*, IBCA 1945, 87-1 BCA ¶19,461, the board stated at 98,368:

> The law on service contracts is relatively well settled . . . . Appeals boards have recognized that cleaning services are a vital function that the contractor must perform satisfactorily, or else the contractor must be replaced. If properly documented, termination can be accomplished very quickly.

Failure to perform services on time and in accordance with specifications has been held to justify an immediate termination for default only when there has been a "substantial failure of performance." See *Suburban Indus. Maint. Co.*, ASBCA 23570, 85-2 BCA ¶18,148, stating that for a service contract to be terminated for specific failures to perform on time, "a sufficient number of such failures must accumulate such that it could be said that there had been a substantial failure of performance." This rule was followed in *Plum Run, Inc.*, ASBCA 46091, 05-1 BCA ¶32,977 (recurring lack of performance a substantial failure); *Swanson Group, Inc.*, ASBCA 44664, 98-2 BCA ¶29,896 (government failed to prove substantial failures); *William Howard Wilson*, ASBCA 47831, 97-1 BCA ¶28,911 (failure to work for two weeks clearly a substantial failure); *CardioMetrix v. Department of the Treasury*, GSBCA 13462-TD, 97-1 BCA ¶28,775 (substantial failure when contractor failed to secure the status of the physicians as its employees as proposed, failed to notify the government of subcontracting relationships, and failed to provide proof of adequate insurance coverage); and *Handyman Bldg. Maint. Co.*, IBCA 1335-3-80, 83-2 BCA ¶16,646 (no substantial failure in specific omissions of janitorial services). Earlier decisions had stated a stricter rule permitting default termination upon a single failure of performance. See *Utah Waste Paper Co.*, VACAB 1104, 75-1 BCA ¶11,058 (some garbage pickups were made late and some were not made at all). In *Ortec Sys., Inc.*, ASBCA 43467, 92-2 BCA ¶24,859, the board sustained a termination where the asbestos abatement project was to be completed. The board noted the importance of timely completion to the government and that time was "of the essence." The contractor had left the site seven days earlier and the government was unable to reach the contractor prior to the termination. See also *Decatur Realty Sales*, HUDBCA 75-26, 77-2 BCA ¶12,567, in which the board held that the government had the right to "summarily" terminate for failure to provide management brokerage services according to the contract schedule. Even where only a portion of the required services are not performed on time, it has been held that the entire contract may be terminated, *Al's Enters., Ltd.*, ASBCA 13576, 70-1 BCA ¶8080 (less than one-half of the containers emptied). The right to terminate immediately may also be limited by specific contract provisions, *Mr.'s Landscaping & Nursery*, HUDBCA 75-6, 76-2 BCA ¶11,968 (default overturned where government failed to observe provision entitling the contractor to notice of deficiencies and an opportunity to correct). In *Itra Coop Ass'n*, GSBCA 7974, 90-1 BCA ¶22,410, the board found a default termination improper because the contractor's performance was within the terms of an informal "side agreement" with the agency receiving the service. Although the contractor failed to perform a number of typewriter repair services within the 10-hour period specified by the contract, it did meet the requirements of the side agreement requiring a technician to be present for repairs only two days a week. The board held that the side agreement established a course of dealing upon which the contractor relied and that the government was not free to find the contractor in default for proceeding in accordance with established practice. In addition, the board noted that it was not appropriate to terminate the entire contact since the majority of documented complaints occurred at only one of approximately 50 service locations. The board stated at 112,564:

> In general, it is not appropriate to terminate an entire contract for default where it is possible to terminate only a severable portion of the work as to which an actual default has been demonstrated.

b. Timely Delivery of Defective Supplies

In *Radiation Tech., Inc. v. United States*, 177 Ct. Cl. 227, 366 F.2d 1003 (1966), the court invoked the doctrine of "substantial compliance" as a limitation of the government's broad termination rights under a supply contract. Under this doctrine, summary default termination may be prevented when supplies have been delivered on time and substantially comply with the contract requirements.

The substantial compliance doctrine is similar to U.C.C. § 2-508(2), which gives a seller reasonable time to cure a defective shipment of goods provided that it had reasonable grounds to believe that the goods would be accepted, *Environmental Tectonics Corp.*, ASBCA 20340, 76-2 BCA ¶12,134. Substantial compliance differs from the concept of substantial completion (as discussed in detail below) in two respects. First, under the *Radiation Technology* rule of substantial compliance, the right to terminate the entire contract will revive unless the defect in the goods is cured within a reasonable time, *Levelator Corp. of Am.*, VACAB 738, 71-1 BCA ¶8721, while substantial completion bars termination of the completed work. Second, the supply contractor's state of mind is relevant to application of the *Radiation Technology* rule, whereas state of mind is not a factor in assessing a contractor's substantial completion. Despite these differences, the *Radiation Technology* rule has occasionally been cited in evaluating a construction contractor's substantial completion, *R.M. Crum Constr. Co.*, VABCA 2143, 85-2 BCA ¶18,132; *Samuel Quarno & Co.*, HUDBCA 76-21, 77-2 BCA ¶12,599; *Corway, Inc.*, ASBCA 20683, 77-1 BCA ¶12,357; *Capitol City Constr. Co.*, DOTCAB 74-29, 75-1 BCA ¶11,012; *K & M Constr.*, ENGBCA 2998, 73-2 BCA ¶10,034.

The *Radiation Technology* rule has also been applied to service contracts that require, in part, the delivery of goods, *Metzger Towing, Inc.*, ENGBCA 5862, 94-2 BCA ¶26,651 (substantial compliance doctrine made default termination improper where the deficiencies were remedied quickly and the dredge plant substantially complied with the contract requirements); *Itra Coop Ass'n*, GSBCA 7974, 90-1 BCA ¶22,410 (board stated that "[t]he principle of 'substantial compliance' places a considerable limitation upon an agency's exercise of its right to terminate for default a service contract"); *Palmetto Enters., Inc.*, ASBCA 19588, 76-2 BCA ¶12,139 (default termination of a contract to provide refueling services held proper due to numerous, complex deficiencies; no substantial compliance with requirements found). In addition, the substantial compliance doctrine has been applied to limit the government's right to default terminate for submission of a defective "first article" or "preproduction" model.

(1) Timely Tender

In order to take advantage of the substantial compliance rule, the contract articles must be received by the due date, *SCM Corp.*, ASBCA 19941, 75-2 BCA ¶11,508. Thus, the doctrine does not apply where there has been no delivery. See *Nash Metalware Co.*, GSBCA 11951, 94-2 BCA ¶26,780 (default termination proper because contractor failed to tender goods that conformed to the specifications, failed to propose corrective action, and ultimately failed to deliver by the due date); *Norwood Precision Prods., Textron Inc.*, ASBCA 38095, 90-3 BCA ¶23,200 (government justified in terminating contract for default if the contractor fails to deliver supplies within the time specified); *Hedlund Lumber Sales, Inc.*, ASBCA 14815, 71-1 BCA ¶8782 (default termination for failure to make timely delivery proper despite failure of government to notify contractor of its intent to deny request for time extension); and *Fitzgerald Labs., Inc.*, ASBCA 15205, 71-2 BCA ¶9029 (no persuasive evidence that strikes caused contractor's failure to deliver). It also does not apply when there is a late delivery of less than the required quantity, *Forest Scientific, Inc.*, ASBCA 17822, 74-1 BCA ¶10,447 (contractor had 96 of the required 98 items ready for one delivery deadline but had already missed two prior deadlines). It has been stated, but not held, that *Radiation Technology* might apply even where goods are tendered after the due date, *Franklin E. Penny Co. v. United States*, 207 Ct. Cl. 842, 524 F.2d 668 (1975). However, to date, the only clear exception to the requirement for delivery by the due date is where waiver of the due date has rendered time no longer of the essence. See *Astro Dynamics, Inc.*, ASBCA 28381, 88-3 BCA ¶20,832, in which the board stated at 105,366:

> When a due date has passed and the contract has not been terminated for default within a reasonable time, the inference is created that time is no longer of the essence so long as the constructive election not to terminate continues and the contractor proceeds with performance.

In such cases, the *Radiation Technology* rule has been relied on to reverse a default, *Video Research Corp.*, ASBCA 14684, 71-2 BCA ¶9006 (due-date extensions had been given to allow for correction of defects).

(2) Reasonable Belief That the Goods Conform

Another prerequisite for use of the substantial compliance doctrine is that the contractor must have had a reasonable belief that the tendered goods conformed to the stated requirements, *Hannon Elec. Co. v. United States*, 31 Fed. Cl. 135 (1994) (contractor knew goods did not conform to specifications); *Kurz-Kasch, Inc.*, ASBCA 32486, 88-3 BCA ¶21,053 (substantial compliance not applicable where the contractor submitted the units knowing that they did not comply with the contract specifications); *Environmental Tectonics Corp.*, ASBCA 20340, 76-2 BCA ¶12,134 (no substantial compliance where the contractor knowingly shipped defective sterilizers with the expectation that it would be permitted additional time to rework the units and correct defects at the delivery site). Thus, the *Radiation Technology* rule will not apply if the contractor knows that the goods do not comply or if the contractor's belief that the goods comply is unreasonable. For example, knowledge of noncompliance defeats application of the doctrine, *Meyer Labs, Inc.*, ASBCA 18347, 77-1 BCA ¶12,539 (tendered bomb release units contained various components that had previously been rejected as nonconforming); and *Century Hone Div. of Desert Labs., Inc.*, ASBCA 18360, 78-1 BCA ¶12,990, *recons. denied*, 78-2 BCA ¶13,343 (delivery of metal honing device with knowledge of 90 percent failure of metal removal tests). Similarly, an unreasonable belief that the goods conformed also defeats application of the doctrine, *Gillett Mach. Rebuilders, Inc.*, ASBCA 28341, 89-3 BCA ¶22,021 (where three of four spindles did not meet spindle runout tests, contractor could not reasonably conclude that the spindles conformed to the contract requirements or that the defects were minor or readily correctable); *Vanbar*, ASBCA 20762, 77-2 BCA ¶12,798 (breach of requirement to notify government prior to conducting first article test upon which nonconforming test report was based); *Filcon Corp.*, ASBCA 19578, 75-1 BCA ¶11,303, *recons. denied*, 75-2 BCA ¶11,527 (quantity of defects supported inference of no reasonable belief that the goods would conform); *Solar Labs., Inc.*, ASBCA 19269, 74-2 BCA ¶10,897, *recons. denied*, 75-1 BCA ¶11,049 (failure to conduct testing of articles even though not required by contract); *Kain Cattle Co.*, ASBCA 17124, 73-1 BCA ¶9999 (failure to inspect at origin as required by contract); *Frank A. Pellicia v. United States*, 208 Ct. Cl. 278, 525 F.2d 1035 (1975) (shipment of noncomplying goods under erroneous belief that specifications had been waived). Contrast *Products Eng'g Corp. v. General Servs. Admin.*, GSBCA 12503, 98-2 BCA ¶29,851, where the contractor did not know of the tests used by the government to establish the defects, and *Argent Indus., Inc.*, ASBCA 15207, 71-2 BCA ¶9172, where reasonable belief was found because assembly was made by very experienced workers and testing performed at all production stages.

(3) Defects Minor in Nature and Readily Correctable

In order to take advantage of the additional time to correct under the substantial compliance doctrine, the contractor must demonstrate that the defects are minor and readily correctable. Whether a defect is minor is a question of fact, based on a consideration of (1) whether the items are usable, (2) the nature of the product, (3) the urgency of the government's needs, and (4) the extent of repair and adjustment necessary to produce a fully conforming product, *Kain Cattle Co.*, ASBCA 17124, 73-1 BCA ¶9999.

Defects were found to be minor in *Radar Devices, Inc.*, ASBCA 43912, 99-1 BCA ¶30,223, *recons. denied*, 99-2 BCA ¶30,396 (items repaired in less than one hour); *Trident Indus. Prods. Corp.*, DOTBCA 2807, 98-1 BCA ¶29,619 (slightly less than specified quantity of cloth); *Metzger Towing, Inc.*, ENGBCA 5862, 94-2 BCA ¶26,651 (remaining dredge plant deficiencies were remedied within a few days); *Cosmos Eng'g, Inc.*, ASBCA 19780, 77-2 BCA ¶12,713 (only 10 days needed to correct minor work on complex audiovisual); *Orion Elecs. Corp.*, ASBCA 18010, 75-1 BCA ¶11,006 (packing and packaging defects could be corrected in one day); *National Aviation Elecs., Inc.*, ASBCA 18256, 74-2 BCA ¶10,677 (instruments could easily be packaged to meet dimensional requirements); *Video Research Corp.*, ASBCA 14684, 71-2 BCA ¶9006 (one hour of work and $10.00 per unit would allow tape recorders to pass "drift" test); and *Argent Indus., Inc.*, ASBCA 15207, 71-2 BCA ¶9172 (even the most serious defect could have been corrected in 10 minutes).

In *Defense Tech. Corp.*, ASBCA 39551, 91-3 BCA ¶24,189, the board found a default termination unjustified because defects in first articles were easily correctable and enough time remained in the first article schedule to allow timely correction. The board stated at 120,988:

> We have consistently held that the Government may not demand strict compliance with the [first article] specifications as with supplies tendered for final delivery. The purpose of a First Article is to discover defects. Therefore, if defects are discovered and are easily correctable in production the Government may not reject the [first article].

See *National Aviation Elecs., Inc.*, ASBCA 18256, 74-2 BCA ¶10,677, in which the board noted that the substantial compliance doctrine of *Radiation Technology* applied "a fortiori" to a first article submission and overturned the default where the only defects were "correctable in production." See also *Advanced Precision Indus., Inc.*, ASBCA 34676, 89-2 BCA ¶21,597; *Acudata Sys., Inc.*, DOTCAB 1198, 84-1 BCA ¶17,046; and *Argent Indus., Inc.*, ASBCA 15207, 71-2 BCA ¶9172. The Court of Claims also held that the validity of termination for submission of a defective preproduction model that was to become the first production item upon approval following "acceptance testing" would be judged according to the *Radiation Technology* standard, *Astro Sci. Corp. v. United States*, 200 Ct. Cl. 354, 471 F.2d 624 (1973). Compare *Flight Refueling, Inc.*, ASBCA 46846, 97-2 BCA ¶29,000, holding that the doctrine does not apply when the contractor delivers only one of two required prototypes.

Defects are not minor when they affect the "efficiency" and "inherent functioning" of an item, *Technical Sys. Assocs., Inc. v. Department of Commerce*, GSBCA 13277-COM, 00-1 BCA ¶30,684. See also *Integrated Sys. Group, Inc.*, ASBCA 46918, 97-2 BCA ¶29,316, finding no substantial compliance when the defects went to the functioning and servicability of the computers being procured. For other cases finding that defects were not minor or readily correctable, see *Halifax Eng'g, Inc. v. United States*, 915 F.2d 689 (Fed. Cir. 1990) (contractor could not show that guard services deficiencies could be remedied within a short time); *Shiffer Indus., Inc.*, ASBCA 30919, 91-3 BCA ¶24,316; *Introl Corp.*, ASBCA 27610, 85-2 BCA ¶18,044 (modification of rotor shaft assembly to reduce its height would be a costly operation requiring 18 to 20 weeks to complete); *Astro Sci. Corp. v. United States*, 200 Ct. Cl. 354, 471 F.2d 624 (1973) (numerous minor defects when considered together were major nonconformity); *Reach Elecs., Inc.*, VACAB 1375, 79-2 BCA ¶14,048 (proposed corrections would not have complied); *Environmental Tectonics Corp.*, ASBCA 20340, 76-2 BCA ¶12,134 (sterilizers had major problems with doors and locking devices as well as numerous minor defects in workmanship that, taken together, were major); *Sperry-Vision Corp.*, ENGBCA 3489, 76-2 BCA ¶12,055 (television monitors failed eight different tests); *K-Square Corp.*, NASABCA 1271-23, 76-1 BCA ¶11,867, *recons. denied*, 76-2 BCA ¶12,093 (electron microscope failed intermittently and daily performance was essential); *Inforex, Inc.*, GSBCA 3859, 76-1 BCA ¶11,679 (contractor asked for two months to cure); *Frequency Elecs, Inc.*, ASBCA 17917, 74-2 BCA ¶10,792 (previous nonconforming cesium beam clocks with similar defects had taken several months to correct); *Levelator Corp.*, VACAB 1069, 74-2 BCA ¶10,763 (seven weeks needed to correct defects, and hospital was scheduled to open in one week); *Kain Cattle Co.*, ASBCA 17124, 73-1 BCA ¶9999 (excess fat rendered shipment of beef significantly defective); *Nuclear Equip. Corp.*, NASABCA 1170-18, 73-1 BCA ¶9815 (after two-day investigation, contractor could not propose a solution to various complex technical problems); *Echo Sci. Corp.*, NASABCA 671-9, 72-2 BCA ¶9755 (contractor needed one week to determine why tape recorder failed vibration test); *Renwin Metal Prods., Inc.*, ASBCA 15413, 72-1 BCA ¶9233, *recons. denied*, 72-1 BCA ¶9329 (powder separators deviated from dimensional tolerances to such a degree that equipment was not compatible with equipment manufactured by others); *Consolidated Mach. Corp.*, ASBCA 14176, 72-1 BCA ¶9212 (sterilizers were wired to operate on wrong voltage, had improperly placed controls, and contained exposed wiring); *Bardeen Mfg. Co.*, ASBCA 14381, 71-2 BCA ¶9007 (aircraft link assemblies could have failed at high temperatures since tensile strength requirements were not met and copper brazing was not performed); and *Filtron Co.*, DCAB ESSA-3, 70-1 BCA ¶8086 (electromagnetically shielded enclosure contained numerous defects including defective doors that required redesign, refabrication, and reinstallation).

(4) The Cure Period

When the contractor meets the above requirements, the *Radiation Technology* rule entitles it to cure the defect within a reasonable period of time, which may extend beyond the contract delivery schedule. The length of the cure period may vary depending on the nature of the defects and urgency of the government's needs. There is no right to any specific cure period, although at least one board has indicated that a 10-day cure period would apply, *Inforex, Inc.*, GSBCA 3859, 76-1 BCA ¶11,679 (default termination proper where the contractor asked for an "inordinate" time extension). A contractor that has already been afforded a reasonable opportunity to cure the defects may not later invoke the *Radiation Technology* rule, *Technics EMS, Inc.*, GSBCA 6679-COM, 84-1 BCA ¶17,060 (contractor failed to meet performance specifications for dual chamber ion mill after three opportunities to cure defects); *Electro-Neutronics, Inc.*, ASBCA 12947, 71-2 BCA ¶8961 (contractor was given four chances to correct the goods). There is no requirement for the contracting officer to direct that goods be corrected, and the absence of a contractor's expression of willingness to cure may defeat application of the doctrine, *Frequency Elecs., Inc.*, ASBCA 17917, 74-2 BCA ¶10,792 (contractor "never undertook to make the corrections"). See also *Donald C. Hubbs, Inc.*, DOTBCA 2012, 90-1 BCA ¶22,379 (contractor failed to take corrective action to remedy the defect); *Appli Tronics*, ASBCA 31540, 89-1 BCA ¶21,555 (contractor neither offered nor undertook corrective action with respect to substantiated defects); and *Kain Cattle Co.*, ASBCA 17124, 73-1 BCA ¶9999 (absence of willingness to cure defective meat was one factor in denying application of the doctrine).

c. *Limitations on Termination of All Work*

The right of the government to terminate all the work when only a part is in default is limited in certain situations.

(1) Accepted Work

The right to terminate for default is limited to the executory portion of a contract. Thus, acceptance of work bars default termination of that work in construction contracts, *Sentell Bros., Inc.*, DOTBCA 1824, 89-3 BCA ¶21,904; *Building Contractors, Inc.*, ASBCA 14840, 71-1 BCA ¶8884; *Hogan Constr., Inc.*, ASBCA 39014, 95-1 BCA ¶27,398; and in supply contracts, *K Square Corp.*, IBCA 959-3-72, 73-2 BCA ¶10,363. In *Donat Gerg Haustechnick*, ASBCA 41197, 97-2 BCA ¶29,272, termination for default was not available for a contractor's refusal to provide records for examination and audit, because no contract work remained to be performed nor any outstanding demand by the government for performance of work. Under those circumstances, the contract could fairly be said to have been complete. Compare *Aerometals, Inc.*, ASBCA 53688, 03-2 BCA ¶32,295, stating that a termination would be proper after the delivery schedule had been waived if the contractor delivered items that were substantially nonconforming, citing *Louisiana Lamps & Shades*, ASBCA 45294, 95-1 BCA ¶27,577; *Northeastern Mfg. & Sales*, ASBCA 35493, 89-3 BCA ¶22,093; and *Appli Tronics*, ASBCA 31540, 89-1 BCA ¶21,555.

Likewise, acceptance precludes imposition of other default remedies, such as excess costs of reprocurement on the accepted portion of the work, *Onus Co.*, ASBCA 16706, 72-2 BCA ¶9722. However, proper revocation of acceptance may revive the government's right to terminate for default, *Cross Aero Corp.*, ASBCA 14801, 71-2 BCA ¶9075 (discovery of latent defects allowed revocation of acceptance and subsequent termination for default); *Spandome Corp. v. United States*, 32 Fed. Cl. 626 (1995) (termination for default upheld when acceptance revoked more than one year after final acceptance); *Chilstead Bldg. Co.*, ASBCA 49548, 00-2 BCA ¶31,097 (termination effected without a cure notice upon discovery of contractor's gross mistake amounting to fraud). See Chapter 9 for a discussion of revocation of acceptance.

(2) Substantial Completion

The principle of "substantial completion" is often applied when the contractor has substantially but not completely performed the contract requirements. The term "substantial completion" is used synonymously with the term "substantial performance" to mean performance that is in good faith and in compliance with the contract but that falls short of complete performance due to minor and relatively unimportant deviations. The doctrine of substantial completion prevents the government from assessing liquidated damages or terminating the contract without giving the contractor reasonable time to correct deficiencies. However, it does not prevent the government from demanding strict compliance and full completion of the work, or from obtaining an equitable adjustment in the contract price if strict compliance is not attained.

Contractors bear the burden of proving substantial completion. If the contractor's assertions at trial conflict with its contemporaneous documents (daily reports), it is more difficult to sustain this burden, *Dixon Contracting, Inc.*, AGBCA 98-191-1, 00-1 BCA ¶30,766.

(A) CONSTRUCTION CONTRACTS

Occasionally, government construction contractors who have undertaken considerable efforts but have failed to complete all of the specified work by the due date have successfully invoked the doctrine of "substantial completion" to avoid the consequences of default termination. Although the boards have sometimes indicated that the government has no right to terminate for default where the work has been substantially completed, it is clear that the government retains full rights to terminate the contractor's right to proceed with that portion of the work that has not been completed by the due date. See *G.A. Karnavas Painting Co.*, VACAB 992, 72-1 BCA ¶9369; *Southland Constr. Co.*, VABCA 2217, 89-1 BCA ¶21,548, and *Environmental Data Consultants, Inc. v. General Servs. Admin.*, GSBCA 13244, 96-2 BCA ¶28,614. This rule was explained in *PCL Constr. Servs. Inc. v. United States*, 47 Fed. Cl. 745 (2000), *aff'd*, 96 Fed. Appx. 672 (Fed. Cir. 2004), as follows at 810:

> PCL's second argument regarding the propriety of the termination for default asks the court to adopt a rule that a construction contractor cannot be terminated for default after in fact substantially completing the contract. It is true that some cases in the Board of Contract Appeals have allowed a construction contractor to avoid a termination for default because it had substantially performed the contract. See *Metzger Towing, Inc.*, E.N.G.B.C.A. No. 5862, 94-2 B.C.A. (CCH) ¶26,651 (1994); *Wolfe Constr. Co.*, E.N.G.B.C.A. Nos. 3607-3611, 3853, 4752, 84-3 B.C.A. (CCH) ¶17,701 at 88,329 (1984); *Cosmos Eng'rs, Inc.*, A.S.B.C.A. No. 19780, 77-2 B.C.A. (CCH) ¶12,713 at 61,710-11 (1977); *Edward S. Good, Jr.*, A.S.B.C.A. No. 10514, 66-1 B.C.A. (CCH) ¶5362 at 25,157 (1966). The doctrine of substantial performance, however:
>
> > should not be carried to the point where the non-defaulting party is compelled to accept a measure of performance substantially less than had been bargained for. Substantial performance "is never properly invoked unless the promisee has obtained to all intents and purposes all benefits which he reasonably anticipated receiving under the contract."

> *Blinderman Constr. Co. Inc. v. United States*, 39 Fed. Cl. 529, 572 (citing *Franklin E. Penny Co. v. United States*, 207 Ct. Cl. 842, 857-58, 524 F.2d 668, 677 (quoting *In re Kinney Aluminum Co.*, 78 F. Supp. 565, 568 (S.D. Cal. 1948)), *aff'd*, 178 F.3d 1307 (Fed. Cir. 1998) (table)); see also *M.C. & D. Capital Corp. v. United States*, 948 F.2d at 1256.
>
> In the instant case, the legally supportable and sensible approach appears to be to simply follow the language of the FAR and the contract and to allow the government to terminate the "separable portion" of the contract, the separable portion being the uncompleted work. See 48 CFR § 52.249-10(a) (1990). The result is to prevent the government from avoiding its obligation to pay provable monies owed on the contract, while allowing an appropriate reduction for the uncompleted work and any consequences normally associated with a default termination on that portion of the contract the plaintiff refused to perform.

Thus, the better-reasoned decisions recognize that the true effect of substantial completion is to prevent the government from avoiding the obligation to pay the contract price for the substantially completed work, less an appropriate reduction for uncompleted work, *Edward S. Good, Jr.*, ASBCA 10514, 66-1 BCA ¶5362.

The basic rationale for invoking the "substantial completion" doctrine in construction contracts has been to avoid a forfeiture where the contractor has made permanent improvements on government property. See *H.L.C. & Assocs. Constr. Co. v. United States*, 176 Ct. Cl. 285, 367 F.2d 586 (1966), and *Cosmos Eng'g, Inc.*, ASBCA 19780, 77-2 BCA ¶12,713. In *R.M. Crum Constr. Co.*, VABCA 2143, 85-2 BCA ¶18,132, the board stated the reasoning behind the "substantial completion" doctrine at 91,009:

> We agree that often construction contracts are not fully completed to perfection by the due date, often having minor discrepancies and problems needing correction. The existence of those incomplete items or deviations often do not necessarily deprive the Government of what it contracted for and anticipated as a complete project. When that is the case, those deficiencies should not be available to sustain the harsh remedy of termination. While forfeiture is an element to be considered in analyzing a default, we do not consider it an essential element if the project has otherwise been substantially performed.

Such reasoning has occasionally been questioned, however, because construction contractors have consistently recovered at least the fair value of work performed prior to the time of default, *G.A. Karnavas Painting Co.*, VACAB 992, 72-1 BCA ¶9369. See *Keyser Roofing Contractors, Inc.*, ASBCA 32069, 90-3 BCA ¶23,024 (substantial completion doctrine not applicable where contractor was paid 86 percent of the contract price, which was the percentage of work done), and *Cosmic Constr. Co.*, ASBCA 24014, 88-2 BCA ¶20,623 (substantial completion doctrine not applicable where contractor had been paid or credited for the work it performed on percentage of completion basis and the termination for default affected only the uncompleted or remaining work). In *General Ship & Engine Works, Inc.*, ASBCA 19243, 79-1 BCA ¶13,657, which involved a ship repair contract having attributes of both a construction and a supply contract, the board stated at 67,022:

> [W]here a contractor has been paid or given credit for all work properly performed or corrected, there is less likelihood that a showing of forfeiture may be made so as to call for the application of the doctrine of substantial performance and to upset an otherwise proper termination for default.

See also *Mark Smith Constr. Co.*, ASBCA 25058, 81-2 BCA ¶15,306, in which the board concluded that the substantial completion doctrine was "not for application" since the contractor had been paid for the work performed on a "percentage of completion" basis and the default termination affected only the "uncompleted or remaining work."

The basic test for substantial completion is generally stated to be whether the product is capable of being occupied or used by the government for its intended purpose, *Dimarco Corp.*, ASBCA 28529, 85-2 BCA ¶18,002. In *Barton & Sons Co.*, ASBCA 14097, 70-2 BCA ¶8429, substantial completion warranted reversal of a default termination where airport runways being repaired were operational despite the need to perform minor capping of approximately 3 percent of total runway joints. In *Corway, Inc.*, ASBCA 20683, 77-1 BCA ¶12,357, the board found substantial completion where deficiencies in tennis courts were "primarily of a cosmetic nature" and were "mostly outside of the playing area" of the courts.

However, see *M.C. & D. Capital Corp. v. United States*, 948 F.2d 1251 (Fed. Cir. 1991), finding no substantial completion where the roofing was not installed by a certified roofer and was not warranted as required by the contract. See also *Joseph Morton Co.*, GSBCA 4876, 82-2 BCA ¶15,839, where various defects in a courthouse heating and cooling system denied the government beneficial occupancy of the building and thereby precluded a determination of substantial completion. Accord, *Nagy Enters.*, ASBCA 48815, 98-1 BCA ¶29,695 (facility could not be used for its intended purpose because the filtration system was not operational when the contractor stopped working).

In *Two State Constr. Co.*, DOTCAB 78-31, 81-1 BCA ¶15,149, involving a contract to construct an airport control tower, the government terminated because of the contractor's failure to diligently correct "punchlist" items. The contractor contended that the project had been substantially completed at the time of the termination, noting that the government had entered the building to begin installation of air traffic control equipment. In upholding the termination, the board emphasized that the listed deficiencies "in their totality" constituted a significant amount of work that "impaired" and rendered "hazardous" the FAA's use of the facility, stating at 74,939:

> We cannot equate the entry of FAA personnel to commence installation with substantial completion. That an owner is willing to risk hazards to expedite ultimate availability of a project for the intended use does not mean the project is capable of intended use.

Although the boards have occasionally looked to the "percentage of completion" of total contract work as an indication of substantial completion, *Highland Constr. Corp.*, GSBCA 2470, 68-1 BCA ¶6966; *Edward S. Good, Jr.*, ASBCA 10514, 66-1 BCA ¶5362, it has also been stated that application of a "rigid percentage of completion test" is not appropriate, *Two State Constr. Co.*, DOTCAB 78-31, 81-1 BCA ¶15,149.

The substantial completion doctrine has been applied to contracts that represent a hybrid between supply and construction, *Cosmos Eng'rs, Inc.*, ASBCA 19780, 77-2 BCA ¶12,713 (contract for design, fabrication, and installation of an audiovisual system apparently using a supply contract clause); *Pacific Coast Refrigeration, Inc.*, ASBCA 14546, 71-2 BCA ¶9146 (contract to furnish and install refrigerated display cases contained both supply and construction default clauses). See also *General Ship & Engine Works, Inc.*, ASBCA 19243, 79-1 BCA ¶13,657, in which the board indicated that the substantial completion doctrine has some limited applicability to supply contracts but qualified its potential impact by stating at 67,021:

> How often [the doctrine of substantial completion] may properly be applied in view of the competing rules that time is of the essence in any case where fixed dates for performance are specified, and that the government is entitled to require strict compliance with its specifications, is another question.

(B) SERVICE CONTRACTS

Although the boards have occasionally stated that a contractor's failure to perform all specified services in a timely fashion establishes a government right to immediately terminate for default, *Marble & Chance*, HUDBCA 85-908-C2, 87-1 BCA ¶19,337; *Utah Waste Paper Co.*, VACAB 1104, 75-1 BCA ¶11,058, the doctrine of "substantial completion" has become a significant limitation on this right. See *Reliable Maint. Serv.*, ASBCA 10487, 66-1 BCA ¶5331, *recons. denied*, 67-1 BCA ¶6194, in which the board stated at 25,044:

> The failure to perform a daily task is not cured by the performance of a similar task which is also required on a following day. Each individual failure is technically a default, though not necessarily the basis for a default termination, and when a sufficient number of individual defaults accumulate then it can be said the contract has not been substantially performed, the contract is then terminable under subparagraph [(a)(1)(i)] of the Default clause.

See *Contract Maint., Inc.*, ASBCA 18528, 75-1 BCA ¶11,247, in which the board invoked the "substantial completion" doctrine to overturn a default termination where the number of omitted tasks was "inconsequential" compared to the total number of janitorial tasks called for under the contract. In reaching this conclusion, the board found it significant that the contract provided the remedy of deductions from contract billings for "insubstantial elements of nonperformance and uncorrected substandard tasks." Similarly, in *Handyman Bldg. Maint. Co.*, IBCA 1335-3-80, 83-2 BCA ¶16,646, the board overturned a default termination based on repeated nonperformance of various janitorial tasks, stating at 82,775:

> The presence of the inspection clause and the accompanying schedule of deductions in the contract indicate a recognition on the part of the Government that janitorial service is not likely to be the one perfect aspect of an otherwise imperfect world. The clause provides a mechanism, short of default, for dealing with anticipated omissions of services.

See *C.S. Smith Training, Inc.*, DOTCAB 1273, 83-1 BCA ¶16,304, where a contractor's failure to promptly pay subjects being furnished for biomedical experiments was found not to be of sufficient magnitude to justify summary termination. The board stated at 81,016:

> Elementary fairness dictates that when a contractor is actually performing, and is actually performing a substantial portion of the required services, as was the case here, he is entitled to receive formal notification if the Contracting Officer considers the work to be substandard and a termination for default to be a real possibility.

See also *W.M. Grace, Inc.*, ASBCA 23076, 80-1 BCA ¶14,256, overturning a default in similar circumstances, holding that the government, by taking deductions for performance deficiencies, "effectively waived the performance failures . . . as a basis for default termination, while still preserving its right to terminate the contract for default if these failures were not cured in the future."

However, see *Cervetto Bldg. Maint. Co. v. United States*, 2 Cl. Ct. 299 (1983), rejecting the contractor's contention that the government was precluded from relying on, as grounds for default, any deficiencies for which deductions had been taken, stating at 301:

> Despite its elegance, [the contractor's] argument must be rejected as leading to an absurd result. The contract plainly contemplates that minor deficiencies in performance will be addressed through remedies short of termination for default. Equally plainly, it was intended that minor deficiencies be the exception and that performance be satisfactory on most days. When deficiencies become the rule, as they did in this case, necessitating corrections or deductions virtually every day, overall performance under the contract can be deemed unsatisfactory even though individual problems are resolved. See *Pride Unlimited*, 75-2 BCA at 54,500. In such a case, the repeated need for correction may itself serve as the default, making termination an appropriate remedy.

(3) Severability

The concept of severability, sometimes referred to as divisibility, is that there are, in reality, two or more contractual agreements in a single document. When it is concluded that the document is severable or divisible, the government's right to terminate for default is limited to those severable or divisible parts that are in default, *Murphy v. United States*, 164 Ct. Cl. 332 (1964). There, the language in the construction contract clause was held not to permit the government to terminate the entire contract when only a separable part of the work is in default. The case involved a lump sum contract for construction of the Fort Sumner Diversion Dam on the Pecos River. The contract specified a completion date for the entire project and interim dates for the release of irrigation waters. A series of financial and supervisory difficulties led the contracting officer to terminate for failure to prosecute the work "with such diligence as will insure its completion within the time specified in Article I," which required overall completion within 450 days from the date of notice to proceed. However, the evidence did not indicate that the contractor could not meet the final deadline, but only that it would be unable to release the irrigation waters on time. The court concluded that the contract terms made the release of irrigation waters separate from and incidental to the construction of the dam. The contracting officer was permitted to terminate the right to proceed on that portion of the contract but not on the entire contract. See *Brett Arnold, P. C. v. United States*, 98 Fed. Appx. 854 (Fed. Cir. 2004), which distinguished *Murphy* on the grounds that the deficiency was a critical function of the contract. See also *Plum Run, Inc.*, ASBCA 46091, 05-1 BCA ¶32,977 (one CLIN in maintenance contract severable from 21 other CLINs); *Itra Coop Ass'n*, GSBCA 7974, 90-1 BCA ¶22,410 (default termination of entire contract for typewriter maintenance not warranted since most of documented complaints took place at only one of approximately 50 service locations);

and *Overhead Elec. Co.*, ASBCA 25656, 85-2 BCA ¶18,026 (default termination of entire contract containing three work items—two involving electrical work and one requiring chemical disposal services—on the basis of the contractor's failure to perform the chemical removal was improper because the work items were separable).

Determining whether portions of the work are severable or the contract is entire is often difficult. The presence or absence of separate item numbers, prices, and delivery dates is not conclusive. See *Pennsylvania Exch. Bank v. United States*, 145 Ct. Cl. 216, 170 F. Supp. 629 (1959), finding a contract with four items of work an entire contract because the separately priced items were incidental to the ultimate aim of volume production. The fact that a contract contained a single bid item and a lump sum price was considered significant in holding a telephone engineering study not to be severable even though some work could be done independently, *Telecommunication Consultants*, ASBCA 13801, 69-2 BCA ¶7925. In *Spartan Aircraft Co. v. United States*, 120 Ct. Cl. 327, 100 F. Supp. 171 (1951), the contractor was required to perform 14 items of inspection, repair, and maintenance of government aircraft, including a 100-hour inspection. There was no total contract price stipulated, and of the 14 items, three were at a fixed hourly rate, 10 had a net cost specified, and one flight testing was to be free. The court reasoned that the payment provisions could be apportioned, which was evidence of divisibility. However, the court also found that the government would not have entered into the contract without the 100-hour inspection and concluded that this was evidence of indivisibility. Based on this latter finding, the court held that the contract was probably entire. With considerable candor, the court stated that severability is "a very vexing problem. . . . The authorities hold that the question is essentially one of the intention of the parties; examination of some of the many cases on the point suggests rather that resolution of the question has more commonly been a matter of the intention of the court." See also *Capitol City Constr. Co.*, DOTCAB 74-29, 75-1 BCA ¶11,012 (government could not terminate entire building repair contract for contractor's refusal to provide "chillers," which were unrelated to the other work and had been added by a change order). However, in *Phillip Bradley & Sons*, AGBCA 314, 71-2 BCA ¶9002, where a contractor leasing earth-moving equipment was unable to provide the specified multi-use equipment, the board found the contract not to be severable even though a portion of the work could have been completed on time using substitute equipment offered by the contractor, emphasizing that the contractor's obligation was to provide "all of the equipment required for performance."

The board may find the contract severable to prevent forfeiture. See *Nestos Painting Co.*, GSBCA 6945, 86-2 BCA ¶18,993, where an entire painting contract was terminated for default because of the contractor's failure to comply with the specified method in preparing 65 percent of the surfaces to be painted. The board converted the default termination to a termination for convenience for the 35 percent of the surfaces that were acceptably prepared and painted, stating at 95,916:

> Termination of the entire contract for default would enable GSA to benefit from the acceptable portion of [the contractor's] work without any payment and would result in a forfeiture. . . . Such a result is not favored.

(4) Installment Contracts Excepted

Although many government contracts call for delivery in installments, the individual installments are not necessarily treated as severable contracts. Thus, when one due date has been missed, the right to terminate extends to both the delinquent quantity and all future installments if the future installments are not severable, *Guenther Sys., Inc.*, ASBCA 14032, 72-1 BCA ¶9443 (failure to make first delivery as specified endangered performance of the entire contract). The right to terminate accrues each time an installment due date is missed, *Raytheon Serv. Co.*, ASBCA 14746, 70-2 BCA ¶8390 (government permitted to delay issuance of a partial default termination until the final delivery date, although the contractor failed to meet several prior delivery dates). Even where late deliveries of installments have been accepted, the government retains the right to terminate for subsequent delinquencies, *Lapp Insulator Co.*, ASBCA 13303, 70-1 BCA ¶8219, *recons. denied*, 70-2 BCA ¶8471 (government had accepted late deliveries on the first two installments before terminating for default). See also *Container Sys. Corp.*, ASBCA 40611, 94-1 BCA ¶26,354 (despite government acceptance of late deliveries of installments under a contract for missile containers, termination for failure to deliver was proper because each successive increment represented a severable obligation to deliver on the contract delivery date); *Papco Tool Corp.*, GSBCA 5679, 81-1 BCA ¶15,077 (despite waiver of delinquency in delivery of past increments, the government retains the right to terminate for delinquencies on subsequent increments); and *Phoenix Petroleum Co.*, ASBCA 42763, 96-2 BCA ¶28,284 (termination proper for late delivery even though prior delinquencies under an incremental delivery contract were waived). However, when a contractor catches up on past due installments, it is no longer in default, and the right to terminate is extinguished until another due date is missed, *Gibraltar Fabrics, Inc.*, ASBCA 15709, 73-1 BCA ¶9905. In *Consumers Oil Co.*, ASBCA 24172, 86-1 BCA ¶18,647, the board found that an indefinite delivery, indefinite quantity contract calling for delivery in installments was a separable contract using the "agreed equivalents" reasoning of *Restatemen, Second, Contracts* § 240, Part Performance of Agreed Equivalents.

The federal contract rule permitting termination of the entire contract for a missed installment differs from commercial contract principles, which permit termination only when the missed installment constitutes a substantial impairment of the whole contract, in accordance with U.C.C. § 2-612. The federal contract rule was defended in *Artisan Elecs. Corp. v. United States*, 205 Ct. Cl. 126, 499 F.2d 606 (1974), in which the court stated that "the plain language of the contract," which incorporated the standard default clause, obviated the need to consider the application of U.C.C. principles.

d. *Preproduction Items*

FAR 52.209-3 and -4 provide special clauses to be used when government or contractor first article testing and approval are required. Paragraph (d) of these clauses provides:

> If the contractor fails to deliver any first article on time, or the Contracting Officer disapproves any first article, the Contractor shall be deemed to have failed to make delivery within the meaning of the "Default" clause of this contract.

Similar clauses were called for by DAR 1-1903. In *Electro-Neutronics, Inc.*, ASBCA 12947, 71-2 BCA ¶8961, such a clause was found to have the effect of making the "make delivery" language in subparagraph (a)(i) of the default clause applicable in situations where first articles were properly disapproved by the contracting officer. See also *FJW Optical Sys., Inc.*, ASBCA 33885, 87-2 ¶19,905 (default termination justified where contract included a First Article Approval–Government Testing clause, and the contractor failed to timely deliver the first article for inspection).

Thus, when such a clause is used, failure to deliver the first article justifies summary termination without the 10-day cure period set out by ¶(a)(2) of the default clause, *H.N. Bailey & Assocs.*, ASBCA 21300, 77-2 BCA ¶12,681 (contract terminated for default when contractor failed to deliver first article because of a subcontracting complication for which contractor was responsible); *Kit Pack Co.*, ASBCA 33135, 89-3 BCA ¶22,151 (contract properly terminated for default without government providing cure notice after contractor failed to timely deliver first article because of financial difficulties in acquiring materials and components). Even without a first article clause, the conduct of the parties may impliedly modify the contract to provide that failure to deliver acceptable preproduction quantities will justify summary termination under paragraph (a)(1)(i). In *Monitor Sys.*, ASBCA 14261, 71-1 BCA ¶8885, the contractor induced the government to extend the date for preproduction testing by repeatedly promising that a conforming article would be tendered, and the government repeatedly asserted that a nonconforming item would result in default rather than another extension. A first article clause will not justify termination for nondelivery of required first article test procedures, *AAR Corp.*, ASBCA 16486, 74-2 BCA ¶10,653 (board specifically stated that termination was allowed because of a lack of progress rather than the failure to submit test procedures). However, the definition of first article was more broadly construed in *Inforex, Inc.*, GSBCA 3859, 76-1 BCA ¶11,679, where a preproduction demonstration was considered a first article.

However, absent such a clause, failure to deliver acceptable preproduction items (e.g., first articles and prototypes) is not a failure to deliver "supplies" within the meaning of ¶(a)(1)(i) of the supply contract default clause, since "supplies" refers to the end items required by the contract, *Bailey Specialized Bldgs., Inc. v. United States*, 186 Ct. Cl. 71, 404 F.2d 355 (1968) (preproduction tower that was required to be ready for inspection on a certain date, but was not required to be ready for delivery until four weeks later, was not an end item). See also *System Dev. Corp.*, VABCA 1976, 87-2 BCA ¶19,946 (failure to deliver computer unit for acceptance testing was not a failure to deliver an end item under ¶(a)(1)(i) of the default clause, even though the unit would ultimately be used as a functioning item). Likewise, such failures do not constitute a failure to deliver "services," since ¶a(1)(i) refers to "services" as an end item, *Dubrow Elec. Indus., Inc.*, ASBCA 8464, 65-1 BCA ¶4859. Thus, absent a special clause, such terminations can only be supported under a theory of failure to make progress or failure to perform some "other provision" of the contract, *Lorch Elecs. Corp.*, ASBCA 21496, 78-1 BCA

¶12,911 (termination for default was improper where the government did not show that the contractor had failed to make progress in any aspect of performance other than making a preproduction item ready for inspection). See *System Dev. Corp.*, VABCA 1976, 87-2 BCA ¶19,946, in which the board stated at 100,951:

> In the absence of a first article approval clause, it is well established that failure to deliver a timely preproduction or test unit is a failure "to make progress" under paragraph (a)(ii) of the disputes clause and not a breach of contract under (a)(i).

As discussed earlier, the "substantial compliance" doctrine of *Radiation Technology* may operate to limit the government's right to default terminate for timely delivery of a slightly nonconforming first article or preproduction item, *National Aviation Elecs., Inc.*, ASBCA 18256, 74-2 BCA ¶10,677. For example, a default termination was not upheld where first article defects were easily correctable, in *International Foods Retort Co.*, ASBCA 34954, 92-2 BCA ¶24,994 (blandness of packaged chicken à la king was a minor defect easily remediable by the addition of salt); *Penjaska Tool Co.*, ASBCA 31836, 89-2 BCA ¶21,700 (excessive discoloration of rifle firing pins was easily correctable by use of special devices for production runs). However, the board did not find the defects minor or readily correctable in *Sonora Mfg. Co.*, ASBCA 31587, 91-1 BCA ¶23,444 (discrepancies in dimensions of actuator piston not a minor defect because part was crucial to the safe operation of aircraft); *Idaho Norland Corp.*, ASBCA 33487, 90-2 BCA ¶22,858 (failure of a first article snow-removal machine to meet the contract requirements in three separate tests was not minor in nature or easily correctable).

2. Progress Failures

The standard clauses contain somewhat different language concerning default termination for failure to make progress. The supply and service contract clause permits termination if the contractor fails to "[m]ake progress, so as to endanger performance of this contract." The construction contract clause permits termination if the contractor "refuses or fails to prosecute the work or any separable part, with the diligence that will insure its completion within the time specified in this contract." Most litigation has occurred under the supply and service contract language.

a. *Basic Principle*

The necessity for and impact of a reservation of the right to terminate before the due date was discussed in *United States v. O'Brien*, 220 U.S. 321 (1911), in which Justice Holmes stated at 327:

> The sole material express promise of the contractors was to complete the work by July 1, 1902. If the work was done at that date that promise was performed, no matter how irregularly or with what delays in the earlier months. Under its terms the United States was not concerned with the stages of performance, but only with the completed result. See *Bacon v. Parker*, 137 Massachusetts, 309, 311. Its interest in the result, however, made it reasonable to reserve the right to employ someone else if, when time enough had gone by to show what was likely to happen, it saw that it probably would not get what it bargained for from the present hands. But it would be a very severe construction of the contract, a contract, too, framed by the United States, to read the reservation of a right to annul, for want of a diligence not otherwise promised, as importing a promise to use such diligence as should satisfy the judgment of the engineer in charge. It is one thing to make the right to continue work under the contract depend upon his approval, another to make his dissatisfaction with progress conclusive of a breach. In this case it was admitted that there was time enough left to finish the work under the contract when the [contractors] were turned off. It would be a very harsh measure to pronounce the contract broken when but for the prohibition of the United States the [contractors] might have done the work in time.

b. *Evaluating Progress Failures*

Early default cases did not clearly enunciate a test for evaluating the propriety of progress failure terminations. See Speidel, Default for Failure to Make Progress, Government Contractor Briefing Paper No. 64-5, October 1964. Although the supply contract default clause uses the phrase "endanger performance," a test requiring the government to prove that it was impossible for the contractor to complete by the due date was used in early cases.

(1) The "Impossible" Test

Initially, in order to justify termination for progress failures, the government was required to prove that it was not possible for the contractor to complete the contract work within the schedule. See *Emsco Screen Pipe Co. of Tex., Inc.*, ASBCA 11917, 69-1 BCA ¶7710 (government has burden of establishing that contractor was in fact incapable of performing the contract); *Midwest Eng'g & Constr. Co.*, ASBCA 5801, 1962 BCA ¶3289 (cure notice affords the contractor "an opportunity to demonstrate that timely completion was possible"); *Northeastern Eng'g, Inc.*, ASBCA 6504, 61-2 BCA ¶3108 (termination improper "when delivery is not shown to have been beyond [the contractor's] power"); and *Manhattan Lighting Equip. Co.*, ASBCA 5113, 60-1 BCA ¶2646 (default improper unless the contractor "had deprived itself of power to make enough progress . . . to permit performance" by the due date). Impossibility was found in *Samuel M. Wagner*, GSBCA 2722, 69-2 BCA ¶7776 (over 60 percent of the time for performance had passed but only 10 percent of the work was complete, no second shift was added, and contractor expressly stated performance was impossible unless time extensions were granted); *Isolation Prods., Inc.*, AECBCA 19-11-65, 66-1 BCA ¶5505 (state court enjoined contractor from using manufacturing process essential to performance); *General Prods. Co.*, ASBCA 6522, 61-1 BCA ¶3003 (even assuming maximum productivity, timely completion was unattainable, and it was "highly unlikely" that another supplier could be found).

(2) The "No Reasonable Likelihood" Test

The Court of Claims apparently rejected the impossibility test in favor of a demonstrated lack of diligence test. In *Universal Fiberglass Corp. v. United States*, 210 Ct. Cl. 206, 537 F.2d 393 (1976), the court upheld a default termination after waiver of the right to default terminate when no schedule existed, based on the lack of progress, without evidence of impossibility, stating at 217:

> [The contractor] was making no progress at all, had never manufactured a vehicle under the new specifications it had agreed to, did not have the necessary parts and could not obtain them and had allowed its labor force to wither away. If this situation is not what this failure to make progress clause is about and is not the exact case for which it was written, we are at a loss to understand why it was put in the contract at all.

In *Globe Eng'g Co.*, ASBCA 23934, 83-1 BCA ¶16,370, *recons. denied*, 84-1 BCA ¶16,941, the board expressly rejected the impossibility test, citing *Universal Fiberglass* as representing the "correct rule" in progress failure cases. See also *RFI Shield-Rooms*, ASBCA 17374, 77-2 BCA ¶12,714, concluding that the test was that "there was no reasonable likelihood that appellant could perform the entire contract effort within the time remaining for contract performance." Later cases have upheld progress failure terminations without a specific finding that timely performance was impossible, *California Dredging Co.*, ENGBCA 5532, 92-1 BCA ¶24,475; *Stephen-Leedom Carpet Co.*, GSBCA 4835, 79-1 BCA ¶13,570; *John F. Lehnertz*, AGBCA 77-132, 78-1 BCA ¶12,895. See also *Ranco Constr., Inc. v. General Servs. Admin.*, GSBCA 11923, 94-2 BCA ¶26,678, in which the board overturned the default termination on other grounds, stating at 132,703:

> GSA is not required to establish that timely performance by Ranco was impossible. Rather, GSA is required to establish that, at the time of the termination, there was a reasonable, valid basis for concluding that there was no reasonable likelihood that Ranco could perform within the time remaining for performance.

In *Santee Dock Builders*, AGBCA 96-161-1, 99-1 BCA ¶30,190, the board held that to terminate for lack of diligent prosecution of work, the government need not prove impossibility but must show that the contractor's performance was so lacking as to establish either an intention not to complete the work or lack of ability to timely complete the work. In *Morganti Nat'l, Inc. v. United States*, 49 Fed. Cl. 110 (2001), *aff'd*, 36 Fed. Appx. 452, (Fed. Cir. 2002), the court upheld the default termination although the contractor was entitled to additional time because schedule analyses made it clear that contract completion would not be achieved by the modified completion date. Evidence indicated that at the time of default, when approximately 75 percent of the contract was complete, the contractor was progressing at 1 percent per month, hardly sufficient to complete the project in the remaining eight months. See also *Bender GmbH v. Brownlee*, 106 Fed. Appx. 728 (Fed. Cir. 2004) (repeated delays and contractor's inability to prove it could meet the completion schedule), and *R. F. Lusa*

& Sons Sheet Metal, Inc., LBCA 2000-BCA-00002, 04-2 BCA ¶32,780 (contractor had completed only 45 percent of the work by the substantial completion date—termination upheld).

(3) Failure to Comply with the Contract Quality and Other Requirements

Factual considerations supporting termination for failure to make progress include consistent failure to meet industry standards, *Engineering Serv. Sys.*, PSBCA 2933, 92-3 BCA ¶25,146; failure to provide quality work consistent with the acceptable skill and workmanship standards of the contract, *Dozie I. Rienne*, ENGBCA 5711, 91-1 BCA ¶23,432; failure to give a meaningful response to a cure notice, *Midwest Eng'g & Constr. Co.*, ASBCA 6171, 61-2 BCA ¶3125; failure to submit data and drawings for approval, *C.C. Galbraith & Son, Inc.*, ASBCA 10769, 67-2 BCA ¶6488; failure to deliver preproduction model and procurement of only 3 percent of components although over half the performance period had passed, *Telecomputing Corp.*, ASBCA 7154, 1962 BCA ¶3620, *recons. denied*, 65-2 BCA ¶5223; and failure to timely initiate preproduction testing, *Midwest Eng'g & Constr. Co.*, ASBCA 5390, 1962 BCA ¶3460. In *Santee Dock Builders*, AGBCA 96-161-1, 99-1 BCA ¶30,190, the failure was demonstrated by showing failure to meet acceptable standards of skill and workmanship. Throughout the project, the contractor's progress was less than diligent, and the contractor had inadequate workers, inadequate equipment, failed to comply with contract provisions, and had inadequate supervision.

Work can be so defective that a termination will be upheld even if a suspension of work order has been issued. In *Pipeline Constr., Inc.*, ASBCA 50744, 98-2 BCA ¶29,991, the board held that such a default termination would be invalid only "when the suspension is not lifted so as to permit a contractor to make simple corrections by the contract completion date." Where the contractor's work is so "gravely deficient" that it could not be performed by the completion date, the default termination is proper and the suspension justified. Similarly, in *Zimcon Prof'ls*, ASBCA 49346, 00-1 BCA ¶30,839, the government, after a show cause notice, directed the contractor to perform no further work on the project. Twelve days later the government default terminated for failure to complete by the completion date. The board upheld the termination based in part on the amount of outstanding work (43 percent) and the contractor's past performance.

c. *Proof of Endangered Performance*

Although the government is not required to show that contractor performance was impossible, it must reasonably believe that the contractor could not perform the entire contract within the time remaining for performance, *Lisbon Contractors, Inc. v. United States*, 828 F.2d 759 (Fed. Cir. 1987); *McDonnell Douglas Corp. v. United States*, 182 F.3d 1319 (Fed. Cir. 1999), *cert denied*, 529 U.S. 1097 (2000), 50 Fed. Cl. 311 (2001), *aff'd in part & rev'd in part*, 323 F.3d 1006 (Fed. Cir. 2003). The government may reasonably find performance to be endangered when the contractor's monthly progress reports indicate that delivery will be late and a time extension is sought, *Fitzgerald Labs., Inc.*, ASBCA 15205, 71-2 BCA ¶9029. Likewise, actual on-site inspection of the contractor's efforts may indicate that performance is endangered, *Ubique, Ltd.*, DOTCAB 71-28, 72-1 BCA ¶9340 (virtually no work was done in the 30 days following first cure notice). See also *Sach Sinha & Assocs., Inc.*, ASBCA 47594, 00-1 ¶30,735 (failure to make progress justified a default termination because it was clear that the contractor was not making progress and had all but abandoned the contract).

Another indication of endangered performance is inconsistent contractor representations as to the time that delivery will be made, *Guenther Sys., Inc.*, ASBCA 14032, 72-1 BCA ¶9443 (following oral discussion of potential revised delivery schedule, contractor's written request the next day recommended a different schedule that further delayed deliveries). However, in *T.C. & Sarah C. Bell*, ENGBCA 5872, 92-3 BCA ¶25,076, poor attitude, uncooperativeness, and failure to interpret contract policies did not endanger the performance, because these deficiencies were "readily remediable."

In determining that the rate of progress is "endangering" timely performance, all circumstances should be considered, *Michigan Joint Sealing, Inc.*, ASBCA 41477, 93-3 BCA ¶26,011. In *Omni Dev. Corp.*, AGBCA 97-203-1, 01-2 BCA ¶31,487, the board described the factors to consider when reviewing a default decision: "the status of the project at the time [of default], how much time remained to complete [the project], the resources available to the contractor, the ability of the contractor to execute steps needed to perform the work and the materiality of any interim failures to meet milestones." See *Arrowhead Starr Co.*, AGBCA 81-236-1, 83-1 BCA ¶16,320 (contractor had completed only 42 percent of tree planting work in 66 percent of allotted time and could offer no plan for timely completion). A contractor's failure to make business arrangements vital to performance may also be grounds for a progress failure termination. In *ABC Knitwear Corp.*, ASBCA 22575, 81-1 BCA ¶14,826, a termination was upheld where the contractor failed to secure financing for acquisition of raw materials.

In the following cases, the government failed to sustain its burden: *SAE/Americon-Mid Atl., Inc. v. General Servs. Admin.*, GSBCA 12294, 98-2 BCA ¶30,084 (contractor had sufficient resources to complete performance without the schedule as extended to compensate for government-caused delays); *CJP Contractors, Inc. v. United States*, 45 Fed. Cl. 343 (1999) (contractor could meet the contract completion date as extended by 47 days for excusable delays); *Haselrig Constr. Co.*, PSBCA 4148, 00-1 BCA ¶30,674 (although the contractor was clearly behind schedule and failed to meet an interim milestone, it could still have accelerated its performance and finished the project on time, especially in view of the government's failure to cooperate in resolving a latent subsurface design problem, which contributed to the delays); *Hillebrand Constr. of the Midwest, Inc.*, ASBCA 45853, 95-1 BCA ¶27,464 (contractor's failure to submit shop drawings within the required 30 days after award not proof that the contractor was unable or unwilling to perform the contract within the remaining period of completion); *American Sheet Metal Corp. v. General Servs. Admin.*, GSBCA 14066, 99-1 BCA ¶30,329 (agency prematurely terminated before calculating the extended completion date). Curiously, in *American Sheet Metal Corp v. General Servs. Admin.*, GSBCA 15165-C, 00-2 BCA ¶31,126, requesting recovery of attorneys' fees, the board nevertheless held that the government's position in defaulting the contractor was substantially justified, precluding recovery under the EAJA, because of a "lack [of] confidence in the ability of [the] contractor to complete the job on time . . . numerous time extensions, performance problems, [and] insufficient progress in a time which should have been a time of considerable acceleration."

Failure to meet pre-due-date milestones or interim submission requirements is often significant, *Dubrow Elec. Indus., Inc.*, ASBCA 8464, 65-1 BCA ¶4859; *Melcor Elecs. Corp.*, ASBCA 17211, 73-1 BCA ¶10,015 (contractor repeatedly failed to meet performance milestones that it had suggested to the government). Such milestones may be the requirement to submit test plans, *Allied Tech., Inc.*, ASBCA 18101, 74-1 BCA ¶10,621 (default proper since nonconforming test plan was not corrected); *AAR Corp.*, ASBCA 16486, 74-2 BCA ¶10,653; a preproduction model, *Fitzgerald Lab., Inc.*, ASBCA 15205, 71-2 BCA ¶9029; or a first article, *Ubique, Ltd.*, DOTCAB 71-28, 72-1 BCA ¶9340.

Even though the government allows a progress milestone to pass without taking action to terminate for progress failure, the missed milestone may be relied on at a later date if performance has in fact become endangered, *AAR Corp.*, ASBCA 16486, 74-2 BCA ¶10,653 (date for submission of test procedures had passed and government delayed seven months before issuing a cure notice; termination was proper since, absent the test procedures, the pending first article due date was endangered). When the government has a reasonable basis to expect that a progress milestone will be missed, it is proper to issue the cure notice for progress failure in advance of the milestone date, *Melcor Elecs. Corp.*, ASBCA 17211, 73-1 BCA ¶10,015. However, although progress milestones may indicate that performance is endangered, the right to terminate does not necessarily arise from a missed milestone, *Ubique, Ltd.*, DOTCAB 71-28, 72-1 BCA ¶9340. See *McDonnell Douglas Corp. v. United States*, 182 F.3d 1319 (Fed. Cir. 1999), *cert denied*, 529 U.S. 1097 (2000), 50 Fed. Cl. 311 (2001), *aff'd in part & rev'd in part*, 323 F.3d 1006 (Fed. Cir. 2003), finding termination for failure to make progress improper when it was based on the contractor's prospective inability to deliver the initial prototype on a contract calling for delivery of a number of aircraft.

d. Construction Contracts

In *Discount Co. v. United States*, 213 Ct. Cl. 567, 554 F.2d 435, *cert. denied*, 434 U.S. 938 (1977), the court expressly rejected the argument that the construction contract clause requires a showing that timely performance is impossible in order to justify a pre-due-date termination. Rather, the court noted that the overall evidence of dilatory performance made the government "justifiably insecure" and that default was proper upon a finding that a "demonstrated lack of diligence indicated that the Government could not be assured of timely completion." See *Lisbon Contractors, Inc. v. United States*, 828 F.2d 759 (Fed. Cir. 1987), holding that the standard is whether the contracting officer had a "reasonable belief" that the contractor could not complete performance within the remaining time.

In assessing the construction contractor's diligence and evaluating the reasonableness of the government's insecurity, the boards frequently have compared the percentage of completion with the percentage of time remaining for performance. Where the resulting comparison showed that the contractor was ahead of schedule, default termination was found improper, *Mishara Constr. Co.*, ASBCA 8604, 1964 BCA ¶4345 (over half the time for performance remained and over 60 percent of the work was complete). Similarly, where the time remaining approximated the amount of work to be done, default was found improper even though the board itself had some doubt whether the contractor would have completed on time, *G.A. Karnavas Painting Co.*, ASBCA 19569, 76-1 BCA ¶11,837.

Direct comparison of percentage of time remaining may not be solely determinative where remaining work is likely to be done at a faster rate. In a situation similar to construction, the board found that remaining tree planting was to take place in soil conducive to a better rate of progress, *Robert Hart*, IBCA 659-8-67, 68-1 BCA ¶6984.

Most decisions upholding progress failure terminations consider all the circumstances, including percentage of completion, time remaining, and other pertinent factors. See *Bender GmbH*, ASBCA 52052, 03-2 BCA ¶32,292, *aff'd*, 106 Fed. Appx. 728 (Fed. Cir. 2004) (repeated delays, inability to protect work site from flooding, and unwillingness to work after partial suspension); *Cox & Palmer Constr. Corp.*, ASBCA 38739, 92-1 BCA ¶24,756 (contractor lost some key personnel, returned part of the required materials, failed to provide a revised schedule and management plan, and was only 58 percent complete instead of 80.8 percent); *Dozie I. Rienne*, ENGBCA 5711, 91-1 BCA ¶23,432 (contractor failed to acquire professional masons and masonry tools); *TMI, Inc.*, ENGBCA 5524, 89-3 BCA ¶22,029 (contractor had completed only 4 percent of the project when 70 percent of the time for performance had passed); *W.B. Branin Constr. Co.*, AGBCA 313, 73-1 BCA ¶9887 (only 15 percent of the work was completed in 60 percent of the time for performance, and the contractor was behind in payments to employees and materialmen); *J.E. DeKalb Co.*, VACAB 1317, 79-2 BCA ¶13,939 (job only 75 percent complete, superintendent but no workforce on job, and no performance for several weeks); *Community Window Shade Co.*, ASBCA 13675, 72-2 BCA ¶9587 (contractor failed to furnish data to indicate that storm windows would meet specifications, thus precluding the government from ordering fabrication and installation to commence); *Olympic Painting Contractors*, ASBCA 15773, 72-2 BCA ¶9549 (more than one-third of the time for performance had passed but only 7 percent of the work was done, and there were many discrepancies); and *Airco Eng'rs*, AGBCA 245, 72-1 BCA ¶9215 (contractor had been granted an extended date to complete in return for an agreement to average $2,760 worth of work per day but averaged only $1,650). Compare, however, *Western Contracting Corp.*, ENGBCA 3835, 82-1 BCA ¶15,486, overturning a default termination of a dam construction contract for failure to make progress where the contractor was only 5 percent behind schedule and had increased its efforts, and the dam was already providing the intended protection.

Failure to submit a proposed progress schedule can also be a significant factor in evaluating the contractor's lack of diligence, *Discount Co. v. United States*, 213 Ct. Cl. 567, 554 F.2d 435, *cert. denied*, 434 U.S. 938 (1977) (failure to furnish revised work schedule coupled with prior unsatisfactory performance showed that contractor was not "ready, willing and able to make progress"); *K & M Constr.*, ENGBCA 2998, 72-1 BCA ¶9366, *recons. granted*, 73-2 BCA ¶10,034 (no submission of revised progress schedule and failure to comply with speed-up orders).

3. Failure to Comply with Other Provisions

Government contracts impose many duties on contractors that are in addition to the contract requirements for the delivery of supplies, performance of services, or completion of construction. Failure to comply with a contract's "other provisions" may result in the contract being terminated for default even though the contractor is complying with the contract requirements for delivery or performance of the supplies, services, or construction.

a. Scope of Right

The FAR Default (Fixed-Price Supply and Service) clause specifically provides that the government may terminate for default based on the contractor's failure to comply with "other provisions of this contract." The construction contract clause is silent on this matter. The significance of the "other provisions" language in the default clause is to give the government the right to terminate prior to the delivery date without the necessity of establishing a progress failure. However, the provision does require a 10-day cure notice before termination. Thus, the government cannot summarily terminate a supply or service contract for failure to comply with another provision.

Generally, in order to sustain a default termination for failure to perform some other provision of the contract, that provision must represent a "material requirement" of the contract, *Brandywine Prosthetic-Orthotic Serv., Ltd.*, VABCA 3441, 93-1 BCA ¶25,250. In *Brandywine*, the board stated, at 125,765:

> To sustain a default for failure to perform other provisions of the contract, the Government must establish that the Contractor breached a material provision of the contract and that the Contractor has been given the opportunity to rectify or cure its breach. *Corban Industries, Inc.*, VABCA Nos. 2181, 2559T, 88-3 BCA ¶20,843.

In *Precision Prods.*, ASBCA 25280, 82-2 BCA ¶15,981, the board held that the contractor's violation of a clause requiring production items to be produced at the same facility as a first article did not justify default termination, stating at 79,247:

> However, to sustain a default termination, the Government must demonstrate that the breach of other provisions, not pertaining to accomplishment of the contract work itself, constituted a material breach. See *Universal Fiberglass Corp. v. United States*, 210 Ct. Cl. 206, 537 F.2d 393 (1976); *Conway Electric Co.*, ASBCA 6256, 61-1 BCA 2991.
>
> In our opinion, [the contractor's] contract non-compliance did not constitute a material breach of the contract.

The board relied heavily on the following facts: (1) government officials administering the contract "knew or should have known" that the contractor intended to subcontract for production units, (2) the contracting officer admitted that it would have accepted units that were produced by the subcontractor and that were exactly like the first article, and (3) the production units did in fact duplicate the first article.

b. Application of Rule

Examples of failures to perform other material provisions include *Kelso v. Kirk Bros. Mech. Contractors, Inc.*, 16 F.3d 1173 (Fed. Cir. 1994) (failure to maintain pay records); *Ann Riley & Assocs., Ltd.*, DOTBCA 2418, 93-3 BCA ¶25,963 (failure to provide records); *Old Dominion Sec., Inc.*, GSBCA 8563, 88-2 BCA ¶20,785 (failure to provide a state security contractor license); *Johnson & Gordon Sec., Inc.*, GSBCA 7804, 87-3 BCA ¶20,074 (failure to obtain a state license); *P.A. Arrietta*, GSBCA 4650, 77-1 BCA ¶12,334 (failure to provide performance bonds required by ash removal services contract); *Airport Indus. Park, Inc. d/b/a P. E. C. Contracting Eng'rs v. United States*, 59 Fed. Cl. 332 (2004) (inadequate bond); *Denny Furniture*, GSBCA 4502, 76-2 BCA ¶12,095 (required brochure not furnished); *Conncor, Inc.*, GSBCA 3932, 74-1 BCA ¶10,563 (failure to furnish preproduction sample); *K Square Corp.*, IBCA 959-3-72, 73-2 BCA ¶10,363 (failure to perform duties under Warranty clause); *White Lines, Inc.*, ASBCA 17756, 73-2 BCA ¶10,126 (bus transport contractor failed to furnish ICC certificate); *Genisco Tech. Corp.*, NASABCA 1068-18, 69-2 BCA ¶7802, *recons. denied*, 69-2 BCA ¶7999 (failure to deliver property under termination for convenience clause); *Inter-Continental Equip., Inc.*, ASBCA 37422, 96-1 BCA ¶28,048 (failure to demonstrate compliance with the "Cargo Preference" clause (U.S.-flag vessels)); *Airtronics, Inc.*, ASBCA 12608, 69-1 BCA ¶7757 (tender of nonconforming sample); *Samuel A. Moore*, PSBCA 1063, 83-1 BCA ¶16,376 (plea of nolo contendere to embezzlement charge where contract clause authorized agency to terminate for "conviction of a crime"); *American Bus. Sys.*, GSBCA 5140, 80-2 BCA ¶14,461 (failure to maintain adequate records as required by the Examination of Records clause); and *Christina Corp.*, PSBCA 762, Dec. 24, 1980, *Unpub.* (failure to provide required insurance certificates).

In some cases, the failure to perform in accordance with specifications has been characterized as a failure to perform other provisions. See, for example, *Nash Metalware Co.*, GSBCA 11951, 94-2 BCA ¶26,780 (contractor failed to respond to cure notice and to deliver conforming ladles); *Maywood Cab Serv., Inc.*, VACAB 1210, 77-2 BCA ¶12,751 (contractor's drivers lacked proper licenses); *Vaqueria Tres Monjitas, Inc.*, VACAB 1120, 75-1 BCA ¶11,308 (milk failed to meet sanitary standards); and *Long Island Nuclear Serv. Corp.*, ASBCA 12454, 69-1 BCA ¶7492 (spilling radioactive waste violated specifications requiring caution during performance). In *Space Dynamics Corp.*, ASBCA 13376, 71-1 BCA ¶8853, the failure to timely deliver conforming end items was apparently treated as a breach of another provision. The classification in these cases is questionable. Failures to meet specifications in end items should be treated as delivery failures if they occur after the scheduled delivery date or as progress failures if they occur before the scheduled delivery date.

Since the construction contract default clause does not specifically refer to "other provisions," there are relatively few decisions dealing with the government's right to terminate for such failures in such contracts. However, the failure to furnish bonds required by the Invitation for Bid has been held to be a sufficient basis for default termination, *Gupta Carpet Prof'ls*, GSBCA 5229, 79-1 BCA ¶13,834; *Walsh Constr. Co. of Ill.*, ASBCA 52952, 02-2 BCA ¶32,004.

Various other contract clauses provide independent bases for terminating a contractor's right to proceed with the work when the provisions of such clauses are breached. For example, the Covenant Against Contingent Fees clause, FAR 52.203-5, permits the government to "annul" the contract. Likewise, the Equal Opportunity clause, FAR 52.222-26, provides that a contract may be "cancelled, terminated, or suspended." In addition, there are other statutes and regulations that provide similar sanctions for improper conduct. See FAR 52.203-3 (anti-gratuities clause) and 41 U.S.C. §§ 51-54 (Anti-Kickback Act, prohibiting any subcontractor from making a gift to a contractor or higher-tier subcontractor as inducement for the award of a subcontract). When the violation of such provisions is at issue, the government's right to terminate may be derived from the particular clause or statute concerned. Thus, there is apparently no need to rely on the provisions of a default clause to justify such a termination. However, as a practical matter, the government may issue a default termination as the procedural mechanism for effectuating the substantive rights created by such clauses or statutes. For example, in *Joseph Morton Co. v. United States*, 757 F.2d 1273 (Fed. Cir. 1985), the Federal Circuit held that fraud in connection with one change order in a very large contract enabled the government to terminate the contract for default.

Default terminations have been used to enforce the right to terminate for violations of the Buy American Act, *H&R Machinists Co.*, ASBCA 38440, 91-1 BCA ¶23,373; *Ballantine Labs., Inc.*, ASBCA 35138, 88-2 BCA ¶20,660; *Integrated Sys. Group, Inc. v. Social Sec. Admin.*, GSBCA 14054-SSA, 98-2 BCA ¶29,848; the Walsh-Healey Act, *SanColMar Indus., Inc.*, ASBCA 15339, 73-2 BCA ¶10,086; the Service Contract Act, *Giltron Assocs., Inc.*, ASBCA 14561, 70-1 BCA ¶8316; and the Davis-Bacon and Contract Work Hours Standards Acts, *Edgar M. Williams*, ASBCA 16058, 72-2 BCA ¶9734. However, in *Herman B. Taylor Constr. Co. v. Barram*, 203 F.3d 808 (Fed. Cir. 2000), the court held that a contractor's consent decree with the Department of Labor was not a final adjudication of Davis-Bacon Act violations and could not be the basis for a default termination since neither party admitted or determined anything about the alleged violation.

Although difficult to categorize, terminations are sometimes justified on the basis of outrageous conduct by the contractor. In *Tom Kime*, PSBCA 3480, 95-1 BCA ¶27,490, a contractor was properly terminated because of his abusive behavior toward a postal clerk and the postmaster as well as a failure to obey the postmaster's instructions. Other contracts were terminated after the contractor assaulted the postmaster and a postal clerk. In *Larry J. Miller*, PSBCA 3632, 95-1 BCA ¶27,448, a postal delivery contractor's intentional disposal of extra advertising mail in a trash bin was a serious enough violation of the contract requirements to merit a default termination.

False certifications also justify a default termination. In *National Med. Staffing Inc.*, DOTBCA 2568, 95-1 BCA ¶27,341, the contractor's knowingly false certification that it had not been terminated for default in the prior three years by any federal agencies was sufficient basis for default termination of a contract. See also *Spread Info. Sciences, Inc.*, ASBCA 48438, 96-1 BCA ¶27,996. In *Ricmar Eng'g, Inc.*, ASBCA 44260, 97-2 BCA ¶29,084, the contract was terminated because the contractor and its president had been convicted of conspiring to submit a fraudulent progress payment request. Compare *Technical Sys. Assocs., Inc. v. Department of Commerce*, GSBCA 13277-COM, 97-2 BCA ¶30,684 (government's motion for summary judgment to uphold the default termination based on the contractor's false certification regarding previous default terminations denied because the contractor alleged that the government knew of the prior terminations for default before the contract was awarded).

4. Failure to Proceed

The Contract Disputes Act of 1978, 41 U.S.C. § 605(b), authorizes agencies to include clauses requiring contractors to proceed with performance pending "final decision of an appeal, action or final settlement." The standard Disputes clause set forth at FAR 52.233-1 for contracts subject to the Disputes Act implements this authority in ¶(i), as follows:

> The Contractor shall proceed diligently with performance of this contract, pending final resolution of any request for relief, claim, appeal, or action arising under the contract, and comply with any decision of the Contracting Officer.

Language requiring the contractor to proceed with performance during pendency of disputes was also included in the standard pre-Act Disputes clauses:

> Pending final decision of a dispute hereunder, the Contractor shall proceed diligently with the performance of the contract and in accordance with the Contracting Officer's decision.

The basic rationale for imposing such a "duty to proceed" was articulated by the Armed Services Board in *Detroit Designing & Eng'g Co.*, ASBCA 8807, 1964 BCA ¶4214, at 20,452:

> Regardless of the merits of a [contractor's] dispute, the plain provisions of the contract and the public interest do not for a moment permit us to countenance possible hampering of operations which might involve the lives of servicemen or the political position of the country in its myriad world-wide commitments and responsibilities. Yet, this might be the precise effect of prolonged suspension of contract performance even in connection with the most commonplace item of supply.

The contractor's rights are in theory protected by permitting the contractor to subsequently assert a claim and challenge a contracting officer's adverse decision through an appeal to a board of contract appeals or suit in the U.S. Court of Federal Claims. See *Dyanamics Corp. of Am. v. United States*, 182 Ct. Cl. 62, 389 F.2d 424 (1968).

The contractor's duty to proceed in the standard Disputes clause is applicable only to disputes "arising under the contract." This phrase means that there must be a remedy-granting clause in the contract applicable to the matter in dispute for the duty to proceed to be binding. Thus, if there is no remedy-granting clause applicable, the contractor would be entitled to abandon the work upon a material breach by the government. However, the wide class of government breaches, such as many constructive changes, which are covered by remedy-granting clauses, has severely narrowed the universe of government misconduct that can be characterized as a material breach and upon which a contractor rescission or abandonment of performance could therefore properly be based.

An even greater limit on the contractor's right to abandon the work on the government's breach is contained in the alternate version of the Disputes clause provided in FAR 52.233-1, which calls for the contractor to proceed diligently with performance "pending final resolution of any request for relief, claim, appeal, or action arising under or relating to the contract." DFARS 233.013 requires this alternate to be used in Department of Defense contracts for aircraft, ships, and major defense systems. This language may also be included in DOD contracts where performance is vital to national security or public health or welfare. NFS 1833.104 authorizes inclusion of this alternate provision "where continued performance is vital to national security, the public health and welfare, critical/major agency programs, or other essential supplies or services whose timely procurement from other sources would be impracticable." Note that FAR 33.213(b) states that the agency should consider providing financial assistance to contractors being instructed to proceed pending resolution of claims not arising under, but related to, the contract. Under this alternate provision, arguably, the contractor would have a duty to proceed even in the event of a "material breach" that would otherwise constitute grounds for rescission or abandonment under contracts containing either the pre-Act or standard Disputes Act disputes clauses. See the discussion of "material breach" that follows.

The requirement to proceed pending resolution of a dispute is also stated in the supply contract Changes clause at FAR 52.243-1, which states in part, "nothing in this clause shall excuse the contractor from proceeding with the contract as changed." Similar language appeared in earlier versions of the construction contract Changes clause, but it was removed in 1968 as unnecessary, Hiestand, *A New Era in Government Construction Contracts,* 28 Fed. B.J. 165, 180-81 (1968). The Changes clause requirement to proceed has been relied on in whole or in part to uphold defaults in *Nasco Prods. Co.*, VACAB 974, 72-2 BCA ¶9556 (contractor's failure to proceed pursuant to "a clear and unambiguous contract requirement" resulted in default), and *Telecommunication Consultants*, ASBCA 13801, 69-2 BCA ¶7925 (contractor failed to continue performance when it felt that certain drawings were not required by specifications despite the contracting officer's directions). The duty to proceed in accordance with the Changes clause has been infrequently cited as the specific ground for upholding a default.

While neither the Disputes clauses nor the standard default clauses specify the contractor's failure to proceed as a grounds for default termination by the government, a contractor's failure to proceed has occasionally been cited as proper grounds for default termination. While it has been suggested that, under the supply contract default clause, a contractor's failure to proceed provides a grounds for default as a failure to perform another provision of the contract, it would seem that a failure to proceed with the work in accordance with contracting officer's directions should properly provide a basis for default termination only where default would otherwise be justified based on failure to make progress or anticipatory repudiation.

The failure to proceed pending resolution of a dispute has sometimes been equated with anticipatory repudiation. See, for example, *Ortec Sys., Inc.*, ASBCA 43467, 92-2 BCA ¶24,859 (contractor abandonment is actual repudiation); *Aero Prods. Co.*, ASBCA 44030, 93-2 BCA ¶25,868 (contractor refusal to perform according to directions constituted a material breach); *Twigg Corp.*, NASABCA 62-0192, 93-1 BCA ¶25,318 (contractor refusal to remove and replace concrete slabs supported a termination for anticipatory breach); and *Kirk Casavan*, AGBCA 76-192, 78-2 BCA ¶13,459 (contractor, by refusing to perform during a dispute, "exhibited no inclination, and in fact refused, to prosecute the work with such diligence as to insure its completion within the contract time," thereby repudiating the contract).

Contractors often condition their continued performance upon the granting of other relief such as the payment of money or changes of technical requirements. Agencies properly terminated contracts for default on the grounds of anticipatory breach when the contractor conditioned the continuation of its performance on the authorization of a price adjustment, and the agency had not required work beyond the scope of the contract. See *Starghill Alternative Energy Corp.*, ASBCA 49612, 98-1 BCA ¶29,708; *Brenner Metal Prods. Corp.*, ASBCA 25294, 82-1 BCA ¶15,462 (contractor refused to proceed with work unless it was granted a price increase for alleged government-caused delays); and *Howell Tool & Fabricating, Inc.*, ASBCA 47939, 96-1 BCA ¶28,225. However, although failure to proceed pending resolution of a dispute is analogous to repudiation, there are some distinctions. Failure to proceed pending resolution of a dispute does not necessarily involve abandonment or repudiation but may involve merely work stoppage that the contractor believes to be justified.

a. *Notification to Proceed*

The contractor's duty to proceed under the Disputes clause requires an indication from the contracting officer that the government expects continued performance. This most clearly exists where the contracting officer has issued an appealable final decision concerning a matter in dispute, *RFI Shield-Rooms*, ASBCA 19005, 77-1 BCA ¶12,237. Although it has been argued that absent a contracting officer's final decision pursuant to the Disputes clause the duty to proceed does not attach, the contractor's duty has not been so narrowly construed. Thus, the duty to proceed also "embraces the period when the dispute is in the `embryonic stage' before the contracting officer's formal decision," *Winder Aircraft Corp.*, ASBCA 4364, 59-1 BCA ¶2257 (contractor complained of inadequacy of specification drawings); *Stoeckert v. United States*, 183 Ct. Cl. 152, 391 F.2d 639 (1968) (contractor's refusal to follow contracting officer's directions in a stop-work order to remove and replace previously laid tile).

The direction from the contracting officer may take the form of a unilateral order directing the contractor to proceed with stated contract work, *Eriez Constr., Inc.*, VACAB 1273, 78-2 BCA ¶13,547; *Aero Prods. Co.*, ASBCA 44030, 93-2 BCA ¶25,868 (clear direction to provide plotting board carrying cases that added 20 percent to cost of performance, pending resolution of interpretation dispute); or a notice directing some specific action, *RFI Shield-Rooms*, ASBCA 19005, 77-1 BCA ¶12,237 (explicit direction that full-load test plan be submitted); *Colangelo Constr. Co.*, ENGBCA 3313, 74-2 BCA ¶10,853 (specific order to correct defective asphalt in accordance with the construction contract inspection clause); *Sanders Assocs., Inc.*, ASBCA 17653, 75-1 BCA ¶11,043 (cure notice required contractor to correct numerous technical discrepancies). Specific notice would appear to be required if the requirement to proceed is questionable, *Seven Sciences, Inc.*, ASBCA 21079, 77-2 BCA ¶12,730 (default termination without specific notice improper where the government failed to supply all the drawings needed for fabrication of battery chargers).

However, where the facts and circumstances clearly indicate that the contractor should proceed, a formal unilateral order is unnecessary. See *American Dredging Co.*, ENGBCA 2920, 72-1 BCA ¶9316, where, following the contracting officer's denial of a channel-dredging contractor's claim for adjustment due to differing site conditions, the contractor became aware that only blasting and drilling would accomplish the required results but did not proceed with the work.

In addition to explicit orders or the existence of a clear requirement to proceed, other factors may place the contractor on notice that continued performance is expected. Such factors include issuance of a cure notice for failure to make progress, *APCO Mossberg Co.*, GSBCA 3440, 72-1 BCA ¶9403; explicit notification that the delivery schedule remains in effect, *Geophysical Instrument & Supply Co.*, IBCA 996-6-73, 74-1 BCA ¶10,404; and clear statements as to the government's interpretation of contract language, *Charles Bainbridge, Inc.*, ASBCA 15843, 72-1 BCA ¶9351. The government's indication that work should proceed may also be found where the contracting officer has made statements of intended future actions that are consistent only with continued performance, *Campbell Keypunch Serv.*, GSBCA 3123, 71-1 BCA ¶8800 (contractor required to proceed when, following overpayment on a requirements contract, contracting officer expressed intent to set off against amounts payable on future orders).

b. Scope and Nature of Obligation

The nature of the duty to proceed is broad. See *Essex Electro Eng'rs, Inc.*, ASBCA 49115, 02-1 BCA ¶31,714, stating at 156,699:

> After the Contracting Officer has given an interpretation of the contract requirements, the contractor must perform as directed and may not stop work. If the contractor believes the interpretation erroneous, the determination may be appealed in the claims procedure. *Benju Corporation,* ASBCA 43648, et al. 97-2 BCA 29274 at 145, 654-55. In *Benju* we made clear that even if the Government's interpretation were wrong, the contractor is not justified in refusing to do as directed since the merits of the controversy have no effect on the requirement that a contractor continue performance. A contractor may disagree with the Government's representative as to how the work is to be completed, but nevertheless is under a duty to proceed diligently with performance. *Advanced Mechanical Services, Inc.* ASBCA 38832, 94-3 BCA 26964.

The contractor must proceed even where the government erroneously advises that no relief for its claim is possible, *Accu-Met Prods., Inc.*, ASBCA 19704, 75-1 BCA ¶11,123 (following clarification of a defective specification, the government denied responsibility for delays and cost increases due to the defect); *Mai Huu An Co.*, ASBCA 14953, 71-1 BCA ¶8874 (default upheld where a Vietnamese contractor, who was "apparently" able to read and write English, was initially advised that there would be no price adjustment to compensate for adverse impact of an austerity tax, although the contracting officer later stated "relief might be granted" and the form contract in use contained an explicit right to an adjustment).

The contractor must also proceed even though it believes the government's action to be wrong. If the contractor refuses to proceed, it risks termination even if its belief concerning the dispute is correct, *Schmid Plumbing & Heating Co. v. United States,* 173 Ct. Cl. 302, 351 F.2d 651 (1965) (contractor had the duty to install more expensive boilers erroneously demanded by the contracting officer even though the department head later ruled in the contractor's favor); *Scientific Book Serv., Inc.*, GSBCA 3096, 70-1 BCA ¶8357 (contractor refused to deliver publications, although it was able to do so, because of a disagreement over the meaning of a list price provision); *Benju Corp.*, ASBCA 43648, 97-2 BCA ¶29,274, *aff'd,* 178 F.3d 1312 (Fed. Cir. 1999) (refusal to furnish test procedures that contractor believed were not required); *Protech Atlanta,* ASBCA 52217, 01-2 BCA ¶31,434 (refusal to continue when contracting officer refused to consider deviation requests); *George F. Marshall & Gordon L. Blackwell,* ENGBCA 6066, 00-1 BCA ¶30,730 (refusal of takeover contractor to continue, in belief that additional payments were due).

The Disputes clause duty to proceed provision also precludes a contractor from stopping work on one contract because of a pending dispute on another contract, *Kirk Casavan,* AGBCA 76-192, 78-2 BCA ¶13,459 (tree-thinning contractor improperly refused to perform until "positive action" was taken on claims under other contract); *Clinical Supply Corp.*, ASBCA 15466, 72-1 BCA ¶9452 (contractor required to continue performance despite improper government claim under the warranty provisions of other contracts ultimately adjudicated in the contractor's favor).

Default terminations for breach of the duty to proceed have been found proper regardless of the time at which the refusal to proceed occurs. See, for example, *Skip Kirchdorfer, Inc.*, ASBCA 32637, 91-1 BCA ¶23,380 (undue lapse of time between default and actual termination did not affect valid termination); *Campbell Keypunch Serv.*, GSBCA 3123, 71-1 BCA ¶8800 (requirements contractor refused to accept job orders that were, in effect, notices to proceed); *Hackett Corp.*, GSBCA 3942, 75-1 BCA ¶11,060 (after award but prior to the due date); *Accu-Met Prods., Inc.*, ASBCA 19704, 75-1 BCA ¶11,123 (the due date was apparently uncertain since a defective specification had delayed performance for some time and no revised date had been established); and *Kirk Casavan*, AGBCA 76-192, 78-2 BCA ¶13,459 (prior to due date). Where the due date has passed prior to termination, defaults have been upheld in part because of the contractor's failure to proceed pending resolution of a dispute. See *Eriez Constr., Inc.*, VACAB 1273, 78-2 BCA ¶13,547 (contractor's refusal to install casework classified as a failure to proceed pending resolution of a dispute even though the date for completion had passed). In finding defaults proper in such cases, the boards have implicitly held that the contractor's untimely performance, which is an independent basis for default, cannot be excusable merely because there was a dispute during the period of performance. The nonexcusability of such delays was explicitly recognized in *Pennsylvania Testing Lab.*, ASBCA 6185, 61-2 BCA ¶3234 (contractor's allegations of deficient government preliminary drawings were not an excusable cause for delay).

In one case, the court held that the contractor was required to proceed to perform an option that had been invalidly exercised by the contracting officer by specifying a rate of delivery not required by the contract, *Alliant Techsystems, Inc. v. United States,* 178 F.3d 1260 (Fed. Cir. 1999). There the court upheld a termination for default for failure to perform the option at a rate that had been specified by the Court of Federal Claims in a declaratory judgment, stating at 1276:

> Alliant's obligations under the Disputes clause are independent of its obligations under the Option clause. Because we have determined that the Disputes clause requires Alliant to perform the option as directed pending resolution of its challenge to the Contracting Officer's order, we hold that Alliant was obligated to deliver the option quantities until and unless it obtained a court order excusing it from its performance obligations. The Court of Federal Claims issued its declaratory judgment prior to the first delivery of option quantities required by the contracting officer's decision. Alliant was therefore not obligated to perform at the contracting officer's rate, but absent reversal or interim relief from this court, Alliant was required by the disputes clause to perform at the rate specified by the Court of Federal Claims.

Although the Disputes clause in the contract required the contractor to proceed only when claims met the "arising under" standard, the decision contains no reference to any remedy-granting clause that applied to improperly exercised options. However, the decision does reject the contractor's contention that the option exercise was a "cardinal change"—perhaps indicating that the court believed that the Changes clause was the applicable remedy-granting clause.

In *Dae Shinn Enters., Inc., d/b/a Dayron,* ASBCA 50533, 03-1 BCA ¶32,096, the board ruled that even in the face of its allegation of commercial impracticability, Dae Shinn should have proceeded with performance while pursuing extra compensation under the Changes and Government Property clause.

c. *Exceptions to the Duty to Proceed*

The courts and boards have excused the contractor from its duty to proceed where it would be unfair or illogical to require it to continue contract performance. A failure to proceed may be excused where government actions materially breach the contract or make performance impractical or impossible, or where the government does not provide the contractor with clear direction necessary to perform the contract.

(1) Government Material Breach

Under a well-established common law principle, a contracting party is under no duty to continue rendering required performance in the face of an "uncured material failure" or "material breach" by the other party, *Restatement, Second, Contracts* § 237. The standard pre-CDA and post-CDA clause would appear to severely limit a contractor's ability to rely on this doctrine by making many kinds of government misconduct subject to resolution under the disputes procedures and specifically directing the contractor to proceed with the work pending resolution of such disputes. Nevertheless, the doctrine of "material breach" remains applicable to government contracts and serves as an important exception to the duty to proceed.

Since the government's major obligation in its contracts is to pay the contractor, most material breaches occur when timely payment in accordance with the contract provisions is not made. In *General Dynamics Corp.*, DOTCAB 1232, 83-1 BCA ¶16,386, the board held that the government's failure to pay five invoices under a cost-reimbursement contract, based on the contractor's alleged failure to make progress, constituted a material breach justifying the contractor's suspension of performance. In reaching this conclusion, the board relied on a contract provision stating that the contractor was entitled to be paid its incurred costs up to a certain ceiling without regard to its success in performing. In *Drain-A-Way Sys.*, GSBCA 6473, 83-1 BCA ¶16,202, the board explicitly recognized that, while the government's failure to pay for services performed was "clearly a dispute of fact arising under the contract," the contractor was nevertheless under no duty to continue with performance, stating that "where the Government has itself committed a material breach, it may not compel its contractor to continue performance under the Disputes clause." In *Seven Sciences, Inc.*, ASBCA 21079, 77-2 BCA ¶12,730, the board stated that the discharge of a contractor's duty to perform "depends on the seriousness of the Government's breach, both the nature of the breach and the impact on the contractor's ability to perform." A serious breach was found in *Northern Helex Co. v. United States*, 197 Ct. Cl. 118, 455 F.2d 546 (1972), in which the court stated at 124:

> [M]ere delay in payment, for a while, would not be a material breach but there is a clear distinction between delay of that kind and a total failure to pay over many months. Our jurisprudence strongly suggests that the latter sort of breach by the Government is material, just as it would be in the case of a private party.

Where government failure to make payments justifies a contractor's failure to proceed, default termination is improper. See *U.S. Servs. Corp.*, ASBCA 8291, 1963 BCA ¶3703, in which the board stated at 18,509:

> Under the circumstances, the Government's attempt to terminate the contract for default was ineffective because the [contractor] had already exercised its right to rescind the contract.

In *H.E. & C.F. Blinne Contracting Co.*, ENGBCA 4174, 83-1 BCA ¶16,388, the board overturned a default termination, holding that the government's failure to remit the proper amount of progress payments constituted a "Government breach." In *Building Maint. Specialist, Inc.*, ENGBCA 4115, 83-2 BCA ¶16,629, the board held that unauthorized deductions from payments for services performed justified abandonment of work even though the underpayment did not render the contractor financially incapable of performing. The contractor's right to stop performance for payment failures was also upheld in *Contract Maint., Inc.*, ASBCA 19409, 75-1 BCA ¶11,207 (four-month failure to pay amounts admittedly due); *Robert O. Redding*, AGBCA 272, 69-2 BCA ¶7888 (withholding one month's progress payment); *R. H. J. Corp.*, ASBCA 9922, 66-1 BCA ¶5361, *recons. denied*, 66-1 BCA ¶5625 (progress payments were to be calculated on the basis of incurred costs, but government suspended payments pending submission of an acceptable first article); *Valley Contractors*, ASBCA 9397, 1964 BCA ¶4071 (failure to pay janitorial services contractor where at least 51 percent of monthly fee was admittedly due); and *U.S. Servs. Corp.*, ASBCA 8291, 1963 BCA ¶3703 (one month's progress payment wrongfully withheld). Following work stoppage, the contractor may have no obligation to return to work even where the government subsequently offers to make the payments, *Suburban Contracting Co. v. United States*, 76 Ct. Cl. 533 (1932). However, the government's withholding of payment excuses the contractor's default only where it is both improper and the primary or controlling cause of default, and not where the contractor has repudiated its contractual obligations, *Graham Int'l*, ASBCA 50360, 01-1 BCA ¶31,222. Moreover, a wrongful withholding may still be reasonable under the circumstances. In *Bill J. Copeland*, AGBCA 1999-182-1, 02-2 BCA ¶32,049, *aff'd*, 350 F.2d 1230 (Fed. Cir. 2003), the agency properly withheld progress payments based on a Department of Labor investigator's recommendation even though a subsequent DOL decision found the withholding to be grossly excessive. The board found that since the agency's reliance on the investigator's recommendation was both reasonable and in accordance with applicable law, the default termination was proper.

Another type of material breach that may justify refusal to proceed is action by the government in excess of that authorized by the contract, *United States v. Spearin*, 248 U.S. 132 (1918). For example, it has been held that a "cardinal change"—defined as a change that fundamentally alters the contractual undertaking—constitutes a material breach and that in such circumstances "there is no contractual duty on the part of the contractor to comply with the change or continue performance," *Kakos Nursery, Inc.*, ASBCA 10989, 66-2 BCA ¶5733, *recons. denied*, 66-2 BCA ¶5909. Unreasonable and untimely inspections by the government may also justify a failure or refusal to proceed, *Wayne Welding Equip. Co.*, GSBCA 4560, 77-1 BCA ¶12,532. In *Brand S. Roofing*, ASBCA 24688, 82-1 BCA ¶15,513, a three-month government delay in informing the contractor of defects in performance greatly increased costs of correction and constituted a material breach that justified refusal to perform as directed. Furthermore, government failure to follow the procedures required by the Disputes clause was found to be so egregious that refusal to perform was justified, *Penker Constr. Co. v. United States*, 96 Ct. Cl. 1 (1942) (perfunctory administrative review of the contractor's claim so denied the contractor's right to an effective hearing that the court characterized the process as a "travesty of justice").

The contractor may elect to waive a material breach by the government and continue performance, but in such situations the contractor should notify the government of this election and reserve the right to seek redress for the breach, *Ling-Temco-Vought, Inc. v. United States*, 201 Ct. Cl. 135, 475 F.2d 630 (1973). See also *Empire Energy Mgmt. Sys., Inc.*, ASBCA 46741, 03-1 BCA ¶32,079; *aff'd*, 362 F.3d 1343 (Fed. Cir. 2004), holding that the government retained the right to terminate a utility construction contract for default because, although the contractor ceased work for a year citing alleged site contamination, it resumed work after the performance period had lapsed. The board reasoned that although the contractor alleged that the government breached the contract, the rights and obligations of the parties remained in effect for as long as the contractor continued performance.

The alternate Disputes clause, requiring the contractor to proceed in the event of disputes "relating to" as well as those "arising under" the contract, may compel the contractor to continue with performance even in the face of a "material breach" by the government. See *Metric Sys. v. McDonnell Douglas Corp.*, 850 F.Supp. 1568 (N.D. Florida 1994), in which the judge upheld a termination based on the failure to proceed because, inter alia, the contract clause was modeled after the Disputes clause, Alternate 1, and required performance even in the face of a breach.

(2) Impractical to Proceed

Government acts may excuse a contractor from the duty to proceed even though the disputes process provides administrative relief for the effects of such actions if the contractor is unable to perform or is delayed by the government's conduct. See *E.L. Cournand & Co.*, ASBCA 2955, 60-2 BCA ¶2840, in which the board stated that the clauses requiring the contractor to proceed must be read "together with the words in the 'Default' article which in effect excuse a failure to perform any provision of the contract if the failure arises out of causes beyond the control and without the fault or negligence of the contractor. Acts of the Government are included in such causes." Thus, a wrongful failure to pay may excuse a subsequent default if the failure to pay caused the default, *Pilcher, Livingston & Wallace, Inc.*, ASBCA 13391, 70-1 BCA ¶8331, *recons. denied*, 70-2 BCA ¶8488 (default excused since failure to make progress payments deprived contractor of funds essential to pay subcontractors, and subsequent failure to complete work was due to subcontractors' failure to proceed absent payment); *Q.V.S., Inc.*, ASBCA 3722, 58-2 BCA ¶2007 (default excused since government failure to make payments precluded timely performance).

When the government requires a contractor to follow detailed plans and specifications, it impliedly warrants that if the specifications are followed the results will be adequate, *United States v. Spearin*, 248 U.S. 132 (1918). Defects in government design or specifications may excuse the contractor from its duty to proceed. See *D.E.W., Inc.*, ASBCA 35896, 94-3 BCA ¶27,182, in which the board found that defects in a bearing bolt design made it impossible for the contractor to proceed with hanger construction in accordance with the government's plans and specifications. Thus, the termination for default was converted to a termination for the convenience of the government. Impossibility of performance may also be found if the contractor can establish that performance of the contract could not be accomplished without commercially unacceptable costs and time input far beyond that contemplated in the contract, *Foster Wheeler Corp. v. United States*, 206 Ct. Cl. 533, 513 F.2d 588 (1975). See *Soletanche Rodio Nicholson (JV)*, ENGBCA 5796, 94-1 BCA ¶26,472, in which a contractor's failure to complete its excavation contract was excusable because a differing site condition "made it legally, commercially, and practically impossible to continue performance." The contractor proposed the use of a rock mill as a performance method based on an assumption that it would encounter normal ground stress. However, the contractor encountered unusual ground stress at the site, and the excavation could not be performed with a rock mill. In converting the default termination to a termination for the convenience of the government, the board stated that the evidence established "the classic case for legal, practical and commercial impossibility." See *Defense Sys. Corp. & Hi-Shear Tech. Corp.*, ASBCA 42939, 95-2 BCA ¶27,721, holding that the government improperly terminated a contract for default when the contractor stopped work because an inadequate technical data package coupled, with unrealistic acceptance criteria, combined to make performance of an ammunition production contract commercially impracticable.

Even if continued performance is possible and the contractor has a clear idea of what the government desires in the way of performance, there may be no duty to proceed if the circumstances make continued performance impractical, *Ned C. Hardy*, AGBCA 74-111, 77-2 BCA ¶12,848 (denial of permission for workers to camp at worksite rendered national forest site preparation contractor's performance impractical since unattended equipment was subject to vandalism and contractor reasonably suspected that a single night watchman would be in personal danger from ecology activists); *Hempstead Maint. Serv., Inc.*, GSBCA 3127, 71-1 BCA ¶8809 (cleaning services contractor encountered severe difficulty in opening numerous windows, and employees' union advised workers not to push pivot windows for fear of falling from the fifth floor).

It is also considered impractical to proceed with performance where the contractor knows that the resulting work will be defective or useless, *Seven Sciences, Inc.*, ASBCA 21079, 77-2 BCA ¶12,730; *Ascani Constr. & Realty Co.*, VABCA 1572, 83-2 BCA ¶16,635. In *Puma Chem. Co.*, GSBCA 5254, 81-1 BCA ¶14,844, the contractor's refusal to proceed was justified where government imposition of improper inspection methods and test procedures was likely to lead to rejection of finished supplies. See also *Astro Dynamics, Inc.*, ASBCA 28320, 83-2 BCA ¶16,900, where a high rate of rejections resulting from demanding tolerance specifications made it reasonable for the contractor to seek a solution rather than proceed with work in the hope that the government would grant "waivers" as to definitive items. Moreover, it has been stated that a contractor may not proceed with performance when it knows the resulting work will be defective. In *J.D. Hedin Constr. Co. v. United States*, 171 Ct. Cl. 70, 347 F.2d 235 (1965), the court stated at 77:

> [A]n experienced contractor cannot rely on government-prepared specifications where, on the basis of the government furnished data, he knows or should have known that the prepared specifications could not produce the desired result for ". . . he has no right to make a useless thing and charge the customer for it." *R.M. Hollingshead Corp. v. United States*, 124 Ct. Cl. 681, 683, 111 F. Supp. 285, 286 (1953).

However, in *Switlik Parachute Co. v. United States*, 216 Ct. Cl. 362, 573 F.2d 1228 (1978), the court indicated that recovery was appropriate when the contractor proceeded with the work even though the government failed to take corrective action after being notified of the alleged defect, stating at 374:

> Even if it be assumed that [the government's] design specifications were deficient, [the contractor] in notifying the defendant on May 3, 1973 of the alleged design deficiencies, had discharged its duty not to knowingly produce defective items without first contacting [the government]. *See Blount Brothers Construction Co. v. United States*, 171 Ct. Cl. 478, 495-97, 346 F.2d 962, 972-73 (1965). Thereafter, given the absence of either an order by [the government] immediately to suspend production or of a change order modifying the design specifications, it was [the contractor's] right to go forward with production, even though in so doing [the government] might incur liability for defective products. After all, it is the [government] who warrants that compliance with its design specifications will result in an acceptable product. *United States v. Spearin*, 248 U.S. 132 (1918). *See*, also, *R.E.D.M. Corp. v. United States*, 192 Ct. Cl. 891, 901-02, 428 F.2d 1304, 1309-10 (1970).

In *S.W. Elecs. & Mfg. Corp. v. United States*, 228 Ct. Cl. 333, 655 F.2d 1078 (1981), a contractor was denied an equitable adjustment for increased costs attributable to defective work after the contracting officer had issued instructions to substitute a workable switch for the inadequate switch identified in the specifications. The court rejected the contractor's attempt to rely on *Switlick*, stating at 345:

> Nor does this court's opinion in *Switlik Parachute Co. v. United States*, 216 Ct. Cl. 362, 573 F.2d 1228 (1978), support the [contractor's] position. Rather, that case tends to support the position that a contractor would be entitled to continue production of what the contractor believed were defective units, once the contractor had advised the Government of the problem and the Government had failed to take corrective action. In *Switlik* the Government believed that the vests which [the contractor] was producing met the contract requirements and

> concluded that corrective action was not necessary. *Switlik* stated that under those circumstances the contractor had a right to continue production. In this case, everyone agreed that the radios which incorporated the Ledex switch did not function. More importantly, the contracting officer instructed the [contractor] on the appropriate action to take, *i.e.*, use the Oak switch. It is clear that the reasoning in *Switlik* would not justify [the contractor's] continued production using the Ledex switch on the facts of this case. [The contractor's] reliance on *Switlik* assumes that [the contractor] was following the Government's instructions in producing all of the defective radios, whereas [the contractor] clearly was not.

The risk of stopping performance to avoid producing defective work is illustrated by *Martin & Turner Supply Co.*, ASBCA 16809, 72-2 BCA ¶9610, in which the board upheld a default termination, stating at 44,936:

> [The contractor's] position was simply that it could have provided an item that would conform to specifications but that it refused to do so since it knew that the item was not what the Government intended to acquire. However praiseworthy [the contractor's] motives may have been, it had the duty to perform under the contract just as the Government had the duty to accept the item if it conformed to specifications even were the item different from what it desired. On failure to perform, the Government had no choice but to terminate for default and quite properly so.

See also *Al-Cal Painting Co.*, GSBCA 2806, 70-1 BCA ¶8319 (total abandonment of job was not justified by allegation that government specifications calling for a single coat of white paint over green paint would not produce satisfactory results).

Even where performance is impossible, a contractor generally may not abandon performance and repudiate the contract unless the government has been adequately informed of the problem and afforded an opportunity to relax the specifications, *Wise Instrumentation & Control, Inc.*, NASABCA 1072-12, 75-2 BCA ¶11,478, *recons. denied*, 76-1 BCA ¶11,641; *Suffolk Envtl. Magnetics, Inc.*, ASBCA 17593, 74-2 BCA ¶10,771; or to assist the contractor by providing special equipment, *Thermovac Indus. Corp.*, AECBCA 64-11-69, 70-1 BCA ¶8157.

Once performance is again practicable, the duty to proceed revives, *D.H. Dave & Gerben Contracting Co.*, ASBCA 6257, 1962 BCA ¶3493. Likewise, contractors must proceed with severable portions of the work that are not impracticable, *James G. Henderson*, ASBCA 15353, 72-2 BCA ¶9567. However, the contractor does not have to proceed if the government has specifically indicated that it will not accept performance of the severable work absent completion of the impracticable work, *Stamell Constr. Co.*, DOTCAB 68-27J, 75-1 BCA ¶11,334.

(3) Lack of Clear Direction

Lack of clear direction necessary for performance can justify a failure to proceed in accordance with the Disputes clause, *Industrial-Denver Co.*, ASBCA 13735, 70-1 BCA ¶8118 (failure to provide design criteria to meet government's interpretation of specification); *Foremost Mech. Sys., Inc. v. General Servs. Admin.*, GSBCA 12335, 95-1 BCA ¶27,382 (failure to give timely response to requests to resolve numerous technical issues); *Turbine Aviation*, ASBCA 51323, 98-2 BCA ¶29,945 (failure to provide crucial technical information in a timely manner); *Alsace Indus., Inc.*, ASBCA 50720, 98-1 BCA ¶29,576 (government failed to answer an unnecessary but good faith query on technical requirements); *SAE/Americon-Mid Atl., Inc. v. General Servs. Admin.*, GSBCA 12294, 98-2 BCA ¶30,084 (failure of government's architect to answer technical inquiries). Whether directions are so unclear that the contractor need not continue is a factual question. Thus, contractors must be certain that there is a significant uncertainty and must make some attempt to resolve the problem, *Florida Sys. Corp.*, ASBCA 12443, 69-2 BCA ¶8028 (contractor requested no information despite the contracting officer's express willingness to clarify disputed items). In *Robert R. Marquis, Inc.*, ASBCA 38438, 92-1 BCA ¶24,692, the government failed to tell a contractor how to proceed in the face of a potential conflict with another contractor's work despite repeated requests. Thus, the contractor was unable to proceed in the absence of direction.

Requests for clarification must be reasonable. See *Electromagnetic Indus., Inc.*, ASBCA 11485, 67-2 BCA ¶6545, in which the board stated at 30,410:

> It is true that [the contractor] cannot, by continually writing letters requesting information and clarification, impose an obligation on the Government to answer every letter thereby postponing indefinitely the "day of reckoning"—default termination.

In *Pennsylvania Testing Lab., Inc.*, ASBCA 6185, 61-2 BCA ¶3234, the board discussed the reasonableness of the contractor's requests for clarification, stating at 16,765-66:

> [The contractor] could have obtained the information claimed to be indispensable to performance at any time by resort to published industry data of general circulation. He chose instead to compel the Government to assemble such information for him, losing many months in the process. When [the contractor] received the essential data he was so entrenched in contumacy that he declined to use them on the pretext that the data came into his possession indirectly. Rather than proceed he insisted upon contract amendments for the avowed objective of vindicating his opinions on the questions of interpretation. [The contractor] did not want information; he wanted change orders.

See also *Dynatran Elecs. Corp.*, ASBCA 8371, 1963 BCA ¶4006 (board found that the contractor "did not want a solution to the problems of manufacture but change orders vindicating its point of view"); *Fraya, S.E.*, ASBCA 52222, 02-2 BCA ¶31,975 ("the duty to cooperate is a duty not to hinder or interfere with the contractor's performance. It 'is not a duty to do whatever a contractor demands,'" citing *Tri-Indus., Inc.*, ASBCA 47880, 99-2 BCA ¶30,529 at 150,765). However, in *Bison Trucking & Equip. Co.*, ASBCA 53390, 0l-2 BCA ¶31,654, the board held that the contractor was justified in stopping performance when the government failed to respond to its request for testing locations.

Where a reasonable request for clarification has been made, the contractor need not inform the government that work has stopped so long as such stoppage could reasonably be anticipated, *Milwaukee Transformer Co.*, ASBCA 10814, 66-1 BCA ¶5570. Likewise, performance may be stopped even where the government has not issued a stop-work order, so long as there has been a reasonable request for clarification, *Pacific Devices, Inc.*, ASBCA 19379, 76-2 BCA ¶12,179. Obviously, where a stop-work order has been issued, the contractor need not proceed, *Delta Eng'g & Sales, Inc.*, ASBCA 16326, 72-1 BCA ¶9373 (default improper where termination was issued while stop-work order was still in effect). A request for clarification may justify stopping work even though the specifications are not in fact defective, *Monitor Plastics Co.*, ASBCA 11187, 67-2 BCA ¶6408. Once lack of clear direction is proven, a default may be excused whether it was based on a missed due date, *Stockwell Rubber Co.*, ASBCA 20952, 76-2 BCA ¶12,130; *Henry Spen & Co.*, ASBCA 16296, 74-2 BCA ¶10,651; or failure to make progress, *CML-Macarr, Inc.*, ASBCA 19950, 76-2 BCA ¶12,047; *Avco Corp.*, NASABCA 869-18, 76-1 BCA ¶11,736. Likewise, a default based on nonconforming goods will be overturned where lack of clear direction precluded the contractor from correcting alleged discrepancies, *Remm Co.*, ASBCA 18430, 74-2 BCA ¶10,876.

5. Anticipatory Repudiation

An additional ground for default termination of a government contract arises where a contractor "repudiates" its obligations under the contract. The well-settled rule for invoking the doctrine of "anticipatory repudiation" is that there must be a "definite and unequivocal manifestation of intention on the part of the repudiator that he will not render the promised performance when the time fixed for it in the contract arrives," *Corbin on Contracts* § 973. Although standard default clauses do not specifically enumerate anticipatory repudiation as a basis for default termination, the right to terminate in such cases is an established common law remedy that the government retains.

Generally, the government may treat the contractor's repudiation as a total breach of contract, *Restatement, Second, Contracts* § 253. If the government elects to terminate the contract because of the repudiation, the common law right of rescission may be used. However, the government normally exercises this common law right by issuance of a notice of "default termination." The anticipatory repudiation must be expressed clearly, absolutely, and unequivocally, *Western States Mgmt. Serv. Inc.*, ASBCA 40212, 92-1 BCA ¶24,714; *Scott Aviation*, ASBCA 40776, 91-3 BCA ¶24,123. The repudiation must manifest either the contractor's clear refusal to perform or an unequivocal expression of its inability to perform the contract, *Beeston, Inc.*, ASBCA 38969, 91-3 BCA ¶24,241; *Premier Microwave Corp.*, ASBCA 36546, 88-3 BCA ¶20,984. Since repudiation must be "definite and unequivocal," there is no anticipatory breach where the professed inability to perform can be overcome and the contractor "expresses a willingness to continue performance," *Fairfield Scientific Corp.*, ASBCA 21151, 78-1 BCA ¶13,082, *recons. denied*, 78-2 BCA ¶13,429, *aff'd*, 228 Ct. Cl. 264, 655 F.2d 1062 (1981). There, the board also noted that such manifestation may be expressed either orally or through action. The contractor's refusal to perform in the presence of a government material breach is not an anticipatory repudiation, *Murdoch Mach. & Eng'g Co. of Utah v. United States*, 873 F.2d 1410 (Fed. Cir. 1989). See also *Marine Constr. & Dredging, Inc.*, ASBCA 39246, 95-1 BCA ¶27,286. However, see *United States v. DeKonty Corp.*, 922 F.2d 826 (Fed. Cir. 1991), reversing a board decision holding that a contractor was justified in stopping work based on the government's withholding of a greater amount than permitted by the contract's payment clause. The court found that the government's actions were not an unequivocal refusal to make payments.

a. *Timing of the Remedy*

Default termination is an available remedy for anticipatory repudiation regardless of the stage of contract performance. Thus, anticipatory repudiation has justified default termination before issuance of a notice to proceed, *Aireborne Sec., Inc.*, GSBCA 3333, 71-1 BCA ¶8872 (determined a progress failure, but since no cure notice apparently was sent, repudiation was implicitly found); prior to the date services were to begin, *What Mac Contractors, Inc.*, GSBCA 4766, 78-2 BCA ¶13,279; prior to execution of the written contract, *Urban Indus. Corp.*, GSBCA 3050, 72-2 BCA ¶9604; before any attempted performance had begun, *Central Fire Truck Corp.*, ASBCA 12715, 72-1 BCA ¶8946; after the due date where no "waiver of due date" had occurred, *Drillmation Co.*, ASBCA 12501, 69-1 BCA ¶7632; *Transdyne Corp.*, ASBCA 12834, 69-1 BCA ¶7615; where the delivery date was disestablished but the contractor insisted on a change order and payment as conditions to resuming work, *Polyurethane Prods. Corp.*, ASBCA 42251, 96-1 BCA ¶28,154; where nine months passed after the due date had been "waived," *Giannini-Voltex*, ASBCA 15077, 72-1 BCA ¶9199; *Simplex Mfg. Co.*, ASBCA 13897, 71-1 BCA ¶8814; where the due date had been "waived" but no new due date had been set, *B.F. Goodrich Co.*, ASBCA 19960, 76-2 BCA ¶12,105; *Menches Tool & Die, Inc.*, ASBCA 21469, 78-1 BCA ¶13,167; and where the government had expressly allowed a delinquent contractor to continue after the due date, *Bobco Mfg. Co.*, ASBCA 13430, 69-1 BCA ¶7537. When the due date has passed, the contractor's present failure alone would apparently support a default termination. However, if the due date has been "waived," there is no right to default terminate unless there is some independent ground to support the termination. Repudiation, being such a ground, will thus defeat the contractor's claim of "waiver."

The government's flexibility in the timing of an anticipatory repudiation default reflects the fact that a contractor's words or acts may amount to repudiation at any stage of performance. When repudiation has occurred, a notice of termination is not required, *Imperial Van & Storage Co.*, ASBCA 11462, 67-2 BCA ¶6621 (notification of the termination would have constituted a "vain and futile act"). Rather, the government may take immediate action to safeguard its interests, *James E. Kennedy v. United States*, 164 Ct. Cl. 507 (1964) (government promptly relet the contract to another contractor after repossessing the government-furnished material from the defaulting contractor). However, good contract administration would seem to call for the sending of a termination notice to the contractor to avoid subsequent misunderstandings.

b. *Evidence Considered*

Generally, the contracting officer may consider any acts or words of the contractor in evaluating whether a repudiation has occurred. However, in order to find repudiation, the acts and words of the contractor must indicate at the time of termination an "unequivocal manifestation of the contractor's intention not to perform." See *Fairfield Scientific Corp.*, ASBCA 21151, 78-1 BCA ¶13,082, *recons. denied*, 78-2 BCA ¶13,429, *aff'd*, 228 Ct. Cl. 264, 655 F.2d 1062 (1981), in which the board stated that the government "is not permitted the luxury of establishing through hindsight that the cure notice may have been useless. To permit this would effectively nullify the contractual requirement for a cure notice." In *Fairfield*, the board held that, since the government reestablished the due date, only subsequent contractor actions or words should be considered. The boards may always weigh the words and actions of both parties to determine whether a clear repudiation was present, *Mountain State Constr. Co.*, ENGBCA 3549, 76-2 BCA ¶12,197 (the contracting officer's "defensive approach" in evaluating work accomplished was considered in deciding that the contract was improperly terminated); *Hubbard Trucking, Inc.*, PSBCA 3701, 04-2 BCA ¶32,667 (default termination for abandonment was upheld because the contractor failed to apply for a medical release, which was required under the contract).

c. Examples of Anticipatory Repudiation

Anticipatory repudiation is commonly found when a contractor clearly expresses its intention not to perform the contract or unequivocally states that it is unable to perform the work. It can also be found in actions indicating that the contractor is unable to perform.

(1) Express Refusal to Perform

The classic example of anticipatory repudiation occurs when a contractor expressly refuses to perform the work. Such an express repudiation has been found in *Betakut USA, Inc. v. General Servs. Admin.*, GSBCA 12512, 94-2 BCA ¶26,945 (refusal to supply items in excess of estimated quantity as required by contract); *Gerald M. Davy*, PSBCA 3270, 94-2 BCA ¶26,690 (refusal to perform followed by failure to appear on job); *Twigg Corp.*, NASABCA 62-0192, 93-1 BCA ¶25,318 (contractor refused to remove and replace concrete); *Cox & Palmer Constr. Corp.*, ASBCA 38739, 92-1 BCA ¶24,756 (contractor sent letter to its surety, with copies to the government, stating that it would leave the project and allow the surety to take over performance); *Interstate Indus., Inc.*, GSBCA 5252, 79-2 BCA ¶13,954 (repeated refusal to accept orders under requirements contract); *North Am., Ltd.*, ASBCA 22718, 79-2 BCA ¶13,894 (contractor abandoned work and telegraphed government "to take any action you deem necessary for operation of mess facilities"); *Big 3 Contracting Corp.*, ASBCA 20929, 79-1 BCA ¶13,601 (contractor left job, removed equipment, and stated it would resume performance only upon a condition contrary to contract requirements); *Sharjon, Inc.*, ASBCA 22954, 79-1 BCA ¶13,585 (contractor's contract manager, who had "full authority," stated that the work was being abandoned, equipment was removed, and no personnel were at the site); *Rex Conklin Reforestation,* AGBCA 76-155, 78-1 BCA ¶13,070 (following a unilateral bid mistake, contractor advised the COR that it would not perform and sent a mailgram stating, "We rejected the contract by phone and reassigned our crews"); *TS Reforestation Co.,* AGBCA 414, 76-1 BCA ¶11,780 (contractor's letter to contracting officer stated, "I have terminated the . . . contract"); *Wear Ever Shower Curtain Corp.,* GSBCA 4360, 76-1 BCA ¶11,636 (express refusal to perform following government refusal to increase contract price to compensate for the lifting of price controls); *Video Eng'g Co.*, DOTCAB 72-5, 72-1 BCA ¶9432 (contractor failed to qualify the bid "all or none," refused to accept single-item award, returned the purchase order, and denied the authority of the agent who signed the bid); *LTD Indus. Corp.*, ASBCA 16565, 72-1 BCA ¶9332, *recons. denied,* 72-2 BCA ¶9499 (refusal to perform following denial of relief under Pub. L. No. 85-804); and *Hawaii Fence & Iron Works,* ASBCA 15242, 71-1 BCA ¶8690 (contractor used abusive language to a government official, agreed that the contract should be cancelled, and stated it neither cared about nor wanted the work).

Anticipatory repudiation may be found if the contractor mistakenly believes it does not have to perform. See *EFG Assocs., Inc.,* ASBCA 50546, 01-1 BCA ¶31,324, in which a § 8(a) contractor's misinterpretation of a regulation, leading it to believe that its contract ended when the contractor was sold, was considered an anticipatory repudiation.

Anticipatory repudiation is commonly found when a contractor clearly expresses that it is not required to do the work, either by arguing that the contract was never formed or that it has ended. In *Integrated Sys. Group, Inc. v. Social Sec. Admin.*, GSBCA 14056-SSA, 98-2 BCA ¶29,848, the contractor asserted that it did not have to proceed because the contract was voidable because of a mistake in bid. The board disagreed and concluded that that did not justify failure to proceed. Such an express repudiation believing that the contractual obligations had ended has been found in *Betakut USA, Inc. v. General Servs. Admin.*, GSBCA 12512, 94-2 BCA ¶26,945 (refusal to supply items in excess of estimated quantity as required by contract).

Lack of an unequivocal refusal to perform was found in *McKenzie Marine Constr. Co.*, ENGBCA 3245, 74-2 BCA ¶10,673 (contractor's letter stated, "I have no moral or contractual obligation . . . to pursue . . . such an insane project," but the board found that government actions gave the contractor "reason to vent his frustrations"); *Michael J. Gotskind,* GSBCA 4999R, 78-1 BCA ¶13,144 (high bidder on surplus sale requested to withdraw bid but later asked to discuss the matter with the contracting officer); *Martin Suchan*, ASBCA 22521, 83-1 BCA ¶16,323 (statement that difficulty with suppliers would render contractor unable to "honor" prices in its bid). In *HBS Nat'l Corp. v. General Servs. Admin.*, GSBCA 14302, 98-2 BCA ¶29,935, the board held that a copy the contractor sent to the contracting officer of a draft letter required under the Worker Adjustment and Retraining Notification Act notifying its employees that it planned to discontinue performance and that the employees would be terminated, and a second letter the contractor sent to the contract administrator indicating that the contractor would soon request a "no cost" termination but would not leave the government without services or supplies, did not establish a positive, definite, unconditional, and unequivocal intent not to perform necessary to justify the default termination.

(2) Failure to Give Adequate Assurances

Failure to give adequate assurances after the government has issued a cure notice indicating that it has grounds to believe that the contractor will not complete the work as required can provide grounds for a default termination. See *Danzig v. AEC Corp.*, 224 F.3d 1333 (Fed. Cir. 2000), *cert. denied,* 532 U.S. 995 (2001), sustaining a default termination based on lack of adequate assurances and stating at 1337:

> The law applicable to a contractor's failure to provide assurances of timely completion is a branch of the law of anticipatory repudiation. See, e.g., *Discount Co.*, 554 F.2d at 441 (when the government was not assured of timely completion, the court could properly "rely upon cases involving abandoned or repudiated contracts"). At common law, anticipatory repudiation of a contract required an unambiguous and unequivocal statement that the obligor would not or could not perform the contract. See *Dingley v. Oler,* 117 U.S. 490, 503, 29 L. Ed. 984, 6 S. Ct. 850 (1886); *Cascade Pac. Int'l v. United States,* 773 F.2d 287, 293 (Fed. Cir. 1985). As the Restatement of Contracts has recognized, however, modern decisions do not limit anticipatory repudiation to cases of express and unequivocal repudiation of a contract. Instead, anticipatory repudiation includes cases in which reasonable grounds support the obligee's belief that the obligor will breach the contract. In that setting, the obligee "may demand adequate assurance of due performance" and if the obligor does not give such assurances, the obligee may treat the failure to do so as a repudiation of the contract. *Restatement, Second, Contracts* § 251 (1981). The Uniform Commercial Code has adopted a similar rule for contracts involving the sale of goods. See U.C.C. § 2-609.
>
> The law of government contracts has adopted that doctrine, expressing it as a requirement that the contractor give reasonable assurances of performance in response to a validly issued cure notice. See *Tubular Aircraft Prods., Inc. v. United States,* 23 Cont. Cas. Fed. (CCH) ¶81,327, at 86,619 (Ct. Cl. Trial Div. Nov. 29, 1976) (recommended decision) (citing the Restatement and stating that "parties are entitled to ask for reassurances when persons with whom they have contracted have by word or deed created uncertainty about their ability or intent to perform and they are entitled to treat the failure to provide such assurances as a repudiation of the contract"), *approved and op. adopted by court, id.* at 86,610, 213 Ct. Cl. 749 (1977); *National Union Fire Ins.*, 90-1 B.C.A. (CCH) P22,266, at 111,855, ASBCA No. 34744 (Aug. 23, 1989); *Salzburg Enters.*, 87-2 B.C.A. (CCH) ¶19,761, at 99,994, ASBCA No. 29509 (Mar. 30, 1987). That rule, as the Restatement explains, rests "on the principle that the parties to a contract look to actual performance 'and that a continuing sense of reliance and security that the promised performance will be forthcoming when due, is an important feature of the bargain.'" *Restatement, Second, Contracts* § 251 cmt. a (quoting U.C.C. § 2-609 cmt. 1).

See also *L&M Thomas Concrete Co.*, ASBCA 49198, 03-1 BCA ¶32,194, finding a valid termination for default because the contractor failed to provide adequate assurances, but not characterizing this as an anticipatory repudiation, and *NECCO, Inc.*, GSBCA 16354, 05-1 BCA ¶32,902, finding a valid termination for default when the contractor failed to provide adequate assurances, characterizing it as a failure to make progress. Compare *Omni Dev. Corp.*, AGBCA 97-203-1, 05-1 BCA ¶32,982, in which the board refused to find an anticipatory repudiation where the contractor's assurances were somewhat equivocal but stated that it would complete the contract on time.

(3) Express Statement of Inability to Perform

Anticipatory repudiation is also commonly found where a contractor has unequivocally stated that it cannot perform, *Nation-wide Reporting & Convention Coverage*, GSBCA 8309, 88-2 BCA ¶20,521. Often such statements of inability are coupled with other factors that further substantiate the finding of a repudiation. Some common examples of such factors are acts of abandonment, *Ortec Sys., Inc.*, ASBCA 43467, 92-2 BCA ¶20,521; or nonperformance and claims for payments or relief from matters as to which the contractor had assumed the risk. For cases finding anticipatory repudiation for stated inability to perform, see *Bendix Corp.*, GSBCA 4352, 77-2 BCA ¶12,656 (stated inability to meet accuracy requirements for oceanographic data system and request for specification waiver indicated inability to cure); *Comdata Sys., Inc.*, ASBCA 19893, 77-1 BCA ¶12,463 (inability to perform following explosion in plant unless extraordinary financial assistance was provided); *J. W. Bibb, Inc.*, ASBCA 19589, 76-2 BCA ¶12,135 (road construction contractor admitted performance could not be completed on time, requested the balance of contract work be deleted, and advised the government to send future communications to a law firm); *L & W Contracting*, AGBCA 416, 76-2 BCA ¶12,023, *recons. denied*, 76-2 BCA ¶12,165 (contractor's letters stated essential equipment was unobtainable absent government guarantee of payment to subcontractors); *B.F. Goodrich Co.*, ASBCA 19960, 76-2 BCA ¶12,105 (contractor claimed that the specifications for coated fabric tanks were beyond the state of the art and requested a convenience termination); *Jesse W. Wayne*, AGBCA 410, 75-2 BCA ¶11,394 (contractor letter stated in part, "I am not qualified to complete the job. I'm sorry it has to be this way."); *SRM Mfg. Co.*, IBCA 1032-4-74, 75-1 BCA ¶11,279 (due to rising materials costs, contractor stated performance was impossible absent 33 percent price increase); *R & O Indus., Inc.*, GSBCA 4094, 75-1 BCA ¶11,061 (two contractor letters requested immediate termination since no qualified supplier could be found); *National Cleaners & Laundry, Inc.*, ASBCA 16186, 74-2 BCA ¶10,978, *recons. denied*, 75-1 BCA ¶11,035 (stated inability to perform since IRS had seized plant and equipment); *National Farm Equip. Co.*, GSBCA 3833, 73-2 BCA ¶10,300 (stated inability to manufacture goods absent specification waiver); *Amexicana Corp.*, ASBCA 14417, 71-1 BCA ¶8886, *recons. denied*, 71-2 BCA ¶8990 (contractor advised that production facility would close absent progress payments that were specifically precluded by the IFB); *Hellmuth, Obata & Kassabaum, Inc.*, PSBCA 524, 73-1 BCA ¶9894 (contractor admitted inability to design a building that could be constructed within the cost limitations set by the contract); *Pacific Electro Dynamics, Inc.*, ASBCA 16805, 72-1 BCA ¶9380 (contractor admitted financial incapacity and sought no-cost termination); *Giannini-Voltex*, ASBCA 15077, 72-1 BCA ¶9199 (contractor admitted financial incapacity, stated intention to sell product line to another company, and failed to commit to a new delivery schedule); *Aireborne Sec., Inc.*, GSBCA 3333, 71-1 BCA ¶8872 (guard services contractor failed to provide performance bonds and insurance and to obtain security clearances, stated inability to perform, and returned contract documents to the government); *Sparkadyne, Inc.*, ASBCA 15162, 71-1 BCA ¶8854 (contractor admitted going out of business and gave the status of outstanding orders in order to assist the government to reprocure); *Hydro-Space Sys. Corp.*, ASBCA 15275, 71-1 BCA ¶8739 (contractor admitted it could not perform because of the government's "tight money" policy); *Clean Sweep, Inc.*, ENGBCA 2967, 71-1 BCA ¶8701 (contractor stopped work, removed equipment, and wrote a letter to the contracting officer expressly admitting inability to complete performance); *Mission Valve & Pump Co.*, ASBCA 13552, 69-2 BCA ¶8010 (contractor letter stated in part, "We regret we will be unable to furnish the valves on subject contract"); *Ringer Co.*, ASBCA 13654, 69-2 BCA ¶7938 (shirt manufacturer claimed inability to find a satisfactory subcontractor, stopped production, made a final shipment, returned necessary cloth to the government, and admitted being on the verge of bankruptcy); *Drillmation Co.*, ASBCA 12501, 69-1 BCA ¶7632 (stated inability to continue manufacture following denial of Pub. L. 85-804 relief for "grave error" in cost estimate); and *Bobco Mfg. Co.*, ASBCA 13430, 69-1 BCA ¶7537 (refusal to sign modification reflecting price increase granted under Pub. L. 85-804, refusal of no-cost settlement, and stated inability to continue).

Stated inability to perform may constitute a repudiation even where the statement is made by someone other than the contractor. See *Menches Tool & Die, Inc.*, ASBCA 21469, 78-1 BCA ¶13,167, where in response to the government's unilateral reestablishment of the due date, the contractor's attorney sent a letter stating, "this corporation is unable to produce the contract item." A carbon copy of the letter was sent to the contractor, who did not deny the attorney's authority until after a default termination was issued. Furthermore, repudiation by stated inability to perform may be found where the statements originate from a successor in interest to the contractor, *Aerospace Support Equip., Inc.*, ASBCA 13579, 71-1 BCA ¶8904 (stated inability to perform coupled with request for convenience termination or no-cost settlement).

No clear indication of inability to perform was found in *Production Serv. & Tech., Inc.*, ASBCA 53353, 02-2 BCA ¶32,026 (letter addressed difficulties being encountered but implied that contractor would continue performing); *Talano Transp.*, PSBCA 3812, 97-1 BCA ¶28,898 (contractor threatened to cease performance, but continued to perform); *Paul E. McCollum, Sr.*, ASBCA 20120, 77-1 BCA ¶12,271 (stated intent to file a claim under the Changes clause or an appeal under the Disputes clause); *Norfolk Air Conditioning Serv. & Equip. Corp.*, ASBCA 14080, 71-1 BCA ¶8617 (contractor data submission indicated nonspecification equipment would be provided and contractor requested an unwarranted equitable adjustment); *C.T.M. Co.*, ASBCA 7332, 65-1 BCA ¶4757, *recons. denied*, 65-2 BCA ¶5219 (contractor characterized "catch up" order as impossible but continued trying to perform); and *Denison Research Found.*, ASBCA 7653, 1963 BCA

¶3651 (contractor's statement that proceeding with a specification modification would be useless amounted to an "honest professional opinion expressed in an effort to obtain reconsideration").

(4) Actions Indicating Inability to Perform

There have been a number of cases indicating that a contractor may demonstrate, even unintentionally, that it is unable to perform and that such a demonstrated likelihood of inability to perform may amount to a repudiation. See, for example, *Pennsylvania Exch. Bank v. United States*, 145 Ct. Cl. 216, 170 F. Supp. 629 (1959) (contractor's assignment for the benefit of creditors constituted a total breach, since the contractor was disabled from performing); *Hampton Business Forms, Inc.*, GSBCA 4026, 75-2 BCA ¶11,532 (contractor required to supply 74,174 boxes of paper within one year, but by seventh month only 2,561 boxes were delivered, the facility was abandoned, and contractor failed to secure necessary machinery or supplies); *Wyodak Enters., Inc., dba Healthmart*, VABCA 3678, 95-1 BCA ¶27,493, (with eight months remaining on the contract, the contractor's president repudiated it by stating that he could not be in compliance even if the government gave him a year); *Atronix, Inc.*, ASBCA 16644, 72-2 BCA ¶9763 (contracting officer became aware that, in addition to passage of the due date without a conforming delivery, the contractor's plant had been padlocked due to an IRS lien); *Protective Coating Co.*, ENGBCA 3205, 72-1 BCA ¶9431 (contractor returned rented equipment that was essential to performance and walked off the job); *Simplex Mfg. Co.*, ASBCA 13897, 71-1 BCA ¶8814 (following a conference concerning failure to make progress, contractor reduced the work force and cut labor and material expenditures); *Transdyne Corp.*, ASBCA 12834, 69-1 BCA ¶7615 (following waiver of due date and a government request for a revised delivery schedule, contractor responded that performance would resume four months after approval of its request for relief under Pub. L. 85-804). However, a contrary result was reached in *Reliable Bay Ridge Car Serv., Inc.*, VACAB 1127, 75-1 BCA ¶11,276 (even though only two days remained until performance was to commence, there was conflicting evidence whether the contractor could clear its vehicles through local licensing officials); *Donald R. Schlueter*, GSBCA 3232, 71-1 BCA ¶8700 (contractor filed bankruptcy petition and failed to commence work as promised, but bankruptcy trustee stated that contractor had necessary equipment and capability to perform); *Therm-Air Mfg. Co.*, NASABCA 180-2, 82-2 BCA ¶15,881 (letter informing contracting officer of suspension of manufacturing operations did not constitute grounds for default where contractor was "actively trying to resolve its financial problems . . . so that it could resume normal manufacturing operations"); and *Milo Werner Co.*, IBCA 1202-7-78, 82-1 BCA ¶15,698 (contractor repeatedly expressed intention to complete work, left some equipment at the work site, and sought to obtain additional funding).

d. Retraction of Repudiation

Under *Restatement, Second, Contracts* § 256 and U.C.C. § 2-611, a repudiation may be retracted before the injured party materially changes its position or makes it known that it considers the repudiation to be final. In *Nation-wide Reporting & Convention Coverage*, GSBCA 8309, 88-2 BCA ¶20,521, the contractor's unequivocal repudiation could not later be retracted, since the government considered the repudiation to be final. Thus, if the contracting officer has issued a termination notice following the repudiation, it may not be retracted, *What Mac Contractors, Inc.*, GSBCA 4766, 78-2 BCA ¶13,279. In *Gerald M. Davy*, PSBCA 3270, 94-2 BCA ¶26,690, the contractor's attempted retraction was too late because the government had already contracted with an emergency replacement.

6. Subcontractor Termination

A contractor is responsible for contract performance and thus is subject to default termination if its subcontractor fails to perform or deliver or fails to proceed and endangers timely performance. If a subcontractor is in default, the government and contractor can agree to substitute alternative performance in lieu of terminating the contractor for default. In *McLain Plumbing & Elec. Serv. v. United States*, 30 Fed. Cl. 70 (1993), the contractor claimed that the government improperly ordered the default termination of a subcontractor during the performance of a contract. This claim arose after the defaulted subcontractor prevailed against the contractor in a contract arbitration proceeding for improper default termination. The court held that the contractor's claim was barred by accord and satisfaction and that there was no basis for economic duress, stating at 82:

> [T]he [contractor] contends that it had no choice but to accept the terms of the proposed alternative to default termination. The result, the [contractor] states, constituted economic duress.
>
> In contrast, the [government] contends that the United States sought no remedies other than those conferred under the terms of the contract. Thus, upon untimely performance, the [government] cites the right to terminate under the Default clause of the contract. The [government] points out: "At worst, the VA merely insisted upon its rights under the contract and reminded [the contractor] of the consequences of nonperformance. Such conduct is neither offensive not illegal." As such, the [government] argues that the offer to consider an alternative performance, in the form of a recovery schedule and upon the replacement of the subcontractor, constituted nothing more than an attempt at settlement. Further, as the [contractor] purportedly presents no evidence of coercion, the [government] denies any showing of economic duress. Based on the evidence presented, this Court finds the [government's] arguments persuasive.

B. Waiver of the Right to Terminate

If the government does not exercise its right to terminate for default within a reasonable time, and the contractor relies to its detriment on such forbearance by continuing with performance, the government will be held to have waived the right to terminate, *De Vito v. United States*, 188 Ct. Cl. 979, 413 F.2d 1147 (1969); *S.T. Research Corp.*, ASBCA 39600, 92-2 BCA ¶24,838; *Motorola Computer Sys., Inc.*, ASBCA 26794, 87-3 BCA ¶20,032. In *De Vito*, the court explained this rule at 990-91:

> The Government is habitually lenient in granting reasonable extensions of time for contract performance, for it is more interested in production than in litigation. Moreover, default terminations—as a species of forfeiture—are strictly construed. *Murphy, et al., v. United States*, 164 Ct. Cl. 332 (1964); *J.D. Hedin Construction Co. v. United States*, 187 Ct. Cl. 45, 57, 408 F.2d 424, 431 (1969).
>
> Where the Government elects to permit a delinquent contractor to continue performance past a due date, it surrenders its alternative and inconsistent right under the Default clause to terminate, assuming the contractor has not abandoned performance and a reasonable time has expired for a termination notice to be given. This is popularly if inaccurately referred to as a "waiver" of the right to terminate. 5 Williston, *Contracts, Third Ed.*, § 683. The election is sometimes express, but more often is to be inferred from the conduct of the non-defaulting party. McBride and Wachtel, *Government Contracts*, § 31.170. The determination of what conduct constitutes such an election is more conjectural than to prescribe the proper method of effecting a valid termination once the election has occurred.
>
> * * *
>
> The necessary elements of an election by the non-defaulting party to waive default in delivery under a contract are (1) failure to terminate within a reasonable time after the default under circumstances indicating forbearance, and (2) reliance by the contractor on the failure to terminate and continued performance by him under the contract, with the government's knowledge and implied or express consent.

No waiver was found were the government terminated the contractor when it failed to perform and subsequently terminated the surety when it failed to perform in a timely manner with a replacement contractor, *Florida Dep't of Ins. v. United States,* 81 F.3d 1093 (Fed. Cir. 1996). The court found no waiver because the Government had continually reminded the surety that time was of the essence by pointing out that liquidated damages were continuing to accrue

The government may forbear for a reasonable period of time after the default occurs before taking action, *Eraklis Eraklidis,* ASBCA 40110, 91-3 BCA ¶24,188; *Kit Pack Co.*, ASBCA 33135, 89-3 BCA ¶22,151.

1. The Basic Concept

Use of the term "waiver" to describe the facts that operate to divest the government of its right to terminate creates some confusion. Waiver suggests the voluntary relinquishment of a vested right, which government officials are prohibited from doing, 47 Comp. Gen. 170 (B-160886) (1967). In *General Equip. Co.*, ASBCA 6415, 1964 BCA ¶4166, *recons. denied*, 1964 BCA ¶4307, the board stated at 20,273:

> There was no waiver of the extended delivery schedule in this case because there was no voluntary and intentional relinquishment by the Government of the right to terminate for the failure to deliver and there was no consideration for any such relinquishment. Such matters are necessary to find waiver. *U.S. v. Chichester*, 312 F.2d 275 (1963) upon review of *The Aircraftsmen Company*, ASBCA 3592 et al., 26 March 1958, 58-1 BCA ¶1667.

Contrast this view with U.C.C. § 1-107, which permits waiver without consideration if evidenced by a signed writing delivered to the other party.

In *De Vito*, the court preferred to use the term "election." In addition, the court found that contractor reliance on government action or inaction was an indispensable element of the "waiver" or "election" theory. Thus, the government's waiver or election is binding, not because of consideration, but on principles of fair dealing or estoppel. See U.C.C. § 2-209 for a similar rule.

Waiver has been a more significant issue in supply contracts than in construction contracts, since the supply contractor that continues performance while in default frequently incurs costs that will not be recovered if the government later properly terminates for default. See *Acme Process Equip. Co. v. United States*, 171 Ct. Cl. 324, 347 F.2d 509 (1965), *rev'd on other grounds*, 385 U.S. 138 (1966), in which the court observed that the government "cannot allow an unwary contractor to continue performance and thus incur large expenses, all of which the Government will refuse to reimburse if and when it decides to cancel the contract on the ground of the violation." However, in construction contracts the contractor will be reimbursed for acceptable work performed at the site even if the contract is terminated. For this reason, continued performance of a construction contract will not ordinarily support a claim of waiver or election.

a. *Construction Contracts*

The inapplicability of the waiver rule to construction contracts was explained in *Brent L. Sellick*, ASBCA 21869, 78-2 BCA ¶13,510, as follows at 66,194-95:

> The essence of the waiver of the delivery date doctrine as explained in *DeVito*, *supra*, is that through Government actions or inactions, and contractor reliance thereon, the Government is estopped from enforcing a specified contractual delivery date. However, as explained by this Board in recent cases, this estoppel rationale is not normally applicable where the contract contains the usual provisions applicable to construction contracts entitling the contractor to payment for work performed subsequent to the specified completion date but also entitling the Government to recover liquidated damages for late completion. With such provisions in the contract, detrimental reliance on the contractor's part cannot be found merely from a period of Government forbearance coupled with continued contractor performance in reliance thereon. *Olson Plumbing & Heating Co.*, ASBCA Nos. 17965, 18411, 75-1 BCA ¶11,203; *Fraenkische Parkettverlegung R.*, ASBCA 18453, 75-2 BCA ¶11,388; *Joseph Morton Company, Inc.*, ASBCA 19793, 78-1 BCA ¶13,173. Moreover, with these provisions in the contract Government encouragement to expedite completion during a forbearance period should not be interpreted as a disestablishment of the contractually-prescribed completion date absent further manifestation by the Government that it no longer considered that date to be enforceable. Such a disestablishment was indeed found in *Corway, Inc.*, ASBCA 20683, 77-1 BCA ¶12,357, where the Government neither mentioned nor assessed liquidated damages and otherwise manifested lack of concern with the contractor's late completion. Under those circumstances, the *DeVito* doctrine was invoked with recognition that the case was unusual.

See also *Arens Corp.*, ASBCA 50289, 02-1 BCA ¶31,671, rejecting the application of the doctrine of waiver to a construction contract where there had been a 102-day delay in terminating the contract because the contract was for construction work and the government notified the contractor it was not waiving its rights.

There are a few construction cases that accept the waiver rationale. See, for example, *Nisei Constr. Co.*, ASBCA 51464, 99-2 BCA ¶30,448, in which the board accepted the limited application of *De Vito* in construction cases. It noted that a construction case would have to be "so unusual" to fall within *De Vito.* One such unusual case is *B. V. Constr., Inc.*, ASBCA 47766, 04-1 BCA ¶32,604, finding a waiver when the government allowed the contractor to perform for 20 months after the completion date without expressing concern. See also *Jess Howard Elec. Co.*, ASBCA 44437, 96-2 BCA 28,345, finding an actual waiver when the government offered a later schedule if the contractor met specified conditions. In *American Sheet Metal Corp. v. General Servs. Admin.*, GSBCA 14068, 99-1 BCA ¶30,329, the government nullified a prior completion date and failed to establish a new one. The board considered this to be "tantamount to a waiver." See also *AFV Enters., Inc.*, PSBCA 2691, 01-1 BCA ¶31,388 (board analyzed a construction case as though the doctrine were applicable, but did not find waiver).

A number of cases have held that there can be no waiver in a construction contract if the contractor is told that the government will continue to assess liquidated damages, *Olson Plumbing & Heating Co. v. United States*, 221 Ct. Cl. 197, 602 F.2d 950 (1979); *Indemnity Ins. Co. of N. Am. v. United States*, 14 Cl. Ct. 219 (1988); *LaCoste Builders, Inc.*, ASBCA 29884, 88-1 BCA ¶20,360; *Delta Constr. Co.*, ASBCA 42453, 96-1 BCA ¶28, *recons. granted in part & denied in part*, 96-1 BCA P28,251, *aff'd*, 114 F.3d 1206 (Fed. Cir. 1997); *Nagy Enters.*, ASBCA 48815, 98-1 BCA ¶29,695. In *Olson Plumbing & Heating* the court stated at 204:

> Where the right to terminate has been expressly reserved or when liquidated damages have been imposed by the [government], the [contractor] has a heavier burden of proving that the right to terminate for failure to deliver on time has been waived.

In contrast, waiver of the completion date has been found based on the failure of the contracting officer to either mention or assess liquidated damages, *Overhead Elec. Co.*, ASBCA 25656, 85-2 BCA ¶18,026.

The default termination of a contract to construct and lease a post office was overturned even though the contractor had admittedly failed to submit required bonds. Although the contract called for the submission of bonds within 20 days of acceptance of the lease, the Postal Service did not demand the bonds until more than a year later and never informed the contractor of the penal amount it would require on the bonds, *Upwest Corp.*, PSBCA 4281, 01-2 BCA ¶31,474.

b. Waiver Prior to a Due Date

Although most cases of waiver involve government actions after the delivery date has passed, a waiver may result from government action prior to the due date evidencing that time is not of the essence. See *Delta Marine, Inc.*, ASBCA 39649, 93-3 BCA ¶26,164, where a default based on the contractor's failure to complete work items within the time specified in a cure notice was not proper, because the contracting officer had required the contractor to perform work before the contractually required date; *Lanzen Fabricating, Inc.*, ASBCA 40328, 93-3 BCA ¶26,079, in which default termination was improper because there was no schedule against which to measure progress; and *Baifield Indus., Div. of A-T-O, Inc.*, ASBCA 14582, 72-2 BCA ¶9676, where government waiver of certain performance requirements, which had resulted in production delays five days prior to the due date, was found to have "manifested a Government lack of concern" with the original delivery schedule. See also *Acudata Sys., Inc.*, DOTCAB 1198, 84-1 BCA ¶17,046, where the Government's waiver of the due date for presentation of the preproduction prototype also constituted waiver of the production schedule. Accord, *Heat Exchangers, Inc.*, ASBCA 9349, 1964 BCA ¶4381; *American Sheet Metal Corp. v. General Servs. Admin.*, GSBCA 14066, 99-1 BCA ¶30,329.

In *Polyurethane Prods. Corp.*, ASBCA 42251, 96-1 BCA ¶28,154, the board stated at 140,544:

> It is undisputed that the delivery schedule set by Modification A000001 was disestablished and no new delivery schedule was ever established, thereby foreclosing this default termination resting on either of those subpara-

graphs [(a)(1)(i) and (a)(1)(ii)]. See *Lanzen Fabricating, Inc.*, ASBCA No. 40328, 93-3 BCA ¶26,079 at 129,609; *Motorola Computer Systems, Inc.*, ASBCA No. 26794, 87-3 BCA ¶20,032 at 101,416; *Electronics of Austin*, ASBCA No. 24912, 86-3 BCA ¶19,307 at 97,631.

Similarly, in *Freedom, NY, Inc.*, ASBCA 35671, 96-2 BCA ¶28,328, *decision corrected*, 96-2 BCA ¶28,502, the board overturned the termination for default for failure to make progress because of waiver, stating at 141,478:

> [T]he Government's right to terminate for a contractor's "fail[ure] to make progress" requires the existence of a valid delivery schedule against which the contractor's progress can properly be measured.

2. Reasonable Forbearance

Failure to terminate immediately when the right to terminate accrues does not constitute a waiver, *Frank A. Pelliccia v. United States*, 208 Ct. Cl. 278, 525 F.2d 1035 (1975). The contracting officer has a reasonable period to investigate the facts and determine what course of action will be in the best interests of the government, *Eraklis Eraklidis*, ASBCA 40110, 91-3 BCA ¶24,188. During this period, which is called the forbearance period, the government may terminate at any time, without prior notice, *Raytheon Serv. Co.*, ASBCA 14746, 70-2 BCA ¶8390; *Lapp Insulator Co.*, ASBCA 13303, 70-1 BCA ¶8219, *recons. denied*, 70-2 BCA ¶8471. The determination of what length of time constitutes a reasonable forbearance period depends on the facts and circumstances of each case, *H.N. Bailey & Assocs. v. United States*, 196 Ct. Cl. 156, 449 F.2d 387 (1971). In *Westinghouse Elec. Corp.*, ASBCA 20306, 76-1 BCA ¶11,883, it was observed that there is no clear demarcation between reasonable forbearance and waiver.

If the contractor is incurring costs in continued efforts to perform, the government has an obligation to act expeditiously in making a decision. In contrast, if the contractor has ceased performance, the need for rapid action is not as great since the contractor is not prejudiced by the delay. Cases that have found the delay to be a reasonable forbearance period include *Scandia Mfg. Co.*, ASBCA 20888, 76-2 BCA ¶11,949 (seven-day delay between due date and termination); *Aargus Poly Bag*, GSBCA 4314, 76-2 BCA ¶11,927 (delays of 25 and 35 days between due date and termination); *Cosmos Eng'g, Inc.*, ASBCA 19780, 77-2 BCA ¶12,713 (three-day delay between due date and termination); *Fairfield Scientific Corp.*, ASBCA 21152, 78-1 BCA ¶12,869, *aff'd*, 228 Ct. Cl. 264, 655 F.2d 1062 (1981) (five-day delay "patently reasonable"); and *Honig Indus. Diamond Wheel, Inc.*, ASBCA 46875, 96-1 BCA ¶28,028, *aff'd*, 116 F.3d 1496 (Fed. Cir. 1997) (government reasonably took 19 days to issue show cause letter and two months to terminate).

In *Amecom Div., Litton Sys., Inc.*, ASBCA 19687, 77-1 BCA ¶12,329, *recons. denied*, 77-2 BCA ¶12,554, a 50-day delay was found unreasonable. The board stated that the reasonable forbearance period was confined to the single day on which the right to terminate accrued because "[at] that point in time, the Navy had all the information necessary to make the decision." Also, there were prior government actions indicating that time was no longer of the essence. On reconsideration, and in response to the government's argument that the board's decision would have "detrimental impact on the procurement community because it eliminates the normal forbearance period," the board responded that decisions on forbearance turn on their own facts and are precedent only when applied to similar fact situations.

In *Precision Dynamics, Inc.*, ASBCA 41360, 97-1 BCA ¶28,722, a waiver was found when the contracting officer left the contract "in a delinquent status" and delayed for more than 70 days before terminating the contract while the contractor expended time and money continuing to perform the contract. See also *Ralbo, Inc.*, ASBCA 49541, 99-2 BCA ¶30,438, denying summary judgment for the government because the contractor alleged that it had been allowed to perform for three years after the government had knowledge of the erroneous certification on which the termination was based. Compare *A.R. Sales Co. v. United States*, 51 Fed. Cl. 370 (2002), where, despite a failure to terminate the contract until five months after the contract completion date, and not establishing a new completion date, no indications of waiver were found because the government repeatedly asked for a revised completion date to determine when or if the project could be completed and the contractor could not show any reliance on the government's forbearance.

3. Government Election to Continue Performance

One indispensable element of waiver is that the government indicates a willingness to have the contractor continue performance. This willingness, also often referred to as an election to continue, can be manifested in a number of ways, ranging from unreasonable delay in terminating to express statements or acts of the government.

a. *Unreasonable Delay*

Unreasonable delay in terminating is a frequent basis for finding an election, *H.N. Bailey & Assocs. v. United States*, 196 Ct. Cl. 166, 449 F.2d 376 (1971). In *Westinghouse Elec. Corp.*, ASBCA 20306, 76-1 BCA ¶11,883, the board found that the government's silence for a 57-day period following receipt of the contractor's letter indicating that it was continuing performance constituted an election, stating at 59,964:

> Insofar as the record shows, [the government] did nothing for another 57 days from the date of the [contractor's] letters. [The government's] delay, for which it has furnished no explanation, deprived [the contractor] of the opportunity to stop work and to reduce the loss which it will sustain if the termination for default is permitted to stand. The unexplained delay was unreasonably long. Absent an acceptable explanation for its silence and inaction during the 57-day period, [the government] may not, in light of [the contractor's] continued efforts to perform, be heard to argue that such silence and inaction does not constitute an election to permit continued performance.

See also *Prestex, Inc.*, ASBCA 21284, 81-1 BCA ¶14,882, *recons. denied*, 81-2 BCA ¶15,397 (waiver based on 60-day delay in taking action following show cause letter); *Beta Eng'g, Inc.*, ASBCA 53570, 02-2 BCA ¶31,879, *recons. denied*, 02-2 BCA ¶31,970 (inaction following time extension request waives government's right to default terminate supply contract).

b. *Acts of the Government*

For cases finding an election to continue based on the words or actions of the government, see *S. T. Research Corp.*, ASBCA 39600, 92-2 BCA ¶24,838 (government waived right to terminate where the contracting officer told the contractor to continue and proposed a new delivery schedule); *Marci Enters., Inc.*, GSBCA 12197, 94-1 BCA ¶26,563 (government waived delivery date by telling the contractor to delay shipment for inspection and continuing to encourage the contractor to correct deficiencies); *Vista Scientific Corp.*, ASBCA 25974, 87-1 BCA ¶19,603 (waiver by supporting contractor's efforts to fulfill contract after due date); *Sidney G. Kornegay & Florence Kornegay*, ASBCA 18454, 76-1 BCA ¶11,744 (issuance of speed-up orders); *Aargus Poly Bag*, GSBCA 4314, 76-2 BCA ¶11,927 (acceptance of late partial delivery); *Automated Servs., Inc.*, GSBCA EEOC-2, 81-2 BCA ¶15,303 (acceptance of deliverable items after due date and meetings with contractor to discuss establishing revised delivery schedule); *Menches Tool & Die, Inc.*, ASBCA 19255, 74-2 BCA ¶10,969 (failure to respond to contractor's excuses for delay and government assistance in expediting delivery); *Acorn Specialty & Supply Co.*, GSBCA 4367, 76-2 BCA ¶12,086 (conduct implying late deliveries would be permitted combined with partial acceptance); *Flexonics Div., Universal Oil Prods. Co.*, ASBCA 18485, 74-1 BCA ¶10,525 (acceptance of late deliveries); *Baifield Indus., Div. of A-T-O, Inc.*, ASBCA 14582, 72-2 BCA ¶9676 (urging corrective action to meet specifications); *Lowell Monument Co.*, VACAB 1111, 75-1 BCA ¶11,341, *recons. denied*, 75-2 BCA ¶11,460 (late deliveries continually accepted); *Clavier Corp.*, ASBCA 19144, 75-1 BCA ¶11,241 (government letters encouraged continued performance but disclaimed any intent to waive); *Wayne Group*, HUDBCA 75-24, 77-2 BCA ¶12,727 (encouragement of continued performance); *Corway, Inc.*, ASBCA 20683, 77-1 BCA ¶12,357 (encouragement of continued performance); *Milo Werner Co.*, IBCA 1202-7-78, 82-1 BCA ¶15,698 (letter encouraging "early resumption and completion of remaining work"); *Cecile Indus., Inc.*, ASBCA 24600, 83-2 BCA ¶16,842 (two-month delay where there was history of government acceptance of late deliveries); and *Divecon Servs., LP v. Department of Commerce*, GSBCA 15997, 04-2 BCA ¶32,656 (encouraging contractor to make expensive repairs and keep its personnel on stand-by).

In *Action Support Servs. Corp.*, ASBCA 46524, 00-1 BCA ¶30,701, the board found that the government had waived delivery dates by allowing the contractor to work through several missed deadlines and continuing to pay progress payments. Although the government reserved its right to terminate for default in a show cause letter, the government also gave signals that it would not insist on the contractor's meeting the delivery dates and knew the contractor was continuing to work and incur costs. In *SITCO Servs. & Marine, Inc. v. United States,* 41 Fed. Cl. 196 (1998), the government waived its rights after working with the contractor for over seven months after the contract completion date. In *Radar Devices, Inc.*, ASBCA 43912, 99-1 BCA ¶30,223, waiver was found when, although a show cause notice stated that any acceptance of delinquent goods would be solely to mitigate damages, the contracting officer orally advised the contractor that delivery would not be considered delinquent if the goods were delivered within the 10-day period covered by the notice, and informal departures from contract terms were commonplace between the parties. See also *Ming C. Phua,* PSBCA 4180, 00-1 BCA ¶30,872, where the contracting officer informed the contractor that if he did not provide a satisfactory vehicle by January 16, 1998, his contract would be suspended until he did so. On January 20, 1998, in reliance on this notice, the contractor was en route to present a vehicle for inspection when it was terminated. The board found that the government waived its right to default terminate until the contracting officer imposed a new deadline. Compare *Nisei Constr. Co.*, ASBCA 51464, 99-2 BCA ¶30,448, holding that the government did not waive its right to terminate for default by encouraging the contractor to continue performance past the scheduled completion date because there was no indication that the government considered the completion date unenforceable.

For cases finding that acts of contract administration did not amount to an election, see *Fairfield Scientific Corp.*, ASBCA 21152, 78-1 BCA ¶12,869, *aff'd,* 228 Ct. Cl. 264, 655 F.2d 1062 (1981) (willingness to consider revised delivery schedule for $500 price reduction); *Allied Paint Mfg. Co.*, GSBCA 1488, 67-1 BCA ¶6387 (conference to establish present status and future production plans); and *Precision Prods., Inc.*, ASBCA 14284, 70-2 BCA ¶8447 (inspection of late delivery was only to determine conformity; conforming goods would have been accepted only to mitigate contractor damages). In *H.N. Bailey & Assocs. v. United States,* 196 Ct. Cl. 166, 449 F.2d 376 (1971), the court explained that acts of assistance and encouragement do not always indicate an election to continue, stating at 181-82:

> In sum, we find ample support in the record for the conclusion of the ASBCA that [the government's] actions, quite obviously influenced by [the contractor's] optimistic projections, did not amount to encouragement or inducement to the defaulting contractor to continue production efforts beyond default. In light of [the government's] extensive experience in Government procuring and in the absence of convincing evidence, it cannot be presumed that [the government] waived its right to terminate for default, even impliedly, in a situation where the procured item is urgently needed as part of a vital and high integrity national program, and the contractor has yet to demonstrate satisfactorily that it is capable of successfully producing the article. If we are to penalize [the government] for displaying a benevolent attitude toward the defaulting contractor (a posture, incidentally, which the Government does not frequently assume), we must be prepared for the predictable and undesirable consequence of discouraging [the government] from again rendering any assistance, voluntary or otherwise, beyond that specifically required by the contract, for fear of waiving an essential contractual right.

4. Contractor Reliance

Contractor reliance is an indispensable element for the waiver or election to be binding on the government. See *A.B.G. Instrument & Eng'g, Inc. v. United States*, 219 Ct. Cl. 381, 593 F.2d 394 (1979), stating at 398:

> The *De Vito* decision has no application to the facts of this case. That decision addresses itself only to the situation where the Government's forbearance from pressing its right to demand timely delivery is coupled with continued performance on the contractor's part. In these so-called "waiver-after-breach" situations, it is the contractor's reliance that counts rather than the Government's failure to have insisted upon strict adherence to the terms of the delivery schedule. There was no reliance in this case. The Government's final show cause letter was issued on September 17, 1969; as of October 6, 1969, the contractor's production had ceased altogether and was never thereafter revived.

Further, the contractor's reliance must be induced by the government. See the trial judge's recommended decision, adopted by the court in *Northrop Carolina, Inc. v. United States*, 213 Ct. Cl. 670, 553 F.2d 105 (1977), finding no inducement by the government since the contractor made a "management decision" to continue the work. There was no showing that the contractor was acting under any governmental influence in deciding to continue production.

The reliance must also be reasonable, *General Prods. Corp.*, ASBCA 16658, 72-2 BCA ¶9629. In that case, the contractor's reliance was unreasonable and not justified since the contractor knew that the administrative contracting officer, who had agreed to recommend acceptance of its schedule revision proposal, was not authorized to accept the proposal. See also *Meyer Labs., Inc.*, ASBCA 17169, 73-1 BCA ¶9841 (reliance not reasonable since performance after due date was premised on obtaining a specification waiver), and *Chester Morton Elecs.*, ASBCA 14904, 72-1 BCA ¶9185 (experienced contractor with knowledge that all other extensions had been formally approved through established procedure not justified in proceeding). Compare, however, *ITT Def. Communications Div.*, ASBCA 12964, 69-1 BCA ¶7720, finding the contractor's reliance reasonable where the government's show cause letter indicating that a time extension was pending was considered by the board to be an invitation to negotiate.

Merely incurring additional costs will not constitute reliance unless they are incurred in connection with continued performance or some other activity caused by the government's action. See *Olson Plumbing & Heating Co. v. United States*, 221 Ct. Cl. 197, 602 F.2d 950 (1979), in which the court stated at 205:

> After January 11, 1972, [the contractor] never resumed performance under the contract with the exception of minor housekeeping activities and the joint testing project which ended on May 5, 1972. In *Acme*, the court held it would be unfair to permit the contractor to continue incurring performance costs for which the Government would not make reimbursement. Housekeeping costs which merely attempt to preserve the status quo and are unrelated to continued performance, and which are not caused by the Government's failure or by a condition excusing the delay, are properly placed on [the contractor]. In order to have the costs, incurred after the passage of the due date, considered as a factor weighing in favor of a finding of a waiver, it must be shown that the expenses contributed to performance.

For cases finding sufficient justifiable reliance to support a waiver or election, see *Park Indus., Inc.*, ASBCA 13218, 69-1 BCA ¶7508 (contractor leased new machines, hired new employees, and built a new plant); *Nanofast, Inc.*, ASBCA 12545, 69-1 BCA ¶7566 (attempts to correct defects); *Legion Utensils Co.*, GSBCA 2732, 69-1 BCA ¶7745, *recons. denied*, 69-2 BCA ¶7896 (continued production albeit at lower rate); *Alton Iron Works, Inc.*, GSBCA 2596, 69-2 BCA ¶7841, *recons. denied*, 70-1 BCA ¶8202 (continued performance); *Al Greene, Inc.*, ASBCA 15225, 71-1 BCA ¶8789 (contractor made commitments for labor and material); *ISC/Phonplex Corp., Instrument Sys. Corp.*, ASBCA 16668, 73-2 BCA ¶10,361 (continued performance); *Menches Tool & Die, Inc.*, ASBCA 19255, 74-2 BCA ¶10,969 (production continued); *Hamill Mfg. Co.*, ASBCA 20926, 78-1 BCA ¶13,088 (continued production, negotiation with suppliers, and receipt of material); *American Trans-Coil Corp.*, ASBCA 22233, 78-1 BCA ¶13,157 (production continued after due date); *Prestex, Inc.*, ASBCA 21284, 81-2 BCA ¶15,397 (continued production efforts by subcontractors); and *Pacific Coast Welding & Mach., Inc.*, ASBCA 26105, 83-1 BCA ¶16,398 (subcontractor performance).

The best evidence of reliance is complete or substantial performance. In *Trident Indus. Prods. Corp.*, DOTBCA 2807, 98-1 BCA ¶29,619, the contractor failed to ship fabrics by the contract deadline but tendered substantially all of the items months later, and the government failed to terminate the contract and establish a new delivery schedule, thereby waiving the original delivery schedule. See also *Cadillac Gage Co.*, ASBCA 18416, 75-1 BCA ¶11,210 (completed most of work following due date).

Insufficient evidence of justifiable reliance was found in *Doyle Shirt Mfg. Corp. v. United States*, 199 Ct. Cl. 150, 462 F.2d 1150 (1972) (all work was complete and contractor was just seeking specification waiver); *Lieco., Inc.*, ASBCA 13681, 69-1 BCA ¶7489 (contractor was out of business); *Temco, Inc.*, ASBCA 13907, 71-1 BCA ¶8683 (increased production was in contractor's own best interest to amortize costs and avoid loss on follow-on contract); *Ace Elecs. Assocs., Inc.*, ASBCA 14245, 71-1 BCA ¶8729 (only contractor efforts occurred after default termination); *KDI Precision Prods., Inc.*, ASBCA 17382, 73-2 BCA ¶10,231 (only action involved seeking Pub. L. No. 85-804 relief or no-cost settlement); *Crawford Dev. & Mfg. Co.*, ASBCA 17565, 74-2 BCA ¶10,660 (no reliance because contractor recouped its continuing expenditures on unterminated portion of partially terminated contract); *Westholt Mfg., Inc.*, ASBCA 19519, 75-1 BCA ¶11,196 (production stopped before due date and not resumed); *CTS Knights, Inc.*, ASBCA 20028, 75-1 BCA ¶11,259 (no expenditures during 86-day period following due date); *Belmont Instrument Corp.*, ASBCA 18861, 77-1 BCA ¶12,332 (expenditure of $1,168.80 did not reach level of detriment amounting to reliance); *Electro-Methods, Inc.*, ASBCA 50215, 99-1 BCA

¶30,230 (absent clear proof that the government knew of the contractor's continuing performance, 7 percent progress during forbearance period "not sufficiently material" to establish detrimental reliance); *E.O. Mfg. Co.*, ASBCA 52120, 01-2 BCA ¶31,587 (total lack of action by contractor during the government's eight-month silence concerning the contractor's failure to meet delivery date); and *Comspace Corp.*, DOTBCA 4011, 02-1 BCA ¶31,792 (no evidence of continued performance after delivery date).

5. Reservation of Right to Terminate After Completion Date

The government often attempts to preclude a finding of waiver or election by expressly reserving its right to terminate during the period of reasonable forbearance. See, for example, the show cause letter in FAR 49.607, which includes a provision stating:

> Any assistance given to you on this contract or any acceptance by the Government of delinquent goods or services will be solely for the purpose of mitigating damages, and it is not the intention of the Government to condone any delinquency or to waive any rights the Government has under the contract.

Such a reservation will be considered with all the other facts and circumstances of the case to determine whether a waiver has occurred, *Olson Plumbing & Heating Co. v. United States*, 221 Ct. Cl. 197, 602 F.2d 950 (1979); *Engineering Design & Dev.*, ASBCA 22067, 77-2 BCA ¶12,774; *Belmont Instrument Corp.*, ASBCA 18861, 77-1 BCA ¶12,332; *Obrisco Elecs., Inc.*, ASBCA 18533, 76-2 BCA ¶12,049; *Echo Science Corp.*, NASABCA 671-9, 72-2 BCA ¶9755. See *Roberts Supply Co.*, ASBCA 14775, 70-2 BCA ¶8522, in which the board found that the government made it "unmistakably clear" that it did not wish to waive its right to terminate. See also *Camel Mfg. Co.*, ASBCA 41231, 93-1 BCA ¶25,470, in which the board found that the government had reserved its right to terminate for default while attempting to negotiate a revised schedule after giving a cure notice. However, if the government's actions indicate an election to continue, the mere presence of a reservation will not preclude a finding of election or waiver. In *Flintkote Co.*, GSBCA 4223, 76-2 BCA ¶12,031, the contract contained a supplemental clause to the Default clause. This clause, prescribed for use with General Services Administration contracts, stated:

> (b) Waiver of Delivery Schedule
>
> None of the following shall be regarded as an extension, waiver, or abandonment of the delivery schedule or a waiver of the Government's right to terminate for default: (i) the delay by the Government in terminating for default; (ii) acceptance of delinquent deliveries; and (iii) acceptance or approval of samples submitted either after default in delivery or in insufficient time for the contractor to meet the delivery schedule.
>
> Any assistance rendered to the Contractor on this contract or acceptance by the Government of delinquent goods or services hereunder will be solely for the purpose of mitigating damages, and is not to be construed as an intention of the Government to condone any delinquency, or as a waiver of any rights the Government may have under subject contract.

The board concluded that this provision did not preclude it from finding a waiver, stating at 57,746:

> Government counsel points out on brief that this Board has not heretofore interpreted the Non-waiver clause. However, it argues that since the contract contains an "*express* statement of an intent to forbear, as long as the Government's right to terminate for default was exercised within a *reasonable* period of time, it should be sustained." He further argues that where there is an "express intent to forbear, the delivery schedules can only be waived by an *express* waiver," and that in the absence of such waiver, "the conduct of the parties alone is insufficient to overcome the specific language of a contract clause."
>
> In arguing for a "reasonable period of time" to decide upon a course of action following delivery failure, we think that counsel for the Government recognizes the broad implication of this provision and the Government's failure to define a reasonable period of delay within this provision. Taken literally, the provision permits the Government

> to extend the forbearance period in perpetuity. It eliminates the doctrine of waiver and renders meaningless a long-standing line of Board and Court decisions which charge the Government with the inherent obligation to exercise its discretionary right to terminate or not to terminate, within a reasonable time. It discourages contractors from continuing performance and incurring costs, for there is no way to determine the course which the Government might eventually settle upon. The delay in termination would delay reprocurement, resulting in almost certain increased repurchase costs. It is an attempt to contract away nonfeasance. Thus, notwithstanding the language of clause 11(b)(i) we find that the Government does not have the right to forbear for an indeterminable period.

Accord, *Flexonics Div., Universal Oil Prods. Co.*, ASBCA 18485, 74-1 BCA ¶10,525, dealing with similar language in a show cause letter.

In *Abcon Assocs., Inc. v. United States*, 44 Fed. Cl. 625 (1999), the court upheld the government's avoidance of a waiver when the government notified the contractor, after there had been a failure of performance, that nothing the government does may be construed as a waiver of its rights to terminate for default because it was exercising its rights of forbearance. Thus, the 70-month delay between issuance of the show cause notice and actual termination and the contractor's continued work in reliance on the government's forbearance did not amount to waiver; the court noting that in construction contracts continued performance alone will not ordinarily support a claim of waiver.

6. Reestablishment of the Right to Terminate After Waiver

Following waiver, the right to terminate may be reestablished either by giving the contractor notice of a new date or through a bilateral agreement, *Lumen, Inc.*, ASBCA 6431, 61-2 BCA ¶3210; *Aviation Tech., Inc.*, ASBCA 48063, 00-2 BCA ¶31,046. A new delivery date established by the parties is presumed to be reasonable, *Trans World Optics, Inc.*, ASBCA 35976, 89-3 BCA ¶21,895. However, in order to hold the contractor to the new bilaterally established date, it must be shown that there has in fact been such an agreement. For example, in *Bailey Specialized Bldgs., Inc. v. United States*, 186 Ct. Cl. 71, 404 F.2d 355 (1968), the contractor's revised delivery schedule was accepted by the government. The schedule included a date when a preproduction model would be available for inspection and also listed later dates for delivery. The inspection revealed defects, and the government terminated for default. In reversing the termination, the court held that the only mutually agreed-upon dates in the revised schedule were those relating to final products and that the setting of inspection dates did not mean that the contractor had agreed to deliver goods without defect on those occasions.

In reaching a new schedule by agreement, the government is apparently entitled to use hard bargaining, short of duress. In *Simmonds Precision Prods., Inc. v. United States*, 212 Ct. Cl. 305, 546 F.2d 886 (1976), the contractor agreed to a new date and the insertion of a liquidated damages clause into the contract after the contracting officer had threatened a default termination following what the contractor claimed was a waiver. The court stated at 313:

> [I]n his negotiations, the PCO was not seeking to re-impose the original delivery schedules which, [the contractor] says, the Government had previously "waived." Rather, the PCO sought only to establish a specific new schedule for deliveries. From the facts known to him, a two to three-month time extension seemed adequate and reasonable, and he threatened default if some such reasonable schedule were not forthwith submitted to him by the contractor. In so doing, the contracting officer appears merely to have followed the guidelines developed by this court concerning waiver by the Government of its right to terminate a contract where the contractor has failed to meet the contract delivery date.

When the government unilaterally attempts to reestablish the due date after waiver, it must establish a specific date, *International Tel. & Tel. Corp. v. United States*, 206 Ct. Cl. 37, 509 F.2d 541 (1975); *Sun Cal., Inc. v. United States*, 21 Cl. Ct. 31 (1990). In *International*, following waiver of initial delivery dates, the government attempted to obtain a bilateral agreement setting the new delivery date as February 9, 1968, but because of performance problems the contractor declined to accept. Upon learning of the government's decision to terminate for default, the contractor arranged a meeting on February 15 and informed the government that the system was ready for shipment. At that time the government presented the contractor with a letter containing a blank space for inserting a final test date in February. The contractor refused to sign this letter, but the parties agreed to resume tests on February 19. When the February 19 tests failed, the government terminated for default, contending that February 19 had been unilaterally set as the final delivery date. The court ruled that the February 15 letter containing a blank space for the final test date did not constitute an appropriate notice of a unilateral new delivery date because it failed to set a specific time for performance as required by *De Vito*. The court also found that the agreement to resume testing on February 19 did not establish that as the date upon which the government could default terminate for failure to make delivery. The issuance of a cure notice or a show cause notice is not sufficient, *Lanzen Fabrication, Inc.*, ASBCA 40328, 93-3 BCA ¶26,079 (issuance of a show cause letter is "practically useless" where the delivery schedule has been "disestablished").

The reestablished date must be reasonable in view of the performance capabilities of the contractor at the time the notice is given, *McDonnell Douglas Corp. v. United States*, 182 F.3d 1319 (Fed. Cir. 1999), *cert denied*, 529 U.S. 1097 (2000), *on remand*, 50 Fed. Cl. 311 (2001), *aff'd in part & rev'd in part*, 323 F.3d 1006 (Fed. Cir. 2003). In the latter decision, the Federal Circuit rejected the contractor's contention that the standard for reasonableness was objective, ruling that the date would be reasonable if the contracting officer subjectively believed it was reasonable based on the available evidence at the time it was reestablished. The court stated at 1019:

> If the government opts to act unilaterally, the new date that it sets must be "both reasonable and specific from the standpoint of the performance capabilities of the contractor at the time the notice is given." [*DeVito v. United States*, 413 F.2d 1147, 1154-55, 188 Ct. Cl. 979 (Ct. Cl. 1969)], at 1154. The reasonableness of the action turns on what the government "knew or should have known" at the time it imposed the new schedule. *ITT Corp. v. United States*, 509 F.2d 541, 549-50, 206 Ct. Cl. 37 (Ct. Cl. 1975).
>
> Beyond this standard of reasonableness, our precedent does not impose the additional burdens that the Contractors would impose on the government when the United States unilaterally imposes a new completion date. Contrary to what [the contractor] contends, our precedent neither requires a determination of "what work remained to be completed as of the date the unilateral schedule was issued," nor does it necessitate an inquiry into "how long it likely would have taken the contractor to complete the remaining work, given its actual production capabilities as of the date the schedule was issued." Although those inquiries may be appropriate in certain situations, they are not requisite underpinnings for the DeVito reasonableness determination. Similarly, we reject the "objective achievability" paradigm suggested by the Contractors as not rooted in our precedent. Were we to adopt this new criterion, we would depart from our case law by requiring more than reasonableness; we would compel the government to have perfect prescience and be infallible in its decision. Because such an expectation is unachievable, the touchstone of this inquiry must remain grounded on reasonableness based on what the government knew or should have known when it adopted the unilateral schedule.

Earlier cases had appeared to require that the reestablished date be objectively reasonable, *Oklahoma Aerotronics, Inc.*, ASBCA 25605, 87-2 BCA ¶19,917; *Vista Scientific Corp.*, ASBCA 25974, 87-1 BCA ¶19,603; *Spasors Elecs. Corp.*, ASBCA 12877, 70-1 BCA ¶8119, *recons. denied*, 70-1 BCA ¶8346. A revised delivery schedule suggested by the contractor will probably be considered prima facie evidence of reasonableness, *Mark Assocs., Inc.*, ASBCA 12272, 67-1 BCA ¶6313, no matter how ill-considered the schedule may have been, *Tampa Brass & Aluminum Corp.*, ASBCA 41314, 92-2 BCA ¶24,865. See *National Bag Corp.*, GSBCA 4331, 77-2 BCA ¶12,664 (new time reasonable since performance problems had been solved, the date was based on contractor's estimate, and it allowed one-half the original performance time to complete one-third of the work); *Sidney G. Kornegay & Florence Kornegay*, ASBCA 18454, 76-1 BCA ¶11,744 (unilaterally imposed date, although based on prior estimates by the contractor, was unreasonable where it failed to take account of intervening severe weather); and *Aargus Poly Bag*, GSBCA 4314, 76-2 BCA ¶11,927 (new dates were reasonable because they were based on contractor's estimates and contractor did not complain when new dates were set). See also *Rowe, Inc. v. General Servs. Admin.*, GSBCA 14211, 01-2 BCA ¶31,630 (although the government overlooked the contractor's failure to meet two previously established delivery dates, the contracting officer reasonably established a new delivery date by allowing the extra 15 days requested by the contractor, and adding another 12 days to ensure flexibility in the schedule).

Termination following waiver without a reestablished delivery date will not be improper in the case of an anticipatory repudiation by the contractor. See *Herlo Corp.*, ASBCA 19198, 77-2 BCA ¶12,820, in which the board stated at 62,409:

> An extended examination of the waiver issue would avail the [contractor] nothing because, even if we were to conclude there had been a waiver of delivery schedule, no reestablishment of a reasonable delivery date, and consequently that the Government lost its right to terminate for failure to delivery on time, it would not affect the Government's right to terminate the contract for "anticipatory breach." The contractor's inability to perform, amounting to an anticipatory breach, is a separate basis for terminating a contract for default.

The tender of delivery following a waiver of the contract delivery date establishes a new and enforceable delivery date. In *Louisiana Lamps & Shades*, ASBCA 45294, 95-1 BCA ¶27,577, even if the government had waived the completion date of a contract for floor lights, it was justified in terminating the contract for default because the lights delivered did not substantially comply with the contract specifications.

III. THE TERMINATION DECISION

The fact that the government has the legal right to terminate is only one factor considered in making the business decision to terminate. In determining whether to terminate for default, the contracting officer must first decide if the contractor is in a default status without excuse, and second, whether it is in the government's interest to terminate the contract despite the contractor's being in default. The crucial issue is how best to complete the work called for by the contract. In many instances, evaluation of the situation indicates that working with the delinquent contractor is the most promising means of completing the work. In other instances, an immediate default termination followed by a quick selection of a new contractor may appear to be the most expedient course of action. The government never has to terminate for default, even if the contractor has been placed on the debarment list, FAR 9.405-1(a). But see *Ohio Casualty Ins. Co. v. United States,* 12 Cl. Ct. 590 (1987), where the government was found liable because it had waited too long to terminate a contractor and in so doing had failed in its equitable obligations to the surety.

Default termination may also be improper if the government has already exercised other contractual rights that solve the problem. For example, the agency improperly terminated a lease for failure to maintain the property in accordance with the lease when the agency already had exercised its right to make repairs at the lessor's expense, *Oscar Narvaez Venegas*, ASBCA 49291, 98-1 BCA ¶29,690.

It is well established that "A default termination is a drastic sanction . . . which should be imposed (or sustained) only for good grounds and on solid evidence," *J. D. Hedin Constr. Co. v. United States*, 187 Ct. Cl. 45, 408 F.2d 424 (1969). The government bears the burden to prove a default termination justified. The contracting officer's default decision must not be arbitrary or capricious or an abuse of discretion, *Darwin Constr. Co. v. United States,* 811 F. 2d 593 (Fed. Cir. 1987). The default clause does not require the government to terminate a contract for default but merely gives it the discretion to do so, *Schlesinger v. United States,* 182 Ct. Cl. 571, 390 F.2d 702 (1968). That discretion must be exercised reasonably. In order to prevail, the government must show that the termination for default was correct procedurally, that it was not an abuse of discretion, and that it was proper substantively.

A. Discretionary Decision

This decision is highly discretionary, based on the business judgment of the contracting officer and any advisors in the procuring agency, *Mega Constr. Co. v. United States*, 29 Fed. Cl. 396 (1993). In *Schlesinger v. United States,* 182 Ct. Cl. 571, 390 F.2d 702 (1968), the Court of Claims found a default termination invalid because the government had not exercised discretion in making the decision to terminate. The Navy had terminated in response to pressure from a congressional committee without considering the impact on the contractor or the government. The court found that the contractor was technically in default at the time of the termination, but stated at 581-84:

> Our difficulty is that the default article does not *require* the Government to terminate on finding a bare default but merely gives the procuring agency discretion to do so, and that discretion was not exercised here by the Navy. The existence of discretion is undeniable. The clause says that "the Government *may* . . . terminate" (emphasis added), not "shall" or "must". We have recognized that a decision to terminate for convenience is rooted in discretion (*Commercial Cable Co. v. United States*, 170 Ct. Cl. 813, 821 (1965); *John Reiner & Co. v. United States*,

> 163 Ct. Cl. 381, 390, 325 F.2d 438, 442-43 (1963), *cert. denied*, 377 U.S. 931 (1964)), and though the factors the Government will wish to consider may be different when a default is involved there is no reason to read the default article, contrary to its literal terms and the accepted practice, as compelling termination. We are certain that there have been a great many instances in which the Government has not terminated a contractor in technical default, but has granted an extension or waived the noncompliance. In this very case the [government], as the Board found, excused the earlier non-delivery on May 31st which was, of course, also a default. Our ruling today is not new. More than ten years ago, the court specified that procurement officials had to exercise judgment in terminating an agreement for default and were not automatons. *John A. Johnson Contracting Corp. v. United States*, 132 Ct. Cl. 645, 658-60, 132 F. Supp. 698, 704-05 (1955).
>
> We hold, too, that this discretion was never exercised but the Navy simply surrendered its power of choice. This is so clear from the Board's record that we are warranted in reaching the conclusion despite the Board's failure to consider the point. Although the Congressional communication does not appear to have suggested that the [contractor's] contract be canceled without consideration of [its] rights or situation, or even that it be terminated for default rather than for convenience (which would give the contractor [its] reasonable expenses to date), the Navy acted as if it had no option but to terminate for default (barring all compensation) once the mere fact of non-delivery was found. The Navy did not consider whether an extension should be granted or the June 30th default waived (as that of May 31st had been) so as to allow delivery in July. The guillotine was dropped immediately after the non-delivery of June 30th, and was strongly contemplated even before that day had been reached or passed.

The court in *Schlesinger* restated the rule that in terminating a contract for default, government procurement officials shall not act as "automatons." Rather, the party with default-termination power shall make a "judgment as to the merits of the case before terminating a contract for default."

The *Schlesinger* rule was limited in *McDonnell Douglas Corp. v. United States,* 182 F.3d 1319 (Fed. Cir. 1999), *cert denied,* 529 U.S. 1097 (2000), *on remand,* 50 Fed. Cl. 311 (2001), *aff'd in part & rev'd in part,* 323 F.3d 1006 (Fed. Cir. 2003), where the contracting officer had terminated for default shortly after the Secretary of Defense refused to continue funding of a major weapon system. The court, in its 1999 decision, reversed the decision of the Court of Federal Claims that no discretion had been exercised, stating at 1326:

> Properly understood, then, *Schlesinger* and its progeny merely stand for the proposition that a termination for default that is unrelated to contract performance is arbitrary and capricious, and thus an abuse of the contracting officer's discretion. This proposition itself is but part of the well established law governing abuse of discretion by a contracting official. See, e.g., *United States Fidelity & Guaranty Co. v. United States*, 230 Ct. Cl. 355, 676 F.2d 622, 630 (Ct. Cl. 1982) (listing four factors to be used in determining if conduct by a government official is arbitrary and capricious: (1) evidence of subjective bad faith on the part of the government official, (2) whether there is a reasonable, contract-related basis for the official's decision, (3) the amount of discretion given to the official, and (4) whether the official violated an applicable statute or regulation).

1. Person Exercising Discretion

The court in *Schlesinger* indicated that the person exercising discretion to terminate did not necessarily have to be the contracting officer, stating at 584:

> We do not put our decision on the failure of the contracting officer to exercise his own judgment. This agreement gave the default-termination power to "the Government" and did not single out the contracting officer as the official to decide that particular question. But the record affirmatively shows that nobody in the Navy, neither the contracting officer nor his superiors, exercised the discretion they possessed under the article. [The contractor's] status of technical default served only as a useful pretext for the taking of action felt to be necessary on other grounds unrelated to the [contractor's] performance or the propriety of an extension of time.

However, since the termination notice is described as a final decision under the Disputes clause, FAR 49.402-3(g)(5) and (7), it is generally assumed that discretion must be exercised by the contracting officer issuing the termination notice. See *Fairfield Scientific Corp. v. United States*, 222 Ct. Cl. 167, 611 F.2d 854 (1979), stating at 181-82:

> The default clause does not say that the Government "shall" or "must" terminate the contract in the event of default, only that the Government "may" terminate it. Not only is the contracting officer to consider whether or not the default is excusable, but the regulations require him to consider at least seven factors in addition to the default in deciding whether or not to terminate the contract. "The existence of discretion is undeniable." *Schlesinger v. United States*, 182 Ct. Cl. 571, 581, 390 F.2d 702, 707 (1968). If the contracting officer was improperly influenced by [the contractor's] competitor or by anyone else to terminate the contract for default rather than to exercise his own independent judgment in the light of the factors set out in the regulations, it would represent an abdication rather than an exercise of his discretion.

Fairfield Scientific appears to assume that a contracting officer is required to make the decision to terminate. This question has not been authoritatively decided. One decision has held that the decision to terminate for default need not be a "personal decision" of the contracting officer so long as there was not a complete abdication of discretion, *Square Constr. Co. & LaFera Contracting Co.*, ENGBCA 3494, 76-1 BCA ¶11,747. In *Novelty Prods. Co.*, ASBCA 21077, 78-1 BCA ¶12,989, a termination decision was made despite a recommendation from the administrative contracting officer to negotiate a new delivery schedule based on the contractor's progress. The board found that the contracting officer who terminated the contract did not give any weight to this recommendation and did not bring it to the attention of the Director of the Defense Logistics Agency, who approved the termination. Nevertheless, the board upheld the default, stating that there is "no requirement that the contracting officer must adopt the ACO's recommendations favorable to the contractor." In any event, the contracting officer is entitled to receive advice from others. See the trial judge's recommended decision, 22 CCF ¶80,535, adopted by the court in *Northrop Carolina, Inc. v. United States*, 213 Ct. Cl. 670, 553 F.2d 105 (1977), stating at 85,756:

> The contracting officer (J.C. Darcy) responsible for [the contractor's] default termination testified at the Board hearing. His testimony establishes that the decision to terminate [the contractor's] contract for default was his independent decision based on the failure of [the contractor] to deliver the badly needed flares in a timely fashion. His judgment in this regard involved a review of pertinent documentation and receipt of advice from his subordinate supportive personnel, as well as from a Contract Review Board. He recognized that termination of a contract for default required a high degree of judgment and maturity, and the tenor of his testimony reflected an awareness that a default termination was a drastic sanction. See *J.D. Hedin Constr. Co. v. United States*, 187 Ct. Cl. 45, 57, 408 F.2d 424, 431 (1969). On this record, there is no question but that the contracting officer exercised his independent discretion in terminating [the contractor's] contract for default.
>
> [The contractor's] claim of lack of discretion on the part of the contracting officer rests primarily on the following assertion. [The contractor] argues that Darcy had not conferred with a representative of [the contractor] for a period of almost 2 months prior to default. This is immaterial since representatives of Darcy, including William C. Schreffler, a management and administrative contracting officer on [the contractor's] contract and a subordinate of Darcy, had conferred with [the contractor's] representatives during the pertinent period. Plaintiff complains because Darcy did not participate in the deliberations of the Contract Review Board. This, too, is immaterial. More importantly, Darcy was not a member of this Board. This Board submitted recommendations to Darcy relative to proposed default actions, which recommendations could be accepted or rejected by him. Finally, [the contractor] points to the fact that Darcy was not present at the December 17, 1970, meeting. While [the contractor] alleges that it requested that he be at this conference, it cites no record reference in support thereof. In any event, Schreffler was present at this meeting and [the contractor's] position was fully set forth in writing by [the contractor's] president and made available to and reviewed by Darcy before he reached his decision on the matter. As a result, his unavailability at this meeting was of no importance. In sum, these contentions do not establish in any way that the terminating contracting officer's decision failed to rest on the exercise by him of his discretion.

See also *McDonald Welding & Mach. Co.*, ASBCA 36284, 94-3 BCA ¶27,181 (procurement contracting officer made the decision which was "concurred in" by a board of review). However, in *Dulles Networking Assocs., Inc.*, VABCA 6077, 00-1

BCA ¶30,775, the termination notice was issued by someone other than the contracting officer. Rather than overturn the termination, the board held it had no jurisdiction absent a contracting officer decision.

In *PLB Grain Storage Corp. v. Glickman*, 113 F.3d 1257 (Fed. Cir. 1997), in a nonprecedential decision, the court held that, even though other government officials had instructed the contracting officer to terminate the contract for default, the contracting officer was the final decision maker and had exercised independent, personal judgment. The court did not discuss *Nuclear Research Corp. v. United States*, 814 F.2d 647 (Fed. Cir. 1987), in which the court stated that the contractor had failed to show that the contracting officer's superiors had directed him to terminate, implying that such a direction would have made the termination improper. In *Larry J. Miller*, PSBCA 3632, 95-1 BCA ¶27,448, any representations by postal inspectors to a contractor that he would not be fired if he cooperated and told the truth did not preclude a default termination, because the contract authorized termination for mistreatment of mail and the postal inspectors lacked authority to commit the contracting officer to refrain from acting on information of a contract violation. See also *Fraya, S.E.*, ASBCA 52222, 02-2 BCA ¶31,975.

In *Industrial Design Labs., Inc.*, ASBCA 20369, 78-1 BCA ¶12,945, the termination was found proper since there was no evidence that the termination was due to any influence outside the procuring agency or that the termination was based on grounds other than the contractor's default.

2. Factors to Be Considered

There is considerable guidance, both in the FAR and the case law, on the factors that must be considered in making the decision to terminate for default.

a. *FAR Factors*

FAR 49.402-3 states:

(f) The contracting officer shall consider the following factors in determining whether to terminate a contract for default:
  (1) The terms of the contract and applicable laws and regulations.
  (2) The specific failure of the contractor and the excuses for the failure.
  (3) The availability of the supplies or services from other sources.
  (4) The urgency of the need for the supplies or services and the period of time required to obtain them from other sources, as compared with the time delivery could be obtained from the delinquent contractor.
  (5) The degree of essentiality of the contractor in the Government acquisition program and the effect of a termination for default upon the contractor's capability as a supplier under other contracts.
  (6) The effect of a termination for default on the ability of the contractor to liquidate guaranteed loans, progress payments, or advance payments.
  (7) Any other pertinent facts and circumstances.

* * *

(j) If the contracting officer determines before issuing the termination notice that the failure to perform is excusable, the contract shall not be terminated for default. If termination is in the Government's interest, the contracting officer may terminate the contract for the convenience of the Government.

(k) If the contracting officer has not been able to determine, before issuance of the notice of termination whether the contractor's failure to perform is excusable, the contracting officer shall make a written decision on that point as soon as practicable after issuance of the notice of termination. The decision shall be delivered promptly to the contractor with a notification that the contractor has the right to appeal as specified in the Disputes clause.

In *DCX, Inc. v. Perry*, 79 F.3d 132 (Fed. Cir. 1996), the court held that while compliance or noncompliance with FAR 49.402-3(f) may aid a board or court in determining whether a contracting officer has abused his discretion in terminating a contract for default, the factors "are not prerequisites to a valid termination," and do not confer rights on a contractor. See also *International Elecs. Corp.*, ASBCA 18934, 76-1 BCA ¶11,817, *recons. denied*, 76-2 BCA ¶11,943, *rev'd on other grounds*, 227 Ct. Cl. 208, 646 F.2d 496 (1981), in which the board stated that there was no requirement for the government to prove that each and every factor in DAR 8-602.3 (the predecessor to FAR 49.402-3(f)) was considered before terminating. Thus, there is doubt as to what evidence is necessary to establish discretion or lack thereof. Not every provision must be cited in the default termination, *White Buffalo Constr. Co.*, AGBCA 90-133-1, 93-3 BCA ¶26,236. In *Phoenix Petroleum Co.*, ASBCA 42763, 94-1 BCA ¶26,537, the board stated that failure to consider one or more of the factors stated in FAR 49.402-3(f) does not render the default improper. Accord, *Walsky Constr. Co.*, ASBCA 41541, 94-2 BCA ¶26,698; *AIW-Alton, Inc.*, ASBCA 45032, 96-1 BCA ¶28,232. In *LaFayatte Coal Co.*, ASBCA 32174, 89-3 BCA ¶21,963, the board stated that the failure to consider one or more of these factors was "not an automatic admission to a termination for convenience." Therefore, despite the mandatory terms of FAR 49.402-3(f), the government's failure to comply with the FAR requirement does not automatically invalidate a termination for default.

After *DCX v. Perry*, challenges to default terminations based on claims of abuse of discretion by the contracting officer by failing to consider all of the factors in FAR 49.402-3(b) have had little success. See *Double B Enters., Inc.*, ASBCA 52010, 01-1 BCA ¶31,396; *Imperial Props. Constr., Inc.*, ASBCA 49899, 0l-1 BCA ¶31,382; *Morganti Nat'l, Inc. v. United States*, 49 Fed. Cl. 110 (2001), *aff'd*, 36 Fed. Appx. 452 (Fed. Cir. 2002); *Nisei Constr. Co.*, ASBCA 51464, 99-2 BCA ¶30,448; and *Imperial Properties/Constr., Inc.*, ASBCA 49899, 0l-1 BCA ¶31,382.

b. Other Relevant Considerations

The FAR factors in no way limit the contracting officer. The contracting officer can move beyond the FAR and focus on the totality of the circumstances, *Jamco Constructors, Inc.*, VABCA 3271, 94-1 BCA ¶26,405, *recons. denied*, 94-2 BCA ¶26,792. In *Jamco*, the board stated at 131,361:

> The exercise of discretion involves more that a *pro forma* check off of factors drawn from FAR 49.402-3(f). It presupposes an active and reasoned consideration of available and sometimes contradictory information. Various factors must be evaluated and the totality of circumstances weighed by the Contracting Officer in arriving at a decision which "has the most serious consequences for a contractor." *Executive Elevator Service*, VABCA 2152, 87-2 BCA ¶19,849 at 100,438.

The board concluded that a contracting officer abused his discretion in terminating a contract for default when he failed to analyze independently the input of others. See *L & H Constr. Co.*, ASBCA 43833, 97-1 BCA ¶28,766 (termination decision was based on materially erroneous information regarding the contractor's culpability for delay and the labor and time required to complete the work); *CJP Contractors, Inc. v. United States*, 45 Fed. Cl. 343 (1999) (termination decision based on incorrect understanding of the remaining work and the time left for completion). Compare *Philadelphia Regent Builders, Inc.*, VACAB 1179, 79-1 BCA ¶13,856 (termination of "8(a) minority contractor" proper since decision made only after contractor was irretrievably in default and Veterans Administration and Small Business Administration had made every proper effort to assist contractor with financial problems); and *SCM Corp.*, ASBCA 19941, 75-2 BCA ¶11,508 (termination proper since contracting officer considered that convenience termination would be costly, contractor was in default, and government no longer needed supplies).

Default terminations are improper and, therefore overturned, when contractors demonstrate that, for example, the government had not adequately considered schedule extensions and concurrent delays, *SAE/Americon-Mid Atl., Inc. v. General Servs. Admin.*, GSBCA 12294, 98-2 BCA ¶30,084; and when the government's specifications were defective, *ABS Baumashinenvertieb GmbH*, ASBCA 48207, 00-2 BCA ¶31,090. In *SAE/Americon-Mid Atl.*, the board noted that the termination notice was "terse and gives short shrift to the many pending claims filed by SAE for delay and extra work." In the circumstances, where the contracting officer only visited the site a few times each month, the board was not persuaded that the termination was a "product of the careful assessment of the facts and circumstances contemplated by applicable regulation and the guidance of [applicable case law]." In *American Sheet Metal Corp. v. General Servs. Admin.*, GSBCA 14066, 99-1 BCA ¶30,329, the default termination was also wrongful because the government terminated in the absence of a clear overall completion date before the time expired in the cure notice. Given that the contractor had significantly accelerated its efforts and the potential costs and disruption of bringing on a reprocurement contractor to complete a roof that was almost finished were substantial, the board held that the government should at least have waited until the end of the cure period before terminating.

c. *Alternatives*

FAR 49.402-4 specifies alternative courses of action that may be followed by the contracting officer in lieu of terminating for default:

> Procedure in lieu of termination for default.
>
> The following courses of action, among others, are available to the contracting officer in lieu of termination for default when in the Government's interest:
>
> (a) Permit the contractor, the surety, or the guarantor, to continue performance of the contract under a revised delivery schedule.
> (b) Permit the contractor to continue performance of the contract by means of a subcontract or other business arrangement with an acceptable third party, provided the rights of the Government are adequately preserved.
> (c) If the requirement for the supplies and services in the contract no longer exists, and the contractor is not liable to the Government for damages as provided in 49.402-7, execute a no-cost termination settlement agreement using the formats in 49.603-6 and 49.603-7 as a guide.

(1) Convenience Termination

Although termination for convenience is neither expressly authorized nor proscribed by the regulations or standard default clauses as an alternative to a termination for default, the previously quoted language of the Court of Claims in *Schlesinger v. United States*, 182 Ct. Cl. 571, 390 F.2d 702 (1968), stressing the discretionary nature of the decision to default terminate, arguably authorizes the contracting officer to terminate for convenience instead of default where a contractor is inexcusably in default. However, the Armed Services Board has stated that the regulations prohibit the contracting officer from terminating for convenience where the right to terminate for default exists. In *Artisan Elecs. Corp.*, ASBCA 14154, 73-1 BCA ¶9807, *aff'd*, 205 Ct. Cl. 126, 449 F.2d 606 (1974), the board stated at 45,824:

> Except for no cost cancellations, where the right to terminate for default exists, the contracting officer not only may, but, under the cited regulations of his agency, must terminate for default if he is to terminate at all. Under such circumstances he may not terminate for the convenience of the Government. This has not always been the policy.
>
> * * *
>
> But, as the current regulations show, . . . while individual viewpoints on the merits of the policy may differ, neither a contracting officer nor this Board may, in accordance with those regulations, relieve a contractor in default by means of a convenience termination.

Accord, *Bendix Corp.*, ASBCA 23081, 79-1 BCA ¶13,717; *Trinity Resources*, AGBCA 80-187-1, 83-1 BCA ¶16,505.

On the other hand, it has been held that if the contracting officer does in fact issue a termination for convenience, the government may not change it to a termination for default, even though circumstances justifying default termination are present. See *Roged Inc.*, ASBCA 20702, 76-2 BCA ¶12,018, in which the board stated at 57,653-54:

> Presumably to rectify its procedural misstep, [the government] subsequently issued a notice of termination conversion whereby the initial convenience termination would be converted to a default termination. [The government] argued the original termination constituted a waiver of the Government's rights without legal consideration,

> thus it was an act beyond the scope of the contracting officer's authority and not binding on the Government. However, in those cases where the propriety of attempted conversions of prior terminations for convenience to default terminations have been judicially or administratively reviewed, it has been held the Government may not change a convenience termination to one for default. (*Richardson Camera Co., Inc.*, ASBCA 11930, 68-1 BCA ¶6990; *Line Construction Co. v. United States*, 109 Ct. Cl. 154 (1947); *American Kal Enterprises*, GSBCA 4460, 76-1 BCA ¶11,749.) We see no reason in this appeal to depart from those holdings, particularly since it is not even alleged the PCO did not intend to issue the termination for convenience in the form and at the time she did, nor has it been suggested the [contractor] in any way misled the PCO into issuing the convenience termination.

(2) Negotiating a Schedule Extension

If continued performance by the defaulting contractor is desired, a revised delivery schedule should be negotiated with the contractor to clearly establish the contractor's obligation and to avoid the complications that would arise if a waiver was subsequently found. The preferred method of establishing a new schedule would be the negotiation of a time extension supported by consideration from the contractor, *Comp-Con Tech. & Mfg., Inc.*, ASBCA 21150, 78-1 BCA ¶13,152. However, the government takes the risk that its expression of willingness to extend the delivery schedule for consideration could be construed as an election to continue, *Traders Distrib. Co.*, GSBCA 2718, 69-1 BCA ¶7463, *recons. denied*, 69-1 BCA ¶7677. Further, the demand for consideration, coupled with a threat of default termination, could be grounds for a finding of duress if the government does not in fact have the right to terminate. See *Urban Plumbing & Heating Co. v. United States*, 187 Ct. Cl. 15, 408 F.2d 382 (1969), *cert. denied*, 398 U.S. 958 (1970).

If the contractor refuses to furnish consideration for a delivery extension, the contracting officer apparently can establish a new delivery schedule without consideration. See *Free-Flow Packaging Corp.*, GSBCA 3992, 75-1 BCA ¶11,332, stating at 53,960:

> It is a well-established principle in Government contract law that while the Default clause gives the Government the absolute right to terminate the contract upon failure of the contractor to make timely delivery of the procurement item, the clause permits the Contracting Officer to exercise his right to use discretion in deciding whether to immediately terminate the contract, or any part thereof, or, among other things, to allow the contractor to continue performance under a new delivery schedule. No new consideration is necessary to support what the Default clause already permits the Contracting Officer to do. It is also a principle of law that a waiver of delivery date can be inferred from the Government's behavior after the contractor fails to make delivery as promised. Acceptance of a new delivery date can be established by agreement of the parties or by acts of the Government. Here again, acceptance by the Government can be implied from the circumstances.

See also *Gillet Mach. Rebuilders, Inc.*, ASBCA 28341, 89-3 BCA ¶22,021. Care should be taken to protect the government's rights to damages if the contracting officer grants a schedule extension without consideration.

3. Improper Decision Making

Exercise of discretion appears to require that the decision must not be arbitrary, must be based on a judgment on the merits, must demonstrate a consideration of available alternatives, and must be free from outside influence. In *Switlik Parachute Co. v. United States*, 216 Ct. Cl. 362, 573 F.2d 1228 (1978), the court held that the decision to terminate was fully justified and in no way arbitrary or capricious where the government had offered to extend the delivery schedule for consideration and terminated when the contractor did not accept the offer. Judge Nichols, dissenting, felt that there was no exercise of discretion and stated that a contractor has a right to an "informed and deliberate exercise of discretion." The court has indicated, however, that it may be difficult to find the exercise of discretion if a termination was based on "a few deficiencies of the kind every construction contractor experiences on every job," *J.D. Hedin Constr. Co. v. United States*, 187 Ct. Cl. 45, 408 F.2d 424 (1969).

In *McDonnell Douglas Corp. v. United States*, 182 F.3d 1319 (Fed. Cir. 1999), *cert denied*, 529 U.S. 1097 (2000), *on remand*, 50 Fed. Cl. 311 (2001), *aff'd in part & rev'd in part*, 323 F.3d 1006 (Fed. Cir. 2003), the court referred to the following four factors that should be considered in determining whether there had been an abuse of discretion: "(1) evidence of subjective bad faith on the part of the government official, (2) whether there is a reasonable, contract-related basis for the official's decision, (3) the amount of discretion given to the official, and (4) whether the official violated an applicable statute or regulation." In *Empire Energy Mgmt. Sys., Inc.*, ASBCA 46741, 03-1 BCA ¶32,079, *aff'd*, 362 F.3d 1343 (Fed Cir. 2004), the board analyzed the termination decision following these four factors and found no abuse of discretion. With regard to the issue of "subjective bad faith" the board reasoned that it should follow *Am-Pro Protective Agency, Inc. v. United States*, 281 F.3d 1234 (Fed. Cir. 2002), requiring the contractor to establish bad faith by "something stronger than a 'preponderance of evidence' . . . to overcome the presumption [of] good faith." The board found no bad faith because the contractor did not show with "convincing clarity a high probability that [the contracting officer] acted from personal animus with specific intent to injure Empire." See also *Quality Env't Sys., Inc.*, ASBCA 22178, 87-3 BCA ¶20,060, using the same factors. Compare *Tecom, Inc. v. United States*, 66 Fed. Cl. 736 (2005), concluding, after a detailed analysis, that the presumption of good faith on the part of government officials was not applicable to cases not involving allegations of criminal activity.

Regardless of the category (abuse of discretion, bad faith, arbitrary and capricious) the judges select, default terminations are found to be improper if 1) they are infected with informational deficiencies, i.e., either the contracting officer did not consider all relevant information or considered erroneous data; 2) an improper motive was present; or 3) other objectionable government conduct is present.

a. *Informational Deficiencies*

Abuse of discretion will be found where there is an indication that relevant information has not been considered or evaluated. See *Monaco Enters. v. United States*, 907 F.2d 159 (Fed. Cir. 1990), in which the court in a non-precedential opinion reversed a board decision. The court stated that failure to consider the lack of urgency, the contractor's willingness to perform, and the fact that a substitute contractor would not likely perform any earlier constituted an abuse of discretion. See also *Jamco Constructors, Inc.*, VABCA 3271, 94-1 BCA ¶26,405 (failure to evaluate conflicting information on the time needed for contractor to complete performance). However, the failure to consider a factor will not be an abuse of discretion where other factors indicate a termination to be warranted, *Hannon Elec. Co. v. United States*, 31 Fed. Cl. 135 (1994).

In *Marshall Associated Contractors, Inc.–Columbia Excavating, Inc. (J.V.)*, IBCA 1901, 01-1 BCA ¶31,248, the board found that the contracting officer had abused his discretion in terminating for default because he had not reviewed the claim material presented by the contractor and had relied entirely on the advice of technical personnel, who had performed an inadequate analysis. Moreover, the termination was suspect because the government was not prejudiced by the contractor's delay. See also *Ryan Co.*, ASBCA 48151, 00-2 BCA ¶31,094, *recons. denied*, 01-1 BCA ¶31,151, finding an abuse of discretion when the contracting officer had inaccurate information on which to base the termination decision because other government personnel intentionally withheld crucial information. However, in *Dinah Wolverton Perkins*, PSBCA 3691, 95-2 BCA ¶27,670, the board upheld the termination for default and ruled that a contracting officer is not obligated to investigate numerous complaints against the contractor before terminating for default. Although there might be such a duty if the termination relied on only one or two major irregularities, the significant number of complaints about similar problems justified the termination.

b. *Improper Motive*

In *Darwin Constr. Co. v. United States*, 811 F.2d 593 (Fed. Cir. 1987), the court overturned a default termination because of an abuse of discretion—based on the board's finding that the government's reason for the termination was solely to rid itself of the contractor. The court rejected the government's argument that motive could not be considered in determining whether a default termination was an abuse of discretion. See also *Libertatia Assocs., Inc. v. United States*, 46 Fed. Cl. 702 (2000), ruling that a default termination was improper because of the contracting officer's representative's personal animosity toward the contractor. The court characterized this as "bad faith." See also *ABS Baumaschinenvertrieb GmbH*, ASBCA 48207, 00-2 BCA ¶31,090, in which the board concluded that the termination for default was an abuse of discretion because the government's specifications were defective, a machine built to the IFB's specifications would not have met the performance requirements specified, and the government had engaged in improper conduct by meeting with the contractor's competitor after contract award in a "conflict of interest so patent that the Government cannot be assured of getting unbiased advice as to the content of the specifications." The contracting officer relied on information that "taint[edl the decision process leading to the [default]" such as the advice of technical advisors in determining whether the proposed machine, as submitted by the contractor, met the design specifications. Indicative of this "subjective bad faith" was the advisors' withholding from the contracting officer the fact that the machine was no longer required.

Earlier board cases based on the allegation that the termination was motivated by animosity toward the contractor generally rejected such arguments on the grounds that, if the government has a right to terminate and followed the proper procedures, its motive is irrelevant, *Walsky Constr. Co.*, ASBCA 41541, 94-2 BCA ¶26,698. See *Standard Mfg. Co.*, ASBCA 13624, 72-1 BCA ¶9371, in which the board stated at 43,508-09:

> The [contractor's] final argument is that the termination of the [contractor's] order should be for convenience because the Government terminated the appellant's order for reasons unrelated to [the contractor's] performance thereunder. [The contractor] alleges that the order was terminated because of certain prejudices toward the [contractor's] proprietary designs and because of the fact that the need for [the contractor's] items had been extinguished prior to default termination by the Government's procurement of substitute items from an alternate source of supply. It contended that *Schlesinger v. United States*, 182 Ct. Cl. 571, 390 F.2d 702 (1968) stands for the proposition that termination for reasons unrelated to the contractor's performance can only be the basis for a termination for convenience.
>
> We find nothing in the *Schlesinger* opinion to support a conclusion so broad as that urged by the [contractor]. In that case the court held that the Navy was required to exercise the discretion which the Default clause gives it, and could not terminate for default, although the contractor was in technical default, upon the dictates of a Senate Subcommittee, without the exercise of that discretion. There was no abdication of that responsibility by the Air Force in the present case.
>
> The record indicates that the Air Force representatives were unhappy at being forced to purchase a proprietary product from this [contractor] in view of its recalcitrance in complying with the Truth in Negotiations Act and implementing regulations. The fact that by the time of the [contractor's] default a substitute item was available elsewhere was one of the factors considered in arriving at the decision to terminate.
>
> * * *
>
> The [contractor] defaulted in its delivery requirements, without excusable cause. The Air Force considered the factors specified in ASPR before deciding to terminate for default. Among these were the facts that the [contractor] failed to offer a substitute delivery schedule which indicated any attempt at urgency, and the Air Force could secure the quantity it needed elsewhere at a lower price. The termination for default was proper.

See also *Sach Sinha & Assoc., Inc.*, ASBCA 47594, 00-1 ¶30,735, where allegations of bad faith in the form of conspiracy, prejudice, incompetence, and vindictiveness were unproven because the evidence offered, if any, fell short of "well-nigh irrefragable proof;" *George H. Robertson*, HUDBCA 76-31, 78-1 BCA ¶13,035, in which the board held that, even if the government had been motivated by bias against the contractor, termination was not improper because the contractor was actually in default and proper procedures were followed; and *Nuclear Research Assocs., Inc.*, ASBCA 13563, 70-1 BCA ¶8237, in which the board stated, "[D]efault termination is a matter of right, not motive. If the right clearly exists, the board does not examine into the contracting officer's 'motives' or judgment leading to its exercise."

In *Bob Brottmiller*, AGBCA 94-196-3, 95-1 BCA ¶27,468, default was not excused by the government's alleged failure to afford the contractor the same treatment as other contractors because whether other contractors were guilty of violations of their contracts had no bearing on whether the contract at issue was properly terminated. See also *Adelaide Blomfield Mgmt. Co. v. General Servs. Admin.*, GSBCA 12851, 95-1 BCA ¶27,514, in which a lessor of a building failed to overcome the presumption of governmental good faith in terminating the lease because the government entered the lease with the intention of honoring it but later needed more space to house its tenant agencies. The board concluded that it was not evidence of bad faith that the government did not follow the lessor's suggestion to move one agency out and backfill the vacated space with a smaller agency.

c. *Other Objectionable Conduct by the Government*

Often bases for overturning a default termination do not conveniently fit into any category. In *Riyste & Ricas, Inc.*, ASBCA 51841, 02-2 BCA ¶31,883, the board ruled that the contracting officer's failure to promptly rule on requests for a time extension, coupled with the contracting officer's failure to tell the contractor that the government disagreed with it, constituted an abuse of discretion that warranted converting a default termination into a termination for convenience.

The fact that the government no longer needs the items has been frequently rejected as a basis for overturning an otherwise proper default termination. See *Artisan Elecs. Corp.*, ASBCA 14154, 73-1 BCA ¶9807, *aff'd,* 205 Ct. Cl. 126, 449 F.2d 606 (1974), in which the ASBCA Senior Deciding Group held that the government's need for the supplies and services is irrelevant to its right to terminate for default. In affirming, the Court of Claims noted that the government's requirements were reduced but did not comment on this specific finding of the board. From the decision, it does not appear that the contractor raised the discretion issue to the court. See also *Precision Standard, Inc.*, ASBCA 41375, 96-2 BCA ¶28,461; *American Gen. Fabrication, Inc.*, ASBCA 43518, 92-2 BCA ¶24,955; *Scandia Mfg. Co.*, ASBCA 20888, 76-2 BCA ¶11,949; *Hydraulic Sys. Co.*, ASBCA 16856, 72-2 BCA ¶9742; *Standard Mfg. Co.*, ASBCA 13624, 72-1 BCA ¶9371; *Interspace Eng'g & Support,* ASBCA 14459, 70-1 BCA ¶8263; and *Rowe, Inc. v. General Servs. Admin.*, GSBCA 14211, 01-2 ¶31,630.

B. Reconsideration of Default Termination

FAR 49.102(d) provides that a contract terminated for default "may be reinstated by mutual agreement where the contracting officer determines that such reinstatement is advantageous to the Government." The GAO has held that agencies have "inherent authority" to reinstate a default-terminated fixed-price contract "wherever they determine in good faith that the basis for the default no longer exists and that it is reasonable to expect satisfactory completion of contract performance upon reinstatement," *Stancil- Hoffman Corp.*, Comp. Gen. Dec. B-193001.2, 80-2 CPD ¶226. See *Ohnstad Constr., Inc.*, AGBCA 81-160-1, 83-1 BCA ¶16,144, *recons. denied,* 83-1 BCA ¶16,319, where the contracting officer reinstated a portion of the terminated work and also indicated that the termination of the balance would be "reconsidered" based on contractor progress on the reinstated portion.

In *Ra-Nav Labs., Inc. v. Widnall,* 137 F.3d 1344 (Fed. Cir. 1998), nearly 10 years after being terminated for default, Ra-Nav Laboratories filed an appeal alleging an invalid default termination and breach of contract, claiming that the contract had been reinstated. The court rejected this argument because all of the communications of the government subsequent to the termination had indicated that any further work by the contractor would be only for the purpose of mitigating damages.

IV. TERMINATION PROCEDURES

The mere fact that harsh results may accompany a default termination cannot be used as a basis to deny the government this contractual right. However, the boards and courts have not been hesitant to hold terminations improper when the government has failed to strictly observe rules established to protect the contractor's rights. The contracting officer must follow specific procedures if contemplating a default termination, *Lionsgate Corp.*, ENGBCA 5809, 92-2 BCA ¶24,983. The doctrines of waiver and failure to exercise discretion, discussed in previous sections, are techniques used to limit the government's rights. Excusable delays also operate to limit the government's right to terminate. This section examines the required procedures for default termination and the impact of the government's failure to comply with these procedures.

A. Delinquency Notices

The Default clause for supply and service contracts in FAR 52.249-8 requires that a cure notice be sent to the contractor prior to termination based on a failure to make progress or a failure to perform any other provision of the contract.

A pre-default termination cure notice is also required by the termination clause at FAR 52.249-6 for cost-reimbursement contracts. In addition, the regulations provide for an optional show cause notice, which may be used to obtain information from the contractor prior to default termination, FAR 49.607(b).

1. Cure Notices

Paragraph (a)(2) of the FAR Default clause for supply and service contracts, FAR 52.249-8, provides:

> The Government's right to terminate this contract under subdivisions (1)(ii) and (1)(iii) above, may be exercised if the Contractor does not cure such failure within 10 days (or more if authorized in writing by the Contracting Officer) after receipt of the notice from the Contracting Officer specifying the failure.

FAR 49.607(a) gives the following guidance concerning the use and form of such cure notices:

> *Cure notice.* If a contract is to be terminated for default before the delivery date, a "Cure Notice" is required by the Default clause. Before using this notice, it must be ascertained that an amount of time equal to or greater than the period of "cure" remains in the contract delivery schedule or any extension to it. If the time remaining in the contract delivery schedule is not sufficient to permit a realistic "cure" period of 10 days or more, the "Cure Notice" should not be issued. The "Cure Notice" may be in the following format:
>
> CURE NOTICE
>
> You are notified that the Government considers your . . . [*specify the contractor's failure or failures*] a condition that is endangering performance of the contract. Therefore, unless this condition is cured within 10 days after receipt of this notice [*or insert any longer time that the Contracting Officer may consider reasonably necessary*], the Government may terminate for default under the terms and conditions of the . . . [*insert clause title*] clause of this contract.

Failure to give a cure notice, when required, will result in an improper termination, *T.C. & Sarah C. Bell*, ENGBCA 5872, 92-3 BCA ¶25,076. There, a park attendant's deficiencies in performance did not amount to a failure of performance, so a cure notice was required. Because the contracting officer gave no cure notice, the termination was overturned. In *Cross Petroleum, Inc. v. United States,* 54 Fed. Cl. 317 (2002), the court overturned a termination for default, finding that the required cure notice was not issued. In *Griffin Servs., Inc.*, ASBCA 53802, 03-1 BCA ¶32,200, the default termination was overturned because the government had rescinded its cure notice and then terminated on grounds not mentioned in the cure notice.

A notice in the nature of a cure notice is required in the Postal Service's Inspection of Work clause. See *Green Shack Marketplace,* PSBCA 4557, 01-2 BCA ¶31,595, holding that a postal inspectors' unilateral action in closing down a postal unit with no prior notice as required by this clause was not justified despite later ratification by the contracting officer. However, a contracting officer's failure to comply with this notice requirement to provide the contractor written notice of performance deficiencies did not invalidate a default termination because the contractor had actual notice of the contract violations, took no corrective action during the one-month period it was on notice of these violations, and failed to show any prejudice by the lack of written notice, *Fantastique Ultimatique Nautique'*, PSBCA 3652, 96-1 BCA ¶28,150.

a. *Circumstances for Use*

A 10-day cure notice is to be used only when the delivery (or performance) schedule has not yet expired. Thus, a cure notice is not required when a contract is being terminated under (a)(1)(i) of the Default clause for failure to deliver supplies, *Lafayette Coal Co.*, ASBCA 32174, 89-3 BCA ¶21,963; *Comspace Corp.*, DOTBCA 4011, 02-1 BCA ¶31,792, or to perform services, *Chambers-Thompson Moving & Storage, Inc.*, ASBCA 43260, 93-3 BCA ¶26,033; *NDJ Restoration, Inc. v. General Servs. Admin.*, GSBCA 14487, 98-2 BCA ¶29,987.

A cure notice is not required if there is a repudiation prior to a completion date, since there is no need for the contracting officer to do a "futile act," *Bendix Corp.*, GSBCA 4352, 77-2 BCA ¶12,656. See also *Cox & Palmer Constr. Corp.*, ASBCA 38739, 92-1 BCA ¶24,756; *Fairfield Scientific Corp.*, ASBCA 21151, 78-1 BCA ¶13,082, *recons. denied*, 78-2 BCA ¶13,429, *aff'd*, 228 Ct. Cl. 264, 655 F.2d 1062 (1981); and *De-Luxe Vans, Inc.*, ASBCA 23708, 81-2 BCA ¶15,421.

Another situation in which the 10-day cure notice is not required is when fewer than 10 days remain before the due date, FAR 49.607(a); *Century Hone Div. of Desert Labs., Inc.*, ASBCA 18360, 78-1 BCA ¶12,990, *recons. denied*, 78-2 BCA ¶13,343. In *McQuiston Assocs.*, ASBCA 24676, 83-1 BCA ¶16,187, *recons. denied*, 83-2 BCA ¶16,602, the board held that the government's failure to provide the Small Business Administration with a copy of a cure notice prior to default termination of a small business concern, as specifically called for by DAR 8-602.3(b)(4), was not grounds for overturning the termination where the notice was to be provided to the SBA "as a matter of information," with no response from the SBA required, and where the contractor could not demonstrate how failure to abide by this provision prejudiced its position.

Construction contracts do not require cure notices. In *Professional Servs. Supplier, Inc. v. United States*, 45 Fed. Cl. 808 (2000), the court refused to imply a cure notice requirement in a construction contract and rejected the contractor's argument that common law required a cure notice. However, if the government chooses to issue a cure notice, it should fully evaluate the contractor's response before deciding to terminate for default. See *Omni Dev. Corp.*, AGBCA 97-203-1, 01-2 BCA ¶31,487. In *Empire Energy Mgmt. Sys., Inc.*, ASBCA 46741, 03-1 BCA ¶32,079, *aff'd*, 362 F.3d 1343 (Fed. Cir. 2004), the board determined that a hybrid contract that contained elements of both the supply contract and the construction contract Default clauses did not contain a requirement for a cure notice because the contract was more in the nature of a construction contract.

b. *Form of Cure Notice*

The 10-day cure notice must be in writing, *Electromagnetic Refinishers, Inc.*, GSBCA 5035, 79-1 BCA ¶13,697; and must be specific, *American Marine Upholstery Co. v. United States*, 170 Ct. Cl. 564, 345 F.2d 577 (1965). The mere inclusion of a 10-day provision in a letter will not satisfy the requirements for the notice if the clear intention of the letter is to inform the contractor that the government will await further developments, *Long Island Nuclear Serv. Corp.*, ASBCA 12454, 69-1 BCA ¶7492.

The adequacy of a cure notice must be judged in light of correspondence and conversations preceding the notice, and, accordingly, the failure to specify all performance deficiencies does not necessarily invalidate the termination, *RFI Shield-Rooms*, ASBCA 17374, 77-2 BCA ¶12,714. See *Composite Laminates, Inc. v. United States*, 27 Fed. Cl. 310 (1992), in which the court stated at 318:

> Standards by which to determine the adequacy of a cure notice include the following:
>
> > The notice required by the default clause is intended to inform the contractor that it has failed to meet one or more terms of the contract, except for the delivery clause, as perceived by the government at the time. It need not cite each and every failure, but it must list with enough particularity the performance failures which have placed the contractor in danger of termination for default. Where the [contractor] has received prior notice of its failures, whether by telephone, letter, or word of mouth, that information will be considered properly in conjunction with the cure notice.
>
> *Int'l Verbatim Reporters, Inc. v. United States*, 9 Cl. Ct. 710, 721 (1986) (citing *Finast Metal Products, Inc.*, 77-1 BCA (CCH) ¶12,331 (1977).

In *Integrated Sys. Group, Inc.*, ASBCA 46918, 97-2 BCA ¶29,316, the board rejected the contractor's claim that the notice did not adequately inform it of the deficiencies, because the cure notice was followed by discussions between the contractor and the government, the contractor itself had seen the same deficiencies in its own testing, and no evidence had been presented by the contractor that it had been misled by the notice. However, if the contractor is not made aware of the defects, the cure notice is improper and may not be relied on.

c. *Effect of Denial of Cure Period*

Where the 10-day cure notice is required, failure to give proper notice will invalidate the termination, *Composite Laminates, Inc. v. United States*, 27 Fed. Cl. 310 (1992); *Kovatch Truck Ctr.*, GSBCA 5864, 82-2 BCA ¶15,855; *Mr.'s Landscaping & Nursery*, HUDBCA 75-6, 76-2 BCA ¶11,968; *River City Mfg. & Distrib. Co.*, AGBCA 92-157-1, 93-2 BCA ¶25,881.

Termination prior to the expiration of the 10-day period is also improper, *Swanson Group, Inc.*, ASBCA 44664, 98-2 BCA ¶29,896; *River City Mfg. & Distrib. Co.*, AGBCA 92-157-1, 93-2 BCA ¶25,881; *Introl Corp.*, DOTCAB 1030, 80-1 BCA ¶14,380; *B & C Janitorial Servs.*, ASBCA 11084, 66-1 BCA ¶5355. In *Cervetto Bldg. Maint. Co. v. United States*, 2 Cl. Ct. 299 (1983), the court invalidated a default termination issued on the final day of the 10-day cure period, concluding that the actual "decision" to terminate had been arrived at prior to expiration of the 10-day cure period and that the contracting officer had failed to consider a letter from the contractor responding to cited performance deficiencies apparently received on the final day of the cure period and had also failed to consider the contractor's performance of janitorial services on the last day. However, wrongful conduct or repudiation by the contractor during the cure period may relieve the government of the requirement to wait until the end of the period. See *Lee Maint. Co.*, PSBCA 522, 79-2 BCA ¶14,067, in which the board stated at 69,127:

> Prior decisions have held that once a cure notice is issued, even though a right to terminate a contract may have previously existed, the contract cannot be terminated until expiration of the period afforded the contractor to cure its unacceptable performance. *San Antonio Construction Company*, ASBCA 8110, 1964 BCA ¶4479; *B&C Janitorial Service*, ASBCA 11084, 66-1 BCA ¶5355. However, exceptions to this position have been made. *Soledad Enterprises*, ASBCA 20376, 77-2 BCA ¶12,552.
>
> In this appeal, the period afforded the [contractor] to cure its defective performance was preempted because of the [contractor's] threats to do physical harm to Postal Service personnel. The *Restatement of The Law of Contracts* (1932), § 315 states in part:
>
>> "Sec. 315. Breach By Preventing or Hindering Performance By The Other Party.
>>
>> "(1) Prevention or hindrance by a party to a contract of any occurrence or performance requisite under the contract for the creation or continuance of a right in favor of the other party, or the discharge of a duty by him, is a breach of contract, unless
>>
>> "(a) the prevention or hindrance is caused or justified by the conduct of the other party."
>
> * * *
>
> (Also see § 295 "Excuse of Condition by Prevention or Hindrance" and *Williston on Contracts*, 3rd edition, §§ 1601 et seq.) We conclude that any obligation the Postal Service had to afford the [contractor] the ten day period indicated in the cure notice was terminated by the [contractor's] wrongful conduct.

See also *Ohnstad Constr., Inc.*, AGBCA 81-160-1, 83-1 BCA ¶16,144, *recons. denied*, 83-1 BCA ¶16,319, in which the board upheld a default termination issued prior to the expiration of the designated cure period because the contract did not actually require a cure notice and the contractor had not shown any substantial reliance on the cure notice, and *Contract Auto. Repair & Mgmt.*, ASBCA 45316, 94-1 BCA ¶26,516, in which the board held that a partial default termination during the 10-day cure period was proper because the contractor did not show that it could have or would have cured the deficiencies before the end of the cure period.

d. *Adequate Assurances*

Once a valid 10-day cure notice has been issued, the contractor's failure to advise the government during the period that corrective action will be taken justifies a default termination, *Composite Laminates, Inc. v. United States*, 27 Fed. Cl. 310

(1992). Conversely, if the contractor timely cured its deficiency by providing proof that it had obtained proper insurance coverage, termination was improper, *Hughes Moving & Storage, Inc.*, ASBCA 45346, 98-1 BCA ¶29,693.

The government is entitled to "adequate assurances" of performance similar to those required under U.C.C. § 2-209 and *Restatement, Second, Contracts* § 251. The applicability of these common law and commercial law concepts to the resolution of government contracts progress failure cases was implicitly recognized in *Supertechnology Corp.*, NASABCA 570-9, 72-2 BCA ¶9619, in which the board described the government as an "insecure buyer" and upheld the progress failure termination since the contractor had failed to give "assurances." See *Danzig v. AEC Corp.*, 224 F.3d 1333 (Fed. Cir. 2000), in which the board had overturned the default termination of a construction contract on the basis that the government failed to present evidence that the contractor could not have completed the contract on time and that it had not expressed "unequivocal unwillingness" to perform, where the contractor stated it could not predict when it would finish the job only two months before the scheduled completion date. On appeal, the Federal Circuit reversed, holding that, although the government did not have sufficient cause to terminate the contract for failure to make progress, the contractor's response to the cure notice did not satisfy its obligation to provide assurances to the agency that it could timely complete the contract where the contractor did not dispute that it would be unable to complete the contract by the completion date, removed contract files and office equipment from the worksite. and disconnected telephones at the worksite office. Thus, the agency was entitled to regard the contractor's failure as a breach justifying termination of the contract for default. The court thus enhanced the importance of the U.C.C.'s "adequate assurances," by reasoning that failure to provide adequate assurance was an anticipatory repudiation and reversing the board's decision that no anticipatory repudiation had occurred because there was no "unequivocal statement" that the contractor could not or would not perform. See also *Twigg Corp.*, NASABCA 62-0192, 93-1 BCA ¶25,318 and *National Union Fire Ins. Co.*, ASBCA 34744, 90-1 BCA ¶22,266.

Even though the assurances do not provide a clear indication that the contractor will complete on time, the contracting officer should make an independent analysis before concluding that default termination is proper. See *Omni Dev. Corp.*, AGBCA 97-203-1, 01-2 BCA ¶31,487, in which the board found that shortcomings in the contractor's response to a cure notice did not excuse the contracting officer from performing the detailed analysis of the contractor's ability to complete work in the time remaining, before terminating for failure to make progress. Accord, *Bison Trucking & Equip. Co.*, ASBCA 53390, 01-2 BCA ¶31,654; *Beacon Cyberport*, AGBCA 2002-102-1, 03-1 BCA ¶32,105. Compare *Thomas & Sons, Inc.*, ASBCA 51874, 01-1 BCA ¶31,166, finding a proper default termination where, after the contractor responded to the cure notice by requesting an additional 60 to 90 days to complete the work, the government performed its own independent analysis of the updated schedule and concluded that the contractor could not perform within the time remaining for performance. See also *Automated Power Sys., Inc.*, DOTBCA 2678, 01-1 BCA ¶31,259, in which the board relied in part on the contractor's failure to provide assurances in response to a cure notice in upholding a default termination. Accord, *L&M Thomas Concrete Co.*, ASBCA 49198, 03-1 BCA ¶32,194.

Assurances generally involve both contractor acts (e.g., hiring additional employees, performing additional work) and words (e.g., submission of proposed work schedules or requests for excusable delays). For a discussion of the adequacy of assurances, see *RFI Shield-Rooms*, ASBCA 17374, 77-2 BCA ¶12,714. Assurances were found inadequate in *John F. Lehnertz*, AGBCA 77-132, 78-1 BCA ¶12,895 (90 percent of tree thinning not completed with 10 percent of contract time remaining, and contractor failed to respond to a request for a progress schedule specifying how it intended to finish the work within the contract time); *Building Maint. Specialists, Inc.*, ENGBCA 3540, 77-2 BCA ¶12,810 (contractor failed to commence grounds maintenance and cleaning services on time and was unable to hire employees or secure needed equipment); *Dozie I. Rienne*, ENGBCA 5711, 91-1 BCA ¶23,432 (mere promise to improve insufficient); *John E. Faucett*, AGBCA 396, 76-2 BCA ¶11,946 (failure to provide revised progress schedule); *J. W. Bibb, Inc.*, ASBCA 19589, 76-2 BCA ¶12,135 (contractor's response to cure notice was that further inquiries should be addressed to a law firm); *R.C. Hudson & Assocs., Inc.*, ASBCA 20711, 76-2 BCA ¶12,201 (proposed completion schedule included subcontractor commitments that were contingent on receiving back payments totaling $109,000, pending contractor claims for progress payments were uncertain and amounted to only $85,000, and prior contractor performance was erratic); and *Comdata Sys., Inc.*, ASBCA 19893, 77-1 BCA ¶12,463 (continued performance dependent on relief under Pub. L. No. 85-804, to which contractor was not entitled). In *Lorch Elecs. Corp.*, ASBCA 21496, 78-1 BCA ¶12,911, the progress failure was found to be cured when a breadboard model was successfully demonstrated to the government inspector, who did not report the success to the contracting officer.

2. The Show Cause Notice

FAR 49.402-3 contains the following guidance on the use of show cause notices:

(e)(1) If termination for default appears appropriate, the contracting officer should, if practicable, notify the contractor in writing of the possibility of the termination. This notice shall call the contractor's attention to the contractual liabilities if the contract is terminated for default, and request the contractor to show cause why the contract should not be terminated for default. The notice may further state that failure of the contractor to present an explanation may be taken as an admission that no valid explanation exists. When appropriate, the notice may invite the contractor to discuss the matter at a conference. A format for a show cause notice is in 49.607.

(2) When a termination for default appears imminent, the contracting officer shall provide a written notification to the surety. If the contractor is subsequently terminated for default, a copy of the notice of default shall be sent to the surety.

(3) If requested by the surety, and agreed to by the contractor and any assignees, arrangements may be made to have future checks mailed to the contractor in care of the surety. In this case, the contractor must forward a written request to the designated disbursing officer specifically directing a change in address for mailing checks.

(4) If the contractor is a small business firm, the contracting officer shall immediately provide a copy of any cure notice or show cause notice to the contracting office's small business specialist and the Small Business Administration Regional Office nearest the contractor. The contracting officer should, whenever practicable, consult with the small business specialist before proceeding with a default termination (see also 49.402-4).

FAR 49.607(b) provides the following form of notice and states that "it should be sent immediately upon expiration of the delivery period":

SHOW CAUSE NOTICE

Since you have failed to ______ [*insert "perform Contract No. ___ within the time required by its terms", or "cure the conditions endangering performance under Contract No. ___ as described to you in the Government's letter of ________ (date)"*], the Government is considering terminating the contract under the provisions for default of this contract. Pending a final decision in this matter, it will be necessary to determine whether your failure to perform arose from causes beyond your control and without fault or negligence on your part. Accordingly, you are given the opportunity to present, in writing, any facts bearing on the question to ______ [*insert the name and complete address of the contracting officer*], within 10 days after receipt of this notice. Your failure to present any excuses within this time may be considered as an admission that none exist. Your attention is invited to the respective rights of the Contractor and the Government and the liabilities that may be invoked if a decision is made to terminate for default.

Any assistance given to you on this contract or any acceptance by the Government of delinquent goods or services will be solely for the purpose of mitigating damages, and it is not the intention of the Government to condone any delinquency or to waive any rights the Government has under the contract.

The use of a show cause notice is not mandatory, *Sandia Die & Cartridge*, AGBCA 89-176-1, 94-2 BCA ¶26,927. In *Nisei Constr. Co.*, ASBCA 51464, 99-2 BCA ¶30,448 the board rejected the contractor's argument that FAR 49.607(b) required a 10-day response period to a show cause notice rather than the six days the government actually gave. The board noted that FAR 49.607(b) was merely precatory and did not mandate that the government literally follow it. Moreover, there is no need for a show cause notice in a supply contract after the delivery date has passed. See *Connecttec, Inc.*, ASBCA 51579, 02-2 BCA ¶32,021(issuance of a show cause notice was non-mandatory and was not required because the contractor failed to meet the revised delivery date).

The legal effect of a show cause notice issued after the due date was discussed in *Aargus Poly Bag*, GSBCA 4314, 76-2 BCA ¶11,927, in which the board stated at 57,184:

> The Default clause permits the Government to immediately terminate the whole or any part of a contract where the contractor fails to deliver the supplies within the time specified in the contract. However, it is to the mutual benefit of the parties for the Government to forbear where the contractor appears capable of performance and the Government might be willing to accept late deliveries. Thus, in the administration of supply contracts, it has become almost routine practice for the Government to issue a show-cause notice prior to termination; not so much, in our opinion, to determine excusability, but rather, to gain information relative to the contractor's performance capability. However, the Government is not legally obligated to issue such notice. The notices issued under this contract do not state, nor suggest, that the 10 days constitute an isolated period of immunity from termination. Thus, we conclude that the Government, whatever its motive, may see fit, at any time, to terminate and permit [the contractor] to show excusability at a later date under 11(e) of the Default clause.

Such a notice does not grant the contractor an automatic 10-day extension, *Kan-Du Tool & Instrument Corp.*, ASBCA 23466, 79-2 BCA ¶13,907; *Churchill Chem. Corp.*, GSBCA 4321, 77-1 BCA ¶12,318. The government can, therefore, terminate before the end of the period specified in the notice unless the contractor can show prejudice from an earlier termination, and prejudice will not normally be present when the government has the right to terminate without the notice, *Mission Paint Mfg. Co.*, GSBCA 4914, 78-2 BCA ¶13,389. These show cause rules also appear to apply to extended cure periods, *Litcom Div., Litton Sys.*, ASBCA 13413, 78-1 BCA ¶13,022.

Nor does a show cause waive a prior delivery date. In *Flight Refueling, Inc.*, ASBCA 46846, 97-2 BCA ¶29,000, a contractor's contention that the government's transmission of a show cause letter requesting information on excusable delay constituted a waiver of a prior delivery date was rejected. On the other hand, a contractor's failure to respond to a show cause notice does not waive a contractor's claims, *Roxco, Ltd. v. United States*, 60 Fed. Cl. 39 (2004).

FAR 49.402-3(e)(4) requires that show cause notices and cure notices be immediately provided to the Small Business Administration when they affect a small business. However, in *Baltimoy Mfg. Co.*, ASBCA 47140, 98-2 BCA ¶30,017, the board held that the agency's failure to follow this regulation did not preclude an otherwise proper default termination when the contractor was not prejudiced by the omission because the contract administrator had orally notified the SBA. Accord, *S&W Assocs.*, DOTBCA 2633, 96-2 BCA ¶28,326 (notice is for informational purposes only); *Rowe, Inc. v. General Servs. Admin.*, GSBCA 14211, 01-2 BCA ¶31,630 (government's failure to consult with an SBA specialist prior to terminating a contract for default did not render the termination procedurally defective, because the government put SBA on notice it was considering the action, and consultation with SBA is not a mandatory requirement).

B. Termination Notice

FAR 49.402-3(g) provides the following guidance as to the form of a default termination notice:

> If, after compliance with the procedures in paragraphs (a) through (f) of this 49.402-3, the contracting officer determines that a termination for default is proper, the contracting officer shall issue a notice of termination stating —
>
> (1) The contract number and date;
> (2) The acts or omissions constituting the default;
> (3) That the contractor's right to proceed further under the contract (or a specified portion of the contract) is terminated;
> (4) That the supplies or services terminated may be purchased against the contractor's account, and that the contractor will be held liable for any excess costs;
> (5) If the contracting officer has determined that the failure to perform is not excusable, that the notice of termination constitutes such decision, and that the contractor has the right to appeal such decision under the Disputes clause;

(6) That the Government reserves all rights and remedies provided by law or under the contract, in addition to charging excess costs; and
(7) That the notice constitutes a decision that the contractor is in default as specified and that the contractor has the right to appeal under the Disputes clause.

DAR 8-602(d) and FPR 1-8.602.3(d) contained similar guidance. The Court of Claims held that government failure to strictly observe these formalities in issuing a default termination notice will not necessarily provide grounds for overturning a default termination where the contractor has not been prejudiced by such failures. In *Philadelphia Regent Builders, Inc. v. United States*, 225 Ct. Cl. 234, 634 F.2d 569 (1980), the court upheld the default despite several "formal defects" in the default termination notice, including lack of citation to the proper contract number, lack of statement that it constituted a final decision, and failure of the contracting officer to sign the notice, where the contractor failed to show that it was "harmed in any way by the admitted defects in the notice." Compare *Kisco Co. v. United States*, 221 Ct. Cl. 806, 610 F.2d 742 (1979), in which the court overturned a partial default termination, relying on both the lack of a "cure notice" and the absence of "final decision" notification in the termination notice. The termination notice will be ineffective if it does not clearly indicate that the contract is being terminated for default, *Stroud Realty*, HUDBCA 75-13, 76-1 BCA ¶11,770. In that case, since the "cancellation" notice referred to both the convenience and default clauses, the board declined to hold that the contract had been terminated for default.

A default termination notice, as a contracting officer's final decision, must include information for the contractor on how to appeal the decision. In *George Ledford Constr., Inc.*, VABCA 6630, 02-1 BCA ¶31,662, the contracting officer's failure to put this information in a September 1996 notice of termination caused the board to refuse to dismiss the contractor's notice of appeal filed in May 2001, nearly five years later. Defective notice of appeal rights will not trigger the 90-day appeal period to the board, *Atlantis Constr. Corp.*, ASBCA 44044, 96-1 BCA ¶28,045; *Delta Constr. Co.*, ASBCA 42453, 96-1 BCA ¶28,106. However, in *State of Fla., Dep't of Ins. v. United States*, 81 F.3d 1093 (Fed. Cir. 1996), the court stated that relief may only be granted for the omission of the statement of appeal rights required by the Contract Disputes Act of 1978 if the absence of the notification prejudiced the party. There, the appellant could not show prejudice because it had actual notice of its appeal rights from other documents. See also *Decker & Co. v. West*, 76 F.3d 1573 (Fed. Cir. 1996) (a defect in an otherwise proper termination of default notice will justify relief only when accompanied by detrimental reliance). A contracting officer's final decision is not required for default grounds discovered after termination, *Glazer Constr. Co. v. United States*, 52 Fed. Cl. 513 (2002).

Terminations for present failures have been upheld, even though the reasons cited in the termination notice would not support default termination, so long as proper grounds for default termination did in fact exist at the time of termination, *Shields Enters., Inc. v. United States*, 28 Fed. Cl. 615 (1993); *Joseph Morton Co. v. United States*, 757 F.2d 1273 (Fed. Cir. 1985); *Pots Unlimited, Ltd. v. United States*, 220 Ct. Cl. 405, 600 F.2d 790 (1979); *American Photographic Indus., Inc.*, ASBCA 29272, 90-1 BCA ¶22,491; *Tester Corp.*, ASBCA 21312, 78-2 BCA ¶13,373, *recons. denied*, 79-1 BCA ¶13,725, *aff'd*, 227 Ct. Cl. 648 (1981); *Ralbo, Inc.*, ASBCA 49541, 99-2 BCA ¶30,438. Accord, *Cogefar-Impresit U.S.A., Inc.*, DOTBCA 2721, 97-2 BCA ¶29,188; *CJP Contractors, Inc. v. United States*, 45 Fed. Cl. 343, 379 (1999). The government may rely on other grounds for default unless the government's error in incorrectly specifying the basis for the default action has prejudiced the contractor, *United Detection Sys., Inc.*, ASBCA 46603, 98-1 BCA ¶29,368, *recons. denied*, 98-1 BCA ¶29,369. The government can so rely even if the other ground was known to the contracting officer at the time of termination, *Empire Energy Mgmt. Sys., Inc. v. Roche*, 362 F.3d 1343 (Fed. Cir. 2004). While the government can rely on other factors to justify the termination for default, it cannot do so if it was aware of all of the alleged instances and encouraged and demanded continued performance notwithstanding, *Aptus Co. v. United States*, 61 Fed. Cl. 638 (2004).

This rule has not been applied to progress failure terminations. In *Cross Aero Corp.*, ASBCA 14801, 71-2 BCA ¶9075, the board discussed the different rules, stating at 42,085:

> [The contractor] argues that the dimensional deficiencies of the pins, discovered after termination, may not be used as a basis to justify the TCO's antecedent decision to terminate. This Board held in *Marmac Industries, Inc.*, ASBCA 11861, 69-2 BCA ¶8067, that where default termination is sought for failure to make progress, the subsequent termination action can be based only on those failures of which the contractor had been given notice and

which it had an opportunity to cure or validly excuse. Where default termination is, however, based on default in delivery, the Board has held as long ago as 1955 that assertion of an invalid reason in the termination notice does not void it provided that at the time of termination a valid ground does in fact exist. *Royal Lumber Co., Inc.*, ASBCA 2847 (1955). Both the Court of Claims and this Board have ever since followed the rule laid down in *Royal Lumber. Nesbitt v. United States*, 170 Ct. Cl. 666 (1965); *Telecommunication Consultants*, ASBCA 13801, 69-2 BCA ¶7925; *Logan Electronic Corporation*, ASBCA 13054, 70-1 BCA ¶8083. Accordingly, the default termination, if otherwise permissible, is supported both on the ground that the pins cannot be considered to be the new pins of designated manufacturers and that they were dimensionally defective.

The default termination notice is effective when delivered to the contractor's place of business even if the person who signs the receipt for the notice is not empowered to bind the contractor, *Fred Schwartz*, ASBCA 20724, 76-1 BCA ¶11,916, *recons. denied*, 76-2 BCA ¶11,976. In *National Rag & Waste Co. v. United States*, 237 F.2d 846 (5th Cir. 1956), the court upheld the validity of a termination notice that was issued three weeks ahead of the completion date that clearly and unequivocally stated that the contract was terminated if the date was not met.

V. EXCESS COSTS OF REPROCUREMENT

Excess costs of reprocurement or completion are the unique remedies given to the government upon a valid default termination. The standard default clauses for fixed-price supply, service, and construction contracts state that the right to assess excess costs is "in addition to any other rights and remedies provided by law or under this contract." Thus, if the government loses its right to assess excess costs, it still retains the right to collect actual damages if they can be proved. The ease of proving excess costs, however, makes it a far more desirable remedy in most cases than attempting to prove actual damages.

The specific language giving the government the right to recover excess costs is contained in the Default clause at FAR 52.249-8 for supply and service contracts, which provides:

> If the Government terminates this contract in whole or in part, it may acquire, under the terms and in the manner the Contracting Officer considers appropriate, supplies or services similar to those terminated, and the Contractor will be liable to the Government for any excess costs for those supplies or services. However, the Contractor shall continue the work not terminated.

The Default clause at FAR 52.249-10 for construction contracts provides rights after termination as follows:

> In this event, the Government may take over the work and complete it by contract or otherwise, and may take possession of and use any materials, appliances, and plant on the work site necessary for completing the work. The Contractor and its sureties shall be liable for any damage to the Government resulting from the Contractor's refusal or failure to complete the work within the specified time, whether or not the Contractor's right to proceed with the work is terminated. This liability includes any increased costs incurred by the Government in completing the work.

FAR 49.402-6 contains the following procedures to be followed by the contracting officer in making repurchases against the contractor's account:

> (a) When the supplies or services are still required after termination, the contracting officer shall repurchase the same or similar supplies or services against the contractor's account as soon as practicable. The contracting officer shall repurchase at as reasonable a price as practicable, considering the quality and delivery requirements. The contracting officer may repurchase a quantity in excess of the undelivered quantity terminated for default when the excess quantity is needed, but excess cost may not be charged against the defaulting contractor for more than the undelivered quantity terminated for default (including variations in quantity permitted by the terminated contract). Generally, the contracting officer will make a decision whether or not to repurchase before issuing the termination notice.

(b) If the repurchase is for a quantity not over the undelivered quantity terminated for default, the statutory requirements for formal advertising are inapplicable. However, the contracting officer shall use formal advertising procedures unless there is a good reason to negotiate. If the contracting officer decides to negotiate the repurchase contract, any appropriate negotiation authority in Subpart 15.2 may be used. If none of the negotiation authorities is used, the contracting officer shall cite the Default clause as the authority. If the repurchase is for a quantity over the undelivered quantity terminated for default, the contracting officer shall treat the entire quantity as a new acquisition.

(c) If repurchase is made at a price over the price of the supplies or services terminated, the contracting officer shall, after completion and final payment of the repurchase contract, make a written demand on the contractor for the total amount of the excess, giving consideration to any increases or decreases in other costs such as transportation, discounts, etc. If the contractor fails to make payment, the contracting officer shall follow the procedures in Subpart 32.6 for collecting contract debts due the Government.

A. The Fulford Doctrine

Because the assessment of excess costs does not ordinarily occur at the time of the default termination, a contractor may sometimes choose not to contest the default termination because it does not anticipate any monetary liability. In other instances, a contractor may have simply failed, through inadvertence or otherwise, to make a timely challenge to the default action. In *Fulford Mfg. Co.*, ASBCA 2144, 6 CCF ¶61,815, the board announced the rule that ultimately became known as the "Fulford doctrine." The *Fulford* case allowed the defaulted contractor to challenge the underlying termination on the government's assessment of excess costs of reprocurement only in cases involving excusable delay. Prior to the enactment of the Contract Disputes Act, however, the boards broadened the scope of this doctrine "beyond the issue of excusable delays" so as to "permit the consideration of any challenge to the original [unappealed] default termination," *Fairfield Scientific Corp.*, ASBCA 21151, 78-1 BCA ¶13,082, *recons. denied*, 78-2 BCA ¶13,429, *aff'd*, 228 Ct. Cl. 264, 655 F.2d 1062 (1981). In that case, the board held that a contractor, on timely appeal of the assessment of excess costs, may contest the propriety of any default termination even though there had been no timely appeal of the default action. If the subsequent challenge to the default termination is successful, the improper default termination will be converted into a termination for the convenience of the government, and the contractor may use proof of the impropriety of the default as a basis for defeating an excess cost assessment. Thus, the decision by the government to assess excess costs may present some considerable risk to the government where no timely challenge to the default termination has been made, where the partial liability under termination for convenience is substantial, and where excess costs are not very large. Subsequently, the Fulford doctrine has been held applicable to appeals under the Contract Disputes Act, *Kellner Equip., Inc.*, ASBCA 26006, 82-2 BCA ¶16,077; and "direct access" suits under the Act, *D. Moody & Co. v. United States*, 5 Cl. Ct. 70 (1984). See *Z.A.N. Co. v. United States*, 6 Cl. Ct. 298 (1984), holding that this doctrine permits a contractor to challenge the default termination on the grounds that there was an excusable delay but not to challenge the fact of default or the government's right not to pay the contract price. There is, however, an apparent conflict between the 90-day jurisdictional requirements of the Contract Disputes Act and the Fulford doctrine, which allows issues to be litigated well beyond 90 days following the termination decision by a contracting officer.

Despite this apparent conflict, most of the boards continue to apply the Fulford doctrine to all situations in which the government seeks excess reprocurement costs. See, for example, *Parkway Distrib. & Bldg. Servs., Inc.*, ASBCA 36190, 89-3 BCA ¶22,199; *Primepak Co.*, GSBCA 10514, 90-3 BCA ¶22,280; and *High Tech Group, Inc.*, ENGBCA 5685, 90-2 BCA ¶22,822. In fact, the IBCA has even extended the doctrine to the "reverse Fulford" cases, where the underlying termination for default is timely challenged but the assessment of reprocurement costs is not challenged until more than 90 days after the contracting officer's imposition of those costs, *Tom Warr*, IBCA 2360, 88-1 BCA ¶20,231 (allowing a contractor to bootstrap its otherwise untimely challenge to the government's claim for excess costs to its timely challenge of the merits of the underlying default termination).

However, a broad construction of the doctrine is not employed by the boards uniformly. One board has implied that problems exist with the current state of the law in this area, while another has rejected the Fulford doctrine outright. In *Petroleum Constr., Inc.*, DOTBCA 2533, 93-2 BCA ¶25,760, the board recognized the conflict but did not address the issue because the claim was not one for excess costs of reprocurement. The Agriculture board, however, has employed a stricter interpretation of the Fulford doctrine. The board distinguishes the *Fulford* case, and hence the doctrine that takes its name, on the ground that the Default clause involved there did not require the contracting officer to consider the excusability of the default prior to the termination. Accordingly, the board has determined that, where the Default clause at issue requires an inquiry into excusability prior to the termination, board review of that issue is precluded 90 days after the contracting officer's decision to terminate, *Ace Reforestation, Inc.*, AGBCA 84-272-1, 87-3 BCA ¶20,218 (Default clause akin to FAR 52.249-10 found to require an excusability determination prior to the default decision). See also *Interstate Forestry, Inc.*, AGBCA 89-114-1, 91-1 BCA ¶23,660, and *In Re Bloodgood*, AGBCA 97-178-2, 98-2 BCA ¶29,770. Where the contract does not incorporate this particular FAR clause, the language of the Default clause at issue will be scrutinized to determine whether excusability is a prerequisite to the default decision. In *Mike Horstman*, AGBCA 87-388-1, 89-2 BCA ¶21,752, the board converted a termination for default into a termination for the convenience of the government after ascertaining the merits of the underlying default decision because the language of the clause incorporated into the contract (FAR 52.249-8) did not require an excusability analysis prior to the decision. See also *Paul Evans Co.*, AGBCA 90-198-1, 91-3 BCA ¶24,062. Moreover, if the contracting officer's final decision issuing the termination is not properly worded, the AGBCA will apply the Fulford doctrine regardless of the wording of the Default clause because the contractor is not placed on adequate notice that the jurisdictional clock has begun to run, *B & M Constr., Inc.*, AGBCA 91-132-1, 91-2 BCA ¶23,670; *Theodore R. Korotie*, AGBCA 86-245-1, 89-3 BCA ¶22,214. In sum, while the other boards will apply the Fulford doctrine in all cases regardless of the language of the incorporated Default clause, the AGBCA will carefully analyze the language and, in the process, will strictly construe the application of the doctrine due to its belief that the doctrine is inconsistent with the Contract Disputes Act. The Court of Appeals for the Federal Circuit has yet to hear a case addressing this conflict.

In the post-CDA era, virtually all of the boards of contract appeals have been unwilling to extend the doctrine beyond the situation in which the government subsequently seeks to recover excess reprocurement costs. Thus, the merits of the default termination will not be permitted to be placed at issue where the government later brings a claim for the return of unliquidated progress payments, *Mactek Indus. Corp.*, ASBCA 33277, 87-1 BCA ¶19,345; where the termination for default is timely appealed but not adjudicated on the merits (dismissed with prejudice), *Bulloch Int'l, Inc.*, ASBCA 44210, 93-2 BCA ¶25,692; or where the government attempts to recover for contractor-caused damage to government property under the Permits and Responsibilities clause, *Dailing Roofing, Inc.*, ASBCA 34739, 89-1 BCA ¶21,311; *Smith & Smith Aircraft Co.*, ASBCA 37793, 92-2 BCA ¶24,871. These cases specifically rejected a pre-CDA case that had referred to a "Fulford analogy." See *Pantronics, Inc.*, ASBCA 20982, 78-2 BCA ¶13,285, in which the board stated at 64,984:

> There appears to be no practical difference whether an assessment of costs is made by the Government under paragraph (b) or paragraph (f) of the Default clause, the net effect on the contractor involved is to assess damages against it for allegedly defaulting under [a] Government contract containing a Default clause.

In *Dailing Roofing*, the board specifically confined the reasoning of *Pantronics* to its facts. The board stated at 107,475-76:

> The "*Fulford* analogy" announced in *Pantronics* equated a Government claim for damages under the preservation of all rights (whether common law or contract created) provision in paragraph (f) of the standard supply contract Default clause (and in paragraph (d) of the Default clause in the captioned construction contract) with the assessment of excess reprocurement costs under paragraph (b) of the supply Default clause.
>
> Despite the foregoing sweeping equation, claims for various types of damages arising from deficient contractor performance may be asserted by the Government without necessitating the termination of the contract for default. For example, under a construction contract a contractor may be liable, *inter alia, for damages under the permits and responsibilities clause, as asserted here, or for liquidated damages for late completion of the work. In neither situation does the contractor's right to proceed need to be terminated. By contrast, termination of the work, in whole or in part, is a prerequisite for asserting a claim for excess completion or reprocurement costs.*
>
> * * *
>
> *However, rather than dismiss the "Fulford* analogy" announced in *Pantronics* as mere dictum, we confine its application to the factual setting in which it arose. Judgment on the viability of the *Pantronics* "*Fulford* analogy" can await such time as we are confronted with a "timely" appeal predating the damages claim to which it relates.

Thus, the boards are extremely reluctant to extend the Fulford doctrine any farther than the situations to which it has already been applied. See *Carter Indus., Inc.*, DOTBCA 2995, 98-1 BCA ¶29,625, in which the board refused to apply the Fulford doctrine when excess costs were collected through a proof of claim in a bankruptcy proceeding rather than by a contracting officer decision assessing excess costs. The board also rejected the contractor's contention that it had justifiably waited to appeal the decision because of the contracting officer's stated intention to demand reprocurement—noting that, while the FAR requires that a demand for repayment be made if a contracting officer's final decision results in a finding that the contractor is indebted to the government, a contracting officer has no legal obligation to issue a final decision.

The Fulford doctrine does not permit a contractor to relitigate the propriety of a default termination. See *Premiere Bldg. Servs., Inc.*, ASBCA 51804, 00-1 BCA ¶30,696, granting summary judgment against the contractor when it attempted to question the default termination after the government sought excess reprocurement costs because the contractor had taken the question of the propriety of the default to the Court of Federal Claims prior to the reprocurement cost assessment.

The Fulford doctrine allows a contractor to litigate the propriety of the initial termination for default; it does not afford a contractor the right to recover costs upon showing that the underlying default termination was improper, *American Telecom Corp. v. United States*, 59 Fed. Cl. 467 (2004).

B. Reasonableness of Government Action

In *Cascade Pac. Int'l v. United States*, 773 F.2d 287 (Fed. Cir. 1985), the court established what has now become the general test for determining whether the government's assessment of excess reprocurement costs is reasonable. It stated at 293-94:

> [E]xcess reprocurement costs may be imposed only when the Government meets its burden of persuasion that the following conditions (factual determinations) are met: (1) the reprocured supplies are the same as or similar to those involved in the termination; (2) the Government actually incurred excess costs; and (3) the Government acted reasonably to minimize the excess costs resulting from the default. The first condition is demonstrated by comparing the item reprocured with the item specified in the original contract. *Environmental Tectonics Corp.*, 78-1 BCA at 63,308. The second condition requires the Government to show what it spent in reprocurement. *Fairfield Scientific Corp. v. United States*, [222 Ct. Cl. 167,] 611 F.2d 854, 863-66 (1979). The third condition requires that the Government act within a reasonable time of the default, use the most efficient method of reprocurement, obtain a reasonable price, and mitigate its losses.

Judges typically test whether the contracting officer acted within a reasonable time after the default, obtained a reasonable repurchase price, used a reasonable manner of repurchase, and tried to mitigate the damages caused by the default, *Bertot Indus., Inc.*, ASBCA 41262, 96-1 BCA ¶28,230. Reasonableness is the critical criterion for the recovery of reprocurement costs as well as other expenses incurred that were reasonably foreseeable and the proximate result of the default, *Reddy-Buffaloes Pump, Inc.*, ENGBCA 6049, 96-1 BCA ¶28,111. See *M.D.R.-RIC,* PSBCA 4472, 01-1 BCA ¶31,302, finding a replacement contract reasonable, even though it was awarded at an annual rate nearly double that of the defaulted contractor, because it had to be awarded quickly in light of the emergency nature of the service contract and the government solicited a reasonable number of potential contractors and awarded the contract to the lowest offeror. Conversely, in *ARCO Eng'g, Inc.*, ASBCA 52450, 01-1 BCA ¶31,218, the board found considerable deficiencies, such as the inability to determine whether the reprocurement contract contained provisions impacting price, the absence of evidence indicating whether the reprocurement contract had been analyzed, the absence of evidence of whether the reprocurement contract had been negotiated, and the failure to justify the accelerated nature of the reprocurement contract.

1. Similarity

The determination of similarity is the threshold issue in deciding whether to uphold the assessment of excess costs, *Environmental Tectonics Corp.*, ASBCA 21204, 78-1 BCA ¶12,986; *Old Dominion Sec., Inc.*, GSBCA 9126, 90-2 BCA ¶22,745. The Default clause for supply and service contracts, FAR 52.249-8, contains language explicitly requiring the repurchased supplies and services to be "similar" to the terminated items. The construction contract clause does not contain the word "similar." Instead, it merely provides that the government may take over the work and prosecute it to completion.

The boards have held, however, that a similarity determination under the construction contract clause is "largely analogous" to that under the service and supply contract clause, *Rayco, Inc.*, ENGBCA 4792, 88-2 BCA ¶20,671. In this case, the boards noted that in determining similarity, boards have refused to award reprocurement costs where fragmentation of the work in the reprocurement "materially altered the terms and conditions . . . of the original contract" or resulted in "substantial increase in the reprocurement contract price." See *Alfred L. Scevers, Jr.*, IBCA 1358-5-80, 83-2 BCA ¶16,579 (excess reprocurement costs not awarded where government reprocurement for tree-thinning contract materially altered the terms and conditions of the contract by dividing the remaining acres into two tracts, extending the time of performance, and awarding two separate contracts), and *G. O'Connor*, AGBCA 75-154, 78-1 BCA ¶12,981 (excess reprocurement costs not awarded because the reprocurement contract was almost three times the original price and material differences existed between the services in the original contract and the reprocurement agreement). It has been held that, under the construction contract provisions, the government is not entitled to make "material changes" in the reprocurement specifications resulting in "substantial alterations" in the work, *United States v. Axman*, 234 U.S. 36 (1914); *California Bridge & Constr. Co. v. United States*, 50 Ct. Cl. 40 (1915), *aff'd*, 245 U.S. 337 (1917).

The reprocured supplies or services must meet the similarity test, even though they do not have to be identical to the terminated work, or else the government loses its right to recover excess costs and must recover, if at all, under its common law right to damages. The effect of this rule is that, when a reprocured item is not "similar," the excess costs may not be adjusted to account for dissimilarities. In contrast, when the similarity test is met, but the reprocured item is not identical, the excess costs are adjusted to account for the differences in the items. The rationale for this dichotomy is that when the changes in the reprocured item are substantial and make the work more "onerous," the reprocurement price does not serve as a valid basis for comparison, *Octagon Process, Inc.*, ASBCA 3981, 58-1 BCA ¶1773. See *Romeo P. Yusi & Co.*, ASBCA 19810, 76-1 BCA ¶11,835, holding that the items were "not sufficiently comparable" and that the difference rendered it "impossible to make a rational comparison of the work." In *Cosmos Eng'rs, Inc.*, ASBCA 24270, 88-2 BCA ¶20,795, the board concluded that the differences between the defaulted contract specifications and the reprocurement contract specifications were so substantial that "to require [the contractor] to pay excess reprocurement costs would be patently unfair."

When determining the amount of excess reprocurement costs, the effect contract changes have on the contract price properly may be a fact issue and should not be decided on a motion for summary judgment, *Seaboard Lumber Co. v. United States*, 41 Fed. Cl. 401 (1998), *aff'd*, 308 F.3d 1283 (Fed. Cir. 2002).

a. Changes Reducing Cost of Work

While the lack-of-similarity argument appears to be a sufficient basis for denying excess costs when the effect of changes in the specifications is to make the reprocured article more expensive to produce than the defaulted item, its application would seem not to be called for in cases where the effect of specification changes is to make the reprocured item easier and less expensive to produce than the terminated item. Thus, the relaxation of specifications on reprocurement would appear to cause no harm to the defaulted contractor, would appear to be consistent with the government's requirement to mitigate its damages, and ought to be encouraged if it can clearly be shown that the changed reprocurement was less expensive than reprocurement of identical items would have been. Nevertheless, in some cases involving relaxed specifications, excess costs have been denied on the basis of dissimilarity. In *Hofman Indus., Inc.*, ASBCA 3435, 57-2 BCA ¶1468, the board stated that the specification changes on reprocurement, even though making the item less expensive to produce, showed that the government did not want the original item, never got it, and therefore should not be able to collect damages for not obtaining it on the original contract. In *Lome Elecs., Inc.*, ASBCA 8642, 1963 BCA ¶3833, the board recognized the mitigation argument but rejected it, stating at 19,102:

> The Government contends the change in specifications simplified the item, made it less costly and in effect rendered it an off the shelf item for the reprocurement contractor and therefore saved the defaulted contractor money. That the Government in its repurchase received nothing more than it was entitled to under the [contractor's] contract and received a similar item which it vitally needed, and its effort to simplify the specifications as to the computer, can only be interpreted as an honest effort to obtain the items needed as soon as possible, and at the lowest possible price.

> The board is impressed with the Government's contention and argument with respect to mitigating the amount of the excess cost. However, the board, although it recognizes the laudability of the Government's efforts to minimize the cost of reprocurement, does not believe that the reprocurement of a cheaper type of item is of itself determinative of this appeal.

The board in *B & M Constr., Inc.*, AGBCA 90-165-1, 93-1 BCA ¶25,431, reaffirmed this general rule, stating at 126,669:

> We have little sympathy for a contractor who abandons performance. Given the CO's clear rejection of [the contractor's] proposed design change, [the contractor] had a duty to proceed diligently with performance and file a claim for changed or additional work. [The contractor] did not so do.
>
> Nevertheless, we find that there were material differences between the project to be constructed under [the contractor's] contract and that ultimately delivered on reprocurement. The Government no longer wanted the access ramp removed or the area returned to its pristine pre-construction state. Nor did the Government want a field stone headwall or off-site disposal of construction debris. The terms and conditions of reprocurement differed materially from those under the defaulted contract, and SCS's treatment of [the contractor] and the reprocurement contractor was indeed disparate. We conclude that these factors alone are sufficient to support denial of the Government's claim for excess costs.

The fact that the differences in contracts reduced the difficulty and cost of the project was considered irrelevant in the board's determination of similarity. However, this logic will be inapposite where the relaxation of the contract requirements is found to be immaterial to the "quality, function, or manufacture" of the product. See *Meyer Labs., Inc.*, ASBCA 19525, 87-2 BCA ¶19,810 (allowing recovery of excess reprocurement costs where the relaxation of testing requirements did not relate to the causes of the default termination).

b. Test for Determining Similarity

One aspect of the determination of similarity involves comparing the end item delivered on the reprocurement contract with the item specified in the original contract at the time of default. It is generally stated that similarity requires that the item be similar in "physical and mechanical characteristics as well as functional purpose," *Lome Elecs., Inc.*, ASBCA 8642, 1963 BCA ¶3833. See *AGH Indus., Inc.*, ASBCA 27960, 89-2 BCA ¶21,637, in which the board determined that changes in testing requirements for helicopter skid tube assemblies were significant, stating at 108,863:

> The test to be applied in determining similarity is a comparison of end items delivered under the reprocurement contract with the item specified in the original contract at the time of default. It is well settled that the word "similar" need not be treated as meaning "identical."
>
> Therefore, while it is true that minor variations in the repurchased items will not relieve a contractor of its liability under the DEFAULT clause for excess reprocurement costs, substantial and material differences between the end items in the original contract and reprocurement contract will completely relieve the contractor of its liability for excess costs. [citation omitted]
>
> Moreover, changes in the specifications after the default of [the contractor's] contract do not invalidate the excess reprocurement cost assessment where the changes are corrections of errors or omissions, normal updating of specifications as more production experience leads to simplifying manufacture or product improvement as long as the specification changes do not go to the heart of the procurement by affecting function of the product or by affecting the repurchase price. However, a difference in the reprocurement contract requiring or omitting a stringent test may invalidate the assessment of excess reprocurement costs. Thus, if the difference in testing would cause greater acceptance or rejection of one product over another, the difference would be significant. *Marmac Industries, Inc.*, ASBCA 12158, 72-1 BCA ¶9249.

See also *B & M Constr., Inc.*, AGBCA 90-165-1, 93-1 BCA ¶25,431, in which the board denied the government's claim for excess costs of reprocurement because the government's deletion of a contract requirement to remove an access ramp amounted to a substantial change in the desired end item.

One apparently broader test suggested for determining similarity is whether the changes in specifications would have fallen within the scope of the Changes clause of the defaulted contract. In *Skiatron Elecs. & Television Corp.*, ASBCA 9564, 65-2 BCA ¶5098, the board held that variations in reprocured resistance bridges were similar because they could have been made under the Changes clause, stating at 24,016:

> To hold otherwise would defeat the very purpose of the reprocurement privilege the Default clause allows or it would place the Government in the dilemma of reprocuring obsolete items in order to effect an assessment of excess costs. Obviously, this was never intended. No where in the record do we find any basis for vitiating the entire assessment or working a specific downward adjustment in the amount.

See also *Angler's Co.*, GSBCA 4390, 76-2 BCA ¶12,065, *recons. denied*, 77-1 BCA ¶12,319, *rev'd on other grounds*, 220 Ct. Cl. 727 (1979), in which the board held that the use of commercial rather than specification vinyl did not render the procured portfolios so different that they could not have been ordered under the Changes clause of the original contract. In *Dave's Aluminum Siding, Inc.*, ASBCA 34092, 90-3 BCA ¶23,053, the board found that changes in the degree of painting required under the reprocurement contract did not establish dissimilarity because such a revision fell within the scope of the Changes clause under the original contract. In view of the broad rights given to the government under the Changes clause, it is doubtful that this test is usable in all cases. In practice, the boards rarely even mention this approach as a viable standard for determining similarity.

Where there is no proof that the change caused an increase in the reprocurement price, similarity normally will be found. See *Arjay Mach. Co.*, ASBCA 16535, 73-2 BCA ¶10,179 (slight modifications of the drawings were not material); *Meyer Labs, Inc.*, ASBCA 19525, 87-2 BCA ¶19,810 (substitution of materials and modes of measurement did not preclude a similarity finding as they were minor variations); and *Solar Labs., Inc.*, ASBCA 19957, 76-2 BCA ¶12,115 (revised purchase description neither increased costs nor created substantial or material changes in functional purpose or physical and mechanical characteristics of the pads). Even where there is an increase in cost, similarity may be found where "the material, essential configuration and purpose of the reprocured articles [are] the same" as those that were to be furnished by the defaulted contractor, *H.N. Bailey & Assocs. v. United States*, 196 Ct. Cl. 166, 449 F.2d 376 (1971).

The reprocured work was found to be similar in *Associated Traders, Inc. v. United States*, 144 Ct. Cl. 744, 169 F. Supp. 502 (1959) (although reprocurement contractor furnished a different quality adhesive than defaulted contractor, both items met the same specifications); *Guenther Sys., Inc.*, ASBCA 18343, 77-1 BCA ¶12,501 (reprocured components found functionally, physically, and mechanically similar although manufactured from bar stock rather than from castings); *UMM, Inc.*, ENGBCA 5330, 87-2 BCA ¶19,893 (new contract for lawn mowing work incorporated essentially "the same services . . . on virtually identical terms" as the defaulted contract); *Sequal, Inc.*, ASBCA 30838, 88-1 BCA ¶20,382 (minor dimensional differences in specifications insufficient to find dissimilarity); *Predator Sys., Inc.*, NASABCA 43-0291, 92-2 BCA ¶24,903 (reprocurement modification changing the pounds per square inch on the calibration system did not render the new contract dissimilar); and *Arctic Corner, Inc.*, ASBCA 38075, 94-1 BCA ¶26,317 (similarity found where the reprocurement involved the same specifications and basically the same drawings as the defaulted contract). In *MPT Enters.*, ASBCA 25483, 83-2 BCA ¶16,767, the board upheld an excess cost assessment based on repurchase of "newly manufactured items" following default under a contract that permitted the contractor to provide "surplus" items, even though the repurchase price was three times the original contract price, because "it does not appear unreasonable in the light of the price history and the risk appellant assumed under the Default clause that the respondent might reprocure the more expensive manufactured units in lieu of surplus."

The reprocurement was found dissimilar in *American Sheet Metal Corp., v. General Servs. Admin.*, GSBCA 14066, 99-1 BCA ¶30,329 (reprocurement contractor certified only to install a completely different roof system, with a different number of membranes and a different application process); *Ace Reforestation, Inc.*, AGBCA 84-272-1, 87-3 BCA ¶20,218 (deletion of hand-scalping requirement and clearer indication of the degree of work to be completed under the reprocurement contract rendered it dissimilar to the defaulted contract); *Tenney Eng'g, Inc.*, ASBCA 19289, 75-1 BCA ¶11,249 (added floor support "significantly additional" to that required by specifications); *Suffolk Envtl. Magnetics, Inc.*, ASBCA 17593, 74-2 BCA ¶10,771 (waiver of tolerance specifications rendered reprocured items dissimilar in physical and mechanical characteristics); *Cosmos Eng'rs, Inc.*, ASBCA 24270, 88-2 BCA ¶20,795 (substantial relaxation of specifications on reprocurement of radio transmitters precluded award of excess reprocurement costs); *Star Food Processing, Inc.*, ASBCA 34161, 90-1 BCA ¶22,390 (lack of similarity between reprocured diced beef and terminated ham slices prevented recovery); *G. O'Connor*, AGBCA 75-154, 78-1 BCA ¶12,981 (extension of work area resulting in a price more than twice that of the original contract); *NEH Logging*, AGBCA 76-187, 77-2 BCA ¶12,850 (reduction in work area and government's inability to allow salvage rights to timber on reprocurement constituted material variations); *Aerosonic Corp.*, ASBCA 11718, 72-1 BCA ¶9241 (repurchase contract was "essentially a research and development rather than a production effort"); and *Accutherm, Inc.*, ASBCA 25474, 83-1 BCA ¶16,307 (repurchase specifications called for heat-treat furnaces "more modern in material and design").

The "physical and mechanical characteristics" test has been held not to be applicable to a reprocurement under a terminated two-step formally advertised contract, *Steelship Corp.*, ENGBCA 3830, 78-2 BCA ¶13,478. There, the second low bidder on the two-step procurement was awarded the reprocurement contract for an item that was significantly better and more expensive than the one that was to have been provided under the defaulted contract. The board determined that a two-step procurement differs from the normal procedure in that the competition is on performance specifications. It further noted that, if the physical and mechanical characteristics test for similarity were applied, the government would be unable to recover any excess costs despite its efforts to "cover," stating at 65,943:

> In this situation, we believe that it is sufficient that the replacement item is similar in function and utility, and that variations in physical characteristics need not (subject to the duty of mitigation) bar the Government from recovering reasonable excess costs.

Note, however, that the board did hold the contractor entitled to a $140,000 reduction in the excess cost assessment to account for this "betterment" in design.

c. Changes in Inspection and Testing

The changes do not have to be in the end item specifications for dissimilarity to be found. The addition or deletion of an inspection or test can result in the excess cost assessment being invalidated. In *AGH Indus., Inc.*, ASBCA 27960, 89-2 BCA ¶21,637, the tightening of tolerance specifications on a helicopter assembly contract rendered the reprocurement dissimilar because it would have an effect on the rejection rate of the reprocurement as well as the repurchase price. Similarly, in *Luis Martinez*, AGBCA 86-148-1, 87-3 BCA ¶20,219, the board found the reprocurement dissimilar because the resolicited contract had relaxed the degree of compliance necessary to satisfy the standard for acceptability of grubbing work, which amounted to substantially disparate treatment. However, not all changes in tests or inspections result in dissimilarity. In *Puroflow Corp.*, ASBCA 36058, 93-3 BCA ¶26,191, the board held that the addition in their entirety of several military specifications that had only been referenced in the defaulted contract did not render the reprocurement contract dissimilar. The board found it compelling that the variations were shown neither to have caused any unreasonable expense to the reprocurement contractor nor to have created a different, more expensive product. Likewise, in *Churchill Chem. Corp.*, GSBCA 4353, 77-1 BCA ¶12,318, *aff'd*, 221 Ct. Cl. 284, 602 F.2d 358 (1979), the reprocurement was similar despite the addition of a test for adhesive quality of a sealing compound because there was no evidence that the addition induced increases in the pricing data utilized on reprocurement, and in *Meyer Labs, Inc.*, ASBCA 19525, 87-2 BCA ¶19,810, no dissimilarity was found because the addition of several tests did not affect the function or manufacture of the end items.

d. Changes in Terms and Conditions

The GAO has concluded that there is no regulatory requirement that a reprocurement be conducted using precisely the same terms as the original procurement, *Vereinigte Gebaudereinigungsgesellschaft*, Comp. Gen. Dec. B-280805, 98-2 CPD ¶117. Dissimilarity may be found, however, if the terms and conditions of the reprocurement contract differ materially from those of the defaulted contract, *Seay's Moving & Storage Co.*, ASBCA 12806, 69-1 BCA ¶7639 (reprocurement of moving services through purchase orders given by oral quotations held to be "a clean break" from the original contract); *Allied Sales Co.*, ASBCA 12650, 68-2 BCA ¶7257 (omission of a price warranty clause); *B & M Constr., Inc.*, AGBCA 90-165-1, 93-1 BCA ¶25,431 (deletion of access ramp requirement found to be a material change in terms and conditions). The focus in such cases is usually on whether the different terms and conditions would increase the reprocurement contractor's cost of performance or result in higher bids. Thus, in *Skiatron Elecs. & Television Corp.*, ASBCA 9564, 65-2 BCA ¶5098, the insertion of a liquidated damage clause in the reprocurement contract was held not to make the reprocurement dissimilar because it did not increase the cost of performance and the price was unchanged in alternate bidding—with or without the liquidated damages clause. In *Rhocon Constructors*, AGBCA 86-125-1, 91-1 BCA ¶23,308, the board noted that, despite evidence of similarity, a 25 percent increase in reprocurement price coupled with a lack of evidence addressing the terms and conditions of the reprocurement contract precluded an assessment of excess reprocurement costs.

In *James A. Connor*, ASBCA 10356, 68-2 BCA ¶7409, the government terminated a negotiated fixed-price contract for tracking antennas and awarded a cost-plus-incentive-fee contract on reprocurement. In response to the defaulted contractor's arguments that this change in pricing arrangement should invalidate the excess costs assessment, the board stated at 34,451:

> Further, it does not appear that the use of the cost-plus incentive fee method of contracting enlarged the damages. In fact, based upon the Radiation two-phase proposal, the first phase alone would have been, according to its 26 October 1964 proposal, $187,309 and, as indicated in its 6 October 1964 proposal, the second phase had a "ball park estimate" of $500,000. If this is any indication of what its contingency planning would be, a fixed-price bid may have been considerably higher than the actual cost-plus incentive fee contract turned out to be. It is fairly clear from the record that there were many uncertainties once the Air Force made the decision to take and use the ASI items in their condition at the time of termination. If the solutions were not clear and simple, it is because the problems left with the Air Force as a result of the ASI default were not clear and simple.

Contrast *Matthews Co.*, AGBCA 459, 76-2 BCA ¶12,164, *recons. denied*, 77-1 BCA ¶12,434, in which the board found that a reprocurement contractor working on a cost-reimbursement contract had incurred costs that were "clearly excessive."

Similarity has been found despite a difference in terms and conditions, *Lester Phillips, Inc.*, ASBCA 20735, 77-1 BCA ¶12,447 (although clauses specifying the date for container removal and limiting the number of refuse collection containers were not included in reprocurement contracts, the number actually used did not exceed the original limits, and the reprocurement contractor's bid was slightly lower than its bid on the original contract); *Schmalz Constr. Ltd.*, AGBCA 92-177-1, 94-1 BCA ¶26,423 (modification to reprocurement contract deleting the last 836 feet of road construction found not to be a material change in terms and conditions); *George E. Marshall & Gordon L. Blackwell*, ENGBCA 6066, 00-1 BCA ¶30,730 (reprocurement contract differed from the terminated contract due to "conditions on the ground after [the contractor] abandoned the work and by minor, required updating of the specifications and clauses that have not been shown to have increased the costs to complete").

e. Changes in Method of Procurement

A change in procurement technique is not, in and of itself, a sufficient reason to find dissimilarity in the reprocurement. The courts and boards have held that "[i]n reprocuring items on a defaulted contract, the contracting officer has very broad discretionary powers," and the choice of procurement methods falls within that discretion, *Astro-Space Labs., Inc. v. United States*, 200 Ct. Cl. 282, 470 F.2d 1003 (1972). See *Old Dominion Sec., Inc.*, GSBCA 9126, 90-2 BCA ¶22,745, where reprocurement of a security services contract by negotiation rather than sealed bidding was found to be within the contracting officer's discretion. The board dismissed as speculation the contractor's argument that the use of negotiation rather than sealed bidding drove up reprocurement prices. See also *Orlotronics Corp.*, ASBCA 23287, 79-2 BCA ¶13,912, in which the board rejected as speculative and unsupported a contractor's contention that reprocurement of aircraft barrel assemblies through negotiation rather than formal advertising had resulted in increases in previously submitted offers. In *Rayco, Inc.*, ENGBCA 4792, 88-2 BCA ¶20,671, the fragmentation of a construction contract reprocurement into 13 purchase orders and two solicitations for bids was upheld because, in the circumstances, the fragmentation was reasonable and within the contracting officer's discretion. However, see *Mathews Co.*, AGBCA 459, 76-2 BCA ¶12,164, *recons. denied*, 77-1 BCA ¶12,434, in which the board found that the government had failed to mitigate damages and obtain a reasonable price in reprocuring a fixed-price construction contract on a cost-reimbursement basis. In denying the government's claim for excess reprocurement costs, the board held that the reprocurement contract was inadequately supervised and that the contractor incurred costs that were clearly excessive.

Generally, the statutes and regulations governing federal procurements are not strictly applicable to reprocurement of defaulted contracts. *E. Huttenbauer & Son, Inc.*, Comp. Gen. Dec. B-239142.2, 90-2 CPD ¶140. Rather, the contracting officer may use any terms and acquisition method deemed appropriate under the circumstances that result in a reasonable price and maximum practicable competition. For example, the contracting officer may also choose to reprocure the items by placing an order under an existing Federal Supply Schedule contract rather than conduct a new competition under which the defaulted contractor might have participated, *ATA Def. Indus., Inc.*, Comp. Gen. Dec. B-275303, 97-1 CPD ¶161.

2. Effect of Relaxed Specifications That Contractor Could Have Met

Some boards of contract appeals are reluctant to assess excess costs based on relaxed specifications that the defaulted contractor could have met, even though the default termination is held to be proper. See *Blake Constr. Co.*, GSBCA 4013, 75-2 BCA ¶11,487, stating at 54,806:

> It is an established principle in the law of Government contracts that the contractor will not be liable for the excess costs of reprocurement where the contract requirements are relaxed on reprocurement and where the facts indicate that the contractor could have performed given the same relaxation in requirements. *Appeal of Federal Identification Co.*, ASBCA 9117, 1964 BCA ¶4191.

See also *Luis Martinez*, AGBCA 86-148-1, 87-3 BCA ¶20,219, in which the board further established this principle, stating at 102,407:

> [T]he burden [is] on the [contractor] to show performance could have been accomplished under the relaxed standard. . . . Mere allegations without more are not acceptable as proof. [The contractor] has, however, shown a relaxed standard was applied. We conclude such showing, coupled with the change in contract specifications, evidences so material a difference between the original and reprocurement contracts as written and administered as to preclude assessment of reprocurement costs.

Accord, *Sterling Tool, Inc.*, ASBCA 19790, 75-2 BCA ¶11,577. See *F.R. Schultz Constr. Co.*, AGBCA 455, 79-2 BCA ¶13,890, overturning an excess costs assessment where the government failed to place any time limitation on completion of the work in the reprocurement contract; and *Pervo Paint Co.*, GSBCA 8220, 87-1 BCA ¶19,409, finding that where the reprocurement contractor also failed to maintain proper testing controls that had led to the default of the original contractor, excess reprocurement costs were improper. Compare, however, *Rio Hondo Containers*, GSBCA 3494, 72-2 BCA ¶9514 (no indication that elimination of a sidewall thickness requirement from the reprocurement contract for plastic caps would have prevented the performance difficulties encountered by the defaulted contractor); *Russ Leadabrand*, AGBCA 75-126, 77-2 BCA ¶12,765 (no evidence that the defaulted contractor could have properly written and prepared Forest Service leaflets had it been granted the same time extension); and *Birken Mfg. Co.*, ASBCA 32590, 90-2 BCA ¶22,845 (no evidence that the defaulted contractor could have delivered spacers had first article deliveries not been required). Generally, the contractor bears the burden of proving that it could have performed under the specifications incorporated in the reprocurement contract, *T.M. Indus.*, ASBCA 21025, 77-1 BCA ¶12,400, *recons. denied*, 77-1 BCA ¶12,545; *Butler Enters.*, AGBCA 74-106, 76-2 BCA ¶12,094.

There is authority that the contractor's ability to perform to the reprocurement specifications is not relevant to the issue of excess costs, *American Sur.y Co. of N.Y. v. United States*, 317 F.2d 652 (8th Cir. 1963) (substitution permitted to reprocurement contractor but denied to original contractor); *United States v. McMullen*, 222 U.S. 460 (1912) (government denying permission to defaulted contractor to dump spoil in deep water and granting permission to completing contractor did not preclude assessment of cost since diminished cost was the only change).

3. Variations in Quantity Reprocured

The contracting officer has broad discretion to vary the quantity reprocured, and if increased costs result, the reprocurement cost will be adjusted rather than totally disallowed, *Consolidated Airborne Sys., Inc. v. United States*, 172 Ct. Cl. 588, 348 F.2d 941 (1965). For example, in *M.S.I. Corp.*, VACAB 599, 67-2 BCA ¶6643, where the government contracted for completion of repair of 600 feet of footwalk but the original contractor had been obliged to repair only 400 feet, the board reduced the government's assessment of costs against the contractor by one-third. In many cases, the purchase of a larger quantity tends to reduce the unit price of the items. Thus, the defaulted contractor is often benefited by an increased quantity because the excess costs are measured by the unit price paid on reprocurement for the number of units that were to have been provided under the terminated contract, *Charles Nugent*, AGBCA 92-195-1, 93-3 BCA ¶26,213 (deduction for variation of quantity of acres to be scalped led to reduction of excess cost recovery); *F.P. Pla Tool & Mfg. Co.*, ASBCA 19073, 75-1 BCA ¶11,091 (increase did not prejudice the defaulted contractor).

On the other hand, the impact of purchasing fewer items may be to increase the unit cost. In such cases, the increased unit cost should be offset against the lower number of units. Thus, a case-by-case price comparison must be made. When there is a determination that the reduction in quantities has no impact on the price, the full amount of the excess cost assessment will generally be upheld, *Consolidated Mach. Corp.*, ASBCA 14366, 73-1 BCA ¶9942 (a quantity discount for the original quantity was apportioned equally among those units and subtracted from the total of the reprocurement to arrive at the excess cost assessment); *Bardeen Mfg. Co.*, ASBCA 19128, 75-1 BCA ¶11,036 (no impact on price through repurchase of reduced quantity except for minor errors in computation that were adjusted by the board). However, where the reduction does increase the cost of the reprocurement, a downward adjustment in the excess cost assessment normally will be made, *Agni Eng'g Co.*, ASBCA 10885, 67-1 BCA ¶6250 (reprocurement contractor's quotation for the same quantity reflected a 19 percent increase in unit price but indicated a 43 percent price increase on the reduced quantity); *R & O Indus., Inc.*, GSBCA 4917, 79-1 BCA ¶13,832 (increased price not linked solely to reduction in quantity but also to inflationary market conditions); *Rayco, Inc.*, ENGBCA 4792, 88-2 BCA ¶20,671 (reduction of quantity by a factor of 10 or greater found to be the logical cause of increased prices on reprocurement and did not reduce recovery).

When comparison of unit prices of the original contract items and the reduced quantity of reprocured items is impossible, the excess cost assessment may be completely denied, *Management Servs., Inc.*, ASBCA 11190, 67-1 BCA ¶6103 (price adjustment mechanism in the reprocurement contract indicated that the price of meals varied inversely with the quantity). In *Alfred L. Scevers, Jr.*, IBCA 1358-5-80, 83-2 BCA ¶16,579, the board disallowed an excess cost assessment where terminated work under a tree-thinning contract was divided into two tracts and reprocured under two separate contracts, causing fixed costs to be allocated over a smaller number of acres and resulting in a higher price per acre. See also *B & M Constr., Inc.*, AGBCA 90-165-1, 93-1 BCA ¶25,431, in which the board found that neither the unreasonably low government estimate nor the unreasonably high reprocurement contract price provided a reasonable basis for calculating excess costs. Therefore, the costs were denied completely.

When a requirements contract is terminated, the government is entitled to assess costs not only on the items actually ordered but not delivered under the defaulted contract, but also on items that could have been ordered under the defaulted contract, *Interroyal Corp.*, GSBCA 5439, 83-1 BCA ¶16,339; *Zan Mach. Co.*, ASBCA 39462, 91-3 BCA ¶24,085.

4. Mitigation

In pricing and awarding the reprocurement contract, the government must endeavor to mitigate its damages, *Cascade Pac. Int'l v. United States*, 773 F.2d 287 (Fed. Cir. 1985), and make the reprocurement award at a reasonable price, FAR 49.402-6. Both these requirements will be satisfied if the government acts reasonably in selecting the reprocurement contractor and in establishing the reprocurement price. In *Barrett Ref. Corp.*, ASBCA 36590, 91-1 BCA ¶23,566, the board stated at 118,145:

> The duty the Government owes the defaulted contractor in reprocuring for its account is not one of perfection, but one of reasonableness and prudence under the circumstances. [citations omitted] This duty is to be carried

out within the confines of Federal procurement statutes, regulations, policies and directives and the Government is not required to change such policies to secure a better reprocurement price for a defaulted contractor. *X-Tyal International Corp.*, ASBCA Nos. 24353, 26495, 84-2 BCA ¶17,251. Further, it is not the contracting officer's obligation to do everything that he or she might to secure a lower price for a defaulted contractor, and in the process subordinate the Government's own best interests.

In making this determination, the board will consider both the government's actions and the relationship between the reprocurement price and that of the defaulted contract. In *Solar Labs., Inc.*, ASBCA 19957, 76-2 BCA ¶12,115, the board identified a number of the factors to be considered, stating at 58,196:

> Specifically, in numerous cases upholding assessments of excess costs incurred in a sole-source reprocurement, this Board and others, in determining reasonableness of the reprocurement price and whether the Government had made reasonable efforts to mitigate damages, have considered whether give-and-take negotiations were conducted, whether a cost breakdown was obtained, whether the Government performed any cost or price analysis, and whether the Government obtained a satisfactory explanation for any substantial increase over the reprocurement contractor's bid on the original contract. See, for example, *Consolidated Airborne Systems, Inc.*, ASBCA 5498, 61-1 BCA ¶2933, in which the Board, relying on the facts that the Government obtained cost data and negotiated a price reduction, upheld the assessment of excess costs, in the face of a substantial increase over the original contract price. The decision was sustained by the Court of Claims. *Consolidated Airborne Systems, Inc. v. United States*, [*supra*], 172 Ct. Cl. 588, 348 F.2d 941 (1965). In upholding the reasonableness of the reprocurement price as a basis for measuring excess costs, the Board has also relied on the fact that vigorous, arm's-length negotiations were conducted, even though no price reduction resulted. *Kollsman Instrument Corp.*, ASBCA 10667, 66-1 BCA ¶5696. A similar result was reached in *Applied Scientific Production and Research*, ASBCA 17245, 74-2 BCA ¶10,877, in which the Board noted that the contracting officer had obtained an explanation for the difference between the reprocurement contractor's price as compared with his original bid.
>
> On the other hand, the amount of the Government's excess cost recovery has frequently been reduced where the Government did not show adequate efforts to obtain the lowest reasonable price on the reprocurement, especially where the reprocurement contractor was a sole source. In some cases the Board has relied simply on the absence of an explanation for increases in the reprocurement contractor's price over his bid on the defaulted contract or other earlier contracts. *Standard Engineering & Manufacturing Co.*, ASBCA 3733, 57-2 BCA ¶1477 at p. 5067, *reconsid. denied*, 57-2 BCA ¶1568 (10.1 and 25.9 percent higher, respectively, than two of his previous contract prices); *Dakota Process Equipment Co.*, ASBCA 4435, 58-2 BCA ¶1981 (55 percent increase over original bid one year before); *Agni Engineering Co.*, ASBCA Nos. 10885 and 11535, 67-1 BCA ¶6250 at p. 28,951 (net unexplained increase of 24 percent over original bid 21 months before).
>
> In other cases the Board has emphasized specific actions that the Government could or should have taken, but did not, to assure price reasonableness or mitigate excess costs—sometimes in the face of substantial increases over previous prices, but other times even without mention of such increases. In these cases the Board has emphasized variously the absence of give- and-take negotiations to obtain a lower price or an explanation of price increases; the absence of inquiry as to catalog or market prices; the absence of showing of prices established in earlier Government contracts; the failure to obtain a cost breakdown; the omission of a most-favored customer warranty included in the defaulted contract; the failure to perform price analysis; and the inconsistency of an explanation of a price increase even where a cost breakdown was obtained. *De Lisser Manufacturing Corp.*, ASBCA 1002, 22 September 1952, *reconsid. denied*, 9 January 1953 (reprocurement price 91 percent higher than defaulted contract price and 16 1/3 percent higher than his bid thereon one year before); *General Electronic Laboratories, Inc.*, ASBCA Nos. 8918 and 8926, 1964 BCA ¶4326 at p. 20,932 (25 percent increase over original bid five months before); *Goldhaber*, ASBCA Nos. 8277 and 8370, 65-2 BCA ¶5083 at p. 23,955; *Lutz Company*, GSBCA 2173, 68-1 BCA ¶6762 (10 percent increase over original bid five months before); *Reliable Maintenance Service*, ASBCA 11010, 68-1 BCA ¶6853 (24 percent increase over original bid five months before); *Atlas Manufacturing Co., Inc.*, ASBCA 15177, 71-2 BCA ¶9026 at 41,929; *Fitzgerald Laboratories, Inc.*, ASBCA Nos. 15205 and 15594, 71-2 BCA ¶9029 (40 percent increase over original bid); *Empresas Electronicas Walser, Inc.*, ASBCA 17524, 74-2

BCA ¶10,664 at p. 50,639; *Century Tool Co.*, GSBCA 4000, 76-1 BCA ¶11,855; *Marine Engine Specialties Corp.*, ASBCA Nos. 20418, 20521 and 20522, 76-1 BCA ¶11,891 (in ASBCA 20521, 25 percent increase over original bid); *Marine Engine Specialties Corp.*, ASBCA 21053, 76-2 BCA ¶12,034 (23 July 1976) (19 percent increase over original bid).

The board found that the government had failed to mitigate because, despite a 41 percent increase in cost, it had not demanded cost data, conducted a price analysis, checked catalog prices, negotiated for a lower price, or sought a quantity discount.

a. Lack of Negotiation or Price Analysis

The government must follow reasonable business practices to ensure that the reprocurement price is not inflated. In *Century Tool Co.*, GSBCA 4000, 76-1 BCA ¶11,855, the board found no mitigation where the contracting officer had neither negotiated for a lower price nor attempted to obtain an explanation, despite the fact that the reprocurement unit price was $.03 greater than a bid by the same contractor two weeks earlier. See also *A.L.S. Elec. Corp.*, ASBCA 18417, 74-1 BCA ¶10,589 (failure to investigate reprocurement contractor's much lower bids on previous contracts resulted in a repurchase price that was "grossly excessive and completely out of line"); *Wise Instrumentation & Control, Inc.*, NASABCA 1072-12, 75-2 BCA ¶11,478, *recons. denied*, 76-1 BCA ¶11,641 (no give-and-take negotiations or price analysis though procurement price was 37 percent over the original price); *Associated Cleaning, Inc.*, GSBCA 8360, 91-1 BCA ¶23,360 (use of flawed price estimate found unreasonable where the reprocurement contract price amounted to 30 percent more than the original contract price and was higher than the bids of all those who responded to the original solicitation); *T.M. Indus.*, ASBCA 21026, 77-1 BCA ¶12,451 (no price analysis when reprocurement contractor's bid was 35 percent higher than the price of the defaulted contract); *Birken Mfg. Co.*, ASBCA 32590, 90-2 BCA ¶22,845 (lack of price analysis and negotiation with the reprocurement contractor when price was 67 percent higher than that of the defaulted contractor found unreasonable); *Rhocon Constructors*, AGBCA 86-125-1, 91-1 BCA ¶23,308 (25 percent increase in price with no evidence of efforts by the government to mitigate held unreasonable); *Puroflow Corp.*, ASBCA 36058, 93-3 BCA ¶26,191 (excess costs reduced due to the lack of negotiations with the reprocurement contractor, whose bid was 12.5 percent higher than it had been for the original solicitation); and *Acorn Specialty & Supply Co.*, ASBCA 22710, 79-1 BCA ¶13,820 (failure to adequately explore the technical acceptability of another manufacturer's product that was known to be much lower in price).

For cases finding the reprocurement price to be reasonable because of adequate negotiation, see *Airosal Co.*, GSBCA 4374, 76-1 BCA ¶11,781 (government researched increased performance costs and conducted bona fide negotiations to award contract for accelerated delivery costing 32 percent more on one item and at least 97 percent more on another); *Pinel Tool Co.*, GSBCA 4380, 76-2 BCA ¶12,009 (price analysis conducted and found to justify award where only one offer received); *American Kal Enters., Inc.*, GSBCA 4449, 76-2 BCA ¶11,929 (negotiations for lower price unsuccessful, but the closeness of the three offered prices indicated reasonable market price); *Mattatuck Mfg. Co.*, GSBCA 4847, 80-1 BCA ¶14,349 (reprocurement price 87 percent higher found reasonable based on general increase in steel prices, accelerated delivery requirement, and original contract price that was 32 percent low); *Barrett Ref. Corp.*, ASBCA 36590, 91-1 BCA ¶23,566 (temporary shifting of oil from different suppliers already under contract when other contractors were available at a lower price found reasonable because this was the prior government practice); and *Great Northern Forestry Serv.*, AGBCA 85-260-1, 90-2 BCA ¶22,668 (8 percent increase in price for immediate reprocurement found reasonable given that the reprocurement contractor had been the second low bidder on the original procurement and a substantial amount of rework needed to be done).

b. Lack of Competition

The extent of competition on reprocurement is also important to a determination of reasonableness. See FAR 49.402-6(b), stating that "the contracting officer shall obtain competition to the maximum extent practicable for the repurchase." Nonetheless, each reprocurement is evaluated in terms of the circumstances faced by the government at the time of the reprocurement. See *Old Dominion Sec., Inc.*, GSBCA 9126, 90-2 BCA ¶22,745, in which the board concluded that the method of reprocurement is within the "very broad discretionary powers" of the contracting officer and is not, by itself, sufficient to overcome a claim for excess costs of reprocurement; and *Interstate Forestry, Inc.*, AGBCA 89-114-1, 91-1 BCA

¶23,660, in which the board cited FAR 49.402-6 for the proposition that, for reprocurement, the contracting officer may use "any terms and acquisition method deemed appropriate" as long as it is completed promptly and competition is obtained to the "maximum extent practicable." See also *H & H Mfg. Co. v. United States*, 168 Ct. Cl. 873 (1964), holding that a sole source, negotiated reprocurement was justified by the urgent need although the unit price was nearly 60 percent above that of the original contract. The importance of competition as a factor in determining whether the government acted reasonably may diminish when there is an urgent need for the supplies or services or when other special circumstances preclude full competition, *Erickson Enters.*, AGBCA 77-168, 79-1 BCA ¶13,628 (government efforts to locate contractor sufficient in view of limited time to perform work); *Ross & McDonald Contracting, GmbH*, ASBCA 38154, 94-1 BCA ¶26,316 (contacting firms from original solicitation rather than resoliciting found reasonable given the urgent need for janitorial services on two military bases); *Luther Benjamin Constr. Co.*, ASBCA 40401, 93-1 BCA ¶25,459 (use of sole source negotiations found reasonable given the urgency involved in a contract for an administrative building and the fact that the government had complied with the justification and approval requirements for the establishment of compelling urgency under FAR 6.302-2). In *Ronald L. Collier*, ASBCA 26972, 89-1 BCA ¶21,328, award to a contractor doing similar work in the same region as the defaulted contractor was found reasonable due to the urgent need for the performance of such services at 550 naval bases. The board placed great emphasis on the fact that the prices paid to the reprocurement contractor were the same as those the government would have paid for the same services on a competitive basis.

The standard for determining the adequacy of the solicitation for the reprocurement was set forth in *Camrex Reliance Paint Co.*, GSBCA 6870, 85-3 BCA ¶18,376, at 92,179-80:

> To obtain adequate competition in the reprocurement, offers must be solicited from a sufficient number of competent potential sources to ensure adequate competition. The Government is not required, however, to solicit every known source of supply; nor is it required to solicit all who bid on the original solicitation. Where there is no reason to believe that solicitation of a greater number of potential contractors would have resulted in lower prices, the Government will be found to have fulfilled its duty to mitigate damages.

See *San Antonio Constr. Co.*, ASBCA 8110, 1964 BCA ¶4479 (no indication that costs would have been lower had negotiations been conducted with more than one firm); *Marmac Indus., Inc.*, ASBCA 12158, 72-1 BCA ¶9249 (only 14 of the original 57 bidders were solicited, but no evidence was presented of resultant cost increase or of other firms being qualified); *Brazier Lumber Co.*, ASBCA 18601, 76-2 BCA ¶12,207 (government solicited bids from five regular lumber suppliers on reprocurement of six contracts, and 18 of 23 line item prices were less than those quoted in a trade publication); *Star Food Processing, Inc.*, ASBCA 34161, 90-1 BCA ¶22,390 (solicitation of 10 offerors found reasonable); and *John L. Hartsoe*, AGBCA 88-116-1, 93-2 BCA ¶25,614 (award to lowest of four bidders found reasonable even though the price was 300 percent greater than that of the defaulted contractor, in part because the price was still lower than the government's in-house estimate).

In *A.L.S. Elec. Corp.*, ASBCA 18417, 74-1 BCA ¶10,589, the reprocurement was found deficient where, in addition to other problems, only three firms were orally solicited despite the existence of at least 26 other qualified manufacturers. Similarly, in *Disan Corp.*, ASBCA 21297, 79-1 BCA ¶13,677, the board overturned an excess cost assessment because only one source had been solicited and its price was approximately 200 percent higher than the defaulted contract price. In *JR & Assocs.*, ASBCA 41377, 92-1 BCA ¶24,654, the board substantially reduced a claim for excess costs where the reprocurement contract had been awarded on a sole source basis and there existed neither an urgent need for new windows nor a reasonable basis in the record for the higher price. Failure to publish the repurchase solicitation may also indicate a failure to mitigate costs, *Continental Chem. Corp.*, GSBCA 4483, 76-2 BCA ¶11,948.

Sole source reprocurement will be permitted if required by the circumstances, *Consolidated Airborne Sys., Inc. v. United States*, 172 Ct. Cl. 588, 348 F.2d 941 (1965) (urgent need); *Agni Eng'g Co.*, ASBCA 10885, 67-1 BCA ¶6250 (no evidence that other qualified producers were interested in bidding); *AAR Corp.*, ASBCA 17194, 74-1 BCA ¶10,607 (reprocurement contractor was the only supplier of the items other than the defaulted contractor and another who had been unable to perform a previous contract, the only one on the qualified products list, and the only one who could ensure timely delivery); *EDI Corp.*, ASBCA 21705, 79-1 BCA ¶13,650 (only other firm to respond to original solicitation). However, where evidence exists that other sources are capable of doing the work and are reasonably obtainable, sole source awards are improper,

John L. Hartsoe, AGBCA 88-116-1, 93-2 BCA ¶25,614 (lack of evidence of adequate competition precluded assessment of excess costs of reprocurement, despite price equal to the defaulted contractor's, in part because the reprocurement contractor had not been included in the original procurement).

In *Pastushin Aviation Co.*, ASBCA 21243, 82-1 BCA ¶15,639, the board held that the government could not recover the costs incurred by the reprocurement contractor in completing units using the defaulted contractor's termination inventory where it had never solicited "competing proposals" from other sources. The board did, however, allow the government to recover the difference between the contract price and the fair market value of the uncompleted items at the time of the default. In *Donahines Inv. Co.*, ASBCA 23825, 82-1 BCA ¶15,791, a geographical restriction in the repurchase solicitation was not grounds for upsetting an excess cost assessment where no out-of-state firms had submitted bids on the original contract and there was a question whether the government's "urgent needs" could be met by non-local firms.

c. *Soliciting Original Bidders*

It is a common practice on reprocurement for the government to solicit those firms that bid on the original procurement. See *Ross & McDonald Contracting, GmbH*, ASBCA 38154, 94-1 BCA ¶26,316. Recovery has been allowed where only the original small business bidders were contacted for reprocurement, *American Marine Upholstery Co. v. United States*, 170 Ct. Cl. 564, 345 F.2d 577 (1965). However, when a small business is granted the reprocurement contract award while the other participants are not solicited, the award has been found improper, *Associated Cleaning, Inc.*, GSBCA 8360, 91-1 BCA ¶23,360 (unreasonable to make the reprocurement contract a set-aside and award for a 30 percent higher price when the original solicitation had been an open procurement). Further, failure to make a reasonable effort at contacting the original offerors may result in denial or reduction of the excess costs assessment. See *AAA Janitorial Serv.*, ASBCA 9603, 67-1 BCA ¶6091, in which the board noted at 28,184:

> In effect a presumption has been applied that the repurchase could have been completed at the price previously quoted by a lower bidder if an effort had been made to do so. Such a presumption would clearly be rebuttable since prior bid prices—or bidders for that matter—are not always available on repurchase. But in the absence of any rebuttal evidence [the contractor's] burden of showing a failure to mitigate can be met, prima facie, by showing a failure by the Government to make any effort to reprocure from sources whose prices on the original procurement were lower than those of the repurchase contractor.

See also *Dillon Total Maint., Inc. v. United States*, 218 Ct. Cl. 732 (1978), where the government failed to solicit six of the original bidders, three of whom had submitted bids in the original procurement that were lower than the reprocurement price, which was 68 percent higher than the defaulted contract price; and *American Photographic Indus., Inc.*, ASBCA 29272, 90-1 BCA ¶22,491, *recons. denied*, 90-2 BCA ¶22,728, where the government failed to solicit the second low bidder because it was located out of state and would have further delayed completion. However, the board noted that probable delay "does not excuse the Government's failure to mitigate its damages." In part for this reason, the board denied the government's request for excess reprocurement costs.

The government often attempts to reprocure by approaching the second low bidder on the original contract. However, there is no necessity to do this, particularly when the second low bidder is experiencing difficulties on another procurement, *Zoda v. United States*, 148 Ct. Cl. 49, 180 F. Supp. 419 (1960); *United Microwave Co.*, ASBCA 7947, 1963 BCA ¶3701. Furthermore, absent a showing that the government solicited additional offers, award of a reprocurement contract to the second low bidder on the original contract for a high price may not support a conclusion that the government acted reasonably to mitigate excess costs, *Marine Engine Specialties Corp.*, ASBCA 20521, 76-1 BCA ¶11,891 (reduction of excess cost assessment where repurchase unit price was 25 percent greater than that of the original contract and no effort was made to contact three other contractors who had submitted offers on the original procurement). Compare *Wisconsin Lift Truck Corp.*, AGBCA 82-288-1, 87-2 BCA ¶19,736 (soliciting next best bidder held reasonable because the bid was merely 1 percent greater than the defaulted bid price and lower than the government estimate).

d. Delayed Award of Reprocurement Contract

Failure to mitigate also occurs when the government unreasonably delays in awarding a reprocurement contract. The determination of what is a reasonable time is based on the circumstances of each procurement but focuses on any government explanation for the delay and any prejudice suffered by the defaulted contractor. Timeliness is measured as the time between the default termination and the date of award of the reprocurement contract, *Arctic Corner, Inc.*, ASBCA 38075, 94-1 BCA ¶26,317 (6½-month delay did not prejudice defaulted contractor). The mere existence of a long period of time between default and reprocurement, absent evidence that the price increased due to the delay, is not sufficient to show a failure to mitigate, *Conncor, Inc.*, GSBCA 4654, 77-2 BCA ¶12,857 (4½-month delay in repurchase); *Lee Mfg. & Eng'g Co.*, ASBCA 22866, 79-1 BCA ¶13,814 (eight-month delay); *Jimm Worthington*, AGBCA 77-175, 79-1 BCA ¶13,710 (eight-month delay in issuing first request for proposals was justified because work was not normally performed during that period, and an additional three-month delay in awarding final contract was reasonable); *B.R. Servs., Inc.*, ASBCA 47673, 99-2 BCA ¶30,397 (eleven-month delay but cost was close to government estimate). The excess cost assessment may also be upheld when the defaulted contractor contributes to the delay, *Astro-Space Labs., Inc. v. United States*, 200 Ct. Cl. 282, 470 F.2d 1003 (1972) (default created shortages of urgently needed ring fittings). In *Grimco Pneumatic Corp.*, ASBCA 50977, 00-1 BCA ¶30,727, the board found that the government acted reasonably in soliciting offers within two months following its default termination.

A defaulted contractor bears the burden of proving that the delay prejudiced it in terms of price. See *Standard Eng'g & Mfg. Co.*, ASBCA 3733, 57-2 BCA ¶1477, *recons. denied*, 57-2 BCA ¶1568, in which the board stated that an assessment of excess costs could not be barred by a delay of four months from the time of default when the delay did not increase the amount of the assessment. Similarly, in *Comspace Corp.*, ASBCA 37202, 89-3 BCA ¶22,027, a delay of three months was found reasonable because the record contained no evidence that the delay increased the cost of the end items. However, the ultimate burden of persuasion to establish mitigation is on the government, *Carlyle Rubber Co.*, ASBCA 23070, 79-2 BCA ¶14,117.

For cases in which delays have been found unreasonable, see *Continental Chem. Corp.*, GSBCA 4483, 76-2 BCA ¶11,948 (government delayed four months, failed to rebut the contractor's allegations that the delay increased the reprocurement contract prices by 47.5 percent, and failed to obtain necessary competition); *Disan Corp.*, ASBCA 21297, 79-1 BCA ¶13,677 (unexplained delay of seven months in reprocurement of radar power supplies despite statement in the reprocurement contract concerning the urgency of the need); *AGH Indus., Inc.*, ASBCA 27960, 89-2 BCA ¶21,637 (unexplained 17-month delay in reprocurement); *Sonico, Inc.*, ASBCA 31110, 89-2 BCA ¶21,611 (eight-month delay found unreasonable); and *AAA Eng'g & Drafting, Inc.,*. ASBCA 44605, 96-1 BCA ¶28,182 (unexplained delay of two years in repurchasing a computer software program). An excess cost assessment may be invalidated when the delay in reprocurement encompasses a period of severe inflation. In *American Packers Supply*, ASBCA 20024, 75-2 BCA ¶11,451, the board denied excess costs for the repurchase, which had been "delayed over 10 months during a period of raging inflation." See also *B & M Constr., Inc.*, AGBCA 90-165-1, 93-1 BCA ¶25,431, in which the board denied an excess cost claim, in part because of a government-caused delay between bid opening and award of the reprocurement contract. Due to 100 percent inflation, both bid prices were deemed unacceptable and the government unsuccessfully sought to renegotiate with other contractors.

The actions of the government during the delay are also pertinent to determining whether the government failed to mitigate. See *Consolidated Airborne Sys., Inc.*, ASBCA 5498, 61-1 BCA ¶2933, *aff'd*, 172 Ct. Cl. 588, 348 F.2d 941 (1965) (five-month delay while the government negotiated with the reprocurement contractor for lower prices was reasonable); *AAR Allen Aircraft Corp.*, ASBCA 32702, 88-2 BCA ¶20,581 (four-month delay reasonable because the government needed the time to develop a list of potential offerors and to arrange the new solicitation); and *Mega Constr. Co. v. United States*, 29 Fed. Cl. 396 (1993) (five-month delay found reasonable because the government, rather than sitting idly by, consulted with an architect-engineering firm to set up the resolicitation and negotiated lower prices with potential offerors). Compare *Old Dominion Sec., Inc.*, GSBCA 9126, 90-2 BCA ¶22,745 (delay caused by the government's post-default misinterpretation of labor standards found unreasonable). However, when the procuring agency's internal funding and other problems caused a delay, these problems were not permitted to be "visited upon" the defaulted contractor through an excess cost assessment, *Maitland Bros. Co.*, ASBCA 30089, 90-1 BCA ¶22,367. See also *ASC Sys. Corp.*, DOTCAB 73-37,

78-1 BCA ¶13,119, *aff'd*, 223 Ct. Cl. 672 (1980), where, despite a critical need for the equipment, a 13-month delay in the repurchase was caused by the government's internal procedures for determining the form of purchasing and obtaining approval, and the unit price was nearly twice that under the terminated contract.

Even if it reprocures within a reasonable time after termination, the government may lose the right to assess excess costs if the termination has been delayed for an unreasonable time, *Allied Tech., Inc.*, ASBCA 18101, 74-1 BCA ¶10,621 (the government's urgent need to enter into a sole source negotiated contract and the resultant cost increases had been created by the government's own action in delaying termination of the original contract for default); *Wolverine Diesel Power Co.*, ASBCA 20609, 77-2 BCA ¶12,551 (price rose 51 percent when the contracting officer delayed termination until six months after contract repudiation, delayed solicitation of the reprocurement for three months after termination, and delayed award for three months after solicitation).

In an unusual case, *Ketchikan Pulp Co. v. United States*, 20 Cl. Ct. 164 (1990), the court rejected the contractor's argument that the government should have waited several extra months to resell so that two major companies would be able to take part in the bidding. The court stated at 167:

> [The contractor] seeks to hold the Forest Service to an impossibly high standard for mitigation. Although the agency is charged with administering timber sales, it cannot be expected to predict with perfect accuracy the state of the future market. Carried to its logical extreme, the [contractor's] argument would prevent the Forest Service from ever collecting damages resulting from a defaulted timber sales contract because it might always be able to resell the timber at a higher price some time in the future.

Thus, because any future delay in resale might result in a finding of unreasonableness, the court concluded that the government had acted reasonably in not delaying resale until the two major companies would be available to bid.

e. *Effect of Failure to Mitigate*

There is a conflict of authority on whether the reprocurement cost can be adjusted to compensate for failure to mitigate and obtain a reasonable price on reprocurement. In *Francis M. Marley v. United States*, 191 Ct. Cl. 205, 423 F.2d 324 (1970), the court held that the failure to mitigate completely prohibits recovery of excess costs, even in reduced amount, stating at 221:

> Such phrases as "failure to minimize excess costs" or "failure to mitigate damages" do not make applicable, to questions of excess costs, the law of breach of contract damages, in which failure to mitigate damages need not prevent an award but only affect its amount. A proceeding to pass on excess costs is far different from the trial of an issue of breach-of-contract damages. An award of excess costs is by the terms of the contract clause based on a single reprocurement. A proper reprocurement relieves the Government of the burden of proving market value in a suit for damages for breach of contract. The contractor's pocket must, however, be protected from the consequences of an extravagant or improper reprocurement. The award is therefore conditioned upon proof of a reprocurement action reasonably designed to minimize the excess costs. When the reprocurement relied upon by the Government is found, for a sufficient reason, not to have been so designed, it may not be a basis for an award, and the right to excess costs is lost. *Rumley v. United States*, 152 Ct. Cl. 166, 285 F.2d 773 (1961) (reprocurement too late); *Alabama Shirt & Trouser Co. v. United States*, 121 Ct. Cl. 313 (1952) (insufficient solicitation of bids). See Paul, *United States Government Contracts & Subcontracts*, 481-485 (1964). This is what occurred in this case.

The court also held, however, that the government retained its right to seek a common law remedy of damages for breach of contract despite loss of the express contractual right to excess costs. Accord, *Rumley v. United States*, 152 Ct. Cl. 166, 285 F.2d 773 (1961); *Hideca Trading, Inc.*, ASBCA 24161, 87-3 BCA ¶20,040; *ERG Consultants, Inc.*, VABCA 3223, 92-2 BCA ¶24,905.

The boards never strictly adhered to the *Marley* rule. Where evidence has permitted determination of a fair and reasonable excess cost assessment, the boards have regularly awarded the government reduced excess costs of reprocurement. This rationale was explained in *Cable Sys. & Assembly Co.*, ASBCA 17844, 73-2 BCA ¶10,172, at 47,892-93:

> The amount of excess costs actually incurred by the Government is not necessarily the amount of excess costs for which the [contractor] is liable because, in the event of an improper reprocurement, such amount may include costs which would not have been incurred had a proper reprocurement been made. Questions as to whether the reprocurement was improper and, if so, the amount of excess costs reasonably occasioned thereby are principally factual in nature.
>
> It is, and as shown by the cases cited below for sometime has been, the practice of the Board in excess cost cases to determine whether the evidence shows that the amount claimed is correct and, when the evidence does not so show, to determine the correct amount of excess costs if the evidence permits such a determination. We do not read *Marley as holding that this established practice of the Board is improper and should be discontinued.*
>
> * * *
>
> We find that the term "excess costs" as used in subparagraph (b) of the contract's Default provisions includes any costs that the Government may have incurred in the reprocurement of similar supplies or services. If the reprocurement action was proper in all respects, the Government need not establish a "fair market value" of the similar supplies or services at the time of default. However, if the reprocurement action is defective, the Government then has the burden of establishing that the costs claimed represent what the reprocurement cost reasonably should have been which is sometimes stated as "fair market value" at the time of default or a reasonable period thereafter, such period being that amount of time which may be justified for effecting a reprocurement.

See also *Rayco, Inc.*, ENGBCA 4792, 88-2 BCA ¶20,671 (reductions for rework not included in the first contract price and for significant inflation between contracts found reasonable where evidence of such increased costs was fairly based in the record and the costs were not caused by the default). Moreover, where excess costs are improperly computed, the government does not lose its rights to recover those costs as long as there is a firm basis in the record for their recovery, *Ronald L. Collier*, ASBCA 26972, 89-1 BCA ¶21,328.

In cases where evidence does not permit determination of what a fair excess cost assessment would have been had the government fulfilled its duty to mitigate, the boards have denied the government the right to assess excess costs, *Matthews Co.*, AGBCA 459, 76-2 BCA ¶12,164, *recons. denied*, 77-1 BCA ¶12,434 (cost of completing road construction was clearly excessive); *Barrett Chem. Co.*, GSBCA 4544, 77-2 BCA ¶12,625 (failure to conduct give-and-take negotiations); *ASC Sys. Corp.*, DOTCAB 73-37, 78-1 BCA ¶13,119, *aff'd*, 223 Ct. Cl. 672 (1980) (extended delay and negotiated sole source procurement made prices obtained not reflective of fair market value); *B & M Constr., Inc.*, AGBCA 90-165-1, 93-1 BCA ¶25,431 (100 percent inflation and a five-month delay, coupled with substantial modifications to the specifications, left no basis in the record for determining reasonable costs).

A variety of methods have been used to calculate the reduced excess costs assessment. One frequently used method is to base the assessment on the difference between the original contract price and the second low bid on the original contract, *Fitzgerald Labs., Inc.*, ASBCA 15205, 71-2 BCA ¶9029; *Atlas Mfg. Co.*, ASBCA 15177, 71-2 BCA ¶9026; *Marine Engine Specialties Corp.*, ASBCA 21053, 76-2 BCA ¶12,034; *Wolverine Diesel Power Co.*, ASBCA 20609, 77-2 BCA ¶12,551; *Jefferson Constr. & Demolition Co.*, ASBCA 22787, 79-1 BCA ¶13,606; *American Photographic Indus., Inc.*, ASBCA 29272, 90-1 BCA ¶22,491, *recons. denied*, 90-2 BCA ¶22,728. However, a second low bid will not be used as a basis for computing the excess costs where it appears unreasonable. Thus, in *Solar Labs., Inc.*, ASBCA 19957, 76-2 BCA ¶12,115, the board measured excess costs by the difference between the original contract price and the price at which the reprocurement contractor had accepted a concurrent contract for the same items. See also *Birken Mfg. Co.*, ASBCA 32590, 90-2 BCA ¶22,845, in which the board used the reprocurement contractor's price on a similar contract as the basis for the valuation of excess costs of reprocurement because the government had not provided any evidence that this amount was inappropriately low and it was a fairer basis for measurement.

Other measures used include the difference between the defaulted contract price and what it would have cost the defaulted contractor to produce the items, *R.C. Allen Bus. Machs., Inc.*, ASBCA 12932, 72-1 BCA ¶9325; deduction of a specific amount, *Irvin Fisher*, HUDBCA 77-198-C10, 79-2 BCA ¶14,076 (assessment reduced by that portion of reprocurement price caused by a different manner of contract administration); *Old Dominion Sec., Inc.*, GSBCA 9126, 90-2 BCA ¶22,745 (deduction of costs incurred due to the unreasonable portion of the delay); and a jury verdict method, *Belmont Instrument Corp.*, ASBCA 18861, 77-1 BCA ¶12,332 (determination of what price would have been had the items been repurchased through one rather than two contracts), and *William A. Hulett*, AGBCA 91-230-3, 93-1 BCA ¶25,389, *recons. denied*, 93-2 BCA ¶25,888 (determination of value of work already done by the defaulted contractor).

Some of the confusion surrounding the appropriate measure of damages for a failure to mitigate costs of reprocurement may have been resolved by the Federal Circuit's decision in *Cascade Pac. Int'l v. United States*, 773 F.2d 287 (Fed. Cir. 1985), in which the court concluded that the proper measure of damages should be the "reasonable reprocurement price less the original contract price." In *Interstate Forestry, Inc.*, AGBCA 89-114-1, 91-1 BCA ¶23,660, the board provided further explanation of the appropriateness of this remedy at 118,521:

> This analysis is consistent not only with the recent board decisions reducing excess costs, but also with the Court of Claims' earlier statement that contractual excess cost provisions merely take the common law rule for determining damages and say that if the Government repurchases within a reasonable time, the repurchase price will be accepted as the reasonable cost of obtaining performance without further proof. *Rumley v. United States, supra* at 777.
>
> In the case at bar, it makes little difference whether we consider the Government's claim as one for common law damages or as one for excess costs which should be reduced because of failure to mitigate. In either case, we will look to the reasonableness of the first reprocurement contract price. The price of the second reprocurement contractor, used by the CO, is not a proper measure of damages because, as indicated above, the additional cost did not reasonably flow from [the contractor's] default. In common law terms, it was not a foreseeable, direct, natural or proximate result of [the contractor's] breach of contract. See *Birken Mfg. Co.*, ASBCA 32651, 88-1 BCA ¶20,385, citing *Hadley v. Baxendale*, 9 Exch. 341, 156 Eng. Rep. 145 (1854).

The board concluded that the appropriate method of measuring damages was to subtract the original contract price from the reasonable reprocurement costs or price. See also *Mega Constr. Co. v. United States*, 29 Fed. Cl. 396 (1993), in which the court employed this standard in finding the government entitled to recover as excess reprocurement costs the cost of repairing defective workmanship and consultant's fees as well as the difference in price between the original and reprocurement contracts. Similarly, in *Associated Cleaning, Inc.*, GSBCA 8360, 91-1 BCA ¶23,360, the board found that, where the government had not made a reasonable effort to mitigate damages, excess costs could be recomputed by evaluating the difference between the original contract price and the price of a potential offeror on reprocurement.

f. Refusal to Deal with Original Contractor

There is considerable controversy over whether the government loses the right to excess costs by refusing to deal with the defaulting contractor. In seeking to resist the assessment of excess costs, the contractor often argues that it would be able to perform more quickly and less expensively than other firms. FAR 49.102(d) authorizes the contracting officer, with the contractor's agreement, to reinstate the contract if doing so would be advantageous to the government. However, the government is not required to do so, *Churchill Chem. Corp. v. United States*, 221 Ct. Cl. 284, 602 F.2d 358 (1979); *Lafayette Coal Co.*, ASBCA 32174, 89-3 BCA ¶21,963.

Although the government may not be obligated to deal with a defaulted contractor, failure to do so may be considered a failure to mitigate damages and may result in a loss of the right to assess reprocurement costs. At a minimum, the government must accept completed supplies that meet specifications rather than include such quantities in a reprocurement. See *Guenther Sys., Inc.*, ASBCA 18343, 77-1 BCA ¶12,501, in which the board stated at 60,592:

> After termination the Government accepted 95 completed firing lock assemblies. Since these were all that had been completed at that time, respondent discharged its obligation to mitigate damages in this respect. Once the contract had been terminated, [the Government] was under no obligation to accept further assemblies that [the contractor] offered to complete. Also, neither the default termination nor the reprocurement are tainted, if otherwise proper, by the prospect that it would have been more advantageous for the Government to stay with the

terminated contractor and to obtain from him earlier deliveries than obtainable on reprocurement. *C.W. Wood Mfg., Inc.*, ASBCA 9640, 65-2 BCA ¶4972.

Failure to take completed items can lead to a refusal to allow an excess cost assessment, *United Microwave Co.*, ASBCA 9420, 65-1 BCA ¶4641, *recons. denied*, 65-2 BCA ¶5244 (items repurchased from another firm had no time or price advantage over those that were available from the defaulted contractor subsequent to the default termination and prior to the reprocurement); *Junkunc Bros., American Lock Co.*, ASBCA 12042, 68-1 BCA ¶7059 (items had been completed but not packaged for shipment on the termination date but became available for shipment prior to reprocurement), or to a reduction in excess costs of reprocurement by an estimate of the value of the services already rendered, *William A. Hulett*, AGBCA 91-230-3, 93-1 BCA ¶25,389, *recons. denied*, 93-2 BCA ¶25,888 (employing a jury verdict approach to establish the value of the benefit conferred on the reprocurement contractor by the pre-default work). The government is not required to take such work if doing so would result in a waiver of the government's rights, *Hyland Elec. Supply Co.*, ASBCA 19270, 75-2 BCA ¶11,466 (defaulted contractor's offer to supply additional items was properly rejected since the offer was contingent on a waiver of the excess cost assessment for the remaining defaulted quantity). In *R & O Indus., Inc.*, GSBCA 4804, 80-1 BCA ¶14,196, the board found that the government's failure to use completed items was excused because the contractor did not make a timely tender of the items. Excess costs will also not be reduced when the pre-default work is found to be defective in some way. In *Flooring Co.*, GSBCA 8297, 89-3 BCA ¶22,167, the value of carpeting work done prior to the default did not reduce the amount of recovery because the work did not comply with the specifications.

When a decision to reprocure has been made, the question has been raised as to whether the defaulted contractor should be given an opportunity to participate in the competition. Although the Armed Services Board has asserted that the government may have a contractual right to exclude a defaulted contractor from the reprocurement action, *TYCO Air Spec Div.*, ASBCA 16534, 73-1 BCA ¶9951, the GAO had previously stated that there can be no per se rule excluding the defaulted contractor. Such an exclusion would, in effect, constitute a predetermination of lack of responsibility and would improperly preclude a consideration of all the facts surrounding the default, *Ikard Mfg. Co.*, Comp. Gen. Dec. B-192316, 78-2 CPD ¶315 (contracting officer may not automatically exclude defaulted contractor from reprocurement, but urgent need for parts justified limiting reprocurement competition to prior producers); *Master Sec., Inc.*, Comp. Gen. Dec. B-235711, 89-2 CPD ¶303 (noncompetitive reprocurement improper for option years). The continued vitality of *Ikard* is now questionable since in *Montage, Inc.* Comp. Gen. Dec. B-277923.2, 97-2 CPD ¶176, the GAO ruled that the contracting officer may exclude the defaulted contractor from the competition for reprocurement and overruled previous contrary decisions, stating "To the extent that *PRB Uniforms, Inc.*, [56 Comp. Gen. 976 (1977), 77-2 CPD ¶213], and other decisions citing that case state that a defaulted contractor may not be automatically excluded from the competition for the reprocurement of the requirement as to which it defaulted, those cases will not be followed." Generally, the boards and courts hold that the government is neither required to solicit an offer from nor make an award to a defaulted contractor. However, it may do so. See *Churchill Chem. Corp. v. United States*, 221 Ct. Cl. 284, 602 F.2d 358 (1979), in which the court upheld the government's refusal to award the repurchase contract to a defaulted contractor who had given no indication of interest prior to reprocurement, stating at 293:

> While the Government need not, in all cases, consider a defaulted contractor for reprocurement, the contractor may be permitted to bid on the repurchase solicitation. If the defaulted contractor is found to be responsible and capable of performance, is *responsive* to the solicitation, and is the lowest bidder, it may receive the repurchase contract; on reprocurement, the defaulted contractor, notwithstanding its submission of the lowest bid, may not receive more than the initial contract price for its reprocurement performance. (See, e.g., Opinion of Comptroller General, B-182323, 54 Comp. Gen. 853.)

The contracting officer's refusal to deal with the defaulted contractor has been upheld, *United States v. Thompson*, 168 F. Supp. 281 (N.D. W. Va. 1958), *aff'd*, 268 F.2d 426 (4th Cir. 1959) (defaulted contractor rejected as nonresponsible); *Marmac Indus., Inc.*, ASBCA 12158, 72-1 BCA ¶9249 (defaulted contractor nonresponsible); *Wear Ever Shower Curtain Corp.*, GSBCA 4360, 76-1 BCA ¶11,636 (reliability of defaulted contractor in question); *Ketchikan Pulp Co. v. United States*, 20 Cl. Ct. 164 (1990) (no requirement that the government delay reletting the contract until the defaulted contractor was free to enter); *Birken Mfg. Co.*, ASBCA 32590, 90-2 BCA ¶22,845 (defaulted contractor nonresponsible); *Morton Mfg., Inc.*, ASBCA 30716, 89-1 BCA ¶21,326 (no obligation to solicit the defaulted contractor because its noncompliance caused the need to reprocure in the first place). However, where it appears that the defaulted contractor is clearly a responsible contractor, the failure to deal has resulted in loss of reprocurement costs, *World-Wide Dev. Co.*, ASBCA 16608, 73-2 BCA ¶10,140 (temporary inability cured at time of reprocurement). See also *Tom W. Kaufman Co.*, GSBCA 4623, 78-2 BCA ¶13,288, in which the board held that the government had failed to mitigate costs through its failure to solicit a clearly responsible defaulted contractor who had the greatest ability to deliver promptly, and *Walsh Constr. Go.*, ENGBCA 6325, 98-1 BCA ¶29,683, in which the board denied the government's motion for summary judgment because the agency's refusal to allow a contractor to compete in the reprocurement may have been unreasonable when the agency assumed that the contractor's bid would have been the sum of its original bid plus the amount of its alleged error.

Considerations advanced to justify permitting a defaulted contractor to participate include (1) providing other offerors with notice that the award might go to the defaulted contractor, (2) obtaining an offer lower than the original contract price, and (3) assessing changes in price due to any changes made in the specifications. In *R.H. Pines Corp.*, Comp. Gen. Dec. B-182323, 75-1 CPD ¶224, the defaulted contractor was found to be the "lowest responsive, responsible bidder under the reprocurements" and was properly awarded the contracts. However, the GAO has stated that a repurchase contract may not be awarded to the defaulted contractor at a price greater than that of the original contract because doing so would be tantamount to modifying an existing contract without consideration, *Aerospace Am., Inc.*, Comp. Gen. Dec. B-181553, 74-2 CPD ¶130; *Air, Inc.*, Comp. Gen. Dec. B-233501, 88-2 CPD ¶505. Compare *Western Filament, Inc.*, Comp. Gen. Dec. B-181558, 74-2 CPD ¶320, stating that the government may award a subsequent contract that is not a reprocurement to the defaulted contractor at a price higher than that of the terminated contract if the defaulted contractor is the low bidder on the new contract for similar supplies or services. The GAO has found it reasonable for the contracting officer to take specification changes into account when determining whether the award is actually for a greater price than the defaulted contract, *A.R.E. Mfg. Co.*, Comp. Gen. Dec. B-246161, 92-1 CPD ¶210 (specification alterations between the defaulted contract and the reprocurement solicitation accounted for an almost $6,000 increase in the defaulted contractor's price and thus allowed award to be made to the defaulted contractor). However, the defaulted contractor may not reduce its offer in order to qualify for the reprocurement contract when its offer is not otherwise acceptable and responsible, *F&H Mfg. Co.*, Comp. Gen. Dec. B-184172, 76-1 CPD ¶297. Finally, the GAO has determined that a defaulted contractor may not recover the costs of preparing its offer when it is properly rejected, *Aerospace Am., Inc.*, Comp. Gen. Dec. B-181553, 74-2 CPD ¶130.

The government also has a right to acquire the contractor's inventory but is not required to do so, *Thermodyne Int'l, Ltd.*, ASBCA 21997, 80-1 BCA ¶14,333 (government acted correctly in not taking inventory that contained defective materials). With respect to the use of the contractor's inventory by a reprocurement contractor, it appears that the government satisfies its responsibilities if it makes the reprocurement contractor aware of the inventory and does not impede its use by the reprocurement contractor, *C.W. Wood Mfg., Inc.*, ASBCA 9640, 65-2 BCA ¶4972; *Vanbar*, ASBCA 18488, 76-2 BCA ¶11,924 (no need to use the defaulted contractor's tooling where the reprocurement contractor had existing tooling that could be used and did not increase the repurchase price); *Meyer Labs, Inc.*, ASBCA 19525, 87-2 BCA ¶19,810 (no violation of duty to mitigate when the government disposed of the defaulted contractor's inventory, tools, and materials when the reprocurement contractor implemented different manufacturing and testing techniques that rendered the tools only minimally valuable).

C. The Reprocurement Contract

In order to obtain excess costs of reprocurement, the government must also prove that the reprocurement contract was issued and administered in a way that did not increase the costs assessed.

1. Intent to Reprocure

In order to assess excess costs, the government must show that the contract on which such costs were incurred was intended to be a reprocurement. As long as this intent is shown, it is not necessary that the reprocurement contract be awarded after the termination. See *Olean Case Corp.*, GSBCA 4673, 78-1 BCA ¶12,905, in which the board stated at 62,860:

> Neither the issuance of the invitation for bids for the reprocurement prior to termination of all the purchase orders, nor award of the reprocurement contract five days prior to termination of the last delivery under [the contractor's] contract

> affects our holding. See *Allied Paint Mfg. Co., Inc.*, ENGBCA 3043, 71-1 BCA ¶8765 (issuance of solicitation prior to default); *Tilton Machine & Tool Co.*, GSBCA Nos. 4198, 4199, 76-1 BCA ¶11,750 (repurchase from an existing term contract). In the *Tilton Machine & Tool Co.* opinion, it was stated that ". . . there is nothing sacred in the date of award of the contract under which the Government repurchases supplies against the account of a defaulted contractor." In that case, it was held to be in the [contractor's] best interest to effect the purchase from the existing term contract, as reprocurement costs were clearly mitigated. Here the Contracting Officer issued the solicitation at the earliest possible time. The firm bid was obtained on August 31, 1976, and when it became apparent on September 10, 1976, that [the contractor] was 100 percent in default of its contract, and would probably never perform, the repurchase contract was awarded. The Government clearly acted reasonably and promptly in an effort to mitigate excess costs.

In *Foster Refrigerator Corp.*, ASBCA 32059, 88-1 BCA ¶20,398, the board allowed excess reprocurement cost recovery even though the reprocurement contract had been initiated three months before the prior contract had been terminated. In fact, this added time had enabled the government agency to solicit 59 competitors for the reprocurement, thus improving competition substantially, consistent with its duty to mitigate damages.

Excess costs were also permitted where the reprocurement was effected through exercise of an option that had been included in another procurement in anticipation of the terminated contractor's default, *AAR Corp.*, ASBCA 16486, 74-2 BCA ¶10,653. The exercise of an option under an existing contract may also be appropriate. In *Southwest Safety Prods. Mfg. Co.*, ASBCA 22902, 79-1 BCA ¶13,617, the board found that the government reasonably mitigated its costs by canceling a solicitation that had resulted in high bids and by electing to exercise an option under two existing contracts at lower unit prices. In *Ronald L. Collier*, ASBCA 26972, 89-1 BCA ¶21,328, the board held that the contracting officer had not breached its duty to mitigate damages by reprocuring through the addition of options to the contract of a contractor performing similar services in the same geographic area because (1) there was an urgent need for maintenance services, (2) the completion contract was for services identical to those in the defaulted contract, (3) the contracting officer acted as promptly as practicable to obtain the reprocurement contractor, and (4) the contract price would be equal to that of the defaulted contract. However, in *General Optical, Ltd.*, ASBCA 23835, 84-1 BCA ¶17,026, the board found a failure to mitigate where the government reprocured through exercise of an option under another contract without having solicited offers to determine whether competitive prices would be lower than the option prices. Accordingly, the excess costs were based on a lower price that had been obtained in a related competitive procurement for similar items.

In *Fairfield Scientific Corp. v. United States*, 222 Ct. Cl. 167, 611 F.2d 854 (1979), the court held that it was not necessary to use the same appropriation in the repurchase. So long as it acts reasonably and in a manner designed to mitigate damages, the government may repurchase by placing orders at reasonable prices under existing indefinite quantity or requirements contracts, *Tilton Mach. & Tool Co.*, GSBCA 4198, 76-1 BCA ¶11,750 (expressly overruling previous case disallowing the excess cost assessment for a reprocurement through orders under an existing contract). Thus, where the government shows that an existing requirements contract provides the best price available, an excess cost assessment based on orders under that contract will be upheld, *Woodford Hardware Co.*, ASBCA 16062, 72-1 BCA ¶9445; *Hyland Elec. Supply Co.*, ASBCA 19270, 75-2 BCA ¶11,466; *Barrett Ref. Corp.*, ASBCA 36590, 91-1 BCA ¶23,566.

There is some question as to whether the government has a duty or merely an option to utilize existing contracts for reprocurement. See *American Air Prods. Corp.*, ASBCA 4754, 60-1 BCA ¶2514 (excess costs assessment upheld despite government's failure to attempt placing orders with an existing contractor). But compare *Century Tool Co.*, GSBCA 4006, 76-2 BCA ¶12,030 (government failed to mitigate excess costs by not evaluating prospects for delivery under an existing requirements contract). Excess cost assessments have also been upheld, *American Kal Enters., Inc.*, GSBCA 4449, 76-2 BCA ¶11,929 (government failed to order quantities from an existing term contractor that was having difficulties meeting delivery schedules); *Palmetto Indus., Inc.*, ASBCA 21955, 79-1 BCA ¶13,594 (government failed to exercise an option extended by a prior contractor).

2. Proof of Cost Incurrence

Since reprocurement costs are based on the amount paid to the reprocurement contractor, the government must demonstrate that the costs were in fact incurred by showing that the reprocurement contract has been completed and the contractor paid, *Whitlock Corp. v. United States*, 141 Ct. Cl. 758, 159 F. Supp. 602, *cert. denied*, 358 U.S. 815 (1958). See FAR 49.402-6(c), which states that the demand for excess costs shall be made "after completion and final payment of the repurchase contract." See *Hunt's Janitor Serv.*, ASBCA 27719, 83-1 BCA ¶16,455 (government could not properly withhold amounts due contractor for completed services to cover potential excess costs); *Pyramid Packing, Inc.*, AGBCA 86-128-1, 92-2 BCA ¶24,831 (rejecting claim for excess reprocurement costs because the government had presented no evidence that the contract had been awarded, completed, and paid); *Patty Armfield*, AGBCA 91-185-1, 93-1 BCA ¶25,235 (denying recovery where excess costs were assessed prior to payment of reprocurement price); *Scalf Eng'g Co. & Pike County Constr., J.V.*, IBCA 2328, 89-3 BCA ¶21,950 (lack of evidence of payment precluded excess cost recovery); and *American Photographic Indus., Inc.*, ASBCA 29272, 90-1 BCA ¶22,491 (recovery of excess costs reduced to only those incurred and paid at the time of the assessment—four months). Accord, *What Mac Contractors, Inc.*, GSBCA 5015, 79-2 BCA ¶14,179. Compare *Servicemaster of W. Cent. Ga.*, DOTCAB 1096, 80-2 BCA ¶14,676, upholding a decision to withhold funds to "offset the contractor's potential liability for the excess costs of reprocurement." A demand for payment of excess costs prior to completion of the reprocurement contract is premature and will not be effective as a "final decision" under the CDA, *United Aero, Inc.*, ASBCA 26967, 83-1 BCA ¶16,268.

The government was denied recovery of excess reprocurement costs because the only evidence it put on to support recovery was the first two pages of the reprocurement contract. The board found this inadequate to determine if the government had met its obligation to act reasonably to minimize costs, *ARCO Eng'g, Inc.*, ASBCA 52450, 01-1 BCA ¶31,218.

In *C. Howdy Smith*, AGBCA 90-154-1, 92-2 BCA ¶24,884, the board expressed displeasure at the seemingly harsh and inefficient results created by the implementation of this doctrine, stating at 124,107:

> To deny recovery for excess reprocurement costs simply because the contract had yet to run its natural course to completion may seem anomalous and an impediment to the CO's giving prompt attention to claim presentation. That, nevertheless, appears to be well established law.

Accordingly, the board concluded that the reprocurement costs should be returned to the defaulted contractor because they had been assessed seven months prior to the completion of the reprocurement contract.

3. Poor Administration of Reprocurement Contract

The defaulted contractor may also be able to show that the government's administration of the reprocurement contract was sufficiently different to invalidate the assessment of excess costs, *Irvin Fisher*, HUDBCA 77-198-C10, 79-2 BCA ¶14,076. There, the board found some reprocurement costs to be improper because the contracting officer administered the initial services provision of a lawn maintenance contract differently by allowing the new contractor rather than the agency to determine the need for the services, as had been the case for the defaulted contractor. In order to obtain sufficient information to present such arguments, the defaulted contractor often attempts to inspect the reprocurement contractor's work. However, it has consistently been held that the defaulted contractor has no right to demand such an inspection. In *Industrial Elecs. Hardware Corp.*, ASBCA 10201, 68-2 BCA ¶7174, the board stated at 33,283:

> [T]he Board is aware of no case holding that in order for a buyer to collect excess costs from a defaulting seller the buyer must permit the seller to witness the inspection of the repurchase contractor's tenders. Nor is the Board aware of any case holding that in order to collect excess costs from a defaulting seller the buyer must turn over to the seller for inspection a representative sample of the repurchased items, or permit a joint inspection, so that the seller can satisfy himself that the repurchased items met specifications.

Likewise, in *Betsy Ross Flag Co.*, GSBCA 2786, 69-1 BCA ¶7692, the defaulted contractor "made repeated demands that the Government furnish it with a flag of another manufacturer for its inspection, contending that it had a right to inspect a flag made by another company to substantiate its claim that no other company could produce a better flag." The board affirmed the denial of the demand.

In *Boyd Tools, Inc.*, GSBCA 3469, 73-1 BCA ¶9874, the defaulted contractor's motion for discovery by having samples of the reprocured articles submitted for its inspection was denied. Similarly, in *Ranger Constr. Co.*, DOTCAB 74-32B, 75-2

BCA ¶11,524, the defaulted contractor's efforts to obtain discovery by having its own inspectors observe the conduct of a major cost-reimbursement construction reprocurement were unsuccessful. The government asserted that the facts sought by the defaulted contractor were more discoverable by government supervision, evaluation, and control, that the responsibility for site control was placed on the reprocurement contractor, and therefore the surety could monitor the validity of the completion costs. The board upheld the government's assertions and added that the government's obligation not to impede or interfere with the reprocurement contractor's performance was also a factor. Thus, the board concluded that "good cause" had not been shown for discovery by on-site inspection.

In *Western Contracting Corp.*, ENGBCA 3920, 78-1 BCA ¶12,922, discovery by use of an on-site inspector was allowed. However, the purpose of the inspection was to gather evidence to support the defaulted contractor's claim of changed site conditions as an excuse for default, rather than to observe the performance of the reprocurement contractor.

Where the reprocurement contractor also defaults on the contract, the original contractor will not have to pay excess costs for the administration of the second contract. See *Interstate Forestry, Inc.*, AGBCA 89-114-1, 91-1 BCA ¶23,660, holding that the added costs of the second reprocurement contract did not directly result from the initial default and therefore should not be assessed to the first defaulted contractor. The board limited recovery of reprocurement costs from the original contractor to the reasonable difference in costs between the first and second contracts. The first reprocurement contractor, if anyone, should be held liable for excess costs involved with the second reprocurement contract.

4. Use of Government Personnel

The government may also satisfy its requirements and preserve its rights through the use of government personnel to complete the work. The construction contract clause provides that the government "may take over the work and complete it by contract or otherwise." This language allows the government to use its employees to complete the work and deduct the resulting costs from the contract price. However, the government must act reasonably and incur reasonable costs. Although the standard supply and services contract clause does not specifically permit completion of the contract by the government's own forces as a proper method of reprocurement, the Armed Services Board has apparently recognized that a reprocurement could be effected by the government's in-house completion of the work. In fact, where it is clear that the government has the in-house capability to complete the defaulted contract, the failure at least to explore this alternative will be deemed a breach of the duty to mitigate, *ERG Consultants, Inc.*, VABCA 3223, 92-2 BCA ¶24,905 (rejecting claim for excess costs where the government had on staff professional engineers and industrial hygienists capable of completing the remaining 5 percent of the design contract although this option was not even considered).

In-house performance has been permitted when the need for the defaulted items is urgent and other forms of repurchasing are impractical, *R.A. Miller Indus., Inc.*, ASBCA 16433, 72-1 BCA ¶9409 (critical need for firing cases and lack of evidence that supplies could have been procured in time to obtain a lower price); *Guenther Sys., Inc.*, ASBCA 18343, 77-1 BCA ¶12,501 (urgent need for reliable production); *Star Contracting Co.*, ASBCA 27848, 89-2 BCA ¶21,587 (interim use of on-base personnel for emergency requests for services upheld as reasonable and consistent with the duty to mitigate damages).

The government may not complete the work with its own forces at a cost higher than available elsewhere unless circumstances require such action. See *Brent L. Sellick*, ASBCA 21869, 78-2 BCA ¶13,510, in which the board stated at 66,196:

> Turning to the Government's assessment of excess completion costs, the principal issue raised is whether the Government was justified in using an in-house public works crew without soliciting any bids from potential contractors. In undertaking the completion effort the Government had a duty to mitigate the damages chargeable to [the contractor] and the burden of persuasion is on the Government to establish that it acted reasonably to minimize the damages occasioned by [the contractor's] default. *Environmental Tectonics Corporation*, ASBCA 21204, 78-1 BCA ¶12,986. In prior cases we have upheld Government claims for excess completion costs, based on use of Government employees without prior solicitation of bids or proposals, where there was an urgent need to complete the work and the circumstances allowed no other reasonable alternative. See *Collins Electronics, Inc.*, ASBCA 16956, 72-2 BCA ¶9542; *Superior Disposal*, ASBCA 19910, 75-2 BCA ¶11,464; *Superior Disposal*, ASBCA Nos.

> 19350, 19816 and 20016, 75-2 BCA ¶11,523; *P&B Catering Service, Inc.*, ASBCA Nos. 20726 & 21722, 77-2 BCA ¶12,770. The *Superior Disposal* appeals and *P&B Catering Service, supra*, involved threats to base or mess hall sanitation occasioned by the default of refuse disposal and mess attendant service contractors respectively.
>
> In the instant appeal the Government would have us conclude that the existence of the safety hazard at [the contractor's] work site justified the use of a Government public works crew on a non-competitive basis. However, the facts of record do not support the conclusion that, from an objective standpoint, the need to remove the debris was as urgent as the Government contends. A safety hazard at the site had persisted at the site from 7 September, if not earlier, and once the walls came down in October, the hazard was qualitatively and quantitatively the same until [the contractor's] contract was terminated for default. If the threat to safety was as great as the Government maintains, it was unreasonable for the Government to wait as long as it did to terminate the contract for default. The decision to use public works forces on a non-competitive basis stemmed in large part from pressure exerted by the base commander to remove the debris as quickly as possible. The base commander's perception of an urgent need to eliminate immediately a long persistent safety hazard and eyesore does not support the conclusion that use of public works forces was the only reasonable alternative.

Thus, the government remains obligated to act reasonably and to mitigate excess costs when completing the work with government personnel. In *Elton E. Widdifield & Excavating Unlimited*, AGBCA 81-115-1, 83-2 BCA ¶16,639, the board found a failure to mitigate where the government had the work completed in part by government employees and in part through use of a reprocurement contractor, since the total costs of performing the work in this manner were substantially higher than they would have been had the reprocurement contractor performed the entire job. See *Surf Cleaners, Inc.*, ASBCA 20197, 77-2 BCA ¶12,687 (government failed to solicit another contractor who might have been able to perform defaulted janitorial services immediately); *Made-Rite Tool Co.*, ASBCA 22127, 79-2 BCA ¶13,975 (no proof of reasonableness by government); and *Datronics Eng'rs, Inc. v. United States*, 190 Ct. Cl. 196, 418 F.2d 1371 (1969) (reducing excess cost assessment by travel costs incurred in bringing government personnel from distant location to perform unskilled labor tasks).

As long as the costs incurred by the government employees are those that would not have been incurred in their normal work, they will be recoverable. In *Landmark Interior Builders, Inc.*, GSBCA 8382, 91-1 BCA ¶23,386, the board allowed recovery of excess costs incurred by government employees who worked overtime because overtime was necessary since the straight-time work day was devoted to their normal tasks. In *Sam's Elec. Co.*, GSBCA 9359, 90-3 BCA ¶23,128, the board allowed full recovery because there was no evidence that the government's use of in-house employees to complete the contract had increased the costs of performance.

Taking items out of existing stock and charging the contractor the price the government paid for the stock will not satisfy the requirement for a reprocurement, *Naples Food Prods. Co.*, ASBCA 8191, 1963 BCA ¶3932. However, if the government borrows from stock to satisfy immediate needs and then contracts for items to replenish the stock, such a contract would be a reprocurement, *Rockingham Poultry Mktg. Corp.*, ASBCA 1319 (1953).

D. Computation of Excess Costs

The computation of recoverable excess costs is based on the difference in price between the defaulted contract and the reprocurement contract as adjusted for all increases in the original contract price to which the defaulted contractor is entitled, and for any cost increases resulting from changes in the work or government misconduct under the reprocurement contract.

1. Price Adjustments Under Defaulted Contract

In computing excess costs of reprocurement, the price of the defaulted contract must be adjusted to account for all price increases to which the defaulted contractor is entitled. In *Big Star Testing Co.*, GSBCA 5793, 81-2 BCA ¶15,335, *recons. denied*, 82-1 BCA ¶15,635, the adjustment in price due because of the contractor's "justified" inability to obtain third-party testing services specified in the contract eliminated the entire excess cost assessment. See also *D.H. Dave & Gerben Contracting Co.*, ASBCA 6257, 1962 BCA ¶3493 (assessment reduced to account for price increases due for changes, suspensions, and changed conditions encountered); *Iran B. Tech Enter., Ltd.*, ASBCA 24820, 81-2 BCA ¶15,424 (assessment reduced to account for constructive changes); *American Dredging Co.*, ENGBCA 2920, 78-2 BCA ¶13,494 (assessment reduced to account for differing site condition); *B.R. Servs., Inc.*, ASBCA 47673, 99-2 BCA ¶30,397 (assessment reduced for constructive changes); and *Walsh Constr. Co. of Ill.*, ASBCA 52952, 02-2 BCA ¶32,004 (assessment reduced for increased labor costs attributable to updated wage rate determinations). In *American Kal Enters., Inc.*, GSBCA 4987, 80-2 BCA ¶14,522, the board refused to adjust the defaulted contract price to reflect that it had been evaluated as a foreign bid. By contrast, if the costs are a reasonably foreseeable result of the defaulted contractor's failure to complete the work, the costs will be recoverable, *Milner Constr. Co.*, DOTBCA 2043, 91-3 BCA ¶24,195 (allowing recovery of temporary storage of hazardous waste materials during the resolicitation period as a reasonably foreseeable result of the default); *Sealtite Corp.*, ASBCA 34156, 90-2 BCA ¶22,844 (cost of performance of architect-engineering firm found foreseeable).

2. Adjustments in Reprocurement Contract Costs

If the costs eventually paid by the government under the reprocurement contract increase due to government misconduct during administration of the reprocurement contract, an appropriate downward adjustment in the excess cost assessment should be made. In addition, if the government calls for effort under the reprocurement contract that was not required under the defaulted contract, but the reprocurement constitutes a valid reprocurement of "similar" work, costs attributable to the extra work required under the reprocurement contract must be excluded from any excess cost assessment. See *Datronics Eng'rs, Inc. v. United States*, 190 Ct. Cl. 196, 418 F.2d 1371 (1969) (excluding costs of repairing damage to transmission lines for which the defaulted contractor was not responsible); *Lee Mfg. & Eng'g Co.*, ASBCA 22866, 79-1 BCA ¶13,814 (reprocurement price adjusted to eliminate costs of additional testing); *Steelship Corp.*, ENGBCA 3830, 78-2 BCA ¶13,478 (reprocurement price reduced by $140,627 to account for improvement over defaulted contractor's ship design); *Gardner Constr. Co.*, DOTCAB 70-18, 73-2 BCA ¶10,342 (reprocurement price reduced to reflect work added to reprocurement contract); *Foster Refrigerator Corp.*, ASBCA 32059, 88-1 BCA ¶20,398 (reprocurement price reduced to reflect deletion of first article testing requirement); and *Schmalz Constr. Ltd.*, AGBCA 92-177-1, 94-1 BCA ¶26,423 (deletion of right-of-way timber purchase requirement entitled contractor to a reduction in price).

The price must also be adjusted for specification waivers granted to the reprocurement contractor without price reductions or for the government's failure to obtain consideration for the reprocurement contractor's schedule extensions, *Specialty Wood Prods.*, ASBCA 22324, 79-1 BCA ¶13,815; *RFI Shield-Rooms*, ASBCA 17991, 77-2 BCA ¶12,714 (reduction for schedule extension given without requiring consideration). In *Iran B. Tech Enter., Ltd.*, ASBCA 24820, 81-2 BCA ¶15,424, where a reprocurement contractor performing work in Iran was able to complete only 78 percent of the work because of the Iranian revolution, the excess cost assessment was based on only 78 percent of the reprocurement price even though the government had actually paid the reprocurement contractor 96 percent of the price.

In *Guenther Sys., Inc.*, ASBCA 18343, 77-1 BCA ¶12,501, the board refused to credit the defaulted contractor for its value engineering incentive earnings on the reprocured items. Reasoning that such a credit, if allowed, would only "add to the Government's procurement costs" and thus would increase the liability of the defaulted contractor, the board concluded that reducing the assessment in such circumstances would be inconsistent with the government's rights under the Default clause. In contrast, in *Fairfield Scientific Corp.*, ASBCA 21152, 78-1 BCA ¶12,869, *aff'd*, 222 Ct. Cl. 167, 611 F.2d 854 (1979), the board used the reprocurement price without reductions reflecting value engineering incentives earned by the reprocurement contractor. There, the board also reduced the defaulted contractor's price by an amount for prompt payment discounts that the government would have earned.

3. Time Period Covered

The government is also entitled to recover costs incurred during the entire reprocurement period, including additional option years, as long as the original contractor had agreed to perform for that duration, *Lewis Mgmt. & Serv. Co.*, ASBCA 24802, 85-3 BCA ¶18,416. The government must still comply, however, with the basic option requirements of FAR 17.207 that (1) funds are available; (2) the requirement covered by the option fulfills a government need; and (3) the exercise of the option is the most advantageous method of fulfilling the government's need, price, and other factors considered.

In the reprocurement context, this provision has been interpreted to require the contracting officer to meet the mandates of similarity and mitigation before the option costs will be made allowable aspects of excess reprocurement costs. Thus, in *Ross & McDonald Contracting, GmbH*, ASBCA 38154, 94-1 BCA ¶26,316, the board, acting consistently with this general rule, allowed recovery of excess costs associated with the exercise of an option on the reprocurement contract because the identical option had been included in the defaulted contract and the requirements of FAR 17.207 had been satisfied. However, the board mitigated the recovery by the value of certain options that had been added to the reprocurement contract but not included in the original contract, as these costs had not directly resulted from the default.

E. Right to Other Damages

As noted previously, the standard default clauses for fixed-price contracts state that the government's right to assess excess costs of reprocurement following default termination is "in addition to any other rights and remedies provided by law or under this contract." Thus, in cases where the government loses its right to assess excess costs, such as where the reprocured work is found to be "dissimilar," the government may fall back on its right to common law damages. Common law damages are measured as the reasonable excess costs of completing the work in compliance with the contract regardless of whether or not the work has been completed by the government, *M.C. & D. Capital Corp.*, ASBCA 40159, 91-3 BCA ¶24,084. The government cannot, of course, recover actual damages that have been already recovered through an excess cost assessment. In addition, the government's right to recover actual damages not covered by an excess cost assessment may be limited to the extent that the contract contains a liquidated damages clause covering such damages, *Sorensen v. United States*, 51 Ct. Cl. 69 (1916). But see *Hideca Trading, Inc.*, ASBCA 24161, 87-3 BCA ¶20,080 (the board allowed the government, the aggrieved buyer, the traditional common law or U.C.C. damages, i.e., the difference between the contract price at date of contract delivery and the market price, even though the government did not reprocure.) In *Kirk Bros. Mech. Contractors, Inc.*, ASBCA 47801, 96-2 BCA ¶28,291, the board held that the inspection clause did not limit the government's default clause right to reprocure the defective work and charge the contractor.

The government must credit the contractor for work accepted. A properly defaulted contractor may recover for changed work incorporated into end items delivered to and accepted by the government and also recover for "wasted work" attempting to comply with impossible specifications even though no end items were delivered and the government otherwise received no benefit from the work. In *Dennis Berlin d/b/a Spectro Sort*, ASBCA 53549, 03-1 BCA ¶32,075, a contractor unsuccessfully sought a 20 percent profit added on to the cost of acquisition in determining the correct value of the manufacturing materials accepted by the government after the termination. The board noted that in the past it has approximated the value by adjusting the contractor's cost by the indicated rate of loss on delivered end items or by applying the percentage of completion method and subtracting the price of delivered items or by using the jury verdict valuation. A fixed-profit percentage, however, has no relationship to the market value of the material.

The other remedies mentioned in the clause have been held by the Court of Claims to include the right to collect certain "administrative costs" incurred by the agency in connection with the reprocurement contract, *Southeastern Airways Corp. v. United States*, 230 Ct. Cl. 47, 673 F.2d 368 (1982). Accord, *Tester Corp. v. United States*, 1 Cl. Ct. 370 (1982) (expenses for government inspection, testing, and travel); *Futura Sys., Inc.*, ENGBCA 6037, 95-2 BCA ¶27,654 (costs of observing a reprocurement contractor's contractually required testing and costs of a supervisor who traveled to the reprocurement contractor's facility to ensure that problems experienced in the original procurement would not recur). See also FAR 49.402-7 recognizing the government's right to recover "any other ascertainable damages" resulting from the default; *Birken Mfg. Co.*, ASBCA 32590, 90-2 BCA ¶22,845 (costs of issuing reprocurement purchasing request found to be reasonable administrative costs); *Sealtite Corp.*, ASBCA 34156, 90-2 BCA ¶22,844 (costs of administering funds due to labor violations found recoverable). Such costs can be proven by reasonable and reliable estimates, *Walsh Constr. Co. of Ill.*, ASBCA 52952, 02-2 BCA ¶32,004; *ARCO Eng'g, Inc.*, ASBCA 52450, 01-1 BCA ¶31,218.

In *Sach Sinha & Assocs., Inc.*, ASBCA 50640, 00-2 BCA ¶31,111, the government's recoupment claim for unliquidated progress payments was reduced because the per-item contract price was the proper measure for calculating the amount the contractor was entitled to retain. The government accepted the first two of three equal lots, but terminated for default after the contractor failed to deliver the third lot. The government argued that the contractor only delivered two-thirds of the required quantity and was entitled to retain only two-thirds of the progress payments. However, the Default clause required the government to pay the contract price for items delivered and accepted. Therefore, the proper method of calculating the amount due was to multiply the number of items accepted by the contract's per-item price and to deduct that from the amount of the progress payments.

F. Administrative Requirements for Reprocurement

A reprocurement is technically a purchase for the contractor's account and not a new purchase by the government. See FAR 49.402-6. Thus, reprocurement following a termination for default does not require justification under one of the exceptions to the statutory preference for full and open competition, *Old Dominion Sec., Inc.*, GSBCA 9126, 90-2 BCA ¶22,745; *Conti v. United States*, 158 F.2d 581 (1st Cir. 1946); *American Smelting & Ref. Co. v. United States*, 259 U.S. 75 (1922). FAR 49.402-6(b) limits this exemption from the full and open competition requirement to cases where the repurchased quantity does not exceed the quantity of the defaulted contract. If the repurchased quantity is greater, the regulation requires that the procurement be treated as a new procurement. Analogously, where an original contract is restricted to small businesses, there is no requirement that the reprocurement contract must be so restricted, *Bud Mahas Constr., Inc.*, Comp. Gen. Dec. B-235261, 89-2 CPD ¶160.

The GAO has continued to review protests over the propriety of the reprocurement even though the reasonableness of the reprocurement remains for the board's determination. See *Hemet Valley Flying Serv., Inc.*, Comp. Gen. Dec. B-191922, 78-2 CPD ¶117, upholding the award of a negotiated reprocurement contract on a sole source basis to the third low bidder on the original contract because the normal procurement regulations are not strictly applicable to the reprocurement and the need for the airplanes was urgent. The GAO also found that, because the award of a repurchase contract to the second low bidder is a recognized method of reprocurement, the award to the third low bidder was reasonable where the second low bidder was unable to perform. In determining whether award to the second low bidder is proper, the GAO will examine the time between the original award and the default, the time available after the default to undertake a new solicitation, and the difference between the price of the defaulted contractor and the second low bidder, *DCX, Inc.*, Comp. Gen. Dec. B-232692, 89-1 CPD ¶55. See *International Tech. Corp.*, Comp. Gen. Dec. B-250377.5, 93-2 CPD ¶102, in which award to the second low bidder was upheld as proper due, in part, to the fact that only 80 days had passed between award and default. If, however, the repurchase exceeds the quantity under the defaulted contract, the GAO will treat it as a new procurement, *Euclid Designs & Dev. Co.*, Comp. Gen. Dec. B-186679, 76-2 CPD ¶321.

A reprocurement contract issued in a subsequent fiscal year may be charged to an annual appropriation used for the original contract, *Funding of Replacement Contracts*, Comp. Gen. Dec. B-232616, 88-2 CPD ¶602, citing 34 Comp. Gen. 239 (B-121248) (1954). The requirement that the funds be initially obligated within the appropriate year for bona fide needs occurring during that year still applies. See 32 Comp. Gen. 565 (B-114334) (1953), where a reprocurement contract could not be funded from a prior year's appropriations because the original contract did not reflect bona fide needs when obligated.

The GAO had long held that excess costs recovered following default termination had to be deposited in the Treasury as "miscellaneous receipts" rather than credited to the appropriation out of which the contract had been funded. As a result, the excess cost proceeds were unavailable to the agency for funding the reprocurement work, 14 Comp. Gen. 729 (A-60541) (1935); 52 Comp. Gen. 45 (B-173735) (1972). The GAO has partially reversed this line of cases, stating in *Bureau of Prisons*, Comp. Gen. Dec. B-210160, 84-1 CPD ¶91:

> We therefore decide that to the extent necessary to cover the full costs of a replacement contract, excess reprocurement costs recovered by an agency from a breaching contractor need not be deposited in the Treasury as miscellaneous receipts, but rather may be applied to the costs of the replacement contract. The replacement contract must be coextensive with the original contract; that is, it may procure only those goods or services which would have been provided under the breached contract. Any recovered excess reprocurement costs which are not necessary or used for such a replacement contract must still be deposited into the Treasury as miscellaneous receipts.

VI. LIQUIDATED DAMAGES

Like many other buyers of goods and services, the federal government has made substantial use of liquidated damages—primarily as a method of motivating contractors to perform on time. Such damages are spelled out in a contract clause in specific dollar amounts rather than leaving the parties to determine actual damages if a breach occurs. Liquidated damages clauses are regularly used in construction contracts and occasionally in supply and service contracts. DFARS 211.503 makes their use mandatory in fixed-price construction contracts over $500,000, except for cost-plus-fixed-fee contracts where the contractor cannot "control the pace of the work." The use of liquidated damages leads to substantial judicial intervention because federal contracts are subject to the normal common law rule that liquidated damages will not be enforced if they are a penalty, *Priebe & Sons, Inc. v. United States,* 332 U.S. 407 (1947). However, the contractor has the burden of proof that a liquidated damages clause has been improperly used, *DJ Mfg. Corp. v. United States,* 86 F.3d 1130 (Fed. Cir. 1996).

Since liquidated damages clauses infrequently assess damages that are penal, they are generally enforced. However, the government is required to strictly adhere to the provisions of the clause. See, for example, *Abcon Assocs., Inc. v. United States,* 49 Fed. Cl. 678 (2001), in which an assessment of liquidated damages earlier than the time permitted by the clause was held to constitute a breach by the government that invalidated a default termination. See also *William F. Klingensmith, Inc.*, ASBCA 52028, 01-2 BCA ¶32,072 (liquidated damages only assessable for phases 1-5 of contract, not "final phase).

A. General Policy

FAR Subpart 11.5 provides guidance on when and how liquidated damages clauses are to be used. FAR 11.501 contains the general policy on the use of such clauses:

(a) The contracting officer must consider the potential impact on pricing, competition, and contract administration before using a liquidated damages clause. Use liquidated damages clauses only when –
  (1) The time of delivery or timely performance is so important that the Government may reasonably expect to suffer damage if the delivery or performance is delinquent; and
  (2) The extent or amount of such damage would be difficult or impossible to estimate accurately or prove.

(b) Liquidated damages are not punitive and are not negative performance incentives (see 16.402-2). Liquidated damages are used to compensate the Government for probable damages. Therefore, the liquidated damages rate must be a reasonable forecast of just compensation for the harm that is caused by late delivery or untimely performance of the particular contract. Use a maximum amount or a maximum period for assessing liquidated damages if these limits reflect the maximum probable damage to the Government. Also, the contracting officer may use more than one liquidated damages rate when the contracting officer expects the probable damage to the Government to change over the contract period of performance.

(c) The contracting officer must take all reasonable steps to mitigate liquidated damages. If the contract contains a liquidated damages clause and the contracting officer is considering terminating the contract for default, the contracting officer should seek expeditiously to obtain performance by the contractor or terminate the contract and repurchase (see subpart 49.4). Prompt contracting officer action will prevent excessive loss to defaulting contractors and protect the interests of the Government.

(d) The head of the agency may reduce or waive the amount of liquidated damages assessed under a contract, if the Commissioner, Financial Management Service, or designee approves (see Treasury Order 145-10).

This policy deals only with liquidated damages as a substitute for actual damages for *late delivery or completion of the work.* As a result, the standard contract clauses provide for the concurrent assessment of both liquidated damages and the excess costs of reprocurement that are called for by the default clauses. The only guidance for establishing the rate of liquidated damages pertains to construction contracts. See FAR 11.502, which states:

(b) Construction contracts with liquidated damages provisions must describe the rate(s) of liquidated damages assessed per day of delay. The rate(s) should include the estimated daily cost of Government inspection and superintendence. The rate(s) should also include an amount for other expected expenses associated with delayed completion such as –
  (1) Renting substitute property; or
  (2) Paying additional allowance for living quarters.

There are two standard liquidated damages clauses. The clause for construction contracts in FAR 52.211-12 provides:

LIQUIDATED DAMAGES—CONSTRUCTION (SEP 2000)

(a) If the Contractor fails to complete the work within the time specified in the contract, the Contractor shall pay liquidated damages to the Government in the amount of ____________ [*Contracting Officer insert amount*] for each calendar day of delay until the work is completed or accepted.

(b) If the Government terminates the Contractor's right to proceed, liquidated damages will continue to accrue until the work is completed. These liquidated damages are in addition to excess costs of repurchase under the Termination clause.

The standard clause for other types of contracts in FAR 52.211-11 provides:

LIQUIDATED DAMAGES-SUPPLIES, SERVICES, OR RESEARCH AND DEVELOPMENT (SEP 2000)

(a) If the Contractor fails to deliver the supplies or perform the services within the time specified in this contract, the Contractor shall, in place of actual damages, pay to the Government liquidated damages of $__________ per calendar day of delay [*Contracting Officer insert amount*].

(b) If the Government terminates this contract in whole or in part under the Default-Fixed-Price Supply and Service clause, the Contractor is liable for liquidated damages accruing until the Government reasonably obtains delivery or performance of similar supplies or services. These liquidated damages are in addition to excess costs of repurchase under the Termination clause.

(c) The Contractor will not be charged with liquidated damages when the delay in delivery or performance is beyond the control and without the fault or negligence of the Contractor as defined in the Default-Fixed-Price Supply and Service clause in this contract.

B. Enforceability of Liquidated Damages Clause

The general rule as to whether liquidated damages are enforceable was stated in the first *Restatement of Contracts* § 339 as follows:

> An agreement, made in advance of breach, fixing the damages therefor, is not enforceable as a contract and does not affect the damages recoverable for the breach, unless
>
> (a) the amount so fixed is a reasonable forecast of just compensation for the harm that is caused by the breach, and
>
> (b) the harm that is caused by the breach is one that is incapable or very difficult of accurate estimation.

This two-part test is stated in FAR 11.501(a) and is cited in most government contract cases, *Southwest Eng'g Co. v. United States*, 341 F.2d 998 (8th Cir.), *cert. denied*, 382 U.S. 819 (1965).

To overcome the imposition of liquidated damages, it is usually stated that the contractor has the burden of proving that the amount is an unenforceable penalty, *Mega Constr. Co. v. United States*, 29 Fed. Cl. 396 (1993); *JEM Dev. Corp.*, ASBCA 45912, 94-1 BCA ¶26,407. However, see *Clifford La Tourelle*, AGBCA 93-132-1, 94-1 BCA ¶26,509, stating that the government is obligated to show that the amount is reasonable. See also *DJ Mfg. Corp. v. United States,* 86 F.3d 1130 (Fed. Cir. 1996), indicating that the courts are reluctant to overturn liquidated damages clauses. The court stated at 133-34:

> When damages are uncertain or difficult to measure, a liquidated damages clause will be enforced as long as "the amount stipulated for is not so extravagant, or disproportionate to the amount of property loss, as to show that compensation was not the object aimed at or as to imply fraud, mistake, circumvention or oppression." *Wise v. United States*, 249 U.S. 361, 365, 63 L. Ed. 647, 39 S. Ct. 303 (1919); see *United States v. Bethlehem Steel Co.*,

205 U.S. at 121 ("The amount is not so extraordinarily disproportionate to the damage which might result from the [breach], as to show that the parties must have intended a penalty and could not have meant liquidated damages."). With that narrow exception, "there is no sound reason why persons competent and free to contract may not agree upon this subject as fully as upon any other, or why their agreement, when fairly and understandingly entered into with a view to just compensation for the anticipated loss, should not be enforced." *Wise v. United States*, 249 U.S. at 365; see also *Sun Printing & Publishing Ass'n v. Moore*, 183 U.S. 642, 674, 22 S. Ct. 240, 46 L. Ed. 366 (1902) (except where "the sum fixed is greatly disproportionate to the presumed actual damages," a court "has no right to erroneously construe the intention of the parties, when clearly expressed, in the endeavor to make better contracts for them than they have made for themselves").

Liquidated damages clauses are enforceable so long as the government, at contract formation, reasonably could have anticipated harm flowing from a breach of the contract, and the stipulated amount was a reasonable estimate of the anticipated harm. Whether the stipulated amount represents a penalty instead of compensation is highly fact-specific. Liquidated damages are a creature of contract and must be assessed in accordance with the contract.

The government's motive in using a liquidated damages provision is not relevant to determining the enforceability of the provision. See *DJ Mfg. Corp. v. United States*, 86 F.3d 1130 (Fed. Cir. 1996), in which the court provided one of its more extensive discussions of liquidated damages. The court rejected the contractor's argument that the contracting officer's statement about needing to get the items to the troops quickly showed that the liquidated damages clause was designed to "spur performance" and not for just compensation. The court ruled that a liquidated damages clause is not unenforceable simply because the government hopes that it will encourage the contractor's prompt performance.

1. Reasonableness of the Forecast

At the time the contract is made, a forecast of liquidated damages must be based on a reasonable possibility that the government will sustain damages if the contract is breached, and the stipulated liquidated amount must be a reasonable estimate of the anticipated harm to the government. In *FBS Generalbau GmbH*, ASBCA 44743, 95-1 BCA ¶27,504, liquidated damages were proper because they were based on the German economy.

a. Time of the Forecast

The government contract rule is that the reasonableness of the forecast of liquidated damages is evaluated by looking at the situation at the time the contract is made rather than at the time of breach, *Sunflower Landscaping & Garden Ctr.*, AGBCA 87-342-1, 91-3 BCA ¶24,182; *Downing Elec., Inc.*, ASBCA 37851, 90-3 BCA ¶23,001; *Coliseum Constr., Inc.*, ASBCA 36642, 89-1 BCA ¶21,428; *Rivera-Cotty Corp.*, ASBCA 32291, 86-3 BCA ¶19,148. In several instances, this analysis has led to the enforcement of a liquidated damages clause in a situation where no actual damages were incurred by the government, *William F. Klingensmith, Inc.*, ASBCA 52028, 01-2 BCA ¶31,589 ("the focus of an inquiry concerning the propriety of an LDs rate is at the time of contract award, not LDs assessment"); *Southwest Marine, Inc.*, DOTBCA 1577A, 95-1 BCA ¶27,519 (whether the government suffered actual damage was immaterial); *Mit-Con, Inc.*, ASBCA 42884, 92-1 BCA ¶24,634 (liquidated damages based on the daily costs for one inspector found reasonable even though there was no evidence that the government had been damaged by any delay in awarding the follow-on contract); *Central Ohio Bldg. Co.*, PSBCA 2742, 92-1 BCA ¶24,399 ($250 per day was a reasonable rate at the time of contracting, so it is valid even though the government did not incur actual damages); *American Constr. Co.*, ENGBCA 5728, 91-2 BCA ¶24,009. Likewise, on various occasions, liquidated damages awards have been upheld despite being substantially greater than actual damages, *Connell Rice & Sugar Co.*, AGBCA 85-483-1, 87-1 BCA ¶19,489, *rev'd on other grounds*, 837 F.2d 1068 (Fed. Cir. 1988) (liquidated damages award of $289,549 upheld even though the government's actual out-of-pocket expenses were only $27,645); *First Interstate Bank of Denver, N.A.*, GSBCA 9484, 89-1 BCA ¶21,453 (upholding $67,600 in liquidated damages due to a one-year delay in making land ready for lease to the government even though the contractor had not been receiving the government's rent income during the delay).

In *Triad, Inc.*, VABCA 1774, 89-2 BCA ¶21,661, the contractor argued that the not only had the government failed to incur damages as a result of the contractor's delay, the government had profited from the delay. Accordingly, the contractor argued that the incorporation of the liquidated damages provision in the contract had been improper because any liquidated damages the government could recover would be less than the government's savings in terms of interest payments. More specifically, the contractor asserted that the government was saving 10 percent of the contract price in interest payments for each year of delay, while the liquidated damages payment of $50 per day would yield a substantially lower yearly total. The board rejected this argument on the grounds that it would require the government to take the time value of money into account for every contract and would not be consistent with prior precedent that liquidated damages are to be judged from the time of contracting rather than from the time of assessment. See also *Conner Bros. Constr. Co.*, VABCA 2504, 95-2 BCA ¶27,910, where the government made significant alterations to the project but still assessed liquidated damages at the original rate. The board affirmed the assessment, finding no evidence that the rate was "disproportionately high to the reasonably anticipated damages").

The boards have refused to assess such damages where the government did not incur and should not have anticipated incurring any actual damages, *Sunflower Landscaping & Garden Ctr.*, AGBCA 87-342-1, 91-3 BCA ¶24,182 (rejecting assessment of liquidated damages for failure to make progress default with 130 days left before the completion date because the government reprocured immediately thereafter with a 50-day performance period); *Ford Constr. Co.*, AGBCA 241, 72-1 BCA ¶9275 (liquidated damages could not be collected to cover a period where there was no chance of damage to the government by the contractor's delay); *Garden State Painting Co.*, ASBCA 22248, 78-2 BCA ¶13,499 (liquidated damages of $100 per calendar day a penalty because the government knew that there would be no daily inspection or supervision costs). Compare *Hogan Mech., Inc.*, ASBCA 21612, 78-1 BCA ¶13,164, where the assessment of liquidated damages on a calendar-day basis was upheld even though the personnel who generated the bulk of the administrative costs upon which the assessment was based worked only a five-day week. In *Kingston Constructors Inc.*, ENGBCA 6006, 95-2 BCA ¶27,841, the board found the liquidated damages unreasonable because the facts on which the rate had been determined had changed prior to award of the contract. However, the board reduced the assessment from $1,000 to $500 per day. On appeal the court held that if the liquidated damages amount is not a reasonable forecast, it must be stricken as an unreasonable penalty, *Kingston Constructors, Inc., v. WMATA*, 930 F. Supp. 651 (D.D.C. 1996).

Restatement, Second, Contracts § 356 appears to indicate that the presence or absence of actual damages should also be considered in determining the reasonableness of liquidated damages:

> (1) Damages for breach by either party may be liquidated in the agreement but only at an amount that is reasonable in the light of the anticipated or actual harm caused by the breach and the difficulties of proof of loss. A term fixing unreasonably large liquidated damages is unenforceable on grounds of public policy as a penalty.

However, this statement has had no impact on government contract litigation.

b. Accuracy of Measurement of Forecast Damages

In general, a forecast of damages will be held unreasonable if the contractor can demonstrate that the deductions taken by the government are not reasonably related to the government's anticipated loss or injury such that the damages amount to an unwarranted penalty. The decision of whether or not an award amounts to a penalty depends on the facts and circumstances of each case. Most often, this issue will arise when the liquidated damages assessment is contractually specified as a percentage of the contract price. See *Tommy Nobis Ctr., Inc.*, GSBCA 8988-TD, 89-3 BCA ¶22,112 (40 to 60 percent reduction in contract price rejected as unreasonable); *JEM Dev. Corp.*, ASBCA 42645, 92-1 BCA ¶24,428 (47 percent of contract price found to be based on disproportionate estimates of government expense caused by delays); and *W.H. Smith Hardware Co.*, ASBCA 34532, 89-2 BCA ¶21,606 (assessment of 15 percent of contract price was unreasonable because there was no connection made between that figure and the damages that the government incurred as a result of the contractor's improper use of an other than small supplier). Compare *Winfield Mfg. Co.*, ASBCA 35743, 89-2 BCA ¶21,837 (liquidated damages of 8 percent of the contract price with a mandated cap at 25 percent found reasonable).

If the contractor had substantial involvement in negotiating the liquidated damages rate, a finding of reasonableness will be more likely, *Tricon-Triangle Contractors*, ENGBCA 5553, 92-1 BCA ¶24,667 (because the contractor had negotiated a change in the liquidated damages provision in the contract, a finding of penalty was precluded); *Downing Elec., Inc.*, ASBCA 37851, 90-3 BCA ¶23,001 (contractor's unquestioned knowledge of the formula for the daily rate of liquidated damages rendered assessment proper). However, there is no requirement that a liquidated damages clause must be negotiated for it to have the desired effect, *JEM Dev. Corp.*, ASBCA 45912, 94-1 BCA ¶26,407 (lack of negotiation of liquidated damages rate did not necessitate a finding of penalty).

(1) Proportional Application

Liquidated damages will be held to be a reasonable forecast if the amount assessed varies in proportion to the anticipated harm to the government. Conversely, a liquidated damages rate may well be considered a penalty if it is an "all or nothing" rate; that is, the full rate is applied even though significant portions of the work are complete. In *Charley O. Estes.*, IBCA 1198-7-78, 84-1 BCA ¶17,073, a clause in a tree-planting contract, which provided for no payment when tree-planting efforts were deemed to be below the 85 percent level of performance, was held to be unenforceable as a penalty since it made no allowance for the value of timber in a partially planted unit. Accord, *JMNI, Inc. v. United States*, 4 Cl. Ct. 310 (1984). See also *Green Int'l, Inc.*, ENGBCA 5706, 98-1 BCA ¶29,684 (liquidated damages clause was void as a penalty because the clause required the payment of damages for the entire amount of work due under contract milestones even though significant portions of the work toward the milestones had been completed early). In *Conner Bros. Constr. Co.*, VABCA 2504, 95-2 BCA ¶27,910, the government's decision to drop a renovated building from its inspection requirements under a hospital construction project was tantamount to acceptance of that portion of the project. Thus, the contractor was entitled to a pro rata reduction of liquidated damages.

(2) Fixed Daily Rates

Since almost all liquidated damages clauses cover only delay damages (for an exception, see FAR 19.705-7), they are usually assessed at a fixed rate of dollars per day. On construction contracts, where the government does not usually accept the work until it is substantially completed, the use of such daily rates has generally been held reasonable, *Wise v. United States*, 249 U.S. 361 (1919) (liquidated damages of $200 per day for each day of delay in completion of two laboratories were permissible); *Mitchell Eng'g & Constr. Co.*, ENGBCA 3785, 89-2 BCA ¶21,753 ($85 per day partially based on cost of daily site inspections not unreasonable even though daily inspections did not occur due to the contractor's frequent, unjustified absences from the job site); *Browne-Morse Co.*, IBCA 390, 65-2 BCA ¶5037, *recons. denied*, 65-2 BCA ¶5096 (liquidated damages of $75 per day for each day of delay in completion reasonable); *Triad, Inc.*, VABCA 1774, 89-2 BCA ¶21,661 ($50 per day reasonable despite the contractor's claim that flat liquidated damage rates are per se penalties). But see *Coliseum Constr. Inc.*, ASBCA 36642, 89-1 BCA ¶21,428 (liquidated damages of greater than $1,800 per day found unreasonable).

Liquidated damages assessed at a fixed rate per day are not necessarily reasonable when multiple quantities are to be delivered on supply contracts, *Graybar Elec. Co.*, IBCA 773-4-69, 70-1 BCA ¶8121 (flat rate of $50 per day unreasonable where 10 of 18 items were delivered on time, six items two days late, and two items five days late); *Southern Mapping & Eng'g Co.*, AGBCA 224, 71-2 BCA ¶9040 ($25 per day flat rate for failure to deliver any portion of required photographic prints unreasonable because the government failed to prove that partial deliveries were not of value when received). Accord, *Standard Coil Prods., Inc.*, ASBCA 4878, 59-1 BCA ¶2105; *Marathon Battery Co.*, ASBCA 9464, 1964 BCA ¶4337. In *Southern Mapping*, the board recognized that a liquidated damages rate may remain the same until a construction project is substantially complete and available for use but refused to assume that the parties meant to stipulate the same damages for both total and partial failure to deliver items. See also *Northwestern Terra Cotta Co. v. Caldwell*, 234 F.2d 491 (8th Cir.), *cert. denied*, 242 U.S. 643 (1916). However, one board has specifically rejected a contractor's claim that fixed liquidated damages rates are penalties as a matter of law for multiple quantity contracts. See *Triad, Inc.*, VABCA 1774, 89-2 BCA ¶21,661, in which the board stated at 108,964:

> There is no evidence that the Government's administrative and inspection costs did not continue until completion of the contract. Some degree of reduction of this activity may have been experienced in the later stages of the contract but the extent of the reduction, if any, is not disclosed—the matter is simply not addressed. Furthermore, it is well established that the legality of a liquidated damage provision is to be determined on facts and estimates extant at the outset of the contract, and the actual damages experienced thereafter are generally considered not material.

Accordingly, the board concluded that it was irrelevant whether the contractor had installed only one window or almost all of them prior to the termination. The contractor was charged the $50-per-day rate for the full 186-day delay.

Assessment of liquidated damages at a per-unit per-day rate is generally upheld. In *Henry Angelo & Co.*, ASBCA 44648, 93-3 BCA ¶26,131, the board held that a liquidated damages assessment of $10 per day for each house not renovated was reasonable because the contractor had provided no evidence tending to demonstrate that this figure was not a "reasonable forecast of damages" or that it bore "no reasonable relation to damages for delay." Accord, *Bayou Culvert Mfg., Inc.*, AGBCA 400, 76-1 BCA ¶11,796. In *Simmonds Precision Prods., Inc. v. United States*, 212 Ct. Cl. 305, 546 F.2d 886 (1976), liquidated damages were upheld because the parties had negotiated a per-item per-day rate even though the contract mistakenly included a clause calling for such damages on a per-day rate. However, in *Pre-Con, Inc.*, IBCA 986-3-73, 74-2 BCA ¶10,957, a liquidated damages provision of $3 per unit per day was held unreasonable because the effect of the delayed deliveries was to require special installation of the units at an approximate cost of $50 per unit, regardless of the extent of the delay. In *Lauhoff Grain Co.*, AGBCA 75-120, 80-1 BCA ¶14,192, liquidated damages at a fixed rate per unit per day were held unreasonable because a GAO study stated that they were too high and the government submitted no evidence of either estimated or actual damages.

(3) Inclusion of Administrative Expenses

In accordance with FAR 11.502(b) most contracts set the liquidated damages rate based on anticipated administrative expenses. The courts and boards generally uphold such liquidated damages because such administrative expenses—that is, inspection, superintendence, or engineering costs—can be reasonably anticipated if a delay is encountered, *Downing Elec., Inc.*, ASBCA 37851, 90-3 BCA ¶23,001 (liquidated damages of $265 per day reasonable because they were measured as one-half the daily cost of a typical inspector plus administrative and overhead expenses); *Southland Constr. Co.*, VABCA 2217, 89-1 BCA ¶21,548 ($45 per day upheld because the contracting officer had warned the contractor at a pre-construction conference that liquidated damages would include storage costs); *Robert E. McKee, Inc.*, ASBCA 33643, 90-1 BCA ¶22,391 (liquidated damages assessment based upon delay in only one of 15 construction items not a penalty because such a delay would foreseeably disrupt the inspector's capability to work and the liquidated damages formula was based upon these perceived costs); *FBS Generalbau GmbH*, ASBCA 44743, 95-1 BCA ¶27,504 (liquidated damages properly included increased costs for inspector and for the contracting officer's representative.); *Young Assocs., Inc. v. United States*, 200 Ct. Cl. 438, 471 F.2d 618 (1973) (liquidated damages of $100 per day not unreasonable because they were based on an approximation of administrative and engineering costs that would be incurred by such a delay). Such reasonableness has been found even though the daily rate is established by regulation and based on a sliding scale that lists the dollars of liquidated damages to be used for various contract prices. In *Young*, the court stated at 445:

> Citing the liquidated damages policy section of the Federal Procurement Regulations, 41 CFR § 1-1.315-2(c) (1972), [the contractor] says that the incorporation of FP-61 (promulgated in 1961 by the Commerce Department) into this Interior Department 1964 contract shows that no "case-by-case" consideration was given to the rate of liquidated damages. The answer is, we think, that the regulation does not require a liquidated-damage schedule to be tailor-made for each individual contract. It is enough if the amount stipulated is reasonable for the particular agreement at the time it is made. We have no reason to doubt that that was so here, and [the contractor] suggests none. The court can take judicial notice that costs did not generally decrease from 1961 to 1964, and the [Government] points out that other procuring agencies were using the same charge of $100 per day for a contract of this magnitude. We cannot say, therefore, that in June 1964 it was unreasonable to adopt that amount as daily liquidated damages for delay on this road-building project.

See also *Lane Co.*, ASBCA 21691, 79-1 BCA ¶13,651. In *George F. Marshall & Gordon L. Blackwell*, ENGBCA 6066, 00-1 BCA ¶30,780, the board expressed doubt about the propriety of an "interest" component in the liquidated damages clause. Although it did not determine whether this rendered the clause a penalty per se, it did state that to the extent the government recovers under such a liquidated damages provision, it would be recovering interest on interest. The board called such an "interest" methodology "highly dubious."

(4) Maximum Assessment

Merely because a liquidated damages clause does not contain a time limit or maximum amount of liquidated damages, does not make it unreasonable and a penalty. In *Hughes Bros. v. United States*, 133 Ct. Cl. 108, 134 F. Supp. 471 (1955), the court approved a liquidated damages clause that could have allowed assessed damages on a per-day basis for an indefinite period. Accord, *Bayou Culvert Mfg., Inc.*, AGBCA 400, 76-1 BCA ¶11,796; *Southland Constr. Co.*, VABCA 2217, 89-1 BCA ¶21,548; *Weldon Farm Prods., Inc. v. Commodity Credit Corp.*, 214 F. Supp. 678 (D. Minn. 1963); *Jennie-O Foods, Inc. v. United States*, 217 Ct. Cl. 314, 580 F.2d 400 (1978); 35 Comp. Gen. 484 (B-126434) (1956). This has led to the assessment of liquidated damages in excess of the contract price, *Parker-Schram*, IBCA 96, 59-1 BCA ¶2127; *Ivy H. Smith Co. v. United States*, 154 Ct. Cl. 74 (1961). Contrast *Operational Serv. Corp.*, ASBCA 37059, 93-3 BCA ¶26,190, in which the board, in concluding that the assessment amounted to a penalty, gave substantial weight to the fact that the liquidated damages assessment was greater than the contractor's bid price.

(5) Use of Standard Formulae

The use of certain standard formulas for measuring has not only been upheld as reasonable but has also been accepted by the courts and boards as prima facie evidence of the reasonableness of the liquidated damages assessment. For example, the 20 percent liquidated damages provision incorporated into the SF 114C Default clause used in all government sales of property has been ruled presumptively reasonable and not a penalty, *Baltazar Torres v. General Servs. Admin.*, GSBCA 11472, 92-3 BCA ¶25,178 (no evidence that the failure to pay for four automobiles precluded an assessment of 20 percent of the contract price where the figure represented a reasonable estimate of anticipated damages); *Mike Casey v. General Servs. Admin.*, GSBCA 11570, 92-2 BCA ¶24,882 (20 percent upheld where the bidder failed to demonstrate grounds to void the sale of a truck); *Harry W. Griffith v. General Servs. Admin.*, GSBCA 11571, 93-1 BCA ¶25,421 (20 percent is a reasonable estimation of the government's administrative costs for sales of property); *Spiess Constr. Co.*, ASBCA 48247, 95-2 BCA ¶27,767 (assessment of liquidated damages was enforceable because the daily rate for the assessment was arrived at by using a standard government manual); *Orbas & Assocs.*, ASBCA 48260, 97-2 BCA ¶29,281 (liquidated damages rate of $50 per day was enforceable because the rate in the contract was significantly less than the rate of $200 a day prescribed by the regulation governing the calculation of liquidated damages rates for government contracts of this value); *Valenzuela Eng'g, Inc.*, ASBCA 53936, 04-1 BCA ¶32,517 (daily rate for liquidated damages presumed reasonable because it came from a government contracting manual).

Similarly, the use of tables such as those in the NAVFAC P-68 manual is presumed reasonable because the purpose of these tables is to establish a reasonable estimate of government expense in case of a delay. In *Fred A. Arnold, Inc. v. United States*, 18 Cl. Ct. 1 (1989), *recon.*, 24 Cl. Ct. 6 (1991), *rev'd on other grounds*, 979 F.2d 217 (Fed. Cir. 1992), the court reversed the conclusion that $1,728 per day based on the NAVFAC formula incorporated into the contract was a penalty and upheld that award, stating at 13:

> [T]o hold that the regulation was unreasonable, or in need of substantiation by independent proof, is tantamount to requiring the Government to "reinvent the wheel" each time it enters into a contract for the construction of military housing that is to include a liquidated damages provision. By the Board's reasoning, the Government would be obliged to re-calculate the per diem damage rate for each and every contract. Such a result is impractical, inefficient, and, indeed, unwise because it robs the Government of the more informed decision-making that enters into the development and promulgation of a service-wide regulatory standard. We must presume, therefore, that this regulation, like federal regulations in general, is reasonable absent evidence to the contrary. Here there was no such evidence.

One board followed this decision in *Brooks Lumber Co.*, ASBCA 40743, 91-2 BCA ¶23,984, in which it noted that the utilization of these tables is prima facie evidence that the liquidated damages assessment is reasonable. Accord, *JEM Dev. Corp.*, ASBCA 45912, 94-1 BCA ¶26,407 ($100 per day upheld, though determined by a formula, because the formula was based on properly recoverable administrative costs); *Skip Kirchdorfer, Inc.*, ASBCA 40515, 00-1 BCA ¶30,622 (upholding rates less than those prescribed by Naval Facilities Engineering Command manual). Thus, formulas will generally be upheld unless, of course, doing so would be unreasonable or unconscionable. See *Operational Serv. Corp.*, ASBCA 37059, 93-3 BCA ¶26,190 (penalty found where the use of a contractually mandated formula—hourly rate multiplied by period of delay—led to an assessment greater than the original bid price). If the standard formula is wrongly applied, however, the rate may be rejected. In *George F. Marshall & Gordon L. Blackwell*, ENGBCA 6066, 00-1 BCA ¶30,780, the agency erroneously applied its own internal guidelines, resulting in a liquidated damages rate that grossly exceeded the per diem amount that was computable pursuant to the regulations.

In *Young Assocs., Inc. v. United States*, 200 Ct. Cl. 438, 471 F.2d 618 (1973), the court noted that a liquidated damages schedule is not required to be tailor-made for each individual contract. Similarly, in *DJ Mfg. Corp. v. United States*, 86 F.3d 1130 (Fed. Cir. 1996), the court approved a liquidated damages clause even though the amount was not calculated specifically for the contract. The court rejected the contractor's argument that the regulations in effect at the time, FAR 12.202(b), required the contracting officer specifically to tailor the liquidated damages clause to the particular contract in advance, holding that the regulation provided advice and "internal guidance rather than [creating] rights in contracting parties." In addition, the court found nothing "inherently unreasonable" in the rate reducing the price by 1/15 of 1 percent per day.

2. Difficulty of Accurate Estimation

It is generally stated that liquidated damages will not be enforced unless the harm is difficult to determine, *Robert E. Dineen v. United States*, 109 Ct. Cl. 18, 71 F. Supp. 742 (1947), *cert. denied*, 333 U.S. 842, *reh'g denied*, 334 U.S. 816 (1948); *Broderick Wood Prods. Co. v. United States*, 195 F.2d 433 (10th Cir. 1952); *First Interstate Bank of Denver, N.A.*, GSBCA 9484, 89-1 BCA ¶21,453; *Downing Elec., Inc.*, ASBCA 37851, 90-3 BCA ¶23,001; *Work Force Reforestation, Inc.*, AGBCA 90-131-3, 90-3 BCA ¶23,138; *Jennie-O Foods, Inc. v. United States*, 217 Ct. Cl. 314, 580 F.2d 400 (1978). However, this requirement has rarely been dispositive, and testimony by a government witness to the effect that the government cannot accurately estimate the amount of damages due to delay is usually adequate proof of difficulty. See *Green Int'l, Inc.*, ENGBCA 5706, 98-1 BCA ¶29,684, accepting the government's argument that it was difficult to assess the damage when dealing with a public project such as the construction of a subway station.

C. Relief from Liquidated Damages

Liquidated damages will not be assessed during any period in which the contractor experienced an excusable delay, or after the date on which the contractor substantially completed the work.

1. Excusable Delays

The standard clause used to include liquidated damages in supply, service, or research and development contracts contains a provision relieving the contractor from the assessment of such damages during any period of excusable delay, FAR 52.211-11. The construction contract default termination clause in FAR 52.249-10 accomplishes the same result by granting the contractor schedule extensions for excusable delays. For a detailed discussion of the types of excusable delays, see Chapter 6.

Even if liquidated damages are included in a contract without cross-reference to excusable delays, it is likely that no assessment would be allowed for an excusable delay period. See *North Am. Aviation, Inc.*, ASBCA 11603, 68-1 BCA ¶6998 (target delivery date adjusted for excusable delays in incentive contract with delivery bonus that did not cross-reference excusable delays provision); *General Precision, Inc.*, ASBCA 11071, 66-2 BCA ¶5904 (neither delivery bonus nor penalty assessable in incentive contract without cross-reference to excusable delays provisions where both government delays and excusable delays were concurrent); and *Morganti Nat'l Inc. v. United States*, 49 Fed. Cl. 110 (2001), *aff'd*, 36 Fed. Appx. 452 (Fed Cir. 2002) (because the contractor was entitled to a time extension, which extended beyond the date of the default termination, the court directed the return of the liquidated damages.)

Contractors have the burden of proving that the delay was excusable under the Default clause of the contract, *Sauer Inc. v. Danzig*, 224 F.3d 1340 (Fed. Cir. 2000). Compare *Fire Sec. Sys., Inc. v. General Servs. Admin.*, GSBCA 12120, 97-2 BCA ¶28,994, stating that the government has the "initial burden of establishing the facts upon which the assessment of liquidated damages is based."

Where a contractor is delayed by a series of nonconcurrent causes, liquidated damages will be assessed after the excusable delays are accounted for, *Southwest Eng'g Co. v. United States,* 341 F.2d 998 (8th Cir.), *cert. denied,* 382 U.S. 819 (1965). However, when both excusable and inexcusable causes of delay would have prevented work from being accomplished on a given day, liquidated damages have generally not been assessed, *Vogt Bros. Mfg. Co. v. United States,* 160 Ct. Cl. 687 (1963) (where both parties are responsible for contract delays, neither party has a claim against the other); *Brooks Lumber Co.*, ASBCA 40743, 91-2 BCA ¶23,984 (government changes and delays running concurrently with subcontractor delays in restarting performance precluded recovery for that period). See also *Arrow, Inc.*, ASBCA 39621, 90-3 BCA ¶23,217; *Spectrum Leasing Corp.*, GSBCA 7347, 90-3 BCA ¶22,984, and *ADCO Constr., Inc.*, PSBCA 2355, 90-3 BCA ¶22,944. Thus, concurrent delays will invalidate an assessment of liquidated damages, *Conner Bros. Constr. Co.*, VABCA 2504, 95-2 BCA ¶27,910 (contractor entitled to reimbursement for periods of concurrent government-caused and contractor-caused delay); *Tempo, Inc.*, ASBCA 37589, 95-2 BCA ¶27,618 (liquidated damages reduced because the government failed to meet its burden of proving that any part of the delay period was not concurrent with government-caused delay).

In some cases, it has been stated that concurrent delays will lead to "annulment" of the liquidated damages provision. See *Schmoll v. United States,* 91 Ct. Cl. 1 (1940), in which the court stated at 28:

> In *Levering & Garrigues Co. v. United States,* 73 C. Cls. 566, 578, this court stated that "where a contractor is prevented from executing his contract according to its terms, he is relieved from the obligations of the contract (as to time of completion) and from paying liquidated damages." In several cases we have held that where delays are caused by both parties to the contract the court will not attempt to apportion them, but will simply hold that the provisions of the contract with reference to liquidated damages will be annulled.

See also *Acme Process Equip. Co. v. United States,* 171 Ct. Cl. 324, 347 F.2d 509 (1965), *rev'd on other grounds,* 385 U.S. 138 (1966).

Cases indicate that an effort will be made to avoid annulment by seeking to ascertain the controlling cause of the delay, *Industrial Design Labs., Inc.*, ASBCA 21603, 80-1 BCA ¶14,269. Thus, if the government can prove that the total project delay was caused by contractor fault, concurrent excusable delays not delaying the total project will not be used to relieve the contractor of liquidated damages, *G. Bliudzius Contractors, Inc.*, ASBCA 42366, 93-3 BCA ¶26,074 (despite the lack of a critical path method schedule in the contract, several government-caused delays were found not to require remission of all damages because those delays did not affect final completion); *Central Ohio Bldg. Co.*, PSBCA 2742, 92-1 BCA ¶24,399 (government delay in approval of an additive ruled irrelevant because the contract precluded the use of this additive and the contractor had been responsible for a 41-day delay after receiving the notice to proceed); *Harold J. Younger, Inc.*, ASBCA 38922, 91-1 BCA ¶23,436 (inclusion of alleged extra and unnecessary items on a punch list by the government held not critical to the completion of the overall project); *G.Q. Carmichael Surveyors & Eng'rs, Inc.*, AGBCA 86-186-1, 92-1 BCA ¶24,743 (government's refusal to provide plans and specifications found not the central cause of delay; the contractor's failure to provide a supervisor at the work site was so found). See also Wickwire and Smith, *The Use of Critical Path Method Techniques in Contract Claims,* 7 Pub. Cont. L.J. 1, 43-45 (1974). In each of these cases, the critical path method (CPM) was used to apportion concurrent delays, with the board holding that the delay on the critical path was the causative delay. As this type of accurate evidence of the impact of various delays becomes more widely available, it is likely that there will be more apportionment of delays for purposes of assessing liquidated damages. Without such evidence, however, the boards continue to refuse to assess liquidated damages where concurrent delays have occurred, *H.G. Reynolds Co.*, ASBCA 42351, 93-2 BCA ¶25,797 (conflicting punchlists issued by the government precluded a liquidated damages assessment even though the contractor had also been responsible for the delay). Accord, *Jordan & Nobles Constr. Co.*, GSBCA 8349, 91-1 BCA ¶23,659; *ADCO Constr. Inc.*, PSBCA 2355, 90-3 BCA ¶22,944. See, however, *Lawrence D. Krause*, AGBCA 76-118-4, 82-2 BCA ¶16,129, holding that the contractor has the burden of proof that its delay was not the cause of the late delivery.

In one unique case, the Department of Transportation Board of Contract Appeals apportioned concurrent delays on the basis of comparative fault rather than proof of causation, *Hilltop Elec. Constr., Inc.*, DOTCAB 78-6, 78-2 BCA ¶13,421. The board granted time extensions for one-half the delay period on the theory that the parties were equally at fault. The effect of such time extensions was that the contractor was assessed one-half the liquidated damages.

In recent decisions, seeking the casue of delays has been called "apportionment." Apportionment was allowed in *Sauer, Inc. v. Danzig,* 224 F.3d 1340 (Fed. Cir. 2000), because of clear fault on both sides. See also *R. P. Wallace, Inc. v. United States,* 63 Fed. Cl. 402 (2004) (reviewing decisions and apportioning "sequential delays"), and *Sunshine Constr. & Eng'g, Inc. v. United States,* 64 Fed. Cl. 346 (2005) (agreeing with *Wallace*). In *PCL Constr. Servs., Inc. v. United States,* 53 Fed. Cl. 479 (2002), however, the court continued to adhere to the rule against apportionment, finding that *Sauer* had not overruled *Acme Process Equipment.*

Where apportionment is considered inappropriate, contractors have been relieved from liability for liquidated damages, *Wexler Constr. Co.*, ASBCA 23782, 84-2 BCA ¶17,408; *Powell's Gen. Contracting Co.*, DOTCAB 77-27, 79-1 BCA ¶13,694, *recons. denied,* 79-1 BCA ¶13,702; *Myers-Laine Corp.*, ASBCA 18234, 74-1 BCA ¶10,467; *ICA Southeast, Inc.*, AGBCA 331, 73-1 BCA ¶9969. In *Kirk Bros. Mechanical Contractors, Inc.*, ASBCA 43738, 93-1 BCA ¶25,325, the board relieved a contractor of 37 days of liquidated damages—seven days for government-caused delays and 30 days for concurrent delays. However, in *Acme Process Equip. Co. v. United States,* 171 Ct. Cl. 324, 347 F.2d 509 (1965), *rev'd on other grounds,* 385 U.S. 138 (1966), the court indicated that, even though the contractor is relieved from liquidated damages, it would still be liable for actual damages suffered by the government as a result of a concurrent delay.

2. Substantial Completion

Liquidated damages will not be assessed after the date on which the work is substantially completed. Substantial completion has been defined as the moment when the construction sites or the tendered supplies are capable of being used for their intended purposes, *Theon v. United States,* 765 F.2d 1110 (Fed. Cir. 1985); *Central Ohio Bldg. Co.*, PSBCA 2742, 92-1 BCA ¶24,399. This rule is applied primarily on construction contracts where substantial completion is held to have occurred when a high percentage of the work is completed and the project is available for its intended use, *Lindwall Constr. Co.*, ASBCA 23148, 79-1 BCA ¶13,822 (because building was available for beneficial occupancy, it was substantially complete); *Vern W. Johnson & Sons, Inc.*, ENGBCA 5554, 90-1 BCA ¶22,571 (government had beneficial occupancy of a pumping station for a fish hatchery and could not demonstrate that it was not working as intended); *Long Elevator & Mach. Co.*, VABCA 2246, 90-2 BCA ¶22,637 (substantial completion found where one elevator was returned to service, even though minor punch list items remained to be completed); *Matthew Andrew Kalosinakis*, ASBCA 41337, 91-2 BCA ¶23,744 (substantial completion occurred where the only remaining work was the permanent installation of a receptacle in the bathroom of a house and some minor clean-up items); *R.J. Crowley, Inc.*, GSBCA 11080 (9521)-REIN, 92-1 BCA ¶24,499 (substantial completion found despite lack of installation of a fire alarm); *Batson-Cook of Atlanta, Inc.*, ASBCA 44902, 97-1 BCA ¶28,754 (government failed to prove that deficiencies in the contractor's work precluded use of that phase of the project); *Orbas & Assocs.*, ASBCA 48260, 97-2 BCA ¶29,281 (record strongly suggested that the system was substantially completed when government began withholding only $1,920 as retainage). Conversely, if a building is not available for its intended use, no substantial completion will be found, *Randolph & Co.*, ASBCA 52953, 03-1 BCA ¶32,080, *recons. denied,* ASBCA 52957, 03-1 BCA ¶32,138 (government had not accepted the work and it was not suitable for its intended purpose); *Gassman Corp.*, ASBCA 44975, 00-1 BCA ¶30,720 (building not available for follow-on contractor to perform the interior finish work necessary for the facility to be used as a research laboratory).

While the contractor must show that performance is near completion, there is no set percentage that establishes substantial completion. However, when a significant percentage of the work remains unperformed, substantial completion will not be found, *Wilton Corp.*, ASBCA 39876, 93-2 BCA ¶25,897 (substantial completion rejected where price of unperformed lintel work was 11 percent of total price); *Toombs & Co.*, ASBCA 34590, 91-1 BCA ¶23,403 (government occupation of two buildings did not demonstrate substantial completion because work on the roofs of the buildings had yet to pass the contract testing requirements); *Foremost Mgmt. Sys., Inc.*, ENGBCA-PCC-145, 99-1 BCA ¶30,137 (completion of 9 out of 10 phases was not substantial completion because the parties had planned for each phase to be of equivalent importance). This is true even though the government may be able to derive some benefit from the uncompleted project, *J&A Pollin Constr. Co.*, GSBCA 2780, 70-2 BCA ¶8562 (although classes were held for nine days before heat was provided, building was not substantially complete until heat was provided). See also *Capitol City Constr. Co.*, DOTCAB 74-29, 75-1 BCA ¶11,012, and *Lambert Constr. Co.*, DOTCAB 77-9, 78-1 BCA ¶13,221. The board will determine the percentage of completion from the contractor's progress reports unless evidence exists that they overstate the actual percentage of completion of the project, *Electronic & Missile Facilities, Inc.*, GSBCA 2787, 71-1 BCA ¶8785.

Board decisions place more emphasis on the availability of the work for its intended use than the application of any rigid formula as to the percentage of work that has been accomplished, *Electrical Enters., Inc.*, IBCA 972-9-72, 74-1 BCA ¶10,400. If the product cannot be used as intended, liquidated damages generally are assessed. See *Mit-Con, Inc.*, ASBCA 44509, 93-2 BCA ¶25,570, holding that a building was not substantially complete when the contractor had yet to complete wire mesh cages for safe storage of equipment and had yet to remove nonconforming pavement. The board concluded that, although most of the work had been completed, without these essential components the building could not be used for its intended purpose. See also *Pathman Constr. Co.*, ASBCA 16781, 74-2 BCA ¶10,785, holding that a mess hall was not substantially complete where performance of remaining work would have interfered with food preparation, and *Fisher Constr. Co.*, ASBCA 7264, 1962 BCA ¶3497, finding a facility not substantially complete where deficiencies rendered it unsafe for use. Accord, *Fred Loffredo*, ASBCA 22218, 82-1 BCA ¶15,509 (hangar not fit for intended purpose even though only minor effort was required to correct out-of-line door aperture); *Martell Constr. Co.*, ASBCA 23679, 80-1 BCA ¶14,429 (even though government was able to occupy building, no substantial completion found because building could not be used for its intended purpose as an audiovisual center); *Lane Co.*, ASBCA 21691, 79-1 BCA ¶13,651 (no substantial completion of building where toilets had been installed and used but sewage treatment system not fully operational); *Hof Constr. Co.*, ASBCA 22136, 78-1 BCA ¶13,062 (automatic data processing center not substantially complete without functioning air conditioning system since ADP equipment required a cool temperature to function properly); *Electronic & Missile Facilities, Inc.*, GSBCA 2787, 71-1 BCA ¶8785 (no substantial completion where punchlist totaling 1,200 defects, many of them minor, made building unsuitable for normal business functions); *George A. Grant, Inc.*, IBCA 100-7-73, 74-2 BCA ¶10,851 (defective drain pipes representing only 3.35 percent of the drain line interfered with farming operations in the area).

The doctrine of substantial completion will not be applied in cases where delivery of the item complete and intact is required in order for it to be used at all, *Southwest Welding & Mfg. Div., Yuba Consolidated Indus., Inc.*, IBCA 281, 1962 BCA ¶3564; *Bayou Culvert Mfg., Inc.*, AGBCA 400, 76-1 BCA ¶11,796.

Substantial completion will not be found where the government does not have notice that the work has been substantially completed and beneficial occupancy can take place, *Seaboard Surety Co.*, ASBCA 43281, 93-1 BCA ¶25,510.

D. Relationship with Default Termination

The termination for default of a contract containing a liquidated damages provision may result in the assessment against the contractor of liquidated damages that are in addition to the excess costs of reprocurement or other actual damages not covered by the provision.

1. Concurrent Running of Liquidated Damages and Excess Costs of Reprocurement

When a contract containing a liquidated damages provision is terminated for default, the standard clauses provide that the government may assess liquidated damages until it obtains completion of the work. The time period used to compute such damages begins at the contract completion date, as adjusted for excusable delays, and ends when the work would have been completed had the government acted reasonably in reprocuring the work, *Racine Screw Co. v. United States*, 156 Ct. Cl. 256 (1962). See *Biehler Painting Co.*, ASBCA 18855, 76-1 BCA ¶11,729, in which the government argued that liquidated damages should be assessed starting at the date the contractor abandoned the contract, but the board held that the proper date to begin the running of liquidated damages was the original contract completion date. See also *Frontier Contracting Co.*, ASBCA 33658, 89-2 BCA ¶21,595, in which the board remitted liquidated damages that had been assessed against the contractor for the period between the original completion date and the actual completion date because a time extension had been granted due to government insistence that the contractor fix leaks in the roof.

The contractor is not necessarily liable for the entire time necessary for completion. The reasonableness of the government's reprocurement will be closely scrutinized, and liquidated damages will not be assessed for any period of delay caused by the government, *Arctic Corner, Inc.*, ASBCA 38075, 94-1 BCA ¶26,317 (cost of 6½-month delay in awarding the reprocurement contract must be excluded from liquidated damages assessment); *Biehler Painting Co.*, ASBCA 18855, 76-1 BCA ¶11,729 (liquidated damages would not run to the actual completion date of the reprocurement contract where it was found that "but for unreasonable delay in awarding the reprocurement contract, work thereunder would have been completed one month earlier"). See *Nichols Dynamics, Inc.*, ASBCA 17610, 74-2 BCA ¶10,820, in which liquidated damages were reduced because the government had allowed the contractor to continue to perform for 25 days following termination for default before issuing a solicitation for completion of the work. The board disallowed liquidated damages for the full 25-day period and also denied the contractor payment for work performed during that period. See also FAR 11.501(c), noting that efficient administration of reprocurements is imperative to avoid the loss of liquidated damages.

Liquidated damages may not be assessed unless work is completed or the supplies are reprocured, *Manart Textile Co. v. United States*, 111 Ct. Cl. 540, 77 F. Supp. 924 (1948). The government cannot recover liquidated damages for the period of an attempted but incomplete procurement, *Standard Coating Serv., Inc.*, ASBCA 48611, 00-1 BCA ¶30,725. Here, the government canceled the reprocurement after issuing its solicitation but before award. Thus the contractor was not liable for liquidated damages after the date of termination. See also *Designatronics, Inc.*, ASBCA 10149, 65-1 BCA ¶4812, and *Hydro Flex Inc.*, ASBCA 20352, 77-1 BCA ¶12,353. Accordingly, where the government did not reprocure but instead proposed, as the amount of a liquidated damages assessment, a hypothetical minimum amount that the reprocurement would cost, the board rejected it as improper, *Dave's Aluminum Siding, Inc.*, ASBCA 34092, 90-3 BCA ¶23,053 (no evidence presented establishing the reasonableness of the minimum). Similarly, liquidated damages will be denied where the reprocured items were not similar to those purchased under the original contract, *Milro Controls Co.*, ASBCA 11550, 68-2 BCA ¶7372.

The contractor is not liable for delays encountered by the reprocurement contractor, *Mega Constr. Co. v. United States*, 29 Fed. Cl. 396 (1993); *Matthews Co.*, AGBCA 459, 76-2 BCA ¶12,164, *recons. denied*, 77-1 BCA ¶12,434. See *Olympic Painting Contractors*, ASBCA 15773, 72-2 BCA ¶9549, in which the board held that liquidated damages could be assessed only through the scheduled completion date of the reprocurement contract and not for the 30 days of excusable delay encountered by the reprocurement contractor. If the reprocurement contractor fails to perform and a second reprocurement is awarded, liquidated damages may be assessed against the original contractor only through the scheduled completion date of the first reprocurement contract, *Interstate Forestry, Inc.*, AGBCA 89-114-1, 91-1 BCA ¶23,660. In a questionable decision, the GAO allowed the government to assess liquidated damages for a period beyond the scheduled completion date of the reprocurement contract where the original contract stated that liquidated damages could be assessed up to a "45 day maximum," *California Meat Co.*, Comp. Gen. Dec. B-190150, 78-2 CPD ¶250. When the reprocurement contractor failed to complete the work by the reprocurement scheduled completion date, or within 45 days of the completion date of the original contract, the contracting officer assessed liquidated damages for 45 days. The GAO upheld the contracting officer's decision, stating:

> The fact that the terminated contractor had no control over the replacement contractor's efforts to deliver the goods, required that there be established a maximum period for which liquidated damages could be assessed, but provides no further equitable basis for remitting damages within the agreed maximum period. Equity is implicit in the maximum 45 day period.

2. Effect of Waiver

Waiver of the original completion date by forbearance from default action does not preclude assessment of liquidated damages beginning on the original completion date, *Southland Constr. Co.*, VABCA 2279, 89-1 BCA ¶21,271; *Clifford La Tourelle*, AGBCA 93-132-1, 94-1 BCA ¶26,509; *Robert E. Moore Constr.*, AGBCA 85-262-1, 90-2 BCA ¶22,803; *Instruments for Indus., Inc.*, ASBCA 10543, 65-2 BCA ¶5097, *recons. denied*, 70-1 BCA ¶8246. In the last case, the board reasoned that the liquidated damages provision specifically imposed damages where the government elected to permit the contractor to continue work after the original completion date. In *JEM Dev. Corp.*, ASBCA 42872, 92-1 BCA ¶24,709, the board rejected an assessment of liquidated damages against a construction contractor because the government had knowledge of the causes of the contractor's delay and had acquiesced in the result. In general, however, waiver of delivery date will rarely be found in construction contracts. Similarly, issuance of a change order after the completion date of the contract does not bar the imposition of liquidated damages for any period of inexcusable delay prior to the date of issuance of the order, *Thomas E. Schroyer & Co.*, GSBCA 3465, 72-1 BCA ¶9181; *M.S.I. Corp.*, VACAB 626, 68-1 BCA ¶6773; *Norfolk Shipbuilding & Drydock Corp.*, ENGBCA 3225, 73-1 BCA ¶9950. Contra, *Jan R. Smith, Contractor*, FAACAP 66-21, 65-2 BCA ¶5306. However, where both parties negotiate the time extensions for changes and the date for overall completion of the contract is not affected as a result, liquidated damages will be upheld, *Eurostyle Inc.*, GSBCA 10037, 91-1 BCA ¶23,595.

E. Computation of Time Covered by Liquidated Damages

Under the standard clauses, liquidated damages are assessed for each calendar day of delay. Holidays are included in the computation, *Pressed Steel Car Co. v. Eastern Ry. Co. of Minn.*, 121 F. 609 (8th Cir. 1903); *Hogan Mech., Inc.*, ASBCA 21612, 78-1 BCA ¶13,164; *Winslow Tele-Tronics, Inc.*, ASBCA 15036, 72-1 BCA ¶9234. In *J.H. Strain & Sons, Inc.*, ASBCA 34432, 90-2 BCA ¶22,770, the board denied the contractor's argument that liquidated damages could not be assessed for weekends and holidays, stating at 114,298:

> The fact that the Government assessed liquidated damages for week-ends and holidays does not invalidate the liquidated damages assessment. Both contract performance and liquidated damages were measured in terms of calendar days, not weekdays.

In *Diane Assocs., Inc.*, ASBCA 23836, 80-1 BCA ¶14,453, the board rejected the contractor's argument that because work was permitted only on weekdays, the period of assessment should include only weekdays. In *Steele Contractors, Inc.*, ENGBCA 6043, 95-2 BCA ¶27,653, the government improperly withheld liquidated damages for the final day of the original contract performance period, because the record did not reveal the government's rationale for including that day in its assessment.

In *Fa. Kammerdiener Gmb H & Co. (KG)*, ASBCA 45248, 95-1 BCA ¶27,295, the board rejected the contractor's argument that the word "days" in a contract clause providing for a specific amount of liquidated damages meant working days because the board had held otherwise in *Hogan Mech.* However, in *Monaco Enters., Inc.*, ASBCA 19725, 75-1 BCA ¶11,122, the board limited the assessment of liquidated damages to working days, reasoning that the nature of the contractor's obligations required that it be available for work during weekdays. In *Custom Roofing Co.*, ASBCA 19164, 74-2 BCA ¶10,925, the board avoided the imposition of liquidated damages by computing the contract completion date using working days rather than calendar days.

F. Government Right to Actual Damages

When a contract contains a liquidated damages provision, the damages specified by the provision will generally serve as a substitute for any actual damages that the government may suffer. When such a clause is present, the government may collect only liquidated damages unless the contract specifically authorizes the assessment of actual damages as an alternative or as a supplement. The government does, however, have the right to assess actual damages for any harm not covered by the Liquidated Damages clause.

1. Damages Covered by the Clause

The government gives up the right to obtain actual damages for any harm covered by a liquidated damages provision. In *Sorensen v. United States*, 51 Ct. Cl. 69 (1916), the court held that government inspection costs during the delay period were not recoverable since they were included in liquidated damages, stating at 83-84:

> When they liquidated in advance the amount of the damages they fixed the amount which the one could be required to pay or the other be entitled to recover in case of breach, and the clause as much limits the [Government's] right to recover as it affects the [contractor's] obligation to pay. Both are bound by the liquidated damage clause.

See *Desert Sun Eng'g Corp.*, IBCA 725-8-68, 69-1 BCA ¶7431, where delay damages paid to another contractor because of a contractor's delay were not recoverable because they were included in liquidated damages for delay in performance.

See also *Simmonds Precision Prods., Inc. v. United States*, 212 Ct. Cl. 305, 546 F.2d 886 (1976), and *Nichols Dynamics, Inc.*, ASBCA 17610, 74-2 BCA ¶10,820.

The standard clauses used with liquidated damages do not describe what types of damages they cover. In *Cargill, Inc.*, AGBCA 84-164-1, 88-3 BCA ¶21,064, the board discussed the difficulty of determining what damages are covered by liquidated damages at 106,368:

> It is a long established principle that actual damages cannot be recovered when they are also included in liquidated damages. *Sorenson v. United States*, 51 Ct. Cl. 69 (1916). However, the Government generally retains the right to obtain actual damages for any harm not covered by the liquidated damages clause [citations omitted].
>
> We therefore, turn to the liquidated damages clause (VII C.) to determine what damages are covered by the clause. The clause does not give any indication as to what damages are, or are not, covered in the provision for liquidated damages, in addition to actual damages. The clause could easily state in unequivocal language that liquidated damages, in addition to actual damages, are for impairment to the price support program and to the Government's credibility with warehousemen, or any other intangible elements difficult to quantify as argued in the Government's brief. The clause does not, however, contain any such language. [The government] contends that the clause provides for both liquidated damages and actual damages. [The contractor] contends that the clause is an either or situation, where, if [the government] does not terminate the contract, actual damages cannot be claimed.
>
> We find that the clause is capable of being read both ways, and [the contractor's] contention is reasonable. Under the clause [the government] had an option to either allow continued performance with the imposition of liquidated damages or, if the delivery is not completed within 30 days beyond the last day of the specified period, to default the contractor and exercise its right to resell the quantity undelivered and claim actual damages.

The board concluded that because the government had neither defaulted the contractor nor exercised the right to resell, actual damages could not be recovered and the contractor's interpretation prevailed.

If a liquidated damages provision is held to be unenforceable as a penalty, the government will be entitled to seek common law breach of contract damages, *United States v. Reisman*, 611 F.2d 325 (9th Cir. 1980).

In *ROI Invs. v. General Servs. Admin.*, GSBCA 14402, 99-1 ¶30,353, the government had a right to withhold rent and to assess liquidated damages on the same rental space at the same time because there was no law prohibiting parties from agreeing to a lease that allowed both actions. The withholding of the rent was to ensure that the government paid only for space it occupied, whereas the liquidated damages were intended to compensate the government for administrative costs incurred by the government in inspecting construction progress, communicating with the lessor and local building inspectors, and having to work in overcrowded space while revising plans for its move into new block space.

2. Damages Outside the Clause

The government generally retains the right to obtain actual damages for any harm not covered by a liquidated damages clause. The clause is carefully analyzed to determine what harm is covered, *United States v. American Sur. Co.*, 322 U.S. 96 (1944) (no liquidated damages after default when clause limited their recovery to situation in which contractor was permitted to complete). The present standard clauses provide that a defaulted contractor will be liable for both excess costs of completion or reprocurement and liquidated damages, but they are silent as to what other damages are excluded from liquidated damages. In *Wells Constr.*, IBCA 737-10-68, 69-2 BCA ¶7866, costs of restoring uncompleted work and excess costs of completion were recovered because they were not included in liquidated damages for delay. See *Casson Constr. Co.*, GSBCA 4884, 78-1 BCA ¶13,032, holding that the government's rights under a special clause authorizing recovery of acceleration payments to a follow-on contractor following the first contractor's unexcused delay were not limited by a liquidated damages provision. In *Timberland Paving & Constr. Co. v. United States*, 18 Cl. Ct. 129 (1989), the court allowed the recovery of liquidated damages for untimely performance at the same time as recovery of an offset of the contractor's claims. The court concluded that both recoveries "served a different, non-overlapping function."

In addition to reprocurement costs and liquidated damages, the government is also "entitled to damages, including reasonable administrative expenses," *Grimco Pneumatic Corp.*, ASBCA 50977, 00-1 BCA ¶30,727.

G. Remission of Liquidated Damages

A unique aspect of the use of liquidated damages in government contracts is the statutory authority of the Secretary of the Treasury (formerly the Comptroller General) to remit such damages in accordance with 41 U.S.C. § 256a:

> Whenever any contract made on behalf of the Government by the head of any Federal Agency, or by officers authorized by him so to do, includes a provision for liquidated damages for delay, the Secretary of the Treasury upon recommendation of such head is authorized and empowered to remit the whole or any part of such damages as in his discretion may be just and equitable.

Substantially similar language is contained in 10 U.S.C. § 2312.

The Secretary of the Treasury, as the Comptroller General previously, will not exercise this power except upon receipt of a recommendation from the head of the agency involved, *J. Murray Co.*, Comp. Gen. Dec. B-236673, 90-1 CPD ¶55; *American Constr. & Energy, Inc.*, Comp. Gen. Dec. B-227253, 87-2 CPD ¶186. In addition, before the GAO would provide such relief, the contractor must have exhausted all administrative remedies, *Pine Belt Helicopters, Inc.*, Comp. Gen. Dec B-181787, 74-2 CPD ¶115; Comp. Gen. Dec. B-152201, Sept. 26, 1963, *Unpub.* See, however, Comp. Gen. Dec. B-155678, Aug. 18, 1966, *Unpub.*, holding that a previous decision by the GAO denying remission would not prevent the contractor from appealing under the Disputes clause or preclude the contracting officer or appeals board from granting a time extension for changed work conditions, thereby eliminating any liquidated damages due.

The remitting official may also condition remission on the actions of the contractor. See Comp. Gen. Dec. B-174147, Mar. 12, 1973, *Unpub.*, in which the contractor's claim for $20,200 was reduced to $4,500 provided it accepted that amount as full settlement of the claim.

The merit of a contractor's claim is "dependent upon a showing as to his ability to have prevented the situation in which he finds himself," 34 Comp. Gen. 251 (B-120656) (1954). Strong and persuasive equities must favor the contractor before GAO remission is likely, 36 Comp. Gen. 143 (B-128218) (1956), and remission will not be allowed to rescue the contractor from the consequences of its own negligence and carelessness, 46 Comp. Gen. 252 (B-159546) (1966). The contractor bears the burden of persuading the Comptroller that the reasons for delay merit remission. The GAO has refused remission where there were conflicting facts as to the cause of the delay, Comp. Gen. Dec. B-149899, Oct. 25, 1962, *Unpub.*, and where the contractor was careless in preparing its bid, *Construction Elec. Co.*, Comp. Gen. Dec. B-187820, 77-1 CPD ¶403. The fact that the government suffered little actual damage is not alone sufficient to obtain remission, Comp. Gen. Dec. B-156765, July 7, 1965, *Unpub.*

However, where liquidated damages include damages that are an unforeseeable consequence of a delay, remission will be appropriate. This result has been applied where the liquidated damages assessment included actual damages, *Panama Canal Comm'n*, Comp. Gen. Dec. B-242980, Sept. 20, 1991, *Unpub.*, or where the government had played a substantial role in the delay, *Preston's Legal Support & Court Reporting Serv.*, Comp. Gen. Dec. B-254610, Apr. 20, 1994, *Unpub.* For a discussion of the GAO's previous power to remit liquidated damages, see Preston, *The Role of the Comptroller General in Remitting Liquidated Damages*, 30 Fed. B.J. 144 (1971).

CHAPTER 3

TERMINATION FOR CONVENIENCE

The Termination for Convenience of the Government clause is one of the most unique provisions contained in government contracts. In no other area of contract law has one party been given such complete authority to escape from contractual obligations. This clause gives the government the broad right to terminate without cause and limits the contractor's recovery to costs incurred, profit on work done, and costs of preparing the termination settlement proposal. Recovery of anticipated profit is precluded. Thus, this mandatory provision confers a major contract right on the government with no commensurate advantage to the contractor.

The courts have also fashioned a constructive termination doctrine that applies the clause to prevent recovery of anticipated profit where government acts would otherwise have been material breaches of the contract. In these cases, the contracting officer elects not to use the clause but is still given the benefit of the clause in limiting the contractor's recovery. This is an additional broad limitation on a government contractor's rights.

This chapter addresses the scope of both actual and constructive termination for convenience of the government. It then reviews the rules governing termination settlements.

I. BACKGROUND

The concept of termination for convenience of the government was developed principally as a means to end the massive procurement efforts that accompanied major wars. Although the government had always had the power to terminate its contracts, such action constituted a breach of contract. Questions developed concerning the authority to settle such breach of contract claims and the procedures to be used in negotiating a settlement. These questions have persisted even though the Supreme Court, in *United States v. Corliss Steam Engine Co.*, 91 U.S. 321 (1875), clearly indicated that contracting officials were authorized to settle termination claims. A more important question concerned the contractor's remedy for termination. There were many objections to paying a contractor profits on unperformed work, and yet the contractor was entitled to such a remedy if the government did not have a right to terminate the contract. See *G.L. Christian & Assocs. v. United States*, 160 Ct. Cl. 1, 312 F.2d 418, *reh'g denied* 160 Ct. Cl. 58, 320 F.2d 345, *cert. denied*, 375 U.S. 954 (1963).

A number of regulatory and statutory provisions were developed to resolve these questions concerning settlement authority and the compensation due the terminated contractor. As early as 1863, Rule 1179 of the Army Regulations provided that contracts for subsistence stores "shall expressly provide for their termination at such time as the Commissary-General may direct." See *United States v. Speed*, 75 U.S. (8 Wall.) 77 (1868), for a discussion of this provision. However, it was not until World War I that contracts were terminated in large numbers. Some agencies had already developed termination clauses, but the majority of claims were settled under statutory authority—the most important of which was the Dent Act, 40 Stat. 1272 (1919). During World War II, further statutory and regulatory provisions were developed, including the Contract Settlement Act of 1944, 58 Stat. 649.

After the war, regulatory provisions began to require termination clauses in contracts. The 1950 edition of the Armed Services Procurement Regulation (ASPR) contained mandatory Termination for Convenience clauses to be used in the majority of DoD contracts over $1,000, DAR 8-701-705. In 1964 the first edition of the Federal Procurement Regulations (FPR) contained optional termination for convenience clauses to be used "whenever an agency considered it necessary or desirable . . . ," FPR 1-8.700-2. In June 1967, the FPR was revised to make the Termination for Convenience clauses mandatory, with limited exceptions, in fixed-price supply contracts over $2,500 and fixed-price construction contracts over $100,000, 32 Fed. Reg. 9683 (1967). FAR 49.502 continues to require broad use of Termination for Convenience clauses, with the result that the broad rights developed for war contracts have come to be applied to all types of contracts, civilian as well as military, in times of both peace and war.

II. THE RIGHT TO TERMINATE

Termination for convenience is a government right to be exercised in the best interests of the government. In cases where a contractor is performing at a loss, a termination might be beneficial to the contractor. However, the government has no duty to terminate for convenience to benefit the contractor, *Rotair Indus., Inc.*, ASBCA 27571, 84-2 BCA ¶17,417.

A. Termination Clauses

There are three basic types of convenience termination clauses currently in use in standard federal contracts. For most fixed-price contracts there are "long form" clauses for contracts over $100,000, FAR 52.249-2, and "short form" clauses for contracts that do not exceed $100,000, FAR 52.249-1. The FAR includes specialized versions of these clauses for research and development, services, construction, architect and engineer, dismantling, and nonprofit institution contracts. There is also a "short form" clause for service contracts in FAR 52.249-4. Cost-reimbursement contract clauses are of the "long form" variety, but they differ from fixed-price contract clauses in that they cover both convenience and default terminations, FAR 52.249-6. Prior to the FAR there were suggested clauses for fixed-price subcontracts, DAR 8-706 and FPR 1-8.706, and for cost-reimbursement subcontracts, DAR 8-703. FAR 49.502(e) contains guidance on appropriate modification of the standard clauses for use in subcontracts.

FAR 49.502 prescribes when these clauses are to be used. In general, the "long form" clauses are required to be used in all contracts over $ 100,000, except that the "short form" clause in FAR 52.249-4 is prescribed for use in service contracts over $ 100,000 by FAR 49.502(c) as follows:

> The contracting officer shall insert the clause at 52.249-4, Termination for Convenience of the Government (Services) (Short Form), in solicitations and contracts for services, regardless of value, when a fixed-price contract is contemplated and the contracting officer determines that because of the kind of services required, the successful offeror will not incur substantial charges in preparation for and in carrying out the contract, and would, if terminated for the convenience of the Government, limit termination settlement charges to services rendered before the date of termination. Examples of services where this clause may be appropriate are contracts for rental of unreserved parking space, laundry and drycleaning, etc.

The service contract "short form" clause is very restrictive, providing only for payment "for services rendered before the effective date of the termination." Thus, its use has been challenged in a number of cases and has been held to be an abuse of discretion, *DWS, Debtor in Possession*, ASBCA 29742, 90-2 BCA ¶22,696 ($11.4 million contract requiring extensive construction, repairs, training, parts, and supply purchases); *Carrier Corp.*, GSBCA 8516, 90-1 BCA ¶22,409 (significant start-up costs that could not be recovered in payments for preventative maintenance services on a monthly basis); *Guard-All of Am.*, ASBCA 22167, 80-2 BCA ¶14,462 (use of clause unfair when government knew that termination of guard services might happen shortly after award of contract). Compare *Mid-Atl. Sec. Servs., Inc.*, ENGBCA 6302, 97-2 BCA ¶29,012, finding no abuse of discretion, stating at 144,539-40:

> Factors relevant to our inquiry include: the nature of the services; unusual and substantial "start-up" type costs and other requirements that are not separately priced and are not "common items" which can be reallocated to other work; the nature of the pricing provisions of the solicitation and any elements of "unfairness" in those mechanisms if the contract is terminated early; how the contractor actually priced its offer; Government, pre-award knowledge of the likelihood of early termination; the existence of any protest or concerns expressed to contracting officials during the solicitation process concerning use of the "short form" clause; and the overall fairness of judicially rewriting the contract and, thereby reallocating the termination cost risks to the Government given all the facts and circumstances.

In contracts for commercial items, the Contract Terms and Conditions—Commercial Items clause at FAR 52.212-4 also limits the contractor's recovery, as follows:

> (l) *Termination for the government's convenience.* The government reserves the right to terminate this contract, or any part hereof, for its sole convenience. In the event of such termination, the Contractor shall immediately stop all work hereunder and shall immediately cause any and all of its suppliers and subcontractors to cease work. Subject to the terms of this contract, the Contractor shall be paid a percentage of the contract price reflecting the percentage of the work performed prior to the notice of termination, plus reasonable charges the Contractor can demonstrate to the satisfaction of the government using its standard record keeping system, have resulted from the termination. The Contractor shall not be required to comply with the cost accounting standards or contract cost principles for this purpose. This paragraph does not give the Government any right to audit the Contractor's records. The Contractor shall not be paid for any work performed or costs incurred which reasonably could have been avoided.

FAR 12.403 provides the following general guidance on termination of commercial contracts:

> (a) *General.* The clause at 52.212-4 permits the Government to terminate a contract for commercial items either for the convenience of the Government or for cause. However, the paragraphs in 52.212-4 entitled "Termination for the Government's Convenience" and "Termination for Cause" contain concepts which differ from those contained in the termination clauses prescribed in Part 49. Consequently, the requirements of Part 49 do not apply when terminating contracts for commercial items and contracting officers shall follow the procedures in this section. Contracting officers may continue to use Part 49 as guidance to the extent that Part 49 does not conflict with this section and the language of the termination paragraphs in 52.212-4.
>
> (b) *Policy.* The contracting officer should exercise the Government's right to terminate a contract for commercial items either for convenience or for cause only when such a termination would be in the best interests of the Government. The contracting officer should consult with counsel prior to terminating for cause.

For a case involving termination for convenience of a contract for a commercial item, see *Individual Dev. Assocs., Inc.*, ASBCA 53910, 04-2 BCA ¶32,740.

Periodically, especially in Non-Appropriated Fund Instrumentality contracts, non-standard termination clauses are used. In *Home Entm't, Inc.*, ASBCA 50791, 99-2 BCA ¶30,550, the contract with the Army and Air Force Exchange Service to operate a video rental concession at military installations in Panama did not contain the standard Termination for Convenience clause but provided that the contract could be terminated "without cause" on 30 days' written notice. In *Dart Advantage Warehousing, Inc. v. United States*, 52 Fed. Cl. 694 (2002), the warehousing contract contained both a standard Termination for Convenience clause and a Termination on Notice clause permitting either party to terminate the contract on 180 days' notice. The contractor contended that the Termination on Notice provision modified the Termination for Convenience clause, making an improper termination for default a breach, entitling it to 180 days of anticipated profits. The court held that the two clauses served different purposes and that the contractor would be limited to recovery under the Termination for Convenience clause. In *Poston Logging*, AGBCA 99-143-R, 00-1 BCA ¶30,829, *motion to vacate denied*, 00-2 BCA ¶30,973, rather than the standard Termination for Convenience clause, the timber contract included a special clause providing for termination based on a Forest Service determination that continued performance would damage the environment.

B. Exercising the Right to Terminate

The courts and boards have placed few limitations on the ability of the government to exercise its right to terminate a contract for convenience. This subsection first discusses the factors a contracting officer should consider in deciding whether to terminate a contract for the convenience of the government and then discusses the limitations that have been placed on the contracting officer when making such a decision.

1. The Decision to Terminate

The language giving the government the right to terminate is brief and very broad. For example, the termination clause contained in FAR 52.249-2 states:

> (a) The government may terminate performance of work under this contract in whole or, from time to time, in part if the Contracting Officer determines that a termination is in the government's interest.

If the contracting officer decides to terminate for convenience, the government's liability will be admitted, and the contractor will recover its incurred allowable costs and profit on work done. If another means of severing the relationship is used, litigation over the obligations of the parties is likely. However, even if the contractor wins such litigation, the application of the constructive termination for convenience doctrine will limit its recovery to that permitted under the Termination for Convenience clause. Thus, the government takes little risk, other than the cost of litigation, in choosing some other means of severing the relationship. If such action is upheld, the contractor's recovery may be limited. If it is not, the government pays nothing more than it would have paid had it initially elected to terminate for convenience. It is therefore possible that in many such cases contracting officers "decide" that to terminate for convenience is not in the interest of the government. Thus, it is unlikely that the Termination for Convenience clause will be used if there is a more favorable method of severing the relationship. Whether this is an appropriate policy is another question.

a. *"The Government's Interest"*

The regulations contain no guidance on the factors to be considered in determining "the government's interest." However, FAR 49.101(b) provides that a negotiated no-cost settlement shall be used in lieu of a convenience termination if the contractor will accept such a settlement; if no government property has been furnished to the contractor; and if there are no outstanding payments, debts, or other contractor obligations due the government. If the undelivered balance of the contract is less than $5,000, the contract should normally be allowed to run to completion, FAR 49.101(c).

Termination for convenience is most common when the government no longer needs the contract work, but it often occurs in other situations. For example, if the contractor is in default but has raised potential defenses, the contracting officer must decide whether to terminate for default or convenience. See FAR 49.402-3(j). A contractor's refusal to accept a modification supports a termination for convenience, *Saltwater, Inc.*, Comp. Gen. Dec. B-293335.3, 2004 CPD ¶106. If there are questions concerning the propriety of an award or its continued performance, the award may be canceled or a termination for convenience may be ordered. In *Landmark Constr. Corp.*, Comp. Gen. Dec. B-281957.3, 99-2 CPD ¶75, the GAO held that the immediate termination of an 8(a) set-aside contract (improperly awarded to an ineligible offeror) was permissible but was not required. The agency could allow the contract to remain in place to meet its ongoing requirements until a new contract is awarded. Sometimes a convenience termination may be required if, for example, an 8(a) firm is sold to a large business, *International Data Prods. Corp. v. United States,* 64 Fed. Cl. 642 (2005).

A contract may be terminated for the convenience of the government based on the deterioration of the business relationship between a contractor and the agency, *Embrey v. United States*, 17 Cl. Ct. 617 (1989). In *Bryan D. Highfill*, HUDB-CA 96-C-118-C7, 99-1 BCA ¶30,316, among the factors the board considered in upholding the agency's termination for convenience were the contractor's statements to the contract specialist that "he was about ready to kill a man" and that he would like to hire someone to do it, which the contract specialist interpreted as a reference to another agency employee.

Convenience termination may also be used to restructure multiple contractual arrangements. Northrop-Grumman was one of four contractors on the space station. Subsequently, the program experienced substantial cost overruns and NASA feared that the entire project would be lost if the contractors' management structure and contractual relationships were not adjusted. NASA's administrator met with the CEOs of the four contractors and proposed that one of the contractors would become the single contractor and that the other three would be "novated" as subcontractors to the single contractor. The four contracts were terminated for convenience and Boeing was selected as the contractor. After Northrop-Grumman was awarded a new subcontract with substantially less work, it sued alleging that its contract had been terminated in "bad faith." The court disagreed, noting that the government had acted with the sole intent of saving the space station program, not to acquire a better bargain from another source even if that was the final result. Even if NASA knew that Northrop-Grumman's scope of work would be reduced under the single contract, such knowledge did not establish any intent to injure Northrop-Grumman, *Northrop Grumman Corp. v. United States,* 46 Fed. Cl. 622 (2000).

b. Special Situations

One requirement is that there must be a contract to terminate. If a contract has not been awarded or has legitimately expired, for example, when an option is not exercised, a termination for convenience is inappropriate. In *Sierra Rock v. Regents of Univ. of Cal.,* EBCA C-9705223, 99-2 BCA ¶30,507, the board held that where a contractor cannot show even an implied-in-fact contract with the government, it cannot establish a bad faith termination for convenience. The board also noted that the remedy for bad faith actions by the government is limited to anticipatory profits rather than punitive damages. The latter are unavailable unless the contract allows the same or provides that a particular state law applies that clearly allows the imposition of punitive damages

Neither is there any obligation to terminate an indefinite delivery/indefinite quantity contract after ordering the specified minimum quantity, *J. Cooper & Assocs., Inc. v. United States,* 53 Fed. Cl. 8 (2002), *aff'd,* 65 Fed. Appx. 731 (Fed. Cir. 2003). There the government allowed a letter contract for an ID/IQ contract to expire rather than definitize it or issue a termination for convenience. The court found that since the government's sole obligation in an ID/IQ contract is to order the minimum amount, the government was under no obligation to terminate the contract for convenience, nor was there a constructive termination or bad faith. The contractor was limited to payment for task orders issued, and it could not recover for items such as preparing proposals for anticipated future orders.

Blanket purchase agreements, by themselves, generally need not be terminated formally because the government can simply elect not to issue orders under the agreement. In *BSG Constr. Servs., Inc.,* ENGBCA 6127, 95-1 BCA ¶27,520, the board concluded that the government improperly included a Termination clause in a blanket purchase agreement and then attempted to invoke that clause. The government's errors, however, did not create any rights in the contractor. The government's invocation of the clause gave the contractor notice that it would receive no additional orders under the agreement, which was more notice than the contractor would have been entitled to had the termination clause not been present.

c. Terminations in Support of Competition

One particular justification for a termination for convenience is to uphold the statutory preference for full and open competition by terminating a potentially improper award. While the Competition in Contracting Act (CICA) does not deal with terminations for convenience, correcting a flawed procurement can certainly be considered an appropriate means to further full and open competition. The majority of the cases cited in *Torncello v. United States,* 231 Ct. Cl. 20, 681 F.2d 756 (1982), the leading case limiting the right to terminate for convenience, as demonstrating changed circumstances, were flawed contract awards. Flawed awards might be an irregularity in the award process, such as improper nonresponsibility determinations or specifications not reflecting the government's needs, or cases where the competition was not procedurally flawed but the government later decides that an unwise decision was made. The court in *Torncello* stated at 37:

> The history of cases in this court demonstrates [the use of the clause in changed circumstances]. *John Reiner & Co. v. United States,* 163 Ct. Cl. 381, 325 F.2d 438 (1963), *cert. denied,* 377 U.S. 931 (1964) (irregularity in the bid award); *Brown & Son Elec. Co. v. United States,* 163 Ct. Cl. 465, 325 F.2d 446 (1963) (irregularity in bid award); *Nesbitt v. United States,* 170 Ct. Cl. 666, 345 F.2d 583 (1965), *cert. denied,* 383 U.S. 926 (1966) (refusal of contractor to meet requirements); *Warren Bros. Roads Co. v. United States,* 173 Ct. Cl. 714, 355 F.2d 612 (1965) (irregularity in the bid award); *Coastal Cargo Co. v. United States,* 173 Ct. Cl. 259, 351 F.2d 1004 (1965) (irregularity in bid award); *Schlesinger v. United States,* 182 Ct. Cl. 571, 390 F.2d 702 (1968) (plaintiff under investigation by Senate for procurement irregularities, and in technical default); *Nolan Bros. v. United States,* 186 Ct. Cl. 602, 405 F.2d 1250 (1969) (physical changes at site made performance impossible); *G.C. Casebolt Co. v. United States,* 190 Ct. Cl. 783, 421 F.2d 710 (1970) (irregularity in the bid award).

In *Krygoski Constr. Co v. United States*, 94 F.3d 1357 (Fed. Cir. 1996), the court explained that when faced with an allegation that a contracting officer abused his or her discretion in terminating a contract for the convenience of the government, "this court will avoid a finding of abused discretion when the facts support a reasonable inference that the contracting officer terminated for convenience in furtherance of statutory requirements for full and open competition." *Krygoski* found that one indication that termination was necessary to further competition is whether, if the government had retained the contract, it would have imposed a cardinal change in the scope of the contract to meet its requirements.

In *T&M Distribs., Inc. v. United States*, 185 F.3d 1279 (Fed Cir. 1999), the Federal Circuit determined that CICA, which compels the promulgation of regulations and procedures to ensure full and open competition in contracting, sufficiently addressed the concerns of earlier decisions regarding the government's shopping for lower prices after the contract award. CICA's competitive fairness requirement provides the additional restraint on a contracting officer's contract administration, under which contracting officers have no incentive to terminate a contract for convenience except to maintain full and open competition under CICA. Thus, the court found that the contracting officer did not act in bad faith or abuse his discretion because he had a reasonable basis for terminating the contract and conducting a competitive reprocurement—the increased asbestos removal constituted a cardinal change. See also *EROS Div. of Res. Recycling Int'l., Inc.*, ASBCA 48355, 99-1 BCA ¶30,207 (bad faith or abuse of discretion not present when the contracting officer terminated for convenience because the improper award of the contract, without a synopsis and concurrence of the government's competition advocate, were reasonable grounds for the termination).

A termination for convenience may also be used to get the government out of a lawfully awarded contract that the government realizes contains unbalanced line item prices. In *Custom Printing Co. v. United States*, 51 Fed. Cl. 729 (2002), the government awarded a contract for printing services that included a high-priced line item, then found that it required a high volume of that type work. After failing to negotiate a contract modification lowering the line item price, the contracting officer terminated the contract for convenience. The court held that the circumstances justified the termination and there was an absence of bad faith on the part of the government. See also *Kellie W. Tipton Constr. Co.*, Comp. Gen. Dec. B-281331.3, 99-1 CPD ¶73 (termination for convenience upheld when shortly after award agency determined its award had been based on a mistaken evaluation of another bidder's past performance).

2. Limitations on the Right to Terminate

The Termination for the Convenience of the Government clauses state that the contract can be terminated when it is determined to be "in the Government's interest," with no stated limits on that right. The judicial interpretation of the government's rights under this clause has led some commentators to conclude that there are "virtually no limitations on the Government's right to terminate," Pearlman and Goodrich, *Termination for Convenience Settlements*, 10 Pub. Cont. L.J. 1 (1978). However, an unlimited government right of termination raises serious questions as to whether the government furnishes consideration in a contract containing a termination clause. *Restatement, Second, Contracts* § 77 states:

> A promise or apparent promise is not consideration if by its terms the promisor or purported promisor reserves a choice of alternative performance unless (a) each of the alternative performances would have been consideration if it alone had been bargained for; or (b) one of the alternative performances would have been consideration and there is or appears to the parties to be a substantial possibility that before the promisor exercises his choice events may eliminate the alternatives which would not have been consideration.

See also 1 *Williston, Contracts* § 105 (3d ed. 1957 and Supp. 1979), which states at 418: "[a]n agreement wherein one party reserves the right to cancel at his pleasure cannot create a contract."

Surprisingly, this issue has rarely been raised in relation to current convenience termination clauses. An early government contract case dealing with the question of lack of consideration in a contract containing a termination clause is *Sylvan Crest Sand & Gravel Co. v. United States*, 150 F.2d 642 (2d Cir. 1945). In that case the clause stated: "Cancellation by the Procurement Division may be effected at any time." The appellate court held that the contract was based on consideration and hence was not illusory because it contained an implied promise by the government to give notice of cancellation within a reasonable time if it did not want to accept the goods. In *Torncello v. United States*, 231 Ct. Cl. 20, 681 F.2d 756 (1982), the court discussed the consideration issue extensively and concluded that the scope of termination rights had to be limited to prevent a finding of lack of consideration. The court also indicated that it disagreed with the reasoning in *Sylvan Crest* that the bare requirement to give notice constituted consideration. The Court of Claims concluded, in a plurality opinion, that "a party may not reserve to itself a method of unlimited exculpation without rendering its promises illusory and the contract void."

In *Montana Ref. Co.*, ASBCA 50515, 00-1 BCA ¶30,694, the board rejected the argument that the government's attempt to terminate an IDIQ contract before it had purchased the guaranteed minimum quantity was improper because it would render the contract illusory due to lack of consideration. The board held that the compensation available under the Termination for Convenience clause provides adequate consideration to the contractor.

So, courts and boards are still searching for meaningful limitations that will accommodate the government's legitimate needs and leave the contractor with some rights under this clause. Prior to 1982, the view was that terminations for convenience would be overturned only in the event of bad faith or an abuse of discretion on the part of the government, *Kalvar Corp. v. United States*, 211 Ct. Cl. 192, 543 F.2d 1298 (1976), *cert. denied*, 434 U.S. 830 (1977). However, in 1982, the court in *Torncello v. United States*, 231 Ct. Cl. 20, 681 F.2d 756 (1982), determined that bad faith, as articulated by *Kalvar*, was not a meaningful limitation on the government's right to terminate. The three-judge plurality concluded that the scope of the termination power had to be narrowed so that public contracts would not be illusory for lack of consideration on the part of the government. Accordingly, the plurality opinion held that a convenience termination could only be justified where there was a "change in circumstances" after the contract was awarded from those in existence when the contract was formed. The impact of *Torncello* was undercut in *Krygoski Constr. Co. v. United States*, 94 F.3d 1537 (Fed. Cir. 1996), *cert. denied*, 520 U.S. 1210 (1997). These three decisions, *Kalvar, Torncello,* and *Krygoski*, are basic to understanding the limitations on the government's right to terminate for convenience.

a. The Kalvar Test—Government Bad Faith or Abuse of Discretion

The convenience termination cases give little guidance on abuse of discretion or bad faith. The bad faith and abuse of discretion standards have been, at best, only superficially examined in the opinions, and many inconsistencies exist between the facts of the cases and the language of the decisions. But other areas of government contracting provide guidance. For example, the government may not arbitrarily refuse to grant approval where a clause provides that approval must be obtained by the contractor, e.g., *Hoel-Steffen Constr. Co. v. United States*, 231 Ct. Cl. 128, 684 F.2d 843 (1982). This is one aspect of the implied duty of good faith and fair dealing that all contracting parties are required to observe. In addition, the government is required to exercise discretion in deciding whether to terminate a contract for default, *Schlesinger v. United States*, 182 Ct. Cl. 571, 390 F.2d 702 (1968). It would be appropriate to apply the abuse of discretion standards developed under these other areas to convenience terminations.

Because the plaintiff failed to distinguish between bad faith and abuse of discretion, the *Kalvar* court treated them the same "only for purposes of the decision." The contractor's burden of proving governmental bad faith, however, is quite heavy, *Kalvar Corp. v. United States*, 211 Ct. Cl. 192, 543 F.2d 1298 (1976), *cert. denied*, 434 U.S. 830 (1977). There, the court indicated that "specific intent to injure" the contractor must be demonstrated. An oft-repeated statement indicates that to prove bad faith a contractor must (1) prove specific intent to harm the plaintiff and (2) prove this intent with well-nigh irrefragable proof. But upon analysis, it is unclear whether proof of specific intent to harm the plaintiff is really a requirement. The following statement from *Kalvar* at 198-99 is usually credited with announcing the proposition:

> Any analysis of a question of Governmental bad faith must begin with the presumption that public officials act "conscientiously in the discharge of their duties." *Librach v. United States*, 147 Ct. Cl. 605, 612 (1959). The court has always been "loath to find to the contrary," and it requires "well- nigh irrefragable proof" to induce the court to abandon the presumption of good faith dealing. *Knotts v. United States*, 128 Ct. Cl. 489, 492, 121 F. Supp. 630, 631 (1954).
>
> In the cases in which the court has considered allegations of bad faith, the necessary "irrefragable proof" has been equated with evidence of some specific intent to injure the plaintiff. Thus, in *Gadsden v. United States*, 111 Ct. Cl.

> 487, 489-90, 78 F. Supp. 126, 127 (1948), the court compared bad faith to actions which are "motivated alone by malice." In *Knotts, supra,* at 128 Ct. Cl. 500, 121 F. Supp. 636, the court found bad faith in a civilian pay suit only in view of a proven "conspiracy . . . to get rid of plaintiff." Similarly, the court in *Struck Constr. Co. v. United States,* 96 Ct. Cl. 186, 222 (1942) found bad faith when confronted by a course of Governmental conduct which was "designedly oppressive." But in *Librach, supra,* at 147 Ct. Cl. 614, the court found no bad faith because the officials involved were not "actuated by animus toward the plaintiff."

This specific intent statement in *Kalvar* apparently motivated the *Torncello* plurality to adopt the changed circumstances concept. By contrast, Judge Davis did not believe that proof of specific intent to harm was a necessary ingredient to a finding of bad faith and that *Kalvar* did not necessarily so hold. His concurring opinion in *Torncello* stated at 50-51:

> Third, I do not agree that "bad faith" is as narrow as Judge Bennett says it is. In *Kalvar, supra*—the case he cites—this court said, without in any way seeking to modify our prior holdings: ". . .many of our prior decisions seem implicitly to accept the equivalence of bad faith, abuse of discretion, and gross error." 211 Ct. Cl. at 198, note 1, 543 F.2d at 1301, note 1. *Kalvar* expressly held that that contractor had failed to show either bad faith or abuse of discretion. . .and the limited definition of bad faith quoted in the opinion gave merely one aspect of the concept of "bad faith." Here, too, I would be ready to hold that a contracting officer acted in bad faith when he terminated a contract for convenience to get a better price of which he had full knowledge (and which was available) at the time when he deliberately entered into the contract with plaintiff.

In footnote 3, *Krygoski* cites *Keco Indus., Inc. v. United States,* 203 Ct. Cl. 566, 492 F.2d 1200 (1974), for the proposition that four factors are listed for determining whether discretion has been abused. The first of these is bad faith, followed by "the reasonableness of the decision, the amount of discretion delegated to the procurement official," and finally, whether violations of an applicable regulation or statute alone are arbitrary.

It has been virtually impossible for terminated contractors to demonstrate government bad faith. See *McFadden, Inc. v. United States,* 215 Ct. Cl. 918 (1977) (even if contracting officer followed directions of superiors in canceling award, bad faith not present); *Kalvar Corp. v. United States,* 211 Ct. Cl. 192, 543 F.2d 1298 (1976), *cert. denied,* 434 U.S. 830 (1977) (bad faith not established by failure to disclose information making determinations favorable to another contractor concerning coverage of requirements contracts, or by taking the other contractor's word concerning specifications and evaluating bids based on a different thickness of material); *Gould, Inc. v. Chafee,* 450 F.2d 667 (D.C. Cir. 1971) (termination based on agreement with GAO decision or on acquiescence to avoid conflict unlikely to be found arbitrary and capricious); and *Librach v. United States,* 147 Ct. Cl. 605 (1959) (miscalculation of requirement not bad faith). In *Allied Materials & Equip. Co. v. United States,* 215 Ct. Cl. 902 (1977), the court stated that the contractor "should harbor no illusions that the task of overcoming the presumption that Government officials perform their duty in good faith is less than burdensome." In the absence of bad faith or a clear abuse of discretion, the contracting officer's decision to terminate a contract for convenience is conclusive. Because contracting officers are presumed to act in good faith when performing their procurement functions, a contractor must present virtually irrefutable proof of bad faith before the court will overturn the decision to terminate for convenience, *T&M Distribs., Inc. v. United States,* 185 F.3d 1279 (Fed. Cir. 1999). See also *Melvin R. Kessler,* PSBCA 2820, 92-2 BCA ¶24,857, *recons. denied,* 92-3 BCA ¶25,092 (relying on presumption that public officials discharge their duties conscientiously, board found no bad faith in termination of mail delivery contract resulting from conflict between contractor and postmaster over proposed schedule change). Compare *Benjamin P. Garcia,* ASBCA 18035, 73-2 BCA ¶10,196, in which the board stated that a termination based on discrimination would be improper, but because of discrimination proceedings in another tribunal, dismissed the case pending substantiation of the charges; and *Apex Int'l Mgmt. Servs., Inc.,* ASBCA 38087, 94-2 BCA ¶26,842, *recons. denied,* 94-2 BCA ¶26,852, in which the board found bad faith based on numerous actions designed to injure the contractor.

In a number of cases, it has been stated that a "clear abuse of discretion" would also invalidate a termination for convenience, *A-Transport Northwest Co. v. United States,* 36 F.3d 1576 (Fed. Cir. 1994). However, although this appears to be a lesser standard of proof, it has also been difficult to establish. In *TLT Constr. Corp.,* ASBCA 40501, 93-3 BCA ¶25,978, the government attempted to negotiate a no-cost termination, and when it was unsuccessful, ordered the contractor to perform, then terminated the contract for convenience. The board held that there was no abuse of discretion, even though the government still needed the work.

The ability to show either bad faith or an abuse of discretion is virtually impossible if the contracting officer can show an alternative reason for the termination, *"Quazar,"* ASBCA 23504, 79-1 BCA ¶13,828 (not bad faith to terminate contract for band performance because of poor reception given to band at high school dance). In *Stan Harris dba Harris & Co.*, ASBCA 47771, 95-1 BCA ¶27,585, the government did not act in bad faith in canceling for convenience, a week before the event, a contract for a dance band performance, because the sole reason for the cancellation was disappointing potential audience response. The government held the event but substituted other entertainment that it believed would generate greater revenue for its officers' club. See also *Northrop Grumman Corp v. United States,* 46 Fed. Cl. 622 (2000) (government had acted with the sole intent of saving the space station program, not to acquire a better bargain from another source even if that was the final result.)

Nevertheless, despite the difficulty of proof, the contractor is entitled to present evidence of bad faith, as indicated in *Allied Materials* and *National Factors, Inc. v. United States,* 204 Ct. Cl. 98, 492 F.2d 1383 (1974). But there is a very low likelihood of meeting this standard. For example, the court applied the "well nigh irrefragable proof" standard in refusing to overturn a termination for convenience where the contracting officer determined there was a gross misestimate of quantities in the solicitation, *Custom Printing Co. v. United States,* 51 Fed. Cl. 729 (2002). Accord, *Fields v. United States,* 53 Fed. Cl. 412 (2002).

In 2002, the Federal Circuit attempted once more to clarify its past cases on bad faith. In *Am-Pro Protective Agency, Inc. v. United States,* 281 F.3d 1234 (Fed. Cir. 2002), the contractor alleged that it had signed a release under duress and threats from the contracting officer that its contract would be canceled and options not exercised if it pursued its claim for contract changes. Although the contractor's case was weak on the facts under any standard, the court took the occasion to "clarify" the standard of proof for showing government bad faith. The court held that "clear and convincing" evidence was closest to "well nigh irrefragable proof," and it stated that in the future it would apply the clear and convincing standard, but would include within that standard a requirement that the contracting officer was motivated by malice toward the contractor. See also *Tecom, Inc. v. United States,* 66 Fed. Cl. 736 (2005), concluding that there was no presumption of regularity of government action.

b. The *Torncello* Test—No Change in Circumstances

In 1982 the Court of Claims added a new limitation on the government's right to terminate. In *Torncello v. United States,* 231 Ct. Cl. 20, 681 F.2d 756 (1982), the court held that the government could not terminate for convenience unless there had been a change in circumstances. Although the "changed circumstances" test has been severely weakened after some cases in the late 1990s, it was used for over a decade.

Torncello arose out of a requirements contract for janitorial and other services awarded by the Navy to Soledad Industries, Inc., for multiple items, with bids solicited and award made on an "all or none" basis. During performance, the Navy never issued any calls to Soledad for even one item, but had all of the work performed by an in-house Navy organization. The contract was terminated for default, and one of the defenses raised by Soledad was the government's failure to order the work. The Armed Services Board of Contract Appeals held that even in a requirements contract, the government could have terminated the contract for its convenience and that, therefore, the government's failure to order work would not be a breach of contract, *Soledad Enters., Inc.,* ASBCA 20376, 77-2 BCA ¶12,552. Since the contract included a short form Termination for Convenience clause that permitted recovery only for services performed, this gave Soledad no recovery. The appeal was decided by the full court "because of the exceptional importance of the legal issues involved." Three judges joined in a "plurality opinion." The other three judges wrote individual concurring opinions, each disagreeing to some extent with the opinion of the three judges who had joined together. However, the end result was a determination that the Navy had breached the contract, and the case was remanded to the Trial Division to determine the amount of damages.

In *Torncello,* the court ruled that the Termination for Convenience clause could not be used to avoid paying anticipated profits unless there had been some change in circumstances between the time of award of the contract and the time of termination. The court found that no changed circumstances had occurred and overruled *Colonial Metals Co. v. United States,* 204 Ct. Cl. 320, 494 F.2d 1355 (1974), which had held that a termination for convenience was proper when the government awarded a contract knowing of a lower price and subsequently terminated the contract to obtain that price.

The plurality opinion reasoned that this limitation on the use of the clause was necessary to avoid the creation of an illusory bargain where the government had no obligation to the contractor, stating at 26:

> We note as one of the most elementary propositions of contract law that a party may not reserve to itself a method of unlimited exculpation without rendering its promises illusory and the contract void, and we question if the government's termination for convenience clause should be construed that broadly.

It then traced the development of the concept of termination for convenience, finding that it was a device to get the government out of a contract when circumstances changed after the contract was awarded. The opinion declared that the "history of cases in this court demonstrates this" concept, stating further at 36-37:

> The response in this court was to rely on the risk allocation nature of the concept and to allow termination for convenience only when the expectations of the parties had been subjected to a substantial change. The contractor risked losing the full benefit of his performance if something occurred, apart from the bargain and the expectations of the parties, that made continuance of the contract clearly inadvisable.

It rejected the government's contention that not permitting convenience terminations when motivated by "bad faith" or as a result of an "abuse of discretion" would satisfy the consideration requirement and held that a termination for convenience could only be justified in situations where there was a "change in circumstances" from the time the contract was awarded.

The three concurring opinions assist in understanding *Torncello*. Judge Davis thought it unnecessary to invoke a changed circumstances doctrine because in this case the contracting officer acted in bad faith. In addition, he stated that he "would have no difficulty in holding that it was an abuse of discretion to use the clause to end the contract because lower prices could be obtained elsewhere when the contracting officer already knew that very fact before he consummated the contract with plaintiff."

Judge Nichols went further in his concurring opinion, recognizing the "all or none" basis of the contract award, and would have found an abuse of discretion under the circumstances. He stated at 52 that the government:

> would be estopped to eliminate from the award by termination any items just because, separately considered, they were at unfavorable prices, while retaining all those bid at favorable prices. The administration of the contract must be consistent with the rules used in evaluating the bids, to which the bidders conformed in bidding.

Chief Judge Friedman concurred on the understanding that the decision was limited to the specific facts of the case, stating at 49:

> As I understand the court's opinion, the court holds only that when the government enters into a requirements contract, knowing that it can obtain an item the contract covers for less than the contract price and intending to do so, there cannot be a constructive termination for convenience of the government when the government follows that course. On that basis, I join in the opinion.

This view adds the requirement of government intent to buy at the lower price at the time of contracting. See *David R. Brown, Jr.*, IBCA 1600-7-82, 83-1 BCA ¶16,423; *Tamp Corp.*, ASBCA 25692, 84-2 BCA ¶17,460; and the concurring opinion of Administrative Judge Lieblich in *Drain-A-Way Sys.*, GSBCA 7022, 84-1 BCA ¶16,929. This view appears to be unduly restrictive in that the basic purpose of requiring changed circumstances is to ensure that the government has entered into a real, not illusory, obligation at the time of contract award. See also the discussion in *Federal Data Corp.*, DOTCAB 2389, 91-3 BCA ¶24,063, construing *Torncello* narrowly.

Torncello has been cited numerous times by the boards of contract appeals, Claims Court, Court of Federal Claims, and Court of Appeals for the Federal Circuit, but the focus has generally been solely on the plurality opinion. The scope of the *Torncello* rule has been viewed somewhat restrictively by later decisions. In *Automated Servs., Inc.*, DOTBCA 1753, 87-1 BCA ¶19,459, the board interpreted *Torncello* narrowly, stating that, absent the same fact pattern, invocation of the Termination for Convenience clause is just as valid and enforceable in indefinite-quantity type contracts as it is in other types of supply contracts, even in situations where the goods or services contracted for have not yet been delivered. Compare *S & W Tire Servs., Inc.*, GSBCA 6376, 82-2 BCA ¶16,048, in which the board found that the Termination for Convenience clause did not overcome the government's obligation to pay anticipated profits when it failed to order requirements because of a subsequent decision to contract out the entire government operation that had previously had the requirements. The board reasoned that the government knew of the decision to contract out at the time of the award of the requirements contract and, hence, that there was no change in circumstances between award and termination. See also *Adams Mfg. Co.*, GSBCA 5747, 82-1 BCA ¶15,740, *aff'd*, 714 F.2d 161 (Fed. Cir. 1983), in which the board found that the Termination for Convenience clause precluded anticipated profits where no work had been ordered on a requirements contract because of a moratorium on the further purchase of office furniture, which was imposed after award of the contract with no evidence that officials had known or conceived of it before award. The Federal Circuit decision in *Adams Manufacturing*, however, was unpublished and is not citable as precedent. For additional discussion of the scope of the rule, see *Drain-A-Way Sys.*, GSBCA 7022, 84-1 BCA ¶16,929.

In the years since *Torncello*, the courts and boards have had difficulty deciding whether there is a "changed circumstance" rule, and if so, what constitutes such a change. In *Maxima Corp. v. United States*, 847 F.2d 1549 (Fed. Cir. 1988), the court seemed to adopt the changed circumstance rule. In holding that the government may not use a termination for convenience to avoid obligation on a contract already performed, the court quoted from *Municipal Leasing Corp. v. United States*, 7 Cl. Ct. 43 (1984), saying that the government's right to terminate arises "only in the event of some kind of change from the circumstances of the bargain or in the expectations of the parties." Subsequently, in *Salsbury Indus. v. United States*, 905 F.2d 1518 (Fed. Cir. 1990), *cert. denied*, 498 U.S. 1024 (1991), the court seemed to retreat from such a broad application of *Torncello* and return to the bad faith or abuse of discretion standards as the only limitations on the government's right to terminate. In that case, the government had entered into the contract after determining that another offeror was not responsible. However, the contracting officer had not advised that offeror that the determination was based on allegations that government employees had received kickbacks from that offeror under previous contracts. The contract was terminated to comply with a district court injunction. The court stated at 1521:

> Salsbury's second argument is that under *Torncello v. United States*, 231 Ct. Cl. 20, 681 F.2d 756 (1982), the termination of its contract was improper because it was the foreseeable victim of the Postal Service's illegal conduct . . . in disqualifying Doninger before it awarded the contract to Salsbury, the *Doninger* injunction does not justify allocating the burden of changed circumstances to Salsbury.
>
> *Torncello* has nothing to do with this case. It stands for the unremarkable proposition that when the government contracts with a party knowing full well that it will not honor the contract, it cannot avoid a breach claim by adverting to the convenience termination clause.

Thus, the court essentially imposed an additional intent requirement on contractors seeking to rely on *Torncello*—not only must they establish "changed circumstances," they must also show that the government entered into the contract with the intent to breach it. This "explanation" of *Torncello* was cited with approval in *Caldwell & Santmyer, Inc. v. Glickman*, 55 F.3d 1578 (Fed. Cir. 1995)—another case concerning termination for convenience following a flawed award. The court unequivocally stated that "bad faith . . . is a prerequisite for a *Torncello* claim." Thus, in order to invoke *Torncello*, the contractor faces a formidable burden—that is, it must be able to establish that, before award, the government specifically intended to terminate the contract. In *Caldwell*, the Federal Circuit refused to extend *Torncello* to the situation in which the government contracts in good faith but, at the same time, has knowledge of facts supposedly putting it on notice that, at some future date, it may be appropriate to terminate the contract for convenience. The court declined to apply *Torncello* to limit the government's termination for convenience rights in such circumstances. Accord, *Advanced Materials, Inc. v. United States*, 34 Fed. Cl. 480 (1995). See *Bryan D. Highfill*, HUDBCA 96-C-118-C7, 99-1 BCA ¶30,316 (government's right to terminate a contract for convenience is unlimited unless the termination is motivated by bad faith, the contracting officer abused his discretion in terminating the contract, or the government entered into the contract with no intention of allowing it to be completed); and *C.F.S. Air Cargo, Inc.*, ASBCA 36113, 91-1 BCA ¶23,583 (the *Torncello* rule did not apply to a termination where the government learned of better prices half-a-year after the award).

For a case applying the principles of *Torncello*, see *Operational Serv. Corp.*, ASBCA 37059, 93-3 BCA ¶26,190, holding that a grass mowing requirements contract was improperly terminated for convenience because the government knew at the time of contract formation that it intended to terminate the contract when either the government or a commercial activity contractor took over the work. The contractor was not informed of the government's intentions, nor was it given the opportunity to revise its prices. Relying on *Torncello*, the board held that the termination was an abuse of discretion and breach of contract. See also *Cray Research, Inc. v. United States*, 41 Fed. Cl. 427 (1998) (government may terminate for convenience only in the event of a change in the circumstances or in the parties' expectations).

c. The Krygoski Test—No Intention to Fulfill Promise

In *Krygoski Constr. Co. v. United States*, 94 F.3d 1537 (Fed. Cir. 1996), *cert. denied*, 520 U.S. 1210 (1997), the Federal Circuit again rejected an attempt to challenge a termination for convenience based on the *Torncello* changed circumstances doctrine and held that, when there was no bad faith or abuse of discretion, the government could terminate for convenience unless it had entered into the contract with no intention of fulfilling its promises.

In *Krygoski* the contracting officer decided to terminate for convenience in order to obtain new competition when it was discovered that there was a requirement for far more extensive asbestos removal than anticipated when the contract was awarded. The contracting officer believed that such termination was required because the new work was a "cardinal change" in the contract. The Court of Federal Claims concluded that this was not a changed circumstance with the result that the termination for convenience was improper and a breach of contract. As an alternative basis for overturning the termination, the court found that the government had abused its discretion, presumably because the contracting officer failed to justify the determination that the expansion of the contract work constituted a cardinal change. Accordingly, the court awarded Krygoski $1,456,851.20 in damages, which included anticipatory profits.

The Federal Circuit reversed, holding that, absent bad faith or abuse of discretion, a contracting officer's decision to terminate a contract for the convenience of the government is conclusive and will not be disturbed by the courts. The court concluded that *Torncello* stands only for the narrow proposition that the government may not invoke the Termination for Convenience clause, and thereby avoid breach of contract liability for anticipatory profits, when it enters a contract that it does not intend to honor. The Federal Circuit panel stated: "Although arguably the Government's circumstances had sufficiently changed to meet even the *Torncello* plurality standard, this court declines to reach this issue because *Torncello* applies only when the Government enters a contract with no intention of fulfilling its promises." The panel in *Krygoski* found that the changed circumstances test was merely an application of the *Kalvar* bad faith test and concluded that in *Torncello* the changed circumstances test had been "articulated in dicta."

The *Krygoski* decision appears to be based on the reasoning that with the advent of CICA, the "changed circumstances" test is no longer necessary to protect contractors against improper terminations for convenience. The court viewed a "lenient convenience termination" standard as consistent with the goal of full and open competition. The role of convenience terminations in the "CICA regime" is therefore seen as distinct from pre-CICA cases such as *Torncello*. The court stated at 1544:

> In sum, on two recent occasions after enactment of CICA, this court has expressly repeated the narrow applicability of *Torncello*. [*Caldwell*, 55 F.3d] at 1582; *Salsbury*, 905 F.2d at 1521. Indeed this court's recent pronouncements are fully consistent with the policy goals of CICA and other Government procurement statutes. Under these policies, contracting officers have no incentive to terminate a contract for convenience except to maintain full and open competition under CICA. With an adequate contractor in place, the contracting officer has no interest to reprocure. Moreover, where an officer must choose between modifying or terminating a contract, ease of administration usually imparts a bias in favor of modification. Thus *Salsbury* and *Caldwell* suggest that this court will avoid a finding of abused discretion when the facts support a reasonable inference that the contracting officer terminated for convenience in furtherance of statutory requirements for full and open competition.

A contractor is therefore essentially left with only the theories of bad faith and abuse of discretion to try to support such a challenge. As recognized by the Federal Circuit in *Krygoski*, a contractor's burden of proof in such cases is a heavy one, and "contractors have rarely succeeded in demonstrating the Government's bad faith."

The *Krygoski* court did not have the authority to explicitly overrule *Torncello*, since a panel of the Federal Circuit decided the former and the latter was decided en banc by the Court of Claims. See, for example, *South Corp. v. United States*, 690 F.2d 1368, (Fed. Cir. 1982).

Since *Krygoski*, courts and boards have been reluctant to convert terminations for convenience into breach of contract claims in the absence of strong evidence of bad faith or abuse of discretion in the termination decision. See *T&M Distribs., Inc. v. United States*, 185 F.3d 1279 (Fed. Cir. 1999) (no evidence that government did not intend to fulfill its promise when it terminated after large increase in requirements); *Charles G. Williams Constr., Inc.*, ASBCA 49775, 00-2 BCA ¶31,047, *vacated and remanded on other grounds*, 271 F.3d 1055 (Fed. Cir. 2001) (no bad faith because there was no evidence that the government intended to terminate the contract at the time of the award); and *Max S. Castle*, AGBCA 97-137-1, 00-1 BCA ¶30,871, *recons. denied*, 03-2 BCA ¶32,270 (contractor not entitled to recover costs incurred in remodeling a building for rental to the government because there was no evidence that the government had misled the lessor regarding the length of the lease term).

d. Violation of Paramount Government Policies

The courts have enjoined convenience terminations on the grounds that they violate or avoid other government policies of paramount importance. See *National Helium Corp. v. Morton*, 455 F.2d 650 (10th Cir. 1971), upholding an injunction against termination based on the government's failure to file an environmental impact statement as required by law. The court noted that the action was otherwise "within the discretion of the secretary." In *Art-Metal-USA, Inc. v. Solomon*, 473 F. Supp. 1 (D.D.C. 1978), the contractor was granted a preliminary injunction against a convenience termination on the grounds that the termination, along with actions the government was contemplating on other contracts, would constitute a constructive debarment without required procedural safeguards. The contractor was under investigation for alleged improper dealings but had not been officially accused of wrongdoing. The court found that the termination was based on unfavorable publicity and fear of political pressure. The injunction was made permanent, 25 CCF ¶82,962 (D.D.C. 1979). The case was voluntarily dismissed by both parties on appeal, No. 79-1296 (D.C. Cir. 1979). A termination for convenience was also enjoined when it was based on arbitrary and capricious action during the source selection process, *Vibra-Tech Eng'rs, Inc. v. United States*, 567 F. Supp. 484 (D. Colo. 1983). There, three months after the contracting officer had awarded a contract based on a clearly superior technical proposal, the contract was terminated for convenience and an award was made to an offeror with a lower price. The court found no rational basis for this action and enjoined the termination. Similarly, in *Law Eng'g Testing Co. v. Lee*, 25 Gov't Ctr. ¶26 (D. La. 1982), a termination was enjoined because the contracting officer had based the decision on an arbitrary and capricious recommendation of the GAO in response to a protest from a competitor. In *Gould, Inc. v. Chafee*, 450 F.2d 667 (D.C. Cir. 1971), the court stated that if the contractor could substantiate its claim that the termination was arbitrary and capricious it would be entitled to an injunction against the termination.

C. Partial Terminations

The termination clauses specifically entitle the government to make partial terminations and require the contractor to complete the unterminated work. Although a contracting officer, absent a deviation from the FAR, may not restrict the government's right to partially terminate, other clauses in the contract may control the financial results of a termination, *Raytheon Co.*, DOTCAB 1363, 84-1 BCA ¶16,969, *recons. denied in part, aff'd in part*, 84-2 BCA ¶17,459 (overhead ceiling applicable as long as work varied no more than 15 percent from estimate, but not applicable after partial termination reduced work more than 15 percent). There appear to be no limitations on the extent of a partial termination, which can run to the great majority of the contract work. See *Memheth, Ltd.*, ASBCA 21395, 77-1 BCA ¶12,274, where the government's failure to provide work resulted in a constructive partial termination of 118 units out of 181 units of heat exchangers being overhauled. Further, the character of the work can change drastically as a result of a partial termination. In *Lieb Bros., Inc.*, ASBCA 10007, 73-2 BCA ¶10,131, *recons. denied*, 74-1 BCA ¶10,509, the board upheld a partial termination that removed the major and most attractive portion of the job, explaining that "the Government was simply exercising its contractual rights." Thus, while the termination clauses call for an equitable adjustment in the unterminated portion of the work, the contractor bears a substantial risk of loss if the most profitable portion of the work is terminated.

D. Procedural Requirements

There are relatively few procedural requirements for a termination for convenience.

1. Notice of Termination

In addition to the provisions in the termination clause, FAR 49.102(a) contains the following guidance with respect to the notice of termination:

> The contracting officer shall terminate contracts for convenience or default only by a written notice to the contractor (see 49.601). When the notice is mailed, it shall be sent by certified mail, return receipt requested. When the contracting office arranges for hand delivery of the notice, a written acknowledgement shall be obtained from the contractor. The notice shall state—
>
> (1) That the contract is being terminated for the convenience of the Government (or for default) under the contract clause authorizing the termination;
> (2) The effective date of termination;
> (3) The extent of termination;
> (4) Any special instructions; and
> (5) The steps the contractor should take to minimize the impact on personnel if the termination, together with all other outstanding terminations, will result in a significant reduction in the contractor's work force (see paragraph (g) of the notice in 49.601-2). If the termination notice is by telegram, include these "steps" in the confirming letter or modification.

FAR 49.601 provides model forms to be used for both telegraphic and letter notices of termination. The letter notice contains detailed guidance to the contractor on the procedures to be followed. DFARS 249.102 requires the use of Standard Form 30 for such notices.

A contracting officer's oral statements that he intended to convert a default termination into a convenience termination were not binding on the government because the contract terms and the regulations required notice of a convenience termination to be in writing, *Marshall Assoc. Contractors, Inc.*, IBCA 1901, 98-2 BCA ¶29,756.

Based on the language of the termination clause, in *Okinawa Climate Control Corp.*, ASBCA 19753, 77-2 BCA ¶12,669, the board refused to consider allegations that acts of the contracting officer's superior resulted in a termination for convenience, holding that it is the contracting officer who makes the decision to terminate the contract for convenience.

2. Termination for Default versus Termination for Convenience

In some cases, there has been confusion about whether a contract was being terminated for the contractor's default or the government's convenience. In *Richardson Camera Co.*, ASBCA 11930, 68-1 BCA ¶6990, the board held that if the contractor reasonably believes the notice of termination to be for convenience it will be treated as a termination for convenience even though it lacks the technical language normally found in such notices. Conversely, where the contractor knows that the termination is for default, the mere fact that the notice describes it as a convenience termination will not permit the contractor to treat it as such. See *Hadden v. United States*, 131 Ct. Cl. 326, 130 F. Supp. 610 (1955), where, in order to "save face" for the contractor, the contracting officer agreed to cancel the contract for convenience with the understanding that the contractor's recovery would be limited by the Default clause. When the termination notice was issued, reference to the Default clause limitations was inadvertently omitted. The court refused to permit the contractor to recover under the convenience clause because both parties knew that the termination was really for default. However, where there was genuine uncertainty over the type of termination, the board treated the termination as one for convenience, *Stroud Realty*, HUDBCA 75-13, 76-1 BCA ¶11,770. There, the contractor requested to be informed of the basis for the "cancellation," and the contracting officer replied by referring to both the default and the convenience termination provisions. The board stated that the government had a clear obligation to specify the exact method by which it was terminating the contract and ruled that it would be construed as a termination for convenience.

E. Finality of Termination for Convenience

Once a contract has been terminated for convenience, the act is treated as final, and the contractor's obligations to complete the terminated work are considered to be at an end. Thus, even though grounds for a default termination existed at the time the convenience notice was given, conversion to a default termination is not permitted, *Roged, Inc.*, ASBCA 20702, 76-2 BCA ¶12,018. See also *ITT Def. Communications Div.*, ASBCA 11858, 70-2 BCA ¶8415. Similarly, the contractor is not obligated to correct defective work in the terminated portion of the contract and is entitled to be paid the cost of the defective work, *New York Shipbuilding Co.*, ASBCA 15443, 73-1 BCA ¶9852. In that case, the board stated that "by terminating the contract for convenience the Government deprives the contractor of the opportunity to overcome deficiencies by better performance as the contract is nearing completion." The board also noted that to hold otherwise "would be inconsistent with the nature of a termination for convenience which is not based upon any fault or negligence on the part of the contractor." Finally, the board stated that its holding did not prevent the estimated costs of the contractor for correcting the deficiencies from being considered when reaching a termination settlement. Consideration of such costs would be important in determining whether a loss adjustment was required.

In *Cross Petroleum, Inc. v. United States*, 51 Fed. Cl. 549 (2002), the court held that the termination for default was improper in the absence of a 10-day cure notice. However, the court rejected the contractor's claim that, because the improper termination for default would be converted to a termination for convenience, it had no further liability for the remediation. The court distinguished the usual situation in which an improper termination for default went to the subject matter of the contract from the present case, in which the remediation obligation was ancillary. The court ruled that the damages should be determined under standard contract law, under which the contractor has the burden to show that government-incurred costs were unreasonable.

FAR 49.102(d) states that a terminated contract may be reinstated with the written consent of the contractor. In *Richardson Camera Co.*, ASBCA 11930, 68-1 BCA ¶6990, the government unsuccessfully attempted to change a termination from convenience to a termination for default. Thereafter, the contractor accepted the return of a prototype and attempted corrective action. In holding that such action did not reinstate the contract, the board stated that "performance cannot be construed as agreement to complete the contract."

F. Deletion of Work Through Termination for Convenience, Changes, or Other Clauses

Both the Termination for Convenience of the Government clause and the Changes clause provide mechanisms for deleting work. However, the pricing formulas, claims processing, cost recovery, settlement procedures, and inventory disposition methods may be substantially different depending on which method is selected. FAR 49.002(c) permits the use of termination principles in determining equitable adjustments under the Changes clause—but there is no means for imposing such adjustments on a contractor when they result in less compensation than is available through use of normal equitable adjustment principles. Thus, the basic rights of the parties will be determined by the clause used by the contracting officer to delete the work. The Termination for the Convenience of the Government clause must be used when major portions of the work are deleted and no additional work is substituted. Otherwise, either clause may be used, *Nager Elec. Co. v. United States*, 194 Ct. Cl. 835, 442 F.2d 936 (1971).

J. W. Bateson Co. v. United States, 308 F.2d 510 (5th Cir. 1962) is the leading case for the rule that major deletions may not be accomplished under the Changes clause. The court cited with approval the trial judge's statement that "the proper yardstick in judging between a change and a termination in projects of this magnitude would best be found by thinking in terms of major and minor variations in the plans." See also *John N. Brophy Co.*, GSBCA 5122, 78-2 BCA ¶13,506 (deletion of small amount of instructional services permitted under Changes clause), and *Bromley Contracting Co.*, HUDBCA 75-8, 77-1 BCA ¶12,232 (minor change in amount of work to be considered a constructive change). In *Celesco Indus., Inc.*, ASBCA 22251, 79-1 BCA ¶13,604, the board stated that termination for convenience was more appropriate for eliminating units of work or identifiable work items or tasks, whereas changes were normally used to delete work by changing the specifications. In that case a partial termination was treated as a change. Contrast *G.L. Cory, Inc.*, GSBCA 4383, 77-2 BCA ¶12,824, *recons. denied,* 78-2 BCA ¶13,356, in which a deletion of defective work under the Changes clause was treated as a termination for convenience.

In cases where the contracting officer initially orders the deletion under the Changes clause, it has been held that he or she can subsequently proceed under the termination clause if a binding agreement on the equitable adjustment has not been consummated, *Frederick Constr. Co.*, ASBCA 12241, 68-1 BCA ¶6832; *Gyrodyne Co. of America*, ASBCA 17415, 73-2 BCA ¶10,208. However, in view of the degree of finality accorded a notice of termination, the reverse would not appear to be true.

How the parties treated the deletion at the time is often outcome determinative. In *Honeycomb Co. of Am., Inc.*, ASBCA 44612, 02-1 BCA ¶31,703, the board held that reduction from 116 to 21 units was not a partial termination for convenience because the contractor voluntarily entered into bilateral modification designating the reduction as a change. In *P.J. Dick, Inc. v. General Servs. Admin.*, GSBCA 12215, 95-1 BCA ¶27,574, *modified on recons.*, 96-1 BCA ¶28,017, although the government purported to partially terminate for convenience a building renovation contract, the pricing of the government's credit was based on the cost of the deleted work under the Changes clause rather than under the Termination for Convenience clause because both parties had analyzed the matter and treated it as a deductive change. The board stated that it would not disturb the parties' treatment of the matter in the absence of a compelling reason to do so.

The government may delete work under other clauses. In *Jiminez, Inc.*, VABCA 6351, 02-2 BCA ¶32,019, the government relied on the Inspection of Construction clause to have unsatisfactory work completed by another contractor. The board rejected the contractor's assertion that the work should have been deleted from the contract as a termination for convenience. The use of a particular clause depends on the extent of work being deleted, rather than on which clause provides the greatest benefit to the contractor. Here, since only 2 percent of work was not completed, it was appropriate to use the Inspection of Construction clause.

III. CONSTRUCTIVE TERMINATION

There are significant differences between an express termination and a constructive termination. Express terminations occur when the clause is specifically invoked. Constructive terminations and constructive changes are both judicial constructs in situations when a breach might otherwise result. Constructive changes, however, were designed to provide contractors with an administrative remedy, while a constructive termination insulates the government from breach damages, including anticipated profits.

In *John Reiner & Co. v. United States*, 163 Ct. Cl. 381, 325 F.2d 438 (1963), *cert. denied*, 377 U.S. 931 (1964), the Court of Claims enunciated the principle that any government action preventing a contractor from continuing performance would be adjusted for under the Termination for Convenience clause if the contracting officer could have used the clause at the time of the action. This principle has prevented contractors from recovering anticipated profits in a number of situations where the government elected not to terminate for convenience but rather to end the contractual relationship in some other way. This result might also be obtained even if the clause was omitted from the contract documents but was required by the regulations to be included, under the rationale of *G.L. Christian & Assocs. v. United States*, 160 Ct. Cl. 1, 312 F.2d 418, *cert. denied*, 375 U.S. 954 (1963).

In *Diversified Energy, Inc. v. TVA*, 223 F.3d 328 (6th Cir. 2000), the court refused to apply the constructive termination logic to benefit the contractor. The contractor had argued that the government's exercise of a "reopening" provision, which permitted the parties to reopen the contract at its midway point to renegotiate the contract terms, was a "constructive" termination, thus triggering the Unilateral Termination provision, which permitted the TVA to terminate the contract upon 60 day' notice but imposed a penalty requiring payment of $14 for each ton scheduled for delivery under the remainder of the contract. The court concluded that the purpose of the constructive termination rule was to retroactively justify the government's actions, avoiding breach and limiting liability. See also *Contact Int'l, Inc. v. Widnall*, 106 F.3d 426 (Fed. Cir. 1997), rejecting a contractor's claim that a constructive termination for convenience occurred based on uncertainty created by the government about whether it was going to terminate the contract for convenience.

In *United Techs. Corp.*, ASBCA 46880, 97-1 BCA ¶28,818, the board held that the constructive termination rule does not apply to promises to buy more products in the future. It therefore rejected the government's argument that its breach of an Investment Incentive clause calling for the future award of jet engines should be treated as a convenience termination.

A. Wrongful Default Terminations

For a number of years the government has, by contract clause, provided for the application of the convenience termination provisions to wrongful default terminations. Paragraph (g) of the present fixed-price supply contract Default clause contained in FAR 52.249-8 states:

> If, after termination, it is determined that the Contractor was not in default, or that the default was excusable, the rights and obligations of the parties shall be the same as if the termination had been issued for the convenience of the Government.

Similar provisions are contained in ¶(c) of the fixed-price construction contract Default clause in FAR 52.249-10 and in ¶(g) of the fixed-price research and development contract Default clause in FAR 52.249-9. The default termination will be converted to a convenience termination if the contractor was not in default or if its failure is excusable. Thus, there is little likelihood of a contractor recovering anticipated profits when a contract is improperly terminated for default.

The conversion of default to convenience terminations by boards and courts is a very common practice and has been extended to practically any reason for wrongful default termination. See *Specialty Constr. Co.*, ASBCA 21132, 78-2 BCA ¶13,348 (waiver of right to terminate for default); *Electro-Magnetic Refinishers, Inc.*, GSBCA 5035, 79-1 BCA ¶13,697 (failure to follow procedures—no written cure notice); *Sayers Custom Mowing*, ENGBCA 3950, 79-1 BCA ¶13,695 (contractor excusably delayed); *Mr.'s Landscaping & Nursery*, HUDBCA 75-6, 76-2 BCA ¶11,968 (contracts substantially performed); *A.W. Burton*, AGBCA 431, 77-1 BCA ¶12,307 (contractor not in default); and *Whittaker Corp.*, ASBCA 14740, 79-1 BCA ¶13,805 (contract impossible to perform). See also *Carter Indus.*, DOTBCA 4108, 02-1 BCA ¶31,738, applying the Termination for Convenience clause when the government breached the contract by requiring the bankrupt contractor (acting as a debtor in possession) to either accept or reject the contract in the bankruptcy proceedings. For a case considering but rejecting application of the *Torncello* rule to an improper default termination, see *Drain-A-Way Sys.*, GSBCA 7022, 84-1 BCA ¶16,929.

In *Apex Int'l Mgmt. Servs., Inc.*, ASBCA 38087, 94-2 BCA ¶26,842, *recons. denied,* 94-2 BCA ¶26,852, the board refused to convert an improper default termination into a termination for convenience. It found that the government's actions satisfied all the requirements of bad faith. The government employees, unhappy with the contracting-out involved, attempted to block the award and then "declared war" on the contractor, making false statements and committing numerous acts designed to harass and injure the contractor.

B. Government's Failure to Perform Under an Indefinite Delivery Contract

The government's failure to perform its obligations under a requirements contract has been alternatively treated as a constructive change or a breach of contract. If the government action is considered a breach, the *Reiner* rule has been applied to limit recovery on the theory that a convenience termination was possible and could have been used by the contracting officer, *Nesbitt v. United States*, 170 Ct. Cl. 666, 345 F.2d 583 (1965), *cert. denied,* 383 U. S. 926 (1966). See *Inland Container, Inc. v. United States*, 206 Ct. Cl. 478, 512 F.2d 1073 (1975), and *Kalvar Corp. v. United States*, 211 Ct. Cl. 192, 543 F.2d 1298 (1976), *cert. denied*, 434 U.S. 830 (1977). A constructive termination for convenience has also been found where the government failed to order work under a multiyear contract when funds were available, *Varo, Inc.*, ASBCA 13739, 70-1 BCA ¶8099.

In two cases, the *Reiner* rule has been rejected when the government breached a requirements contract. In *Torncello v. United States*, 231 Ct. Cl. 20, 681 F.2d 756 (1982), and *S & W Tire Servs., Inc.*, GSBCA 6376, 82-2 BCA ¶16,048, anticipated profits were included in the contractor's damages because there had been no change in circumstances leading to the government decision to buy its requirements from another contractor. Compare *Adams Mfg. Co.*, GSBCA 5747, 82-1 BCA ¶15,740, *aff'd*, 714 F.2d 161 (Fed. Cir. 1983), in which the *Reiner* rule was applied when the government had breached a requirements contract by not informing the contractor of a moratorium on its requirements. See also *Atlantic Garages, Inc.*, GSBCA 5891, 82-1 BCA ¶15,479, in which the board held that failure to inform the contractor of reduced requirements was a breach rather than a constructive termination for convenience but did not discuss the measure of damages.

Constructive termination is not available for a completed contract. In *Maxima Corp v. United States*, 847 F.2d 1549 (Fed. Cir. 1988), the court held that the government cannot retroactively terminate a completed contract to avoid a breach. In *Ace-Fed. Reporters, Inc. v. Barram*, 226 F.3d 1329 (Fed. Cir. 2000), the court held that, by ordering services from other vendors in violation of requirements-like contracts, the GSA breached the contracts and was liable for lost profits. The court rejected the GSA's constructive termination argument since the contracts were completed and the contractors stood ready to perform throughout, stating that the "concept is a fiction to begin with, but there has to be some limit to its elasticity." See also *Mid Eastern Indus., Inc.*, ASBCA 53016, 02-1 BCA ¶31,657 (government's failure to order the minimum quantity on an ID/IQ contract not a constructive termination for convenience because contractor maintained its capability until completion of contract period); *T&M Distribs., Inc.*, ASBCA 51279, 01-2 BCA ¶31,442 (applying *Ace-Federal Reporters* to hold that the government's diversion of purchases from a requirements contract constituted a breach that could not be recast by the government as a partial constructive termination for convenience); and *Carroll Autom.*, ASBCA 50993, 98-2 BCA ¶29,864 (denying the government's argument that purchase of some supplies from other sources was a constructive partial termination for convenience because the government first invoked its constructive partial convenience termination theory two years after the contract had been performed, and the contract's termination provisions required an equitable adjustment of the nonterminated portion of the contract in the event of a partial termination). Compare *Hermes Consol., Inc.*, ASBCA 52308, 02-1 BCA ¶31,767, holding that the government's partial termination for convenience reducing the minimum quantity under an IDIQ contract was a permissible termination for convenience even though the termination notice was issued only eight days before the end of one contract.

C. Cancellation of Award

The convenience termination clause has been consistently applied to limit the contractor's recovery when the government wrongfully cancels as a result of an award controversy. In *G.C. Casebolt Co. v. United States*, 190 Ct. Cl. 783, 421 F.2d 710 (1970), the government contended that an award had not been made because the notice of award had been retrieved from the mail and the award canceled. The court held that, even if the award had been consummated, the contractor's recovery would be limited by the convenience termination clause. See also *Albano Cleaners, Inc. v. United States*, 197 Ct. Cl. 450, 455 F.2d 556 (1972) (award canceled on erroneous belief that bid was nonresponsive); *McFadden v. United States*, 215 Ct. Cl. 918 (1977) (all bids rejected because government estimate exceeded but award had already been made to plaintiff); and *Dairy Sales Corp. v. United States*, 219 Ct. Cl. 431, 593 F.2d 1002 (1979) (partial cancellation because award for one item should have gone to another bidder—converted to partial termination).

IV. TERMINATION SETTLEMENTS

Contracts terminated for the convenience of the government may be settled by negotiated agreement, determination of the Termination Contracting Officer (TCO) (only when settlement cannot be reached by agreement), costing out in cost-reimbursement contracts, or a combination of these methods, FAR 49.103. If agreement on a settlement cannot be reached, the "long form" clauses require the government to pay the contractor the costs incurred in performing the terminated work, the costs of settling and paying settlement proposals under terminated subcontracts, and a fair and reasonable profit on work performed. The "short form" clauses and the clause for contracts for commercial items provide for minimal compensation to the contractor.

The terms of a convenience termination recovery are governed by U.S. public contract law, not the law of the country in which the contract is performed. See *Empresa de Viacao Terceirense*, ASBCA 49827, 00-2 BCA ¶31,120, *recons. denied*, 01-1 BCA ¶31,243, rejecting the contractor's argument that Portuguese law should govern whether severance pay costs are allowable and reimbursable as part of the termination settlement.

A. Procedures

After a contract has been terminated for the convenience of the government, the parties are faced with the problem of stopping the work to the extent terminated, disposing of the termination inventory, and adjusting the contract price. These matters are covered in detail in the "long form" termination clauses, and FAR Part 49 contains detailed procedures covering terminations.

1. Obligations of the Parties

The contractor's and contracting officer's duties are summarized at FAR 49.104 and FAR 49.105, as follows:

49.104 Duties of prime contractor after receipt of notice of termination.

After receipt of the notice of termination, the contractor shall comply with the notice and the termination clause of the contract, except as otherwise directed by the TCO. The notice and clause applicable to convenience terminations generally require that the contractor—

(a) Stop work immediately on the terminated portion of the contract and stop placing subcontracts thereunder;
(b) Terminate all subcontracts related to the terminated portion of the prime contract;
(c) Immediately advise the TCO of any special circumstances precluding the stoppage of work;
(d) Perform the continued portion of the contract and submit promptly any request for an equitable adjustment of price for the continued portion, supported by evidence of any increase in the cost, if the termination is partial;
(e) Take necessary or directed action to protect and preserve property in the contractor's possession in which the Government has or may acquire an interest and, as directed by the TCO, deliver the property to the Government;
(f) Promptly notify the TCO in writing of any legal proceedings growing out of any subcontract or other commitment related to the terminated portion of the contract;
(g) Settle outstanding liabilities and proposals arising out of termination of subcontracts, obtaining any approvals or ratifications required by the TCO;
(h) Promptly submit the contractor's own settlement proposal, supported by appropriate schedules; and
(i) Dispose of termination inventory as directed or authorized by the TCO.

49.105 Duties of termination contracting officer after issuance of notice of termination.

(a) Consistent with the termination clause and the notice of termination, the TCO shall—
  (1) Direct the action required of the prime contractor;
  (2) Examine the settlement proposal of the prime contractor and, when appropriate, the settlement proposals of subcontractors;
  (3) Promptly negotiate settlement with the contractor and enter into a settlement agreement; and
  (4) Promptly settle the contractor's settlement proposal by determination for the elements that cannot be agreed on, if unable to negotiate a complete settlement.
(b) To expedite settlement, the TCO may request specially qualified personnel to—
  (1) Assist in dealings with the contractor;
  (2) Advise on legal and contractual matters;
  (3) Conduct accounting reviews and advise and assist on accounting matters; and
  (4) Perform the following functions regarding termination inventory (see Subpart 45.6);
    (i) Verify its existence.
    (ii) Determine qualitative and quantitative allocability.
    (iii) Make recommendations concerning serviceability.
    (iv) Undertake necessary screening and redistribution.
    (v) Assist the contractor in accomplishing other disposition.
(c) The TCO should promptly hold a conference with the contractor to develop a definite program for effecting the settlement. When appropriate in the judgment of the TCO, after consulting with the contractor, principal subcontractors should be requested to attend. Topics that should be discussed at the conference and documented include—
  (1) General principles relating to the settlement of any settlement proposal, including obligations of the contractor under the termination clause of the contract;

(2) Extent of the termination, point at which work is stopped, and status of any plans, drawings, and information that would have been delivered had the contract been completed;
(3) Status of any continuing work;
(4) Obligation of the contractor to terminate subcontracts and general principles to be followed in settling subcontractor settlement proposals;
(5) Names of subcontractors involved and the dates termination notices were issued to them;
(6) Contractor personnel handling review and settlement of subcontractor settlement proposals and the methods being used;
(7) Arrangements for transfer of title and delivery to the Government of any material required by the Government;
(8) General principles and procedures to be followed in the protection, preservation, and disposition of the contractor's and subcontractor's termination inventories, including the preparation of termination inventory schedules;
(9) Contractor accounting practices and preparation of SF 1439 (Schedule of Accounting Information (49.602-3));
(10) Form in which to submit settlement proposals;
(11) Accounting review of settlement proposals;
(12) Any requirement for interim financing in the nature of partial payments;
(13) Tentative time schedule for negotiation of the settlement, including submission by the contractor and subcontractors of settlement proposals, termination inventory schedules, and accounting information schedules (see 49.206-3 and 49.303-2);
(14) Actions taken by the contractor to minimize impact upon employees affected adversely by the termination (see paragraph (g) of the letter notice in 49.601-2); and
(15) Obligation of the contractor to furnish accurate, complete, and current cost or pricing data, and to certify to that effect in accordance with 15.403-4(a)(1) when the amount of a termination settlement agreement, or a partial termination settlement agreement plus the estimate to complete the continued portion of the contract exceeds the threshold in 15.403-4.

2. Basis for Settlement Proposals

Two fundamental approaches are available for use in the submission of settlement proposals: (1) an "inventory" basis, which FAR 49.206-2 states is the "preferred" method; and (2) a "total cost" basis. Under both methods for submission of settlement proposals, the contractor is paid the contract price for items completed and accepted, FAR 49.205, but the accounting treatment of the work in process is quite different.

Under the inventory method the contractor must separately itemize charges to be allocated to the settlement proposal. FAR 49.206-2(a)(1) requires the separation of the following costs:

(i) Metals, raw materials, purchased parts, work in process, finished parts, components, dies, jigs, fixtures, and tooling, at purchase or manufacturing cost;
(ii) Charges such as engineering costs, initial costs, and general administrative costs;
(iii) Costs of settlements with subcontractors;
(iv) Settlement expenses; and
(v) Other proper charges.

Use of the inventory method requires the contractor to have an accounting system that is capable of accurately segregating costs of the partially performed work. If the contractor's accounting system is not sufficiently well developed for this purpose, the total cost basis for submission of settlement proposals will generally be approved for use.

Under the total cost basis for submission of settlement proposals, the contractor itemizes all costs incurred in performance of the contract work. Costs are not segregated between the completed and partially performed portions of the work. FAR 49.206-2(b) provides for use of the total cost approach as follows:

(1) When use of the inventory basis is not practicable or will unduly delay settlement, the total-cost basis (SF-1436) may be used if approved in advance by the TCO as in the following examples:
  (i) If production has not commenced and the accumulated costs represent planning and preproduction or "get ready" expenses.
  (ii) If, under the contractor's accounting system, unit costs for work in process and finished products cannot readily be established.
  (iii) If the contract does not specify unit prices.
  (iv) If the termination is complete and involves a letter contract.

FAR 49.206-2(b) also contains the following guidance concerning use of the total cost method in both complete and partial termination situations:

(2) When the total-cost basis is used under a complete termination, the contractor must itemize costs incurred under the contract up to the effective date of termination. The costs of settlements with subcontractors and applicable settlement expenses must also be added. An allowance for profit (49.202) or adjustment for loss (49.203(c)) must be made. The contract price for all end items delivered or to be delivered and accepted must be deducted. All unliquidated advance and progress payments and disposal and other credits known when the proposal is submitted must also be deducted.
(3) When the total-cost basis is used under a partial termination, the settlement proposal shall not be submitted until completion of the continued portion of the contract. The settlement proposal must be prepared as in [subparagraph (2) above], except that all costs incurred to the date of completion of the continued portion of the contract must be included.

When the inventory approach is used, the contractor must pay careful attention to those costs that were to have been recovered or amortized over all contract work—completed units as well as partially completed and terminated work—especially costs such as engineering and development expenses, preproduction, and starting load costs. Unless the contractor separates and allocates an appropriate portion of such costs to the termination claim, the inventory approach may unfairly limit the contractor's recovery.

For commercial contracts, FAR 12.403 states:

(d) Termination for the Government's convenience.
  (1) When the contracting officer terminates a contract for commercial items for the Government's convenience, the contractor shall be paid—
    (i) The percentage of the contract price reflecting the percentage of the work performed prior to the notice of the termination, and
    (ii) Any charges the contractor can demonstrate directly resulted from the termination. The contractor may demonstrate such charges using its standard record keeping system and is not required to comply with the cost accounting standards or the contract cost principles in Part 31. The Government does not have any right to audit the contractor's records solely because of the termination for convenience.
  (2) Generally, the parties should mutually agree upon the requirements of the termination proposal. The parties must balance the Government's need to obtain sufficient documentation to support payment to the contractor against the goal of having a simple and expeditious settlement.

3. Time of Submission of Proposals

Paragraph (d) of the "long form" termination clause in FAR 52.249-2 requires that the contractor submit its settlement proposal within "1 year from the effective date of termination" unless the period is extended in writing by the contracting officer. If the contractor fails to do so, the contracting officer may make a unilateral determination of the amount due the contractor, although contracting officers do have discretion to act upon late settlement proposals, FAR 52.249-2. Paragraph (j) of the "long form" clause provides that contractors lose their right to appeal a unilateral termination determination of a contracting officer if they have neither submitted their settlement proposal within one year nor requested a time extension. See *England v. Swanson Group, Inc.*, 353 F.3d 1375 (Fed. Cir. 2004), holding that the board had no jurisdiction to consider an appeal of a contracting officer's award of settlement costs after the contractor had failed to submit a settlement proposal within one year. The court reached this conclusion even though the board had found that the contractor had requested an extension of time to submit the proposal within the one-year period. The court reasoned that the Contract Disputes Act did not provide for an appeal of the contracting officer's determination because it was not an appeal from a final decision on a claim that Swanson had submitted. See also *Industrial Data Link Corp.*, ASBCA 49348, 98-1 BCA ¶29,634, *recons. denied,* 98-2 BCA ¶29,775, *aff'd,* 194 F.3d 1337 (Fed. Cir. 1999), and *Rivera Tech. Prods., Inc.*, ASBCA 48171, 96-2 BCA ¶28,564, holding that the contractors had lost the right to appeal the contracting officer's determination of the amount due on their late termination settlement proposals. None of these cases addresses the issue of whether the contractor could challenge the settlement proposal as being arbitrary and capricious. See also *United Elecs. Co.*, ASBCA 21686, 78-1 BCA ¶13,091.

In *Do-Well Mach. Shop, Inc. v. United States*, 870 F.2d 637 (Fed. Cir. 1989), the court held that the requirement that the settlement proposal be submitted no later than one year after the termination was not inconsistent with the Contract Disputes Act. Thus, the failure to file within the time limit was a valid defense that could be raised by the government. See *Dynatech Bldg. Sys. Corp.*, ASBCA 47462, 95-1 BCA ¶27,325, in which the contractor's failure to file a termination for convenience claim within the required one-year period was not excused by a hurricane because the contractor failed to request a time extension from the contracting officer. The purpose in requiring the contractor to present a prompt settlement proposal is to permit the government to close out the terminated contract within a reasonable time, to budget its funds, and to enable it to gather evidence concerning the pricing of the contractor's claims, if necessary.

The one-year period begins to run when the contractor is given notice of the termination. In *Swanson Group, Inc.*, ASBCA 52109, 01-1 BCA ¶31164, the board held that the one-year period for the submission of the proposal or request for extension began when the contractor received notice of the conversion of the default termination to one for convenience. In *Space Dynamics Corp.*, ASBCA 25106, 81-2 BCA ¶15205, the board rejected the argument that the one-year period began with the contractor's receipt of the notice of the default termination. In *Voices R Us, Inc.*, ASBCA 51565, 99-1 BCA ¶30,213, the termination notice specified the effective date as April 15, 1997, and a Federal Express air bill established that the contractor received a hard copy of the notice on April 16, 1997. The board rejected the government's argument that the proposal was untimely because the government had sent the contractor a facsimile of the termination notice on April 14, 1997, finding that the contractor's records for the period showed no facsimile received on April 14, 1997, and the government offered no record of the alleged facsimile.

4. Imperfect Proposals

The primary function of a termination settlement proposal is to foster negotiations between the parties. Therefore, a proposal that is initiated within the one-year period for submission, but that contains flaws, may be valid if the flaws are not so severe as to render the proposal meaningless for purposes of negotiation and are remediable within a reasonable time, *Astor Bolden Enters., Inc.*, ASBCA 52377, 00-2 BCA ¶31,115. In *Marine Instrument Co.*, ASBCA 41370, 97-2 BCA ¶29,082, the government, alleging that the contractor had failed to submit a proper settlement proposal within one year, was denied summary judgment because it failed to show that the contractor's timely submissions "were so deficient as to be meaningless for the purposes of negotiation." In *Consolidated Def. Corp.*, ASBCA 52315, 01-2 BCA ¶31,484, the government was not entitled to summary judgment that a termination settlement proposal not submitted within one year from the termination for convenience was untimely where (a) the contractor's initial proposal, submitted five months after the termination for convenience, was not so flawed as to be meaningless for resolution of the termination for convenience; (b) the contractor had requested additional time to submit a corrected proposal before the one year expired; (c) the contractor did submit a final proposal within 14 months of the termination for convenience; (d) a succession of termination contracting officers made partial payments and negotiated with the contractor on the submittals; and (e) the government waited five years before asserting that the proposal was untimely.

A related issue involves whether claims separate from the termination are waived if they are not presented within one year with the termination settlement proposal. In *Ellett Constr. Co. v. United States,* 93 F.3d 1537 (Fed. Cir. 1996), the court held that a termination for convenience does not subsume within the termination settlement proposal all claims a contractor might have against the government. Therefore, terminating the contract does not eliminate valid contractor claims. Relying on *Ellett*, the Department of Agriculture Board of Contract Appeals vacated part of its prior decision dismissing a terminated contractor's equitable adjustment claims when it denied jurisdiction of the appeal of the contracting officer's determination after a late settlement proposal, *RBW Assocs,* AGBCA 95-208-1, 96-2 BCA ¶28,416, *recons. granted,* AGBCA 96-205R, 96-2 BCA ¶28,616. *Ellett* also appears to have overruled *M-Pax, Inc.*, HUDBCA 81-570-C10, 81-2 BCA ¶15,409, barring appeal of a denial of a constructive changes claim submitted by the contractor after failure to submit a settlement proposal within one year.

5. Terminations for Convenience Settlement Proposals Under a Termination for Default

Contractors often submit a termination settlement proposal even when the contract has been terminated for default in case the default is overturned. One purpose for this course of action is to begin the running of interest. In *Kit Pack Co.*, ASBCA 53155, 01-2 BCA ¶31,479, a contractor whose contract had been terminated for default filed a CDA-certified termination for convenience settlement proposal. The board noted that the date of the submission of the proposal would establish the date on which interest would begin to run in the event the default termination were converted to a convenience termination, but it held that it could not consider the convenience termination claim until it ruled on the propriety of the termination for default. In *Foremost Mech. Sys., Inc. v. General Servs. Admin.*, GSBCA 12335, 95-1 BCA ¶27,382, although the board had denied a default termination, the board was not free to decide the amount of the contractor's recovery and conversion of the action to a convenience termination because the certified convenience termination claim had to be presented to the contracting officer before the board could take jurisdiction.

6. Negotiation of Final Settlement

Following submission of the contractor's termination settlement proposal, ¶(e) of the "long form" clause calls for the contractor and the contracting officer to seek to negotiate a final settlement. See also FAR 49.103, which states:

> When possible, the TCO should negotiate a fair and prompt settlement with the contractor. The TCO shall settle a settlement proposal by determination only when it cannot be settled by agreement.

There is great latitude given to the parties in negotiating the settlement agreement. Paragraph (f) of the "long form" clause in FAR 52.249-2 states:

> Subject to paragraph (e) of this clause, the Contractor and the Contracting Officer may agree upon the whole or any part of the amount to be paid or remaining to be paid because of the termination. The amount may include a reasonable allowance for profit on work done. However, the agreed amount, whether under this paragraph (f) or paragraph (g) of this clause, exclusive of costs shown in paragraph (g)(3) of this clause, may not exceed the total contract price as reduced by (1) the amount of payments previously made and (2) the contract price of work not terminated. The contract shall be modified, and the Contractor paid the agreed amount. Paragraph (g) of this clause shall not limit, restrict, or affect the amount that may be agreed upon to be paid under this paragraph.

FAR 49.107(a) requires the TCO to "refer each prime contractor settlement proposal of $100,000 or more to the appropriate audit agency for review and recommendations." However, FAR 49.107(d) states that the "audit report is advisory only, and is for the TCO to use in negotiating a settlement or issuing a unilateral determination." Formerly, FPR 1-8.211-2(a) required that proposed termination settlements involving $50,000 or more be approved by a settlement review board before a settlement agreement was executed. The DAR at one time also required such review. Air Force DAR Supplement 8-210.1 also required settlement review board approvals for settlements over $100,000. Failure to obtain mandated settlement review board approval has been held to invalidate a settlement agreement, *Atlantic Gulf & Pac. Co. of Manila, Inc. v. United States,* 207 Ct. Cl. 995 (1975). See also *Bromley Contracting Co.*, DOTCAB 1284, 84-2 BCA ¶17,233, *aff'd*, 14 Cl. Ct. 69 (1987), *aff'd*, 861 F.2d 729 (Fed. Cir. 1988), where failure to obtain audit review required by regulations prior to execution of a modification in excess of $100,000 provided the government with grounds for voiding the agreement.

Termination settlement agreements must cover any setoffs that the government has against the contractor, FAR 49.109-1. This provision does not require the termination contracting officer to include setoffs arising from different contracts between the same contractor and the government, although the contractor may negotiate to bar the government from exercising its setoff right against the proceeds of the termination settlement agreement, *Applied Cos. v. United States,* 144 F.3d 1470 (Fed. Cir. 1998).

A contractor's appeal was untimely when it waited 33 months before claiming duress in entering into a no-cost termination for convenience. The board held that the contractor could not challenge the termination for convenience when the government accepted the terms the contractor proposed after refusing to perform in accordance with the contracting officer's direction, *Inca Contracting Co.*, ASBCA 52697, 01-1 BCA ¶31,255.

Where a construction contractor had entered into agreement providing for "no cost settlement (Termination for Convenience)" while stating that all claims related to the contract "remain in force," the board held that claims submitted shortly after the agreement was made were not precluded because the government did not obtain the release for a no-cost termination settlement provided in FAR 49.603-6. The board considered the contractor's claims but denied them on the merits, *Bay Constr. Co.*, VABCA 5594, 02-1 BCA ¶31,795.

Since no finality attaches to an unallowable payment, the government may recover the illegal or improper payment of anticipatory profits and likewise may recover overpayment of a partial payment on a termination proposal before full settlement is achieved. In *Arbor 111 Realty Co.*, HUDBCA 96-C-114-C5, 98-2 BCA ¶29,344, *aff'd*, 914 F.3d 1335 (Fed. Cir. 1999), the board held that a 7 percent commission for sales that occurred after a termination for convenience was an impermissible anticipatory profit even though the contracting officer and a real estate broker providing management and listing services had orally agreed to it.

A contractor was not entitled to collect Contract Disputes Act interest on its termination settlement proposal following a settlement, because the resulting settlement agreement was conclusive evidence that negotiations had not reached an impasse. A settlement agreement is not a final decision by the TCO, but rather, a mutually agreed-upon resolution of termination rights, *Rex Sys., Inc. v. Cohen,* 224 F.3d 1367 (Fed. Cir. 2000).

7. Unilateral Determination

If the contracting officer and the contractor cannot agree, ¶(f) of the "long form" clause requires the contracting officer to make a unilateral determination of the amounts due the contractor. This determination may then be challenged by the contractor pursuant to the Contract Disputes Act procedures. Paragraph (g) provides that such determinations shall include:

(1) The contract price for completed supplies or services accepted by the Government (or sold or acquired under paragraph (b)(9) of this clause) not previously paid for, adjusted for any saving of freight and other charges.
(2) The total of—
  (i) The costs incurred in the performance of the work terminated, including initial costs and preparatory expense allocable thereto, but excluding any costs attributable to supplies or services paid or to be paid under paragraph (g)(1) of this clause;
  (ii) The cost of settling and paying termination settlement proposals under terminated subcontracts that are properly chargeable to the terminated portion of the contract if not included in subdivision (g)(2)(i)of this clause; and
  (iii) A sum, as profit on subdivision (g)(2)(i) of this clause, determined by the Contracting Officer under 49.202 of the Federal Acquisition Regulation, in effect on the date of this contract, to be fair and reasonable; however, if it appears that the Contractor would have sustained a loss on the entire contract had it been completed, the Contracting Officer shall allow no profit under this subdivision (g)(2)(iii) and shall reduce the settlement to reflect the indicated rate of loss.
(3) The reasonable costs of settlement of the work terminated, including—
  (i) Accounting, legal, clerical, and other expenses reasonably necessary for the preparation of termination settlement proposals and supporting data;

(ii) The termination and settlement of subcontracts (excluding the amounts of such settlements); and
(iii) Storage, transportation, and other costs incurred, reasonably necessary for the preservation, protection, or disposition of the termination inventory.

8. Appeal of Convenience Terminations

To appeal a contracting officer decision under the Contract Disputes Act, the contractor must submit a "claim." In *Reflectone, Inc. v. Dalton*, 60 F.3d 1572 (Fed. Cir. 1995), the court held that "routine" requests for payment had to be in dispute to constitute a CDA claim, but that "nonroutine" requests could be appealed immediately. Subsequently, in *Ellett Constr. Co. v. United States*, 93 F.3d 1537 (Fed Cir. 1996), the court held that the appeal of a contracting officer's unilateral determination of the settlement amount met the definition of a "claim" because it was a nonroutine request for payment. The court stated at 1542:

> [I]t is difficult to conceive of a less routine demand for payment than one which is submitted when the government terminates a contract for its convenience. Such a demand, which occurs only in a fraction of government contracts is certainly less routine than a request for an equitable adjustment, several of which a contractor might submit on any one contract. Indeed, in concluding that a request for an equitable adjustment is not routine in *Reflectone*, we pointed to Supreme Court precedent equating a request for an equitable adjustment with an assertion of a breach of contract. That analogue is even more appropriate here, where, but for the convenience termination clause, the government's action would be a breach of contract, and it would be liable for resulting damages.

The court reasoned, however, that nonroutine requests for payment must also be submitted to the contracting officer for a decision to constitute a claim. It concluded that Ellett's termination for convenience proposal, although nonroutine, was not a claim when it was initially submitted for negotiation, but "ripened " into a claim when the parties reached an impasse, requiring the contracting officer to issue a decision. Thus, in *Ellett* the Federal Circuit held that termination settlement proposals are nonroutine submissions that constitute "claims" for the purposes of the CDA, if they (1) make a written demand (2) seeking as a matter of right (3) a sum certain. A settlement proposal must be submitted to the contracting officer for a decision in order to "ripen" into a claim. However, there need not be a preexisting dispute or impasse for the government to issue a final decision on a claim arising out of a termination for convenience, *Eurasia Heavy Indus., Inc.*, ASBCA 52878, 01-2 BCA ¶31,574.

In *Metric Constructors, Inc.*, ASBCA 50843, 98-2 BCA ¶30,088, the board held that a contractor's certified termination settlement proposal became a CDA claim when the parties reached an impasse before the contracting officer's issuance of a unilateral contract modification. The board held that the standard certification contained in the termination settlement proposal is correctable to comply with the certification language required by the CDA. The board acknowledged that it was rejecting its previous decision in *Chan Computer Corp.*, ASBCA 46763, 96-1 BCA ¶28,005, which held that the termination settlement proposal certification language could not be corrected to meet CDA certification requirements. In *Airo Servs., Inc. v. General Servs. Admin.*, GSBCA 14301, 98-2 BCA ¶29,909, the contractor submitted a termination settlement proposal and later asked the contracting officer to consider the proposal as a claim for an equitable adjustment and issue a final decision. The board held that the termination settlement proposal was an equitable adjustment claim for uncompensated costs under a modification, even though it did not include an express demand, because all the facts relevant to the equitable adjustment were incorporated within the facts of the termination claim.

Contract claims are not extinguished by the termination. A contractor whose work has been terminated for convenience may still submit a breach or other claim for costs independent of its termination settlement with the government as long as it follows the applicable jurisdictional requirements for submitting such a claim, such as requesting a final decision. See *Advanced Materials, Inc. v. United States*, 46 Fed. Cl. 697 (2000), holding, however, that the contractor's failure to submit its breach of contract claim to the contracting officer for a final decision meant that the court did not have jurisdiction over the breach claim. See also *Raytheon Co.*, ASBCA 50166, 01-1 BCA ¶31,245, *aff'd in part & remanded in part*, 305 F.3d 1354 (Fed. Cir. 2002), holding that, after a termination for convenience, the contractor was entitled to an equitable adjustment for the government's misrepresentation of the condition of the technical data package and for its failure to disclose its superior knowledge with respect to that condition.

Pursuant to 28 U.S.C. § 1491(b), the Court of Federal Claims possesses jurisdiction over claims relating to the government's obligations in the contract formation process. However, this jurisdiction does not extend to decisions to terminate for convenience in order to comply with these obligations, *Davis/HRGM Joint Venture v. United States*, 50 Fed. Cl. 539 (2001). The court held that such claims are more appropriately brought under the Contract Disputes Act. See also *Writing Co. v. Department of the Treasury*, GSBCA 15097-TD, 00-1 BCA ¶30,840, *recons. denied*, 00-1 BCA ¶30,863, denying jurisdiction of a contractor's letter seeking broad relief including relief from a convenience termination. The board reasoned that a termination for convenience decision "is not in and of itself an appealable contracting officer's decision."

B. Nature and Amount of Settlements

FAR 49.201(a) makes "fair compensation" the guiding principle for termination settlements for fixed-price contracts. The concept of fair compensation and the inconsistent FAR provisions implementing it has resulted in considerable confusion concerning the application of the cost principles to termination settlements. This subsection discusses the principles involved in fairly compensating the terminated contractor and analyzes the applicability of the termination cost principle, FAR 31.205-42.

1. Basic Principles

Perhaps the major impact of the termination for convenience procedure is that it relieves the government of the obligation of paying anticipated profits for unperformed work if it terminates the contractor's performance of the work, *Dairy Sales Corp. v. United States*, 219 Ct. Cl. 431, 593 F.2d 1002 (1979). The result is that the contractor's recovery under a convenience termination is based on incurred costs plus some reasonable amount of profit on those incurred costs. In fact, it has been stated that the effect of a termination for convenience is to convert a fixed-price contract into a cost-reimbursement contract as to the work performed up to the effective date of the termination, *Southland Mfg. Corp.*, ASBCA 16830, 75-1 BCA ¶10,994, *recons. denied*, 75-1 BCA ¶11,272; *International Space Corp.*, ASBCA 13883, 70-2 BCA ¶8519. If the contractor has incurred no cost, there is no recovery. Allowable costs incurred, plus profit, will be recovered, subject to the overall limitation of the contract price and the possible application of the loss adjustment provisions. The contractor's recovery is thus measured by the costs recovered rather than the value of the performance to the government. See *Fil-Coil Co.*, ASBCA 23137, 79-1 BCA ¶13,618, *recons. denied*, 79-1 BCA ¶13,683, where the amounts the contractor paid its employees, rather than the value of the services they rendered, were the proper measure of recovery. Conversely, the government may not use the value of the work completed to avoid reimbursing the contractor's allowable costs, *Scope Elecs., Inc.*, ASBCA 20359, 77-1 BCA ¶12,404, *recons. denied*, 77-2 BCA ¶12,586; *Arnold H. Leibowitz*, GSBCA CCR-1, 76-2 BCA ¶11,930.

The termination for convenience clauses have been held to preclude recovery of "consequential damages." See *Aerdco, Inc.*, GSBCA 3776, 77-2 BCA ¶12,775, *recons. denied*, 78-1 BCA ¶12,926, in which the board stated that "contractual limitations on cost recovery" prevent a contractor from recovering for the cost of bankruptcy, the loss of existing business to the company, and its loss of future profits. In *H & J Constr. Co.*, ASBCA 18521, 75-1 BCA ¶11,171, *recons. denied*, 76-1 BCA ¶11,903, the board also refused to grant recovery to the contractor for any of its damage claims, which included an alleged loss of 13 future contracts, damages to the company's standing and reputation, impairment of the company's credit, and loss of production. See also *William Green Constr. Co. v. United States*, 201 Ct. Cl. 616, 477 F.2d 930, *cert. denied*, 417 U.S. 909 (1973).

2. Recoverable Costs

The Termination for Convenience clauses state that all costs claimed or agreed to shall be in accordance with the applicable contract cost principles in Part 31 of the FAR. The cost principles determine which costs are allowable and which are not. They contain extensive allowability rules as well as specific rules for costs likely to be involved in termination claims. The general allowability rules are discussed here only to the extent that recurring termination cost problems are involved. The specific termination cost principle, FAR 31.205-42, is analyzed in detail. See Cibinic and Nash, *Cost-Reimbursement Contracting* (3d ed. 2004) for a discussion of the cost principles and general applicability. Cost principles substantially identical to those in the FAR were contained in FPR, Part 1-15 and DAR, Section XV.

Proceedings before the board to determine the amount of the settlement following a convenience termination are wholly de novo (i.e., the findings in the contracting officer's final decision are given no weight), *Stanley Aviation, Inc.*, ASBCA 49932, 97-1 BCA ¶28,764. The contractor has the burden of establishing the amount of incurred costs, and, in the absence of evidence to the contrary, the contracting officer's termination allowance will be accepted, *Roberts Int'l Corp.*, ASBCA 15118, 71-1 BCA ¶8869. See also *Delaware Tool & Die Works, Inc.*, ASBCA 14033, 71-1 BCA ¶8860, *recons. denied*, 72-1 BCA ¶9206, where the contractor had no proof of the costs incurred in the terminated portion of the work. It is preferable to establish incurred costs from accounting records.

Although a contractor generally may recover the costs incurred in the performance of terminated work, including initial costs and preparatory work allocable thereto, the contractor bears the burden of establishing the claimed cost with sufficient certainty so that the determination of liability will be more than mere speculation. In *James Greer*, ENGBCA 6283, 97-2 BCA ¶29,013, a terminated contractor was unable to convince the board that it was entitled to additional recovery where there was no support for its claims. In *Nomura Enter., Inc.*, ASBCA 51456, 99-2 BCA ¶30,441, the contractor contended that damages should be determined according to the formula set forth in *C.F.S. Air Cargo, Inc.*, ASBCA 36113, 91-1 BCA ¶23,583, which relied on estimated annual costs for the deleted work. However, because specific cost information was available, it was not necessary to rely on estimates to determine the amount recoverable. On the other hand, if accounting records are not available, due to no fault of the contractor, the costs may be established on the basis of estimates, FAR 49.206-1(c); *Bailey Specialized Bldgs., Inc.*, ASBCA 10576, 71-1 BCA ¶8699.

Even if estimates are used, the contractor still has the burden of proof. See *Clary Corp.*, ASBCA 19274, 74-2 BCA ¶10,947, in which the board stated that, although the burden need not be met through the use of accounting records, it cannot be carried by unsupported allegations. See also *R.G. Robbins & Co.*, ASBCA 27516, 83-1 BCA ¶16,420 (disallowing claim for G&A recovery not supported by cost data or accounting testimony). In *Mediax Interactive Techs., Inc.*, ASBCA 43961, 99-1 BCA ¶30,318, *recons. denied*, 99-2 BCA ¶30,453, the contract was terminated in 1983, and the contractor relied on computer-generated listings of costs to support its claim. When the claimed costs were audited in 1996, the contractor was out of business and the controls on its former computer system could not be validated. The board found that, to the extent the contractor relied on computerized reports and after-the-fact narratives, its proof was insufficient. A contractor that expended time and money in obtaining a requirements contract, preparing its business to fulfill the contract, and completing compliant first articles was entitled to recover its initial costs following the convenience termination of a contract because the amount of time the contractor expended was within the range of reasonableness. Although the hours could seem excessive for particular efforts, the contractor met its burden of establishing that its president, chief financial officer, and general manager expended the time indicated. The government's determinations to reduce the claimed hours were not reasonably supported by the record, *Teems, Inc. v. General Servs. Admin.*, GSBCA 14090, 98-1 BCA ¶29,357.

The application of the cost principles to termination settlement claims is the subject of confusing FAR provisions. FAR 49.113 states that cost principles in Part 31 are to be used in determining termination settlement costs "subject to the general principles in 49.201." However, FAR 49.201 indicates that strict application of the cost principles is not necessary, stating:

> (a) A settlement should compensate the contractor fairly for the work done and the preparations made for the terminated portions of the contract, including a reasonable allowance for profit. Fair compensation is a matter of judgment and cannot be measured exactly. In a given case, various methods may be equally appropriate for arriving at fair compensation. The use of business judgment, as distinguished from strict accounting principles, is the heart of a settlement.
>
> (b) The primary objective is to negotiate a settlement by agreement. The parties may agree upon a total amount to be paid the contractor without agreeing on or segregating the particular elements of costs or profit comprising this amount.
>
> (c) Cost and accounting data may provide guides, but are not rigid measures, for ascertaining fair compensation. In appropriate cases, costs may be estimated, differences compromised, and doubtful questions settled by agreement. Other types of data, criteria, or standards may furnish equally reliable guides to fair compensation. The amount of recordkeeping, reporting, and accounting related to the settlement of terminated contracts should be kept to a minimum compatible with the reasonable protection of the public interest.

Additional uncertainty is created by FAR 49.303-5(d), which states:

> If an overall settlement of costs is agreed upon, agreement on each element of cost is not necessary. If appropriate, differences may be compromised and doubtful questions settled by agreement. An overall settlement shall not include costs that are clearly not allowable under the terms of the contract.

The cases are not very helpful in clarifying these confusing provisions. In *Codex Corp.*, ASBCA 17983, 74-2 BCA ¶10,827, *recons. denied*, 75-2 BCA ¶11,554, *remanded*, 226 Ct. Cl. 693 (1981), which involved essentially the same language in predecessor regulations, the contractor had argued that the cost principles should not be applied in a termination settlement to disallow costs. In this case, the contract was awarded March 25, 1971, with an effective date of April 2, 1971. It was terminated on April 15, 1971, before any deliveries were made. Practically all costs claimed by the contractor were incurred between September 1968 and February 1970 in developing and producing the items that were the subject of the contract. In denying the costs, the board found that they did not come within allowable pre-contract costs under DAR 15-205.30 since they were not incurred directly pursuant to the negotiation of the contract and there was no evidence that they were necessary in order to meet the proposed delivery schedule. The board also held that the costs did not qualify under the initial costs and preparatory expense provisions of DAR 15-205.42. On appeal, the Court of Claims trial judge reversed, concluding that ASPR 8-301 (similar to FAR 49.201) "identifies fundamental fairness as the overriding criterion in the formulation of appropriate terms for the settlement of a convenience termination of a fixed-price contract." The Court of Claims refused to adopt the trial judge's holding but did remand the case to the Armed Services Board, stating at 698-99:

> The proper reconciliation of the strict standard of allowable costs in section 15.205-30 and the fairness concept in section 8.301 is a matter primarily within the discretion of the Board of Contract Appeals. The Board did not decide the question. In its opinion on reconsideration, it stated that it "expresses no opinion as to whether the disputed costs concerned in this appeal would or would not be allowable as a part of the termination settlement if allowability were to be governed by paragraph 8.301." 75-2 BCA ¶11,554, pp. 55,149-50. Our holding is not that section 8.301 governs the [contractor's] claim for the field case costs, but that the application of the cost principles in part 2 of section 15 to that claim must be made "subject to the general policies set forth" in section 8.301.
>
> Accordingly, we shall remand the case to the Board of Contract Appeals to make that determination.

There was no decision on remand because the case was settled.

See, however, *Bennie J. Meeks*, GSBCA 6605-REM, 85-2 BCA ¶17,947, which involved costs of training employees to perform planting services undertaken prior to receipt of notice of award. The board initially found that it was unreasonable for the contractor to have trained its employees before receiving a notice to proceed since there would have been sufficient time to conduct the training after receipt of the notice. On remand, however, the board allowed the training costs, finding the contractor's actions in hiring and training employees reasonable under the circumstances. The board stated at 89,923:

> After bid opening, when [the contractor] knew that he was low bidder and would be awarded the contract, he was "on the hook." The Government could accept his offer at any time, and he could not withdraw it. . . . The costs he incurred in hiring, training, and keeping a group of workmen on a standby basis were legitimately a part of his gearing-up effort, and he would not have incurred them except in anticipation of performing the subject contract.

The board noted that its conclusion was consistent with the Termination for Convenience clause in the contract and with FPR 1-8.301(a), which provided (in language similar to FAR 49.201(a)) that "[a] settlement should compensate the contractor fairly for . . . the preparations made for the terminated portions of the contract."

In *General Elec. Co.*, ASBCA 24111, 82-1 BCA ¶15,725, *recons. denied*, 83-1 BCA ¶16,207, the board relied on *Codex* in holding that the contractor could recover certain post-termination costs, including employee retraining expenses and depreciation on idle equipment, that were subject to question under a strict application of the cost principles. In *Kasler Elec. Co.*, DOTCAB 1425, 84-2 BCA ¶17,374, the board went even further, permitting the contractor to recover clearly unallowable bid and proposal costs in a termination settlement because it was deprived of the opportunity of amortizing them out of "expected overhead and profit recovery." In including the costs in the settlement, the board stated at 86,566:

> [W]hen applied to a termination for convenience settlement, the cost principles of Part 1-15 are general principles only, not of mandatory application in all cases to the extent they would be in administering an ongoing cost reimbursement contract.
>
> The gist of § 1-8.301 is clear: a fair compensation is the goal, within the *general* parameters of the cost guidelines.

See also *General Dynamics Land Sys., Inc.*, ASBCA 52283, 02-1 BCA ¶31,659, holding that a termination settlement between a contractor and its subcontractor should be recognized because (1) in a termination for convenience, the board has discretion to reconcile basic fairness with the strict application of accounting principles (citing *Codex*); (2) recovery for loss of useful value of STE is not limited to the amount that was included in the price (citing *American Elec.*, ASBCA 16635, 76-2 BCA ¶12,151, *modified in part on recons.*, 77-2 BCA ¶12,792); and (3) the subcontractor settlement was competently entered into at arm's length at an amount significantly less than the subcontractor might have obtained in litigation (citing *General Elec. Co.*, ASBCA 24111, 82-1 BCA ¶15,725, *recons. denied*, 83-1 BCA ¶16,207). Thus, while the cases do not provide clear guidance on the applicability of the cost principles in termination settlements, it is clear that FAR 49.201 grants latitude to contracting officers and tribunals in this area, and this latitude should be used appropriately.

One major limitation on costs recoverable in a termination settlement is that the costs must be incurred in performing work authorized by the contract. Thus, in *Derrick Elec. Co.*, ASBCA 21246, 77-2 BCA ¶12,643, *motion for new hearing denied*, 78-1 BCA ¶12,942, the contractor was denied recovery for costs incurred in performing work in accordance with an unapproved value engineering proposal under a Value Engineering Incentive clause. A similar result is obtained where the work is covered by the contract but the contractor has not been authorized to proceed with the work. Construction contracts often provide that a contractor shall not proceed with on-site work until a notice to proceed has been given by the contracting officer. In such cases, on-site costs incurred prior to the notice are not recoverable in the termination settlement, *Sherkade Constr. Corp.*, DOTCAB 68-29, 68-2 BCA ¶7365.

Work authorization problems also occur frequently in contracts containing first article approval clauses. The clauses contained at FAR 52.209-3 and -4 specifically provide that the costs of proceeding with production incurred before first article approval "shall not be allocable to this contract for . . . termination settlements." Identical language was contained in the clauses at DAR 7-104.55. This provision was enforced in *Semco, Inc. v. United States*, 6 Cl. Ct. 81 (1984). However, for an exception to this rule, see *Switlik Parachute Co.*, ASBCA 18024, 75-2 BCA ¶11,434, in which the board acknowledged that "a contractor is not bound by this risk provision when it would be impossible to wait until first article approval before ordering production materials, and still to meet the delivery schedule."

Following a convenience termination, compensation for completed work pursuant to a work order was not to be calculated using the full dollar amount of the work order because the contractor previously received a $50,000 progress payment for that work. The contractor was only entitled to the amount sought in its second progress payment request, which had never been paid. The government was entitled to receive a credit for work left incomplete. *D.L. Kaufman, Inc.*, PSBCA 4159, 00-1 BCA ¶30,846.

a. Common Items

FAR 31.205-42(a) provides as follows:

> *Common items*. The costs of items reasonably usable on the contractor's other work shall not be allowable unless the contractor submits evidence that the items could not be retained at cost without sustaining a loss. The contracting officer should consider the contractor's plans and orders for current and planned production when determining if items can reasonably be used on other work of the contractor. Contemporaneous purchases of common items by the contractor shall be regarded as evidence that such items are reasonably usable on the contractor's other work. Any acceptance of common items as allocable to the terminated portion of the contract

> should be limited to the extent that the quantities of such items on hand, in transit, and on order are in excess of the reasonable quantitative requirements of other work.

This cost principle requires that the costs of common items—those that are reasonably usable on the contractor's other work—be excluded from the settlement. The common item exclusion applies only to items that are usable by the contractor on other work, not to items that simply are commonly used in the industry. See *American Packers, Inc.*, ASBCA 14275, 71-1 BCA ¶8846, rejecting applicability of this principle where the terminated contract was the contractor's only use for the material and the only realizable value of the inventory was resale at secondhand prices. In *Essex Electro Eng'rs, Inc.*, DOTCAB 1025, 81-1 BCA ¶14,838, *recons. denied*, 81-1 BCA ¶15,109, *aff'd*, 702 F.2d 998 (Fed. Cir. 1983), assorted motor generators and electric parts of the same type needed to perform ongoing government contracts were held not to be "common items" since the contractor had already purchased other materials for use in connection with this ongoing work. In *Fiesta Leasing & Sales, Inc.*, ASBCA 29311, 87-1 BCA ¶19,622, the board stated at 73,250:

> The respective burdens placed upon the parties relative to establishing the proper classification of residual equipment is very clearly laid out above in FPR 1-15.205-42(a). As an initial proposition, the contractor must go forward with evidence to demonstrate it could not retain the equipment at cost for use on other work without sustaining a loss. Once this is done, the burden shifts to the Contracting Officer to show that there has been an evaluation of the contractor's current and scheduled work plans, orders and supplies to determine if such residual equipment is in fact reasonably usable by the contractor or in excess of the latter's reasonable needs. The extent to which these requirements are met determines the proper classification of residual equipment.

DCAAM (Defense Contract Audit Agency Manual) 12-304.5(b) suggests that an auditor can determine whether inventory items are properly classified as common items:

> In determining whether common items are reasonably usable by the contractor on other work, review the contractor's plans and orders for current/scheduled production and for current purchases of common items. Also determine whether the contractor properly classified inventory items as common items. Do this by reviewing stock records to see if the items are being used for other work and by reviewing bills of material and procurement scheduled for products similar to those included in the termination inventory. Limit acceptance of common items as part of termination inventory to the quantities on hand, in transit, and on order which exceed reasonable quantities required by the contractor for work on other than the terminated contract. In determining whether the inventory contains common items, the contractor should first assign total available quantity (inventory on-hand, in transit, and on order) to continuing or anticipated government or commercial production and assign the remainder, if any, to the terminated contract. The contractor, therefore, should assign to the terminated contract (1) the least processed inventory, and (2) those purchase commitments that result in the least cost when terminated.

The auditor may also examine "nonstandard" stock items. DCAAM 12-304.5(c) provides that, under certain circumstances, even "complex or specialized items may qualify as common items." For instance, the DCAAM states that "the compressor unit of a military jet engine might qualify as a common item if the contractor also uses the unit in commercial jet engine production."

The boards have also applied the common items analysis to productive assets used in contract work. These costs would more properly be dealt with under the principle covering loss of value of assets. See *Fiesta Leasing & Sales, Inc.*, ASBCA 29311, 87-1 BCA ¶19,622, *modified as recons., (decision as to quantum modified)*, 88-1 BCA ¶20,499 (buses usable in contractor's daily rental business); *Metered Laundry Servs.*, ASBCA 21573, 78-1 BCA ¶13,206, *modified on recons.*, 78-2 BCA ¶13,451 (washers and dryers used in contract to provide automatic laundry); *Globe Air, Inc.*, AGBCA 76-119, 78-1 BCA ¶13,079 (helicopter provided under helicopter rental contract); and *American Packers, Inc.*, ASBCA 14275, 71-1 BCA ¶8846 (pickup trucks usable under contract for packing and hauling household goods).

In *Symetrics Indus., Inc.*, ASBCA 48529, 96-2 BCA ¶28,285, the contractor could not recover for common items when it failed to prove that the items would be retained at a loss.

b. Costs Continuing After Termination

FAR 31.205-42(b) provides the following broad guidance on costs that continue after termination:

> *Costs continuing after termination.* Despite all reasonable efforts by the contractor, costs which cannot be discontinued immediately after the effective date of termination are generally allowable. However, any costs continuing after the effective date of the termination due to the negligent or willful failure of the contractor to discontinue the costs shall be unallowable.

DCAAM 12-305.7(a)(1) provides the following coverage concerning costs continuing after termination:

> Reasonable costs associated with termination activities are allowable. FAR 31.205-42(b) recognizes there may be instances where costs incurred after termination may be allowable. For example, the contractor may have contract personnel at a remote or foreign location or there may be personnel in transit to or from these sites. The cost of their salaries or wages would be allocable to the terminated contract for a reasonable period required to transfer the personnel to sites for termination or used on the contractor's other work. In another example, components or end items may be in a heat-treating or electroplating process when termination occurs and the contractor may elect to complete rather than disrupt the process and risk complete loss of the items.

Costs continuing after termination are often associated with a contractor's facilities, such as contractor-owned and contractor-leased buildings, machinery, and equipment. Recovery for the loss of useful value of facilities is covered in FAR 31.205-42(d), and rental costs under unexpired leases are dealt with in FAR 31.205-42(e).

To be recovered, costs continuing after the termination must have been incurred as a result of performing the terminated work or must flow from the termination, *Aviation Specialists, Inc.*, DOTBCA 1967, 91-1 BCA ¶23,534. There, the government terminated for convenience a requirements contract involving the use of one aircraft by the Federal Aviation Administration. After the termination, the contractor made efforts to sell the plane but was unable to dispose of it for 18 months. As a result, the contractor incurred additional costs in retaining the aircraft. In its settlement proposal, the contractor sought reimbursement for the following costs continuing after termination: depreciation, insurance, maintenance costs, cost of facilities capital, overhead, advertising, general and administrative expenses, and profit. In the settlement proposal the contractor also included a credit for profit earned on commercial leasing of the plane during that period. The board held for the contractor, stating that these incurred costs could not be reasonably discontinued immediately following the termination. The contractor could recover such costs up to the estimated contract price. This case is distinguished from *Chamberlain Mfg. Corp.*, ASBCA 16877, 73-2 BCA ¶10,139, in that the costs claimed in *Aviation Specialists* were incurred as a direct result of obligations the contractor undertook to perform the contract, whereas in *Chamberlain,* which involved a manufacturing contract, the claimed post-termination overhead costs were neither incurred as a result of the work performed on the contract nor generated directly by the termination action.

Many of the costs continuing after a termination are normally charged as indirect expenses by the contractor. In a termination, such charges may be allowable as direct costs if separately identified and properly justified. This does not violate CAS 402, which requires consistency in treatment of like costs incurred for like purposes. Reclassified costs, however, must be withdrawn from their former indirect cost pools to avoid double billing.

A contractor bears the cost of employees retained subsequent to a termination if they are not required to wind up work on the terminated contract. In *Engineered Sys., Inc.*, ASBCA 18241, 74-1 BCA ¶10,492, the board found that costs resulting from a decision to retain key employees were not incurred incidental to the work but related to future work of the contractor. The contractor must also demonstrate a reasonable effort to discontinue the costs. In this respect, salaries for retained employees are not recoverable if the contractor has no binding agreement with the employees and they are available for other work of the contractor, *Globe Air, Inc.*, AGBCA 76-119, 78-1 BCA ¶13,079. Further, a contractor's "moral obligation" to retain employees has been held insufficient to support recovery for their retention, *Kay & Assocs., Inc.*, GSBCA TD-17, 76-2 BCA ¶12,127. Severance payments to employees terminated as the result of a convenience termination may be recoverable provided the contractor makes the payment as part of an established company policy or an employer-employee agreement in existence at the time of the termination, *Columbia Univ.*, ASBCA 15578, 73-1 BCA ¶9777. See also *System Dev. Corp.*, ASBCA 16947, 73-1 BCA ¶9788, in which the board found mass severance costs supported by company policy and therefore allowable.

The contractor's reasonable business judgment will be the criterion used to determine the length of the period for reimbursement after termination. In *Baifield Indus. Div. of A-T-O, Inc.*, ASBCA 20006, 76-2 BCA ¶12,096, *recons. denied*, 76-2 BCA ¶12,203, the contractor was permitted to recover continuing costs, despite having passed up earlier opportunities to dispose of the items, because its attempts to get higher prices for the items were reasonable. The board stated at 58,092 that, in determining allowability of continuing costs, there must be "a clear connection between the costs claimed and the terminated contract and, further, that those costs could not have been reasonably shut off upon the termination." In some cases, the continuing costs may be the subject of express agreements between the parties. See *ITT Fed. Support Servs., Inc. v. United States*, 209 Ct. Cl. 157, 531 F.2d 522 (1976), dealing with post-termination management of a pension fund.

c. *Initial Costs*

FAR 31.205-42 contains the following guidance concerning recovery of initial costs:

(c) *Initial Costs.* Initial costs [see 15.804-6(f)], including starting load and preparatory costs, are allowable as follows:
  (1) Starting load costs not fully absorbed because of termination are nonrecurring labor, material, and related overhead costs incurred in the early part of production and result from factors such as—
    (i) Excessive spoilage due to inexperienced labor;
    (ii) Idle time and subnormal production due to testing and changing production methods;
    (iii) Training; and
    (iv) Lack of familiarity or experience with the product, materials, or manufacturing processes.
  (2) Preparatory costs incurred in preparing to perform the terminated contract include such costs as those incurred for initial plant rearrangement and alterations, management and personnel organization, and production planning. They do not include special machinery and equipment and starting load costs.
  (3) When initial costs are included in the settlement proposal as a direct charge, such costs shall not also be included in overhead. Initial costs attributable to only one contract shall not be allocated to other contracts.
  (4) If initial costs are claimed and have not been segregated on the contractor's books, they shall be segregated for settlement purposes from cost reports and schedules reflecting that high unit cost incurred during the early stages of the contract.
  (5) If the settlement proposal is on the inventory basis, initial costs should normally be allocated on the basis of total end items called for by the contract immediately before termination; however, if the contract includes end items of a diverse nature, some other equitable basis may be used, such as machine or labor hours.

The consideration of initial and preparatory costs in termination settlements has caused considerable confusion. The termination clauses provide that the contractor is to be paid the contract price for "completed supplies or services accepted by the Government." This creates a problem where the contractor has allocated nonrecurring costs to both accepted and terminated items or where the accepted and terminated items are priced the same even though the accepted items may actually have cost more to produce than the terminated items would have cost. This problem is dealt with in either of two ways. When the termination is considered a partial termination, the clause provides that the price of the unterminated items may be equitably adjusted. If the termination is not considered a partial termination, a fair result may be achieved by allocating initial and preparatory costs to the termination settlement. Both of these methods appear to yield the same result, and it appears that they are sometimes used interchangeably. See *Dunbar Kapple, Inc.*, ASBCA 3631, 57-2 BCA ¶1448. But compare *Sternberger v. United States*, 185 Ct. Cl. 528, 401 F.2d 1012 (1968). Care must be taken that double recovery does not result when both methods are applied to the same termination, *Elastic Stop Nut Co. v. United States*, 126 Ct. Cl. 100 (1953).

There is not much conceptual difficulty in allowing the contractor to recover such nonrecurring costs as engineering, tooling, employee training, and plant rearrangement, as it is obvious that these expenditures were made for both the terminated and unterminated work. The contractor has even been permitted to recover these expenses as direct charges to the termination settlement although they were initially treated as overhead expense, *Condec Corp.*, ASBCA 14234, 73-1 BCA ¶9808. There is greater difficulty when the actual costs recorded for producing the unterminated items include labor charges that are higher than those that would have been incurred in producing the terminated items. In allocating such costs to the termination settlement, contractors often use learning curves to establish the average unit cost of the total contract quantity and then request, as initial costs, the difference between that amount and the average unit cost of completed units. This has led to objections by the government on the basis that labor inefficiencies and other factors that result in higher costs of producing earlier units are not "nonrecurring" costs as stated in the termination cost principle for initial costs. Further, the government has argued that, since the costs were incurred in actually producing the accepted items, they cannot be properly considered costs allocable to the terminated items. In *Lockley Mfg. Co.*, ASBCA 21231, 78-1 BCA ¶12,987, the board granted the contractor recovery and explained at 63,319:

> A contractor bidding a fixed price per unit of work for a number of units must include in that fixed unit price all the costs of all the units knowing all the while that the cost experienced during the manufacture of the earlier units will be greater than on the later units. Therefore, lest the contractor is to lose the portion of such costs as yet unrecovered through the price paid for delivered items, it must be permitted to recover it as part of the cost of terminated work.

In *Celesco Indus., Inc.*, ASBCA 21928, 81-2 BCA ¶15,260, the contractor was permitted to recover "unamortized labor costs" on the unterminated portion of the production work through application of a learning curve approach, but the board excluded from such recovery an amount attributable to a "prolonged 'abnormal' production phase" experienced by the contractor. The board reached this result without specifically indicating that the costs attributable to the abnormal production phase were "unreasonable." In *VHC, Inc. v. Peters*, 179 F.3d 1363 (Fed. Cir. 1999), the court held that recovery of unamortized labor learning costs is not "automatically prohibited where the original contract pricing was not level." Equitable adjustments for unamortized labor learning costs are a legitimate form of recovery after a partial termination for convenience where the contractor loses the opportunity to amortize the increased early labor costs over the original life of the contract.

Pre-contract costs, except bid and proposal costs, are recoverable when incurred in anticipation of award to meet the contract delivery schedule, *Orbas & Assocs.*, ASBCA 50467, 97-2 BCA ¶29,107, but such costs are not recoverable if they are not needed to meet the delivery schedule, *Aislamientos y Construcciones Apache S. A.*, ASBCA 45437, 97-1 BCA ¶28,632. Start-up costs excluding bid and proposal preparation costs incurred prior to the formal contract award have been awarded a contractor following a termination for convenience where the contractor showed that it reasonably believed the project was urgent, *Barsh Co.*, PSBCA 4481, 00-2 BCA ¶30,917.

A contractor was entitled to a portion of its costs to move to a larger facility in order to perform a contract because the contractor established that the larger facilities required by the contract precipitated the move. The contractor, however, did not justify its allocation rate, so a percentage based on burden rates calculated by the contractor was utilized to determine the amount allocable, *Teems, Inc. v. General Servs. Admin.*, GSBCA 14090, 98-1 BCA ¶29,357. The termination cost principle for initial costs has also been used to award the costs of setting up a plant to perform the terminated contract. See *Inland Container, Inc. v. United States*, 206 Ct. Cl. 478, 512 F.2d 1073 (1975). It is questionable whether this was a proper application of this cost principle because, since the entire contract was terminated before any work was ordered or performed, there was no need to allocate costs between completed and terminated work.

d. Loss of Value of Assets

FAR 31.205-42 contains the following provision on loss of useful value of assets:

> (d) *Loss of useful value.* Loss of useful value of special tooling, and special machinery and equipment is generally allowable, provided—
> (1) The special tooling, or special machinery and equipment is not reasonably capable of use in the other work of the contractor;
> (2) The Government's interest is protected by transfer of title or by other means deemed appropriate by the contracting officer; and

(3) The loss of useful value for any one terminated contract is limited to that portion of the acquisition cost which bears the same ratio to the total acquisition cost as the terminated portion of the contract bears to the entire terminated contract and other Government contracts for which the special tooling, or special machinery and equipment was acquired.

FPR 1-8.101(t) and DAR 8-101.21 contained a definition of special machinery and equipment that included the requirement that the asset be acquired "solely" for the performance of the terminated contract. This definition is omitted from the FAR, with the result that there is less guidance in this area in the current regulation.

Contractors often acquire productive assets for the performance of a specific contract or group of contracts in anticipation of receiving sufficient revenue from the performance of the contracts to cover the cost of the assets. So long as the contract is a fixed-price contract and its performance is completed, the contractor's expectation will be realized. Whether this expectation will be met where the contract is terminated for convenience depends on the cost allowability rules. If the asset meets the tests for special tooling and special test equipment in FAR 45.101, it is clear that the entire cost of the asset must be charged to the contract or contracts and will be recovered as a part of the termination settlement. If the asset does not meet the FAR 45.101 definition of special tooling or special test equipment, a portion of its costs may still be recovered if it can be classified as "special machinery and equipment." If, on the other hand, the asset is considered to be a general purpose asset for which the contractor has other uses, the only appropriate charge to the termination settlement is depreciation on the asset for the period during which it was used on the terminated contract, *Dairy Sales Corp. v. United States*, 219 Ct. Cl. 431, 593 F.2d 1002 (1979).

In *American Elec., Inc.*, ASBCA 16635, 76-2 BCA ¶12,151, *modified on other grounds*, 77-2 BCA ¶12,792, the board determined that equipment that could not be used by the contractor on other work was properly characterized as "special machinery and equipment" even though other contractors could have used the machinery for other purposes. See also *Southland Mfg. Corp.*, ASBCA 16830, 75-1 BCA ¶10,994, *recons. denied*, 75-1 BCA ¶11,272. In *Tubergen & Assocs., Inc.*, ASBCA 34106, 90-3 BCA ¶23,058, the board determined that a braiding machine was special machinery where it was acquired solely for the performance of the contract and was not used after termination. The board concluded that the contractor was entitled to the loss of the useful value of the braiding machine but because there was no evidence as to its useful value, remanded the issue for determination in accordance with DAR 15-205.42(d). See *Celesco Indus., Inc.*, ASBCA 22460, 84-2 BCA ¶17,295, where specially adapted equipment was treated as general purpose equipment because the contractor had capitalized it, intending to use it for other work, and *General Dynamics Land Sys., Inc.* ASBCA 52283, 02-1 BCA ¶31,659, where a subcontractor's special test equipment fabrication costs were allowable because the subcontract specifically contemplated the fabrication. Although the record did not support a conclusion that a lathe was special tooling under regulatory definitions, a contractor was entitled to fair and reasonable recovery of lathe costs because it would have recouped some of the lathe costs incurred to perform the contract had the contract not been terminated, *Teems, Inc. v. General Servs. Admin.*, GSBCA 14090, 98-1 BCA ¶29,357.

The contractor's intention when the equipment was acquired may operate to deny recovery. In *Contract Maint., Inc.*, ASBCA 20689, 77-1 BCA ¶12,446, there was no recovery since the items were standard equipment used or made available for use in another contract and were written off in full. See also *Metered Laundry Servs.*, ASBCA 21573, 78-1 BCA ¶13,206, *modified on recons.*, 78-2 BCA ¶13,451, in which the contractor recovered the loss of value on some equipment but was denied recovery on other equipment because the sale price was not unreasonably low and the loss was less than depreciation for the period that the items were used. In *Manual M. Liodas*, ASBCA 12829, 71-2 BCA ¶9015, *recons. denied*, 71-2 BCA ¶9120, the board reduced the contractor's allowance by 50 percent because the government's interest had not been sufficiently protected. The contractor had obtained only an exclusive right to use the tooling; title was retained by a subcontractor.

Costs of special equipment to be used for developing microwave technology in anticipation of the government's exercise of an option, but not necessary in performance of the existing contract, were unallowable in a termination settlement, as were the costs of renting and adapting rental premises to accommodate the equipment, *Energy Compression Research Corp.*, ASBCA 46560, 99-2 BCA ¶30,564.

A contractor may recover reasonable standby or idle equipment costs following a termination for convenience, *Walsky Constr. Co.*, ASBCA 52772, 01-2 BCA ¶31,557.

e. Rental Costs

Rental costs under unexpired leases, less the residual value of such leases, are generally allowable when shown to have been reasonably necessary for the performance of the terminated contract, FAR 31.205-42(e). The amount of rental costs claimed, however, must not exceed the "reasonable use value of the property leased for the period of the contract and such further period as may be reasonable." The contractor must also make "all reasonable efforts to terminate, assign, settle, or otherwise reduce the cost of such lease." In determining whether the rental was reasonably necessary for performance of the contract, as required by the cost principle, the facts and circumstances existing at the time of the decision to lease will be examined, *American Elec., Inc.*, ASBCA 16635, 76-2 BCA ¶12,151, *modified on other grounds*, 77-2 BCA ¶12,792. Although the cost principle does not require that the lease be made solely for the performance of the contract, it has been held that rent under leases entered into prior to the date of the contract and available for other uses of the contractor is not reimbursable, *Legislative Res., Inc.*, DCABOMBE-16-74, 76-2 BCA ¶11,951.

American Electric holds that what is a reasonable period of time is a question of fact and is based on the reasonable efforts of the contractor to reduce the lease costs. See also *Southland Mfg. Corp.*, ASBCA 16830, 75-1 BCA ¶10,994, *recons. denied*, 75-1 BCA ¶11,272, holding a period of 29 months following a default termination to be reasonable in view of the contractor's efforts and the existing circumstances. The period may extend beyond the contract completion date if reasonable, *Sundstrand Turbo v. United States*, 182 Ct. Cl. 31, 389 F.2d 406 (1968). Compare *Max S. Castle*, AGBCA 97-137-1, 00-1 BCA ¶30,871, *recons. denied*, 03-2 BCA ¶32,270 (contractor not entitled to recover costs incurred in remodeling a building for rental to the government because there was no evidence that the government had misled the lessor regarding the length of the lease term). See also *Information Sys. & Networks Corp.*, ASBCA 46119, 02-2 BCA ¶31,952 (continuing costs after a termination for convenience were allowable because one-year leases for communication circuits were not unreasonable and gave the government significant cost savings over a monthly lease), and *Aviation Specialists Inc.*, DOTBCA 1967, 02-1 BCA ¶31,788 (costs of maintaining a leased aircraft after a convenience termination were recoverable because they were incurred as a direct result of obligations undertaken to perform the contract).

In *Manuel M. Liodas*, ASBCA 12829, 71-2 BCA ¶9015, *recons. denied*, 71-2 BCA ¶9120, the premises had been used for both the contract work and other work. Therefore, the board allowed the contractor to recover only a portion of the unexpired lease costs, measured by the ratio that the allowable G&A costs allocable to the terminated contract had to the total allowable G&A costs. In *American Electric*, the board deducted a credit for the use of facilities on other work after the termination.

The court limited rental costs for a facility owned by key employee's mother to ownership costs of facility transferred between entities under common control, *Advanced Materials, Inc. v. United States*, 54 Fed. Cl. 207 (2002).

In *Qualex Corp.*, ASBCA 41962, 93-1 BCA ¶25,517, the contractor had made the decision to lease space and equipment based on its expectations that the contract would be extended. The government subsequently terminated the contract for convenience. The contractor sought reimbursement of rental costs associated with the facility until its obligations under the lease were discharged or, alternatively, the amount allegedly saved because of the advantageous five-year lease it had obtained. The board rejected the contractor's first basis for reimbursement, stating that the contractor bore the risk, even if the risk was reasonable, for the augmented period. The board, however, found at 127,089:

> We conclude that the reasonable use value for the space during the contract period was the rental prescribed by the lease for that period, which was less than the amount incurred by [the contractor] over the life of the lease which resulted in the concessions. The Government enjoyed the benefit of the longer lease period by reimbursing [the contractor] only $6,421.50 monthly to reflect a credit for the rent-free 11 months granted by the lessor in consideration of the longer lease. Accordingly, we believe that fairness requires that [the contractor] receive the $45,277.14 it would have incurred and charged the Government for leasehold and parking facilities for the contract period in excess of the lower charges enjoyed under the longer lease—less any sublease payments which it received during that period.

The cost of alterations to leased property, when necessary for the performance of a contract, and the reasonable restoration required by the provisions of the lease are also allowable, FAR 31.205.42(f). However, unexpired lease costs should be adjusted by any residual value of the lease resulting from the termination, assignment, or settlement of the lease agreement, DCAAM 12-305.5(b).

f. Subcontract Claims

Detailed procedures for settling subcontractor termination claims are contained in FAR 49.108. FAR 31.205-42(h) gives the following guidance with regard to allowability of the costs of subcontractor claims:

> *Subcontractor claims.* Subcontractor claims, including the allocable portion of the claims common to the contract and to other work of the contractor, are generally allowable. An appropriate share of the contractor's indirect expense may be allocated to the amount of settlements with subcontractors; provided, that the amount allocated is reasonably proportionate to the relative benefits received and is otherwise consistent with 31.201-4 and 31.203(d). The indirect expense so allocated shall exclude the same and similar costs claimed directly or indirectly as settlement expenses.

The primary standard for allowability of the costs of settling subcontractor claims is reasonableness, *Bos'n Towing & Salvage Co.*, ASBCA 41357, 92-2 BCA ¶24,864. In deciding the reasonableness and prudence of such costs, the boards and courts will consider whether a contractor's settlement with its subcontractor was reached through an "arm's-length" transaction. In *General Elec. Co.*, ASBCA 24111, 82-1 BCA ¶15,725, *recons. denied*, 83-1 BCA ¶16,207, the board found reasonable a bottom-line subcontract termination settlement amount. The board stated at 77,806:

> [The] amount . . . was considered by the parties to be a fair and reasonable compromise price. We have found that the settlement amount was arrived at after arm's length bargaining, without collusion, and reflected a sound exercise of prudent judgment by [the prime contractor].

In *Bos'n Towing*, however, the board disallowed the contractor's claim for costs of terminating the charter of two tugs because it appeared that the contractor's settlement with the subcontractor was not an arm's-length transaction. The board stated that the contractor did not appear to be truly independent in its dealings with its subcontractor.

In *Information Sys. & Network Corp.*, ASBCA 42659, 00-1 BCA ¶30,665, *recons. denied,* 00-1 BCA ¶30,866, the board allowed recovery of legal fees in defense of a subcontractor claim in the convenience termination. In *Spectrum Leasing Corp. v. General Servs. Admin.*, GSBCA 12189, 95-1 BCA ¶27,317, the contractor was not allowed to recover the amount it had paid in settlement of the subcontractor's claim because the contractor's claim was barred by its agreement with the government on a modification that resulted in the termination of the subcontractor. The contractor should have anticipated the possibility that a claim might arise in the termination of the subcontractor and reserved its rights to recover costs it might incur under the subcontract as a result of the modification.

The termination clauses provide that a settlement proposal may include "the cost of settling and paying termination settlement proposals under terminated subcontracts." Substantially identical language in the DAR and FPR termination clauses had been interpreted to mean that the contractor must either have paid the subcontractor the amount of its claim or have reached a binding settlement agreement with the subcontractor, before the contractor can recover the amount of the subcontractor's claim, *Atlantic, Gulf & Pac. Co. of Manila, Inc.*, ASBCA 13533, 72-1 BCA ¶9415, *recons. denied*, 72-2 BCA ¶9698. However, the mere fact that the contractor and subcontractor have reached an agreement does not make the government liable to reimburse the contractor for the amount of the agreement. See *Aerojet Gen. Corp. v. United States*, 209 Ct. Cl. 750 (1976), in which the court refused to accept the contractor's allocation of the costs of three subcontracts to one subcontract and submission of the settlement of that subcontract termination under its contract settlement proposal. The trial judge's opinion, adopted by the court and contained in 22 CCF ¶80,022 (1976), notes that the government's obligation to reimburse for subcontractor settlements is dependent upon privity of contract, such that "the considerations between [the subcontractor and contractor] which justified their reconciliation of accounts on a single program basis would have to apply with equal force to the contractual relationship between [the contractor] and the Government in order to warrant imposition upon the Government."

Similarly, a judgment holding the contractor liable to the subcontractor does not entitle the contractor to recover the cost from the government unless the cost is allowable, *McDonnell Douglas Corp.*, NASABCA 467-13, 68-2 BCA ¶7316 (cost of subcontractor judgment for termination unallowable because contractor had not obtained approval of initial subcontract and price was unreasonable). However, where the contractor's actions in dealing with the subcontractor are reasonable, the subcontractor's judgment will support allowability, *Nolan Bros, Inc. v. United States*, 194 Ct. Cl. 1, 437 F.2d 1371 (1971). FAR 49.108-5 contains the following provisions directing the contracting officer to recognize judgments and arbitration awards:

(a) When a subcontractor obtains a final judgment against a prime contractor, the TCO shall, for the purposes of settling the prime contract, treat the amount of the judgment as a cost of settling with the contractor, to the extent the judgment is properly allocable to the terminated portion of the prime contract, if—
  (1) The prime contractor has made reasonable efforts to include in the subcontract a termination clause described in 49.502(e), 49.503(c), or a similar clause excluding payment of anticipatory profits or consequential damages;
  (2) The provisions of the subcontract relating to the rights of the parties upon its termination are fair and reasonable and do not unreasonably increase the common law rights of the subcontractor;
  (3) The contractor made reasonable efforts to settle the settlement proposal of the subcontractor;
  (4) The contractor gave prompt notice to the contracting officer of the initiation of the proceedings in which the judgment was rendered and did not refuse to give the Government control of the defense of the proceedings; and
  (5) The contractor diligently defended the suit or, if the Government assumed control of the defense of the proceedings, rendered reasonable assistance requested by the Government.

(b) If the conditions in subparagraphs (a)(1) through (5) of this Section are not all met, the TCO may allow the contractor the part of the judgment considered fair for settling the subcontract settlement proposal, giving due regard to the policies in this part for settlement of proposals.

(c) When a contractor and a subcontractor submit the subcontractor's settlement proposal to arbitration under any applicable law or contract provision, the TCO shall recognize the arbitration award as the cost of settling the proposal of the contractor to the same extent and under the same conditions as in paragraph (a) and (b) of this Section.

The amount of the subcontractor's recovery from the contractor will depend on the terms of the termination clause, if any, contained in the subcontract, *Dayton T. Brown, Inc. v. Republic Aviation Corp.*, 7 CCF ¶71,176 (D.C.N.Y. 1959); *General Steel Tank Co.*, ASBCA 7254, 61-2 BCA ¶3098. In this regard, FAR 49.108-2 suggests that for their own protection contractors should include termination clauses similar to those contained in FAR 52.249 in their subcontracts. See also FAR 49.502(e) and FAR 49.503(c). These clauses essentially give the subcontractor the same type of recovery that the contractor would receive from the government, most significantly excluding anticipated profits and consequential damages. FAR 49.108-5 further provides that reimbursement greater than the amount allowed under the contract clauses will be allowed only in unusual cases when the contracting officer is satisfied that "the terms of the subcontract did not unreasonably increase the rights of the subcontractor." These provisions are obviously aimed at preventing a contractor from assuming liability for anticipated profits on the theory that it would be able to pass on the subcontractor's claims to the government. However, if the subcontractor refuses to accept the termination clause and the contractor has made a good faith effort to include it, the subcontractor would be permitted to recover anticipated profits from the contractor, and apparently the contractor could include that amount in its termination claim.

While FAR 49.108-1 emphasizes the lack of privity between the government and the subcontractor, the government does retain the right to approve or ratify subcontract settlements, FAR 49.108-3, unless the contractor has been authorized to settle claims ($100,000 or less) without approval or ratification under FAR 49.108-4. In rare cases, however, the contract may contain a clause giving the subcontractor a right directly against the government where the subcontract termination is based upon the government's termination of the contract, *Compudyne Corp. v. Maxon Constr. Co.*, 248 F. Supp. 83 (D.C. Pa. 1965). In addition, the government could create a contractual relationship by dealing directly with the subcontractor. See, for example, *United States v. Georgia Marble Co.*, 106 F.2d 955 (5th Cir. 1939). In *Steel Improvement & Forge Co. v. United States*, 174 Ct. Cl. 24, 355 F.2d 627 (1966), a subcontractor alleged that the government had entered into such an arrangement by directing it to ship the termination inventory directly to the government and by agreeing to settle the claim directly. The court avoided reaching these issues, holding that, even if valid, any such claim would have been barred by the statute of limitations.

52 Comp. Gen. 377 (B-176596) (1972) demonstrates the kinds of problems a subcontractor can encounter under the no-privity rule. The GAO stated that the subcontractor could not expect the government to enforce the subcontractor's rights by conditioning government payment on contractor payment of subcontractor claims. The termination clauses give the government the right, but not the obligation, to settle subcontractor's claims directly. FAR 49.108-8 provides that this right will be exercised only when in the best interests of the government. In *Universal Fiberglass Corp. v. United States*, 210 Ct. Cl. 220, 537 F.2d 400 (1976), the court held that the government's receipt of a subcontractor claim and rejection "largely on the grounds of lack of privity" did not constitute an election to settle the claim directly with the subcontractor. The court further held that the amounts included in the contractor's settlement claim for subcontract settlements were subject to setoff for contractor debts to the government.

g. Termination Inventory

The costs of producing termination inventory are generally recoverable subject to the overall allowability requirements of the cost principles. See FAR 31.205-26(e) (limitations on allowability for intra-company transfer of materials). A contractor is, however, entitled to recover its incurred costs for work in process inventory in a termination for convenience settlement, even where that inventory was thrown away as scrap, *Industrial Tectonics Bearings Corp. v. United States*, 44 Fed. Cl. 115 (1999). Allowable costs include those costs incurred in producing defective material as well as those incurred for material complying with contract requirements, as long as the amount of defective material is not unreasonable. See *Best Lumber Sales*, ASBCA 16737, 72-2 BCA ¶9661, in which the board stated that costs of defective material may be recoverable if they are "reasonable, allocable and allowable," *Caskel Forge, Inc.*, ASBCA 7638, 1962 BCA ¶3318. In *Best Foam Fabricators, Inc. v. United States*, 38 Fed. Cl. 627 (1997), the court held that the contractor on a constructively terminated contract was entitled to recover its costs for termination inventory—even if that inventory did not comply in all respects with the specification requirements—absent proof that the defects resulted from the contractor's gross disregard of its contractual obligations. See also *New York Shipbuilding Co.*, ASBCA 15443, 73-1 BCA ¶9852, holding that a terminated contractor has no obligation to correct defective work.

The termination clauses provide that the contractor is responsible for preservation of the termination inventory and must tender the inventory to the government. Thus, they provide that the value of property that is "destroyed, lost or stolen" is to be excluded from the termination settlement. In *Best Lumber Sales*, the contractor was held liable for stolen lumber because the board was not convinced "that some reasonable means was not available to [the contractor] to protect the lumber from theft." Disposal of the inventory is subject to the instructions of the government's plant clearance officer. In *Thiokol Chem. Corp.*, ASBCA 17544, 76-1 BCA ¶11,731, the board found that the government was "bound by the plant clearance officer's determination that the residual inventory was allocable to the terminated contract and should be scrapped."

The contractor, however, need not retain the inventory for an unreasonable time. See *Southland Mfg. Corp.*, ASBCA 16830, 75-1 BCA ¶10,994, *recons. denied*, 75-1 BCA ¶11,272, where the contractor was relieved from tendering inventory that had been sold at public auction during the five years that had elapsed before a wrongful default termination was changed to a convenience termination. Where the government first made a claim for the value of inventory seven years after the termination for convenience, the contractor's defenses of laches and estoppel were legally viable and raised triable issues of material fact, so that neither party was entitled to summary judgment, *Eurasia Heavy Indus., Inc.*, ASBCA 52878, 01-2 BCA ¶31,574.

3. Settlement Expenses

FAR 31.205-42 compensates the contractor for expenses caused by the termination. This cost principle provides as follows:

> (g) *Settlement expenses.* (1) Settlement expenses, including the following, are generally allowable:
> (i) Accounting, legal, clerical, and similar costs reasonably necessary for—

(A) The preparation and presentation, including supporting data, of settlement claims to the contracting officer; and

(B) The termination and settlement of subcontracts.

(ii) Reasonable costs for the storage, transportation, protection, and disposition of property acquired or produced for the contract.

(iii) Indirect costs related to salary and wages incurred as settlement expenses in (i) and (ii); normally, such indirect costs shall be limited to payroll taxes, fringe benefits, occupancy costs, and immediate supervision costs.

(2) If settlement expenses are significant, a cost account or work order shall be established to separately identify and accumulate them.

Accounting, legal, and clerical costs may be recovered if they are accurately documented and reasonable, *Unified Eng'g, Inc.*, ASBCA 21565, 81-1 BCA ¶14,940. Contractors often fail to recover total legal fees claimed in connection with termination settlements because of faulty record keeping. For instance, in *Nolan Bros., Inc. v. United States*, 194 Ct. Cl. 1, 437 F.2d 1371 (1971), the court denied the contractor's claim for 2,400 hours of work, stating that the record did not contain evidence showing "either the exact or the approximate time" devoted to the claim by any of the attorneys who worked on it. Instead, the court awarded the contractor expenses for 400 hours of legal work. See also *H & J Constr. Co.*, ASBCA 18521, 76-1 BCA ¶11,903 (contractor awarded only $500 rather than claimed $48,000 in legal fees), and *Air-Cool, Inc.*, ASBCA 32838, 88-1 BCA ¶20,399 ($1.700 of claimed $2.000 fee sustained). Conclusory testimony that legal work was necessary for the preparation and presentation of the settlement claim will be insufficient. In *G.E. Boggs & Assocs.*, ASBCA 34841, 91-1 BCA ¶23,515, the board (using FPR 1-15.205-42(f)) denied the contractor's claim for legal fees where the contractor failed to submit time records or estimates, stating that conclusory testimony that the legal work was necessary was insufficient to carry the burden. Rather, the board concluded that a showing of the "exact or the approximate amount of time" that was devoted to the preparation of the termination claim through "records, estimates or otherwise" was required. This reasoning was affirmed in *Industrial Refrigeration Servs. Corp.*, VABCA 2532, 91-3 BCA ¶24,093, in which the government successfully argued that the contractor's invoices for legal services lacked specificity and there was no corroboration of the contractor's explanation of the context of the services. Settlement expenses may be proven by contemporary records; memoranda; and diary entries maintained by the attorneys, employees, and accountants, *Foremost Mech. Sys., Inc.*, GSBCA 13250, 98-1 BCA ¶29,652.

The number of hours expended in working on the termination claim and the rate charged must be reasonable. The hours and rates are analyzed on a case-by-case basis. See *American Packers, Inc.*, ASBCA 14275, 71-1 BCA ¶8846 (unreasonable for attorney to spend so many hours on small claim); *Bailey Specialized Bldgs., Inc.*, ASBCA 10576, 71-1 BCA ¶8699 (matters not legally complex but effort warranted in view of evidentiary effort required); *Cryo-Sonics, Inc.*, ASBCA 13219, 70-1 BCA ¶8313 ($100 per hour attorney fee reasonable for the practitioner's locality and the work involved); *Transcendental Aircraft Corp.*, ASBCA 5823, 61-1 BCA ¶2952 (accountant's rate accepted based on his testimony that charges were normal); and *Acme Coppersmithing & Mach. Co.*, ASBCA 4473, 59-1 BCA ¶2136, *recons. denied*, 59-2 BCA ¶2314 (accountant's rate accepted but number of days reduced).

Termination settlement costs are allowable whether incurred by the contractor's own employees or by outside personnel, *Douglas Corp.*, ASBCA 8566, 69-1 BCA ¶7578, *recons. denied*, 69-1 BCA ¶7699; *H & J Constr. Co.*, ASBCA 18521, 75-1 BCA ¶11,171, *recons. denied*, 76-1 BCA ¶11,903. However, the contractor cannot bill separately for the "value" of services furnished by a salaried employee, *Fil-Coil Co.*, ASBCA 23137, 79-1 BCA ¶13,618, *recons. denied*, 79-1 BCA ¶13,683. Settlement expenses for work performed by in-house personnel are computed on the basis of salary as an employee rather than as an hourly billing rate, *TRC Mariah Assoc., Inc.*, ASBCA 51811, 99-1 BCA ¶30,386. If the board determines that the contractor's rates are not credible, it may apply "reasonable" hourly rates in determining the appropriate recovery, *Teems, Inc. v. General Servs. Admin.*, GSBCA 14090, 98-1 BCA ¶29,357.

One of the government's arguments has been that it is improper to have settlement costs related to claims that are ultimately disallowed. Generally, this position has been rejected by the boards on the theory that the validity is not determined until after the claim has been submitted. See, for example, *Engineered Sys., Inc.*, ASBCA 18241, 74-1 BCA ¶10,492, and *Contract Maint., Inc.*, ASBCA 20689, 77-1 BCA ¶12,446. However, where the contractor's claim is for anticipated profits—made expressly unallowable by the regulations—the attorneys' fees associated with that claim are unallowable, *Dairy Sales Corp. v. United States*, 219 Ct. Cl. 431, 593 F.2d 1002 (1979); *Topeka Janitor Serv.*, ASBCA 9989, 65-2 BCA ¶4911.

In order to be allowable, professional service costs must also meet the requirements of FAR 31.205-33. Among other restrictions, this regulation, and its predecessors at FPR 1-15.205-31 and DAR 15-205.31, prohibits reimbursement of fees that are contingent upon recovery from the government and fees incurred in the prosecution of claims against the government. The contingent fee limitation was applied in *Manuel M. Liodas*, ASBCA 12829, 71-2 BCA ¶9015, *recons. denied*, 71-2 BCA ¶9120. See also *Hugo Auchter GmbH*, ASBCA 39642, 91-1 BCA ¶23,645, *recons. denied*, 91-2 BCA ¶23,777, in which the board disallowed a claim for legal expenses that the contractor was obligated to pay "only after the case was settled" on the basis that it was a contingent fee. In *Fiesta Leasing & Sales, Inc.*, ASBCA 29311, 87-1 BCA ¶19,622, *modified on recons. (on other grounds)*, 88-1 BCA ¶20,499, the government attempted to prevent recovery of attorneys' fees because they were charged under a deferred billing arrangement, not actually paid. The fees, extensively documented, left no question that they were related to settlement expenses. While noting the prohibition against contingent fees, the board allowed recovery, stating that the government had not rebutted evidence establishing that the fees were deferred rather than contingent. *Hugo Auchter* and *Fiesta Leasing* can be distinguished on the basis of when the obligation to pay the attorneys' fees arose. In *Hugo*, there apparently was no obligation to pay until and unless the settlement claim had been paid by the government. In *Fiesta Leasing*, the obligation arose at the time services were rendered and were, therefore, recoverable. See also *R-D Mounts, Inc.*, ASBCA 17422, 75-1 BCA ¶11,077, *recons. denied*, 75-1 BCA ¶11,237; *Southland Mfg. Corp.*, ASBCA 16830, 75-1 BCA ¶10,994, *recons. denied*, 75-1 BCA ¶11,272; and *Atlantic, Gulf & Pac. Co. of Manila, Inc.*, ASBCA 13533, 72-1 BCA ¶9415, *recons. denied*, 72-2 BCA ¶9698.

The costs of processing board and court actions against the government clearly come within the unallowable category of processing claims against the government, *Robertson Co. v. United States*, 194 Ct. Cl. 289, 437 F.2d 1360 (1971). FAR 31.207-47(f) specifically provides that the cost of prosecuting claims or appeals against the government is clearly unallowable. See *A. T. Kearney, Inc.*, DOTCAB 1580, 86-1 BCA ¶18,613. If an attorneys' fee relates to any other portion of the contract action, it is unallowable as part of the convenience termination settlement.

In determining whether legal fees claimed by a contractor are allowable in the termination settlement, the courts and boards will look at the nature of the work rather than the time at which the work was performed, *Alta Constr. Co.*, PSBCA 1463, 92-2 BCA ¶24,824, *recons. denied*, 92-3 BCA ¶25,128. There, the contractor claimed attorneys' fees incurred in 1985. The contract was terminated for default in 1985 and converted to a termination for convenience in 1990. The government defended against the settlement claim on three grounds. First, it asserted that attorneys' fees incurred before the termination should have been included in the company's general overhead cost rather than attributed to the convenience termination. Second, it argued that the fees should not be allowed because they were incurred before actual termination. Third, it asserted that the fees were actually incurred as part of a claim against the government and were, therefore, unallowable. The board stated that the record did not support the government's third argument. In discussing the timing of the legal work, the board concluded at 123,835:

> It is the nature of the work and not the time at which it was performed which controls whether the associated costs may be recovered as part of a termination for convenience claim. *Kalvar Corp., Inc. v. United States* [22 CCF ¶80,737], 543 F.2d 1298 (Ct. Cl. 1976); *Industrial Refrigeration Services Corp.*, VABCA No. 2532, 91-3 BCA ¶24,093; *Baifield Industries, Division of A-T-O, Inc.*, 76-2 BCA ¶12,096, *recons. denied* 76-2 BCA ¶12,203.

See also *Richerson Constr., Inc. v. General Servs. Admin.*, GSBCA 11161, 93-1 BCA ¶25,239, *modified on recons.*, 93-3 BCA ¶26,206, where the government asserted that the certification of the proposal, coupled with a request for a final decision, followed by a prompt filing of a notice of appeal, demonstrated the contractor's litigation posture. The board disagreed, stating at 125,713:

> The fact that [the contractor] was not unduly optimistic about the prospects for reaching a mutually satisfactory settlement, and thus sought to protect its right to recover interest in the event litigation was ultimately necessary, does not change the nature of the activities for which expenses were incurred. [The contractor's] settlement proposal was just that. Indeed, the Government treated it thus, requesting the customary audit of [the contractor's]

> proposal, so as to enable it to negotiate with [the contractor]. Accordingly, we are not persuaded by the argument that the running of CDA interest, started by the filing of a certified claim, precludes the recovery of legal expenses incurred in preparing the termination settlement proposal and negotiating with the Government in an effort to settle the matter.

Generally, the end of negotiations with the contracting officer and the issuance of a final decision are considered to be the cutoff point for allowable settlement costs, *Western States Painting Co.*, ASBCA 13843, 69-1 BCA ¶7616. However, it has been recognized that settlement negotiations can continue past the filing of an appeal and that costs legitimately incurred in negotiating a settlement can be allowed even though a hearing on the case is in process, *ACME Process Equip. Co. v. United States*, 171 Ct. Cl. 251, 347 F.2d 538 (1965); *Frigitemp Corp.*, VACAB 646, 68-1 BCA ¶6766. In *Vincent Ogonnaya Ofor*, PSBCA 3965, 99-1 BCA ¶30,317, the board rejected the agency's assertions that the contractor's legal and accounting costs, incurred after a termination settlement proposal was converted to a claim, were unallowable costs associated with the prosecution of a claim against the government. The board noted that the nature and form of legal activities are more objective standards for determining if the costs may be reimbursed than is their relationship in time to the filing of an appeal to the board. Thus, the board allowed the contractor to recover the costs of direct labor for preparation of the proposal, as well as costs for legal and accounting time.

When a contractor sues the government for breach of contract and the government action is found to have been a constructive termination and the amount of recovery is determined, it has been stated that "it is only fair to allow the contractor the equivalent of legal expenses he would have incurred in preparing a settlement claim after termination," *Kalvar Corp., Inc. v. United States*, 211 Ct. Cl. 192, 543 F.2d 1298 (1976), *cert. denied*, 434 U.S. 830 (1977). However, in that case the court limited recovery to the costs incurred in responding to a court order for a supplemental brief to determine whether the contractor had incurred costs recoverable under a termination settlement. Subsequently, the court concluded that the contractor had incurred no expenses in connection with the brief because its attorney had not billed it for the preparation of the brief and it had not paid him, *Kalvar Corp. v. United States*, 218 Ct. Cl. 433, 587 F.2d 49 (1978). Expenses incurred in dealing with the contracting officer as part of a genuine attempt to negotiate a settlement are allowable even though the efforts may benefit the subsequent legal prosecution of the claim, *Baifield Indus., Div. of A-T-O, Inc.*, ASBCA 20006, 76-2 BCA ¶12,096, *recons. denied*, 76-2 BCA ¶12,203. However, if the board is convinced that the amount and nature of the settlement efforts are influenced by the likelihood of their being useful in subsequent litigation, they may be disallowed, *Power Equip. Corp.*, ASBCA 5904, 1964 BCA ¶4228.

If the settlement effort is performed by the contractor's own employees, the contractor is entitled to charge overhead to direct labor employees performing the effort in accordance with its normal accounting system, *Worsham Constr. Co.*, ASBCA 25907, 85-2 BCA ¶18,016; *Thiokol Chem. Corp.*, ASBCA 17544, 76-1 BCA ¶11,731; *The Boeing Co.*, ASBCA 12685, 69-2 BCA ¶7795. If the effort is performed by personnel normally charged indirectly, there is authority for the contractor to charge those efforts directly to the termination settlement, *Aydin Corp.*, EBCA 355-5-86, 89-3 BCA ¶22,044; *A. T. Kearney, Inc.*, DOTBCA 1580, 86-1 BCA ¶18,613; *Celesco Indus., Inc.*, ASBCA 22460, 84-2 BCA ¶17,295; *Bermite Div. of Tasker Indus.*, ASBCA 18280, 77-1 BCA ¶12,349, *modified on recons.*, 77-2 BCA ¶12,731. This reclassification on its face appears to violate CAS 402. Settlement costs, however, do not trigger the requisite circumstances of "in like manner" or "for the same purpose" as referenced in CAS 402 because the functions performed by the contractor in settling terminated contracts are different from those required for normal business operations. When reclassifying, the contractor must make appropriate adjustments to overhead to prevent double counting, and the board must be assured that the contractor has not already recovered the costs through overhead allocations.

4. Overhead, Profit, and Loss Contracts

Termination settlements are subject to special rules for post-termination overhead, profit, and loss contracts.

a. Post-Termination Overhead

Except to the extent that it is allocable to direct settlement expenses, recovery of post-termination overhead has been prohibited in termination claims for completely terminated contracts. See *Nolan Bros., Inc. v. United States*, 194 Ct. Cl. 1,

437 F.2d 1371 (1971); *Chamberlain Mfg. Corp.*, ASBCA 16877, 73-2 BCA ¶10,139; *Pioneer Recovery Sys., Inc.*, ASBCA 24658, 81-1 BCA ¶15,059; *Celesco Indus., Inc.*, ASBCA 22460, 84-2 BCA ¶17,295; and *Foremost Mech. Sys., Inc. v. General Servs. Admin.*, GSBCA 13250-C(12335), 98-1 BCA ¶29,652. In *Technology, Inc.*, ASBCA 14083, 71-2 BCA ¶8956, *recons. denied*, 72-1 BCA ¶9281, the board held that such a recovery would be similar to anticipated profits and would not be recoverable as continuing costs. However, in *Southland Mfg. Corp.*, ASBCA 16830, 75-1 BCA ¶10,994, *recons. denied*, 75-1 BCA ¶11,272, the board permitted the contractor to recover unabsorbed overhead for a reasonable time after an improper default termination that directly resulted in the contractor going out of business. Substantially similar results were obtained in *American Elec., Inc.*, ASBCA 16635, 76-2 BCA ¶12,151, *modified on other grounds*, 77-2 BCA ¶12,792, where the contractor was able to recover the costs of facilities established solely for the contract. See also *Baifield Indus., Div. of A-T-O, Inc.*, ASBCA 20006, 76-2 BCA ¶12,096, *recons. denied*, 76-2 BCA ¶12,203, in which the board allowed the contractor to recover continuing costs for a manufacturing plant that, although not been acquired solely for the performance of the contract, "was necessary from the standpoint of maximizing efficiency of production and minimizing plant alteration costs." Following termination, the contractor had no further need for the plant. The proper conclusion may have been reached in the *Baifield* case because some of the costs allowed by the board as continuing costs were rental, depreciation, and other costs that would appear to be allowable under the cost principle dealing with continuing rental costs and loss of useful life.

An increased allocation of fixed indirect costs to the continued portion of the contract based on an allocation to all of the contractor's ongoing work and not solely to the continued work on the contract was held to be allowable in *Cal-Tron Sys, Inc.*, ASBCA 49279, 97-2 BCA ¶28,986.

b. *Profit or Loss Adjustment*

The "long form" termination clauses for fixed-price contracts provide that the termination settlement is to include either a "reasonable allowance for profit on work done" or a loss adjustment in the event that the contractor would have sustained a loss on the entire contract had it been completed.

(1) Profit

The clause for fixed-price supply contracts in FAR 52.249-2 calls for the contracting officer to pay a "fair and reasonable" sum of profit on "costs incurred in the performance of the work terminated, including initial costs and preparatory expense allocable thereto." Alternate I of that clause for fixed-price construction contracts is slightly different, stating that a "fair and reasonable" sum of profit is to be paid on the costs of contract work "performed before the effective date of termination." This difference is most likely not significant, however, since both clauses incorporate FAR 49.202 which expressly states that profit shall be allowed on "preparations made and work done by the contractor for the terminated portion of the contract." Thus, under both types of contracts, the contractor would appear to be entitled to a profit on costs incurred under the contract even though no physical work had been accomplished. The wording of the specific termination clause may, however, restrict the profit. See *Advance Window Sys., Inc.*, VACAB 1276, 78-1 BCA ¶13,126, where the termination clause provided for profit only "on work done." The board allowed the contractor to recover its out-of-pocket costs but refused to allow any profits.

If the contractor has incurred no costs, it is clear that no profit recovery is allowed, *Shin Enters., Inc.*, ASBCA 16542, 72-1 BCA ¶9391. FAR 49.202(a) states that "[p]rofit shall not be allowed the contractor for material or services that as of the effective date of the termination have not been delivered by a subcontractor, regardless of the percentage of completion." Following a partial convenience termination, in *TRW, Inc.*, ASBCA 51003, 00-2 BCA ¶30,992, the board found that a contract's "ship in place" provisions would have allowed materials delivered under its provisions to have been eligible for profit, but that mere completion of a milestone was not synonymous with delivery. The board held, however, that the contractor was entitled to recover profit on data delivered by the subcontractor but not separately priced in the subcontract, provided a reasonable value could be placed on the data. See also *Lockheed Martin Corp.*, ASBCA 53032, 03-2 BCA ¶32,408 (fee not allowed on subcontractor effort even in Leader Company contracting).

FAR 49.202 states that the contracting officer may "use any reasonable method to arrive at a fair profit" and provides the following guidance:

(b) In negotiating or determining profit, factors to be considered include—
- (1) Extent and difficulty of the work done by the contractor as compared with the total work required by the contract (engineering estimates of the percentage of completion ordinarily should not be required, but if available should be considered);
- (2) Engineering work, production scheduling, planning, technical study and supervision, and other necessary services;
- (3) Efficiency of the contractor, with particular regard to—
  - (i) Attainment of quantity and quality production;
  - (ii) Reduction of costs;
  - (iii) Economic use of materials, facilities, and manpower; and
  - (iv) Disposition of termination inventory;
- (4) Amount and source of capital and extent of risk assumed;
- (5) Inventive and developmental contributions, and cooperation with the Government and other contractors in supplying technical assistance;
- (6) Character of the business, including the source and nature of materials and the complexity of manufacturing techniques;
- (7) The rate of profit that the contractor would have earned had the contract been completed;
- (8) The rate of profit both parties contemplated at the time the contract was negotiated; and
- (9) Character and difficulty of subcontracting, including selection, placement, and management of subcontracts, and effort in negotiating settlements of terminated subcontracts.

(c) When computing profit on the terminated portion of a construction contract, the contracting officer shall—
- (1) Comply with paragraphs (a) and (b) of this Section;
- (2) Allow profit on the prime contractor's settlements with construction subcontractors for actual work in place at the job site; and
- (3) Exclude profit on the prime contractor's settlements with construction subcontractors for materials on hand and for preparations made to complete the work.

No profit is allowed on settlement expenses. FAR 49.202(a) states that, although the contractor's efforts in settling subcontractor proposals will be considered in determining the overall rate of profit, profit for such efforts is not to be based on the "dollar amount" of the settlements.

The contractor has the burden of proving both the estimated cost to complete the contract, *Clary Corp.*, ASBCA 19274, 74-2 BCA ¶10,947, and the rate of profit, *John M. Brown*, AGBCA 77-105, 78-1 BCA ¶12,892. Note, however, that when a cost-reimbursement contract is terminated the government has the burden of proof as to the amount of reduction of the fee, *Emerson Elec. Co.*, ASBCA 15591, 72-1 BCA ¶9440. Determination of the rate of profit is done on a case-by-case basis, and the application of the regulatory guidelines is considered a matter of judgment, *Metered Laundry Servs.*, ASBCA 21573, 78-1 BCA ¶13,206, *modified on recons.*, 78-2 BCA ¶13,451. The rates of profit have varied widely. See *Fil-Coil Co.*, ASBCA 23137, 79-1 BCA ¶13,618, *recons. denied*, 79-1 BCA ¶13,683 (20 percent more than fair where contractor had claimed 70 percent of anticipated profit, which amounted to 65 percent of cost incurred); *Lockley Mfg. Co.*, ASBCA 21231, 78-1 BCA ¶12,987 (contractor requested 10 percent but board awarded 4.93 percent, the actual experienced rate calculated by the government); *Metered Laundry Servs.*, ASBCA 21573, 78-1 BCA ¶13,206, *modified on recons.*, 78-2 BCA ¶13,451 (contractor claimed 35 percent but board found 20 percent more than reasonable); *Amplitronics, Inc.*, ASBCA 20545, 76-1 BCA ¶11,760 (contractor's investment, expertise, and actions supported 5 percent rate rather than 4.6 percent suggested by government); and *Switlik Parachute Co.*, ASBCA 18024, 75-2 BCA ¶11,434 (contractor claimed 12 percent as its normal bidding rate, government offered 6 percent, and board balanced risk and job difficulty to award 9 percent). In *E.W. Eldridge, Inc.*, ENGBCA 4879, 93-1 BCA ¶25,355, the contractor claimed 20 percent based on its assertion that the deleted work would have been the most profitable under the contract and that the deceased president of the company always bid on the basis of high profit rates. The board, while noting it "seldom" used a rate higher than 10 percent, found that the contracting officer's earlier estimate of 14 percent was the best estimate of the rate of profit the contractor would have earned had the contract been completed and therefore awarded that amount. In *Marshall Associated Contractors Inc. & Columbia Excavating Inc. (J. V.)*, IBCA 1901, 02-1 BCA ¶31,797, a 30 percent profit was allowed under a terminated contract in light of the "[contractor's] truly remarkable production rate . . . under the most difficult and adverse of situations," especially as compared with the re-procurement contractor's production. The board awarded the contractor $17.5 million, plus 18 years of CDA interest, on a $6.6 million contract. Clearly influenced by the severity of the government's conduct, the board allowed (1) cost of facilities capital on the initial value of special equipment, rather than the value as depreciated during performance; (2) rental rates on pre-owned equipment based on "Blue Book" rates, enhanced by 39 percent to reflect the ultra-harsh performance conditions; and (3) "unabsorbed overhead" at contractor's historical overhead percentage in normal periods (10 percent), rather than the lower 5 percent rate actually incurred during performance caused by increases in the direct base due to the cost of the project. The board rejected application of the loss formula, since the government contributed to the contractor's loss.

When a contract fee is determined at the inception of a cost contract, a contractor has a reasonable expectation of receiving some portion of the fee if the contract is terminated for convenience. In that case, the adjusted fee generally will be computed by measuring the percentage-of-completion at the time of termination. But, when a fee has not been fixed at the beginning of the contract and is subject to periodic discretionary adjustment by the government such as an award fee, percentage-of-completion is not the appropriate formula to determine the fee to be paid upon termination of the contract. In *Textron Def. Sys. v. Widnall,* 143 F.3d 1465 (Fed. Cir. 1998), the court affirmed the board's rejection of Textron's attempt to collect 77.4 percent of its award fee based on the percentage-of-completion formula, when the government terminated the contract for convenience. The court opined that the "plain language of the contract" made the Termination clause inapplicable to award fees. Even if the Termination clause did apply to award fees, "a contractor in a cost-plus-award-fee contract is not entitled to a specific share of an award fee."

(2) Loss Adjustment

The "long form" termination clauses state that, if it appears that the contractor would have incurred a loss had the entire contract been completed, an appropriate adjustment shall be made to reduce the amount of the settlement to reflect the indicated rate of loss. FAR 49.203 provides that the formula for applying the loss adjustment is to multiply the incurred costs of the terminated portion of the contract by the ratio of the contract price to the total of the incurred costs plus the estimate to complete the work. In some cases, such as *G.A. Karnavas Painting Co.*, ASBCA 22281, 78-2 BCA ¶13,312, the board applied this percentage directly to the incurred costs to obtain the cost allowance for settlement. In others, the reciprocal of this ratio is applied to the incurred costs to get an amount to be subtracted from the incurred cost to obtain the cost allowance for settlement. See *Henry Spen & Co.*, ASBCA 20766, 77-2 BCA ¶12,784. These are merely different ways of presenting the figures, and the end results are the same.

In *Boeing Def. & Space Group,* ASBCA 50048, 98-2 BCA ¶29,927, the board applied the Christian doctrine to incorporate the FAR loss adjustment provision under FAR 49.203 into a fixed-price incentive fee contract for use as guidance in interpreting the contract's Termination for Convenience clause. The board held that, although the contract required separate contract item costs for purposes of incentive price revisions, incremental funding, and progress payments, it did not prohibit the use of a combined loss ratio to determine the termination settlement amount.

When a contractor submits a termination settlement proposal on an inventory basis, the percentage of loss ("loss formula") is calculated on the entire contract, but is applied only to the terminated portion. By contrast, where the settlement proposal is on the cost basis, the loss formula is applied to the entire contract, *Voices R Us, Inc.*, ASBCA 51565, 01-1 BCA ¶31,328.

The loss adjustment will not be made if the government is responsible for the cost increase, *R.H.J. Corp.*, ASBCA 12404, 69-1 BCA ¶7587; or if the contractor is excused from performing because of impossibility, *Scope Elecs., Inc.*, ASBCA 20359, 77-1 BCA ¶12,404, *recons. denied*, 77-2 BCA ¶12,586; *D.E.W, Inc.*, ASBCA 50796, 00-2 BCA ¶31,104, *modified on recons.*, 01-1 BCA ¶31,150. The adjustment also will not be made where the contractor is entitled to an equitable adjustment that takes the contract out of the loss position, *Douglas Corp.*, ASBCA 8566, 69-1 BCA ¶7578, *recons. denied*, 69-1 BCA ¶7699.

It is not appropriate to apply the loss adjustment factor or to limit the settlement to the contract price without giving consideration to unpriced changes or other modifications. The most straightforward method of accomplishing this is for the parties to negotiate the appropriate price increase or decrease and amend the contract accordingly. If the parties fail to do so, the board may determine the amount of the adjustment, *Pilcher, Livingston & Wallace, Inc.*, ASBCA 13391, 70-1 BCA ¶8331, *recons. denied*, 70-2 BCA ¶8488. However, in some cases the boards will merely ignore the loss adjustment if the contractor is entitled to price adjustments. See *Scope Elecs., Inc.*, ASBCA 20359, 77-1 BCA ¶12,404, *recons. denied*, 77-2 BCA ¶12,586 (contractor entitled to recover all reasonable costs under terminated loss contracts in view of objective impossibility), and *Douglas Corp.*, ASBCA 8566, 69-1 BCA ¶7578, *recons. denied*, 69-1 BCA ¶7699 (loss adjustment factor held inapplicable due to defective government-furnished specifications). In asserting the right to such adjustments, contractors still must prove their claims. In *Defense Sys. Corp.*, ASBCA 44131R, 00-1 BCA ¶30,851, the board held that a contractor whose default termination had been converted to a termination for convenience due to defective specifications and impossibility of performance was not entitled to recover costs in excess of the adjusted contract price because the contractor failed to demonstrate that the government was responsible for the specified costs. Although the contract price ceiling was adjusted for the increased costs caused by the impossibility, the contractor was denied recovery for costs above the adjusted contract price for which the contractor had shown no government-responsible causation.

The regulations do not contain guidance on adjusting the contract price except in FAR 49.114, which indicates the appropriate contracting officer to negotiate unadjusted changes:

> (a) Before settlement of a completely terminated contract, the TCO shall obtain from the contracting office a list of all related unsettled contract changes. The TCO shall settle, as part of final settlement, all unsettled contract changes after obtaining the recommendations of the contracting office concerning the changes.
>
> (b) When the contract has been partially terminated, any outstanding unsettled contract changes will usually be handled by the contracting officer. However, the contracting officer may delegate this function to the TCO.

In *David Boland, Inc.*, VABCA 5931, 01-2 BCA ¶31,578, the board held that because a termination for convenience converts a fixed-price contract into a cost-reimbursement contract, the contractor's quantum claims for the site condition and other matters would be merged into the termination settlement provisions "insofar as they do not, in the aggregate amount, exceed the contract price." By this language, the board appeared to ignore the fact that, if the claims were recognized, the contract price would be increased, resulting in a potentially greater recovery by the contractor. See *Freedom NY, Inc.*, ASBCA 43965, 01-2 BCA ¶31,585, *recons. denied*, 02-1 BCA ¶31,676, *aff'd in part & rev'd in part*, 329 F.3d 1320 (Fed. Cir. 2003), *cert. denied*, 541 U. S. 987 (2004) (contractor's breach claim, to the extent sustained, constituted an adjustment to the contract price for affecting both the total recovery and application of the termination for convenience loss formula).

The government has the burden of proving that the contractor would have been in a loss position at completion since it is seeking to reduce the contractor's recovery, *Systems & Computer Info., Inc.*, ASBCA 18458, 78-1 BCA ¶12,946. In that case, the board resorted to a "jury verdict" determination and favored the contractor in computing the amount of anticipated loss because the government had not fully met its burden. For another case basing the estimate to complete on a "jury verdict" determination, see *Supreme Equip. & Sys. Corp.*, ASBCA 20079, 76-1 BCA ¶11,858. In determining the estimate to complete, all expected costs are considered, including the costs the contractor would have had to expend to correct defective performance had the contract not been terminated, *Power Generators, Inc.*, ASBCA 7607, 1962 BCA ¶3358.

5. Variable Quantity Contracts and Cost Limitation Clauses

With most types of contract the parties can determine the contract price from the terms of the contract. However, when variable quantity contracts are involved, a number of questions arise. If a requirements contract is terminated for convenience, the contractor's recovery is not limited by the ordered amount or by a nominal minimum quantity, *Albano Cleaners, Inc. v. United States*, 197 Ct. Cl. 450, 455 F.2d 556 (1972). If the contract is an indefinite delivery/indefinite quantity (IDIQ) contract and the government is not bound to place orders, the termination settlement will be limited to the ordered amount or the minimum quantity, whichever is greater. These problems were present in *Okaw Indus., Inc.*, ASBCA 17863, 77-2 BCA ¶12,793, in which the board held that the contract price was to be calculated according to the ordered services, so long as the amount ordered exceeded the contract minimum. It did not matter that the amount ordered was less than the "estimated amount," since there was adequate consideration to bind both parties. In *Unified Eng'g, Inc.*, ASBCA 21565,

81-1 BCA ¶14,940, the agency had failed to order the minimum quantities on four items and had exceeded the minimum on the balance on others. The board allowed the contractor to recover in excess of the price corresponding to the price of the minimum quantities under each category, reasoning that "the contract price would not be reached . . . until an amount equivalent to the value of the under-ordered minimums had been established as due" the contractor.

When an IDIQ contract was allowed to expire without reaching the minimum quantity, the contractor was awarded the entire price of the minimum quantity, *Maxima Corp. v. United States*, 847 F.2d 1549 (Fed. Cir 1988). The court reasoned that a constructive termination had not occurred and that the contractor had fully performed the contract by being available to perform. However, other cases have awarded not the full price for the unordered IDIQ work, but rather the amount the contractor lost as the result of the government's failure to order the minimum quantity, *PHP Healthcare Corp.*, ASBCA 39209, 91-1 BCA ¶23,647; *Apex Int'l Mgmt. Servs. Inc.*, ASBCA 38087, 94-2 BCA ¶26,842. In *Delta Constr. Int'l, Inc.*, ASBCA 52162, 01-1 BCA ¶31,195, *recons. granted*, 01-1 BCA ¶31,242, the board had followed *Maxima* in awarding the difference between the dollar amount of work the government actually ordered and the total minimum dollar amount the contract obligated the government to order. On appeal, *White v. Delta Constr. Int'l, Inc.*, 285 F.3d 1040 (Fed. Cir. 2002), the court reversed, concluding that the board's method was an impermissible basis for calculating damages because it would put the contractor in a more favorable position than it would have been in if the government had performed rather than breached its contractual commitment. Instead, the court stated that the proper basis for damages was the loss the contractor suffered as a result of the government's breach, not the total amount it would have received without the breach.

Where a letter contract is terminated for convenience, the Limitation of Government Liability clause would appear to be applied in the same way as the Limitation of Cost clause in cost-reimbursement contracts. In such a termination claim, the contractor can recover costs in excess of the estimated cost only in cases where it was impossible for the contractor to give the required notice of overrun or where the contracting officer had agreed to fund the overrun, *Frederick Burk Found.*, ASBCA 15728, 73-1 BCA ¶9959. In *Breed Corp.*, ASBCA 14523, 72-1 BCA ¶9304, *rev'd*, 223 Ct. Cl. 702 (1980), the board held that the revised clause precluded a contractor from recovering termination settlement costs in excess of the estimated cost. On appeal, the Court of Claims held that termination costs were included under the Limitation of Cost clause as performance costs but reversed the board's decision, reasoning that the government had "waived" the benefit of the clause by requesting the contractor to take specific termination actions with full knowledge that the contract funds had been exhausted, thereby leading the contractor to reasonably conclude that the government would fund its termination costs. The same result was reached in *General Am. Research Div.*, PSBCA 91, 77-1 BCA ¶12,372. See, however, *American Elec., Inc.*, ASBCA 16635, 76-2 BCA ¶12,151, *modified on other grounds*, 77-2 BCA ¶12,792, in which the limitation was held to have been waived by the contracting officer's settlement offers in excess of the limitation.

If a contract is a cost-sharing one, the contractor will only be entitled to its contractual share of the termination costs, *Jacobs Eng'g Group, Inc. v. United States*, 63 Fed. Cl. 451 (2005). The court reached this conclusion based on the language in the cost-reimbursement termination clause in FAR 52.249-6 calling for payment of "all costs reimbursable under this contract." The court reasoned that the cost-sharing provision survived termination and that the no fee arrangement also survived termination.

6. Partial Termination

A partial termination is defined in FAR 49.001 as "the termination of a part, but not all, of the work which has not been completed and accepted under the contract." This definition envisions that some work will continue after the issuance of the notice of termination. However, in practice, the term also has been applied to cases where a part of the work has already been completed and accepted and the balance terminated. The wrongful failure by the government to place all its orders under a requirements contract has also been referred to as a "constructive partial termination," *Wheeler Bros., Inc.*, ASBCA 20465, 79-1 BCA ¶13,642. Determining whether a termination is partial is important since it affects the method of pricing the termination settlement. The termination clauses provide for an equitable adjustment of the prices of the unterminated work when a partial termination is involved. Paragraph (l) of the termination clause contained in FAR 52.249-2 states:

> If the termination is partial, the Contractor may file a proposal with the Contracting Officer for an equitable adjustment of the price(s) of the continued portion of the contract. The Contracting Officer shall make any equitable

adjustment agreed upon. Any proposal by the Contractor for an equitable adjustment under this clause shall be requested within 90 days from the effective date of termination unless extended in writing by the Contracting Officer.

If the termination is not considered a partial termination, the contractor's remedies for the effect of the reduced volume of work must be obtained under the termination cost principle for initial costs.

The equitable adjustment is computed by increasing the price of the unterminated work by the amount of costs that would have been recovered in the prices of the terminated work. In *Wheeler Bros.*, the board permitted the contractor to recover fixed overhead that would have been allocated to the terminated portion of the work, even though the contractor would have made a profit at the unadjusted prices notwithstanding the termination. The board specifically distinguished fixed overhead from anticipatory profit. In *Celesco Indus., Inc.*, ASBCA 22460, 84-2 BCA ¶17,295, the board refused to apply higher overhead rates caused by the termination to the equitable adjustment for the unterminated units on the questionable theory that this amounted to compensation for unabsorbed overhead. See also *Contract Maint., Inc.*, ASBCA 18595, 74-2 BCA ¶10,963, and *Space Age Eng'g, Inc.*, ASBCA 16525, 73-1 BCA ¶9921, where the government terminated lower cost work that the contractor had anticipated using to recoup expenses of the higher cost work, which was not terminated. In these cases, the contractors' offers had been conditioned on being awarded both parts of the work. However, where the government completely terminates a severable item, there is no equitable adjustment to the remaining items, *Gregory & Reilly Assocs., Inc.*, FAACAP 65-30, 65-2 BCA ¶4918. The contractor has the burden of proof that costs have been "increased by the termination," *Askenazy Constr. Co.*, HUDBCA 78-2, 78-2 BCA ¶13,402.

An equitable adjustment for partial contract termination can raise issues of the amount of unrecovered fixed overhead costs associated with the terminated portion of the work. In *Jay Auto. Specialties, Inc.*, ASBCA 50036, 99-1 BCA ¶30,186, the board held that the contractor was entitled to recover fixed overhead costs based on a rate that accounted for the difference between the contractor's actual revenues and the revenues that would have resulted in the absence of the partially terminated work.

The equitable adjustment arising out of partial termination is for the increased cost of continued work due to the partial termination and not for claimed increased cost that would have been incurred in the absence of the termination, *Aeronca, Inc.*, ASBCA 51927, 01-1 BCA ¶31,230. In that case, a contractor's claim for additional indirect costs allocated to the unterminated portion of a contract was unproven. The contractor's calculation included both fixed and variable costs and indirect costs properly allocable to all of its remaining work. Although the contractor was entitled to recover any increased allocation of fixed costs to the unterminated portion of the contract, it could not recover the increased allocation to other work resulting from the termination, *Hunter Mfg. Co.*, ASBCA 48693, 97-1 BCA ¶28,924.

C. Short Form Termination Settlements

FAR 52.249-1 sets forth a "short form" termination clause to be used in fixed-price contracts of $100,000 or less:

TERMINATION FOR CONVENIENCE OF THE GOVERNMENT
(FIXED-PRICE) (SHORT FORM) (APR 1984)

The Contracting Officer, by written notice, may terminate this contract, in whole or in part, when it is in the Government's interest. If this contract is terminated, the rights, duties, and obligations of the parties including compensation to the Contractor, shall be in accordance with Part 49 of the Federal Acquisition Regulation in effect on the date of this contract.

Another "short form" termination clause is available for use in fixed-price service contracts of any amount where the contracting officer determines that "the successful offeror will not incur substantial charges in preparation for and in carrying out the contract." This clause, set forth in FAR 52.249-4, provides as follows:

TERMINATION FOR CONVENIENCE OF THE GOVERNMENT (SERVICES) (SHORT FORM) (APR 1984)

> The Contracting Officer, by written notice, may terminate this contract, in whole or in part, when it is in the Government's interest. If this contract is terminated, the Government shall be liable only for payment under the payment provisions of this contract for services rendered before the effective date of termination.

As long as the contracting officer makes the prescribed determination, the use of this "short form" clause is appropriate regardless of contract value when a fixed-price service contract is contemplated, *Arrow, Inc.*, ASBCA 41330, 94-1 BCA ¶26,353. In that case, the contractor's claim for the useful value of special machinery and equipment was denied because the short form clause, which limits settlement charges to services rendered before the date of termination, was included in the contract. The contractor unsuccessfully argued that the long form clause (FAR 52.249-2) should have been used because the contract for grounds maintenance exceeded $100,000 in value.

Clauses substantially identical to FAR 52.249-4, which were set forth in DAR 7-1902.16 and FPR 1-8.705-1, had consistently been interpreted as precluding recovery of start-up and post-termination costs. See *Trans-Student Lines, Inc.*, ASBCA 20230, 75-1 BCA ¶11,343, *recons. denied*, 75-2 BCA ¶11,419, in which the board stated at 54,348:

> [T]he Termination for Convenience clause provides for no recovery except for payment in accordance with the payment provisions of the contract for services rendered prior to the effective date of termination. In other words, [the contractor] agreed to a contract that permitted the Government to terminate at any time and pay only for the bus service tendered at the stipulated price with no payment to be made for start-up costs or other costs normally paid pursuant to a termination for convenience.

See *Tefft, Kelly & Motley, Inc.*, GSBCA 6562, 83-1 BCA ¶16,177, *recons. denied*, 83-1 BCA ¶16,279, and *Maibens, Inc.*, ASBCA 25915, 82-1 BCA ¶15,668, *recons. denied*, 82-1 BCA ¶15,796. But see *Grover Contracting Corp.*, GSBCA 4115, 75-2 BCA ¶11,550, *recons. denied*, 76-1 BCA ¶11,906, involving a contract to unload copper ore where, after it was able to make available only one-third of the amount of ore stated in the contract, the government terminated the contract for convenience. The contractor was entitled to recover for the work actually performed at a higher unit price than that stated in the contract, based on the government's negligent failure to accurately approximate its unloading requirements. See also *Steelcare, Inc.*, GSBCA 5491, 81-1 BCA ¶15,143.

CHAPTER 4

DISPUTES

Disputes between a contractor and the government are resolved under the procedures prescribed by the Contract Disputes Act of 1978 (CDA), 41 U.S.C. § 601 *et seq.*, which codified and broadened existing disputes procedures. In the early part of the 20th century, prior to the adoption of contract disputes procedures, contractors could assert claims against the government under the Tucker Act, 28 U.S.C. § 1346(a) and § 1491, which waived sovereign immunity for "any claim against the United States, founded either upon the Constitution, or any Act of Congress, or any regulation of an executive department, or upon any express or implied contract with the United States."

As procurement became a significant factor in the operations of the government in the twentieth century, contractors' rights to use the waiver of sovereign immunity through suits in court were significantly limited by the incorporation of disputes provisions into contracts with the government. These clauses required that the contracting officer make the initial decision on a dispute. The contractor could then appeal this decision to the head of the agency or a board designated by the agency head. Contractors were required to exhaust these administrative remedies before bringing suit on any case within the purview of the disputes clauses, *United States v. Holpuch Co.*, 328 U.S. 234 (1946). Under the Wunderlich Act, 41 U.S.C. §§ 321 and 322, such clauses were prohibited from making agency decisions final on questions of law but were permitted to limit judicial review by making agency decisions final on questions of fact, as long as those decisions were supported by substantial evidence and were not "fraudulent or arbitrary or capricious or so grossly erroneous as to necessarily imply bad faith." Considerable litigation arose under these disputes clauses concerning the types of claims covered and the jurisdiction of agency boards of contract appeals and the courts.

The disputes procedure was restructured and made statutory by the CDA, which introduced two major changes. First, the Act broadens the scope of the disputes procedure by removing the need for a "remedy granting clause" as a prerequisite for jurisdiction. Second, it gives the contractor the right to appeal a contracting officer's decision to either an agency board of contract appeals or the Court of Federal Claims, but not U.S. District Courts, *Campanella v. Commerce Exch. Bank*, 137 F.3d 885 (6th Cir. 1998).

To have a viable contract claim under the Tucker Act, a plaintiff must establish privity of contract with the government or a contractual relationship with the government as a third-party beneficiary. To determine whether plaintiff is an intended third-party beneficiary under a contract, the court will examine the entire contractual relationship and determine whether the beneficiary would be reasonable in relying on the promise as intending to confer a right on him, *Sallee v. United States*, 41 Fed. Cl. 509 (1998).

This chapter provides an overview of the disputes process and discusses in detail the types of controversies subject to the CDA, the procedures for asserting claims, the role of the contracting officer in the disputes process, the contractor's options of litigating before the boards of contract appeals or the Court of Federal Claims, alternative dispute resolutions, and judicial review of board or court decisions by the United States Court of Appeals for the Federal Circuit. The last section briefly reviews several types of relief outside the scope of the CDA.

The Disputes process is resorted to when the parties cannot settle their problems by agreement. It can be initiated by either the contractor or the government and involves a number of steps from the initial presentation of a matter to the possible (but rare) review by the Supreme Court. However, once the parties begin the process they are not obligated to continue. Either party can capitulate by abandoning the process at any stage. Hopefully they will be able to resolve the matter through negotiation. Figure 4-1 illustrates the procedures followed in the presentation, request, or litigation of claims. As will be noted, the parties have the choice at each stage of the process to conclude the matter through negotiation.

I. COVERAGE OF DISPUTES PROCESS

Although Congress, in passing the CDA, broadened the coverage of the Disputes clause, the Act does not make all disagreements between the government and a contractor subject to the process. The language delineating the scope of the Disputes clause is the phrase *relating to the contract*. This section deals with the criteria for determining whether a claim is one relating to the contract and thus subject to the disputes process.

Some, but not all, of the coverage issues are discussed in the following Chapter. To aid in determining coverage of specific issues, a summary of the Act's coverage is in Figure 4-2.

Figure 4-1

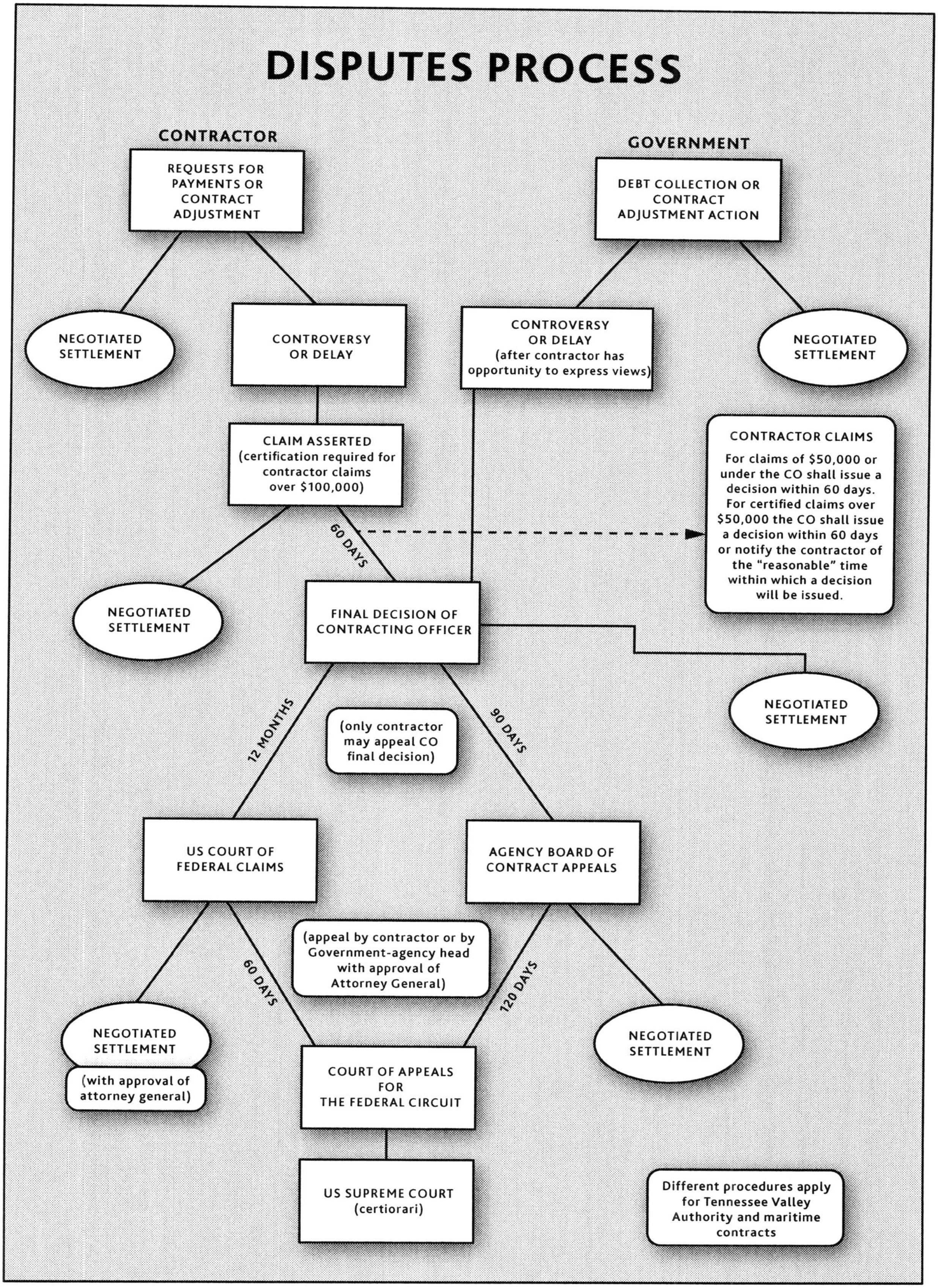
DISPUTES PROCESS
CONTRACTOR
REQUESTS FOR PAYMENTS OR CONTRACT ADJUSTMENT
GOVERNMENT
DEBT COLLECTION OR CONTRACT ADJUSTMENT ACTION
NEGOTIATED SETTLEMENT
CONTROVERSY OR DELAY
CONTROVERSY OR DELAY (after contractor has opportunity to express views)
NEGOTIATED SETTLEMENT
CLAIM ASSERTED (certification required for contractor claims over $100,000)
CONTRACTOR CLAIMS
For claims of $50,000 or under the CO shall issue a decision within 60 days. For certified claims over $50,000 the CO shall issue a decision within 60 days or notify the contractor of the "reasonable" time within which a decision will be issued.
60 DAYS
NEGOTIATED SETTLEMENT
FINAL DECISION OF CONTRACTING OFFICER
NEGOTIATED SETTLEMENT
12 MONTHS
(only contractor may appeal CO final decision)
90 DAYS
US COURT OF FEDERAL CLAIMS
AGENCY BOARD OF CONTRACT APPEALS
(appeal by contractor or by Government-agency head with approval of Attorney General)
60 DAYS
120 DAYS
NEGOTIATED SETTLEMENT
(with approval of attorney general)
COURT OF APPEALS FOR THE FEDERAL CIRCUIT
NEGOTIATED SETTLEMENT
US SUPREME COURT (certiorari)
Different procedures apply for Tennessee Valley Authority and maritime contracts

Figure 4-2

CDA Coverage	Mandatory Coverage	Coverage Excluded or Optional
Date of Contract	Contracts entered into after March 1, 1979[1]	Contracts entered into prior to March 1, 1979 excluded unless contractor elects coverage on final decisions issued after March 1, 1979[2]
Government Organization	Executive agencies[3] and exchange services[4]	Nonappropriated fund activities[5] other than exchange services[6]
Nature of Transaction	Procurement of property;[7] services;[8] construction, alteration, repair or maintenance of real property.[9] Disposal of personal property.[10] Leases of real property.[11] Maritime contracts involving procurement of property or services.[12]	Procurement of real property in being,[13] contracts with foreign governments or agencies[14]
Type of Agreement	Express or implied-in-fact contracts[15]	Implied-in-law contracts and implied contracts to consider bids or proposals fairly[16]
Type of Claim	Arising under or relating to a contract[17]	Restitution (quasi-contract)[18] claims not related to contract,[19] claims involving fraud,[20] claims involving statutory penalties or forfeitures under specific jurisdiction of another federal agency[21]
Nature of Relief	Money in a sum certain, adjustment or interpretation of contract terms, or other relief[22]	Injunctive relief[23] and declaratory judgment[24]

1 92 Stat. 2391.

2 92 Stat. 2391.

3 41 U.S.C. § 602(a). Executive agencies include independent establishments, military departments, wholly owned government corporations, the United States Postal Service and the Postal Rate Commission, 41 U.S.C. § 601(2). An entity's receipt of federal funds does not make it a federal agency for CDA purposes, Morgan v. United States, 55 Fed. Cl. 706 (2003). An agency selecting and buying for exchanges is an exchange, McDonald's Corp. v. United States, 926 F.2d 1126 (Fed. Cir. 1991).

4 28 U.S.C. § 1491.

5 Contracts of nonappropriated fund activities other than exchange services are not subject to 28 U.S.C. § 1491, Research Triangle Inst. v. Board of Governors of the Fed. Reserve Sys., 132 F.3d 985 (4th Cir. 1997) (Federal Reserve Board); Kyer v. United States, 177 Ct. Cl. 747, 369 F.2d 714 (1966), cert. denied, 387 U.S. 929 (1967) (agricultural marketing committee using no appropriated funds). For other nonappropriated fund activities not covered, see Furash & Co. v. United States, 252 F.3d 1336 (Fed. Cir. 2001) (Federal Housing Finance Board); AINS, Inc. v. United States., 56 Fed. Cl. 522 (2003), aff'd, 365 F.3d 1333 (Fed. Cir. 2004) (United States Mint); Core Concepts of Fla., Inc. v. United States, 327 F.3d 1331 (Fed. Cir. 2003) (Federal Prison Industries); and Trent Jones, Inc., AGBCA 98-104-1, 99-1 BCA ¶30,196 (United Soybean Board). But see MDB Communications, Inc. v. United States, 53 Fed. Cl. 245 (2002), holding that the Public Enterprise Fund of the United States Mint was an appropriated fund activity because it was a revolving fund.

6 41 U.S.C. § 602(b) (TVA may use CDA for contracts except those for sale of power or fertilizer).

7 41 U.S.C. § 602(a)(1). See City of Adelanlo, ASBCA 48202, 96-2 BCA ¶28,422 (procurement of water rights, because water is severable from real estate without material harm and, therefore, is personalty).

8 41 U.S.C. § 602(a)(2). See Enrique (Hank) Hernandez, ASBCA 53011, 01-1 BCA ¶31,220 (commissary agreement for grocery bagging services, even though the baggers were to be compensated solely by tips from shoppers at the commissary, is procurement of services).

9 41 U.S.C. § 602(a)(3).

10 41 U.S.C. § 602(a)(4). A dispute arising from a lease was subject to CDA jurisdiction because a lease involved the disposal of personal property rather than the sale of real property, William P. Schnaetzel, ENGBCA 6365, 98-2 BCA ¶29,937. Data used in exchange for services qualified the contract as a disposal of personal property contract so the CDA applied, Marketing & Mgmt. Info., Inc. v. United States, 57 Fed. Cl. 665 (2004).

11 6800 Corp., GSBCA 5880, 81-2 BCA ¶15,388; George Ungar, PSBCA 935, 82-1 BCA ¶15,549. See Up State Fed. Credit Union v. Walker, 198 F.3d 372 (2d Cir. 1999) (contract to build and operate a facility under a one-year land lease is a lease of real property giving CDA jurisdiction).

12 Marine Logistics, Inc. v. England, 265 F.3d 1322 (Fed. Cir. 2001) (appeals from boards of contract appeals decisions are to U.S. district courts, not the Federal Circuit, 41 U.S.C. § 603). Maritime contracts subject to admiralty jurisdiction are not under the CDA, 41 U.S.C. § 609. See Thrustmaster of Tex., Inc. v. United States, 59 Fed. Cl. 672 (2004) (ship repair contract).

13 41 U.S.C. § 602(a)(1).

14 41 U.S.C. § 602(c).

15 41 U.S.C. § 602(a). See Roy v. United States, 38 Fed. Cl. 184 (1997); National Micrographics Sys., Inc. v. United States, 38 Fed. Cl. 46 (1997); Charles Hartlerode, ASBCA 52634, 02-1 BCA ¶31,716 (appeal from a re-offer of an auction item was dismissed for lack of jurisdiction because there was no binding contract with the government); and D&N Bank v. United States, 331 F.3d 1374 (Fed. Cir. 2003) (no proof of mutuality of intent to contract and therefore no jurisdiction). In Gould, Inc. v. United States, 67 F.3d 925 (Fed. Cir. 1995), the court stated that, even when an express contract is illegal, a contractor may recover under an implied-in-fact contract in some circumstances.

16 Coastal Corp. v. United States, 713 F.2d 728 (Fed. Cir. 1983). In Barrett Ref. Corp. v. United States, 242 F.3d 1055 (Fed. Cir. 2001), the Federal Circuit held that the COFC had jurisdiction over the government's implied-in-law claim because the Tucker Act's prohibition on implied-in-law claims does not extend to counterclaims. See 28 U.S.C. §§ 1503, 2508.

[17] 41 U.S.C. § 605.

[18] Dean Prosser & Crew, IBCA 1471681, 81-2 BCA ¶15,294; Rowdybush, ASBCA 24955, 83-1 BCA ¶16,188, recons. denied, 83-1 BCA ¶16,442, recons. denied, 83-2 BCA ¶16,549.

[19] Western Pine Indus. Inc. v. United States, 231 Ct. Cl. 885 (1982).

[20] 41 U.S.C. § 605(a).

[21] 41 U.S.C. § 605(a). The Interstate Commerce Act, 31 U.S.C. § 3726, preempts the CDA regarding a contract for transportation of perishable foods, Inter-Coastal Xpress, Inc. v. United States. 49 Fed. Cl. 531 (2001).

[22] Pub. L. 102-572, § 907.

[23] Ulrich McMillan, GSBCA 7029COM, 83-2 BCA ¶16,595; Maria Manges, ASBCA 25350, 81-2 BCA ¶15,398, recons. denied, 82-1 BCA ¶15,665; Applied Ordnance Tech., Inc., ASBCA 51297, 98-2 BCA ¶30,023. See Western Aviation Maint., Inc. v. General Servs. Admin., GSBCA 14165, 98-2 BCA ¶29,816 (no jurisdiction over claims for specific performance). See also Veda, Inc. v. Department of the Air Force, 111 F.3d 37 (6th Cir. 1997) (District Court, not the Court of Federal Claims, had jurisdiction over the declaratory and injunctive relief sought by the contractor).

[24] A provision granting the Court of Claims jurisdiction under the Declaratory Judgments Act was deleted during the floor debate on the Contract Disputes Act, 124 Cong. Rec. S18,63941 (daily ed. Oct. 12, 1978). See Alaska Pulp Corp. v. United States, 38 Fed. Cl. 141 (1997) (contractor's claim for declaratory relief was not encompassed by the contractor's claims for monetary relief). Relief in the nature of declaratory relief is available through contract interpretation, Alliant Techsystems, Inc. v. United States, 178 F.3d 1260 (Fed. Cir. 1999). When the real issue is money and not the contract's terms, however, the board will refuse such declaratory relief, McDonnell Douglas Corp., ASBCA 50592, 97-2 BCA ¶29,199, recons. denied, 98-1 BCA ¶29,504. See also SUFI Network Servs., Inc., ASBCA 54503, 04-1 BCA ¶32,606. A contractor was not entitled to seek an advance determination of its liability before performing disputed work in Valley View Enters., Inc. v. United States, 35 Fed. Cl. 378 (1996).

A. Claims Relating to the Contract

Prior to the CDA, the Disputes clause stated that disputes procedures would apply to any dispute "concerning a question of fact arising under the contract." This was interpreted to mean that the court and boards had jurisdiction over a dispute only when the contract contained a "remedy granting" clause providing for the remedy requested by the contractor, *United States v. Utah Constr. & Mining Co.*, 384 U.S. 394 (1966).

The CDA, 41 U.S.C. § 605, broadened this coverage to all disputes "relating to the contract," providing:

> (a) All claims by a contractor against the Government relating to a contract shall be in writing and shall be submitted to the contracting officer for a decision. All claims by the Government against a contractor relating to a contract shall be the subject of a decision by the contracting officer . . ..

This "all-disputes" language encompasses both contract claims covered by remedy granting clauses and claims not covered by specific clauses in the contract. The Disputes clause at FAR 52.2331 incorporates both types of claims as follows:

> (b) Except as provided in the Act, all disputes arising under or relating to this contract shall be resolved under this clause.

The sweep of this language is pervasive. In *Burnside-Ott Aviation Training Ctr. v. Dalton,* 107 F. 3d 854 (Fed. Cir. 1997), the court held that a contract provision stating that the agency's award fee determination was not subject to the CDA was invalid. The court said that, by enacting the CDA, Congress, in effect, prohibited the use of such provisions. In *Rig Masters, Inc. v. United States*, 42 Fed. Cl. 369 (1998), a contracting officer's value engineering decision as to the contractor's share of savings was subject to the Contract Disputes Act and was therefore disputable despite the fact that the Value Engineering clause, FAR 52.248-1, states that such determinations are subjective and not subject to the Disputes Act. Compare *NI Indus., Inc. v. United States*, 841 F.2d 1104 (Fed. Cir. 1988) (holding that rejection of a value engineering proposal was an abuse of discretion), with *RCS Enters., Inc. v. United States,* 46 Fed. Cl. 509 (2000) (holding that rejection of a value engineering proposal was not subject to the CDA). See also *D&R Mach. Co.,* ASBCA 50730, 98-1 BCA ¶29,462, taking jurisdiction over an appeal from a contracting officer's decision to deny a contractor's claim for attorneys' fees and costs incurred in defending a trade misappropriation lawsuit in a U.S. District Court, notwithstanding the contractor's agreement in a previous District Court settlement waiving its right to appeal to the board. The board held that the parties could not, by agreement, override the plain dictates of Congress.

1. Remedy Granting Clauses

Most contracts contain a number of standard clauses granting remedies to either the government or contractor. For example, a contractor may be granted compensation or other remedies if the government orders additional work (Changes—Cost-Reimbursement, FAR 52.2432; Changes—Fixed-Price, FAR 52.2431), or if the government delays the contractor (Suspension of Work, FAR 52.21212). In addition, construction contracts contain a clause calling for an equitable adjustment if the contractor encounters unforeseen physical conditions (Differing Site Conditions, FAR 52.2362). Other clauses granting remedies include the Termination for the Convenience of the Government, FAR 52.2496 (applicable to both fixed-price and cost-reimbursement type contracts); Government Property (Fixed-Price Contracts), FAR 52.2452; Government Property (Cost-Reimbursement, Time-and-Material, or Labor-Hour Contracts), FAR 52.2455; Price Reduction for Defective Cost or Pricing Data, FAR 52.21522; Inspection of Services—Fixed-Price, FAR 52.2464 and Inspection of Services—Cost-Reimbursement, FAR 52.2465. The result is that most events leading to a claim are covered by contract clauses providing for the remedy sought.

2. Breach of Contract Claims

Under the pre-CDA procedure, "breach of contract" was a term of art used to refer to contractor claims alleging that the government failed to perform an express or implied duty for which no relief was available under the terms of the contract and which thus fell outside the scope of the pre-Act disputes process, *Globe Eng'g Co.*, ASBCA 23934, 83-1 BCA ¶16,370, *recons. denied*, 84-1 BCA ¶16,941. Since such breach of contract claims are related to the contract, they are within the scope of the statutory disputes process, *Essex Electro Eng'rs, Inc. v. United States*, 702 F.2d 998 (Fed. Cir. 1983); *Mega Constr. Co. v. United States*, 29 Fed. Cl. 396 (1993); *Stephens Assocs.*, PSBCA 1049, 84-1 BCA ¶16,921; *Tefft, Kelly & Motley, Inc.*, GSBCA 6562, 83-1 BCA ¶16,177, *recons. denied*, 83-1 BCA ¶16,279.

3. Mistakes Alleged After Award

Prior to the CDA, the appeals boards consistently held that they lacked jurisdiction over mistake allegations, other than as a basis for excusing a default. Such claims, however, are clearly related to the contract. Thus, FAR 33.205(b) now specifically provides that for postaward mistakes "[a] contractor's allegation that it is entitled to rescission or reformation of its contract in order to correct or mitigate the effect of a mistake shall be treated as a claim under the [Contract Disputes] Act." See *Paragon Energy Corp. v. United States*, 227 Ct. Cl. 176, 645 F.2d 966 (1981), *relief denied*, 230 Ct. Cl. 884 (1982), in which the court held that procuring agencies have authority under the CDA to reform contracts and award monetary relief to mitigate the effect of a unilateral bid mistake of which the government knew or had reason to know. See also *Gentex Corp.*, ASBCA 24040, 80-2 BCA ¶14,732. In *John J. Eufemio, M.D.*, ASBCA 26625, 82-2 BCA ¶15,990, *aff'd*, 702 F.2d 998 (Fed. Cir. 1983), the board held that, in spite of the fact that the contractor previously sought relief from the agency under Pub. L. 85-804, the board's jurisdiction to reform or rescind a contract after award (due to a bid mistake) was not affected. The board stated at 79,287:

> Since our consideration of all appeals is de novo, the fact that [the contractor] may have pursued his claim before the agency under a different theory than that now presented does not defeat his rights to have his appeal considered by us under a proper theory of recovery.

B. Government–Contractor Controversies Not Subject to Disputes Process

Although the coverage of the CDA has sometimes been referred to as an "all disputes" process, the Act does not extend to all controversies between the government and the contractor. Further, not all government instrumentalities are covered under the Act, and certain types of agreements are excluded. For instance, the Act does not cover nonappropriated fund activities other than exchange services; Tennessee Valley Authority (TVA) contracts, 41 U.S.C. § 602(b); the sale of real property, 41 U.S.C. § 602(a); or contracts with foreign governments or agencies, 41 U.S.C. § 602(c).

1. Independent Torts

The Court of Federal Claims and the boards have no jurisdiction to hear tort cases that are not also breaches of contract. The CDA did not expand the court's jurisdiction, which is limited by the Tucker Act, 28 U.S.C. § 1491, to "any claim against the United States founded . . . upon any express or implied contract with the United States . . . in cases not sounding in tort," *Allbritton v. United States*, 178 F.3d 1307 (Fed. Cir.1998); *H.H.O., Inc. v. United States*, 7 Cl. Ct. 703 (1985). The boards' jurisdiction is similarly limited, *Asfaltos Panamenos, S.A.*, ASBCA 39425, 91-1 BCA ¶23,315; *Aulson Roofing, Inc.*, ASBCA 37677, 91-2 BCA ¶23,720.

If, however, the purported tort relates to or arises out of an express or implied contractual obligation, the disputes process applies. See *Chain Belt v. United States*, 127 Ct. Cl. 38, 115 F. Supp. 701 (1953), in which the court stated at 54:

> Inasmuch as we found that [the government's] removal methods resulted in unnecessary and excessive damage to the floors, we discuss briefly [the government's] contention that this claim is beyond the court's jurisdiction because it sounds in tort. While it is true that this court does not have jurisdiction over claims sounding primarily in tort, an action may be maintained in this court which arises primarily from a contractual undertaking regardless of the fact that the loss resulted from the negligent manner in which [the government] performed its contract. *Chippewa Indians of Minnesota v. United States*, 91 Ct. Cl. 97, 130, 131. A tortious breach of contract is not a tort independent of the contract so as to preclude an action under the Tucker Act. *United States v. Huff*, 165 F.2d 720, 723.

See also *Awad v. United States*, 301 F.3d 1367 (Fed. Cir. 2002), stating "where a tort claim stems from a breach of contract, the cause of action is ultimately one arising in contract, and thus is properly within the exclusive jurisdiction of the Court of Federal Claims"; *Wood v. United States*, 961 F.2d 195 (Fed. Cir. 1992) (quoting *San Carlos Irrigation & Drainage Dist. v. United States*, 877 F.2d 957, 960 (Fed. Cir. 1989) "If an action arises 'primarily from a contractual undertaking,' jurisdiction lies in the Claims Court 'regardless of the fact that the loss resulted from the negligent manner in which defendant performed its contract.'").

Thus, even though a contractor alleges that a government employee has engaged in tortious conduct, the key question is whether that conduct was related to a contract. See, for example, *Thomas S. Rhoades & Stephen L. Schluneger*, ENGBCA 6097, 95-1 BCA ¶27,375, in which the board refused to dismiss as a tort claim a claim of a subcontractor that government employees were responsible for sinking a barge. The board construed the claim as a violation of the contractual duty to cooperate. Similarly, in *Richard T. Gannon*, ASBCA 47332, 95-1 BCA ¶27,422, the board held that the contractor's allegation that "a safe working environment is understood under the contract" sufficiently alleged an implied contractual obligation, which gave the board jurisdiction to decide the claim. See also *Maron Constr. Co. v. General Servs. Admin.*, GSBCA 13625, 98-1 BCA ¶29,497 (claim for fraud and deceit during contract formation a contract claim for nondisclosure of information and failure to cooperate); *L&M Thomas Concrete Co.*, ASBCA 49198, 98-1 BCA ¶29,560 (claims that government improperly assessed liquidated damages, improperly withheld payments, and improperly collected reprocurement costs not tort claims but had a contractual nexus to the defaulted contract); *Polaris Travel, Inc.*, EBCA C-9401166, 96-2 BCA ¶28,518 (subcontractor claims that contractor on behalf of the government converted drafts and misused proprietary information are both based on contract provisions); *Morris v. United States*, 33 Fed. Cl. 733 (1995) (misrepresentation during sale a contract claim); *Kolar, Inc.*, ASBCA 28482, 84-1 BCA ¶17,044 (contractor's allegation of fraudulent inducement, although containing elements of a tort action, was based on the contract); *Act IV Constr. Co.*, ASBCA 26378, 82-1 BCA ¶15,621 (government claim for damages for fire loss not a tort claim but under the Permits and Responsibilities clause); *Sierra Pac. Airlines*, AGBCA 821121, 82-1 BCA ¶15,710 (alleged tortious conduct of government employees who instructed the contractor to park its aircraft in an area covered with volcanic ash was contract claim under clause that allocated risk between the parties and placed the contractor under the government's control during performance); and *Electrospace Corp.* ASBCA 19742, 78-1 BCA ¶12,949 (claim that government and bank financing the contractor's performance had conspired to compel the contractor to accept settlement of a claim far below its fair value not a claim sounding in tort but a contract claim based on economic duress).

Although the court and boards have no jurisdiction under the CDA to hear pure tort claims, a contractor can resubmit a petition to "conform with the requirements of a contract claim," *Western Pine Indus., Inc. v. United States*, 231 Ct.

Cl. 885 (1982). Merely alleging, however, that the tort relates in some general sense to the contractual relationship is not sufficient to confer jurisdiction on the court or board: "Contractors must demonstrate a direct nexus between the Government's alleged tortious conduct and its obligations under the contract," *Asfaltos Panamenos, S.A.*, ASBCA 39425, 91-1 BCA ¶23,315. See also *H.H.O., Inc. v. United States*, 7 Cl. Ct. 703 (1985), and *L'Enfant Plaza Props., Inc. v. United States*, 227 Ct. Cl. 1, 645 F.2d 886 (1981).

The Court of Appeals for the Fourth Circuit held that U.S. District Courts lack jurisdiction over government tort claims against a contractor where the tort claims require examination and resolution of issues under the contract itself, *United States v. J&E Salvage Co.*, 55 F.3d 985 (4th Cir. 1995).

2. Fraud

The CDA provides that agency heads are not authorized to "settle, compromise, pay or otherwise adjust any claim involving fraud," 41 U.S.C. § 605(a). The Federal Circuit has held that this provision precludes the issue of fraud from being litigated under the CDA because fraud is assigned to the Department of Justice, *Martin J. Simko Constr. Co. v. United States*, 852 F.2d 540 (Fed. Cir. 1988). Similarly, the Court of Federal Claims lacks jurisdiction over a contractor's appeal from a contracting officer's decision that was based on his belief that the contractor had submitted fraudulent invoices for payment, *Medina Constr., Ltd. v. United States*, 43 Fed. Cl. 537 (1999). Boards also refuse to litigate contentions of fraud in the formation of a contract, *Thomas S. Rhoades*, ENGBCA 6025, 97-1 BCA ¶28,672.

The Act also provides at 41 U.S.C. § 604 that:

> If a contractor is unable to support any part of his claim and it is determined that such inability is attributable to misrepresentation of fact or fraud on the part of the contractor, he shall be liable to the Government for an amount equal to such unsupported part of the claim in addition to all costs to the Government attributable to the cost of reviewing said part of his claim. Liability under this subsection shall be determined within six years of the commission of such misrepresentation of fact or fraud.

Under both pre-Act and post-Act procedures, the boards have refused to litigate directly the issue of fraud but have frequently continued to process claims by severing the fraud element from the contract claim, *Time Contractors, (JV)*, DOTCAB 1669, 86-2 BCA ¶19,003. In determining whether to stay proceedings, the boards balance the contractor's right to an expeditious resolution of its dispute, 41 U.S.C. § 607(e), against the harm to the parties of trying fraud issues in a CDA case rather than in a civil or criminal fraud case. The current rule is summarized as follows in *Hardrives, Inc.*, IBCA 2319, 91-2 BCA ¶23,769, at 119,064:

> Traditionally, Boards have identified at least four situations in which they "should give consideration to suspending proceedings. . .balancing the estimated duration of the suspension against each party's right to a timely resolution." *Fidelity Construction Co.*, DOTCAB Nos. 1113, 1123, 80-2 BCA ¶14,819 at 73,142. They are: (1) when a criminal or civil action has been filed in a competent court involving issues directly relevant to the claims before the Board; (2) when [the Department of Justice] or other authorized investigatory authority formally has requested suspension to protect a civil action or to avoid conflict with a criminal investigation; (3) when the Government can demonstrate that a real possibility of fraud exists of such a nature effectively to preclude a Board from ascertaining the facts and circumstances surrounding a claim; and (4) when [a contractor] requests a suspension to avoid compromising rights in a potential or actual criminal proceeding.

In *Hardrives*, the government alleged fraud in every element of the claim and filed suit under the Civil False Claims Act, 31 U.S.C. § 3729, in a federal district court. Weighing the facts of the case, the board suspended the CDA proceedings. In contrast, the DOTBCA held it would not suspend proceedings on a mere allegation of fraud but would consider the particular circumstances presented in deciding whether to do so, *American Constr. Servs., Inc.*, DOTBCA 2993, 97-1 BCA ¶28,641. See also *Mayfair Constr. Co.*, NASABCA 4786, 80-1 BCA ¶14,261, in which the board suspended the case pending a court action. In *Northrop Corp., Northrop Elecs. Sys. Div. v. United States*, 27 Fed. Cl. 795 (1993), the contractor sought to have a Court of Federal Claims stay lifted for the limited purpose of allowing discovery on the contractor's CDA claims. Previously, the district court had issued an order staying a related case involving an allegation of false claims initiated by qui tam plaintiffs against Northrop Corporation. The district court subsequently lifted the stay. In the Court of Federal Claims case, the government argued that comity and judicial economy required continuance of the court's stay until the resolution of the district court proceeding. The court agreed with the government stating that the "close bond between the two litigations favors deferral of the instant proceeding." The court also stated that judicial economy "demanded" resolution of the district court action prior to continuance of the CDA claim.

Stays have been denied even though a fraud case is pending in a district court. In *Meridith Relocation Corp.*, GSBCA 9124, 90-2 BCA ¶22,677, *recons. denied,* 90-3 BCA ¶23,129, the board denied a stay even though a civil fraud case had recently been filed in a district court. The board reasoned that the issues were not identical and that the contractor had a right to an expeditious resolution of its appeal of a default termination. Similarly, in *TDC Mgmt. Corp.*, DOTBCA 1802, 90-1 BCA ¶22,627, the board declined to suspend an appeal, pending resolution of a concurrent civil action under the False Claims Act, noting that the issues on appeal were separate from those under the False Claims Act proceeding. The board stated that the False Claims Act proceeding involved falsified progress reports whereas the appeal before the board involved a claim for reimbursement of a cost overrun.

Stays are more likely to be denied if the government has not filed a criminal or civil fraud case in court. See, for example, *Triax Co.*, ASBCA 33899, 88-3 BCA ¶20,830, in which the board refused to grant a stay upon the "mere allegation" of fraud by the government, and *Fleischzentrale Sudwest GmbH*, ASBCA 37273, 89-3 BCA ¶21,956, in which the board refused to stay the proceedings even though the government had submitted an affidavit stating that a criminal investigation was underway. In *Fleischzentrale*, the board stated a stringent test for the government at 110,444:

> [T]he Government . . . is obliged to show a compelling "need in terms of protecting the criminal litigation" which "overrides the injury to the parties being stayed" and that "there are `substantially similar' issues, facts and witnesses in both proceedings," *E-Systems, Inc.*, [ASBCA 32033, 88-2 BCA ¶20,753] at 104,868. "[T]he supplicant for a stay must make out a clear case of hardship or inequity in being required to go forward, *if there is even a fair possibility* that the stay for which he prays will work damage to someone else," [emphasis added] *Landis v. North American Company*, 229 U.S. 248, 255 (1936).

The ASBCA has been the most aggressive board in determining that fraud does not totally deprive it of jurisdiction. In *Nexus Constr. Co.*, ASBCA 51004, 98-1 BCA ¶29,375, the board held that an allegation that the contractor submitted a fraudulent claim does not deprive the board of jurisdiction under the CDA. In *Donat Gerg Haustechnik*, ASBCA 41197, 96-2 BCA ¶28,333, the board held that it is not prohibited from considering assertions of fraud in a counterclaim against a contractor because the prohibition against consideration of issues involving fraud in the CDA, 41 USC § 605(a), applies to agency heads, not boards. Similarly, the government was permitted to raise fraud as an affirmative defense to the contractor's claim even though the board would not have jurisdiction over a counterclaim of fraud unless it had been set forth in the contracting officer's final decision, *ORC, Inc.*, ASBCA 49693, 96-2 BCA ¶28,371; *Westphal GmbH & Co.*, ASBCA 39401, 96-1 BCA ¶28,194, *recons. denied,* 96-2 BCA ¶28,466, *aff'd in part, remanded in part,* 135 F.3d 778 (Fed. Cir. 1998) (case remanded so board could consider unpriced work claims). In *TRW, Inc.*, ASBCA 51172, 99-2 BCA ¶30,407, the board held that it had jurisdiction over a contractor's contract interpretation claim although the underlying facts were also the subject of two parallel U.S. District Court qui tam lawsuits under the False Claims Act.

If a board decides a case in which the government contends that fraud is present, the contractor probably will not collect on the decision until the fraud allegation is resolved, *TDC Mgmt. Corp.*, DOTBCA 1802, 88-1 BCA ¶20,242. In *TDC*, the board stated at 102,466 that:

> Government agencies have legal authority to withhold payment from a contractor of amounts which a Board determines to be due that contractor on a claim, in the nature of set-off, until issues of fraud have been disposed of by a court having jurisdiction over Government claims for civil or criminal penalties.

In *United States v. Marovic*, 69 F.Supp. 2d 1190 (N.D. Cal. 1999), the government argued that its breach of contract and unjust enrichment claims were properly before the District Court because the CDA's exclusive jurisdiction does not apply to any claim "involving fraud," 41 USC § 605(a). Noting that the CDA was established to foster administrative resolution of government contract disputes, the District Court adopted a narrow reading of the "involving fraud" exception to CDA jurisdiction and held that the exception did not apply in this case because the government could prove its contract claims against the contractor without proving that the contractor itself committed fraud.

Although in most cases the contract and fraud claims are heard in separate forums, the Court of Federal Claims can take jurisdiction over both civil fraud and contract claims when the contractor asserts a contract claim and the government subsequently asserts the civil fraud as a counterclaim, *Young-Montenay, Inc. v. United States*, 15 F.3d 1040 (Fed. Cir. 1994). In this situation, the decision of whether to merge the claims in a single court is in the hands of the Department of Justice. For cases in which both civil fraud and contract claims were merged in the Court of Federal Claims, see *Godley v. United States*, 26 Cl. Ct. 1075 (1992), *vacated and remanded on other grounds*, 5 F.3d 1473 (Fed. Cir. 1993), and *Sterling Millwrights, Inc. v. United States*, 26 Cl. Ct. 49 (1992). In these cases, although the court heard the government's fraud counterclaims, it dismissed all of the charges as either late or insufficiently supported by the evidence. Fraud counterclaims also may be filed by the government without first obtaining a contracting officer decision on the counterclaims, *Martin J. Simko Constr., Inc. v. United States*, 852 F.2d 540 (Fed. Cir. 1988). This rule is premised on the fact that a contracting officer has no authority under the CDA to handle fraud claims. One of the outcomes of this procedure is that the contractor gives up its right to a jury trial on the fraud claim, which has been held to be a consequence of the contractor's election to file its contract claim in the Court of Federal Claims, *BMY-Combat Sys. Div. of Harsco Corp. v. United States*, 26 Cl. Ct. 846 (1992). See also *Daff v. United States*, 78 F.3d 1566 (Fed. Cir. 1996), in which the court ruled that the Court of Federal Claims had jurisdiction of a default termination even though the contracting officer's decision referred to contractor fraud because there were other grounds for the termination. Having such jurisdiction also gave the court jurisdiction over the government's counterclaim under the False Claims Act even though there had been no contracting officer decision on that issue.

Section 2354 of the Federal Acquisition Streamlining Act of 1994, Pub. L. 103-355, amended the CDA to give U.S. District Court judges authority to obtain advisory opinions from boards of contract appeals by adding the following to 41 U.S.C. § 609:

> (f)(1) Whenever an action involving an issue described in paragraph (2) is pending in a district court of the United States, the district court may request a board of contract appeals to provide the court with an advisory opinion on the matters of contract interpretation at issue.
>
> (2) An issue referred to in paragraph (1) is any issue that could be the proper subject of a final decision of a contracting officer appealable under this Act.
>
> (3) A district court shall direct any request under paragraph (1) to the board of contract appeals having jurisdiction under this Act to adjudicate appeals of contract claims under the contract or contracts being interpreted by the court.
>
> (4) After receiving a request for an advisory opinion under paragraph (1), a board of contract appeals shall provide the advisory opinion in a timely manner to the district court making the request.

This authority could be used to obtain advisory opinions on contract issues involved in fraud cases.

3. Penalties or Forfeitures Administered by Other Agencies

41 U.S.C. § 605(a) provides:

> The authority of this subsection shall not extend to a claim or dispute for penalties or forfeitures prescribed by statute or regulation which another federal agency is specifically authorized to administer, settle or determine.

The legislative history is silent on the meaning of this statutory language, the primary effect of which has been to exclude certain labor-related disputes from the scope of the disputes process. Historically, the boards have refused to exercise jurisdiction over matters that involve determining the contractor's obligations under a variety of statutes prescribing labor standards for contractors. These statutes include the Davis-Bacon Act, 40 U.S.C. § 276; the Service Contract Act, 41 U.S.C. § 351; and the Contract Work Hours and Safety Standards Act, 40 U.S.C. § 327. See *Imperator Carpet & Interiors, Inc.*, GSBCA 6167, 81-2 BCA ¶15,266; *Wickham Contracting Co.*, GSBCA 6579, 82-2 BCA ¶15,883; and *James B. Nolan Investigative & Protective Co.*, GSBCA 5905, 82-2 BCA ¶15,943. In addition, boards held that they lacked jurisdiction to consider a maritime subcontractor's claim, despite District Court precedent to the contrary, *Southwest Marine, Inc.*, ASBCA 49617, 96-2 BCA ¶28,347.

In *Dalton v. Sherwood Van Lines, Inc.*, 50 F.3d 1014 (Fed. Cir. 1995), the court concluded that the CDA provided no jurisdictional basis for disputes concerning transportation services obtained from common carriers through government bills of lading. See *Merchants Moving & Storage, Inc.*, ASBCA 48308, 95-2 BCA ¶27,789, which relied on *Dalton* and held the board had no jurisdiction. This undercuts the validity of *Merchants Moving & Storage Inc.*, ASBCA 47370, 95-1 BCA ¶27,298, which held the board had subject matter jurisdiction over a dispute arising out of a contract to transport household goods because the CDA contains broad language in covering contracts for vehicular services and does not specifically exempt agreements that might also be covered by the Interstate Commerce Act or the Transportation Act of 1940. See also *Stapp Touring Co.*, ASBCA 48375, 96-2 BCA ¶28,293 (a dispute under a bulk fuel transportation contract was governed by the Interstate Commerce Act and deprived the board of jurisdiction). See *Custom Blending & Packaging, Inc.*, ASBCA 49819, 00-2 BCA ¶31,083, holding that the board had no authority to consider a claim that Department of Agriculture inspectors had delayed performance because they were functioning under a separate statute calling for inspection of plants processing food products.

The matters that other agencies have cognizance over are usually issues in the Labor Department. Service contracts subject to the Service Contract Act contain the following provision in the Service Contract Act of 1965, As Amended clause, FAR 52.222-41:

> (t) *Disputes Concerning Labor Standards.* The U.S. Department of Labor has set forth in 29 CFR parts 4, 6, and 8 procedures for resolving disputes concerning labor standards requirements. Such disputes shall be resolved in accordance with those procedures and not the Disputes clause of this contract. Disputes within the meaning of this clause include disputes between the Contractor (or any of its subcontractors) and the contracting agency, the U.S. Department of Labor, or the employees or their representatives.

See *J.R. Cheshier Janitorial*, ENGBCA 5487-Q, 95-1 BCA ¶27,376 no board jurisdiction over dispute on requirement to pay overtime); *Ball, Ball & Brosamerr Inc.*, IBCA 3542-95, 98-1 BCA ¶29,637 (no board jurisdiction over a dispute involving the proper classification of laborers for wage purposes); and *Midland Maint., Ins.*, ENGBCA 6080, 96-2 BCA ¶28,302 (no board jurisdiction over a dispute involving wage classification). Compare *Inter-Con Sec. Sys., Inc.*, ASBCA 46251, 95-1 BCA ¶27,424, in which the board took jurisdiction to decide whether a modification of a collective bargaining agreement was part of a wage determination by the Department of Labor because the board's decision was neither the making of a wage determination nor a ruling on the propriety of a wage determination.

Construction contracts contain the following Disputes Concerning Labor Standards clause, FAR 52.222-14:

> The United States Department of Labor has set forth in 29 CFR parts 5, 6, and 7 procedures for resolving disputes concerning labor standards requirements. Such disputes shall be resolved in accordance with those procedures and not the Disputes clause of this contract. Disputes within the meaning of this clause include disputes between the Contractor (or any of its subcontractors) and the contracting agency, the U.S. Department of Labor, or the employees or their representatives.

See *Emerald Maint., Inc. v. United States*, 925 F.2d 1425 (Fed. Cir. 1991) (no board jurisdiction over application of wage determination). Compare *MMC Constr. Inc.*, ASBCA 50863, 99-1 BCA ¶30,322, taking jurisdiction to decide a contractor's breach of contract claim against the government based on excessive withholding of Davis-Bacon Act wages because the Department of Labor had completed its investigation of the alleged wage underpayments and the government had withheld those amounts from contract progress payments due the contractor. The board concluded that, although DOL wage determinations generally may be disputed only through DOL's administrative process, where that process is completed and a contractor "claims a price adjustment for the effects of the DOL wage determination," the boards (or Court of Federal Claims) have jurisdiction of the claim under the CDA. The GSBCA reached the same conclusion in *Twigg Corp. v. General Servs. Admin.*, GSBCA 14639, 99-1 BCA ¶30,217.

4. Contract Award Controversies and Mistakes Alleged Prior to Award

Challenges to procurement contract award procedures are not subject to the CDA. The Act covers disputes between the contractor and the government that arise during or after the performance of a contract but does not cover contract award controversies that result when an offeror or prospective contractor contests the award of the contract or the conduct of the solicitation process itself, *Coastal Corp. v. United States*, 713 F.2d 728 (Fed. Cir. 1983). The Competition in Contracting Act (CICA) establishes protest procedures for challenging the conduct of an agency procurement process. For a discussion of these protest procedures, see *Formation of Government Contracts* (3d ed. 1998), Chapter 11. See also *Meyers Co.*, ENG-BCA 6360, 98-1 BCA ¶29,473 (board lacked jurisdiction over a bid protest involving a solicitation for outleases because the Secretary of the Army had delegated authority to consider only appeals concerning leases and lessees, not protests by disappointed bidders); *Integrated Sys. Group Inc.*, GSBCA 11336-C (11214-P), 95-1 BCA ¶27,308 (board had no jurisdiction over intervenor's motion to recover costs of defending a protest brought in bad faith because it lacked authority to adjudicate rights between private parties); *Ammon Circuits Research*, ASBCA 50885, 97-2 BCA ¶29,318 (no jurisdiction over agency's failure to award contract); and *RC 27th Ave. Corp.*, ASBCA 49176, 97-1 BCA ¶28,658 (no jurisdiction of claim for lost profits because of failure to award contract).

Preaward mistakes also are not covered by the CDA. Suspected mistakes in contractors' proposals are dealt with either as clarifications or discussions, depending on the circumstances. For a discussion of this process, see *Formation of Government Contracts* (3d ed. 1998), Chapter 6, and *Cost-Reimbursement Contracting* (3d ed. 2004), Chapter 5.

5. Violation of Statutory or Constitutional Rights

The boards lack jurisdiction to consider claims of racial discrimination under the Fifth Amendment or any federal statute, *Starghill Alternative Energy Corp.*, ASBCA 49612, 98-1 BCA ¶29,708; *Duran Constr. Co.*, AGBCA 19991712, 00-1 BCA ¶30,758 (no jurisdiction over contractor's claim for "racial prejudice"); *Northeast Air Group, Inc.*, ASBCA 46350, 95-2 BCA ¶27,679 (no jurisdiction over alleged violation of contractor's civil rights). The boards have also held that they have no jurisdiction over claims under other statutes. See *McKirch & Co.*, ASBCA 51824, 99-2 BCA ¶30,468 (no jurisdiction over alleged violations of the Constitution, the Trade Secrets Act, the Copyright Act, state Trade Secrets Acts, and the common law), and *Data Enters. of the Northwest v. General Servs. Admin.*, GSBCA 15607, 04-1 BCA ¶32,539 (no jurisdiction over alleged violations of the Copyright Act or Fifth Amendment takings). Compare *Ervin & Assocs., Inc. v. United States*, 59 Fed. Cl. 267 (2004), in which the Court of Federal Claims ruled on a claim for copyright infringement.

Although the Court of Federal Claims has jurisdiction over "taking" claims under the Fifth Amendment pursuant to the Tucker Act, the boards of contract appeals have no such jurisdiction under the CDA, *United Techs. Corp.*, ASBCA 46880, 95-1 BCA ¶27,456, *recons. denied*, 95-2 BCA ¶27,698; *Sermor, Inc.*, ASBCA 46956, 95-2 BCA ¶27,748.

C. Subcontractor Controversies

Generally, subcontractors have no right to use the disputes process in their own name. See *Lockheed Martin Corp. v. United States*, 50 Fed. Cl. 550 (2001), *aff'd*, 48 Fed. Appx. 752 (Fed. Cir. 2002); *Detroit Broach Cutting Tools, Inc.*, ASBCA 49277, 96-2 BCA ¶28,493; *Southwest Marine, Inc.*, ASBCA 49617, 96-2 BCA ¶28,347; and *Department of Army v. Blue Fox*, 525 U.S. 255 (1999). However, in the rare case where a subcontractor is in privity of contract with the government, it may file a claim directly against the government. If there is no privity, the subcontractor's claim must be sponsored by the contractor.

1. Direct Subcontractor Claims

It is against the government's policy to deal directly with subcontractors. See FAR 44.203(b)(3), which prohibits contracting officers from giving their consent to "subcontracts obligating the contracting officer to deal directly with the subcontractor." As a result, direct subcontractor claims are very rare.

There are several possible—but not often successful—ways for a subcontractor to establish privity. In some cases, the government has entered into a direct contractual relationship with a subcontractor. See *United States v. Georgia Marble Co.*, 106 F.2d 955 (5th Cir. 1939), in which the court found that the government entered into an implied contract to pay the subcontractor for material the government took from the subcontractor. Such cases are extremely rare. In addition, direct subcontractor claims have been permitted if the contractor is an agent of the government, *Kern-Limerick v. Scurlock*, 347 U.S. 110 (1954). Here, too, the likelihood of a contractor being considered an agent of the government is remote. In *United States v. Johnson Controls, Inc.*, 713 F.2d 1541 (Fed. Cir. 1983), *aff'd*, 827 F.2d 1554 (Fed. Cir. 1987), the court held that a contractor that served as a construction manager was not, for that reason, an agent of the government. The court stated that the contractor was not a purchasing agent, that there was no contractual designation of an agency relationship with the government, and that the government was not bound to pay the subcontractor directly. See also *United States v. New Mexico*, 455 U.S. 720 (1982), in which the Court stated that contractors operating government facilities had a substantially independent role in making purchases, were not agents of the government, and, therefore, were not immune from taxation. Similarly, in *Parsons Brinckerhoff Quade & Douglas, Inc.*, DOTCAB 1299, 84-2 BCA ¶17,309, the board denied a subcontractor's claim, holding that the subcontractor had no privity with the government. The board stated at 86,266:

> It is a general rule that, under the Tucker Act, a subcontractor cannot recover directly from the Government as there is no contractual relationship. *Merritt v. United States*, 267 U.S. 338 (1925). However, if some type of contract can be found to exist between a subcontractor and the Government, an action may be directly brought. *United States v. Munsey Trust Co.* [4 CCF ¶60,304], 332 U.S. 234, 241 (1947). In *Kern-Limerick Inc. v. Scurlock* [6 CCF ¶61,498], 347 U.S. 110 (1954) and *Western Union Telegraph Co. v. United States*, 66 Ct. Cl. 38 (1938), the courts permitted a subcontractor to bring an action directly against the United States since the prime contractor was simply acting as the Government's agent. Both of these cases have carved out narrow exceptions to the general rule that waivers of sovereign immunity are to be strictly construed. *United States v. Mitchell*, 445 U.S. 535 (1980).

The board found that the government had made it clear that it could not deal directly with Parsons and that Parsons assented to this relationship by executing its contract with the contractor and by requesting payment from the contractor. Thus, the board found that there was no contractual relationship between the government and the subcontractor. For a discussion of agency relationship between the government and a contractor, see Chapter 1.

The most feasible way of establishing privity is for the subcontractor to make its claim as a third-party beneficiary of the government's agreement with a contractor. See *Maneely v. United States*, 68 Ct. Cl. 623 (1929). See also *D & H Distrib. Co. v. United States*, 102 F.3d 542 (Fed. Cir. 1996), in which the court found that a subcontractor had a third-party beneficiary relationship with the government when the contracting officer had modified the contract to make the contractor and the subcontractor joint payees. In addition, despite the statutory prohibition on the assignment of rights in government contracts, the court found that the contract modification at issue could be viewed as a valid assignment of payment rights from the contractor to the subcontractor because the contracting officer assented to the assignment. The government's subsequent failure to make payments according to the modified contract was a breach entitling the subcontractor to damages. See also *FloorPro, Inc.*, ASBCA 54143, 04-1 BCA 32571 (board has jurisdiction of subcontractor appeal as third-party beneficiary). But see *JGB Enters., Inc. v. United States,* 63 Fed. Cl. 319 (2004), stating that the Federal Circuit in D&H had only allowed third-party jurisdiction on the basis of the Tucker Act, not the CDA but granting relief as a third-party beneficiary on one contract. See also *Flexfab, L.L.C. v. United States,* 62 Fed. Cl. 139 (2004), *aff'd*, 424 F.3d 1254 (Fed. Cir. 2005), denying recovery as third-party beneficiary because the government employee that authorized the payment to an agent of the subcontractor had no contracting officer authority.

Contracts administered through the Small Business Administration (SBA) 8(a) Program are technically contracts between the procuring agency and the SBA; the SBA then subcontracts out to preferred 8(a) contractors. However, the boards have uniformly held that such SBA subcontractors are in privity with the government and, therefore, able to bring claims directly against the government under the Disputes Act, *Decorama Painting, Inc.*, ASBCA 25299, 81-1 BCA ¶14,992, *modified on other grounds*, 82-1 BCA ¶15,746. Some Department of Energy Management and Operations (M&O) contracts contained provisions authorizing subcontractors to obtain decisions by contracting officers and to take appeals to the Department's board of contract appeals. See, e.g., *Lafollette Coal Co.*, EBCA 336585, 87-3 BCA ¶20,099. Where the M&O contract does not contain such a provision, the board will not take the subcontractor's appeal, *Johnson Tank & Tower Co.*, EBCA 9302148, 93-3 BCA ¶26,251.

2. Indirect (Sponsored) Subcontractor Claims

Sponsored claims are permitted only if the contractor can charge the cost of the subcontractor's claim to the government contract or make a claim against the government based on the subcontractor's recovery. This practice, developed under the pre-statutory process, has been continued under the CDA. The contractor sponsors the subcontractor's claim by bringing an appeal on the subcontractor's behalf or by permitting the subcontractor to bring an appeal in the contractor's name. FAR 44.203(c) explicitly allows indirect subcontractor appeals and provides that:

> Contracting officers should not refuse consent to a subcontract merely because it contains a clause giving the subcontractor the right of indirect appeal to an agency board of contract appeals if the subcontractor is affected by a dispute between the Government and the prime contractor. Indirect appeal means assertion by the subcontractor of the prime contractor's right to appeal or the prosecution of an appeal by the prime contractor on the subcontractor's behalf. The clause may also provide that the prime contractor and subcontractor shall be equally bound by the contracting officer's or board's decision. The clause may not attempt to obligate the contracting officer or the appeals board to decide questions that do not arise between the Government and the prime contractor or that are not cognizable under the clause at 52.2331, Disputes.

The Severin Doctrine limits a subcontractor's right to have its claim sponsored by the contractor. It is based upon the theory that if the contractor has not paid the subcontractor and has no possible liability to the subcontractor, the contractor has suffered no harm at the hands of the government. See *Severin v. United States*, 99 Ct. Cl. 435 (1943), *cert. denied*, 322 U.S. 733 (1944), holding that, if the subcontract contains a clause exculpating the contractor from liability for damages to the subcontractor, the contractor may sue on behalf of its subcontractor only if the contractor has reimbursed its subcontractor for the latter's damages or remains liable for such reimbursement in the future. Later cases have limited the application of the *Severin* doctrine by interpreting exculpatory clauses as applying only to breach of contract claims. Thus, the doctrine has been held inapplicable to claims covered by contract clauses, such as those for constructive changes, for equitable adjustment under the Changes clause. See *F.E. Constructors*, ASBCA 25784, 82-1 BCA ¶15,780, and *Aydin Corp.*, EBCA 355586, 89-3 BCA ¶22,044. Similarly, see *CWC, Inc.*, ASBCA 26432, 82-2 BCA ¶15,907, in which the board held that the *Severin* Doctrine was inapplicable to a contractor's sponsorship of a claim for a price adjustment because the claim was redressable under the contract's Suspension of Work clause. The same result has been reached for claims based on the Differing Site Conditions clause, *Turner Constr. Co.*, ASBCA 25602, 87-3 BCA ¶20,192; *Tutor-Saliba-Parini*, PSBCA 1201, 87-2 BCA ¶19,775, *aff'd*, 847 F.2d 842 (Fed. Cir. 1988). If the exculpatory clause does not completely free the contractor from liability, sponsorship will be permitted. Thus, when the subcontract provides that the contractor will pass subcontractor claims through to the government but will have no further liability, it has been held that the *Severin* doctrine does not bar the claim, *Castagna & Son, Inc.*, GSBCA 6906, 84-3 BCA ¶17,612. See also *Folk Constr. Co. v. United States*, 2 Cl. Ct. 681 (1983), and *Pan Arctic Corp. v. United States*, 8 Cl. Ct. 546 (1985). A clause that relieves the contractor from responsibility to the subcontractor for price increases, damages, and additional compensation as a consequence of delay does not necessarily preclude the contractor from recovering against the government on behalf of its subcontractor; *Roberts, JR. Corp.*, DOTBCA 2499, 98-1 BCA ¶29,680. In *Ball, Ball & Brasamer, Inc.*, IBCA 2841, 97-1 BCA ¶28,897, the board held that the doctrine did not apply because the contractor was liable to the subcontractor for any payment the contractor received from the government, and the subcontractor had not released its claim against the contractor.

The Severin Doctrine will not apply if the agreement between the parties conditions the contractor's liability to the subcontractor on recovery from the government, *J.L. Simmons Co. v. United States*, 158 Ct. Cl. 393, 304 F.2d 886 (1962). In *W.G. Yates & Sons Constr. Co. v. Caldera*, 192 F.3d 987 (Fed. Cir. 1999), both the contractor and a subcontractor pursued their claim against the government pursuant to a "Liquidation and Consolidation Claim Agreement" where the contractor agreed to sponsor the claims and pay the subcontractor the amount it recovered. In exchange, the contractor received a promise to pay the contractor's reprocurement costs regardless of the board's decision. The court determined that this agreement making the contractor "conditionally liable" to the subcontractor avoided the application of the Severin Doctrine.

Although the Severin Doctrine has infrequently precluded sponsored claims, it still has vitality in those cases in which the contractor has paid the subcontractor no money and is not even conditionally liable. See *James Reeves Contractor, Inc. v. United States*, 31 Fed. Cl. 712 (1994), in which an arbitration binding under state law denied the subcontractor's claim against the contractor without reservation. In *George Hyman Constr. Co. v. United States*, 30 Fed. Cl. 170 (1993), *aff'd*, 39 F.3d 1197 (Fed. Cl. 1994), the subcontractor executed a general release in favor of the contractor. The court held that this release was unconditional and that sponsorship was not permitted. The court rejected the contractor's argument that the parties had not intended to include the particular claim in the release. It also rejected a later release excepting the claim. The court held that even if the later release were binding under state law, sponsorship would not be permitted because it depended on "continuing" not "revived" liability.

The right of a subcontractor to appeal in the name of a contractor has been affirmed, even when the contractor has neither paid the claim nor admitted liability, as long as the claim is made in good faith, *TRW, Inc.*, ASBCA 11373, 66-2 BCA ¶5882, and the contractor intends to be held liable for any possible fraud attributable to assertion of the claim, *Transamerica Ins. Corp., Inc. v. United States*, 973 F.2d 1572 (Fed. Cir. 1992); *Blake Constr. Co. v. United States*, 28 Fed. Cl. 672 (1993), *aff'd*, 29 F.3d 645 (Fed. Cir. 1994). However, the fact that the contractor does not agree with the subcontractor may be used as evidence of the reasonableness of the government's position, *Willard-Brent Co.*, GSBCA 3651, 73-2 BCA ¶10,134. Sponsorship is considered an evidentiary rather than a jurisdictional matter. Thus, it is sufficient if sponsorship is alleged by statements in the complaint. Proof of sponsorship is not necessary at the time of filing the notice of appeal, although a complete failure to plead sponsorship would give rise to the jurisdictional question, *Dawson Constr. Co.*, EBCA 155281, 81-2 BCA ¶15,162. See *Coastal Drilling, Inc.*, ASBCA 54023, 03-1 BCA ¶32,241 (board refused to take jurisdiction of an unsponsored claim of a subcontractor even where fraud on the part of the contractor is alleged); *Malaspina Invs., Inc. (Sampson Steel Co., Subcontractor)*, AGBCA 2003-180-1, 04-1 BCA ¶32,418 (board took jurisdiction based on letter from contractor's president, sent after 90-day appeal period had expired, stating that contractor's project coordinator had requested subcontractor to send appeal directly to the board); and *J. E. McAmis, Inc.* ASBCA 54455, 04-2 BCA ¶32,746 (appeal was proper when contractor certified and forwarded subcontractor's Notice of Appeal and requested that it be sent a Rule 4 file even though contractor did not specifically state that it was appealing the contracting officer's decision).

Although a contractor may sponsor the claim of a subcontractor, the subcontractor has no privity of contract with the government and is not a proper party before a board of contract appeals. See *Zenith Data Sys.*, ASBCA 49611, 98-1 BCA ¶29,721, in which the board denied a contractor's request to add its subcontractor as a "co-appellant." See also *McPherson Contractors, Inc.*, ASBCA 50830, 98-1 BCA ¶29,349 (board has no jurisdiction over an appeal by a contractor on behalf of its subcontractor after the contractor withdrew its sponsorship). After a termination for default, a surety took over and entered into a subcontract with the original contractor to complete the job. On appeal, the default termination was overturned and converted to a termination for convenience. The board held it did not have jurisdiction over that part of the termination settlement proposal covering costs incurred while contractor was acting as subcontractor to the surety because the claim was not sponsored by the surety, *Walsky Constr. Co.*, ASBCA 52772, 01-2 BCA ¶31,557.

II. ASSERTION OF CLAIMS

The submission of a claim initiates the disputes process. The contractor's claim triggers the contracting officer's obligation to make a timely decision, 41 U.S.C. § 605(c), and begins the running of interest, 41 U.S.C. § 611. The CDA contains no definition of the word *claim*. It does, however, at 41 U.S.C. § 605(a), specify two requirements for a claim: "All claims by a contractor against the Government relating to a contract shall be in writing and shall be submitted to the contracting officer for a decision." The Disputes clause at FAR 52.233-1 provides additional guidance on the definition of *claim*, as follows:

> Claim, as used in this clause, means a written demand or written assertion by one of the contracting parties seeking, as a matter of right, the payment of money in a sum certain, the adjustment or interpretation of contract

terms, or other relief arising under or relating to this contract. . . . A voucher, invoice, or other routine request for payment that is not in dispute when submitted is not a claim under the Act. The submission may be converted into a claim under the Act, by complying with the submission and certification requirements of this clause, if it is disputed either as to liability or amount or is not acted upon in a reasonable time.

The following discussion considers the essential elements of a claim by examining the requirement that a claim be a nonroutine request for payment; the assertion of nonmonetary claims; the elements of a contractor claim; the assertion of a government claim; and the time for submittal of claims.

A. Nonroutine Requests for Price Adjustment

The early interpretation of the term "claim" had treated the first two sentences of the FAR definition as establishing the full requirements governing whether a contractor had properly asserted a claim under the CDA. However, in *Dawco Constr., Inc. v. United States*, 930 F.2d 872 (Fed. Cir. 1991), the Federal Circuit read the entire definition to require that no contractor claim (not just undisputed requests for payment) could be properly asserted unless there had been a "preexisting dispute." Since there was virtually no support for this interpretation in the history of the drafting of the CDA or its implementation in the FAR, the issue was reconsidered by the court in *Reflectone, Inc. v. Dalton*, 60 F.3d 1572 (Fed. Cir. 1995). That decision overruled *Dawco* and held that only claims for routine requests for payment had to be based on preexisting disputes. Thus, a contractor submitting a "nonroutine" request for additional compensation or other action under the Disputes clause is not required to bring the matter to "dispute" between the parties before it can submit a valid claim under the CDA.

1. Distinguishing Routine and Nonroutine Requests for Payment

All requests for price adjustment called for by contract clauses constitute nonroutine requests—including a request for equitable adjustment for a constructive change, *AAA Eng'g & Drafting, Inc.*, ASBCA 47940, 99-2 BCA ¶ 30,443; *McDonnell Douglas Corp.*, ASBCA 46582, 96-2 BCA ¶ 28,377; a request for equitable adjustment for ordered changes, *Triad Microsystems, Inc.*, ASBCA 39478, 99-1 BCA ¶ 30,234; a request for an equitable adjustment for a recognized differing site condition, *J.S. Alberici Constr. Co.*, ENGBCA 6179, 97-1 BCA ¶ 28,639; a claim for lost revenue, *Schleicher Cmty. Corrections Ctr., Inc.*, DOTBCA 3046, 98-2 BCA ¶ 29,941; a request for a contract rate adjustment to reflect wage and fringe benefit changes made by a contractor in accordance with a wage determination issued by the Department of Labor, *Keydata Sys., Inc. v. Department of the Treasury*, GSBCA 14281-TD, 97-2 BCA ¶ 29,330. In such cases, the contractor has the choice of submitting a request for equitable adjustment ("REA") to the contracting officer—calling for a negotiated settlement—or of submitting a CDA claim requesting a contracting officer decision and starting the running of interest. See *Twigg Corp. v. General Servs. Admin.*, GSBCA 13345, 97-2 BCA ¶ 29,088, where the board held that the contractor was not entitled to CDA interest because it had submitted a proposal for pricing a contract modification rather than a CDA claim.

Claims for damages for breach of contract or a cardinal change are nonroutine requests for payment, *Kentucky Bridge & Dam, Inc. v. United States*, 42 Fed. Cl. 501 (1998). A request for interpretation of the cost principles to determine the allowability of designated costs (unquantified) is also a nonroutine request, *TRW, Inc.*, ASBCA 51172, 99-2 BCA ¶30,407.

Routine requests for payment include billing of the contract price for articles delivered or services rendered, billing for progress payments, *American Serv. & Supply, Inc.*, ASBCA 50606, 00-1 BCA ¶30,858, and submitting a voucher for allowable costs or fee under a cost-reimbursement contract, *Moshman Assocs., Inc.*, ASBCA 52320, 00-1 BCA ¶30,906 (final voucher). However, invoices sent requesting payment for modifications that had not been negotiated were not routine requests but were claims, *MDP Constr., Inc.*, ASBCA 52769, 01-1 BCA ¶31,359.

2. Routine Request Converted Into a Claim

A routine request for payment may be "converted" into a claim. However, it will not be converted automatically, *Martin Marietta Corp.*, ASBCA 25828, 84-1 BCA ¶ 17,119 ("transformation of a routine voucher into a claim does not take place automatically, as if by osmosis, or upon the mere passage of time"). For a conversion to take place, the contractor must make a formal demand subsequent to an unreasonable delay in payment or disagreement with the Government, *JWA Emadel Enters., Inc.*, ASBCA 51016, 98-2 BCA ¶ 29,765, *recons. denied*, 98-2 BCA ¶ 29,960 (*resubmission* of a voucher which had previously been submitted and denied will be considered a nonroutine request for payment); *TRS Research*, ASBCA 50086, 98-2 BCA ¶ 29,780 (claim filed after nonpayment of legitimate invoices a valid CDA claim); *Falcon Research & Dev. Co.*, ASBCA 27002, 82-2 BCA ¶ 16,049 (invoice converted to claim only after contractor made formal demand subsequent to an unreasonable delay in payment). But see *Sprint Communications Co. v. General Servs. Admin.*, GSBCA 15139, 01-2 BCA ¶31,464 (no claim for Prompt Payment Act interest submitted to contracting officer); *A. T. Kearney, Inc.*, DOTCAB 1263, 83-2 BCA ¶ 16,835, *recons. denied*, 84-1 BCA ¶ 17,052 (invoice never converted into a claim by a request for a written decision); and *Granite Constr. Co.*, ASBCA 26023, 83-2 BCA ¶ 16,843 (long Government delay in payment of undisputed amounts not converted without further action by the contractor).

3. REA Submissions Converted Into Claim

Many contractors submit their initial request as a proposal rather than a claim to facilitate a negotiated settlement. The primary reason for proceeding in this manner is that costs incurred during the negotiation process generally will be considered administration costs and will most likely be allowable costs. By proceeding in this manner contractors forgo the commencement of interest on a claim. However, costs incurred during the negotiation process will most likely exceed what the contractor would have received in interest on the claim. Another reason for submitting a proposal such as an REA rather than a claim is that the submission of a claim may chill negotiations. If the contracting officer does not act on the proposal or there is a breakdown in negotiations, then the contractor can submit a claim. Generally the necessary steps to covert the REA proposal into a claim is requesting a contracting officer's final decision and certifying the claim, if it is over the $100,000 threshold. See *AAA Eng'g & Drafting, Inc.*, ASBCA 47940, 99-2 BCA ¶ 30,443 (proposal subsequently converted into claim when contractor requested final decision and certified claim).

4. Convenience Termination Settlement Proposals

The Federal Circuit has held, in *James M. Ellett Constr. Co. v. United States*, 93 F.3d 1537 (Fed. Cir. 1996), that a convenience termination settlement proposal is a nonroutine request for payment and that, if the proposal is not submitted as a claim, it will be automatically converted into a claim if the parties reach an impasse in attempting to reach a settlement. The court stated at 1543–44:

> When a contractor submits a termination settlement proposal, it is for the purpose of negotiation, not for a contracting officer's decision. A settlement proposal is just that: a proposal. *See* 48 C.F.R. § 49.001 (1995) ("a proposal for effecting settlement of a contract terminated in whole or in part, submitted by a contractor or subcontractor in the form, and supported by the data, required by this part"). Indeed, it is a proposal that Ellett contractually agreed to submit in the event of a convenience termination. The parties agreed that they would try to reach a mutually agreeable settlement. If they were unable to do so, however, it was agreed, consonant with the FAR's requirements, that the contracting officer would issue a final decision, *see id.* §§ 52.249-2(f) (Alternate I), 49.103, 49.105(a)(4), which Ellett could appeal to the court or to the Department of Agriculture Board of Contract Appeals, *id.* § 52.249-2(i). Consequently, while Ellett's termination settlement proposal met the FAR's definition of a claim, at the time of submission it was not a claim because it was not submitted to the contracting officer for a decision.
>
> Once negotiations reached an impasse, the proposal, by the terms of the FAR and the contract, was submitted for decision; it became a claim. In other words, in accordance with the contract's prescribed method of compensating Ellett for a convenience termination, a request that the contracting officer issue a decision in the event the parties were unable to agree on a settlement was implicit in Ellett's proposal. After ten months of fruitless negotiations, Ellett explicitly requested that the contracting officer settle its claim. This demand is tantamount to an express request for a contracting officer's decision.

See *Rapid Movers & Forwarders Co.*, ASBCA 48194, 98-2 BCA ¶ 29,339, where the board, following *Ellett*, held that a certified settlement proposal ripened into a CDA claim when the settlement negotiations reached an impasse. See also *Ad-*

vanced Materials, Inc. v. United States, 46 Fed. Cl. 697 (2000), finding a valid CDA claim when the contractor submitted a second termination settlement proposal labeled a "claim" and meeting all of the requirements for a claim.

Some appeals boards have construed this language to require that the parties reach an impasse in negotiations before there can be a CDA claim for termination for convenience settlement costs. For example, in *Central Envtl., Inc.*, ASBCA 51086, 98-2 BCA ¶ 29,912, the contractor filed a termination for convenience settlement proposal on April 29, 1997. A week later, on May 6, 1997, the contractor submitted a letter advising the contracting officer that it considered the matter "in dispute," requesting the contracting officer's final decision on its "claim" and providing a CDA certification. The contractor also stated that it would not appeal its "claim" so long as the parties were negotiating a termination settlement. The board ruled that the letter was not a CDA claim because no impasse had been reached, stating at 148,080:

> When a contractor submits a termination for convenience settlement proposal to the Government, the proposal first must ripen into a claim before we have jurisdiction to review that submission. *James M. Ellett Construction Company, Inc. v. United States*, 93 F.3d 1537, 1444 (Fed. Cir. 1996). A termination settlement proposal is not a CDA claim when it is first submitted to the contracting officer even though it otherwise meets the requirements of the CDA because the proposal is not submitted to the contracting officer for a final decision. *Id.*, 93 F.3d 1537 (Fed. Cir. 1996). Instead, the proposal represents an instrument of negotiation. *Id.*, 93 F.3d at 1543-1544; *Mid-America Eng'g and Mfg.*, ASBCA No. 48831, 96-2 BCA ¶ 28,558 at 142,585. Only after the negotiations reach an impasse, at a point when the contractor demands a final decision, does the termination proposal convert to a CDA claim. *Ellett*, 93 F.3d at 1544; *National Interior Contractors, Inc.*, ASBCA No. 46012, 96-2 BCA ¶ 28,560 at 142,588 (finding no jurisdiction without evidence of an impasse).

See also *Voices R Us, Inc*, ASBCA 51565, 01-1 BCA ¶31,328 ("Notwithstanding its submission . . . as a certified claim, the proposal did not become a claim until there was an impasse in negotiation"). In *Rex Sys., Inc.*, ASBCA 49502, 99-1 BCA ¶ 30,179, *recons. denied*, 99-1 BCA ¶ 30,377, *aff'd*, 224 F.3d 1367 (Fed. Cir. 2000), and *Mediax Interactive Techs., Inc.*, ASBCA 43961, 99-1 BCA ¶ 30,318, *recons. denied*, 99-2 BCA ¶ 30,453, the board discussed the impasse requirement but found that the contractor had not submitted a claim because it had not requested a contracting officer's decision when it submitted the settlement proposal. In contrast, in *Mid-America Eng'g & Mfg.*, ASBCA 48831, 96-2 BCA ¶ 28,558, the board found that a claim had been filed when the contractor, after submitting a settlement proposal, specifically requested a contracting officer's decision after the contracting officer failed to respond to a request for a meeting to negotiate a settlement. See also *McDonnell Douglas Corp. v. United States*, 37 Fed. Cl. 285 (1997), *rev'd on other grounds*, 182 F.3d 1319 (Fed. Cir. 1999), where the court found that an impasse had been reached immediately when the contractor demanded a termination for convenience settlement after its contract had been terminated for default. See also *Kit Pack Co.*, ASBCA 53155, 01-2 BCA ¶31,479, where the board stated that interest would begin to run from the date of the termination settlement proposal submitted as a CDA claim shortly after a termination for default. The board also held that it would not rule on the termination claim until it had determined whether the contract had been improperly default terminated.

In *Ellett*, the court held that requests for equitable adjustment submitted as CDA claims after the contract had been terminated for convenience were valid claims without regard to the requirements pertaining to termination settlement proposals. This same result was reached in *Kentucky Bridge & Dam, Inc. v. United States*, 42 Fed. Cl. 501 (1998).

5. Continued Negotiations

Contractors and the government need not cease talking to each other after submission of a claim because they disagree on its merits. In fact, the continuation of negotiations benefits both parties and is in the spirit of the CDA. Continued offers to negotiate a settlement do not impair an existing CDA claim, *Transamerica Ins. Corp. v. United States*, 973 F.2d 1572 (Fed. Cir. 1992). See also *AAA Eng'g & Drafting, Inc.*, ASBCA 47940, 99-2 BCA ¶ 30,443; and *Holmes & Narver Servs., Inc.*, ASBCA 40111, 92-3 BCA ¶ 25,052.

B. Nonmonetary Claims versus Declaratory Relief

Under certain circumstances, claims can also be nonmonetary in nature. However, there has been considerable confusion over the distinction between nonmonetary claims and requests for declaratory relief. A declaratory judgment is a court ruling that declares the rights and other legal relations of the parties without awarding any further relief. The Declaratory Judgment Act, 28 U.S.C. § 2201, confers jurisdiction upon federal courts to hear and decide such cases. But the United States Court of Claims and its successor, the Court of Federal Claims, were never granted jurisdiction over declaratory judgments. See *United States v. King*, 395 U.S. 1 (1969).

Nonetheless, both the Court of Federal Claims and the boards of contract appeals can take jurisdiction over nonmonetary claims. The appeals boards traditionally ruled on such claims and the CDA does not restrict the practice, *Malone v. United States*, 849 F.2d 1441 (Fed. Cir. 1988). The Court of Federal Claims was given this jurisdiction in 1992 when § 907 of the Federal Courts Administration Act, Pub. L. 102-572, amended 28 U.S.C. § 1491(a)(2) to provide for jurisdiction over disputes

> concerning termination of a contract, rights in tangible or intangible property, compliance with Cost Accounting Standards, and other nonmonetary disputes on which a decision of the contracting officer has been issued under the [CDA].

See *Information Sys. & Networks Corp. v. United States*, 48 Fed. Cl. 265 (2000), exercising this jurisdiction and stating that, "A complaint for declaratory judgment appealing a denial of claims by a final decision of a contracting officer falls within the jurisdiction of the Court of Federal Claims over nonmonetary claims." The jurisdiction to rule on nonmonetary claims is recognized in FAR 33.201 and the definition of "claim" in the Disputes clause which included a demand for "the adjustment or interpretation of contract terms, or other relief arising under or relating to the contract."

The exercise of this jurisdiction is discretionary. In *Alliant Techsystems, Inc. v. United States,* 178 F.3d 1260 (Fed. Cir. 1999), *reh'g denied*, 186 F.3d 1379 (Fed. Cir. 1999), the court stated at 1271:

> [Neither] the Court of Federal Claims (or an agency board of contract appeals) is required to issue a declaration of rights whenever a contractor raises a question of contract interpretation during the course of contract performance. In responding to such a request, the court or board is free to consider the appropriateness of declaratory relief, including whether the claim involves a live dispute between the parties, whether a declaration will resolve that dispute, and whether the legal remedies available to the parties would be adequate to protect the parties' interests.
>
> While a contractor may want to know ahead of time how a contract issue will be resolved—such as whether the contractor will be entitled to additional compensation under the changes clause for a particular item of work directed by the contracting officer—such cases do not ordinarily put into question whether the contractor is obligated to perform at all. In such a case, the dispute typically concerns whether the government will be obligated to grant an equitable adjustment after the ordered performance is completed. It would normally be appropriate in such cases for the court or board to decline to issue a declaratory judgment and to await a later equitable adjustment claim by the contractor. In refusing a request for declaratory relief in the absence of a need for an early declaration of the parties' rights, the court or board would be applying a principle analogous to the traditional rule that courts will not grant equitable relief when money damages are adequate.
>
> The discretion to grant declaratory relief only in limited circumstances allows the court or board to restrict the occasions for intervention during contract performance to those involving a fundamental question of contract interpretation or a special need for early resolution of a legal issue.

In *Alliant* the court took jurisdiction of the question of whether the contractor was required to perform an invalidly exercised option. In *Garrett v. General Elec. Co.*, 987 F.2d 747 (Fed. Cir. 1993), the court agreed that the appeals board properly took jurisdiction over the contracting officer's revocation of acceptance of purportedly, latently defective goods and direction to the contractor to replace the goods at no additional cost. See also *CW Gov't Travel, Inc. v. United States*, 63 Fed. Cl.

:ing jurisdiction but denying summary judgment on the issue of whether special contract language required to exercise an "option," and *Tiger Natural Gas, Inc. v. United States*, 61 Fed. Cl. 287 (2004), taking juris- ...ut denying summary judgment on issue of whether the contract guaranteed a saving when furnishing natural gas.

The most common nonmonetary claim, over which the boards have always taken jurisdiction, is the validity of a default termination. See *Sharman Co. v. United States*, 30 Fed. Cl. 231 (1994), *aff'd*, 41 F.3d 1520 (Fed. Cir. 1994), in which the Court of Federal Claims took jurisdiction, retroactively, to decide this issue after the statutory change in 1992.

Another common situation where jurisdiction has been granted is claims involving the proper accounting of costs. See *Information Sys. & Networks Corp. v. United States*, 48 Fed. Cl. 265 (2000), ruling that state income taxes on the corporate income of a S corporation are reimbursable under the FAR. See also *TRW, Inc.*, ASBCA 51172, 99-2 BCA ¶30,407, in which the board took jurisdiction of the contractor's request for interpretation of several provisions of the cost principles, and *Robert Orr–SYSCO Food Serv. Co.*, ASBCA 51430, 97-1 BCA ¶28,903, interpreting the contract's Rebate clause. Compare *McDonnell Douglas Co.*, ASBCA 50592, 97-2 BCA ¶29,199, in which the board denied jurisdiction of the contractor's appeal of the contracting officer's disallowance of costs because the contractor did not explicitly "seek the adjustment or interpretation of contract terms." The boards have also taken jurisdiction of disputes concerning the interpretation of the Cost Accounting Standards, *Litton Sys., Inc.*, ASBCA 45400, 94-2 BCA ¶26,895 (CAS 405 & 410); *Litton Sys., Inc.*, ASBCA 37131, 94-2 BCA ¶26,731 (CAS 418); *Martin Marietta Corp.*, ASBCA 38920, 90-1 BCA ¶22,418 (change in accounting practice).

The court and boards have frequently denied jurisdiction when a request for contract interpretation can be readily resolved by the submission of a monetary claim. See *Westinghouse Elec. Corp.*, ASBCA 47868, 95-1 BCA ¶27,364, and cases cited therein. See also *Westar Eng'g, Inc.*, ASBCA 52484, 02-1 BCA ¶31,759, refusing to rule on whether the contractor had properly priced its equitable adjustment. The contractor had asked for this ruling as a means of overcoming a fraud investigation. See *Hamilton Secs. Advisory Servs., Inc. v. United States*, 60 Fed. Cl. 144 (2004) (refusing to rule on issue of whether government had right to withhold funds when case was scheduled for trial on contractor's monetary claim and government counterclaim), and *Aeronca, Inc.*, ASBCA 51927, 01-1 BCA ¶31,230 (refusing to declare whether an equitable adjustment was due because of a partial termination and whether contract modifications were binding). Compare *William D. Euille & Assocs., Inc. v. General Servs. Admin.*, GSBCA 15261, 00-1 BCA ¶30,910, in which the board ruled that a letter disputing the contracting officer's directive to replace conduit constituted a "claim" because it sought an adjustment or interpretation of the contract terms, even though the contractor also estimated the cost of the change to be "somewhere between $ 1 and $ 99,999.

The jurisdiction to rule on nonmonetary claims does not extend to the granting of specific performance, *Sabbia Corp.*, VABCA 5557, 99-2 BCA ¶30,394; *Western Aviation Maint. Inc. v. General Servs. Admin.*, GSBCA 14165, 98-2 BCA ¶29,816.

C. Assertion of Contractor Claim

A claim does not arise upon the mere occurrence of a dispute or controversy. The party asserting the claim must make a "demand" or "assertion" to the other party. The Disputes clause provides in ¶(c) that a claim is a "written demand or written assertion by one of the contracting parties." Paragraph (d)(1) of the clause further provides that a claim by the contractor "shall be made in writing and submitted to the contracting officer for a written decision." Because it is the contractor's claim that triggers the running of interest and starts the time running for the contracting officer's final decision, the primary focus has been on determining what type of contractor demand or assertion constitutes a claim. The following discussion examines what parties can assert claims and what information must be included in such claims.

1. Party Entitled to Assert Claim

Appeals often involve threshold issues of 1) whether the dissolved contractor can file a suit; 2) whether a separate entity is entitled to sue on behalf of the contractor; or 3) who can speak for the contractor.

a. Dissolved Contractors

State law determines whether an individual is authorized to act on behalf of an otherwise incapacitated business entity and, therefore, has standing to file an appeal under the CDA. See *RMS Tech., Inc.,* ASBCA 50954, 00-1 BCA ¶30,763 (former manager of a terminated corporation lacked standing to file appeal because only directors were authorized to file suit in the corporate name under Virginia law); *Frénce Mfg. Co.*, ASBCA 46233, 95-2 BCA ¶27,802 (involuntarily dissolved contractor that was reinstated under Illinois law can file appeal); and *Microtool Eng'g, Inc.*, ASBCA 31136, 86-1 BCA ¶18,680 (dissolved corporation could not sue under New York law). In *Weststar, Inc.,* ASBCA 52837, 03-1 BCA ¶32,248, the board held an assignee is not a real party in interest to prosecute an appeal where the contractor has become insolvent and been liquidated under state law. On reconsideration, 04-1 BCA ¶32,501, the board reinstated the appeal based on California law which allowed the contractor to recover its corporate status.

Administrative dissolution does not necessarily preclude the dissolved corporation from proceeding with a claim. State law often provides that a dissolved corporation may continue its corporate existence and may wind up and liquidate its business, including the collecting of its assets and discharging its liabilities. See *DCO Constr, Inc.*, ASBCA 52701, 02-1 BCA ¶31,851 (an administrative dissolution at the time appeal notices were filed did not deprive a contractor of capacity to sue because Florida law allows a defunct entity to continue certain dealings), and *International Crane Co.*, ASBCA 49604, 00-1 BCA ¶30,624, *recons. denied,* 00-2 BCA ¶31,085 (trustee of dissolved corporation had standing to file appeal because he was entitled to bring suit in the corporate name under Maryland law).

A contractor undergoing liquidation under Chapter 7 of the Bankruptcy Code has no right to conduct business, including the prosecution or defense of claims, outside the bankruptcy estate, *Microscience, Inc.*, ASBCA 45264, 98-1 BCA ¶29,480 (holding that president and sole shareholder of a defunct corporation did not have the capacity to prosecute an appeal); *Terrace Apartments, Ltd.*, ASBCA 40125R, 95-1 BCA ¶27,458. For various views on whether bankrupt corporations are subject to state law or bankruptcy law with regard to their corporate status, see *Caesar Constr. Co.*, ASBCA 46023, 97-1 BCA ¶28,665.

b. Separate Entities

There are a number of separate entities that have been denied the right to assert a claim for the contractor. The inability to assert such contractor claims does not necessarily preclude them from asserting claims on their own behalf such as claims of an assignee for payment of contract funds to the contractor.

(1) Assignees

Assignees of the right to receive payment under the Assignment of Claims Act, 31 USC § 3727, may not assert contract claims because an assignee is not a "contractor" within the meaning of the CDA, *Produce Factors Corp. v. United States*, 199 Ct. Cl. 572, 467 F.2d 1343 (1972; *Thomas Funding Corp. v. United States*, 15 Cl. Ct. 495 (1988); *Innovative Tech. Sys., Inc. v. Department of the Treasury*, GSBCA 13474-TD, 97-1 BCA ¶28,971, *recons. denied,* 97-2 BCA ¶29,086; *Barnes, Inc.*, AGBCA 97-111-1, 97-2 BCA ¶29,237; *Banco Disa, SA*, ASBCA 49167, 96-2 BCA ¶28,728; *First Commercial Funding, L.L.C.,* ENGBCA 6447, 00-1 BCA ¶30,769. One board has held, in *John E. Gallno*, AGBCA , 97-146-1, 98-1 BCA ¶29,616, that a contractor may file an appeal after making an assignment, because the appellant's status as a "contractor" under the CDA at the time the claim arose was not changed by the assignment agreement. The board also noted that the question whether the contractor waived its rights against the government when it assigned the contract was related to the merits of the case rather than the contractor's status or the board's jurisdiction. The board found that the assignment agreement was not a release of claims because the transfer did not clearly and specifically set out a release, and the government, as a party to the assignment agreement, could not receive the benefit of inferences or ambiguous language.

(2) Sureties

Performance bond sureties can sue for the unpaid balance on a contract if they assume responsibility for the work and incur costs in that amount, *Aetna Cas. & Sur. Co. v. United States*, 845 F.2d 971 (Fed. Cir. 1988). The theory of such suits is equitable subrogation, *Balboa Ins. Co. v. United States*, 775 F.2d 1158 (Fed. Cir. 1985), and the basis for such suits is the Tucker Act, not the CDA, *Fireman's Fund Ins. Co. v. England*, 313 F.3d 1344 (Fed. Cir. 2002). The impact of *Fireman's Fund* is that the boards have no jurisdiction over such claims. Further, such suits may not encompass claims for additional compensation on the contract.

If such a surety enters into a takeover agreement with the government, it will become a contractor and will be able to assert claims in the Court of Federal Claims to the extent that the terms of the agreement permit such claims. This would allow recovery on post-takeover claims and pre-takeover claims to the extent allowed by the agreement. See *Employers Ins. of Wausau v. United States*, 23 Cl. Ct. 579 (pre-takeover claims are viable if "the takeover agreement . . . encompass[es] the prior contract's rights and obligations), and *Reliance Ins. Co. v. United States*, 27 Fed. Cl. 815 (1993) (considering pre-takeover claims). See also *Roxco, Ltd. v. United States*, 60 Fed. Cl. 39 (2004), taking jurisdiction of a suit by a contractor for claims based on events before its default termination when a surety had completed the project without entering into a takeover agreement.

Boards of contract appeals do not have this broad authority. See *United Pac. Ins. Co. v. Roche*, 380 F.3d 1352 (Fed. Cir. 2004), holding that under the CDA the boards have no authority to grant relief on pre-takeover claims even when the takeover agreement is broadly worded. The court stated at 1356-57:

> United contends that it has a "contractual right" to assert its overpayment claim before the Board because the takeover agreement states that the "SURETY expressly reserves all prior rights including but not limited to the Government's overpayment to" Castle. *United Pac. Ins. Co.*, 03-2 B.C.A. ¶32,267 at 159,613. Contrary to United's argument, however, this provision did not give the Board jurisdiction over the claim. The Board's jurisdiction is defined by the Contract Disputes Act. Parties cannot, by agreement, confer upon a tribunal jurisdiction that it otherwise would not have. See *Fla. Power & Light Co. v. United States*, 307 F.3d 1364, 1370 (Fed. Cir. 2002) ("Contractual language . . . cannot confer jurisdiction" under the Contract Disputes Act.) Thus, a "reference to the [Contract Disputes Act] in the contract" could not vest the Board with "jurisdiction over the . . . claim[] if it was not otherwise authorized" to adjudicate it. *Id.* at 1371. The provision of the takeover agreement upon which United relies reserves only its "prior" rights, i.e., those that existed before the takeover agreement. Under *Fireman's Fund*, the Board had no jurisdiction over claims based upon those rights.
>
> United also cites the following language of the takeover agreement as a basis for Board jurisdiction: the "SURETY shall be entitled to exercise such rights as are afforded by the . . . Contract Disputes Act." *United Pac. Ins. Co.*, 03-2 B.C.A. ¶32,267 at 159,613. That contractual provision merely recognized that United retained whatever rights it otherwise had under the Contract Disputes Act. As we have explained, United had no right under that Act to maintain before the Board a claim based on pre-takeover agreement events.

No jurisdiction attaches to an appeal of a surety that had paid the penal sum of its payment bond but had not assumed contract performance or made any payments under its performance bond. See *Admiralty Constr., Inc.*, ASBCA 48627, 96-2 BCA ¶28,280, *aff'd*, 156 F.3d 1217 (Fed. Cir. 1998). See also *Brent M. Davies*, ASBCA 51938, 00-1 BCA ¶30,678 (where a surety pays out under its payment bond to the defaulted contractor's creditors but neither enters into a takeover agreement with the government nor finances the contract's completion, it lacks privity as a "contractor" and cannot rely on subrogation to support its standing before the board to appeal excessive reprocurement costs and liquidated damages).

A surety also has no rights to recover where the contractor agrees to a no-cost settlement to convert a default termination to a termination for convenience, *Intercargo Ins. Co. v. United States*, 41 Fed. Cl. 449 (1998), *aff'd*, 215 F.3d 1348 (Fed. Cir. 1999).

(3) Merged Contractors

Although a surviving company that has succeeded to a contract by a valid merger may assert contract claims, a company that has purchased a contractor's assets may have no such rights. In *Siracua Moving & Storage*, ASBCA 51433, 99-2 BCA ¶30,447, the board held that it lacked jurisdiction of a claim asserted by a company that had purchased a contractor's assets because the company was not a "contractor" as defined by the CDA. The board reached this conclusion because the transfer of the contractor's assets violated the Anti-Assignment Act and there was no valid, completed novation agreement. In contrast, the same board held in *Omega Envtl., Inc.*, ASBCA 51639, 99-1 BCA ¶30,253, that the transfer of rights in connection with mergers gives the status of "contractor" within the CDA and is not precluded by the anti-assignment statutes. Thus, a successor by merger has standing to appeal an adverse contracting officer's decision.

A company that the government had agreed (in a novation agreement) to look upon as a contractor's successor for all purposes had the right to pursue claims for events that predated the novation, *Vought Aircraft Co.*, ASBCA 47357, 95-1 BCA ¶27,421. See also *General Dynamics Corp. v. United States*, 47 Fed. Cl. 514 (2000), holding that a corporation, rather than its wholly owned subsidiary, was the real party in interest and therefore entitled to bring suit on a contract claim.

(4) Agents of a Contractor

Agents of a contractor with power of attorney may assert claims, *Rudolf Bieraeugel, Stahl-und Metallbau, Gesellschaft mit beschraenkter Haftung*, ASBCA 47145, 95-1 BCA ¶27,536, *aff'd*, 91 F.3d 167 (Fed. Cir. 1996). Compare *Blakely Crop Hall, Inc. & Farmer Alliance Mut. Ins. Co.*, AGBCA 2001-153-F, 02-1 BCA ¶31,796, holding that a crop insurer's managing general agent did not have standing to assert the claim to the board. See also *Hubsch Industrieanlagen Spezialbau GmbH*, ASBCA 51937, 02-1 BCA ¶31,740 (contractor could not recover an affiliate's lost profits or costs relating to a foreclosure on its director's home, because neither the affiliate nor the director were parties to the contract).

2. Claim Content

A valid CDA money claim must contain (1) a written demand (2) seeking as a matter of right (3) the payment of money in a sum certain, *Scientific Mgmt. Assocs., Inc.*, ASBCA 50956, 98-1 BCA ¶29,656. Although the CDA prescribes no particular format, a claim must contain sufficient detail to permit the contracting officer to give meaningful, reasoned consideration to the claim, and the sufficiency of claims will be determined on a case-by-case basis, *Metric Constr. Co. v. United States*, 1 Cl. Ct. 383 (1983). In *Marine Constr. & Dredging, Inc.*, ASBCA 38412, 90-1 BCA ¶22,573, the board stated that the claim "must contain sufficient detail to notify the contracting officer of the factual allegations upon which the claim is premised." In *Tecom, Inc. v. United States*, 732 F.2d 935 (Fed. Cir. 1984), a claim was found to have been filed by a letter asserting that the government's order was beyond the contract's requirements and specifically asking "compensation of $11,000.04 per year, to be billed at $916.67 per month." See *Blake Constr. Co.*, ASBCA 34480, 88-2 BCA ¶20,552, in which the board stated that "the statement of claim must provide a basis for meaningful dialogue between the parties aimed toward settlement or negotiated resolution of the claim if possible, or for adequate identification of the issues to facilitate litigation should that become necessary." See also *ECC Int'l Corp. v. United States*, 43 Fed. Cl. 359 (1999) (the submission of a valid claim requires the contractor to specify its bases for relief, although there is no requirement that a claim be submitted in any particular form or use any particular verbiage), and *Clearwater Constructors, Inc. v. United States*, 56 Fed. Cl. 303 (2003) (a contractor and subcontractor's letters combined constituted a valid, non-monetary claim because the subcontractor's letter clearly outlined its position that the government's demand for "explosion-proof" doors constituted extra work while the contractor's letter sought a contracting officer's final decision concerning the contract's meaning).

As long as the contractor's assertion contains the minimum information necessary to inform the contracting officer of what is being claimed and the grounds of the claim, the contracting officer must act on the claim and deny it if the information is insufficient to approve it, *Fred A. Arnold, Inc.*, ASBCA 27151, 83-2 BCA ¶16,795, *modified on other grounds*, 84-3 BCA ¶17,517.

Claims should have adequate supporting documentation. In *Aerojet Gen. Corp.*, ASBCA 48136, 95-1 BCA ¶27,470, the contracting officer requested full cost or pricing data approximately a month and a half after a claim had been submitted. Rather than providing the data, the contractor appealed to the board arguing that it should take jurisdiction under 41 U.S.C. § 605(c)(5) which states that failure of a contracting officer to provide a timely decision will be "deemed" to be a decision denying the claim (a "deemed" denial). The board found that the contractor had failed to comply and in fact violated both the letter and the spirit of the statute. See *Environmental Chem. Corp.*, ASBCA 53958, 03-1 BCA ¶32,254 (no jurisdiction where appellant had not identified the contract in its claim and there was no indication that contracting officer had prior or concurrent information of the contract(s) affected); *Holk Dev., Inc.*, ASBCA 40579, 90-3 BCA ¶23,086 (no claim because the supporting data were general cost information not connected to the contract in question); and *I.B.A. Co.*, ASBCA 37182, 89-1 BCA ¶21,576 (no claim where the contractor claimed that the government had not made proper payment in the amount of $25,000 and refused to furnish any documentation in support of its claim). However, compare *Bridgewater Constr. Corp.*, VABCA 2866, 90-2 BCA ¶22,764, and *Marshall Constr., Ltd.*, ASBCA 37014, 90-1 BCA ¶22,597, in which proper claims were found even though the contractor submitted almost no supporting data. In *H.G. Smith, Inc. v. Dalton,* 49 F.3d 1563 (Fed. Cir. 1995), the court rejected any requirement for a contractor to submit substantiation for the dollar amount requested in a claim at the time of claim submission. See also *John T. Jones Constr. Co.,* ASBCA 48303, 96-1 BCA ¶27,997, holding that if the claim is sufficient, the contracting officer's desire for more information does not change the "claim" status of the contractor's submission.

In *Bio-Temp Scientific, Inc.*, ASBCA 41388, 91-1 BCA ¶23,548, the board held that a letter by the contractor's attorney that he had been retained "to prosecute . . . a dispute with respect to the full contract amount" failed to constitute "a clear and unequivocal statement that gives the contracting officer adequate notice of the basis and amount of the claim." In *Natural Landscape Contractors, Inc.*, GSBCA 9187, 91-2 BCA ¶23,886, *recons. denied*, 93-1 BCA ¶25,422, the government asserted that the contractor had never filed a claim for a differing site condition. The contractor argued that "the general site condition claim was included in its more general certified claim for 'GSA's failure to properly and timely administer the contracts.'" The board disagreed with the contractor, stating at 119,656:

> The specifics of the claim concerned alleged wrongful reductions for work performed under the contract with payment subsequently disallowed, not for extra work that had to be performed because of a differing site condition or constructive change. The equitable adjustment claimed as a result of the alleged differing site condition is not mentioned in the claim letter. As the differing site condition claim was not presented to the contracting officer for decision, we lack jurisdiction to decide it. 41 U.S.C. § 605(a) (1988); *Modular Devices Inc.*, ASBCA No. 24198, 82-1 BCA ¶15,536.

See, however, *General Constr. Co.*, ASBCA 39983, 91-1 BCA ¶23,314, *recons. denied*, 93-1 BCA ¶25,275, in which the board held that the contractor's claims stating that its increased costs were due to either a differing site condition or defective specifications provided sufficient facts to permit the contracting officer to render a final decision. Similarly, in *R&R Enters.*, ASBCA 41382, 91-2 BCA ¶23,707, the contractor's letter seeking compensation for additional staffing of a mess hall constituted a claim because it provided sufficient information for the contracting officer to give the claim meaningful review. In *Mendenhall v. United States*, 20 Cl. Ct. 78 (1990), the court found that the contractor's letter making a claim for "changed conditions" qualified as a claim. The court stated that the submission was a clear, unequivocal notice of the basis for the claim since the contracting officer understood what was referred to as a result of earlier discussions with the contractor.

3. Request for Sum Certain

A contractor must state a sum certain if that is possible at the time the claim is filed, *RCS Enters., Inc. v. United States,* 46 Fed. Cl. 509 (2000); *Writing Co. v. Department of Treasury,* GSBCA 15097, 00-1 BCA ¶30,840, *recons. denied,* 00-1 BCA ¶30,910; *Colon v. United States* 35 Fed. Cl. 337 (1996); *Harris Mgmt. Co.*, ASBCA 27291, 84-2 BCA ¶17,378; *Logus Mfg. Co.*, ASBCA 26436, 82-2 BCA ¶16,025; *Harnischfeger Corp.*, ASBCA 23918, 80-2 BCA ¶14,541. Failure to quantify a claim will render the claim ineffectual if the essence of the dispute is increased costs, *Winding Specialists Co.*, ASBCA 37765, 89-2 BCA ¶21,737; *Endless Gutter & Sheetmetal Co.*, ASBCA 39369, 90-1 BCA ¶22,474. Thus, if a monetary amount can be determined, that amount must be stated. See *Liberty Painting Co.*, ASBCA 39562, 91-1 BCA ¶23,561 (no claim found where contractor filed a claim for extra compensation for painting but made no estimate of the amount of the claim), and *Rixie Iron & Metal Co.*, ASBCA 40835, 90-3 BCA ¶23,238, *recons. denied,* 91-1 BCA ¶23,453 (no claim found where contractor gave some monetary information but did not clearly state the amount it was requesting). See also *Metric Constr. Co. v. United States*, 14 Cl. Ct. 177 (1988) (a claim "exceeding" a specified dollar amount did not meet the test); *Godwin Equip. Inc.*, ASBCA 53462, 02-1 BCA ¶31,674 (claim "in excess of" $5 million did not constitute a sum certain). In *SEA CON Corp.*, AGBCA 812041, 81-2 BCA ¶15,316, the board dismissed without prejudice a claim alleging mistake in bid because the contractor had submitted no specific dollar claim and had provided no certification. Similarly, a contractor was required to clarify language requesting "more or less than $50,000" before proceeding with an uncertified claim, *Ernest Zapanta*, ASBCA 27633, 83-1 BCA ¶16,259, *recons. denied*, 83-2 BCA ¶16,622.

A claim in which the amount can be easily determined by simple mathematical calculation or from the contractor's submission to the contracting officer is sufficient for purposes of the CDA, *Mendenhall v. United States*, 20 Cl. Ct. 78 (1990) (claim requested return of all the money paid to government under timber sale contract); *Metric Constr. Co. v. United States*, 1 Cl. Ct. 383 (1983) (amount of request for 7.5 percent for bond premium on all changes ordered easily determinable by contracting officer since amount of change orders were known); *Dillingham Shipyard*, ASBCA 27458, 84-1 BCA ¶16,984 (sum determinable by simple arithmetic since government knew both the number of hours and the rate). See *Automated Power Sys., Inc.*, DOTBCA 2925, 98-1 BCA ¶29,568, stating that this requirement will be met if the claim states either the exact amount or a description that would enable the contracting officer to determine the specific amount through the use of simple arithmetic. Thus, the sum certain requirement can be met by setting forth a finite amount but also with data that allow for reasonable determination of the recovery available at the time the claim is presented or decided by the contracting officer, such as at a fixed rate, *Mulunesh Berhe*, ASBCA 49681, 96-2 BCA ¶28,339.

A claim will meet the sum certain requirement even if it demands two different sums if the sums are clearly stated as alternatives and each is based upon a different legal theory but the same factual circumstances, *Heyl & Patterson, Inc. v. O'Keefe*, 986 F.2d 480 (Fed. Cir. 1993), *overruled on other grounds*, *Reflectone, Inc. v. Dalton*, 60 F.3d 1572 (Fed. Cir. 1995). Similarly, the requirement will be met if the claim seeks different sum certain amounts under alternative theories of recovery, *United Techs. Corp.*, ASBCA 46880, 96-1 BCA ¶28,226.

The sum certain need not be the total claim of a contractor. In *MDP Constr., Inc.*, ASBCA 52769, 01-1 BCA ¶31,359, each of several invoices qualified as a "claim" under the CDA, even though the contractor also expressed an intent to submit at some future time a claim for unabsorbed home office overhead expenses. Because each invoice stated a specific monetary amount, the invoices represented a sum certain. The fact that a contractor has not completed all work under a particular contract modification or change does not mean that the contractor is prohibited from submitting one or more claims for the portions of the work that have been completed. See *J.S. Alberici Constr. Co.*, ENGBCA 6179, 97-1 BCA ¶28,639, *recons. denied*, 97-1 BCA ¶28,919, *aff'd*, 153 F.3d 1381 (Fed. Cir. 1998), where the contractor's submission of estimated costs was a valid claim even though it represented a demand for payment for work not yet performed and of costs not yet incurred, and *Fairchild Indus. Inc.*, ASBCA 46197, 95-1 BCA ¶27,594, in which the board held that the decision in *Servidone Constr. Corp. v. United States*, 931 F.2d 860 (Fed. Cir. 1991), implied that a claim that included amounts for not-yet-incurred costs could be properly filed under the CDA. See also *Sentara Health Sys.*, ASBCA 51540, 99-1 BCA ¶30,323, *recons. denied*, 99-2 BCA ¶30,454, (although a valid contractor's claim must include a demand for the "payment of money in a sum certain," the reservation of a right to seek additional "acquisition savings" does not render an existing claim in a specified amount uncertain), and *Writing Co. v. Department of the Treasury*, GSBCA 15117-TD, 00-2 BCA ¶31,076 (submittal of invoice partially disputed by the DCAA constitutes a CDA claim for disputed amount).

4. Request for Contracting Officer Decision

The requirement that the contractor request a contracting officer decision is in neither the CDA nor the FAR but rather derives from case law. See *Mingus Constructors, Inc. v. United States*, 812 F.2d 1387 (Fed. Cir. 1987). In *Mingus*, the court held that the contractor's letters did not constitute a claim because they did not request a decision from the contracting officer. See also *Robert Irsay Co. v. United States Postal Serv.*, 21 Cl. Ct. 502 (1990), in which the court held that there was no claim because the letter lacked a request for a contracting officer decision on the contractor's request for equitable adjustment.

The request for a decision may be either explicit or implied. In *James M. Ellett Constr. Co. v. United States*, 93 F.3d 1537 (Fed. Cir. 1996), the court clarified that a contractor need not explicitly request a final decision "'as long as what the contractor desires by its submissions is a final decision . . . .'" citing *Transamerica Ins. Corp. v. United States*, 973 F.2d 1572 (Fed. Cir. 1992). The court recognized that "'a request for a final decision can be implied from the context of the submission." See *CleanServ Executive Servs., Inc.*, ASBCA 47781, 96-1 BCA ¶28,027; *Rex Sys., Inc.*, ASBCA 49065, 96-1 BCA ¶27,967. In *Mendenhall v. United States*, 20 Cl. Ct. 78 (1990), the court found an implied request when the contractor requested in a letter that the contracting officer take action on specific issues that had arisen between the parties. An implied request was also found in a series of letters between the contractor and the contracting officer followed by a meeting on the "claim" at which the parties could not agree on a resolution of the issues, *Mitchco, Inc.*, ASBCA 41847, 91-2 BCA ¶23,860. See also *Cable Antenna Sys.*, ASBCA 36184, 90-3 BCA ¶23,203, in which the board found an implied request for a contracting officer decision in a demand that the contracting officer promptly respond to the asserted claims and in a statement that the claim was being submitted "pursuant to Disputes clause." In *Transamerica Ins. Corp. v. United States*, 973 F.2d 1572 (Fed. Cir. 1992), the court stated that, although the contractor did not use the explicit words "we request a final decision from the contracting officer," it was obvious that the contractor wanted a final decision on its equitable adjustment claim. Similarly, in *Atlas Elevator Co. v. General Servs. Admin.*, GSBCA 11655, 93-1 BCA ¶25,216, the board held that a letter seeking payment for a contractor's elevator repairs constituted a claim, even though the contractor did not explicitly demand payment as a matter of right or explicitly request final payment. The board stated that a "common sense analysis should be applied to ascertain whether a particular submission" constitutes a request for a final decision. See also *Intercontinental Mfg Co.,* ASBCA 51005, 98-1 ¶29,459, finding an implied request when the contractor submitted a request for equitable adjustment but called it a "claim" and included the CDA certification.

A request for contract interpretation also is a demand for a final decision (even though it is not a request for a sum certain) because nonmonetary claims are within the jurisdiction of the board, *Procontrols Corp.*, VABCA 5477, 98-1 BCA ¶29,622. However, the court will not find an implied request for a contracting officer decision if the contractor requests a meeting to discuss the matter, *Sun Eagle Corp. v. United States*, 23 Cl. Ct. 465 (1991), or requests continued discussions, *M.A. Mortenson Co. v. General Servs. Admin.*, GSBCA 13570, 96-2 BCA ¶28,451. Compare *Kevin J. LeMay*, GSBCA 16093, 03-2 BCA ¶32,345, holding that a request that the contracting officer order an agency to perform was a request for a decision.

Mere precatory language will not suffice, *Jones, Inc.*, VACAB 1708, 84-2 BCA ¶17,382 (letter stating "your prompt payment will be appreciated" in response to government rejection of progress-payment request was insufficient). See also *Robert Irsay Co. v. United States Postal Serv.*, 21 Cl. Ct. 502 (1990) (request that an equitable adjustment be made to the contract did not constitute a request for a final decision), and *Wayne R. Hilf*, PSBCA 2800, 91-1 BCA ¶23,628 (letter appealing an implicit contracting officer decision was held not to be a claim because the letter did not request a contracting officer decision). See *Fisherman's Boat Shop, Inc.*, ASBCA 50324, 97-2 BCA ¶29,257 (no final decision possible if contractor's letter explicitly states it is not seeking a final decision). In *Heyl & Patterson, Inc. v. O'Keefe*, 986 F.2d 480 (Fed. Cir. 1993), *overruled on other grounds, Reflectone, Inc. v. Dalton*, 60 F.3d 1572 (Fed. Cir. 1995), the Federal Circuit upheld a board decision that a contractor had not manifested an intent to bring a claim under the CDA. The court seemed to rely on the fact that there was no request for a final decision in reaching this conclusion. The court stated at 485:

> Each of the three earlier submissions, November 3, 1987, January 28, 1988, and March 23, 1988, suggests in one way or another that *Heyl & Patterson* and the government were still negotiating. In the November 3, 1987 submission, *Heyl & Patterson* indicated that it awaited the government's "preliminary position." In the January 28, 1988 submission, *Heyl & Patterson* indicated that it would submit a "formal request" at a later date. In the March 23, 1988 submission, *Heyl & Patterson* indicated that it was "anxious to proceed with the settlement." None of the submissions requested a final decision, explicitly or implicitly. The third submission, though styled a "claim," merely continued the dialogue of the first two. Indeed, as late as the March 23, 1988 submission, *Heyl & Patterson* inquired whether "any other information [was] needed before the Audit [could] begin." While we agree that "[t]here is no necessary inconsistency between the existence of a valid CDA claim and an expressed desire to continue to mutually work toward a claim's resolution," *Transamerica*, 973 F.2d at 1579, where, as here, "there is no implication that the [contractor] desired a final decision," *id.* at 157778, no claim exists under the CDA as implemented by the FAR.

This case demonstrates the difficulty of discerning the precise element that the contractor failed to establish in bringing a "claim" under the CDA.

5. Submittal to the Contracting Officer

Under 41 U.S.C. § 605(a) "all claims by a contractor against the Government relating to a contract shall be in writing and shall be submitted to the contracting officer for a decision." Thus, claims submitted to other government officials will not qualify as claims. See *White Sands Corp.*, ASBCA 53056, 01-1 BCA ¶31,348 (submission to government lawyer not a claim); *D.L. Braughler Co., Inc. v. West*, 127 F.3d 1476 (Fed. Cir. 1997) (submission to Resident Engineer not seeking contracting officer decision not a claim); and *J&F Salvage Co.*, 37 Fed. Cl. 256 (1997), *aff'd*, 152 F.3d 945 (Fed. Cir. 1998), *cert. denied*, 525 U. S. 827 (1998) (letter to Department of Justice rather than contracting agency not a claim).

Some cases have held that submittal to a person that can be expected to send the claim to the contracting officer will meet the submittal requirement. See *Gardner Zemke Co.*, ASBCA 51499, 98-2 BCA ¶29,997, in which the board held that the contractor's submission of its claim to a private company acting as the primary contact of the government satisfied the requirements of the CDA because the contractor reasonably expected that the private company would forward the claim to the contracting officer. Similarly, in *CACI, Inc.-Fed. v. General Servs. Admin.*, GSBCA 15588, 02-1 BCA ¶31,712, the contractor had filed a claim on an Federal Supply Shedule contract with the ordering agency, with a copy to the GSA contracting officer. After the ordering agency and the contractor reached an impasse, and having received no response from the GSA contracting officer, the contractor filed an appeal. The board held that submitting the claim both to the ordering agency and the GSA "is consonant with the operational realities of FSS contracting, under which the ordering agencies and contractors are expected to make initial attempts to resolve disputes." See also *United Partitions Sys., Inc. v. United States.*, 59 Fed. Cl. 627 (2004), in which the Court of Federal Claims ruled that both the Air Force and GSA's contracting officers had partial authority on FSS contracts.

After a default termination has been converted to a termination for convenience, the contractor must submit a new claim to the contracting officer before the board can take jurisdiction, *Foremost Mech. Sys., Inc. v. General Servs. Admin.*, GSBCA 12335, 95-1 BCA ¶27,382.

6. Certification

A number of certifications may be required of a contractor seeking money from the government. The determination of whether a certification is required and the time when it is to be submitted depends upon the agency involved, whether the request is a claim under the CDA, and whether the matter is settled through negotiation. The most prominent certificate requirements are contained in the CDA, 41 U.S.C. § 605(c), and the Truth in Negotiations Act, 10 U.S.C. § 2306a(a)(2), and 41 U.S.C. § 254b(a)(2). DOD's Contract Claims Certification, 10 U.S.C. § 2410e, was repealed by The Federal Acquisition Streamlining Act of 1994, Pub. L. No. 103-355. As amended, 10 U.S.C. § 2410 applies only to requests for equitable adjustment and relief under Pub. L. 85-804. The new legislation makes clear that provisions of the CDA regarding the certification of claims governs claims on a government-wide basis. Figure 13-3 summarizes the dollar threshold and the timing of these certificates.

Figure 4-3

Statute	Threshold	Time of Certificate	Material Certified
Contract Disputes Act	Over $100,000	Submission of claim	Good faith, supporting data, accuracy, and authority of signer
Truth in Negotiations Act	Over $550,000	Conclusion of negotiation arriving at settlement of dispute	Cost or pricing data current, accurate and complete
10 U.S.C. § 2410	Over Simplified Acquisition threshold	Submission of request for Equitable Adjustment or relief under Pub. L. 85-804	Good faith and supporting data

Certifications are also required by the standard forms for termination settlement proposals, Standard Forms 1435, 1436, 1437, and 1438 in FAR 53.301-1435 though -1438 respectively.

In *Paul E. Lehman, Inc. v. United States*, 230 Ct. Cl. 11, 673 F.2d 352 (1982), the court held that the CDA certification requirement was jurisdictional. Thus, in the absence of the required certificate, the court stated that "there is simply no claim that this court may review." The result was hundreds of cases in which a technical defect in the certification required the contractor to begin the disputes process all over again no matter what stage the proceedings were in. In these cases, the contractor was deprived of interest, which did not begin to accrue until a proper claim was filed. The Federal Courts Administration Act of 1992, Pub. L. 102-572, § 907, corrected this unfair procedure by amending 41 U.S.C. § 605(c) so that the contracting officer and a board or court are no longer required to start over because of a technical defect in the certification. As amended, 41 U.S.C. § 605(c) provides:

> (1) A contracting officer shall issue a decision on any submitted claim of $100,000 or less within sixty days from his receipt of a written request from the contractor that a decision be rendered within that period. For claims of more than $100,000, the contractor shall certify that the claim is made in good faith, that the supporting data are accurate and complete to the best of his knowledge and belief, that the amount requested accurately reflects the contract adjustment for which the contractor believes the government is liable, and that the certifier is duly authorized to certify the claim on behalf of the contractor.
>
> * * *
>
> (6) The contracting officer shall have no obligation to render a final decision on any claim of more than $100,000 that is not certified in accordance with paragraph (1) if, within 60 days after receipt of the claim, the contracting officer notifies the contractor in writing of the reasons why any attempted certification was found to be defective. A defect in the certification of a claim shall not deprive a court or an agency board of contract appeals of jurisdiction over that claim. Prior to the entry of a final judgment by a court or a decision by an agency board of contract appeals, the court or agency board shall require a defective certification to be corrected.

Paragraph (6) of the statute makes it clear that the contracting officer can permit correction of any certification problems when a claim is initially submitted. Thus, contracting officer should review claims for proper certification and immediately notify the contractor if the certification does not fully comply with the statutory requirement. See FAR 33.211(e) stating:

> The contracting officer shall have no obligation to render a final decision on any claim exceeding $ 100,000 which contains a defective certification, if within 60 days after receipt of the claim, the contracting officer notifies the contractor, in writing, of the reasons why any attempted certification was found to be defective.

This new procedure is retroactively effective for all claims submitted before the amendment, except those claims that have been appealed to an agency board or filed in court before the date of enactment of the amendment. These claims are still subject to the old certification rules. See *Blake Constr. Co. v. United States*, 28 Fed. Cl. 672 (1993), *aff'd*, 29 F.3d 645 (Fed. Cir. 1994) (litigation filed prior to date of legislative enactment and, therefore, strict certification rules applied to determine that contractor met prior certification requirements), and *McDonnell Douglas Corp.*, ASBCA 46582, 96-2 BCA ¶28,377 (claim filed prior to legislative enactment but new certification rules applied because appeal filed after enactment).

a. Threshold

When enacted, the CDA required certification of all contractor claims over $50,000. In 1994, Pub. L. 103-355 changed this threshold to $100,000. In determining the dollar amount of a claim, the increased and decreased costs involved in the claim must be aggregated, FAR 33.207(d). Thus, a contract of $70,000 with a change involving $60,000 of added work and $45,000 of deleted work would be required to be certified since the combined amount of the addition and deletion ($105,000) exceeded the $100,000 threshold. A contractor cannot avoid the certification requirement by splitting what is, in fact, one claim into several sub$100,000 claims. See, for example, *Warchol Constr. Co. v. United States*, 2 Cl. Ct. 384 (1983), and *Walsky Constr. Co. v. United States*, 3 Cl. Ct. 615 (1983).

Whether there is one "claim" that exceeds $100,000 and, therefore, must be certified, or multiple claims, each for less than $100,000 that need not be certified, depends on whether the claims or demands arise out of essentially interrelated conduct or services and the same or closely connected operative facts, in which case they comprise a unitary claim. Thus, multiple contract administrative claims involving separate and distinct facts and circumstances are not a unitary claim, *Dunlap Enters.*, AGBCA 94-126-1, 96-1 BCA ¶28,024, but they are unitary when they arise out of virtually identical facts, *Columbia Constr. Co.,* ASBCA 48536, 96-1 BCA ¶27,970. See also *D & K Painting Co.*, DOTBCA 4014, 98-2 BCA ¶30,064, in which the contractor improperly fragmented claims that amounted to less than $100,000 individually but more than $100,000 together. The claims were not "separate and independent," as the contractor argued, but rather a "single unitary claim." Hence the claims were dismissed because the contractor did not certify them as required by the Contract Disputes Act. In *Velia Flying Horse v. United States,* 49 Fed. Cl. 419 (2001), several members of an Indian tribe filed collective claims totaling more than $100,000. Because the claim letter stated, "we are filing individual contract claims with you, as the contracting officer," the contracting officer considered each contract dispute as a separate claim and each plaintiff as a separate contractor. The court thus found that no individual claim was for more than $100,000 and that separate certification was not required.

b. Significance of Defective Certification or Absence of Certification

Under the new CDA certificate requirements, a defective certification will not deprive the court or board of jurisdiction. FAR 33.201 contains the following definition:

> Defective certification means a certificate which alters or otherwise deviates from the language in 33.207(c) or which is not executed by a person duly authorized to bind the contractor with respect to the claim. Failure to certify shall not be deemed to be a defective certification.

This distinction between a defective certification and failure to certify is a key distinction because defective certifications can be corrected without adverse consequences to the contractor, such as loss of interest, whereas failure to submit a certification deprives the court or board of jurisdiction.

(1) Correctable Defective Certifications

If a contractor submits a certification that meets most of the four CDA requirements it is likely that it will be found to be a defective certification that is subject to correction. See *JSA Health Care Corp.*, ASBCA 48262, 97-2 BCA ¶29,126, stating that a certification that omits "some, but not all, of the required statements" must be corrected before the board issues a decision. See *also Rosinka Joint Venture*, ASBCA 48143, 97-1 BCA ¶28,653 (only one of the four required CDA statements missing); *Sprint Communications Co. v. General Servs. Admin.*, GSBCA 15139, 01-2 BCA ¶31,464 (substantial increase in amount certified to); and *Thomas Creek Lumber & Log Co.*, IBCA 4020-1999, 00-2 BCA ¶31,077 (statement that signer had authority missing). However, a certification that contains almost none of the required statements will not be subject to correction. See *Sam Gray Enters., Inc. v. United States*, 32 Fed. Cl. 526, 529 (1995) (statement that included "I acted in good faith" did not remotely resemble required CDA certification so as to permit correction).

There were a few important cases prior to the CDA amendments in 1993 that held that certifications with minor defects met the prior strict certification requirement. See *W.H. Moseley Co. v. United States*, 230 Ct. Cl. 405, 677 F.2d 850, *cert. denied,* 459 U.S. 836 (1982) (specific statutory words need not be used as long as the certification and documents referenced by it contain the essence of the required statements); *United States v. General Elec. Corp.*, 727 F.2d 1567 (Fed. Cir. 1984) (certification met statutory requirement even though it did not state that "the amount requested accurately reflects the contract adjustment for which the contractor believes the government is liable") *Fischbach & Moore Int'l Corp. v. Secretary of State*, 987 F.2d 759 (Fed. Cir. 1993) (certification stating that the supporting data were accurate and complete to the best of the contractor's "understanding and belief" rather than "knowledge and belief" substantially complied with the CDA); and *Heyl & Patterson, Inc. v. O'Keefe*, 986 F.2d 480 (Fed. Cir. 1993), *overruled on other grounds, Reflectone, Inc. v. Dalton*, 60 F.3d 1572 (Fed. Cir. 1995) (certification omitting the word "supporting" was in substantial compliance with CDA). Compare *Aeronetics Div., AAR Brooks & Perkins Corp. v. United States*, 12 Cl. Ct. 132 (1987), in which the court found that the certification did not comply with the requirements of the CDA because it substituted the words "without fraud or misrepresentation" for the required good-faith assertion, omitted the assertion regarding the accuracy of data, and for the third assertion stated that the "amount fairly reflects what the Government owes."

The submission of only the certification on one of the termination settlement forms has been held to be a correctable CDA certification. See *James M. Ellett Constr. Co. v. United States*, 93 F.3d 1537 (Fed. Cir. 1996), holding that only a technical defect was present when the contractor submitted the termination settlement proposal certification in Standard Form 1436 in lieu of the required CDA certification. Because many elements of the CDA certificate are missing from the Standard Form 1436 certification, *Ellett* effectively reversed prior decisions holding that the Standard Form 1436 certificate was an inadequate substitute for CDA certification. The *Ellett* rule has been followed in *Metric Constructors, Inc.*, ASBCA 50843, 98-2 BCA ¶30,088, and *J&E Salvage Co. v. United States*, 37 Fed. Cl. 256 (1997), *aff'd*, 152 F.3d 945 (Fed. Cir.), *cert. denied*, 525 U. S. 827 (1998). In *Medina Constr., Ltd. v. United States*, 43 Fed. Cl. 537 (1999), the court reached the same conclusion in a situation where the contractor had asserted that it had never submitted a valid CDA claim in an effort to avoid a fraud counterclaim by the government. The court held that it was bound by the *Ellett* ruling even though the contractor had refused to correct the certificate so that it contained the CDA language.

The Standard Form 1411, the form previously used for certified cost or pricing data, is not a correctable CDA certificate. See *Scan-Tech Sec. L.P. v. United States*, 46 Fed. Cl. 326 (2000), holding that the statement on this form did "not contain language that remotely corresponds to that of the CDA."

An unsigned certificate is not a defective certification subject to correction. See *Hawaii CyberSpace*, ASBCA 54065, 04-1 BCA ¶32,455; *AT&T Communications v. General Servs. Admin.*, GSBCA 14932, 99-2 BCA ¶30,415; *Eurostyle Inc.*, ASBCA 45934, 94-1 BCA ¶26,458.

(2) Intentional or Negligent Disregard

Correction is not permitted if the contractor's claim reflects "an intentional or negligent disregard" of the CDA certification requirements. Thus, no correction was permitted in *Walashek Indus. & Marine, Inc.*, ASBCA 52166, 00-1 BCA ¶30,728, where the contractor failed with "knowing and intentional disregard of the applicable certification requirements" to include only two prongs of the CDA language after being explicitly told of the requirement by the contracting officer. See also *Keydata Sys. Inc. v. Department of Treasury*, GSBCA 14281-TD, 97-2 BCA ¶29,330 (correction not permitted when there was "negligent disregard" of the CDA certification requirements and the contractor took no action to submit a proper certificate after being told of the specific requirements by the contracting officer); *Production Corp.*, ASBCA 49122-812, 96-1 BCA ¶28,053 (affidavit that was intentionally and deliberately drafted to avoid all of the essential requirements of a CDA certification).

(3) Absence of Certificate

The lack of any certification deprives the court or board of jurisdiction even if the contracting officer has issued a decision on the "claim," *Hemmer—IRS Ltd. Partnership v. General Servs. Admin.*, GSBCA 16134, 04-1 BCA ¶32,509; *AMR Group, Inc., t/a Landmark Allied*, ASBCA 51330, 01-1 BCA ¶31,361; *Golub-Wegco Kansas City 1, LLC v. General Servs. Admin.*, GSBCA 15387, 01-2 BCA ¶31,553; *Hamilton Sec. Advisory Servs., Inc. v. United States*, 43 Fed. Cl. 566 (1999), *vacated*, 46 Fed. Cl. 718 (2000); *Vanalco, Inc. v. United States*, 48 Fed. Cl. 68 (2000); *Twigg Corp. v. General Servs. Admin.*, GSBCA 13345, 97-2 BCA ¶29,088; *Denro Inc.*, DOTBCA 3070, 97-2 BCA ¶29,099; *TGMI Contractors, Inc. v. General Servs. Admin.*, GSBCA 14488, 98-2 BCA ¶29,890; *D&K Painting Co.*, DOTBCA 4014, 98-2 BCA ¶30,064; *CDM Int'l Inc.*, ASBCA 52123, 99-2 BCA ¶30,467; *Hamza v. United States*, 31 Fed. Cl. 315 (1994).

The absence of a contractor's certification when submitting a claim on behalf of a subcontractor is also not correctable. See *Lockheed Martin Tactical Defense Sys. v. Department of Commerce*, GSBCA 14450-COM, 98-1 BCA ¶29,717 (the submission of a subcontractor's CDA certificate with a statement that the claim was certifiable was not a correctable defective certification).

The rule barring correction when there is no certificate does not apply if the absence of the certificate is attributable to the fact that the original claim was under the $100,000 threshold for certification and the claim is later amended to exceed $100,000, *William P. Schaetzel*, ENGBCA 6365, 98-2 BCA ¶29,937; *Pevar Co. v. United States*, 32 Fed. Cl. 822 (1995).

(4) Certification by Combination

The certificate does not have to be signed on the same date as the claim if it is, in fact, certifying the elements of the claim as well as its supporting data. In *D.L. Braughler Co. v. West,* 127 F.3d 1476 (Fed. Cir. 1997), the Federal Circuit held that a submission from a contractor may be a CDA "claim" even if it is not certified where an earlier "letter claim" submitted by the contractor (to an engineer rather than the contracting officer) had been certified and the two submissions were substantially identical and based on the same supporting data. See also *P.I.O. GmgH Bau und Ingenieurplanung v. International Broadcasting Bureau,* GSBCA 15934-IBB, 04-1 BCA ¶32,592 (certificate signed several months before claim but covered essentially same facts and supporting data). Compare *Loral Fairchild Corp.,* ASBCA 45719, 95-1 BCA ¶27,425, where the contractor submitted a claim and certification in 1992 bearing a certification date of 1990 (the date of a previous claim submission). The board rejected application of the certification to the first claim, which had been the subject of an appeal before the revisions to the CDA. The board considered the 1992 submission to be a new claim, however, and permitted the contractor to correct the certification to reflect the 1992 submission date.

c. *Revision of Claim*

It is generally accepted by the courts and boards that a contractor can increase the amount of its claim on appeal after certifying the claim for a lesser amount to the contracting officer, so long as the revised claim involves no new claim, *J.F. Shea Co. v. United States,* 4 Cl. Ct. 46 (1983) (there is no bar to the court's jurisdiction over increased damages flowing from a factual claim that has been submitted to the contracting officer and certified by the contractor); *Rocky Mountain Constructors, Inc.,* AGBCA 82-256-1, 83-2 BCA ¶16,704; *Central Indus. Elec. Co.,* GSBCA 5607, 83-1 BCA ¶16,273. In *Tom Shaw, Inc.,* ASBCA 28596, 95-1 BCA ¶27,457, *recons. denied,* 96-1 BCA ¶28,007, a contractor's revisions over an extended period of time of the amount of some of its multiple claims did not constitute new claims requiring new certifications because the underlying claim allegations remain the same. The revisions were simply attempts at accuracy with the dollars claimed for specific items both increasing and decreasing.

In *Newell Clothing Co.,* ASBCA 24482, 80-2 BCA ¶14,774, the board stated at 72,916:

> Even after a certification has been submitted, a contractor is not precluded from changing the amount of the claim or producing additional data. The only requirements are that the contractor certify to the amount he then honestly believes is due and that the data furnished at the time are accurate and complete to the best of his knowledge and belief.

Newell was followed in *Computer Sciences Corp.,* ASBCA 27275, 83-1 BCA ¶16,452, in which the board stated that "certification under the CDA does not preclude subsequent proof of a higher amount." Compare *Fort Vancouver Plywood Co.,* AGBCA 83-139-1, 84-1 BCA ¶16,982, the board held that the Act requires certification of any increase in the amount of a contractor's claim. The board declined to follow *Computer Sciences,* although the facts were similar, and noted that, although *Newell* held that certification does not bar subsequent proof of higher damages, it also holds that such an increase needs to be certified to be recovered. The prevalent view is that recertification is not required, *Essex Electro Eng'rs., Inc.,* ASBCA 40553, 91-2 BCA ¶23,712 (increase from $881,569 to $1,065,932 did not require recertification); and *Miya Bros. Constr. Co. v. United States,* 12 Cl. Ct. 142 (1987). See *Modeer v. United States,* 68 Fed. Cl. 131 (2005), stating at 137:

> [I]f the dollar value of a claim increases based on new information available only after the claim was submitted to the contracting officer, it is the same claim, not a new claim, as long as it arises from the same operative facts as the original claim and claims the same categories of relief. See, e.g., *Cerberonics, Inc. v. United States,* 13 Cl. Ct. 415, 418 (1987) (testing for new claims by determining whether a claim "is based on a different set of operative facts or seeks different categories of relief"); *Miya Bros. Constr. Co. v. United States,* 12 Cl. Ct. 142, 146 (1987) (holding that "the increased amount of plaintiff's claim that was not submitted to the contracting officer for decision does not represent a new 'claim' . . . [because] the factual basis for the [increased] claims are identical to the claims that were . . . certified to the contracting officer") (citing *Curley, Inc. v. United States,* 6 Cl. Ct. 274, 276-78 (1984); *Spradlin Corp.,* ASBCA No. 23,974, 81-2 BCA ¶15,423 (Sept. 30, 1981)); *Kunz [Constr. Co. v. United*

> *States*], 12 Cl. Ct. [74 (1987)] at 79 (stating that increased claim amounts in this court are permitted if the operative facts are the same as those presented to the contracting officer and "the court finds that the contractor neither knew nor reasonably should have known, at the time when the claim was presented to the contracting officer, of the factors justifying an increase in the amount of the claim" (citations omitted)); *J.F. Shea Co. v. United States*, 4 Cl. Ct. 46, 55 (1983) (finding jurisdiction over a claim when "the factual basis of the claim before this court is identical to the claim which was certified to the contracting officer").

A claim that does not require certification because it is under the threshold when submitted to the contracting officer, need not be certified if it increases to over the threshold during the disputes process but still is not a new claim, *Tecom, Inc. v. United States*, 732 F.2d 935 (Fed. Cir. 1984). In that case, the claim grew in amount when the government exercised an option after appeal of the contracting officer's decision. The court pointed out that this rule would not cover claims deliberately or carelessly uncertified. The same result was reached in *Burgett Inv., Inc.*, AGBCA 811081, 83-2 BCA ¶16,695. But compare *The Vemo Co.*, ASBCA 27048, 83-1 BCA ¶16,194, in which the board, when the additional amount of a claim resulted in an amount exceeding the threshold, permitted interest to run on the additional claim only from the time the government received a certificate.

d. *Claims Not Involving Quantum*

The boards have concluded that claims for nonmonetary relief are not required to be certified. See *Summit Contractors*, AGBCA 811361, 81-1 BCA ¶14,872, and *Sims Paving Corp.*, DOTCAB 1822, 87-2 BCA ¶19,928. Apparently, this same conclusion was reached by the Court of Federal Claims in an unpublished decision. See *Alliant Techsystems, Inc. v. United States*, 178 F.3d 1260 (Fed. Cir. 1999), *reh'g denied*, 186 F.3d 1379 (Fed. Cir. 1999), stating at 1267:

> The CDA requires certification for claims that exceed $ 100,000. See 41 U.S.C. § 605(c)(1) (1994). The government argued before the Court of Federal Claims that Alliant's claim required certification. The court decided otherwise, and the government has not challenged that aspect of the court's decision. For purposes of this case, we therefore take as correct the trial court's ruling that certification was not necessary and that the contracting officer's conclusion on the issue of finality, which was based on the absence of certification, was accordingly in error.

Claims seeking to overturn a default termination or asserting rights under the contract's Patent Rights clause are examples of claims that might be found not to involve quantum. Note, however, that if the contractor subsequently seeks to recover over $ 100,000 from the government as a result of a holding against the government, it would then be required to submit a certified claim to the contracting officer.

The certification requirement cannot be avoided however, by failing to seek a determination of quantum when the claim is essentially a monetary claim, *Newell Clothing Co.*, ASBCA 24482, 80-2 BCA ¶14,774; *Woodington Corp.*, ASBCA 37272, 89-2 BCA ¶21,602; *Eaton Contract Servs., Inc.*, ASBCA 52888, 02-2 BCA ¶32,023.

e. *Authorized Signature*

Paragraph (7) of amended 41 U.S.C. § 605(c) provides a simple rule on authorized signatures, stating that "[t]he certification required by paragraph (1) may be executed by any person duly authorized to bind the contractor with respect to the claim." See also FAR 33.207(e). Although simplified, the new provisions state that an individual who certifies a claim or request must be authorized to bind the contractor and must have *knowledge* of the basis for the claim or request, *knowledge* of the accuracy and completeness of the supporting data, and *knowledge* of the claim or request. See *Metric Constructors, Inc.*, ASBCA 50843, 98-2 BCA ¶30,088 (senior project manager authorized to sign certification); *Home Entm't , Inc.*, ASBCA 50791, 98-1 BCA ¶29,641 (contractor's attorney authorized to sign certification); and *Donat Gerg Haustechnik*, ASBCA 41197, 97-2 BCA ¶29,272 (general manager of individual proprietorship authorized to sign certification in place of owner because he had a power of attorney). In *Stradedile/Aegis Joint Venture*, ASBCA 39318, 95-1 BCA ¶27,397, the presidents of two companies in a joint venture had authority, together, to certify the venture's claim, even though the venture agreement did not expressly authorize them to represent the venture. Compare *I.J. Chung Assocs.*, LBCA 89-BCA -1, 98-2 BCA ¶30,014, holding that a certification was fatally flawed because it was signed by only one member of a joint venture. In contrast, in *McDonnell Douglas Corp.*, ASBCA 46582, 96-2 BCA ¶28,377, the board held that the execution of a CDA certification by an improper person is a correctable defect.

7. Conversion Into a Claim

If a contractor's initial request for relief does not constitute a claim when submitted, it may be "converted" into a claim. This occurs most frequently when the contractor initially submits a routine request for payment which is not honored by the government. In such case, for a conversion to take place, the contractor must make a formal demand subsequent to an unreasonable delay in payment or disagreement with the government, *Falcon Research & Dev. Co.*, ASBCA 27002, 82-2 BCA ¶16,049. See also *Martin Marietta Corp.*, ASBCA 25828, 84-1 BCA ¶17,119 ("transformation of a routine voucher into a claim does not take place automatically, as if by osmosis, or upon the mere passage of time"); *Raimonde Drilling Corp.*, IBCA 1359-5-80, 83-1 BCA ¶16,294; *Fred A. Arnold, Inc.*, ASBCA 27151, 83-2 BCA ¶16,795, *modified on other grounds*, 84-3 BCA ¶17,517 (both delay and a written demand for a decision essential); *A. T. Kearney, Inc.*, DOTCAB 1263, 83-2 BCA ¶16,835, *recons. denied*, 84-1 BCA ¶17,052 (invoice never converted into a claim by a request for a written decision); and *Granite Constr. Co.*, ASBCA 26023, 83-2 BCA ¶16,843 (long government delay in payment of undisputed amounts not converted without further action by the contractor).

In several cases, the General Services Board of Contract Appeals indicated that conversion would take place automatically. See *Dawson Constr. Co.*, GSBCA 5777, 80-2 BCA ¶14,817; *Joseph Fusco Constr. Co.*, GSBCA 5717, 81-1 BCA ¶14,837; and *Capital Sec. Servs., Inc.*, GSBCA 5722, 81-1 BCA ¶14,923. However, in *Safeguard Maint. Corp.*, GSBCA 6054, 83-1 BCA ¶16,276, the board refused to acknowledge a dispute because of the mere nonpayment of an invoice and distinguished *Safeguard* from its decision in the *Dawson* case. The basis for the distinction was that, in *Dawson*, the invoice was based upon an oral agreement on the settlement of an equitable adjustment that was the subject of the claim. In *Federal Elec. Corp.*, ASBCA 24002, 82-2 BCA ¶15,862, *aff'd*, 2 FPD ¶9 (Fed. Cir. 1983), an invoice submitted following the negotiation of a settlement agreement demanded payment within 60 days and a decision of the contracting officer if payment was not forthcoming. The board found that the invoice was sufficient to constitute a claim of nonpayment, without additional action by the contractor. See also *Kirk Bros. Mech. Contractors, Inc.*, ASBCA 43347, 93-1 BCA ¶25,372, in which the board found that, although the contractor's original submissions were not CDA claims, a later request by the contractor for a final decision converted an earlier submission into a claim.

The concept of "automatic conversion" has also been applied to termination for convenience settlement proposals. See *James M. Ellett Constr. Co. v. United States*, 93 F.3d 1537 (Fed. Cir. 1996), holding that the proposal was a nonroutine request for payment that was not a claim because it did not ask for a contracting officer's decision but which was converted into a claim when the contracting officer had completed review of the proposal and reached a conclusion on the amount due. The court stated at 1543-44:

> When a contractor submits a termination settlement proposal, it is for the purpose of negotiation, not for a contracting officer's decision. A settlement proposal is just that: a proposal. See 48 CFR § 49.001 (1995) ("a proposal for effecting settlement of a contract terminated in whole or in part, submitted by a contractor or subcontractor in the form, and supported by the data, required by this part"). Indeed, it is a proposal that Ellett contractually agreed to submit in the event of a convenience termination. The parties agreed that they would try to reach a mutually agreeable settlement. If they were unable to do so, however, it was agreed, consonant with the FAR's requirements, that the contracting officer would issue a final decision, see *id.* §§ 52.249-2(f) (Alternate I), 49.103, 49.105(a)(4), which Ellett could appeal to the court or to the Department of Agriculture Board of Contract Appeals, *id.* § 52.249-2(i). Consequently, while Ellett's termination settlement proposal met the FAR's definition of a claim, at the time of submission it was not a claim because it was not submitted to the contracting officer for a decision.
>
> Once negotiations reached an impasse, the proposal, by the terms of the FAR and the contract, was submitted for decision; it became a claim. In other words, in accordance with the contract's prescribed method of compensating Ellett for a convenience termination, a request that the contracting officer issue a decision in the event the parties were unable to agree on a settlement was implicit in Ellett's proposal. After ten months of fruitless negotiations,

Ellett explicitly requested that the contracting officer settle its claim. This demand is tantamount to an express request for a contracting officer's decision.

D. Assertion of Government Claims

Prior to the CDA, the government followed a variety of methods for asserting and adjudicating claims against its contractors. It issued final decisions under the Disputes clause, *United States v. A.L. Ulvedal*, 372 F.2d 31 (8th Cir. 1967); *A. Padilla Lighterage*, ASBCA 17288, 75-2 BCA ¶11,406; sued in state courts, *Cotton v. United States*, 52 U.S. (11 How.) 229 (1850); *United States v. Bank of New York & Trust Co.*, 296 U.S. 463 (1936); sued in federal courts under 28 U.S.C. § 1345, *United States v. Franklin Steel Prods., Inc.*, 482 F.2d 400 (9th Cir. 1973), *cert. denied*, 415 U. S. 918 (1974); *United States v. Systron-Donner Corp.*, 486 F.2d 249 (9th Cir. 1973); asserted counterclaims to contractor suits, *Horton J. Brown v. United States*, 207 Ct. Cl. 768, 524 F.2d 693 (1975); and set off its claims against payments due the contractor, thereby forcing the contractor to bring suit, *Project Map, Inc. v. United States*, 203 Ct. Cl. 52, 486 F.2d 1375 (1975). The CDA now limits the government's options by requiring that "all claims by the Government against a contractor relating to a contract shall be the subject of a decision of the contracting officer," 41 U.S.C. § 605(a). Thus, the adjudication of entitlement on government claims relating to a contract must now occur under the disputes procedure.

The major question that has arisen with regard to the application of the CDA to government claims is whether the government is now deprived of the common law right of setoff without the issuance of a contracting officer's decision under the CDA. *Cecile Indus., Inc. v. Cheney*, 995 F.2d 1052 (Fed. Cir. 1993), appears to hold that setoffs relating to the contract must be accomplished under the CDA procedures. However, *Kearfott Guidance & Navigation Corp.*, ASBCA 49263, 99-2 BCA ¶30,518, reached the opposite conclusion, permitting an agency finance officer to setoff overpayments on the instant contracts as well as other contracts without obtaining a contracting officer's decision. See also *Applied Cos. v. United States*, 144 F. 3d 1470 (Fed. Cir. 1988), permitting a setoff without following CDA procedures because a government claim for erroneous payment was not a claim relating to the contract. The court reasoned that, to be related to a contract, a claim has to have "some relationship to the terms or performance of a government contract." There are also a number of cases in which contracting officers have reduced the contract price without issuing a final decision under the CDA and the board has taken jurisdiction of the case based on an appeal of the contractor. See *Sea-Land Serv., Inc.*, ASBCA 47200, 94-3 BCA ¶27,226 (deduction from invoices for allegedly improper billings); *General Motors Corp.*, ASBCA 35634, 92-3 BCA ¶25,149 (unilateral modification reducing price to reflect allegedly inapplicable state tax); *Triasco Corp.*, ASBCA 42465, 91-2 BCA ¶23,969 (deduction in payments to reflect alleged overpayment for materials not used); and *Blosam Contractors, Inc.*, VABCA 2305, 88-1 BCA ¶20,370 (unilateral modification reducing price to reflect alleged deductive change orders). See *A.J. Fowler Corp.*, ASBCA 28965, 86-2 BCA ¶18,970, explaining that such actions by the government are not government claims, as such, but are merely the proper refusal to pay amounts considered not due and, therefore, can be taken without issuing a contracting officer's decision under the CDA.

Government claims subject to the CDA procedures include those for reimbursement of costs of reprocurement, *Defense Techs., Inc.*, GSBCA 9570, 90-1 BCA ¶22,406; excess costs due to defects in performance, *Ruhnau-Evans-Ruhnau Assocs. v. United States*, 3 Cl. Ct. 217 (1983); *Chandler Mfg. & Supply*, ASBCA 27030, 82-2 BCA ¶15,997; recovery of overpayments provisionally paid to a contractor, *American Mfg. Co. of Texas*, ASBCA 25816, 83-2 BCA ¶16,608 (goods); *Dodd Frazier & Co.*, IBCA 1591-6-82, 83-1 BCA ¶16,231 (services); recovery of payments made on undelivered goods, *Unimatic Mfg., Co.*, ASBCA 25212, 81-1 BCA ¶15,095, *recons. denied*, 84-1 BCA ¶17,099; setoff against provisionally paid costs later claimed to be unallowable, *General Dynamics Corp., Elec. Boat Div.*, ASBCA 25919, 82-1 BCA ¶15,616; *Martin Marietta Corp.*, ASBCA 25828, 84-1 BCA ¶17,119; setoff for unauthorized contract adjustment, *Space Age Eng'g, Inc.*, ASBCA 26028, 82-1 BCA ¶15,766; claims for defective pricing, *Honeywell Fed. Sys., Inc.*, ASBCA 39974, 92-2 BCA ¶24,966; failure to comply with cost accounting standards, *Aydin Corp.*, ASBCA 50301, 97-2 BCA ¶29,260; *Brunswick Corp.*, ASBCA 26691, 83-2 BCA ¶16,794; *International Tel. & Tel. Corp.*, ASBCA 27802, 83-2 BCA ¶16,773; assessment of liquidated damages, *R.F. Lusa & Sons Sheetmetal, Inc.*, LBCA 2000, 04-2 BCA ¶32,780; *Evergreen Int'l Aviation, Inc.*, PSBCA 2468, 89-2 BCA ¶21,712; demands for warranty work, *Outdoor Venture Corp.*, ASBCA 49756, 96-2 BCA ¶28,490; and a request for remission of alleged overpayments for work not required by the contract, *Bean Horizon-Weeks Marine (J.V.)*, ENGBCA 6398, 99-1 BCA ¶30,134.

A few cases have held that there no jurisdiction over an alleged government claim because the contracting officer had not issued a final decision. See *Computer Network Sys., Inc. v. General Servs. Admin.*, GSBCA 11368, 93-1 BCA ¶25,260; *Diamond Envelope Corp.*, GSBCA 10752, 91-3 BCA ¶24,138; and *Iowa-Illinois Cleaning Co. v. General Servs. Admin.*, GSBCA 12595, 95-2 BCA ¶27,628. In the latter case, a dissenting opinion commented that it was unfair for the contracting officer to avoid adjudication by merely making the demand without characterizing it as a final decision.

The court in *J&E Salvage, Co. v. United States*, 37 Fed. Cl. 256 (1997), *aff'd*, 152 F.3d 945 (Fed. Cir. 1999), *cert. denied*, 525 U.S. 827 (1998), held that a government claim against a contractor need not be documented in a writing separate from the contracting officer's final decision. In *McDonnell Douglas Corp.*, ASBCA 50592, 98-1 BCA ¶29,504, the board declined to reconsider its previous ruling that a contracting officer's premature final decision disallowing a claim for overhead costs did not constitute a government claim because the decision did not seek payment of money (as required by the FAR definition of a claim), and it did not request interpretation of contract terms.

In some cases it is difficult to distinguish between government and contractor claims. See *Fortec Constructors*, ASBCA 27601, 83-1 BCA ¶16,402, where, when the government withheld "potential liquidated damages" from final payment, the contractor's claim for this amount was held to be a contractor claim. In *Fullerton Ctr. Ltd. P'ship*, GSBCA 6833, 83-1 BCA ¶16,348, the government's withholding of payment for liquidated damages was characterized as a government claim, but when the contractor later brought a claim to recover the withheld amount and interest, the board apparently considered it to be a contractor claim. See also *Security Assocs. Int'l, Inc.*, DOTCAB 1340, 84-2 BCA ¶17,444, in which the withholding of payment was characterized as a government claim that was converted to a contractor claim through the issuance of a formal demand for payment. In *Martin Marietta Corp.*, ASBCA 25828, 84-1 BCA ¶17,119, the contractor's failure to submit a formal demand following the government's disallowance of cost prohibited the claim from being characterized as a contractor claim.

As with contractor claims, there must be a properly asserted claim in order for the court and boards to have jurisdiction over the matter. A request for a payment that was not in dispute did not constitute a government claim within the meaning of 41 U.S.C. § 605(a), *A.E. Finley & Assoc., Inc. v. United States*, 898 F.2d 1165 (1990). Similarly, a letter from a contracting officer, stating that if repairs were not completed in a specified time the government would take remedial action, did not constitute a claim, *RSH Constructors, Inc. v. United States*, 14 Cl. Ct. 655 (1988). The government is required to give the contractor prior notice before and an opportunity to respond before issuing a final decision. In *Instruments & Controls Serv. Co.*, ASBCA 38332, 89-3 BCA ¶22,237, the contracting officer issued a decision demanding payment of $144,300 to compensate for defective work. The board dismissed for lack of jurisdiction because the contracting officer had made no attempt to negotiate a settlement or even discuss the problem with the contractor. It is not necessary for the government to make a money claim. It is sufficient if it directs the contractor to perform a contractual obligation. See *Secretary of the Navy v. General Elec. Co.*, 987 F.2d 747 (Fed. Cir. 1993), in which the court held that a demand for the contractor to repair or replace defective engines constituted a government claim. This decision apparently overrules decisions such as *H.B. Zachry Co.*, ASBCA 39202, 90-1 BCA ¶22,342, in which the board held that a demand that a contractor repair defective work was not a government claim because the government did not demand payment for the defective work but merely sought performance of the contract as specified.

Generally, nonmonetary claims deal with instances where the contracting officer has asserted a government right and the contractor is contesting the contracting officer's legal theory. See *McDonnell Douglas Corp.*, ASBCA 26747, 83-1 BCA ¶16,377, *aff'd in part & rev'd on other grounds*, 754 F.2d 365 (Fed. Cir. 1985) (government right to examine records); *Systron Donner, Inertial Div.*, ASBCA 31148, 87-3 BCA ¶20,066 (compliance with cost accounting standards); and *General Elec. Automated Sys. Div.*, ASBCA 36214, 89-1 BCA ¶21,195 (government assertion of unlimited rights in technical data).

The certification requirement does not apply to government claims. See *Brunswick Corp.*, ASBCA 26691, 83-2 BCA ¶16,794; *General Dynamics Corp., Elec. Boat Div.*, ASBCA 25919, 82-1 BCA ¶15,616; *Fruit Growers Express Co.*, ASBCA 28951, 84-1 BCA ¶17,158; and *Martin Marietta Corp.*, ASBCA 25828, 84-1 BCA ¶17,119. A contractor cannot recover interest on a government claim, *Ruhnau-Evans-Ruhnau Assocs. v. United States*, 3Cl. Ct. 217 (1983), because 41 U.S.C. § 611 does not authorize payment of interest on a contractor award stemming from an underlying government claim. Thus, to recover interest the contractor must convert the government claim to a contractor claim and certify the claim if it exceeds

$100,000, *Security Assocs. Int'l, Inc.*, DOTCAB 1340, 84-2 BCA ¶17,444. In *TEM Assocs., Inc.*, NASABCA 330990, 91-2 BCA ¶23,730, the board held that a contracting officer's letter disallowing certain salary costs and notifying the contractor that the government would deduct the unreasonable amounts from future contract payments constituted a final decision even though the contractor did not certify the claim. The board found that the letter pertained to a government claim and therefore did not require certification.

E. Time for Submittal

41 U.S.C. § 605(a) includes the following time limitations on the submission of both contractor and government claims:

> Each claim by a contractor against the government relating to a contract and each claim by the government relating to a contract and each claim by the government against a contractor relating to a contract shall be submitted within 6 years after the accrual of the claim. The preceding sentence does not apply to a claim by the government against a contractor that is based on a claim by the contractor involving fraud.

The six-year requirement for contractor claims is included in ¶(d)(1) of the Disputes clause in FAR 52.233-1 and in FAR 33.206(a), which also notes that the rule does not apply to claims relating to contracts awarded prior to October 1, 1995. See *Walsh Constr. Co.*, ENGBCA 6325, 98-1 BCA ¶29,683. The clause does not implement the statutory requirement that the six-year rule also applies to government claims but this rule is stated in FAR 33.206(b).

The Act does not define what constitutes "accrual" of a claim. However, FAR 33.201 contains the following definition:

> Accrual of a claim means the date when all events, that fix the alleged liability of either the Government or the contractor and permit assertion of the claim, were known or should have been known. For liability to be fixed, some injury must have occurred. However, monetary damages need not have been incurred.

The CDA's statute of limitations, not the two-year statute of limitations in the Suits in Admiralty Act, governs disputes involving maritime contracts subject to the CDA, *Dalton v. Southwest Marine, Inc.*, 120 F.3d 1249 (Fed. Cir.1997).

Under the antifraud provision of the CDA, 41 U.S.C. § 604, a contractor's liability to the government for a fraudulent claim and the government's costs of reviewing the claim must be determined "within six years of the commission of such misrepresentation of fact or fraud." In *UMC Elecs. Co. v. United States*, 45 Fed. Cl. 507 (2000), the court concluded that the government's claim for costs attributable to the review of a claim pursuant to the CDA's antifraud provision was not time barred. The contractor argued that because more than six years had elapsed since the contracting officer denied its fraudulent equitable adjustment claim, the claim was barred by the six-year statutory limitation period. The court indicated that Congress did not intend to allow a contractor to engage in lengthy pretrial and trial procedures to escape liability when a court eventually finds that the contractor committed fraud. Furthermore, the court found that the fraud was ongoing and repeated in submissions presented by contractor to the bankruptcy court and the Court of Federal Claims as well as through the testimony of the contractor's witnesses.

Other time limitations involve different statutes or circumstances. The Supreme Court held a contract claim under the Tucker Act timely even though the suit was filed more than six years after legislation repudiated plaintiff's contract because the claim did not accrue until the government dishonored a prepayment, *Franconia Assocs. v. United States*, 536 U.S. 129 (2002). See also *Rocky Mountain Log Homes, Inc.*, AGBCA 97125-1, 98-1 BCA ¶29,716 (claim not precluded by provision in a timber sales contract imposing a 60-day time limit for filing a road construction claim with the contracting officer because the contractor's claim also related to other contract provisions), and *United States v. American States Ins. Co.*, 252 F.3d 1268 (11th Cir. 2001) (demand that surety pay reprocurement costs on a defaulted bonded contract subject to six-year statute of limitations in 28 U.S.C. § 2415(a) not the CDA because the government was not a party to the defaulted contractor's performance bond).

Claims can also be time-barred under the doctrine of laches. See *LaForge & Budd Constr. Co. v. United States*, 48 Fed. Cl. 566 (2001), stating at 570:

> Fundamental to laches is the maxim that equity aids the vigilant, not those who slumber on their rights. *Cornetta v. United States*, 851 F.2d 1372, 1375 (Fed. Cir. 1988). Laches is a fairness doctrine that implements the public policy of discouraging stale claims by barring recovery when a plaintiff's delay prejudices the proponent of laches by jeopardizing the court's ability "to arrive at safe conclusions as to the truth." *Deering v. United States*, 223 Ct. Cl. 342, 347, 620 F.2d 242, 244 (1980).
>
> To invoke laches a party must show (1) that the delay from the time the claimant knew or reasonably should have known of its claim against the party was unreasonable and inexcusable; and (2) that the delay caused either economic prejudice or injury to the party's ability to mount a defense. *A.C. Aukerman Co. v. R.L. Chaides Constr. Co.*, 960 F.2d 1020, 1032 (Fed. Cir. 1992) (en banc); accord *Cornetta*, 851 F.2d at 1377-78. The proponent of a laches defense has the burden of proving both elements, and the failure to do so will prevent the application of laches. *Costello v. United States*, 365 U.S. 265, 282, 5 L. Ed. 2d 551, 81 S. Ct. 534 (1961). The application of laches is within the discretion of the court and should not be made by application of "mechanical rules." *Aukerman*, 960 F.2d at 1032 (citing *Holmberg v. Armbrecht*, 327 U.S. 392, 396, 90 L. Ed. 743, 66 S. Ct. 582 (1946)). Thus, the court must examine the facts against the well-established laches standards to determine if defendant has met its burden of proving both delay and prejudice.

See also *Staff, Inc.*, AGBCA 99-138-1, 00-1 BCA ¶30,617, in which a claim submitted five years after contract completion was not barred by laches, because the government's contract file remained open during the period, the government was aware that the file remained open, and the government was not prejudiced by any unavailability of witnesses. The government did nothing during the five-year period to finalize the contract after performance. Moreover, all necessary government personnel were available as witnesses. But in *Perkin-Elmer Corp. v. United States*, 47 Fed. Cl. 672 (2000), the court granted summary judgment for a contractor, holding "as a matter of law, that the Air Force did not assert its claim against [the contractor] within a reasonable time when it waited over six years between discovering the alleged latent defect and finally revoking acceptance."

III. CONTRACTING OFFICER'S ROLE

One of the major duties of a contracting officer is to deal with disagreements between the government and contractors. In performing this function, a contracting officer should first attempt to dispose of such matters through negotiated settlement agreements that bind the parties involved. If such an agreement cannot be reached and the contractor submits a claim, the contracting officer must issue a final decision from which the contractor is entitled to appeal to a board of contract appeals or the Court of Federal Claims. A contracting officer's final decision becomes binding on both parties (finality attaches) unless a timely appeal is taken from the decision. In *United States v. Holpuch Co.*, 328 U.S. 234 (1946), the court held that a contractor's claim was "outlawed" by reason of the contractor's failure to appeal to the board of contract appeals within the time period prescribed in the Disputes clause. Under the CDA, a contracting officer's final decision becomes "final and conclusive and not subject to review by any forum, tribunal or Government agency," 41 U.S.C. § 605(b), unless appeal is taken to a board of contract appeals within ninety days after receipt of the contracting officer's decision, 41 U.S.C. § 606, or to the Court of Federal Claims within 12 months following receipt of the decision, 41 U.S.C. § 609(a).

Thus, the contracting officer functions in a dual capacity—acting as (1)the government's advocate while conducting negotiations with the contractor and (2) a quasi-judicial official when rendering a final decision under the Disputes clause. A contracting officer's final decision serves a dual function—it is the final settlement offer of the government and a prerequisite to the contractor's use of the adjudicatory proceedings called for by the CDA.

This section explores these dual roles of the contracting officer. First, the extent of the contracting officer's negotiation responsibilities and authority are considered. The section then focuses on the final decision process.

A. Negotiated Settlement

Negotiations between the contractor and the contracting officer may take place at various times during the administration of the contract. Settlement of routine requests for contract adjustment by mutual agreement will dispose of such matters before a claim ever arises. The vast majority of contract administration issues are settled in this manner. Negotiated settlements also frequently take place following assertion of the claim and prior to the formal rendering of a final decision. Once a final decision is issued, negotiated settlements may still be accomplished unless the contractor has allowed the appeal time on the final decision to run out. Finally, settlement can also occur during the various stages of litigation. Following is a discussion of the government's policy favoring negotiated settlement and an examination of the scope of the contracting officer's settlement authority.

1. Policy Favoring Settlement

It has generally been understood that the contracting officer's initial obligation with regard to claims by or against the government is to attempt to negotiate a settlement with the contractor. Hence, a final decision under the Disputes clause has always been regarded as a last resort. The legislative history of the CDA contains the following statement at 124 Cong. Rec. H10,725 (1978):

> It is still the policy of Congress that contractor claims should be resolved by mutual agreement, in lieu of litigation, to the maximum extent possible.

The policy favoring settlements without litigation was furthered by the Administrative Dispute Resolution Act of 1996 (ADRA), 5 U.S.C. §§ 571-584. In an effort to increase the use of ADR, the Federal Acquisition Streamlining Act of 1994, Pub. L. 103-355, amended the Contract Disputes Act, 41 U.S.C. § 605 by adding the following ¶(e):

> In any case in which the contracting officer rejects a contractor's request for alternative dispute resolution proceedings, the contracting officer shall provide the contractor with a written explanation, citing one or more of the conditions in section 572(b) of title 5, United States Code, or such other specific reasons that alternative dispute resolution procedures are inappropriate for the resolution of the dispute. In any case in which a contractor rejects a request of an agency for alternative dispute resolution proceedings, the contractor shall inform the agency in writing of the contractor's specific reasons for rejecting the request.

FAR 33.214 implements this policy. In addition, FAR 33.204 states:

> The Government's policy is to try to resolve all contractual issues in controversy by mutual agreement at the contracting officer's level. Reasonable efforts should be made to resolve controversies prior to the submission of a claim. Agencies are encouraged to use ADR procedures to the maximum extent practicable.

The ADRA defines "alternative means of resolving disputes" to include but not be limited to such procedures as settlement negotiations, conciliation, facilitation, mediation, fact-finding, mini-trials, and arbitration, 5 U.S.C. § 571(3). With the exception of binding arbitration, all of those ADR techniques are methods of facilitating settlement which can be used by contracting officers or higher level officials to carry out the government's settlement policy without recourse to the authority conferred by the ADRA. See Executive Order 12988, 61 Fed. Reg. 4729, Feb. 7, 1996, on Civil Justice Reform, stating at § 1(c):

> (1) Whenever feasible, claims should be resolved through informal discussions, negotiations, and settlements rather than through utilization of any formal court proceeding. Where the benefits of Alternative Dispute Resolution ("ADR") may be derived, and after consultation with the agency referring the matter, litigation counsel should suggest the use of an appropriate ADR technique to the parties.
>
> (2) It is appropriate to use ADR techniques or processes to resolve claims of or against the United States or its agencies, after litigation counsel determines that the use of a particular technique is warranted in the context of a particular claim or claims, and that such use will materially contribute to the prompt, fair, and efficient resolution of the claims.

The new ADR method for government contracting—binding arbitration—has limited application. However, it is permitted by 5 U.S.C. § 575 after the head of an agency, in consultation with the Attorney General, issues "guidance on [its] appropriate use." Prior to the ADRA, such binding arbitration was believed to be impermissible, *Tenaska Wash. Partners II, L.P. v. United States*, 34 Fed. Cl. 434 (1995); *Dames & Moore*, IBCA 1308-10-79, 81-2 BCA ¶15,418. However, an opinion of the Office of Legal Counsel of the Department of Justice on September 7, 1995 ruled that there are no constitutional impediments to the use of binding arbitration and the ADRA provides positive authority for its use. The opinion concludes that an agency can consent to binding arbitration as long as an Article III court can review constitutional issues and can review the arbitration decisions for fraud, misconduct, or misrepresentations.

The Interior Board of Contract Appeals has held that the government may not agree to settle a dispute by binding arbitration and then challenge the arbitrator's decision, *Lac Courte Oreilles Band of Lake Superior Chippewa Indians*, IBCA 4102-99, 00-1 BCA ¶30,774 ("ADR is not a trial balloon or a means of gaining a better grasp of the other party's position, or merely an opportunity to practice arguments on a neutral third party prior to the real contest").

2. Settlement Authority

The authority to enter into contracts carries with it the implied authority to agree to contract modifications, *Gene Peters v. United States*, 694 F.2d 687 (Fed. Cir. 1982); *LDG Timber Enters. v. Glickman*, 114 F.3d 1140 (Fed. Cir. 1997). Thus, courts have recognized that contracting officers have authority to reach binding mutual agreements with contractors, conclusively disposing of claims for unliquidated damages, *Cannon Constr. Co. v. United States*, 162 Ct. Cl. 94, 319 F.2d 173 (1963). At one time, the GAO took the position that the contracting officer's settlement authority was limited to claims "arising under" the contract, 44 Comp. Gen. 353 (B-155343) (1964). But in *Perez & Assocs., Inc.*, Comp. Gen. Dec. B-187003, 77-1 CPD ¶48, the GAO specifically reversed prior decisions and recognized the authority of the procuring agencies to settle "breach of contract" claims.

The initial drafts of the CDA contained language that would have expressly authorized each agency to "settle, compromise, pay or adjust any claim by or against, or dispute with, a contractor relating to a contract," H.R. 11,002, 124 Cong. Rec. H10725 (1978). This section was deleted from the Act by the Senate, with the following statement at 124 Cong. Rec. S18,641 (1978):

> Executive agency compromise and settlement authority is not addressed in this Act as this is a matter considered to be included in their existing procurement/acquisition authority under the established precedents.

FAR 33.210 contains the following broad settlement authority language:

> Except as provided in this section, contracting officers are authorized, within any specific limitations of their warrants, to decide or resolve all claims arising under or relating to a contract subject to the Act. In accordance with agency policies and 33.214, contracting officers are authorized to use ADR procedures to resolve claims. The authority to decide or resolve claims does not extend to—
>
>> (a) A claim or dispute for penalties or forfeitures prescribed by statute or regulation that another Federal agency is specifically authorized to administer, settle, or determine; or
>>
>> (b) The settlement, compromise, payment or adjustment of any claim involving fraud.

The limitations incorporated into FAR 33.210(a) and (b), above, derive from the statutory limitations contained in § 6(a) of the CDA, 41 U.S.C. § 605(a). Requests for relief that have been held to be outside the contracting officer's jurisdiction because they are "penalties or forfeitures" include disputes concerning Davis-Bacon Act wage classifications, *Prime Roofing, Inc.*, ASBCA 25836, 81-2 BCA ¶15,203, *recons. denied*, 84-2 BCA ¶17,253; *Emerald Maint., Inc. v. United States*, 925 F.2d 1425 (Fed. Cir. 1991); Service Contract Act violations, *Imperator Carpet & Interiors, Inc.*, GSBCA 6167, 81-2 BCA ¶15,266; *Kass Mgmt. Servs., Inc.*, GSBCA 8819, 88-3 BCA ¶20,891; and Contract Work Hours and Safety Standards Act violations, *Nolan Investigative & Protective Co.*, GSBCA 5905, 82-2 BCA ¶15,943; *Wickham Contracting Co.*, GSBCA 6579, 82-2 BCA ¶15,883; *Mobile Calibration Serv., Inc.*, GSBCA 6217, 82-1 BCA ¶15,532.

The CDA states at 41 U.S.C. § 605(a) that the Act "shall not authorize any agency head to settle, compromise, pay, or otherwise adjust any claim involving fraud." FAR 33.210(b) interprets this provision as barring contracting officers from negotiating settlements on any claim where fraud is alleged.

a. *Negotiation after Issuance of Final Decision*

The issuance of a final decision and the filing of an appeal before an agency board of contract appeals by the contractor do not deprive the contracting officer of authority to negotiate and execute an agreement settling the claim, *Purvis Constr. Co.*, GSBCA 905, 69-1 BCA ¶7723. However, if a contracting officer enters into settlement negotiations after issuing a proper final decision, but before the time for appeal has expired, the decision may lose its finality. In such cases, a board may reason that the contracting officer is inviting further discussion or otherwise indicating that the matter "decided" is still an open question. In *Continental Chem. Corp.*, GSBCA 2986, 69-2 BCA ¶7926, a contracting officer's agreement to submit samples of rejected soap for retesting prevented finality from subsequently attaching to the contracting officer's letter to the contractor informing it of the termination of the contract. Similarly, in *Precision Tool & Eng'g Corp.*, ASBCA 16652, 73-1 BCA ¶9878, the board held that no finality attached to a default termination notice where the contractor subsequently tendered items for delivery before the appeal period expired and was informed by the contracting officer that the termination would be rescinded if the items were satisfactory. In *Sach Sinha & Assocs., Inc.*, ASBCA 46916, 95-1 BCA ¶27, 499, the board held that the finality of a contracting officer's decision to terminate the contract for default was vitiated by his discussion of the termination and his request that the contractor submit, in writing, settlement alternatives proposed during the parties' meeting. The board held that this result could occur if the contractor could have reasonably concluded that the contracting officer was reconsidering his prior final decision, stating at 137,042:

> We have determined repeatedly that the issue to be resolved with respect to vitiation of "finality" is whether the contractor presented evidence showing it reasonably or objectively could have concluded the CO's decision was being reconsidered. E.g., *Royal International Builders Co.*, ASBCA No. 42637, 92-1 BCA ¶24,684 (finality vitiated where CO actions created sufficient uncertainty that contractor could reasonably believe decision not final); *Birken Manufacturing Co.*, ASBCA No. 36587, 89-2 BCA ¶21,581 (finality attached where contractor not reasonably led to believe decision being reconsidered); *Johnson Controls, Inc.*, ASBCA No. 28340, 83-2 BCA ¶16,915 (finality vitiated where CO granted contractor audience to discuss decision and did not "make it very clear" that original appeal period was running); *Precision Tool & Engineering Corp.*, ASBCA No. 16652, 73-1 BCA ¶9878 (use of word "reconsider" not "a sine qua non"; issue is whether contractor "reasonably concluded" CO was "reconsidering his final decision").
>
> Other tribunals have determined likewise. *Edward R. Ester and Lorraine Ester*, PSBCA No. 3051, 92-2 BCA ¶24,822 (reasonable interpretation of letter was CO willing to reconsider; contractor led to believe decision would be reconsidered); *Summit Contractors v. United States*, 15 Cl. Ct. 806 (1988) (post-decision review of same record vitiated finality); *Jen-Beck Associates*, VABCA No. 1988, 85-2 BCA ¶18,086 ("test is not limited to the subjective state of the [contractor's] mind but is an objective one considering all the facts"; finality not vitiated where meetings were to discuss matters other than decision); *Riverside General Constr. Co.*, IBCA No. 1603-7-82, 82-2 BCA ¶16,127 at 80,049 (issue is what CO caused contractor to believe after issuance; finality vitiated because CO "held out the prospect . . . that what was described as a 'final decision' would be subject to further discussion and possibly reconsideration").

In *Sach Sinha* the board also concluded that once a final decision has been vitiated, the appeal period can only be reinstated by the issuance of a new final decision complying fully with the CDA. This result was originally reached in *Roscoe-Ajax Constr. Co. v. United States*, 198 Ct. Cl. 133, 458 F.2d 55 (1972), in which the court reversed an appeals board's ruling that contracting officer's agreement to discuss the matter after a final decision had been issued merely "tolled" the running of the appeal period. See also *Summit Contractors v. United States*, 15 Cl. Ct. 806 (1988), holding that the operative decision after reconsideration was the new decision. In *Arono, Inc. v. United States*, 49 Fed. Cl. 544 (2001), the contracting officer's letter advising contractor that the government would continue to pay rent pending resolution of the contractor's breach of lease claim implied that the contracting officer was reconsidering the final decision terminating the lease for default. Therefore the contractor's appeal, filed 19 months after the contracting officer's initial final decision but nine months after the contracting officer's letter affirming that decision was timely. Similarly, in *DK&R Co.*, ASBCA 53451, 02-1 BCA ¶31,769, the contracting officer's willingness to meet with the contractor was evidence of reconsideration of the final decision. Compare *Ra-Nav Labs., Inc. v. Widnall*, 137 F.3d 1344 (Fed. Cir. 1998), rejecting the contractor's contention that the contracting officer's correspondence after a termination for default had indicated that he was reconsidering the termination decision. The court held that the latter correspondence was only for the purpose of allowing the contractor to mitigate the damages flowing from the termination and that the correspondence clearly so indicated.

Various types of conduct have led to the conclusion that the contracting officer has decided to reconsider a final decision. See *Nationwide Postal Mgmt.*, PSBCA 5043, 04-1 BCA ¶32,492 (discussion with "Manager" led contractor to believe that decision was being reconsidered even though contracting officer did not participate); *DK&R Co.*, ASBCA 53451, 02-1 BCA ¶31,769 (after decision parties met and contractor furnished additional documentation at the request of the contracting officer). However, requests for additional efforts at settlement by the contractor with no response from the contracting officer will not demonstrate that the contracting officer is reconsidering the decision, *D'Tel Communications,* ASBCA 50093, 97-2 BCA ¶29,251; *Propulsion Controls Eng'g*, ASBCA 53307, 01-2 BCA ¶31,494.

b. Settlement During Litigation

The contracting officer retains settlement authority during litigation before the boards of contract appeals. For example, a bilateral settlement agreement entered into after a decision by the Armed Services Board but prior to the expiration of time for a motion for reconsideration was held to constitute an accord and satisfaction binding both parties, *American Bosch Arma Corp.*, ASBCA 10305, 67-2 BCA ¶6564. See also *E-Systems, Inc.*, ASBCA 21091, 79-1 BCA ¶13,806, in which the board stated at 67,702:

> The cases cited by the [contractor] confirm the authority of the contracting officer to settle and compromise a claim in dispute even while an appeal is *pending before a board*. However, in all of these cases, the boards considered that the matter was still pending before a board while, at the same time, permitting the Government through its contracting officer to settle and compromise the claims under dispute, either in part or in whole, and then dismissed such claims and, in an appropriate situation, vacated a decision as barred by an accord and satisfaction. [emphasis added]

An agency may be bound by a settlement agreement executed by its attorneys during litigation of an appeal before the agency board, *United States v. Bissett-Berman Corp.*, 481 F.2d 764 (9th Cir. 1973). See, however, *Defoe Shipbuilding Co.*, ASBCA 17095, 74-1 BCA ¶10,537, in which the board, in view of an agency regulation that precluded any final settlement agreement without the written approval of the contracting officer, held the government not bound to a stipulation of liability in the nature of a settlement signed only by the Navy trial attorney. See also *Marino Constr. Co.*, VABCA 2752, 90-1 BCA ¶22,553, in which the board rejected the validity of a settlement agreement negotiated by the government's attorney. The board ruled that the contracting officer had not approved the settlement and that the attorney did not have the authority to bind the government to the settlement. Boards may not reject a settlement that has been agreed to by a contracting officer, *Federal Data Corp. v. SMS Data Prods. Group*, 819 F.2d 277 (Fed. Cir. 1987).

The contracting officer's authority to settle claims does not extend to cases in which litigation has commenced in a court. In *United States v. Newport News Shipbuilding & Dry Dock Co.*, 571 F.2d 1283 (4th Cir.), *cert. denied*, 439 U.S. 875 (1978), the court held that the government was not bound by a settlement entered into by a contracting officer, because the matter was pending in the courts. The court noted that 28 U.S.C. § 516 and § 519 and Executive Order 6166 gave the Attorney General sole authority to settle cases being litigated in the courts. However, this authority has been narrowly construed, *Hughes Aircraft Co. v. United States*, 209 Ct. Cl. 466, 534 F.2d 859 (1976) (authorization to infringe a patent in future given after suit filed); *PBI Elec. Corp. v. United States*, 17 Cl. Ct. 128 (1989) (progress payment made by government after suit filed).

B. Final Decision of the Contracting Officer

If the parties are unable to dispose of a dispute through settlement, the issuance of a contracting officer's final decision is the first step in the litigation process. Once a contractor asserts a claim, the CDA requires the issuance of a final decision,

41 U.S.C. § 605(a). However, no final decision may be issued on a matter that is already in litigation. See *Sharman Co. v. United States*, 2 F.3d 1564 (Fed. Cir. 1993), *overruled in part, Reflectone, Inc. v. Dalton*, 60 F.3d 1572 (Fed. Cir. 1995), in which a final decision demanding the return of progress payments after a default termination was held invalid because the contractor had already filed suit contesting the default termination. Compare *Case, Inc. v. United States*, 88 F.3d 1004 (Fed,. Cir. 1996), in which a final decision denying a contractor's claim for equitable adjustments for constructive changes was found valid even though suit was pending on the validity of the default termination of the same contract. The court reasoned that the second decision concerned different matters than those involved in the pending suit.

A contracting officer's decision is a jurisdictional requirement for the court or board to hear an appeal. This is generally not a problem with contractor claims because contractors can appeal the lack of a contracting officer's decision as a "deemed denied" decision, as discussed below. However, contractors are not permitted to bring new claims into an appeal when they have not be subject to a contracting officer's decision. See *J. Cooper & Assocs., Inc. v. United States*, 47 Fed. Cl. 280 (2000), in which the contractor filed an appeal of a contracting officer's decision denying a constructive termination claim. The contractor's suit included a breach of contract claim. The court dismissed the breach claim because the termination and breach claims did not involve the same operative facts, legal theories, or damage demands. Jurisdiction has also been denied when a purported decision was issued by a person without the proper contracting officer authority, *United Partition Sys., Inc.*, ASBCA 53915, 03-2 BCA ¶32,264 (decision to default terminate order on Federal Supply Service contract issued by contracting officer in ordering agency when regulations required it to be issued by GSA contracting officer); *Dulles Networking Assocs., Inc.* VABCA 6077, 00-1 BCA ¶30,775 (default termination by government employee without authority); *John C. Grimburg, Co.*, AGBCA 96141-1, 96-2 BCA ¶28,503 (decision issued by administrative contracting officer); *Diversified Energy, Inc. v. TVA*, 223 F.3d 328 (6th Cir. 2000) (letter purporting to terminate the parties' business relations issued by official with no contracting officer authority).

The jurisdictional bar because of lack of a contracting officer's decision has posed greater problems with regard to government claims. See *Blinderman Constr. Co. v. United States*, 39 Fed. Cl. 529 (1997), *aff'd*, 178 F.3d 1307 (Fed. Cir. 1998), in which the court ruled it had no jurisdiction of a government counterclaim that had not been the subject of a decision by the contracting officer. The court distinguished *Placeway Constr. Corp. v. United States*, 920 F.2d 903 (Fed. Cir. 1990), which had held that there was jurisdiction over a counterclaim for a setoff because the contracting officer's decision on the contractor's claim had necessarily considered the setoff because the contracting officer had denied the claim based on the agency's intention to make a setoff. See also *Kit-San-Azusa, JV v. United States*, 32 Fed. Cl. 647 (1995), in which the court took jurisdiction of a case where the contracting officer failed to issue any decision on the contractor's claim, and the contractor appealed on the basis of a deemed denial. The court held that the contracting officer's constructive denial of the contractor's claim for a release of a retainage was logically equivalent to a decision to grant a government claim to keep the retainage. The court, therefore, permitted the government to assert a setoff up to the amount of the retainage based on a liquidated damages provision of the contract. But see *Volmar Constr., Inc. v. United States*, 32 Fed. Cl. 746 (1995), denying jurisdiction over several government counterclaims because of a lack of a contracting officer's decision dealing with the issues involved and extensively analyzing the confusing rules on government counterclaims. See also *D.L. Kaufman, Inc.*, PSBCA 4159, 00-1 BCA ¶30,846, (no jurisdiction over a government counterclaim for anticipated recoveries in a False Claim Act suit because the contracting officer had not issued a final decision asserting that claim); *Larry J Miller*, PSBCA 3632, 95-1 BCA ¶27,448 (government's asserted counterclaim for reprocurement costs had not been the subject of a final decision and, thus, was not appropriate for litigation during the contractor's appeal of a termination for default decision); and *Frankstown Fish Co.*, AGBCA 94-188-1, 95-1 BCA ¶27,579, (no jurisdiction because the contracting officer's memorandum to the contracting agency asserting government claims, with a copy to the contractor, was not designated as a final decision and did not include advice as to appeal rights). Compare *Kearfott Guidance & Navigation Corp.*, ASBCA 49263, 99-2 BCA ¶30,518, holding that a final decision was not required to assert a government setoff because the government could rely on a common-law right of setoff without complying with the CDA requirement for a contracting officer's final decision.

The following material deals with the time for making final decisions and the criteria for a valid decision.

1. Time for Issuance of Decision

Prior to the CDA, the timing of the issuance of a final decision was within the discretion of the contracting officer, subject only to the broad requirement that a decision be issued within a reasonable time following submission of a claim. The CDA deals with this topic variously, based upon the dollar value of a claim.

41 U.S.C. § 605(c) requires a contracting officer to issue a decision "on any submitted claim of $100,000 or less within sixty days from his receipt of a written request from the contractor that a decision be rendered within that period." Since the running of the 60-day period is triggered by the submission of a claim, the contractor has the ability to defer the start of the 60-day period while settlement negotiations are being undertaken, H.R. 1556, 95th Cong., 2d Sess. (1978) at 18.

41 U.S.C. § 605(c)(2) contains different procedures for claims exceeding $ 100,000:

A contracting officer shall, within sixty days of receipt of a submitted certified claim over $100,000—

(A) issue a decision; or

(B) notify the contractor of the time within which a decision will be issued.

A further requirement at 41 U.S.C. § 605(c)(3) states:

> The decision of a contracting officer on submitted claims shall be issued within a reasonable time, in accordance with regulations promulgated by the agency, taking into account such factors as the size and complexity of the claim and the adequacy of the information in support of the claim provided by the contractor.

FAR 33.211(d) implements this statute.

The court and boards have ruled that the specified time for issuing a decision must be a date certain. Thus, in *Obras & Assocs. v. United States*, 26 Cl. Ct. 647 (1992), the court held that a contracting officer's statement in a letter to the contractor that it should not expect a final decision prior to June 30 failed to satisfy the notification provision of § 605(c)(2) and, thus, the claim was "deemed denied." See also *Boeing Co. v. United States*, 26 Cl. Ct. 257 (1992), finding inadequate the contracting officer's statement that he would "endeavor to respond" to the claims by a stated date but if unable "I will advise you . . . when I will respond." In *Northrop Grumman Corp.*, ASBCA 52263, 00-1 BCA ¶30,676, the specific date requirement was not met when the contracting officer stated that a final decision would be issued "no later than 90 days after termination of the ADR if the ADR process does not result in resolution of all issues." Similarly, in *Aerojet Gen. Corp.*, ASBCA 48136, 95-1 BCA ¶27,470, a notice stating that the contracting officer did not anticipate issuing a final decision until the early March time frame and that his ability to meet that date was contingent on the claimant's cooperation in supplying cost and pricing data was deemed to be subjective, indefinite, and a conditional response which did not satisfy the CDA's requirements. See also *McDonnell Douglas Corp.*, ASBCA 48432, 96-1 BCA ¶28,166, in which the contracting officer's statement that the agency would issue a final decision promptly if and when the board dismissed the contractor's pending appeal was found deficient. Compare *Defense Sys. Co.*, ASBCA 50534, 97-2 BCA ¶28,971, in which the board held adequate a contracting officer's statement that a decision would be issued "on or before" a date nine months after the date of the claim.

The "reasonable time" requirement for claims over $ 100,000 will be assessed by considering the complexity of the issues in the claim. See *Defense Sys. Co.*, ASBCA 50534, 97-2 BCA ¶28,971, reasoning that nine months was not an undue amount of time to review a $ 71 million claim for breach of contract. In *Suburban Middlesex Insulation, Inc.*, VABCA 4896, 96-2 BCA ¶28,481, the board found that it was reasonable to set a decision time seven months after submission of a claim because it had been referred to the agency inspector general for criminal investigation. The board ruled, however, that it was unreasonable to extend the decision date by over three more months because the investigation was not yet completed. Compare *Dillingham/ABB-SUSA, J.V.*, ASBCA 51195, 98-2 BCA ¶29,778, finding 14 months far too long for deciding "a relatively small, straightforward construction claim." See also *Fru-Con Constr. Corp.*, ASBCA 53544, 02-1 BCA ¶31,729 (13 months an unreasonable time). In *Adventure Group, Inc.*, ASBCA 52687, 00-2 BCA ¶30,994, the board held that it was improper for the contracting officer to postpone indefinitely the issuance of a contracting officer's decision while waiting for the Department of Labor to issue a wage determination. The board concluded that if the absence of a wage determination precluded the issuance of a decision on the merits, the contracting officer should deny the claim for lack of information.

The fact that a claim submission may be inadequate will not relieve the contracting officer from his or her statutory duty to choose between issuing a timely decision or forecasting the date for a decision, and failure to do so is an appealable decision properly before a board, *Westlox Military Prods.*, ASBCA 25592, 81-2 BCA ¶15,270. If a contracting officer considers information submitted by a contractor to be insufficient, the contracting officer's proper course is to deny the claim for lack of proof, not to decline to issue a decision, *Scott Timber Co.*, IBCA 3771-97, 99-1 BCA ¶30,184; *MK-Ferguson Co.*, ASBCA 42435, 91-3 BCA ¶24,308. See, however, *Gauntt Constr. Co.*, ASBCA 33323, 87-3 BCA ¶20,221, in which the board focused on the contractor's requirement to submit a claim in sufficient detail to allow the contracting officer to form a reasoned position. In that case, the board established a standard that, in order to at least support an appeal from a contacting officer's failure to issue a timely decision, the claim must contain sufficient information to allow the contracting officer to make a meaningful review of the claim. Subsequently, in *Blake Constr. Co.*, ASBCA 34480, 88-2 BCA ¶20,552, the board attempted to balance the appeals burden between contractor and contracting officer by establishing a predictable policy for dealing with allegedly inadequate claim submissions. The board stated at 103,891:

> When a contractor's claim submission fails to contain the requisite specificity, the contractor may appeal, in the absence of a decision, when it can be shown that the CO not only failed to render the decision but also failed to take other responsible action such as properly advising the contractor that the submittal was inadequate and required additional information before a decision could be made

See also *Dewey Elecs. Corp.*, DOTCAB 1224, 82-2 BCA ¶15,828 in which the board directed the contracting officer to issue a final decision 10 months after submission of the claim since the government had not challenged the adequacy of the contractor's submissions.

The contracting officer may decide distinct parts of a claim when they are susceptible of separate consideration and may reserve other portions of a claim for different or later treatment, In *Omni Abstract, Inc.*, ENGBCA 6254, 96-2 BCA ¶28,367, the board ruled that, as to those separate matters decided by the contracting officer, the contractor's time to appeal the matters decided begins to run even though other distinct parts were not decided. As to the latter, the contractor may appeal these portions when decided or deemed denied.

In *Logicvision, Inc. v. United States*, 54 Fed. Cl. 549 (2002), the court ruled that the CDA 60-day time limit for extending the final decision deadline was satisfied when the contracting officer mailed the notice within the 60-day period informing the contractor that a final decision would be issued later, not when the contractor received the letter, which was two days after the 60-day deadline expired.

2. Failure to Issue a Timely Decision

If a contractor is not willing to wait for a decision of the contracting officer, it has two alternatives when faced with a contracting officer's failure to issue a decision. The contractor may request that the board or the Court of Federal Claims order the contracting officer to make a decision, 41 U.S.C. § 605(c)(4), or process the case as an appeal of a "deemed denied" decision, 41 U.S.C. § 605(c)(5). Prior to the Federal Acquisition Streamlining Act, Pub. L. 103-355, this authority was vested only in the boards. Section 2351 of the Act extended the authority to a "tribunal concerned," thereby including the Court of Federal Claims.

These provisions only apply to decisions on contractor claims. The court or board cannot direct issuance of a final decision on a government claim, *McDonnell Douglas Corp. v. United States*, 754 F.2d 365 (Fed. Cir. 1985); *Carter Indus., Inc.*, DOTBCA 2997, 96-2 BCA ¶28,548; *MGM Contracting Co.*, ASBCA 26895, 83-1 BCA ¶16,191.

a. *An Order to Issue a Decision*

41 U.S.C. § 605(c)(4) states:

> A contractor may request the tribunal concerned to direct a contracting officer to issue a decision in a specified period of time, as determined by the tribunal concerned, in the event of undue delay on the part of the contracting officer.

If a contractor proceeds under this section, the case is not regarded as an appeal on the merits but merely the request for an order to issue a decision, *Dewey Elecs. Corp.*, DOTCAB 1224, 82-2 BCA ¶15,828. Therefore, once a contracting officer's decision is issued, the contractor must file a new appeal if it wants to challenge the decision, *Dillon Constr., Inc*, ENGBCA PCC-195, 99-2 BCA ¶30,471.

If the claim is for $100,000 or less, it would appear that the court or board has no authority to give the contracting officer more than the required 60 days to issue the decision. Nonetheless, in *DHR, Inc.*, EBCA 4011287, 88-1 BCA ¶20,451, the board directed a contracting officer to issue a decision within four weeks of its decision even though the claim was submitted four months prior to the issuance of the board decision. The board stated at 103,430:

> We are . . loath to take actions which diminish]the] role [of the contracting officer in resolving claims] or which may result in an appeal without the Contracting Officer having first considered and decided the claim and without the Contractor having thereafter reviewed the decision and concluded that it is wrong. Such interplay delineates the issues and fosters responsible deliberation and careful assessment by each party of its own position. It requires each party to take affirmative actions based upon carefully made determinations. Most importantly, it provides a last clear chance to avoid litigation. We recognize that when we issue an order directing a Contracting Officer to issue a decision we set the stage for an appeal without the benefit of this last clear chance, since one consequence of a failure to comply would be to obviate the jurisdictional requirement for a Contracting Officer's decision.

If the claim is for over $ 100,000, the board will assess the facts and give the contracting officer a reasonable time to issue a decision. See *VECO, Inc.*, DOTBCA 2961, 96-1 BCA ¶28,108, in which the board directed a contracting officer to issue a final decision by a date that was approximately one year after the contractor's initial request for an equitable adjustment. The contractor had submitted 23 volumes of documentation in support of its claim for $ 5.7 million. In *Washington Constr. Co.*, DOTBCA 3026, 96-2 BCA ¶28,582, the board directed a contracting officer to issue a decision on an equitable adjustments claim on a date approximately eight months after the submission of a claim, in contrast to the ten months requested by the contracting officer.

Section 605(c)(4), however, does not entitle a contractor to obtain a board directive requiring a more detailed decision than the one already issued, *Sentry Ins.*, VABCA 2617, 88-1 BCA ¶20,236; *A.D. Roe Co.*, ASBCA 26078, 81-2 BCA ¶15,231.

b. Appeal of "Deemed Denied" Decisions

Alternatively, when the contracting officer does not issue a timely decision, a contractor may appeal a "deemed denied" decision under 41 U.S.C. § 605(c)(5) which states:

> Any failure by the contracting officer to issue a decision on a contract claim within the period required will be deemed to be a decision by the contracting officer denying the claim and will authorize the commencement of the appeal or suit on the claim as otherwise provided in this Chapter. However, in the event an appeal or suit is so commenced in the absence of a prior decision by the contracting officer, the tribunal concerned may, at its option, stay the proceedings to obtain a decision on the claim by the contracting officer.

For claims of $100,000 or less, a contractor may immediately appeal once the contracting officer has failed to issue a decision by the end of the 6o-day period, *GPA-I, LP v. United States*, 46 Fed. Cl. 762 (2000). Although the boards will take jurisdiction of such cases, they have noted that the contracting officer may still issue a decision after the appeal has been filed, *Gardner Zemke Co.*, ASBCA 51499, 98-2 BCA ¶29,997; *Sayco, Ltd.*, ASBCA 39366, 92-1 BCA ¶24,573.

The 60-day time limit is a statutory requirement. In *Voices R Us, Inc.*, ASBCA 50373, 97-1 BCA ¶28,768, the contracting officer neither paid nor denied claims within the 60-day period. The board denied the government's motion to dismiss without prejudice for the purpose of "allowing the contracting officer to issue a meaningful final decision or negotiate resolution of the claims," holding that the failure to issue a decision within the 60-day period was a deemed denial from which the contractor was entitled to appeal. Moreover, the board stated that the fact that the decision was delayed because of a lack of cooperation between the contracting personnel and the government's legal department did not excuse the government's delay. See also *Viktoria Schaefer Internationale Spedition*, ASBCA 47792, 97-1 BCA ¶28,805, *aff'd*, 168 F.3d 1316 (Fed. Cir. 1998), in which the board refused to dismiss an appeal after a deemed denial on the basis that the contractor's failure to provide supporting data had precluded any meaningful review of the claim by the contracting officer. Instead, the board stated that all that is required for a claim is a clear and unequivocal written statement that gives adequate notice of the basis and amount of the claim, without accounting for each cost component. In *Landmark Constr. Corp.*, ASBCA 53139, 01-1 BCA ¶31,372, the government claimed that the contracting officer was not obligated to issue a decision on a claim because the claim was replaced and superseded by amended claims and thus that the board had no jurisdiction over the claim. The board found, however, that the contractor expressly included the claim in the amended claims and sought a final decision. Where the contracting officer neither issued a decision nor informed the contractor when a decision would be issued, the contractor was entitled to take a "deemed denial" appeal.

For claims exceeding $100,000, a claim will not be deemed denied until a reasonable time to issue a decision has expired, *Defense Sys. Co.*, ASBCA 50534, 97-2 BCA ¶28,981. However, a claim will be deemed denied if the contracting officer fails to specify a time in which a decision will be issued, *McDonnell Douglas Corp.*, ASBCA 48432, 96-1 BCA ¶28,166; fails to issue a timely decision, *Steve P. Rados, Inc.*, ENGBCA 6130, 96-1 BCA ¶27,982; or specifies an unreasonable time, *Cessna Aircraft Co.*, ASBCA 43196, 92-1 BCA ¶24,425. In *Briggs Eng'g & Testing Co. v. United States*, 230 Ct. Cl. 828 (1982), the court refused to dismiss a direct access suit filed 14 months after the claim was submitted to the contracting officer and ordered a stay of proceedings until the contracting officer rendered a decision. Compare *Fru-Con Constr. Corp.*, ASBCA 53544, 02-1 BCA ¶31,729, in which the board considered a decision "deemed denied" after the contracting officer had been considering the claim for 7½ months and had stated that a decision would not be issued for another six months. See also *Macsons, Inc.*, DOTBCA 4049, 00-2 BCA ¶31,037, in which a decision was deemed denied because the contracting officer had issued no decision after settlement negotiations broke down.

The boards have also considered nonmonetary claims to be deemed denied when the contracting officer failed to issue a decision within a reasonable time, *Holmes & Narver, Inc.*, ASBCA 51430, 99-1 BCA ¶30,131; *Martin Marietta Corp.*, ASBCA 38920, 90-1 BCA ¶22,418.

In some cases in which the contractor has appealed in the absence of a final decision, it is not always clear whether the contractor had properly submitted a claim or whether the contracting officer had a reasonable opportunity to decide the claim. In such cases, the proceedings will be stayed to obtain a decision, *Gentex Corp.*, ASBCA 24040, 79-2 BCA ¶14,007, *recons. denied*, 79-2 BCA ¶14,139. See also *6800 Corp.*, GSBCA 5880, 81-2 BCA ¶15,388, in which the board ordered a stay of proceedings for a reasonable period to allow a contracting officer to consider the claim because it was not clear whether the contractor's tort/contract claim had been submitted to a contracting officer. Compare, however, *Boeing Co.*, ASBCA 27396, 83-1 BCA ¶16,256, in which the board dismissed a contractor's appeal as premature because the contractor had never submitted either a claim or the requisite certifications to a contracting officer for final decision. See also *Data Sys. Div. of Litton Sys., Inc.*, ASBCA 27684, 83-1 BCA ¶16,334, in which the board dismissed the appeal rather than staying proceedings because the contractor failed to certify its claim to the contracting officer.

Although "deemed denied" decisions give jurisdiction to the court or boards, they do not start the twelve-month limitation period for filing direct access suits under the CDA or the 90-day limitation period for filing appeals in the agency board. See *Pathman Constr. Co. v. United States*, 817 F.2d 1573 (Fed. Cir. 1987), holding that this period does not begin to run "until the contracting officer renders an actual written decision on the contractor's claim." The court stated at 1578:

> In view of the detailed specification Congress provided for the content and furnishing of the contracting officer's decision to the contractor, it is most unlikely Congress intended the twelve-month limitation period to start running on the 'deemed denial' of the claim, which by definition the contracting officer never furnished to the contractor and which the contractor therefore never received.

For cases applying this rule, see *Information Handling Servs., Inc. v. General Servs. Admin.*, GSBCA 14318, 98-1 BCA ¶29,620; *Carter Indus., Inc.*, DOTBCA 2995, 98-1 BCA ¶29,625; *Omni Abstract, Inc.*, ENGBCA 6254, 96-2 BCA ¶28,367; and *Bravo Mfg., Inc.*, ASBCA 45293, 94-3 BCA ¶27,236.

3. Form and Content of Decision

Since the failure to appeal from a contracting officer's decision within the time required can result in the loss of all the contractor's rights, the boards and courts have paid particular attention to the form and content of the decision to see that the contractor has been sufficiently protected.

a. *Written Decision*

The CDA requires that final decisions be made in writing, 41 U.S.C. § 605(a). Oral notification by a contracting officer of a decision on a contractor's claim will generally not constitute a proper final decision for purposes of starting the appeal period, *Brookfield Constr. Co. v. United States*, 228 Ct. Cl. 551, 661 F.2d 159 (1981). A telegraphic message will satisfy the requirement for a written decision, *Avondale Shipyards, Inc.*, DOTCAB 6718B, 68-1 BCA ¶7030, *recons. denied*, 68-2 BCA ¶7196. Similarly, in *Tyger Constr. Co.*, ASBCA 36100, 88-3 BCA ¶21,149, the board ruled that a facsimile copy sent by telecopier served as effective notice of the contracting officer's decision.

The boards of contract appeals have occasionally accepted jurisdiction of contractor appeals from oral notification of denial of a claim, *Bay Hardware*, ASBCA 7119, 61-2 BCA ¶3114. In *Ray & Ray's Carpet & Linoleum, Inc.*, GSBCA 5666, 83-1 BCA ¶16,184, the board took jurisdiction of a contractor's request for contract reformation even though there had been no written claim and no contracting officer's decision on the issue. The board found that the parties had in effect waived the statutory requirements for a written claim and decision and held that "even under the CDA there are situations in which the statutory formalities need not be observed." The board stressed, however, that there had been both a written claim and a contracting officer's decision on other aspects of the case and the government had characterized referral of the reformation issue to a contracting officer as a "useless act." See also *Cosmic Constr. Co.*, VACAB 1504, 82-1 BCA ¶15,696, and *Mid-America Prot., Inc.*, GSBCA 5476, 83-1 BCA ¶16,341.

The decision may be sent only to the contractor. See *F.E. Constructors, JV*, ASBCA 24488, 80-2 BCA ¶14,505, rejecting a contractor's contention that the government's failure to send a copy of the final decision to the contractor's lawyer excused an untimely filing of appeal.

b. *Notification*

For many years the regulations have required that final decisions contain language expressly notifying the contractor that the communication constitutes a final decision within the disputes procedures and stating the contractor's appeal rights. FAR 33.211(a)(4)(v) provides that a paragraph substantially similar to the following must be included in the decision:

> This is the final decision of the Contracting Officer. You may appeal this decision to the agency board of contract appeals. If you decide to appeal, you must, within 90 days from the date you receive this decision, mail or otherwise furnish written notice to the agency board of contract appeals and provide a copy to the Contracting Officer from whose decision this appeal is taken. The notice shall indicate that an appeal is intended, reference this decision, and identify the contract by number. With regard to appeals to the agency board of contract appeals, you may, solely at your election, proceed under the board's small claim procedure fix claims at $50,000 or less or its accelerated procedure for claims of $100,000 or less. Instead of appealing to the agency board of contract appeals, you may bring an action directly in the United States Court of Federal Claims [now the Court of Federal Claims] (except as provided in the Contract Disputes Act of 1978, 41 U.S.C. 603, regarding Maritime Contracts) within 12 months of the date you receive this decision.

Following the guidance of *Pathman Constr. Co. v. United States*, 817 F.2d 1573 (Fed. Cir. 1987), the boards consistently held that a contracting officer's decision that does not contain language substantially similar to that above was procedurally defective with the result that the time limitations on appeals did not apply. However, in *Decker & Co. v. West*, 76 F.3d 1573 (Fed. Cir. 1996), the court held that an incorrect notification of appeal rights would not excuse an untimely appeal unless the contractor could demonstrate "detrimental reliance on that defect." In that case, the court held that the agency appeals board had no jurisdiction to hear an appeal filed two years after the contracting officer's decision even though the notification was incorrect in stating that a default termination could be challenged in the Court of Federal Claims.

Detrimental reliance has been found in several cases. See *Eastern Computers, Inc.*, ASBCA 49185, 96-2 BCA ¶28,343 (board, citing *Decker*, stated that the appeal was timely because the contractor was misled as to whether the copy of the final decision sent by facsimile or the copy sent by mail started the appeal time running); *SRM Mfg. Co.*, ASBCA 44750, 96-2 BCA ¶28,487, *recons. granted*, 98-1 BCA ¶29,471, *recons. denied*, 00-1 BCA ¶30,618 (contractor's counsel had advised it that contracting officer's defective notification permitted deferral of appeal); and *TPI Int'l Airways, Inc.*, ASBCA 46462, 96-2 BCA ¶28,373, *recons. denied*, 96-2 BCA ¶28,602, *aff'd*, 135 F.3d 776 (Fed. Cir. 1998), *cert. denied*, 525 U. S. 874 (1998) (testimony of a contractor's president that he did not appeal within 90 days of receiving the final decision because of the erroneous advice in the notice that he had one year to appeal to the Claims Court).

Some boards have concluded that if the contracting officer's decision lacks "critical" or "essential" information, there will be no need to prove detrimental reliance. See *George Ledford Constr., Inc.*, VABCA 6630, 02-1 BCA ¶31,662 (decision provided no information as to when, where or how an appeal could be taken), and *Lawrence Harris Constr., Inc.*, VABCA 7219, 05-1 BCA ¶32,830 (decision did not inform the contractor of the critical 90-day time limit). In *Harris* the board stated that since the small disadvantaged business had indicated that it did not realize there was a 90-day appeal period, it would find detrimental reliance if that were necessary.

Following *Decker*, there have been some decisions dismissing late appeals because of the lack of detrimental reliance. See *State of Fa., Dep't of Ins. v. United States*, 81 F.3d 1093 (Fed. Cir. 1996) (surety had actual notice of appeal rights); *Carter Indus., Inc.*, DOTBCA 2995, 98-1 BCA ¶29,625 (contractor did not prove that it relied on the decision's failure to state to which agency board an appeal should be sent); *Medina Contracting Co.*, ASBCA 52783, 02-2 BCA ¶31,979 (contractor's statement that it would appeal default termination indicated lack of reliance on missing information in contracting officer's decision); and *American Renovation & Constr. Co.*, ASBCA 54039, 03-2 BCA ¶32,296 (contractor had actual knowledge of its appeal rights). See also *Int'l Air Response v. United States*, 49 Fed. Cl. 509 (2001), in which the court dismissed the contractor's complaint for failure to appeal the contracting officer's final decision within one year. The contractor argued that the U.S. District Court of Arizona had stayed all deadlines relevant to its claims under the CDA. The court held, however, that a district court has no power, inherently or statutorily, to derogate the jurisdiction of the court or to toll the CDA's limitations provisions. Moreover, because the district court lifted its stay six weeks before the original CDA 12-month filing deadline. the court found that the contractor had ample time to file its complaint at the court. The Federal Circuit reversed, holding that the stay order tolled the running of the appeal period because the government did not appeal the order, but did not decide whether the district court had jurisdiction to issue it, *Int'l Air Response v. United States*, 302 F.3d 1363 (Fed. Cir. 2002).

Since the notification is for the contractor's benefit, it will be permitted to appeal the decision even if it contains a defective notification. See *J. Fiorito Leasing, Ltd.*, PSBCA 1102, 83-1 BCA ¶16,546, in which the board held that a contractor who received a procedurally defective contracting officer's decision could either continue the board appeal, choose to appeal to the Claims Court, or request a new final decision. See also *Outdoor Venture Corp.*, ASBCA 49756, 96-2 BCA ¶28,490 (contractor entitled to appeal government demand that the contractor proceed with warranty work even though the demand was defective); *Sprint Communications Co. v. General Servs. Admin.*, GSBCA 13182, 96-1 BCA ¶28,068 (contractor entitled to appeal from letter detailing contractor's deficiencies and the amount of deductions the agency would take, even though it did not expressly state that it was a final decision, because it unequivocally informed the contractor that payment was due); and *Midwest Props., LLC v. General Servs. Admin.*, GSBCA 15822, 03-2 BCA ¶32,344 (contractor entitled to appeal government claim because contracting officer's letter was tantamount to a final decision). Similarly, a contracting officer's letter rejecting the entire amount claimed by the contractor constituted a final decision sufficient to trigger an appeal even though the contracting officer's letter did not state that it was a final decision, *The Writing Co. v. Department of the Treasury*, GSBCA 15117-TD, 00-2 BCA ¶31,076.

Procedurally defective decisions returned by the boards to the contracting officers with orders to issue a new decision include *Lucerne Constr. Corp.*, VACAB 1494, 82-2 BCA ¶16,101 (contracting officer's decision held invalid because it did not inform contractor of its right to proceed under the CDA), and *Imperator Carpet & Interiors, Inc.*, GSBCA 6156, 81-2 BCA ¶15,248 (contracting officer's letter was not a final decision because it did not inform the contractor of its appeal rights).

In some cases boards have rendered decisions on timely appeals from procedurally defective contracting officer's decisions, *Daiei Denki Co., Ltd.*, ASBCA 28499, 84-1 BCA ¶16,954; *Vepco, Inc.*, ASBCA 26993, 82-2 BCA ¶15,824; *Habitech, Inc.*, ASBCA 26388, 82-1 BCA ¶15,794.

c. Responsive to the Claim

Although the Act is silent on the matter, it has long been held that a contracting officer's decision must be responsive to the contractor's claim. In other words, the decision must contain an unequivocal expression dealing with the matter in dispute, *AVANTE Int'l Sys. Corp.*, ASBCA 26649, 83-1 BCA ¶16,416. In *Fred A. Arnold*, ASBCA 10886, 65-2 BCA ¶5151, a decision that confused the location of disputed items in a construction plan was not a proper final decision from which timely appeal had to be taken. The board stated at 24,248:

> The Board observes initially that in large part the confusion in this case is attributable to [the contractor] because [the contractor's] claim letters were obscure as to the location of the conduit with which appellant was concerned. It would also appear that the contracting officer made no investigation with respect to the claim, at least insofar as any contacts with [the contractor] were concerned. As a result there has been no meeting of the minds on the alleged factual basis for the claim.

An ambiguous decision by a contracting officer will not be afforded finality. In *Lakeview Lumber Prods. Co. v. United States*, 215 Ct. Cl. 914 (1977), a contracting officer's decision that granted the contractor's claim for direct costs but was entirely silent on the contractor's claim for indirect costs was not a final decision as to the latter types of costs. See also *E.P. Cline*, PSBCA 2926, 91-2 BCA ¶23,992, where the contracting officer's letter was not a final decision because it did not clearly communicate the government's intentions concerning costs associated with the proposed modification of the perimeter wall of a leased facility.

If a decision covers only part of the claims submitted, it will not be effective as to the omitted claims, *Omni Abstract, Inc.*, ENGBCS 6254, 96-2 BCA ¶28,367. See also *JWA Emadel Enters., Inc.*, ASBCA 51016, 98-2 BCA ¶29,765, *recons. denied*, 98-2 BCA ¶29,960, in which the board rejected the government's argument that denial of a claim for a cost overrun should be read as a denial of subsequent overrun claims based on different facts. Although a partial decision constitutes a valid final decision for those matters that are clearly decided, substantial confusion may result from such "piecemeal" decisionmaking and lead to the conclusion that an otherwise proper final decision is ambiguous, *Skyline Constr. Co.*, DOTCAB 7417, 75-1 BCA ¶11,147.

d. Reasons for the Decision

41 U.S.C. § 605(a) provides that a final decision "shall state the reasons for the decision reached" and that "specific findings of fact are not required." FAR 33.211(a)(4) amplifies these provisions by requiring supporting rationale and a statement of factual areas of agreement and disagreement. However, boards have been reluctant to find that decisions contained too little reasoning. See *RMTC Sys., Inc.*, ASBCA 46496, 94-2 BCA ¶26,743 (contracting officer's decision adequate even though tersely worded and sparse in detail). In *Inca Contracting Co.*, ASBCA 52171, 00-1 BCA ¶30,672, the board stated that the decision was sufficient if its "analysis is sufficient to place the dispute in its appropriate contractual context."

Where a contractor disputes the content of the contracting officer's decision rather than its sufficiency, the board will not issue a directive requiring a more detailed decision. In *A.D. Roe Co.*, ASBCA 26078, 81-2 BCA ¶15,231, the board refused a contractor's request to issue a directive requiring a more detailed contracting officer's final decision because the statute only authorized a direction to issue a final decision when there had been undue delay, which was not the case there. The board reasoned that where the contracting officer had actually issued a final decision, a request for more information went to the merits of the claim and could be properly resolved as part of the appeals process.

A contracting officer may amend a final decision on a CDA claim even after the contractor has appealed the decision to an appellate board, *Space Age Eng'g, Inc.*, ASBCA 26028, 82-1 BCA ¶15,766.

e. *Decision in Wrong Form May Bind the Government*

Although a contracting officer decision that fails to satisfy these formal requirements will not normally result in a forfeiture of a contractor's rights under the Disputes clause, it may bind the government. In *Bell Helicopter Co.*, ASBCA 17776, 74-1 BCA ¶10,411, a contracting officer sent a letter informing the contractor of his determination that certain defective pricing allegations made by the DCAA were "unfounded." A successor contracting officer sought to "withdraw" this decision, arguing that the government was not bound by the letter since it failed to contain the terminal language required in final decisions. The board responded at 49,192:

> This statement clearly and unequivocally is a decision intended to resolve a dispute between the parties.

In *General Elec. Co. v. United States*, 188 Ct. Cl. 620, 416 F.2d 1215, *recons. denied*, 189 Ct. Cl. 116 (1969), a contracting officer's endorsement of a recommendation from the chief legal officer of the procurement activity that a contractor's cost overrun be funded was held to be a binding final decision. See *Texas Instruments, Inc. v. United States*, 922 F.2d 810 (Fed. Cir. 1990), in which an administrative contracting officer's signature on a Price Negotiation Memorandum (PNM) was found to constitute a final binding decision to approve the negotiated price. Following *General Electric*, the court concluded that by signing the PNM, the contracting officer had decided to express a definite opinion on the merits of the claim and in the absence of contrary testimony or evidence had in fact made a decision. Likewise, in *Sperry Gyroscope Co.*, ASBCA 9700, 1964 BCA ¶4514, a letter informing a contractor of the contracting officer's decision to allow reimbursement for certain cost items bound the government even though the letter was not intended to constitute a "final and binding determination" on the allowability of the cost items. The board stated that since the contracting officer's intention—not to have the letter interpreted as a determination—"had not been communicated to Sperry, it can have no effect upon the parties' agreement."

4. Quality of the Decisional Process

The courts and various boards of contract appeals have construed the standard Disputes clause as requiring a contracting officer to make a "personal and independent" judgment on the merits of a contractor's claim, *Climatic Rainwear Co. v. United States*, 115 Ct. Cl. 520, 88 F. Supp. 415 (1950); *Byrd Foods, Inc.*, VACAB 1679, 83-1 BCA ¶16,313. See also *Dravo-Groves*, ENGBCA 4801, 83-1 BCA ¶16,158, in which the board dismissed government counterclaims raised in a contractor's appeal because the counterclaims had not been subject to a decision of a contracting officer exercising independent judgment.

a. *Replacement of Contracting Officer*

The requirement for a personal and independent decision generally does not prevent the government agency from replacing the original contracting officer. However, a proper final decision of a contracting officer cannot be reversed by a successor contracting officer. See *General Elec. Co. v. United States*, 188 Ct. Cl. 620, 416 F.2d 1215 (1969), *reh'g denied*, 189 Ct. Cl. 116, 416 F.2d 1320 (1969); *Liberty Coat Co.*, ASBCA 4119, 57-2 BCA ¶1576; and *Airmotive Eng'g Corp.*, ASBCA 15235, 71-2 BCA ¶8988. See also *Bell Helicopter Co.*, ASBCA 17776, 74-1 BCA ¶10,411, in which the board held that a valid settlement agreement cannot be reversed by a successor contracting officer issuing a "final decision." Compare *Kirschner Assocs.*, ASBCA 25824, 81-2 BCA ¶15,304, holding that a successor contracting officer is not bound by a modification agreement drafted by a predecessor contracting officer once the original agreement has been rejected by the parties. In *Kirschner*, the successor contracting officer was permitted to reassess the contractor's claim for payment of a cost overrun, determine that the contractor had failed to comply with the contract's Limitation of Cost clause, and deny the claim based upon the reassessment.

Replacement of the contracting officer may be improper if the contract designates a particular government official (either by name or office) to make the decision. In *New York Shipbuilding Corp. v. United States*, 180 Ct. Cl. 446, 385 F.2d 427 (1967), the contract designated a particular government official, the Nuclear Projects Officer, as the person who would initially decide contract disputes. The government subsequently abolished that post and transferred its functions to a newly created research and development office whose chief had responsibility over all types of merchant vessels as well as nuclear ships. The Court of Claims declared that a decision on a contractor's claim made by the chief of the R&D office was without legal effect as a final decision.

b. Advice from Other Officials

The courts and boards have also recognized that the contracting officer is entitled to rely upon the opinions and conclusions of technical and legal advisors in arriving at a final decision under the Disputes article. See *Barringer & Botke*, IBCA 428364, 65-1 BCA ¶4797, *modified on other grounds*, 66-1 BCA ¶5458, in which the board stated at 22,775:

> While it is well settled that a decision of a contracting officer must represent his own judgment and not that of another, it is also recognized that a contracting officer may, for the purpose of forming his independent judgment, obtain information and advice from his staff officers and advisors, particularly in the areas of law, accounting and engineering, in which fields he may have little or no expertise. We consider that it would be poor judgment on his part if he did not do so.

In *Pacific Architects & Eng'rs, Inc. v. United States*, 203 Ct. Cl. 499, 491 F.2d 734 (1974), the contracting officer was found to have made a personal and independent judgment in exercising his discretion even though his decision was based principally upon legal advice given by government attorneys. The court stated at 517:

> On the other hand, it is unreasonable to construe the requirement for decision by the contracting officer to preclude the obtaining of legal advice, and particularly where the contracting officer is not a lawyer. Even if an overly liberal grant by a contracting officer would not be reviewable on the government's appeal, it would have to be assumed that the contracting officer like any other officer of the United States would do his best to follow the requirements of law. It was contemplated that after receiving recommendations, legal opinions and advice, "in the end he put his own mind to the problems and render his own decisions." *New York Shipbuilding Co. v. United States*, . . . , 385 F.2d at 435. But there was no implied prohibition against his first obtaining or even agreeing with the views of others.

See also *Nuclear Research Corp. v. United States*, 814 F.2d 647 (Fed. Cir. 1987), finding a valid decision where the contracting officer initially argued against a termination for default, but changed his mind after discussions with personnel in the affected agency. Similarly, in *AirOPlastik Corp.*, GSBCA 4802, 81-2 BCA ¶15,338, a contracting officer's reliance on secondhand information, a recommended course of action, and preparation of correspondence by a subordinate reflected no more than routine government procedure and did not provide grounds for overturning a final decision on the basis that the contracting officer has not exercised independent judgment. In *American Transparents Plastics Corp.*, GSBCA 7006, 91-1 BCA ¶23,349, three contracting officers administering separate contracts for plastic bags sought reimbursement for payments made under identical price adjustment clauses found in each contract. The contractor contended that the contracting officers did not exercise independent judgment because they were intimidated by a strong recommendation made by the agency Inspector General or, in one case, because the contracting officer relied on the opinion of a subordinate. In denying the contractor's contention, the board stated at 117,086:

> In this case, the Inspector General provided advice, and that advice the Contracting Officer is required to consider as an important aspect of the litany of advice provided, viz., legal advice, accounting advice, and advice from subordinates and colleagues.

In *Mike Gibson & Mike Bearden, Co-Trs. in Dissolution of Delta Prods. Co.*, AGBCA 88-139-1, 93-2 BCA ¶25,615, the board considered the extent of personal involvement required of the contracting officer when rendering decisions. In that case, a decision issued by a contracting officer but written by others was held to be a properly rendered decision. The board stated at 127,509:

> [I]t is clear that while the CO was not the primary decision maker and had little or no role in actually preparing the decision, he read it in detail, consulted with others within the agency, and agreed with the decision before signing it. . . . The fact that the CO did not know who prepared the initial draft of the decision, or that he was

not made aware of a relevant fact at the time he signed the decision, is irrelevant. . . . The CO need only make the decision.

The same conclusion was reached in *PLB Grain Storage Corp.*, AGBCA 89-152-1, 92-1 BCA ¶24,731, where the decision was written by the agency's counsel but signed by the contracting officer. See also *Kearfott Guidance & Navigation Corp.*, ASBCA 49271, 04-2 BCA ¶32,757 (reliance on DCAA in cost matters permissible).

Although a contracting officer is entitled to rely upon the recommendations of advisors in formulating a final decision, the contracting officer may not substitute the judgments and conclusions of those advisors for his or her own independent consideration of the merits of a claim. See *J.E. Peters, Inc.*, ASBCA 4198, 57-2 BCA ¶1375. In *Beals Plumbing & Heating, Inc.*, GSBCA 1163, 1964 BCA ¶4358, the board held that a personal and independent decision had not been rendered where a construction engineer, acting as an authorized representative of the contracting officer, had "acquiesced completely" in an interpretation of the specifications urged upon him by a third party. Similarly, in *CEMS, Inc. v. United States*, 65 Fed. Cl. 473 (2005), the court found that the contracting officer "failed to conduct an independent review and take ownership" of his decision when he relied almost entirely on a consultant that had been hired by the agency to work on the matter. See also *Digital Simulation Sys., Inc.*, NASABCA 1751, 75-1 BCA ¶11,336, in which the board held that no finality would attach to a contracting officer's decision where the record indicated that the decision had been based upon a "down the line" adoption of recommendations by the Defense Contract Audit Agency without determinable input by the contracting officer or any other NASA official. Similarly, in *Edmund Leising Bldg. Contractor, Inc.*, VACAB 1428, 81-1 BCA ¶14,925, the board invalidated a contracting officer's final decision, which had been imposed upon the contracting officer by the Veterans Administration's central office staff. See also *Equitable Constr. Co.*, GSBCA 2642, 70-1 BCA ¶8196, *recons. denied*, 70-1 BCA ¶8327, in which the decision issued by the contracting officer was denied finality because a project engineer testified that all letters and the final decision regarding the dispute were written by him personally or under his direction.

In a split decision of the ASBCA, the panel majority held that a contracting officer is entitled to rely on his subordinates in reaching a final decision and is not required to investigate independently the facts of a claim. Instead, the contracting officer need only exercise independent discretion in deciding the claims before him, which the majority considered to have been satisfied by the contracting officer's testimony that the decision represented his independent judgment. The board member who presided over the appeal dissented on the basis that the decision neither resulted from the contracting officer's personal and independent consideration of the issues and records nor reflected his own independent judgment, *Prism Constr. Co.*, ASBCA 44682, 97-1 BCA ¶28,909, *recons. denied*, 97-2 BCA ¶29,004.

c. *Orders of Superior*

A decision by a contracting officer who follows the command direction of a superior without making a personal and independent judgment on the merits of a contractor's claim will not be a valid final decision under the Disputes clause. In *John A. Johnson Contracting Corp. v. United States*, 132 Ct. Cl. 645, 132 F. Supp. 698 (1955), the court denied legal effect to a decision of a contracting officer denying a contractor's claims for time extensions and terminating the contract for default. The court found that the contracting officer had initially intended to grant the time extensions but instead abdicated his contractual responsibility to the commanding officer of the base where the work was being performed by complying with the commander's demand that the contract be terminated and the work redesigned. See also *International Builders of Fla., Inc.*, FAACAP 675, 69-1 BCA ¶7706, *recons. denied*, 71-1 BCA ¶8790, in which the board stated that "[d]ecisions by contracting officers under the Disputes clause must be their own independent determinations, subject to advice by others, but not subject to command direction." The board went on to deny a motion to require the contracting officer to issue an independent decision, however, because it found that the direction to the contracting officer from a superior concerned a proposed settlement agreement rather than the final decision eventually issued. Compare *Jack Graham Co.*, ASBCA 4585, 58-2 BCA ¶1998, where a letter signed by the contracting officer that informed the contractor of a decision of "Headquarters, First United States Army" was deemed a proper final decision since both parties to the dispute "accepted the decision as that of the contracting officer." Similarly, in *Kilgore v. United States*, 121 Ct. Cl. 340 (1952), a decision by a district engineer who was himself a contracting officer and a superior of the contracting officer of record was afforded finality under the Disputes clause. The court concluded that although the contractor would have had the right to insist upon a decision from the contracting officer of record, its failure to object to the decision of the district engineer amounted to a waiver of its right to have that decision declared a nullity.

d. *Review of Decisions*

Certain agency regulations require contracting officers to refer proposed final decisions to superiors for review. It has been held that a contracting officer's decision submitted to a superior for "approval" will constitute a valid final decision. In *Jacob Schlesinger, Inc. v. United States*, 94 Ct. Cl. 289 (1941), the court stated at 307:

> [The contractor] now complains that the contracting officer did not, individually and without consulting his superiors, decide the question. In fact he did, although he did not communicate his decision until he had submitted it to his superior officer in the form of a recommendation, as was the usual practice. His letter to [the contractor] did attribute his decision to the War Department which, perhaps, gave it an air of finality which would discourage an appeal. . . . As to his consulting his superior, we see no objection to that, if the contracting officer, in fact, put his mind on the problem as it existed at the place where the contract was being carried out, and if, as here, the decision which he communicated to the contractor was his own, although it also had the approval of his superior. The question had not, in fact, been submitted to the head of the department, as [the contractor] could have learned if it had inquired or shown any desire to appeal as provided in the contract.

See *Systems Tech. Assocs., Inc.*, IBCA 1108476, 81-1 BCA ¶14,934, *recons. denied*, 81-1 BCA ¶15,084, *aff'd*, 699 F.2d 1383 (Fed. Cir. 1983) (agency procedure mandating review by superiors of contracting officer's decisions involving substantial amounts of money does not destroy the independence of a decision so long as the contracting officer independently determined the amount of settlement offered).

e. *Unbiased and Impartial Decision*

The contracting officer is required to make an unbiased and impartial judgment of the merits of the contractor's claim. In *Penner Installation Corp. v. United States*, 116 Ct. Cl. 550, 89 F. Supp. 545, *aff'd*, 340 U.S. 898 (1950), the court stated at 56364:

> In other words, the contracting officer must act impartially in settling disputes. He must not act as a representative of one of the contracting parties, but as an impartial, unbiased judge. If the evidence shows he has failed so to act, there can be no doubt that we have jurisdiction to set aside his decision. *Northern Pacific Railway Co. v. Twohy Bros. Co.*, 86 F.2d 220, 225; *Anderson v. Imhoff, et. al.*, 34 Neb. 335, 51 N.W. 854, 856. The duty to act impartially was imposed upon him by the contract. If we are convinced he has failed to discharge this contractual obligation, then his decision cannot have that finality provided for in the contract, and we are free to decide the case as we see it.
>
> Some contracting officers regard themselves as representatives of the [government], charged with the duty of protecting its interests and of exacting of the contractor everything that may be in the interest of the Government, even though no reasonable basis therefor can be found in the contract documents; but the Supreme Court has said that in settling disputes this is not his function; his function, on the other hand, is to act impartially, weighing with an even hand the rights of the parties.

IV. LITIGATION OF DISPUTES ACT CLAIMS

The CDA permits contractors to litigate disputes in either the agency board of contract appeals or the Court of Federal Claims. This election applies to both contractor claims and government claims with the result that the government has no right to determine the forum in which its claims will be litigated. This section focuses on the factors that contractors should consider when litigating claims. The first section discusses the decision to contest the contracting officer's findings. Next, the choice of forum is covered followed by a discussion of the time constraints for filing appeals or bringing suit. The chapter concludes with a summary of the organization and roles of the boards and courts involved in the Disputes process.

A. The Decision to Appeal or Bring Suit

As with any litigation, CDA appeals or suits should be undertaken only after full consideration of such factors as chance of success, cost of litigation, impact on customer relations, possible disruptive influence on operations, and desirability of creating precedent. In addition, the scope of any appeal or suit should be carefully analyzed because the boards and the court judges will analyze whether the operative facts are the same. If, in an appeal, the claims described in the pleadings arise from operative facts different from those that form the basis of the claim presented to the contracting officer, or if the claims are not contained within the scope of the claim previously presented to the contracting officer, the board lacks jurisdiction to consider them, *Wilson v. General Servs. Admin.*, GSBCA 13152, 96-1 BCA ¶28,266. However, the court or board will carefully scrutinize the operative facts to determine if they are the same as a seemingly new appeal. See *William L. Crow Constr. Co.*, ASBCA 41508, 97-2 BCA ¶29,124 (contractor permitted to raise new legal theories on appeal arising from the same operative facts as its certified claim); *Scott Timber Co. v. United States*, 333 F.3d 1358 (Fed. Cir. 2003) (although plaintiff presented different legal theories to the court than it had to the contracting officer, the underlying operative facts and remedies requested were the same); and *Peter Bauwens Bauunternehmung GmbH & Co. KG*, ASBCA 44679, 98-1 BCA ¶29,551, *aff'd*, 194 F.3d 1338 (Fed. Cir. 1999) (changing the amount demanded and revising the number of days of alleged government-caused delay based on further information not reasonably available when the initial claim was submitted, and not the result of any deliberate understatement or careless initial appraisal of the claim, are properly before the board on appeal). If the scope of the appeal is less than the issues covered by the final decision of the contracting officer, the portions of the final decision not covered in the notice of appeal will be dismissed, *Cafritz Co. v. General Servs. Admin.*, GSBCA 13525, 97-1 BCA ¶28,969 (rule applied even though contractor attached the contracting officer's entire decision to its notice of appeal).

The findings of fact and legal conclusions in final decisions of contracting officers will play virtually no role in the subsequent litigation. Under 41 U.S.C. § 605(a), specific findings of fact made by the contracting officer "shall not be binding in any subsequent proceeding." The CDA also provides that suits in the Court of Federal Claims shall proceed de novo, 41 U.S.C. § 609(a)(3). Thus, the contracting officer's decisions will be affirmed or reversed based upon the evidence introduced in the proceedings before the agency board or the Court of Federal Claims and the law as interpreted by the forum involved. In the past, findings of fact and legal conclusions adverse to the contractor were not entitled to any presumption of validity in proceedings before a board of contract appeals. See *Southwest Welding & Mfg. Co. v. United States*, 188 Ct. Cl. 925, 413 F.2d 1167 (1969). In contrast, decisions in favor of the contractor have in the past been held to constitute an "evidentiary admission" of liability entitled to presumptive validity, *Norair Eng'g Corp.*, GSBCA 3473, 73-2 BCA ¶10,288. The Court of Claims had apparently endorsed this view, *Dean Constr. Co. v. United States*, 188 Ct. Cl. 62, 411 F.2d 1238 (1969); *George A. Fuller Co. v. United States*, 108 Ct. Cl. 70, 69 F. Supp. 409 (1947); *J.D. Hedin Constr. Co. v. United States*, 171 Ct. Cl. 70, 347 F.2d 235 (1965). However, in *Wilner Constr. Co. v. United States*, 24 F.3d 1397 (Fed. Cir. 1994), the court, in an in banc decision, overruled this line of decisions stating that "once an action is brought following a contracting officer's decision, the parties start in court or before the board with a clean slate." See *Heyl & Patterson, Inc.*, ASBCA 43307, 96-2 BCA ¶28,515, in which the board followed the *Wilner* decision, stating that it could weigh the evidence anew, without regard to the contracting officer's decision. Similarly, in *Airo Servs., Inc. v. General Servs. Admin.*, GSBCA 14301, 98-2 BCA ¶29,909, the board held that a contracting officer's concession in her deposition testimony that a contractor was entitled to compensation under a termination settlement proposal did not presumptively impute liability to the government. The board reasoned that, although the contracting officer's stance was a factor to consider in resolving the case, it was not controlling because, if the contracting officer's final decision does not constitute an evidentiary admission, neither can statements of lesser importance, such as those given in a deposition. See also *White v. Delta Constr. Int'l, Inc.*, 285 F.3d 1040 (Fed. Cir. 2002) (contractor cannot rely on contracting officer's interpretation of amount due in the event of a government breach); *Kinetic Builders, Inc. v. Peters*, 226 F.3d 1307 (Fed. Cir. 2000) (contracting officer's findings of fact entitled to no deference); *Conner Bros. Constr. Co. v. United States*, 65 Fed. Cl. 657 (2005) (contracting officer's findings of fact are not evidence); and *C.F. Electronics Inc.*, ASBCA 43212, 95-1 BCA ¶27,394, *recons. denied*, 95-2 BCA ¶27,719 (contracting officer's decision granting partial recovery to a contractor entitled to no presumptive evidentiary weight). See also *Roxco, Ltd. v. United States*, 60 Fed. Cl. 39 (2004), holding that the contractor is not bound by an unappealed default termination in asserting claims that could have been asserted as a defense to the termination.

The *Wilner* reasoning was followed in *England v. Sherman R. Smoot Corp.*, 388 F.3d 844 (Fed. Cir. 2004), holding that the so-called "McMullen presumption," that if the government grants time extensions for delays, it is presumed to be at fault for the delays, was "at odds" with the CDA. Thus, this presumption will no longer be available to contractors appealing contracting officer decisions.

B. Choice of Forums

Numerous consequences can result from the contractor's election of a forum, including the degree of formality of the proceedings, availability of accelerated procedures, possibility of recovery of Equal Access to Justice Act attorneys' fees, scope of review by the Court of Appeals for the Federal Circuit, and presence or absence of precedent or recent decisions on similar issues. Thus, the selection of a forum is an important decision. This section discusses the binding nature of the contractor's election.

1. Election of Forum Binding

After filing an appeal or bringing suit with notice of the available options, the contractor is precluded from changing forums. This rule is known as the Election Doctrine. See *Tuttle/White Constructors, Inc. v. United States*, 228 Ct. Cl. 354, 656 F.2d 644 (1981), where a contractor appealed a contracting officer's final decision to the Armed Services Board of Contract Appeals and was precluded from appealing the adverse decision directly to the court. See also *Diamond Mfg. Co. v. United States*, 3 Cl. Ct. 424 (1983); *Whited Co.*, VABCA 1776, 83-1 BCA ¶16,295, *recons. denied,* 83-2 BCA ¶16,734; and *Stewart-Thomas Indus., Inc.*, ASBCA 38773, 90-1 BCA ¶22,481. Compare *National Elec. Coil v. United States*, 227 Ct. Cl. 595 (1981), holding an election of the appeals board not binding because the final decision had not notified the contractor of the right to elect.

Contractors should carefully consider the Election Doctrine before choosing a forum. In one case a contractor filed a timely appeal to the GSA Board of Contract Appeals but then decided that the case was more properly lodged in the Claims Court (now the Court of Federal Claims). Although the board dismissed the contractor's appeal without prejudice, the court dismissed the appeal because the case had been originally filed in the board and that decision was affirmed on appeal, *Bonneville Assocs. v. United States*, 43 F.3d 649 (Fed. Cir. 1994). The contractor's subsequent request to the board to reinstate its voluntarily dismissed appeal was denied on the grounds that this new appeal was untimely, *Bonneville Assoc. v. General Servs. Admin.*, GSBCA 13134, 96-1 BCA ¶28,122, *aff'd,* 165 F.3d 1360 (Fed. Cir. 1999), *cert. denied,* 528 U.S. 809 (1999).

The Election Doctrine does not apply if the forum that is originally chosen does not have jurisdiction at the time the appeal or suit is filed, *National Neighbors, Inc. v. United States*, 839 F.2d 1539 (Fed Cir. 1988). See *Ball & Brosamer, Inc.*, IBCA 3542-95, 98-1 BCA ¶29,637, holding that the Election Doctrine did not preclude a contractor from timely appealing to the board after first electing the Court of Federal Claims because that court dismissed the case for lack of jurisdiction. The contractor consented to dismissal of the case on the basis that the court lacked jurisdiction to consider wage matters within the purview of the Department of Labor. See also *Hettich GmbH*, ASBCA 42602, 93-3 BCA ¶26,035 (board took appeal after Claims Court had dismissed prior suit for lack of jurisdiction), and *Warchol Constr. Co. v. United States*, 2 Cl. Ct. 384 (1983) (court took suit after board dismissed case for lack of certification of claim).

The untimely appeal to a board of contract appeals does not preclude the contractor from filing a timely suit in the Court of Federal Claims, *Olsberg Excavating Co. v. United States*, 3 Cl. Ct. 249 (1983).

2. Fragmentation and Consolidation of Claims

A contractor may appeal different claims, even those under a single contract, to different forums. See *American Nucleonics Corp.*, ASBCA 27894, 83-1 BCA ¶16,520, where the contractor appealed a default termination to the Claims Court and appealed an excess reprocurement cost assessment claim under the same contract to the board. However, a contractor's attempt to fragment such claims can be defeated by exercise of the Court of Federal Claims' consolidation powers. 41 U.S.C. § 609(d) provides:

> If two or more suits arising from one contract are filed in the United States Court of Federal Claims and one or more agency boards, for the convenience of parties or witnesses or in the interest of justice, the United States Court of Federal Claims may order the consolidation of such suits in that court or transfer any suits to or among the agency boards involved.

The decision to consolidate or transfer is solely within the court's discretion, *Marshall Associated Contractors, Inc. v. United States*, 31 Fed. Cl. 809 (1994). Moreover, an agency board cannot decline to accept a transfer, *Technical Servs. GmbH*, ASBCA 44457, 96-2 BCA ¶28,338. The Court of Federal Claims weighs the positions of both parties and refuses to give controlling weight to the contractor's preference in deciding which forum shall hear a consolidated appeal, *E.D.S. Fed. Corp. v. United States*, 1 Cl. Ct. 212 (1983).

3. Bankrupt Contractors

If a contractor becomes bankrupt, its claims under the CDA can be lodged with a bankruptcy court, *Quality Tooling, Inc. v. United States*, 47 F.3d 1569 (Fed. Cir. 1995). However, the court in *Quality Tooling* held that the district court with cognizance of the bankruptcy proceeding had discretion to transfer the CDA claim to the Court of Federal Claims for resolution, acknowledging that "prudence will often counsel such a transfer." See also *United States v. Bagley*, 990 F.2d 567 (10th Cir. 1993), agreeing that the decision of the district court to retain jurisdiction of the claims against the government or transfer them to the Court of Federal Claims was a discretionary one. Compare *Gary Aircraft Corp. v. United States*, 698 F.2d 775 (5th Cir.), *cert. denied*, 464 U.S. 820 (1983), holding that the court should have allowed the board of contract appeals before which the case was pending to resolve the appeal because it was a forum with specialized competence.

C. Timely Appeal or Suit

The CDA provides that a "contracting officer's decision on the claim shall be final and conclusive and not subject to review by any forum, tribunal, or Government agency, unless an appeal or suit is timely commenced," 41 U.S.C. § 605(b). This is a codification of the rule that was developed under the contractual disputes procedure. See *United States v. Holpuch*, 328 U.S. 234 (1946), holding that a contractor's claim was "outlawed" by reason of the contractor's failure to appeal within the prescribed time.

There are different times for filing an appeal before a board of contract appeals and for bringing suit in the Court of Federal Claims. However, both times begin on the same date—the date the contractor receives the final decision of the contracting officer. The contractor is given 90 days from the receipt of the decision to "appeal such decision to an agency board," 41 U.S.C. § 606, while 41 U.S.C. § 609(a) provides that an action in the Court of Federal Claims "shall be filed within twelve months from the date of the receipt."

The time provisions are considered to be jurisdictional and the boards and the Court of Federal Claims do not have authority to waive them. See *Cosmic Constr. Co. v. United States*, 697 F.2d 1389 (Fed. Cir. 1982. In *Gregory Lumber Co. v. United States*, 229 Ct. Cl. 762 (1982), the court stated at 763:

> Congress has set the twelve-months limit, and this court cannot and should not read into it exceptions and tolling provisions Congress did not contemplate or authorize.

See also *Construcciones Electromecanicas*, ENGBCA PCC65, 90-2 BCA ¶22,864, in which the board dismissed a Panamanian contractor's appeal because the 90-day filing period was jurisdictional and could not be waived even though the contractor claimed the notice of appeal was mailed late due to the United States' military invasion of Panama. The boards will not consider personal circumstances or equitable considerations or in any other way exercise discretion as to acceptance of an appeal filed later that the statutory deadline, *D.L. Woods Constr., Inc. v. General Servs. Admin.*, GSBCA 13882, 97-2 BCA ¶29,009. See also *Devcomm Sys., Inc.*, ASBCA 50127, 98-1 BCA ¶(no jurisdiction of appeal filed on 91st day afer receipt of decision); *Gateway El Paso Bus. Ctr. Assocs. v. General Servs. Admin.*, GSBCA 13883, 97-1 BCA ¶28,777 (no jurisdiction of appeal filed three day late); and *Glenna Romero*, PSBCA 5137, 04-2 BCA ¶32,790 (mental disability not an excuse for failure to meet 90-day filing period). See also *L&D Servs., Inc. v. United States*, 34 Fed. Cl. 673 (1996), finding no jurisdiction and rejecting the contractor's argument that it did not file within one year because it received the contracting officer's decision very quickly after it submitted the claim.

If a contractor files an appeal before the expiration of 60 days after its claim was submitted and there has been no contracting officer's decision, it will be found to be premature, *Max Castle*, AGBCA 97-128-1, 97-1 BCA ¶28,833; *Procontrols Corp.*, VABCA 5477, 98-1 BCA ¶29,622; *Zbigniew Ostaszewski & Ryszard Grabowski v. Department of State*, GSBCA 16319-ST, 04-2 BCA ¶32,640. However, if a contractor's appeal is premature when filed but the contracting officer subsequently fails to comply with the 60-day requirement for issuing either a decision or a notice of decision date, the appeal will not be dismissed but will be treated as an appeal of a "deemed denied" decision, *La Belle Indus., Inc.*, ASBCA 49307, 96-1 BCA ¶28,158; *Dennis Anderson Constr. Corp.*, ASBCA 48780, 96-1 BCA ¶28,075.

1. Receipt of Decision

Oral notification of a contracting officer's decision does not start the appeal period, *Lone Star Multinational Dev. Corp.*, ASBCA 20126, 75-2 BCA ¶11,530; *Gonzalez Constr. Co.*, NASABCA 67816, 79-1 BCA ¶13,663. The government bears the burden of proving when the contractor actually received the final decision. The government must prove "actual physical receipt of [the] decision by the contractor [or his representative]," *Pathman Constr. v. United States*, 817 F.2d 1573 (Fed. Cir. 1987); *Borough of Alpine v. United States*, 923 F.2d 170 (Fed. Cir. 1991)

Proof of receipt is generally accomplished by sending the final decision by certified mail. Furthermore, the boards have generally engaged in a presumption that mail properly addressed and bearing necessary postage is received by the addressee in due course, *SanColMar Indus., Inc.*, ASBCA 16879, 73-1 BCA ¶9812. See also *Hawkins v. United States*, 1 Cl. Ct. 221 (1983), in which the court relied on affidavits of a postal service official and provisions of the Domestic Mail Manual Regulations to conclude that the contractor received the decision on a specified date. The board also took note of the fact that the duties of the secretary who signed the postal receipts included receiving incoming mail. In *SAI Indus. Corp.*, ASBCA 51575, 98-2 BCA ¶29,913, the government presented return receipts to verify the delivery date and the contractor did not present any evidence in response. Similarly, in *Nielsen Dillingham Builders, Inc.*, VABCA 5255, 97-2 BCA ¶29,005, the government met it burden by establishing that it had properly addressed the final decision to the contractor's principal place of business, mailed it by certified mail, and that it had been subsequently signed for by a mail delivery service company. See *Omni Abstract, Inc.*, ENGBCA 6254, 96-2 BCA ¶28,367, holding that a government attorney's affidavit was sufficient to show the date of receipt. Compare *National Interior Contractors, Inc.*, VABCA 4561, 95-2 BCA ¶27,695, holding that the government did not meet its burden when the decision had been sent by a private mail service. The Department of Veterans Affairs regulations specifically provide that the 90-day period for appealing a final decision does not begin to run until a contractor's receipt of the final decision transmitted by U.S. Postal Service certified mail, *Kimberly Constr., Inc.*, VABCA 4542, 96-1 BCA ¶28,136.

Proof of transmission of a facsimile of a final decision is not adequate evidence of receipt. See *Riley & Ephriam Constr. Co. v. United States*, 408 F.3d 1369 (Fed. Cir. 2005), stating at 1372-73:

> [W]e cannot infer receipt from evidence of transmission. Proof of message exit from a transmitting machine cannot serve as a proxy for proof of actual receipt of the sent message by a remote receiving terminal. Simply put, the evidence offered by the government is not the type of "objective indicia of receipt" that the CDA requires to begin the limitations period. The fax cover sheet is only evidence that the fax was prepared. The phone records and contracting officer's statement indicate a fax was transmitted but do not evidence receipt of the fax by the contractor's attorney. The Boards of Contract Appeal have similarly found that a fax transmission sheet is insufficient to show receipt by the contractor stating "we have held that a 'successful' transmission report for a fax transmission was not reliable evidence of receipt of the final decision where the Government did not otherwise confirm receipt." *Pub. Serv. Cellular, Inc.*, ASBCA No. 52,489, 2000-1 BCA (CCH) ¶30,832. Fax receipt was usually confirmed in these cases by calling the intended recipient of the decision. See, e.g., *Tyger Constr. Co.*, ASBCA Nos. 36,100, 36,101, 88-3 B.C.A. (CCH) ¶21,149 (Aug. 25, 1988). The Boards of Contract Appeal have also been reluctant to "make the quantum leap and infer from the Government's transmission report's statement 'Transmission OK' that the final decision was received by [the contractor]." *Pub. Serv.*, ASBCA No. 52,489. We correspondingly find

that receipt by the contractor cannot be inferred from the contracting officer's statement that the machine indicated a successful transmission. In essence, the government has not offered any evidence that the fax was actually received by the contractor's attorney.

In *Mid-Eastern Indus., Inc.*, ASBCA 51287, 98-2 BCA ¶29,907, sufficient proof of receipt was found when the contractor had requested that the final decision be sent by facsimile and there was evidence showing successful transmission to contractor's facsimile number. See also *Leixab, S.A.*, ASBCA 51581, 98-2 BCA ¶29,962, in which the government presented unrebutted evidence that the facsimile was received and the contractor acknowledged receipt of the decision. However, see *David Grimaldi Co.*, ASBCA 49795, 97-2 BCA ¶29,201, in which the board held that proof of the facsimile transmission was inadequate to establish the date of the contractor's receipt of the decision. The board rejected the contention that a "circled x" appearing on each page of the transmitted decision proved receipt.

Although the usual destination for a final decision is the place of business through which the contract was made, delivery to places other than the contractor's place of business has sometimes been considered sufficient to commence the running of the appeal period. In *Pleasant Logging & Milling Co.*, AGBCA 79-172 CDA, 80-2 BCA ¶14,605, the board held that time began to run when an agency employee hand delivered a final decision to the home of the president of the contractor even though the president was on vacation at the time. The board took note that the president did not object to such delivery when notified by telephone and that this was the past practice between the parties in the small town involved. See also *M.D. Willner*, DOTCAB 739, 75-1 BCA ¶11,011, in which delivery to a contractor's wife was held to be proper. In *Fred Schwartz*, ASBCA 20724, 76-1 BCA ¶11,916, *recons. denied*, 76-2 BCA ¶11,976, the board stated at 57,121:

It is not a prerequisite to the effectiveness of a notification sent to an unincorporated business concern that the notification be received only by an official of the concern authorized to bind the company contractually.

Compare *Idela Constr. Co.*, ASBCA 50222, 97-2 BCA ¶29,256, in which the board held that the government did not meet its burden of proof when the decision was sent to the contractor's attorney as a previous address and it was rerouted to the wrong forwarding address by the Postal Service. See also *Riley & Ephriam Constr. Co. v. United States*, 408 F.3d 1369 (Fed. Cir. 2005), finding inadequate proof of receipt the fact that the certified contracting officer's decision was delivered to the post office where the contractor maintained a box. The Post Office had returned the letter to the government and there was no evidence that the contractor had consented to its receipt of certified mail.

A contractor's refusal to accept a hand delivered final decision cannot preclude its "receipt" of the decision within the meaning of the CDA, *CWU Consultants & Servs. v. General Servs. Admin.*, GSBCA 13889, 98-1 BCA ¶29,343.

If there is more than one final decision related to a single claim, the 90-day appeal period will run from the later final decision. See *William P. DeLacy*, AGBCA 82-213-1, 82-2 BCA ¶15,810, where, although the decision to terminate a contract for default was received by the contractor on July 27, 1981, a letter of April 3, 1982 appealing the default was timely; on February 8, 1982 there had been a subsequent final decision issued with respect to excess reprocurement costs, and the appeal on April 3 was made within 90 days from receipt of the second decision. Compare *Gregory Lumber Co.*, IBCA 1237-12-78, 80-1 BCA ¶14,322 (the contracting officer's response to a contractor's letter does not "toll" the 90-day appeal period where the response was an informal reiteration of the original final decision, rather than a reconsideration of the original decision).

2. Date of Appeal or Suit

In addition to the difference in the time periods, the method of determining compliance with the filing date differs among the boards of contract appeals and the Court of Federal Claims.

a. Boards of Contract Appeals

Rule 1 of the Uniform Rules of Procedure for boards of contract appeals requires that written notice of an appeal be mailed or delivered to the board within 90 days following a contracting officer's decision. A copy of the appeal notice must also be furnished to the contracting officer from whose decision the appeal is taken. Oral notice to the contracting officer of an intent to appeal will not satisfy the requirement, *Lows Enter., Inc.*, ASBCA 51585, 99-1 BCA ¶30,623.

Some boards have embraced a liberal policy regarding misdirected appeal notices. Constructive notice has been upheld when the contractor has sent a timely notice of intent to appeal to the Secretary of the Air Force through the contracting officer, *ContravesGoerz Corp.*, ASBCA 26317, 83-1 BCA ¶16,309, or directly to the contracting officer, *Thompson Aerospace, Inc.*, ASBCA 51548, 99-1 BCA ¶30,232; *Rex Sys., Inc.*, ASBCA 50456, 98-2 BCA ¶29,956; *Sharp Constr. Co.*, DOTBCA 3094, 98-1 BCA ¶29,567; *Yankee Telecomm. Lab., Inc.*, ASBCA 25240, 82-1 BCA ¶15,515; *Dawson Constr. Co.*, EBCA 155-2-81, 81-2 BCA ¶15,162. A timely appeal was also found when the contractor's letter of intent to appeal was delivered to the contracting officer prior to the final decision, *Richard A. Guthrie*, GSBCA 5721, 80-2 BCA ¶14,612. See also *P&L Mgmt. & Consulting, Inc.*, DOTBCA 4086, 00-1 BCA ¶30,759, in which the board found a contractor's appeal timely notwithstanding the fact that it was not received by the board until 94 days after receipt of the final decision. The board noted that the contracting officer's failure to respond to the contractor's misdirected notice of appeal to that office, the inaccurate information given by the agency as to the proper place to send the appeal, and the dilatory action of the agency's chief of procurement in waiting until after the 90-day period had elapsed to inform the contractor that his office was the wrong place to send the appeal all violated the "spirit" of the CDA and were themselves sufficient to hold the 90-day limitation period in abeyance.

The Agriculture Board does not follow this liberal policy. See *American Agrisurance, Inc.*, AGBCA 98-169-F, 99-1 BCA ¶30,237, in which the board dismissed an appeal as untimely because it was sent to the agency not the board. See also *Dan Nelson*, AGBCA 97-130-1, 97-1 BCA ¶28,967, dismissing an appeal that had been received by the contracting officer, but not the board, within the 90-day period. The board distinguished an earlier case, *Frank Dufour*, AGBCA 95-170-1, 96-1 BCA ¶27,964, in which it had followed the precedent of the other boards. Compare *Malaspina Invs., Inc.*, AGBCA 2003-180-1, 04-1 BCA ¶32,418, in which the board took jurisdiction of an appeal timely filed by subcontractor where a letter from contractor sent after the 90-day appeal period had expired stated that it had requested the subcontractor to send the appeal directly to the board. The board reasoned that the subcontractor could appeal directly with the permission of the contractor and that the contractor's letter indicated that it had granted permission at the time of the subcontractor's appeal.

Unless the contracting officer withdraws the decision, extensions of the appeal period cannot be granted. See *Lamb Enters.*, ASBCA 48314, 95-1 BCA ¶27,559, holding that a request for an extension did not excuse an untimely filing of an appeal. See also *JWA Emadel Enters., Inc.*, ASBCA 51016, 98-2 BCA ¶29,765, *recons. denied*, 98-2 BCA ¶29,960, holding that a letter to a contracting officer attempting to keep the contractor's options open to elect to appeal to the board or file suit in the Court of Federal Claims was ineffective.

If Federal Express or another delivery service is used, the notice of appeal must actually be received by the board within the 90-day period, *Leixab, S.A.*, ASBCA 51581, 98-2 BCA ¶29,962; *Elaine Dunn Realty*, HUDBCA 98-C-101-C1, 98-1 BCA ¶29,581; *CWI Consultants & Srevs. v. General Servs. Admin.*, GSBCA 13889, 98-1 BCA ¶29,343; *C & S Managing Serv.*, AGBCA 96-184-1, 97-1 BCA ¶28,625; *Innovative Refrigeration Concepts*, ASBCA 48869, 96-1 BCA ¶28,231. In *Tiger Nat'l Gas, Inc.*, GSBCA 16039, 03-2 BCA ¶32,321, the fact that a Federal Express courier could not find the offices of the board did not excuse late delivery.

In computing this time limitation, the boards exclude the date on which the contractor received the contracting officer's final decision and include the date on which the contractor mailed or delivered its appeal, *Lincoln Gage Co.*, ASBCA 3781, 57-1 BCA ¶1261. Thus, the date of dispatch determines the timeliness of a notice of appeal to a board, *Western Adhesives*, GSBCA 6868, 83-1 BCA ¶16,182, *recons. denied*, 83-1 BCA ¶16,493. An appeal mailed on the first working day following the 90th day after the contractor received the contracting officer's final decision is timely, *Pacific Steel Bldg. Sys., Inc.*, ASBCA 26346, 83-1 BCA ¶16,362. An appeal is also timely when filed on the 91st day from receipt of the final decision when the ninetieth day is a Sunday, *Interstate Constr., Inc.*, ASBCA 43261, 91-3 BCA ¶24,338; *Vappi & Co.*, PSBCA 924, 81-1 BCA ¶15,080, or a federal holiday, *Bushman Constr. Co.*, IBCA 193, 59-1 BCA ¶2148 (construing the pre-CDA 30-day appeal period), and perhaps if it is a Saturday. Most board rules state that Saturday, Sunday, and legal holidays are not included in the calculation of the last day of the filing period. Thus, in *Peninsula Marine, Inc.*, ENGBCA 3219, 75-1 BCA ¶11,130, the board, in construing the pre-CDA 30-day appeal period, held that when the 30th day falls on a Saturday, an appeal is timely if it is mailed on the next succeeding business day. Compare *Wyman P. Guye*, ASBCA 4756, 59-1 BCA ¶2060, holding, in construing the pre-CDA 30day appeal period, that when the 30th day is a Saturday, the appeal must be mailed on that date or it is too late.

Evidence of mailing is established by the postmark on the envelope, *SMS Agoura Sys., Inc.*, ASBCA 50926, 97-2 BCA ¶29,325 (board rejected argument that computer records established that drafts of the appeal notices were created over the weekend prior to the deadline and office procedures were such that notices would have been signed and placed in the company mail for postmarking before the deadline); *Bradley Constr., Inc.*, ENGBCA 6004, 93-2 BCA ¶25,631 (board rejected contractor's counsel's statement that he believed appeal notice was mailed on the date it was prepared).

Under the "Fulford Doctrine," a contractor may dispute an underlying default termination as part of a timely appeal from a government demand for excess improvement cost, even though the contractor failed to appeal the underlying default termination in a timely manner, *Fulford Mfg. Co.*, ASBCA 2143, 6 CCF 61,815 (May 20, 1955); *Deep Joint Venture*, GSBCA 14511, 02-2 BCA ¶31,914; *Delta Constr. Co.*, ASBCA 42453, 96-1 BCA ¶28,106; *Southwest Marine, Inc.*, DOTBCA 1891, 96-1 BCA ¶27,985. But see *Phoenix Petroleum Co.*, ASBCA 45414, 02-1 BCA ¶31,835 (Fulford Doctrine did not apply to an attempt to reinstate an appeal from a contracting officer's decision assessing excess reprocurement costs because the doctrine permits an untimely default appeal only if the contractor appealed the excess costs claim in a timely manner). The Fulford Doctrine allows one to litigate the propriety of the initial termination of a default; it does not afford a contractor the right to recover costs upon showing that the underlying default termination was improper, *American Telecom Corp. v. United States*, 59 Fed. Cl. 467 (2004).

If a contractor declares bankruptcy during the appeal period, the trustee may extend the appeal period pursuant to 11 USC § 108(a). See *Carter Indus., Inc.*, DOTBCA 2995, 98-1 BCA ¶29,625, analyzing the statute and concluding that it did not apply to the situation where the contractor filed for bankruptcy prior to the contracting officer's decision to terminate the contract for default because no appeal was pending at the time of the bankruptcy petition.

After an appeal is filed, the contracting officer cannot divest the board of jurisdiction by unilateral decision, such as attempting to withdraw his final decision, *Holmes & Narver, Inc.*, ASBCA 51430, 99-1 BCA ¶30,131; *West State, Inc.*, DOTBCA 2817, 96-1 BCA ¶28,268; *Triad Microsystems, Inc.*, ASBCA 48763, 96-1 BCA ¶28,078. See also *World Computer Sys., Inc.*, DOTBCA 2802, 95-1 BCA ¶27,399, stating that "parties may not by negotiation, agreement, or stipulation bestow or withhold Board jurisdiction." In *General Eng'g Corp.*, ENGBCA 6369, 98-2 BCA ¶29,948, the board rejected the government's argument that it lacked jurisdiction because the contracting officer would allow entitlement on another basis than that claimed by the contractor. The board characterized the government's position as an "affirmative defense" and ruled that affirmative defenses defeat claims and appeals, if at all, on substantive, not jurisdictional grounds.

b. Court of Federal Claims

The Court of Federal Claims does not follow the liberal policy of the boards regarding receipt of an appeal by the agency. Hence, suit in the court is only timely if a complaint is received within the statutory one-year period. Rule 3 of the court provides that a civil action "shall be commenced by filing a complaint with the clerk of the court," whose records are final and conclusive evidence of the date of filing subject to a corrective order by the court. Rule 3(b)(C) permits consideration of complaints mailed by certified or registered mail in sufficient time to be received before the due date if the sender exercised no control over the complaint after mailing. In *B.D. Click Co. v. United States*, 1 Ct. Cl. 239 (1982), the contractor's counsel was not permitted to file a complaint because it did not conform to court rules. Since the subsequent corrected complaint was not mailed in sufficient time to be received by the due date, it was untimely.

D. Organization and Function of Forums

The trial forums, the agency board of contract appeals or the Court of Federal Claims, have unique organizations and function in different ways. Appeals for decisions of these forums are heard by the United States Court of Appeals for the Federal Circuit, which is a specialized circuit court functioning within the federal judicial establishment. This section contains a brief overview of the organization and function of these forums.

1. Boards of Contract Appeals

Prior to the CDA, the boards of contract appeals were established by the heads of agencies for the purpose of carrying out their function of reviewing contracting officers' final decisions. Under 41 U.S.C. § 607, however, the boards acquired independent statutory status, with their jurisdictions determined by the CDA. This statute gives the agency head the right either to appoint a board consisting of at least three members if sufficient workload is anticipated or to have appeals decided by the board of another agency.

The 2004 composition of the 10 boards of contract appeals was as follows:

Board	Number of Members
Armed Services Board of Contract Appeals (ASBCA)	30
Department of Energy Board of Contract Appeals (EBCA)	3
Department of Agriculture Board of Contract Appeals (AGBCA)	3
Department of Interior Board of Contract Appeals (IBCA)	2
Department of Transportation Board of Contract Appeals (DOTBCA)	3
General Services Administration Board of Contract Appeals (GSBCA)	8
Postal Service Board of Contract Appeals (PSBCA)	4
Department of Veterans Affairs Board of Contract Appeals (VABCA)	6
Department of Labor Board of Contract Appeals (LBCA)	3
Department of Housing and Urban Development Board of Contract Appeals (HUDBCA)	3

Effective January 6, 2007, the boards of contract appeals for the Departments of Agriculture, Energy, Housing and Urban Development, Labor, Transportation, and Veterans Affairs will be combined with the General Services Board of Contract Appeals to create a single Civilian Board of Contract Appeals. This change is the result of a provision in the 2006 Department of Defense Appropriations Act, Pub. L. No. 109-163, § 847.

The appeals boards conduct trials at locations most convenient to the parties. The general procedure is for the hearing to be conducted by a single administrative judge who normally writes the decision. Subsequently, this decision is adopted by a panel of judges as the decision of the full board. These procedures are an attempt to maintain uniformity of decision within each board. From their inception, the agency boards of contract appeals have been thought of as administrative bodies that should hear and decide contractor appeals quickly and inexpensively. See 41 U.S.C. § 607(3) stating that boards "shall provide, to the fullest extent practicable, informal, expeditious, and inexpensive resolution of disputes." However, this goal has been thwarted, in considerable measure, because the boards give full due process including discovery and trial-type hearings. The ability of the boards to give full due process is enhanced by 41 U.S.C. § 610, which allows boards the quasi-judicial power to "administer oaths to witnesses, authorize depositions and discovery proceedings, and require by subpoena the attendance of witnesses and production of books and papers."

Efficiency in resolution of disputes is promoted by mandating an "accelerated" procedure for handling claims of $100,000 or less, 41 U.S.C. § 607(f), and an "expedited" procedure for claims of $50,000 or less, 41 U.S.C. § 608(a). Both procedures are available solely at the election of the contractor. Under the accelerated procedure, the board is required to make a decision, "whenever possible, within 180 days from the date the contractor elects to utilize such procedure," and "appeals under the small claims procedure shall be resolved, whenever possible, within 120 days from the date the contractor elects to utilize such procedure." The boards have also adopted alternative dispute resolution procedures in an effort to enhance the efficiency of the appeals process. The ADR procedures most commonly available are settlement judges, mini-trials, and summary trials with binding decisions.

The Act also formalizes the appointment process for board members by requiring that they be "selected and appointed to serve in the same manner as administrative law judges appointed pursuant to section 3501 of Title 5 of the United States

Code," 41 U.S.C. § 607(b)(1). This section also provides that board members must have a minimum of five years' public contract law experience and specifies that compensation for board chairmen, vice chairmen, and members "shall be determined under section 5372a of Title 5 of the United States Code."

The boards of contracts appeals are not bound by decisions of the GAO. However, the ASBCA noted that it is appropriate for the board to look to GAO opinions for guidance and that the GAO's decisions are helpful in matters involving the award of a contract, *Dante Calcagni*, ASBCA 49903, 98-1 BCA ¶29,554.

2. Court of Federal Claims

The Federal Courts Improvement Act of 1982, Pub. L. 97-164, created the U.S. Claims Court pursuant to Article I of the Constitution. The court was renamed the Court of Federal Claims by the Federal Courts Administration Act of 1992, Pub. L. 102-572. The Court of Federal Claims is composed of sixteen judges, appointed for fifteen-year terms by the President, and fourteen "senior judges" whose fifteen-year term has expired, 28 U.S.C. Chapter 7. As Article I judges, the Court of Federal Claims judges are vested with authority to "enter dispositive judgments," including orders on dispositive motions. Pursuant to 28 U.S.C. § 2503(b) the proceedings of the Court of Federal Claims are conducted according to the Federal Rules of Evidence. The court is not bound by the Federal Rules of Civil Procedure, but it has incorporated them "to the extent that they appropriately can be applied to the proceedings in this court," U.S.C.C. Rule 1(b).

The Court of Federal Claims sits in Washington, D.C. and may hold a trial at any location depending upon the convenience of the parties and witnesses, 28 U.S.C. § 173. Cases before the Court of Federal Claims are heard and decided by one judge, 28 U.S.C. § 174(a). The Court of Federal Claims judges have not hesitated in refusing to follow each other's decisions. Compare *Big Bud Tractors, Inc. v. United States*, 2 Cl. Ct. 195 (1983), with *Dean Forwarding Co. v. United States*, 2 Cl. Ct. 559 (1983). Conflicts between the decisions of individual judges on the court are resolved by the Court of Appeals for the Federal Circuit.

Congress may refer cases to the Court of Federal Claims for a report, 28 U.S.C. § 1492. The procedures for these "Congressional reference" cases are set forth in 28 U.S.C. § 2509. These cases are heard first by a Court of Federal Claims judge sitting as a hearing officer. After the hearing officer's decision, the parties may bring any exceptions to a review panel consisting of three judges. The review panel is authorized by statute to review the findings and conclusions of the hearing officer and the record in the case. The hearing officer's findings of fact are not reviewed de novo and may not be set aside unless clearly erroneous. See *INSLAW, Inc. v. United States,* 40 Fed. Cl. 843 (1998), for a discussion of this procedure.

3. Court of Appeals for the Federal Circuit

The Court of Appeals for the Federal Circuit hears appeals directly from both board decisions and Court of Federal Claims decisions, pursuant to their respective CDA jurisdictions. The Federal Courts Improvement Act amended 41 U.S.C. § 609(c) to require that if the trial record is insufficient for court review, the case must be remanded to the trial forum. Prior to these amendments, the Court of Claims could, in its discretion and in lieu of remand, retain the case and take such additional evidence or action as necessary for final disposition of the case.

a. *Review of Board Decisions*

The CDA was amended by the Federal Courts Improvement Act to give the Federal Circuit exclusive jurisdiction to hear government or contractor appeals filed with the court within 120 days of a board of contract appeals decision. This authority is stated in 41 U.S.C. § 607(g)(1) (see also 28 U.S.C. § 1295(a)(10) and § 1295(b)):

The decision of an agency board of contract appeals shall be final, except that—

> (A) a contractor may appeal such a decision to the United States Court of Appeals for the Federal Circuit within one hundred twenty days after the date of receipt of a copy of such decision, or

(B) the agency head, if he determines that an appeal should be taken, and with the prior approval of the Attorney General, transmits the decision of the board of contract appeals to the Court of Appeals for the Federal Circuit for judicial review under section 1295 of Title 28, within one hundred and twenty days from the date of the agency's receipt of a copy of the board's decision.

The 120-day appeal period runs from the date on which an appeals board denies a contractor's timely petition for reconsideration, not from the date of the board's initial decision, *Precision Piping, Inc. v. United States*, 230 Ct. Cl. 741 (1982). This rule is consistent with the predominant rule prior to the Federal Courts Improvement Act which stated that the old 90-day period for appealing an adverse board decision to the Court of Claims ran from the board's denial of a timely request for reconsideration, *B. D. Click Co. v. United States*, 222 Ct. Cl. 290, 614 F.2d 748 (1980). In order to be timely, an appeal must be received by the clerk for the Federal Circuit within the 120-day statutory period, *Placeway Constr. Corp. v. United States*, 713 F.2d 726 (Fed. Cir. 1983). Note that this receipt rule is contrary to the rule generally adopted by the boards, that an appeal from a contracting officer's final decision is considered filed in a board of contract appeals for purposes of the 90-day statutory period when the contractor mails its appeal notice, 41 U.S.C. § 606. In small claims appeals, the court's jurisdiction is limited to board decisions tainted by fraud, 41 U.S.C. § 608(d). See *Palmer v. Barram*, 184 F.3d 1373 (Fed. Cir. 1999).

Appeals to the court are only proper when the appeals board has rendered a "final" decision. The court has ruled that board decisions are not final when they decide only entitlement and remand to the parties to allow them to negotiate quantum, *AAA Eng'g & Drafting Inc. v. Widnall*, 129 F.3d 602 (Fed. Cir. 1997); *United Pac. Ins. Co. v. Roche*, 294 F.3d 1367 (Fed. Cir. 2002). Thus, the court will not accept appeals of entitlement decisions when quantum has not yet been determined. The result of this procedure is that when quantum has been decided and the appeal is filed, the party will have the right to challenge entitlement as well as quantum, *Brownlee v. Dyncorp*, 349 F.3d 1343 (Fed. Cir. 2003) (government appeal); *J. C. Equip. Corp. v. England*, 360 F.3d 1311 (Fed. Cir. 2004) (contractor appeal). See *Kinetic Builders, Inc. v. Peters*, 226 F.3d 1307 (Fed. Cir. 2000), holding that some claims in which the board has decided both entitlement and quantum can be appealed even though other claims have been remanded to negotiation of quantum. See also *Dewey Elecs. Corp. v. United States*, 803 F.2d 650 (Fed. Cir. 1986), permitting appeal of a board decision denying some claims even though the board had ruled favorably on other claims and remanded them for negotiation of entitlement.

Review of board decisions by the Federal Circuit on questions of law is "de novo" with the result that the court can overturn any ruling with which it disagrees. Review of questions of fact is conducted pursuant to the "substantial evidence" standard which was previously contained in the Wunderlich Act, 41 U.S.C. §§ 321, 322. See *Systems Tech. Assocs., Inc. v. United States*, 699 F.2d 1383 (Fed. Cir. 1983). This standard of review is stated in 41 U.S.C. § 609(b) (see also 28 U.S.C. § 1295(c)), which provides:

> In the event of an appeal by a contractor or the Government from a decision of any agency board pursuant to section 607 of this title, notwithstanding any contract provision, regulation, or rules of law to the contrary, the decision of the agency board on any question of law shall not be final or conclusive, but the decision on any question of fact shall be final and conclusive and shall not be set aside unless the decision is fraudulent, or arbitrary, or capricious, or so grossly erroneous as to necessarily imply bad faith, or if such decision is not supported by substantial evidence.

See *Phoenix Control Sys., Inc. v. Babbitt*, 113 F.3d 1255 (Fed. Cir. 1997), and *Conner Bros. Constr. Co. v. Brown*, 113 F.3d 1256 (Fed. Cir. 1997), in which the court concluded that the contractor challenging the board's findings had failed to meet this heavy burden and noted that the mere fact that the record contains conflicting evidence does not mean that the board's findings are unsupported by substantial evidence.

b. Review of Court of Federal Claims Decisions

The Federal Circuit has exclusive jurisdiction to hear appeals from final decisions of the Court of Federal Claims, 28 U.S.C. § 1295(a)(3). These appeals must be received by the clerk of the court within 60 days of entry of the Court of Federal Claims' judgment, 28 U.S.C. § 2107. See *Sofarelli Assocs., Inc. v. United States*, 716 F.2d 1395 (Fed. Cir. 1983).

The Court of Federal Claims' findings of fact will only be set aside if "clearly erroneous," § 52(a), Federal Rules of Civil Procedure. In *United States v. United States Gypsum Co.*, 333 U.S. 364 (1948), the Court stated that "A finding is 'clearly erroneous' when although there is evidence to support it, the reviewing court on the entire evidence is left with the definite and firm conviction that a mistake has been committed."

APPENDIX A
Contract Administration

While the principal goal of contract administration in both fixed-price and cost-reimbursement contracts is to ensure the effective and efficient satisfaction of government needs at fair and reasonable prices, there are fundamental differences in the nature of contract administration activity under these types of contracts. These differences stem from the fact that the government agrees to reimburse the contractor for its expenditures in the cost-type contract. Another basis for a different contract administration focus is that cost-type contracts usually contain less firm and less detailed statement of work compared to the more exact description of work under fixed-price contracts.

In fixed-price contracts, a major focus is on ensuring that the work conforms to the specifications. The government's major goal is to see that it does not get less than it bargained for and that the contractor is not paid the contract price without earning it. In contrast, in cost-reimbursement contracts the government is primarily concerned with ensuring that the contractor expends funds to most effectively accomplish the government's objectives. This frequently involves extensive communication between the government and the contractor during performance. Thus, the government's contract administration effort is directed at establishing the precise methods and manner of performance as the work progresses and controlling the level and nature of the contractor's expenditures. Similarly, the contractor's cost-type contract administration effort is different from that involved with fixed-price contracts. The contractor must keep the government advised of the progress of the work in relation to the contract funding requirements and maintain a close working relationship with the government. The necessity of this type of relationship is discussed in Chapter 1.

The fundamental rules of contract administration have evolved over the years in extensive litigation concerning problems that have arisen under fixed-price type contracts. These rules are considered in great detail in Cibinic, Nash & Nagle, *Administration of Government Contracts* (4th ed. 2006), and will not be repeated in this chapter. Rather, this discussion of cost-type contract administration centers on the principal contract clauses that give the cost-reimbursement contract its unique character. The first section considers funding control under the Limitation of Cost (LOC) and Limitation of Funds (LOF) clauses. The second section examines the rights and obligations of the parties under the Changes and Technical Direction, Inspection and Correction of Defects, Termination, and Government Property clauses.

I. CONTROL OF FUNDING

The most difficult and important responsibility faced by the parties in administering cost-reimbursement contracts is the monitoring and controlling of funds. Legal and practical considerations require that both parties continually focus on contract funding and its relationship to performance. In order to carry out its obligations in this respect, the government requires that the contractor's right to reimbursement of its costs and the concomitant government obligation to make payment are limited to the amount set forth in the contract.

From a legal standpoint, contractual funding limitations are necessary in order to ensure compliance with the Anti-Deficiency Act, 31 U.S.C. § 1341, which states:

> (a)(1) An officer or employee of the United States Government or of the District of Columbia government may not
>
> > (A) make or authorize an expenditure or obligation exceeding an amount available in an appropriation or fund for the expenditure or obligation; or

(B) involve either government in a contract or obligation for the payment of money before an appropriation is made unless authorized by law.

These requirements are restated in FAR 32.702, as follows:

No officer or employee of the Government may create or authorize an obligation in excess of the funds available, or in advance of appropriations (Anti-Deficiency Act, 31 U.S.C. 1341), unless otherwise authorized by law. Before executing any contract, the contracting officer shall (a) obtain written assurance from responsible fiscal authority that adequate funds are available or (b) expressly condition the contract upon availability of funds in accordance with 32.703-2.

Compliance with these rules requires accurate and up-to-date record keeping by government fiscal officers, which would not be possible without definable limits on the amount of the government's obligation.

Maintaining accurate and timely records of actual and estimated costs is also of practical importance. Both the timely identification and reporting of potential situations where the contractor anticipates expending more funds than predicted to accomplish the work (an "overrun") provide the parties the opportunity to take alternative courses of action. After-the-fact recognition and notification of overruns preclude cost-saving changes in work statements and result in delays while additional funding is sought or cancellation of the project is considered.

If a contracting officer decides to fund an overrun, the agency may have to use current appropriations, not the appropriation that was in effect when the contract was awarded. See *National Science Found.—Potential AntiDeficiency Act Violation by the National Science Board Office*, Comp. Gen. Dec. B-317413, 2009 CPD ¶94, stating that funding an overrun was a "new obligation" because it arose from a change to the work ordered by an agency technical person which was settled by the contracting officer. The GAO considered this a "settlement" which had to be paid for with current appropriations—noting that if the agency had treated it as a ratification of an unauthorized commitment, it could have used the expired funds.

This section considers the contractual provisions used by the government to limit or control contractor expenditures under cost-type contracts. It focuses on the legal and practical problems encountered in administering these clauses.

A. Standard Contract Clauses

The clause incorporated into the contract depends upon whether the entire estimated cost and fee are to be obligated upon award of the contract (a fully funded contract) or only a portion of the estimated cost and fee is obligated at time of award (an incrementally funded contract).

1. Limitation of Cost Clause

FAR 32.705-2(a) requires that the following FAR 52.232-20 LOC clause be incorporated into fully funded cost-reimbursement contracts:

LIMITATION OF COST (APR 1984)

(a) The parties estimate that performance of this contract, exclusive of any fee, will not cost the Government more than (1) the estimated cost specified in the Schedule or, (2) if this is a cost-sharing contract, the Government's share of the estimated cost specified in the Schedule. The Contractor agrees to use its best efforts to perform the work specified in the Schedule and all obligations under this contract within the estimated cost, which, if this is a cost-sharing contract, includes both the Government's and the Contractor's share of the cost.

(b) The Contractor shall notify the Contracting Officer in writing whenever it has reason to believe that—

(1) The costs the contractor expects to incur under this contract in the next 60 days, when added to all costs previously incurred, will exceed 75 percent of the estimated cost specified in the Schedule; or

(2) The total cost for the performance of this contract, exclusive of any fee, will be either greater or substantially less than had been previously estimated.

(c) As part of the notification, the Contractor shall provide the Contracting Officer a revised estimate of the total cost of performing this contract.

(d) Except as required by other provisions of this contract, specifically citing and stated to be an exception to this clause—

(1) The Government is not obligated to reimburse the Contractor for costs incurred in excess of (i) the estimated cost specified in the Schedule or, (ii) if this is a cost-sharing contract, the estimated cost to the Government specified in the Schedule; and

(2) The Contractor is not obligated to continue performance under this contract (including actions under the Termination clause of this contract) or otherwise incur costs in excess of the estimated cost specified in the Schedule, until the Contracting Officer (i) notifies the Contractor in writing that the estimated cost has been increased and (ii) provides a revised estimated total cost of performing this contract. If this is a cost-sharing contract, the increase shall be allocated in accordance with the formula specified in the Schedule.

(e) No notice, communication, or representation in any form other than that specified in subparagraph (d)(2) above, or from any person other than the Contracting Officer, shall affect this contract's estimated cost to the Government. In the absence of the specified notice, the Government is not obligated to reimburse the Contractor for any costs in excess of the estimated cost or, if this is a cost-sharing contract, for any costs in excess of the estimated cost to the Government specified in the Schedule, whether those excess costs were incurred during the course of the contract or as a result of termination.

(f) If the estimated cost specified in the Schedule is increased, any costs the Contractor incurs before the increase that are in excess of the previously estimated cost shall be allowable to the same extent as if incurred afterward, unless the Contracting Officer issues a termination or other notice directing that the increase is solely to cover termination or other specified expenses.

(g) Change orders shall not be considered an authorization to exceed the estimated cost to the Government specified in the Schedule, unless they contain a statement increasing the estimated cost.

(h) If this contract is terminated or the estimated cost is not increased, the Government and the Contractor shall negotiate an equitable distribution of all property produced or purchased under the contract, based upon the share of costs incurred by each.

The present LOC clause is substantially the same as the LOC clause adopted by military and civilian agencies in October 1966. Under the LOC clause in use prior to that time, contractors were often able to obtain court and board decisions requiring the government to fund overruns based upon express and constructive orders of government officials even though no mention was made concerning additional funding. The clause was changed, to avoid such results, by adding precise language in ¶(e) and ¶(g). Consequently, it is very difficult for a contractor to recover any amount expended in excess of the contractual expenditure limitation, absent a written notification from the contracting officer providing additional funding.

The board, in *ITT Defense Communications Div.*, ASBCA 14270, 70-2 BCA ¶8370, describes the purpose of the clause at 38,920:

> The purpose of the standard Limitation of Cost clause made mandatory for inclusion in cost-type contracts is to implement policies based upon Acts of Congress to prevent overruns of expenditures on contracts, maintain budget controls and eliminate one cause of deficiency appropriations. *Weinschel Eng'g Co., Inc.*, ASBCA 7046, 1962 BCA ¶3348.

This purpose is implemented by the provisions of the clause that (1) require the contractor to give notice concerning the status of actual and estimated costs and (2) provide that the government is not obligated to reimburse the contractor in excess of the estimated cost set forth in the contract.

2. Limitation of Funds Clause

When a cost-reimbursement contract is incrementally funded, FAR 32.705-2 requires that the FAR 52.232-22 LOF clause be incorporated into the contract. This clause reads as follows:

LIMITATION OF FUNDS (APR 1984)

(a) The parties estimate that performance of this contract will not cost the Government more than (1) the estimated cost specified in the Schedule or, (2) if this is a cost-sharing contract, the Government's share of the estimated cost specified in the Schedule. The Contractor agrees to use its best efforts to perform the work specified in the Schedule and all obligations under this contract within the estimated cost, which, if this is a cost-sharing contract, includes both the Government's and the Contractor's share of the cost.

(b) The Schedule specifies the amount presently available for payment by the Government and allotted to this contract, the items covered, the Government's share of the cost if this is a cost-sharing contract, and the period of performance it is estimated the allotted amount will cover. The parties contemplate that the Government will allot additional funds incrementally to the contract up to the full estimated cost to the Government specified in the Schedule, exclusive of any fee. The Contractor agrees to perform, or have performed, work on the contract up to the point at which the total amount paid and payable by the Government under the contract approximates but does not exceed the total amount actually allotted by the Government to the contract.

(c) The Contractor shall notify the Contracting Officer in writing whenever it has reason to believe that the costs it expects to incur under this contract in the next 60 days, when added to all costs previously incurred, will exceed 75 percent of (1) the total amount so far allotted to the contract by the Government or, (2) if this is a cost-sharing contract, the amount then allotted to the contract by the Government plus the Contractor's corresponding share. The notice shall state the estimated amount of additional funds required to continue performance for the period specified in the Schedule.

(d) Sixty days before the end of the period specified in the Schedule, the Contractor shall notify the Contracting Officer in writing of the estimated amount of additional funds, if any, required to continue timely performance under the contract or for any further period specified in the Schedule or otherwise agreed upon, and when the funds will be required.

(e) If, after notification, additional funds are not allotted by the end of the period specified in the Schedule or another agreed-upon date, upon the Contractor's written request the Contracting Officer will terminate this contract on that date in accordance with the provisions of the Termination clause of this contract. If the Contractor estimates that the funds available will allow it to continue to discharge its obligations beyond that date, it may specify a later date in its request, and the Contracting Officer may terminate this contract on that later date.

(f) Except as required by other provisions of this contract, specifically citing and stated to be an exception to this clause—

(1) The Government is not obligated to reimburse the Contractor for costs incurred in excess of the total amount allotted by the Government to this contract; and

(2) The Contractor is not obligated to continue performance under this contract (including actions under the Termination clause of this contract) or otherwise incur costs in excess of (i) the amount then allotted to the contract by the Government or, (ii) if this is a cost-sharing contract, the amount then allotted by the Government to the contract plus the Contractor's corresponding share, until the Contracting Officer notifies the Contractor in writing that the amount allotted by the Government has been increased and specifies an increased amount, which shall then constitute the total amount allotted by the Government to this contract.

(g) The estimated cost shall be increased to the extent that (1) the amount allotted by the Government or, (2) if this is a cost-sharing contract, the amount then allotted by the Government to the contract plus the Contractor's corresponding share, exceeds the estimated cost specified in the Schedule. If this is a cost-sharing contract, the increase shall be allocated in accordance with the formula specified in the Schedule.

(h) No notice, communication, or representation in any form other than that specified in subparagraph (f)(2) above, or from any person other than the Contracting Officer, shall affect the amount allotted by the Government to this contract. In the absence of the specified notice, the Government is not obligated to reimburse the Contractor for any costs in excess of the total amount allotted by the Government to this contract, whether incurred during the course of the contract or as a result of termination.

(i) When and to the extent that the amount allotted by the Government to the contract is increased, any costs the Contractor incurs before the increase that are in excess of (1) the amount previously allotted by the Government or, (2) if this is a cost-sharing contract, the amount previously allotted by the Government to the contract plus the Contractor's corresponding share, shall be allowable to the same extent as if incurred afterward, unless the Contracting Officer issues a termination or other notice and directs that the increase is solely to cover termination or other specified expenses.

(j) Change orders shall not be considered an authorization to exceed the amount allotted by the Government specified in the Schedule, unless they contain a statement increasing the amount allotted.

(k) Nothing in this clause shall affect the right of the Government to terminate this contract. If this contract is terminated, the Government and the Contractor shall negotiate an equitable distribution of all property produced or purchased under the contract, based upon the share of costs incurred by each.

(l) If the Government does not allot sufficient funds to allow completion of the work, the Contractor is entitled to a percentage of the fee specified in the Schedule equaling the percentage of completion of the work contemplated by this contract.

This clause contains the same strict language precluding recovery of overruns unless notice has been received from the contracting officer providing additional funds.

The use of an LOF clause makes it clear to the contractor that the initial funding provided will not be sufficient to cover all of the work described in the contract. Hence, the contractor must perform in a manner that keeps its costs within the funds provided because the government has no obligation to fully fund the contract. See *Law, Mathematics & Tech., Inc.*, ASBCA 29714, 85-1 BCA ¶17,765, *aff'd*, 779 F.2d 675 (Fed. Cir. 1985), holding that the government had not breached the contract by deciding not to provide funds beyond the initial increment of funding. See also *Sociotechnical Res. Applications, Inc.*, IBCA 3969-98, 01-1 BCA ¶31,235, finding that an agency had no contractual duty to fully fund an incrementally funded contract. Compare *American Elec. Labs., Inc. v. United States*, 774 F.2d 1110 (Fed. Cir. 1985), holding that the contractor was entitled to compensation for an overrun where the contracting officer had prepared an internal document indicating that more funding should be provided and had indicated to the contractor during negotiations that funding was available.

3. Applicability of Clauses

FAR 32.705-2 indicates that either the LOC clause or the LOF clause will be incorporated into the contract, depending upon whether the contract is partially or fully funded. However, some agencies used both clauses in the same contract. See *International Science & Tech. Inst., Inc. v. United States*, 53 Fed. Cl. 798 (2002), and *TEM Assocs., Inc.*, DOTCAB 2556, 93-2 BCA ¶25,759, holding that, in that circumstance, the LOC clause superseded the LOF clause when the contract was fully funded. See also *Analytical Assessments Corp.*, ASBCA 52393, 01-2 BCA ¶31,483, where, when the contract was fully funded, the LOF clause was removed and the LOC clause was added to the contract. Since the LOF clause provides the government and the contractor the same protection as the LOC clause, it is redundant to include both clauses in the contract.

A number of decisions have held that the LOF clause is applicable to the entire contract amount once the contract is fully funded, *George G. Sharp, Inc.*, ASBCA 55385, 09-1 BCA ¶34,117; *Moshman Assocs., Inc.*, ASBCA 52868, 02-1 BCA ¶31,852; *Defense Sys. Concepts, Inc.*, ASBCA 45920, 94-2 BCA ¶26,721, *aff'd*, 41 F.3d 1520 (Fed. Cir. 1994).

When a cost-reimbursement contract is fully funded, the government obligates the full amount of the estimated cost and fee, if any, that are set forth in the Schedule, and the LOC clause clearly states that its limitation relates only to the costs of performance—with no application to the fee. The LOF clause is written in the same way except that it anticipates the incremental allotment of funds to the contract. If such incremental allotments are separated into cost and fee, the limitation in the clause will relate only to the cost with the fee being treated as a separate issue, *Parsons-UXB Joint Venture*, ASBCA 56481, 11-1 BCA ¶34,680; *Textron Defense Sys.*, ASBCA 47352, 96-2 BCA ¶28,332, *aff'd*, 143 F.3d 1465 (Fed. Cir. 1998). The Contract Funding clause in NFS 1852.232-81 requires this result by providing separate allotments for cost and fee. However, if the funds are allotted in a single figure, the contractor can apply the full allotment to performance costs, *Allied-Signal Aerospace Co.*, ASBCA 46890, 95-1 BCA ¶27,462. See also *McMullen Assocs., Inc.*, ASBCA 22450, 79-1 BCA ¶13,818, *recons. denied*, 79-2 BCA ¶13,920, holding that the contractor was entitled to apply the entire amount of funds that exceeded earned fee toward reimbursement of its performance costs.

The clauses relate only to payment for allowable costs under the contract. Thus, they do not apply to any and all government liabilities under the contract. See *Solar Turbines, Inc. v. United States*, 23 Cl. Ct. 142 (1991), where the court appeared to find valid the contractor's argument that a "ceiling" amount added to the contract when an overrun was funded would not pertain to the contractor's claims for damages for breach of contract but found no government breach. Another exception to their coverage is when the government agrees to indemnify the contractor for unusually hazardous risks. See FAR 52.228-7 Insurance—Liability to Third Persons clause and NFS 1852.250-70 Insurance—Liability Indemnification Under Pub. L. No. 85-804 (NASA's clause covering unusually hazardous risks). These clauses state that the LOC and LOF clauses do not apply to the government's indemnification obligations.

B. Contractor Obligation

As discussed in Chapter 2, the contractor in a cost-reimbursement contract has very limited obligations. Paragraph (d)(2) of the LOC clause and ¶(f)(2) of the LOF clause clearly state that once the funds that have been provided in the contract are exhausted, the contractor has no obligation to continue performance under the contract. The clauses are silent as to the contractor's obligation to continue work if there is a lapse in funding followed by the allocation of more funds to the contract. However, it would appear that the contractor is obligated to continue to work within the new funding limitation and ¶¶(f) and (i) of the LOC and LOF clauses respectively state that costs incurred in the funding lapse are allowable costs once overrun funding has occurred.

It would appear that a contractor cannot refuse to allocate overrun funds to costs incurred during a lapse in funding. See *American Nucleonics Corp.*, ASBCA 1370, 73-1 BCA ¶10,025, denying a contractor's claim that it was entitled to the rights to a patent on an invention that it had allegedly made during a "funding hiatus" on a fixed-price best efforts contract.

Paragraph (a) of the LOC and LOF clauses require the contractor to use its "best efforts" to perform the work and "all obligations under the contract" within the cost estimate in the contract. There is no reported decision indicating that the government has attempted to impose any sanction on a contractor for failing to meet this vague requirement.

C. Notice Requirements

The LOC and LOF clauses require the contractor to give two types of notice to the contracting officer. These notices are intended to keep the government advised of the costs incurred and the funds needed to perform the contract and to permit it to take timely action when expenditures are out of line with the funding. Such action might include modification of the estimated cost (upward or downward), modification of the work required under the contract to avoid expenditure of funds in excess of the amount allocated for the contract work, delay or acceleration of the project, or termination of the contract for the convenience of the government.

These notice provisions are strictly enforced because the contractor has a right under the standard LOC and LOF clauses to stop work when funds are no longer available, *Advanced Materials, Inc. v. Perry*, 108 F.3d 307 (Fed. Cir. 1997). Thus, if a non-standard clause does not contain a provision giving the contractor the right to stop work, the notice requirement will not be strictly enforced. See *Applied Tech. Assocs., Inc.*, ASBCA 49200, 98-1 BCA ¶29,633, where a Limitation of Government Obligation clause (similar to an LOF clause) inadvertently omitted a sentence giving the contractor the right to stop work and the contractor, a very small company, did not have the experience to recognize the omission or to understand that notice of a pending overrun should have been given to the contracting officer. A similar result was reached in *Chromalloy Am. Corp.*, ASBCA 22119, 80-2 BCA ¶14,566.

1. Incurred Cost Notice

The incurred cost notice is required by ¶(b)(1) of the LOC clause and ¶(c) of the LOF clause. The contractor is required to give notice when its incurred cost, plus cost to be incurred within a stated period (FAR 52.232-20 permits the use of a period from 30 to 90 days), will exceed a stipulated percentage (FAR 52.232.20 allows agencies to use a percentage between 75% and 85%) of the estimated cost of the contract or the funds allotted to the contract. These notices are intended to warn the contracting officer that actual costs will soon approach the estimated cost or allotted cost. The contracting officer can then determine if the work has progressed accordingly and, if not, take appropriate steps. No significant controversies have arisen concerning the incurred cost notice. However, in *Advanced Materials, Inc. v. Perry*, 108 F.3d 307 (Fed. Cir. 1997), the court held that notice under this paragraph did not meet the requirements of the estimated cost notice.

2. Estimated Cost Notice

The estimated cost notice is often referred to as the "overrun" notice. However, the LOC clause requires notice of both overruns and underruns. Paragraph (b)(2) of the LOC clause requires the contractor to notify the contracting officer "at any time" it has reason to believe that the costs at completion will be either "greater or substantially less" than previously estimated. Paragraph (d) of the LOF clause requires notice only of overruns, stating that the contracting officer must be given notice of "the estimated amount of additional funds required" and "when the funds will be required." This notice is to be given 60 days before the end of the current fund allotment period.

The LOC clause requires notification of even relatively minor increases. See *Kaman Sciences Corp.*, ASBCA 18072, 74-1 BCA ¶10,604, holding that notice of a 1.5% overrun was required. The board stated that the language requires notice of "any increase, substantial or not." In contrast, notice of a cost decrease is required only if it would be substantial.

a. Nature of Notice

Since there are no prescribed procedures or forms for giving the overrun notice, this issue has been litigated frequently. What appears to be required is that the government be fairly apprised that an overrun will occur, enabling the government to timely decide what action to take under the contract, *Marquardt Corp.*, ASBCA 10154, 66-1 BCA ¶5576.

(1) Notice to Contracting Officer

The clauses require that written notice be given to the contracting officer. Thus, notice to administrative personnel will be ineffective in meeting this requirement, *Manpower Program Analysis Consultation & Training, Inc.*, 80 BCA-113, 81-2 BCA ¶15,436. Some agencies place specific provisions in their contracts warning the contractor that notice given to government officials other than the contracting officer is insufficient. See HHSAR 352.202-1, ALT I(c), which states that the project officer who represents the government in technical monitoring of contract performance is "not authorized to receive or act upon the Contractor's notification of revised cost estimate." See *JJM Sys., Inc.*, ASBCA 51152, 03-1 BCA ¶32,192, applying such a clause and upholding the government's refusal to fund the overrun.

(2) Notice That Overrun Will Occur

The notice requirement must specifically indicate that the "estimated cost of the contract" is insufficient for contract performance. That the contractor must indicate that an overrun will occur is underscored by the following statement by the board in *TDC Mgmt. Corp.*, DOTCAB 1802, 91-2 BCA ¶23,815, *recons. denied*, 91-3 BCA ¶24,061, at 119,310:

> TDC argues that two written statements made on December 10, 1984, constituted the requisite notice. The first was in the covering letter to the November progress report. "I would appreciate your immediate attention to the transfer of the additional funds already committed under this contract." The second was in the report itself. "Another administrative matter which requires your immediate attention is the transfer of the additional one hundred sixty-two thousand ($162,000) into our contract. Your immediate attention to this detail is requested."
>
> Neither statement says that TDC had reached or was about to reach the 75% plateau. Neither statement said that TDC was running out of contract money or that it ever expected to run out of contract money, essential ingredients of the contractually-prescribed notice. One reasonable interpretation of these statements is that, although over two months had elapsed since the new fiscal year began, UMTA had still not obligated the additional $161,376 called for by the contract for the new fiscal year and that it ought to do so. While the clause allows a contractor some freedom of expression, nevertheless the contractor must communicate clearly that funds will soon be exhausted, jeopardizing further performance. Something so vital as a contractually-required notice to a Contracting Officer cannot be left to implication. Rather, such a notice must be presented in such a manner that the recipient and its personnel may, in the exercise of reasonable care, grasp its significance. See *Wind Ship Development Corporation*, DOTBCA No. 1215, 83-1 BCA ¶16,135 (1982); *Sperry Univac Division, Sperry Rand Corporation*, DOTBCA No. 1144, 82-2 BCA ¶15,812 at page 78,340; *M-R-S Manufacturing Company v. United States*, 203 Ct. Cl. 551,564,492 F.2d 835 (1974). Appellant's statements in connection with the November progress report did not meet that test.
>
> While the Contracting Officer would have had access to TDC's invoices and conceivably could have ascertained from them the status of cost incurrences, this is not determinative for two reasons: (i) by accepting paragraph (c) of Clause 72, TDC accepted the burden in this regard, and this agreement should not be casually discarded by the Board; (ii) merely knowing the amount of costs incurred does not apprise the Contracting Officer of expected cost incurrences thereafter, so that he would have no way of knowing when, or even whether, the ceiling could be expected to be exceeded.

See also *Carltech Ass'ns, Inc.*, ASBCA 42576, 93-1 BCA ¶25,267 (mere notice of higher indirect cost rates not notice of overrun); *Human Resources Mgmt., Inc.*, ASBCA 27444, 83-2 BCA ¶16,797 (mere notice of proposed overhead rates insufficient); *Consulting Servs. Corp.*, ASBCA 20288, 76-2 BCA ¶12,124 (submission of monthly invoices not the notice required by the LOC clause); and *Greenwich Int'l, Inc.*, ASBCA 14728, 71-2 BCA ¶8922 (mere notice that overhead rate will be increased not adequate). Compliance with the incurred cost notice requirement will not excuse failure to give the overrun notice, *Advanced Materials, Inc. v. Perry*, 108 F.3d 307 (Fed. Cir. 1997); *Seaco, Inc.*, DOTCAB 1686, 86-2 BCA ¶18,933.

(3) Notice of Amount

Paragraph (c) of the LOC clause calls for a revised estimate of costs to perform the contract, *JWA Emadel Enters., Inc.*, ASBCA 51016, 98-2 BCA ¶29,765, *recons. denied*, 98-2 BCA ¶29,960. In that case the contract required a monthly submission to the contracting officer of "contractor's billing vouchers" and "performance and cost reports." The contractor submitted billing vouchers under the contract, each stating costs incurred in the current billing period and cumulative costs incurred since contract inception. Funding of the overrun was denied because no voucher stated a revised estimate of total costs to perform the contract. See also *Applied Theory, Inc.*, ASBCA 49725, 97-1 BCA ¶28,670, *aff'd*, 152 F.3d 944 (Fed. Cir. 1998), where a contractor was denied recovery of a cost overrun exceeding the cost estimate in a CPFF contract because, although it gave notice of the cost overrun during performance, it did not provide a revised estimate of the total cost of performance as required by ¶(c) of the LOC clause. The same result was reached in *Falcon Research & Dev. Co.*, ASBCA 26853, 87-1 BCA ¶19,458, *aff'd*, 831 F.2d 1056 (Fed. Cir. 1987); *International Science & Tech. Inst., Inc. v. United States*, 53 Fed. Cl. 798 (2002), and *Optical E.T.C., Inc.*, ASBCA 53350, 04-1 BCA ¶32,608.

There may be situations where it is apparent that an overrun will occur but the amount of the overrun will be difficult or impossible to determine. In such cases the contractor should not wait until the amount becomes certain before giving notice because the inability to make an accurate projection of the overrun will not excuse failure to give the required notice, *Institute of Comparative Social & Cultural Studies*, ASBCA 32282, 87-3 BCA ¶20,009; *J.J. Henry Co.*, ASBCA 13835, 71-1 BCA ¶8898. In these circumstances, the contractor should furnish as accurate a projection as possible and should update that projection as more information becomes available. The failure to update such an estimate of costs when the contractor has reason to believe additional costs will be incurred will result in a failure to recover those costs, *American Standard, Inc.*, ASBCA 15660, 71-2 BCA ¶9109. See also *Eyler Assocs., Inc.*, ASBCA 16804, 75-1 BCA ¶11,320, where letters sent by the contractor and "accepted as notices of an impending overrun" by the contracting officer were held to apply only to the specific amount mentioned and not to additional amounts. Thus, the contractor should continually update its estimated cost as new information becomes available and not depend upon an initial notification in support of recovery.

b. Government Not Required to Make Computations

The notice requirement has been strictly enforced even though the contractor has furnished the contracting officer with sufficient knowledge of the financial status of the contract to understand that an overrun would occur. In *Industrial Tech. Assocs., Inc.*, ASBCA 16075, 72-2 BCA ¶9531, the board held that the notice requirement would not be waived even though the Defense Contract Administrative Services Region kept a tabulation of the contractor's vouchers from which it could have determined that an overrun would occur. The government is not required to make computations or analyses of data submitted by the contractor to determine whether an overrun will occur, *Consulting Servs. Corp.*, ASBCA 20288, 76-2 BCA ¶12,124. In that case, the board held that submission of monthly vouchers does not excuse notice when detailed analysis of the vouchers is required by the government to predict an overrun. In *Optonetics, Inc.*, ASBCA 17015, 73-2 BCA ¶10,173, the board stated at 47,897:

> The fact that the appellant provided the Government with its expenditures through monthly vouchers submitted for purposes of reimbursement does not excuse its—failure to render the required notice. The Government could not reasonably predict an overrun without making a detailed analysis of the appellant's incurrence of direct and indirect costs. The Government had no obligation to perform this audit analysis during the performance period of the contract.

3. Contractor's Budget and Accounting System

In order to comply with the notice requirements and avoid incurring an overrun, the contractor must maintain accurate records of incurred costs, present commitments, and current estimates of the cost at completion. DCAAM 11-103 requires the auditor to ascertain whether the contractor has the financial management tools necessary to adequately identify potential contract overruns or underruns. Contractor reliance solely on accounting records of incurred costs or amounts invoiced to the government is insufficient. The necessity for factoring in additional information can be illustrated by assuming a fully funded cost-reimbursement contract with an estimated cost of $500,000, incurred cost of $400,000, and billings to the government of $350,000. See Figure 5-1. The lesser billing to the government would be accounted for by the terms of a payment clause that provides for reimbursement of certain costs only if cash disbursements had been made to the contract or other billing lags. Without more information, the government might assume that there is $150,000 remaining for contract performance while a contractor might conclude that $100,000 remains. It is almost a certainty that both would be wrong. The $400,000 would not include potential liabilities to subcontractors or vendors who have not yet completed performance or have not received progress payments. Thus, the amount the contractor would have to pay its subcontractors or vendors if the contract were terminated at this point would have to be added to the $400,000. Further, the contractor may have obligations to give severance notice or pay to its employees if the work is discontinued. The amount of such costs would also have to be added to the incurred cost. Similar potential termination liabilities or costs for other areas would also have to be added to the incurred cost to give an accurate picture of the total current costs of performance. Finally, the contractor must continually update its estimate at completion by considering possible increases in cost, whether for direct labor or material or indirect expense. Only then will the cost-reimbursement contractor have sufficient information to comply with the notice provisions and protect itself from unfunded overruns.

Figure 5-1

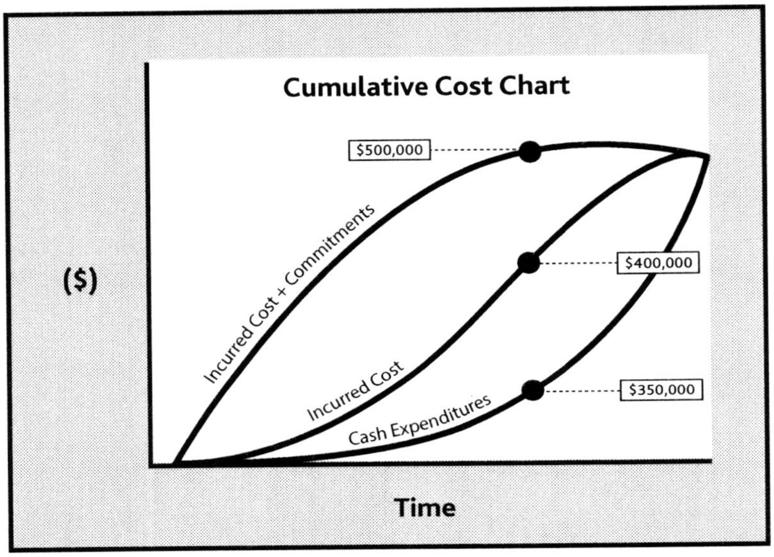

D. Overrun Notice Excused

There are two circumstances where failure to submit an overrun notice has been excused—when the overrun was unforeseeable and when the lack of notice was caused by government fault. As discussed in the following material, overrun costs have been required to be paid in these circumstances.

1. Unforeseeability of the Overrun

The failure to give notice of an overrun has been excused when it was unforeseeable. In *General Elec. Co. v. United States*, 194 Ct. Cl. 678, 440 F.2d 420 (1971), the Court of Claims held that since the overrun was entirely unforeseeable, the contractor could not have given adequate notice. In these circumstances, the court held that the overrun costs should be paid, stating at 687-88:

> In summary, we hold that a contracting officer abuses his discretion under paragraph (b) of the Limitation of Cost clause if he refuses to fund a cost overrun where the contractor, through no fault or inadequacy on its part, has no reason to believe, during performance, that a cost overrun will occur and the sole ground for the contracting, officer's refusal is the contractor's failure to give proper notice of the overrun.

In the substantial number of cases which have addressed this issue, the courts and boards have focused on the facts of each case to determine if a contractor with an adequate accounting system could have foreseen the overrun that occurred. The analysis applied has been stringent, with the result that most overruns have been found to be foreseeable.

a. *Proof of Unforseeability*

The burden of establishing that an overrun was not reasonably foreseeable is on the contractor, *RMI, Inc. v. United States*, 800 F.2d 246 (Fed. Cir. 1986); *Lansdowne Steel & Iron Co.*, ASBCA 41110, 95-1 BCA ¶27,506. Thus, general allegations including those about the shortness of the performance period and the absence of detailed accounting data are insufficient to meet the burden of showing that an overrun was not reasonably foreseeable, *International Tech. Corp.*, ASBCA 48759, 96-2 BCA ¶28,335.

Contractors have generally been found to have sufficient information to have foreseen that an overrun might occur. In *J.J. Henry Co.*, ASBCA 13835, 71-1 BCA ¶8898, the board found that monthly management reports showed an increase from estimated to expended man-days for the project. Such information supported the conclusion that the contractor had actual knowledge sufficient to put it on notice of the overrun. See also *Planning & Human Sys., Inc.*, ASBCA 29725, 90-2 BCA ¶22,821, where the contractor argued that it could not have predicted an overrun since it was only able to determine its overhead costs after it negotiated the rate agreement. The board denied the appeal, holding that the contractor should have been aware of its actual rates and expenditures and should have known that an overrun would occur. In *F2 Assocs., Inc.*, ASBCA 52397, 01-2 BCA ¶31,530, the board found that, in spite of a poor accounting system, the contractor knew it was working in an overrun status on an incrementally funded contract. Similarly, in *Advanced Materials, Inc. v. Perry*, 108 F.3d 307 (Fed. Cir. 1997), the court found that the contractor knew or had reason to know its year-to-date direct and general and administrative costs. In *Lansdowne Steel & Iron Co.*, ASBCA 41110, 95-1 BCA ¶27,506, the board held that the contractor knew or should have known that the termination of its related larger contract would affect the overhead rates on the present contract but took no steps to determine the impact. Instead, the contractor continued to report a fairly constant overhead rate through contract completion. In *Applied Theory, Inc.*, ASBCA 49725, 97-1 BCA ¶28,670, *aff'd*, 152 F.3d 944 (Fed. Cir. 1998), the court affirmed the board's holding that the fact that the DCAA accepted the contractor's proposed final overhead rates without change indicated that it knew or should have known of the overrun. Similarly, in *Titan Corp. v. West*, 129 F.3d 1479 (Fed. Cir. 1997), a subcontractor contended that it had no reason to know of the overrun until after the DCAA audit. The court held that the subcontractor should have known of the impending overrun because its DCAA-determined overhead costs were essentially the same as those submitted to DCAA 17 months earlier. In *JWA Emadel Enters., Inc.*, ASBCA 51016, 98-2 BCA ¶29,993, the board found that the contractor was aware of a substantial underpayment of indirect costs due to its erroneous G&A rate. Thus, the board held that the contractor's overruns did not come as a surprise and thus did not come within the precedents allowing recovery of unforeseeable indirect costs. In *Cal-Tron Sys., Inc.*, ASBCA 49159, 97-1 BCA ¶28,841, the board found that the contractor had knowledge of the overrun because its accounting system showed, within a month of contract award and on a monthly basis thereafter, that its indirect rates varied from the provisional rates it used in billing the government.

Although almost all of the decisions pertain to indirect costs issues, the strict notice requirement has also been applied to subcontractor costs. See *International Tech. Corp.*, ASBCA 54136, 06-2 BCA ¶33,348, *recons. denied*, 2006 ASBCA LEXIS 107, *aff'd*, 523 F.3d 1341 (Fed. Cir. 2008), denying an overrun claim where the contractor did not notify the government that it had a subcontractor claim on which it had done insufficient analysis to arrive at the amount of the claim. See also *Varigas Research, Inc.*, ASBCA 28610, 84-1 BCA ¶17,154, where the board denied an overrun claim because the contractor should have monitored a subcontractor more closely to ensure that it was performing within its estimated cost.

A few cases have found unforeseeability. See *Magnavox Co.*, ASBCA 17455, 74-1 BCA ¶10,495, where the contractor successfully established the unforeseeability of its overrun based on a number of complex changes that had "far reaching effects" on the cost of performance. When the contractor sought to recover "unforeseeable" overrun costs attributable to the changes, the government argued that foreseeability of the overrun was evidenced by a previous overrun notice. The board held for the contractor, concluding that the ordered changes rendered the notice "inoperative" and that overrun costs attributable to the changes were unforeseeable and thus recoverable. See also *Metametrics, Inc.*, IBCA 1552-2-82, 82-2 BCA ¶16,095, where an overrun claim consisting entirely of a post-performance increase in indirect costs rates was unforeseeable when projected additional sales did not materialize. The board stated that, although the contractor had an adequate accounting system, it would have been an unreasonable burden to require the contractor to foresee the failure to secure expected business many months before the opportunity was actually lost. In *Dames & Moore*, IBCA 2553, 93-1 BCA ¶25,487, the board found that the overrun resulted from unforeseeable causes, including the resolution of cost issues in the contractor's favor following delays in government audits and the loss of business due to the Iranian conflict. In *Johnson Controls World Servs., Inc. v. United States*, 48 Fed. Cl. 479 (2001), the court held that the contractor could not foresee an overrun caused by higher insurance costs under a government-sponsored insurance program that determined the premiums retroactively based on past losses.

Failure to give overrun notice of a small, foreseeable portion of an otherwise unforeseeable overrun may preclude recovery of the entire amount. This result was reached in *Data Dynamics, Inc.*, ASBCA 15468, 73-1 BCA ¶9774. In this case, the contractor did not give notice of a predictable overrun of between $780 and $1,260. As a result of an overhead increase, due presumably to a lower volume of post-completion business than anticipated, the total overrun was $5,469. Apparently, over $4,000 of this amount was unforeseeable. The board, however, refused to allow any of the overrun, because the contractor failed to give notice of the portion of the overrun that it could foresee. Note that this case was submitted on the record without a hearing and that the board did not discuss the fact that the actual overrun was substantially greater than what was anticipated. This case points up the risk a contractor runs by electing to absorb a small, anticipated overrun. See also *Spectrum Research, Inc.*, ASBCA 22304, 78-2 BCA ¶13,371, denying recovery of overrun costs to a contractor who intentionally refrained from giving notice of an existing overrun in order to increase its chances of receiving a "phase two" award.

b. Accounting/Budgeting System Inadequacy

The contractor will not be excused from the notice requirement if its accounting and budgeting system did not project the overrun but an adequate system would have predicted the overrun. In *Stanwick Corp.*, ASBCA 14905, 71-1 BCA ¶8777, *modified on recons.*, 71-2 BCA ¶19,115, the board held that the contractor should have been aware of the potential overrun under the doctrine of reasonable foreseeability. The contractor argued that no matter how excellent an accounting system it might have the actual indirect costs of performance could not be determined until after the end of the fiscal year. In explaining the rule, the board stated at 42,244:

> As this Board has stated many times, the Limitation of Cost clause imposes a duty of notice upon the contractor, with the consequent duty of maintaining an accounting and financial reporting system adequate to apprise it of the possibility of a cost overrun before the overrun is incurred. *United Shoe Machinery Corporation*, ASBCA No. 11936, 68-2 BCA ¶7328 and cases cited. In cases such as the present, where the contractor is or should be aware that post-performance events may have an impact on allowable costs, we regard the contractor as having the corollary duty of reasonably endeavoring to predict those events in sufficient time to provide the requisite notice where an overrun is foreseen. We do not perceive in the Court's *General Electric* decision a less rigorous requirement.

The fact that the contractor's accounting system is inadequate to alert the contractor to an impending or actual overrun will not excuse the failure to give notice. See *Advanced Materials, Inc. v. Perry*, 108 F.3d 307 (Fed. Cir. 1997), where the contractor argued that its change of accounting firms and the accounting system used left it unable to calculate that it would exceed the estimated cost. The court stated that the contractor recognized the inadequacy of its accounting system and should have adjusted its cost calculations to reflect the impact of postponed and canceled contracts. In *Optonetics, Inc.*, ASBCA 17074, 73-2 BCA ¶10,174, the board stated at 47,899:

> There is no question that a contractor is obliged, as a consequence of the requirements and risk imposed by the Limitation of Cost clause, to maintain an accounting and financial reporting system adequate to apprise it of the possibility of a cost overrun before the overrun is incurred.

See also *Eyler Assocs., Inc.*, ASBCA 16804, 75-1 BCA ¶11,320, where the board observed at 53,933:

> The situation in which Appellant found itself, i.e., operating without bookkeeping help, did not authorize it to fail to live up to its contractual obligations and cannot serve to excuse its failure to give the requisite notice pursuant to the LOCC.

However, there is some question as to the level of accounting and budgeting sophistication required of small contractors. One board decision allowed the contractor, a small business without a permanent bookkeeper, to recover an overrun even though the contractor had not maintained an adequate accounting system, *California Earth Sciences Corp.*, IBCA 1138-12-76, 78-1 BCA ¶13,045. In contrast, in *Eastman Assocs.*, DOTCAB 75-9, 76-2 BCA ¶12,015, the board held, in a two-to-one decision, that even when the government contracted with a small company with an inadequate accounting system, the notice requirement was not excused since the contractor had the ability to ascertain the overrun at the time it occurred. The dissenting opinion, however, argued that some of the burden of the overrun should be borne by the government because, had the contracting officer ensured that the contractor's accounting system was adequate prior to award of the contract as required under FPR 1-3.703(b) (now FAR 16.301-3(a)(3)), the problem that led to the overrun would have been eliminated. Similarly, in *McLeod Corp.*, ASBCA 29568, 85-2 BCA ¶18,048, a new 8(a) contractor was not entitled to recover a cost overrun since it failed to maintain an adequate accounting system, which would have alerted it to the likelihood of the overrun before it occurred.

Even if the contractor thinks that overruns in some cost areas may be absorbed by reallocation of its budget, the contractor will be held to knowledge of the events or circumstances leading to the overrun, since its accounting system apprised it of such costs. If offset proves insufficient, the overrun will be considered foreseeable, *AVANTE Int'l Sys. Corp.*, ASBCA 26649, 83-1 BCA ¶16,416. In *Opportunity Sys., Inc.*, GSBCA EEOC-1, 80-2 BCA ¶14,537, the contractor sought to recover a portion of an overrun that it claimed was unforeseeable because the government decided to allow, two months after completion of the work, over $7,000 in previously disallowed costs. The board rejected the contention that the overrun was unforeseeable, noting that the contractor's accounting records had never reflected the initial disallowance. The board stated at 71,663:

> Since appellant's own accounts continuously, though inaccurately, reflected the precise amount subsequently allowed by the Government, those accounts must have indicated that a cost overrun was imminent. Appellant's assertion that the sudden allowance of those costs unforeseeably resulted in an overrun is, therefore, untenable. Such an allowance would merely have confirmed and substantiated what appellant's accounts had continuously reflected.

c. *Post-Determined Overhead Rates*

Although almost all overhead rates are established long after work is completed, in accordance with ¶(d) of the Allowable Cost and Payment clause in FAR 52.216-7, this is generally not an acceptable reason for failing to predict or compute an overrun until final rates are determined, *Datex, Inc.*, ASBCA 24794, 81-1 BCA ¶15,060. In *General Time Corp.*, ASBCA 18962, 75-2 BCA ¶11,462, the board stated at 54,588:

> The notice requirement in the LOC clause operates independently of the determination of final overhead rates, which by definition must occur after completion of contract work, and requires notice of possible overrun during contract performance so as to permit the Government to stop work under the contract and so as to avoid the expenditure of more funds than have been allocated for the contract work.

See also *International Science & Tech. Inst., Inc. v. United States*, 53 Fed. Cl. 798 (2002); Lansdowne Steel & Iron Co., ASBCA 41110, 95-1 BCA ¶27,506; *Planning & Human Sys., Inc.*, ASBCA 44013, 94-1 BCA ¶26,376; *Forge Aerospace, Inc.*, ASBCA 22157, 79-2 BCA ¶13,922; and *University of Col.*, ASBCA 18750, 75-1 BCA ¶11,288.

In some instances, however, events will establish unforeseeability. In *Aerojet-General Corp.*, NASABCA 675-6, 77-1 BCA ¶12,295, the contractor appealed the disallowance of certain overhead costs while performance continued. The decision on appeal, made after completion of the contract, reinstated the disputed costs, which effectively increased the contractor's G&A rate and resulted in the cost overrun. The board held that the disposition of the appeal was not foreseeable and that it would be unreasonable and of little benefit to require the contractor to inform the government of costs under each possible disposition of the appeal. See also *Cosmic, Inc.*, ASBCA 15078, 72-1 BCA ¶9278, where the contractor completed the work in January and should have known by March that its overhead rates had increased. Although it did not give notice until later in the year, the notice requirement was not enforced because all funds allocated to the project had been expended prior to the time that the contractor could first predict the overrun. The board held that enforcement of the notice requirement would serve no purpose since notice at that late date would not have permitted the government to exercise its option to stop work before the funding limit was exceeded. The board stated at 42,998:

> Under these circumstances, notice to the Government would have been nugatory. The law does not require the doing of useless acts, and appellant consequently should not be substantially penalized because it failed to take an action which, though required by the contract, was useless to the Government.

The same reasoning was applied in *Marine Design Techs., Inc.*, ASBCA 43142, 99-1 BCA ¶30,224, where the board held that the contractor could not have foreseen the higher annual indirect cost rate until after the first five months of performance because it could not have reasonably foreseen that the decline in its business volume would lead to an increased overhead rate until then. Similarly, in *Moshman Assocs., Inc.*, ASBCA 52868, 02-1 BCA ¶31,852, the board found that the contractor could not have foreseen higher indirect costs when it completed work in the first four months of its fiscal year and subsequently did not receive an anticipated contract.

d. Inaccurate Business Projections

A contractor will generally not be able to overcome the burden necessary to excuse the notice requirement merely by showing that its anticipated business did not materialize, *Astrosystems Int'l, Inc.*, ASBCA 14590, 70-2 BCA ¶8420; *Inter-National Research Inst.*, ASBCA 24212, 80-1 BCA ¶14,345; *Kirschner Assocs., Inc.*, ASBCA 24958, 81-1 BCA ¶14,834; *Datex, Inc.*, ASBCA 24794, 81-1 BCA ¶15,060. A contractor must be realistic in its business projections. The mere hope of obtaining new or additional business is not sufficient, *George G. Sharp*, ASBCA 32338, 89-3 BCA ¶22,103. In *Systems Assocs., Inc.*, ASBCA 17060, 73-2 BCA ¶10,121, the contractor used an overhead rate based on the anticipation of being awarded two additional contracts during the same fiscal year. This projection was found unrealistic, particularly because the contractor was aware, prior to contract completion, that its actual overhead rate for the year would exceed its projected rate. Similarly, in *Messer Assocs. Inc.*, ASBCA 22365, 78-1 BCA ¶13,059, a contractor was not entitled to additional payment for the increases in its costs of performing a CPFF contract because the increases in cost were reasonably foreseeable and the contractor did not give notice of the increases as required by the LOC clause in its contract. The board stated that the contractor (1) knew that its overhead would increase if it did not obtain new contracts and (2) had no basis for concluding that such new business was a certainty. In *Defense Sys. Concepts, Inc.*, ASBCA 45920, 94-2 BCA ¶26,721, a contractor did not prove the reasonableness of its expectation that additional contract awards would offset known overhead and general and administrative cost overruns. In contrast, in *Metametrics, Inc.*, IBCA 1552-2-82, 82-2 BCA ¶16,095, the board held for the contractor and refused to place the cost risk of higher overhead rates on the contractor. The board found that the contractor's obligation to reduce overhead costs, which was consistent with its reduced business, must be tempered by the obvious necessity that it continue in business to meet its remaining contract commitments.

A few cases have found that notice should be excused because the contractor was reasonable in projecting new business. See *Moshman Assocs., Inc.*, ASBCA 52868, 02-1 BCA ¶31,852, excusing the lack of overrun notice where the contractor had projected new business in the months of its fiscal year after the completion of the current contract but that work had not been awarded until the subsequent fiscal year. The board found that the contractor's rates during contract performance indicated that there were sufficient funds to cover its costs and concluded that the contractor could not have reasonably foreseen that its indirect cost rates would increase drastically after completion of the contract because of the slippage in the award of a new contract. The board distinguished the cases denying overruns as follows at 157,411:

> With respect to those cases where the Board has addressed the issue of expected future business, the Board's statements must be understood in the context of contractors hoping to eliminate current overruns, due to higher than expected current indirect overhead rates, by obtaining new business that would lower the indirect rates. In those cases, the Board found that the current monthly and cumulative indirect costs revealed that the current indirect rates were higher than the provisional rates used for billing purposes. When the current monthly and

cumulative indirect rates were applied to the direct costs, it was apparent that there would be an overrun. The contractor failed to provide a notice of that foreseeable overrun, arguing that it expected that new business would so increase the direct billings that the indirect costs would be spread among the larger pool of direct costs, thus lowering the indirect rates and eliminating the overrun.

In *Bissett-Berman Corp.*, NASABCA 1270-19, 73-2 BCA ¶10,346, the contractor anticipated a follow-on contract for more work of the kind it had been doing. When a new contract was not forthcoming, the contractor directed its technical team to charge overhead for two months while it sought new business. Consequently, the overhead rate increased and resulted in an overrun. The board found that such an overrun was not foreseeable and that the contractor's action in keeping the technical team on board and directing it to charge overhead costs was not unreasonable, stating at 48,873:

> We consider that Appellant acted in the same manner as a normal business concern would act in retaining its team of engineers for a short time after completion of the contract and transferring their salaries to its overhead account while it sought new business when it did not receive a follow-on contract. To have immediately laid off its engineers, which it considered the wrong thing to do, might have resulted in the demise of the company. It was not until the contract was nearly completed that it knew definitely it was not going to receive a follow-on contract and not until it was unable to get new business, after completion of the contract, that it foresaw there was going to be an overrun.
>
> A Government contractor, like any business concern in our economic system, has certain management prerogatives which are accepted when a contractor is selected to perform Government work. The contractor must of course perform within the terms of the contract. One of the terms of the present contract was that the period for computing overhead rates was Appellant's fiscal year which extended two months beyond the end of contract performance. We consider Appellant's management reasonably exercised its prerogative in the manner in which it allocated its overhead during this short period under the circumstances confronting it.

In *ARINC Research Corp.*, ASBCA 15861, 72-2 BCA ¶9721, the contractor recovered a cost overrun caused by increased overhead rates due to a loss of business. The contractor had foreseen the loss of business and had adjusted its overhead rates upward to reflect such reduced volume. However, the actual impact of the loss of business was greater than anticipated with the result that an overrun occurred. The board held that the contractor's projection was sufficiently accurate, stating:

> ARINC's awareness of a probable overhead rate increase . . . cannot be equated with foresight of an actual cost overrun." The board also allowed a contractor to recover its cost overruns without notice when overhead increases occurred after contract completion. The increases occurred because the contractor lost business when the General Accounting Office (GAO) reversed the award of an unrelated satellite-development contract, *General Elec. Co.*, ASBCA 18980, 75-1 BCA ¶11,287.

e. Cost Accounting Standard Adjustments

The notice requirement does not apply to accounting adjustments for pension liability for closed segments of contractors that are required under Cost Accounting Standard 413. See *General Motors Corp. v. United* States, 66 Fed. Cl. 153 (2005), stating at 160:

> The Limitation of Cost and Limitation of Funds clauses were designed to provide the government with various protections in connection with cost-overruns in connection with a specific contract. The Limitation of Cost and Limitation of Funds clauses "protect both the contractor and the government" by ensuring that both can make informed decisions regarding whether to continue with a specific contract. *Advanced Materials, Inc. v. Perry*, 108 F.3d 307, 310 (Fed. Cir. 1997). The CAS 413 segment-closing adjustment is not contract specific. The CAS 413 adjustment does not involve a cost adjustment of any individual contract. Accordingly, the court agrees with GM that the Limitation of Cost and Limitation of Funds clauses do not apply to a CAS 413 adjustment and therefore GM's claim is not barred by application of these clauses.

The same result was reached in *Raytheon Co. v. United States*, 96 Fed. Cl. 549 (2011), and *Viacom, Inc. v. United States*, 70 Fed. Cl. 649 (2006). In *Viacom* the court also reasoned that the inapplicability of the notice requirement could also be based on the decisions that have found that a contractor could not have been able to foresee overhead rate increases that were not determinable at contract completion.

f. Pending Legal Proceedings

If the contractor is involved in legal proceedings of which the government is aware, the failure to give notice under the LOC or LOF clauses will be excused, *Parsons-UXB Joint Venture,* ASBCA 56481, 2013 BCA ¶35,378. Thus, if the contractor subsequently loses the case, the government will have to reimburse any amount over the estimated cost of the contract if the costs are allowable. In *Parsons-UXB* the board ruled that the government was liable for overrun costs due to a state excise tax that had been in litigation, stating at 173,597:

> [T]he Navy's attempts to claim inadequate notice under the LOC and LOF clauses are simply unfounded. The Navy knew all about the [tax] dispute and the potential exposure it presented. Indeed, it was the Navy's desire to minimize its [tax] liability that led to the dispute in the first place. The JV kept the Navy informed of its best estimates of that potential liability. The JV was not obligated to predict the dispute's outcome to be entitled to the additional [tax] that has now arisen. *See Aerojet-Gen. Corp.*, NASA BCA No. 675-6, 77-1 BCA ¶12,295 (holding that the contractor is not required to predict the outcome of legal proceedings that could retroactively increase its costs of performance); *see also* ARINC Research Corp., ASBCA No. 15861, 72-2 BCA ¶9721. Given that the purpose of the LOC and LOF clauses is to permit the parties to prospectively determine their future dealings, the Navy was given all the notice it needed.
>
> Finally, it would also be inequitable to employ the LOC and LOF restrictions to bar recovery. At the outset, the JV could have acceded to Hawaii's demands and paid the additional [tax] the State sought. It could have then invoiced the Navy for the increased [tax] contemporaneously with its performance of the associated task orders, while funds were still available, avoiding any overruns. However, immediately paying the State's higher [tax] assessment and billing it to the Navy would have reduced the total funds available to the Navy to acquire the JV's services on the island.

2. Government Fault

The notice requirement will be excused where the government has been at fault in preventing the contractor from determining its costs. In *Scherr & McDermott, Inc. v. United States*, 175 Ct. Cl. 440, 360 F.2d 966 (1966), the government failed to conduct an audit of the contractor's records as it had agreed to do. As a result, the contractor was unable to predict the overrun. The court excused the notice requirement. However, unless the government has clearly undertaken an obligation to conduct the audit, the notice requirement will not be excused. Thus, in *J.J. Henry Co.*, ASBCA 13835, 71-1 BCA ¶8898, the failure to give notice barred overrun recovery, notwithstanding a contract clause stating that the contractor's costs would be "subject" to audit. In *Lansdowne Steel & Iron Co.*, ASBCA 41110, 95-1 BCA ¶27,506, the contractor argued that the government's failure to perform the final audit on the contract abrogated the funding limitations under the LOF clause. The board disagreed, stating that this was not a situation where a government failure to conduct an audit resulted in the contractor's inability to determine actual overhead.

Government fault in the contract administration process has also excused the overrun notice. In *Nash Janitorial Servs., Inc.*, GSBCA 6390, 84-1 BCA ¶17,135, *recons. denied*, 84-2 BCA ¶17,355, the board found that the contracting officer improperly administered the contract by not obtaining funds for constructive changes and not answering the mail, thus breaching the government's implied duty of good faith and fair dealing. In contrast, in *Ling-Temco-Vought, Inc. v. United* States, 201 Ct. Cl. 135, 475 F.2d 630 (1973), the contractor exceeded the contract cost limitation without stopping work when it relied on a statement by the Navy officials that the agency was not considering any device other than the contractor's. The contractor thereafter discovered that a competing device was being developed. However, the contractor continued to perform in an overrun status for four months. The court stated that, even assuming that the government was guilty of actionable misrepresentation, the contractor waived its right to claim breach of contract by remaining silent and performing (during the four-month period) until the government selected the competitor's product over the contractor's.

E. Action on Overruns

The clauses provide that the contractor can stop work rather than incur overrun costs and that the government is not required to fund an overrun. Thus, assuming that timely and appropriate notice has been given, the parties should work out just how the contractor should proceed. FAR 32.704 directs the contracting officer as follows:

> (a)(1) When a contract contains the clause at 52.232-20, Limitation of Cost; or 52.232-22, Limitation of Funds, the contracting officer, upon learning that the contractor is approaching the estimated cost of the contract or the limit of the funds allotted, shall promptly obtain funding and programming information pertinent to the contract's continuation and notify the contractor in writing that—
>
> > (i) Additional funds have been allotted, or the estimated cost has been increased, in a specified amount;
> >
> > (ii) The contract is not to be further funded and that the contractor should submit a proposal for an adjustment of fee, if any, based on the percentage of work completed in relation to the total work called for under the contract;
> >
> > (iii) The contract is to be terminated; or
> >
> > (iv) (A) The Government is considering whether to allot additional funds or increase the estimated cost, (B) the contractor is entitled by the contract terms to stop work when the funding or cost limit is reached, and (C) any work beyond the funding or cost limit will be at the contractor's risk.
>
> (2) Upon learning that a partially funded contract containing any of the clauses referenced in subparagraph (1) above will receive no further funds, the contracting officer shall promptly give the contractor written notice of the decision not to provide funds.
>
> (b) Under a cost-reimbursement contract, the contracting officer may issue a change order, a direction to replace or repair defective items or work, or a termination notice without immediately increasing the funds available. Since a contractor is not obligated to incur costs in excess of the estimated cost in the contract, the contracting officer shall ensure availability of funds for directed actions. The contracting officer may direct that any increase in the estimated cost or amount allotted to a contract be used for the sole purpose of funding termination or other specified expenses.
>
> (c) Government personnel encouraging a contractor to continue work in the absence of funds will incur a violation of Revised Statutes Section 3679 (31 U.S.C. 1341) that may subject the violator to civil or criminal penalties.

If the contracting officer takes any of the actions specified in subparagraphs (a)(1)(i) through (iii) in a timely fashion, the matter will be settled. However, if there is substantial delay or the contracting officer notifies the contractor under (a)(1)(iv) that the matter is being considered, the contractor is left to determine the course of action. If funds are later forthcoming, stopping performance presents significant problems of work interruption, increased costs due to delays, and potential adverse impact on customer relations. On the other hand, if the contractor proceeds with the work, the contractor takes the risk that the contracting officer will not fund the overrun.

Contractors have attempted, unsuccessfully, to imply contracting officer approval of the overrun by sending communications indicating that they intend to proceed and that failure of the contracting officer to direct stoppage will be considered approval of the overrun. The contracting officer's mere silence after receipt of notification from the contractor does not constitute either approval or inducement, *American Standard, Inc.*, ASBCA 17039, 72-2 BCA ¶9568. The giving of overrun notice by the contractor does not vest in the contractor any right of recovery. The board in *Hoffman Elecs. Corp.*, ASBCA 11352, 68-1 BCA ¶6794, discussed the relationship between the notice requirement and funding overruns at 31,427:

> Under the standard clause, notice by a contractor pursuant to paragraph (a), second sentence group, may obligate the contracting officer to seek and provide new funding if the Government elects that the work be continued beyond the exhaustion of the then obligated funding. However, without more, neither the giving of any such notice nor its omission (with or without explainable cause) alters or affects the reciprocal rights of the parties expressed in clause paragraph (b), third sentence group—i.e., the Government's right to refrain from further funding, and the contractor's right to discontinue further performance.

See also *MTL Sys., Inc.*, IBCA 1648, 84-3 BCA ¶17,618, where the contractor had given notice of both a cost overrun and its intent to continue performance. The board found such notice to be insufficient to impute to the government knowledge that the contractor would thereafter seek additional reimbursement.

1. Contracting Officer Discretion

The determination of whether an overrun should be funded and, if so, in what amount is a discretionary decision of the contracting officer that will be overridden by a court or board only in the rarest of circumstances. Thus, contractors must recognize that, as a general matter, they expend funds in excess of the contract limitations at their own risk. In addition, it has been held that, once a binding release has been signed by a contractor, the contracting officer no longer has the discretion to fund an overrun, *Sheladia Assocs., Inc.*, DOTCAB 1589, 85-2 BCA ¶17,956.

If a contracting officer funds an overrun, it is improper to subsequently unilaterally withdraw the funding because the contractor is not performing adequately, *TEM Assocs., Inc.*, DOTCAB 2556, 93-2 BCA ¶25,759. However, in that case the board held that it was a proper exercise of discretion to limit the overrun funding to work performed after the funding was made available with the result that the contractor would remain liable for the costs incurred in excess of the contract cost limitation before the funding was provided. The board reached this conclusion because the contractor had not complied with the notice requirements of the contract and had not stopped work when the funds ran out.

a. *Prior Notice Given*

When the contractor has given prior notice of an overrun, the government has a number of options available to it. The government may provide additional funds, modify the statement of work to permit performance within the estimated cost of the contract, simply permit the work to continue until the funds are exhausted, or terminate the contract. Normally, no duty is owed to the contractor with regard to this decision since the contractor has the option to stop work. Moreover, the mere fact that a contractor has given notice, as required by the clause, does not automatically entitle the contractor to overrun funding, *Connell-Beach Assocs. Int'l, Inc.*, ASBCA 45318, 97-1 BCA ¶28,753; *ITT Defense Communications Div.*, ASBCA 14270, 70-2 BCA ¶8370; *Research Applications, Inc.*, ASBCA 23834, 79-2 BCA ¶14,120.

If the contracting officer refuses to fund an overrun, after timely notice, but continued performance is urged or directed with government knowledge of the overrun, funding of the overrun will be required. See *American Elec. Labs., Inc. v. United States*, 774 F.2d 1110 (Fed. Cir. 1985), where the court held that the government's actions estopped it from refusing to fund the overrun. The court set forth a four-part test at 1113:

> (1) [T]he party to be estopped must know the facts, i.e., the government must know of the overrun; (2) the government must intend that the conduct alleged to have induced continued performance will be acted on, or the contractor must have a right to believe the conduct in question was intended to induce continued performance; (3) the contractor must not be aware of the true facts, i.e., that no implied funding of the overrun was intended; and (4) the contractor must rely on the government's conduct to its detriment.

The court described the following course of conduct as meeting these requirements at 1115:

> In preparation for the October 23 meeting, a memorandum was prepared by the contract specialist (who was soon to be the CO) and given to the CO on October 19. This memorandum detailed the strategy which was to be used by the government during that meeting with AEL. The Board found that the aim of the government was to negotiate a

> contract amendment of $900,000. The record reveals that the advice of a technical representative was that "it is not in the best interests of the Government for work to stop under the contract and every effort must be made to fund the contract and thus continue performance," and that the contract specialist expected that negotiations would result in a $900,000 increase to the contract. Based on this information the CO determined that a modification to the contract was in the best interests of the government. In making this determination the CO wrote that "the contractor advises that contract funding has been exceed[ed] and additional funding must be made available in order for the contractor to continue its efforts"; the CO then signed the document which authorized the $900,000 modification. As a result of the October 23 meeting the Board expressly found that the government expected AEL's continued performance.

The same result occurred in *SCIENTECH Inc.*, EBCA C-0105327, 03-1 BCA ¶32,095, where the government urged continuing performance and provided incremental funding but ultimately refused to fully fund the contract to cover the contractor's increased indirect cost rates. Two earlier decisions also granted overrun funding based on the logic that it was an abuse of discretion for the contracting officer to refuse to fund the overrun. See *Recon Sys., Inc.*, IBCA 1214-9-78, 79-2 BCA ¶14,058, *recons. denied*, 80-1 BCA ¶14,245, where overrun funding was required because the contracting officer had allowed project personnel to order additional work and accept and use the end product after the contractor had informed the contracting officer that contract funds were exhausted, and *Seaco, Inc.*, DOTCAB 1686, 86-2 BCA ¶18,933, where an overrun was funded because a change was directed with knowledge that overhead rates were understated. Compare *Cal-Tron Sys., Inc.*, ASBCA 49159, 97-1 BCA ¶28,841 (unreasonable to rely on statement of technical person that contractor should delay submission of overrun notice); *HTC Indus., Inc.*, ASBCA 40562, 93-1 BCA ¶25,560 (no knowledge of contracting officer that contractor was continuing performance in response to urging of government technical person); *Mater Mfg., Inc.*, ASBCA 37499, 90-2 BCA ¶22,777 (not warning contractor of consequences of continued performance not estoppel); *Ryckman, Edgerley, Tomlinson & Assocs., Inc.*, IBCA 992-4-73, 73-2 BCA ¶10,343 (contracting officer did not urge performance). The decisions requiring that overruns be funded could also be viewed as constructive funding of the overrun.

b. Denial Improper Where Lack of Prior Notice Excused

In cases where the contractor has been excused from giving the appropriate notice, the government's decision on whether or not to fund the overrun has been subject to much greater scrutiny. In *General Elec. Co. v. United States*, 194 Ct. Cl. 678, 440 F.2d 420 (1971), the court held that since the overrun was unforeseeable it was an abuse of discretion for the contracting officer to refuse to fund the overrun solely on the grounds that the contractor failed to give appropriate notice. For cases following this reasoning see *George G. Sharp, Inc.*, ASBCA 55385, 09-1 BCA ¶34,117; *Moshman Assocs., Inc.*, ASBCA 52868, 02-1 BCA ¶31,852; *Carltech Ass'ns, Inc.*, ASBCA 42576, 93-1 BCA ¶25,267; *Dames & Moore*, IBCA 2553, 93-1 BCA ¶25,487; *Opportunities Industrialization Centers of Am., Inc.*, LBCA 82-BCA-33A, 84-2 BCA ¶17,501; *Metametrics, Inc.*, IBCA 1552-2-82, 82-2 BCA ¶16,095; and *Bissett-Berman Corp.*, NASABCA 1270-19, 73-2 BCA ¶10,346. Although the Armed Services Board originally questioned the abuse of discretion rationale in *ARINC Research Corp.*, ASBCA 15861, 72-2 BCA ¶9721, it has been uniformly held that mere lack of notice is not a valid reason for refusing to fund an overrun when appropriate notice is not possible. It is not clear, however, whether other reasons may support the refusal to fund an overrun in such cases. In *Cosmic, Inc.*, ASBCA 15078, 72-1 BCA ¶9278, the board held that it was improper for the contracting officer to refuse to fund the overrun on the grounds that the contractor's work did not attain the desired technical ends. The contracting officer also cited lack of available funds as a basis for refusing to fund the overrun. The board noted that determining the availability of funds was the responsibility of fiscal officers and that the contracting officer's role with respect to funding was merely "ministerial." The board went on to find that the overrun should be funded, stating: "[I]n determining a contractor's entitlement for payment, the availability or nonavailability of funds is not a proper subject for consideration by the Board." Thus, it appears that the contractor is entitled to recover overrun costs even though funding cannot be provided without the action of fiscal officials.

c. Denial Proper Where Failure to Give Prior Notice Not Excused

Where the contractor has not been excused from giving prior notice, the government may elect to fund the overrun but is not required to do so, *PHI Applied Physical Science, Inc.*, ASBCA 56581, 2013 BCA ¶35,308. See *ITT Defense Communications Div.*, ASBCA 14270, 70-2 BCA ¶8370, where the board stated at 38,920:

Even though there has been a flagrant violation of the notice requirement, the government may still, and frequently does, provide additional funds and continue the work under the contract. On the other hand, even though the contractor has complied fully and completely with the notice requirement, the Government may still exercise its election not to provide additional funds and continue the work under the contract.

In these circumstances, a contractor's unexcused failure to give the required notice deprives the government of the opportunity to pursue alternatives to funding. The government's refusal to fund the overrun in such cases has been held not to be an abuse of discretion. See *Optimal Data Corp.*, NASABCA 976-8, 79-1 BCA ¶13,624, *recons. denied,* 80-1 BCA ¶14,225, finding that the contractor had not given proper notices of overruns. The contracting officer had concluded that notice had been received for a small portion of the total overrun and increased the estimated cost to that extent. The board refused to find an abuse of discretion, stating at 53,934:

> Under paragraph (b) of the LOCC, the contracting officer has the discretion to fund an overrun regardless of whether notice thereof had or had not been given. He exercised his discretion in awarding appellant the sum of $14,270. While we may believe that a much larger award could and should have been made to appellant pursuant to such discretionary authority, it was not our discretion which was being exercised and we would have no basis for concluding that the contracting officer abused his discretion in arriving at the amount he did, even if we had the authority to review the matter.

See also *Cal-Tron Sys., Inc.*, ASBCA 49159, 97-1 BCA ¶28,841, and *Applied Theory, Inc.*, ASBCA 49725, 97-1 BCA ¶28,6670, *aff'd*, 152 F.3d 944 (Fed. Cir. 1998), finding no abuse of discretion when the contracting officer refused to fund a cost overrun.

2. Effect of Prior Overrun Funding

The mere fact that a contracting officer has funded overruns in the past will not prohibit the contracting officer from refusing to fund an overrun. See *Arbiter Sys., Inc.*, ASBCA 47403, 97-2 BCA ¶29,183 (government did not waive its right to deny funding of cost overruns by retroactively funding overruns on another contract); *Textron Defense Sys.*, ASBCA 47352, 96-2 BCA ¶28,332, *aff'd*, 143 F.3d 1465 (Fed. Cir. 1998) (government's funding of cost overruns earlier in a contract not a waiver of its right to refuse to fund later overruns); *Kirschner Assocs., Inc.*, ASBCA 24958, 81-1 BCA ¶14,834 (government's prior funding of an overrun not a waiver of its right to apply the LOC clause); and *Voss Mach. Co.*, ASBCA 28305, 83-2 BCA ¶16,899 (contracting officer's past actions in increasing the contract's estimated cost several times, usually retroactively, did not require the funding of subsequent overruns). In *Planar Corp.*, ASBCA 21060, 77-1 BCA ¶12,269, the board held that the fact that the contractor had previously received a post-completion payment for an overrun under another contract had no effect on its right to receive reimbursement under the present contract. In reaching the same conclusion in *Systems Research Corp.*, ASBCA 16907, 73-1 BCA ¶9931, the board stated that "recovery . . . obtained under one contract does not establish that a contractor is entitled to receive payment for all overruns on all of its contracts. Each contract and situation must be examined and decided on the merits of each individual case." In *Atlantic Science & Tech. Corp.*, ASBCA 49799, 97-2 BCA ¶29,202, the board rejected the contractor's argument that the government waived its right to refuse reimbursement on the basis of past practice because each overrun claim must stand on its own feet. See also *City of Wichita Falls*, HUDBCA 76-13, 77-2 BCA ¶12,764, where the board rejected the contractor's contention that funding of past overruns on the same contract established a pattern of conduct obligating the government to fund a subsequent overrun. Funding part of an overrun does not bind the government to fund the balance of the overrun, *Eyler Assocs., Inc.*, ASBCA 16804, 75-1 BCA ¶11,320.

3. Acts Constituting Approval

Absent express written approval, the contractor must establish that the contracting officer somehow acted to fund the overrun, *ITT Defense Communications Div.*, ASBCA 14270, 70-2 BCA ¶8370. Cases in this area usually turn on whether some action by the contracting officer, or a representative with authority to fund overruns, could lead the contractor to believe that an overrun has been approved.

The cases stress the necessity of having the overrun "approval" come from an authorized official. Work directions by a technical monitor were held insufficient to bind the government to fund the overrun, *Hughes Aircraft Corp.*, ASBCA 24601, 83-1 BCA ¶16,396; *American Standard, Inc.*, ASBCA 15660, 71-2 BCA ¶9109. Statements of a government buyer (without contracting officer authority) and engineer to the effect that funding approval was assumed and that funding was delayed pending an audit were also held insufficient, *Aries Corp.*, ASBCA 14004, 70-1 BCA ¶8249. Similarly, statements by a contracting officer's technical representative have been found insufficient to constitute approval, *Cal-Tron Sys., Inc.*, ASBCA 49159, 97-1 BCA ¶28,841 (statement that the contractor should wait until the completion of performance to submit an "overrun claim"); *HTC Indus., Inc.*, ASBCA 40562, 93-1 BCA ¶25,560, *aff'd*, 22 F.3d 1103 (Fed. Cir. 1994) (statements encouraging contractor to work with agency to evaluate technology and that money could probably be found to fund the overrun).

A statement by the contracting officer that funding of the overrun is being "considered" is insufficient to constitute an act funding an overrun, *Advanced Materials, Inc. v. Perry*, 108 F.3d 307 (Fed. Cir. 1997). Neither has the seeking of additional funding by government personnel been considered an act of funding, *Falcon Research & Dev. Co.*, ASBCA 26853, 87-1 BCA ¶19,458, *aff'd*, 831 F.2d 1056 (Fed. Cir. 1987).

Approval has been found if the government demands performance with knowledge of the overrun status and receives a severable amount of work, *Flight Dynamics Research Corp.*, ASBCA 35248, 88-3 BCA ¶20,861. Compare *JJM Sys., Inc.*, ASBCA 51152, 03-1 BCA ¶32,192, refusing to follow this rule because no authorized official had demanded work after the contractor went into overrun status. Similarly, encouragement of continued contract performance through constant contract administration actions when the contractor was known to be in an overrun status was insufficient to demonstrate that the government had agreed to fund the overrun or was estopped from asserting that the contractor had failed to comply with the LOF clause, *Northrop Grumman Corp. v. United States*, 42 Fed. Cl. 1 (1998). See also *Ebasco Servs., Inc. v. United States*, 37 Fed. Cl. 370 (1997), where no agreement to fund an overrun was found when the government technical monitor stated that the government would "take a look" at the overrun claim and that the contractor would be treated fairly, and *F2 Assocs., Inc.*, ASBCA 52397, 01-2 BCA ¶31,530, where no overrun funding agreement was found from the government's continued negotiations regarding "descoping" the work and ending performance in an orderly manner when it also warned the contractor that the LOF clause was operative.

Approval of vouchers that were submitted by the contractor and subject to audit did not constitute approval of an overrun even though such vouchers reflected the contractor's overrun status, *Community Change, Inc.*, ASBCA 19702, 75-1 BCA ¶11,142. See, however, *Dynamics Concepts, Inc.*, ASBCA 44738, 93-2 BCA ¶25,689, where the board found that the overrun was funded even though the contracting officer did not have notice of the overrun. Payment of invoices by the government was held to have induced the contractor to continue performance. The board stated at 127,804-05:

> It is undisputed that in September 1990 appellant gave respondent no prior oral or written notice of an impending overrun and revised estimate of the total estimated cost on Option Year I as contract 8279 required, and that both parties knew the direct hours and costs appellant invoiced for Option Year I exceeded the total estimated cost for that period. The contracting officer's actual knowledge, per se, of appellant's overrun of the total estimated cost for Option Year I did not waive the LOF clause notice requirement, since she authorized no increase in the total estimated cost and the COTR had no authority to do so. . . . However, respondent paid appellant's Option Year I invoices well aware that appellant continued to perform services and its invoiced amount exceeded the "ceiling price" for Option Year I and respondent received the benefit of appellant's performance through 15 September 1990. Such conduct waived the notice and written authorization requirements of the Limitation of Funds clause. Cf., *Flight Dynamics Research Corp.*, ASBCA No. 35248, 35755, 88-3 BCA ¶20,861 at 105,499 (Government must pay for work done after performance period with overrun funds and whose benefit the Government received, even though the Government knew of no continuing work).

4. Decision to Fund Binding

If a contracting officer makes a firm decision to fund an overrun, the government will be bound by that decision even if the contractor does not receive a formal written notification of the funding. In *General Elec. Co. v. United States*, 188 Ct. Cl. 620, 412 F.2d 1215 (1969), *reh'g denied*, 189 Ct. Cl. 116, 416 F.2d 1320 (1969), the Court of Claims discussed the type of action by a contracting officer that would be considered "approval" of an overrun. In that case the overrun occurred without advance notice. The contracting officer refused to fund the overrun although a government attorney and the administrative contracting officer both recommended that the overrun be funded, as indicated by the following portion of a letter sent by them to the procuring contracting officer:

> It is the opinion of the undersigned that it is within the discretionary authority of the Contracting Officer under the contract article, "Limitation of Costs," to fund the overrun of $12,880.00 [sic], and the undersigned further recommends that the Contracting Officer take such funding action.
>
> FOR THE COMMANDER:
>
> /s/Sumner A. Marcus Sumner A. Marcus Chief, Legal Office
>
> CONCUR WITH RECOMMENDATION:
>
> /s/ R.F. McDermott
>
> R.F. McDermott. Lt Col, Ord Corps
>
> Contracting Officer

The Court of Claims found that the administrative contracting officer (Lt. Col. McDermott) possessed the authority to fund the overrun and concluded that the overrun had been funded on McDermott's authority, stating at 629:

> We disagree with the board's conclusion that Colonel McDermott used the definite language of recommendation merely as an executive notation that the letter had crossed his desk. To conclude, in the absence of any direct evidence, that a contracting officer would so loosely use language embodying his authority conflicts with the mentioned presumption. In this regard, the board's decision is unsupported by substantial evidence and in error as a matter of law. We find, therefore, that Colonel McDermott was aware of the overrun situation and his indication of concurrence meant exactly what it said: that he, as contracting officer, approved the funding of the overrun and favored reimbursing plaintiff for its costs. Under the facts present here, we believe that when an authorized contracting officer expresses a definite opinion concerning the merits of a claim with knowledge of the relevant facts, a "decision" has been made. As we have emphasized numerous times, it is the unfettered opinion of the person delegated as decision-maker by the parties to the contract that is determinative. E.g., *New York Shipbuilding Corp. v. United States*, 180 Ct. Cl. 446, 385 F.2d 427 (1967) (and cases cited); *John A. Johnson Contracting Corp. v. United States*, 132 Ct. Cl. 645, 132 F. Supp. 698 (1955). There is no evidence in this record that Colonel McDermott was not expressing his own opinion when he concurred in Mr. Marcus' recommendation. Cf. *John A. Johnson Contracting Corp. v. United States, supra.* Accordingly, the decision of a duly authorized contracting officer could not be defeated by a funding official at the Army Weapons Command. Nor, by implication, could Colonel McDermott's finding be reversed by a successor contracting officer. See *Climatic Rainwear Co. v. United States*, 115 Ct. Cl. 520, 88 F. Supp. 415 (1950). Mr. Lindblad's determination of September 1966 was therefore a nullity.

For another case holding that a formal notice of overrun funding was not necessary, see *Wind Ship Dev. Corp.*, DOT-CAB 1215, 83-1 BCA ¶16,135, where the contractor elected to continue work voluntarily beyond the estimated contract date. The contracting officer was aware of this fact and initially informed the contractor that the government would not fund continued performance. After the completion of all research, the contracting officer sent a letter to the contractor informing him that he should submit his claim. The board found that the communication was unequivocal and that the government's acts implied an intent to fund the overrun. See also *American Elec. Labs., Inc. v. United States*, 774 F.2d 1110 (Fed. Cir. 1985), holding that the contractor was entitled to compensation for an overrun where the contracting officer had prepared an internal document indicating that more funding should be provided and had indicated to the contractor during negotiations that funding was available.

However, where the contracting officer does not have facts relevant to the exercise of sound discretion, no constructive approval will be found. See *J.J. Henry Co.*, ASBCA 15473, 72-2 BCA ¶9641, where a contracting officer, acting in the capacity of head of the Contract Administration Division, sent a letter to the using agency asking for a determination on the availability of funds or a requested cost overrun. The contractor asserted that this letter constituted a decision to fund the cost overrun. The board held that the contracting officer, in sending the letter either under her own warrant or as acting head of the Contract Administration Division, was not thereby making a decision to fund the cost overrun. See also *TEM Assocs., Inc.*, DOTCAB 2556, 93-2 BCA ¶25,759, where the board held that no constructive notice of funding will be found when a contracting officer is unaware of the contractor's overrun status and subsequently provides additional funding to the contract by modification.

5. Government Failure to Respond to Overrun Notice

It has been held that after a contractor notifies the government that contract funds have been exhausted, the government's failure to respond will not constitute a funding of the overrun, *Falcon Res. & Dev. Co.*, ASBCA 26853, 87-1 BCA ¶19,458; *Work in America Inst.*, LBCA 81-BCA-5, 83-1 BCA ¶16,462. However, failure to promptly inform the contractor that the contract is being allowed to expire under terms of the LOC clause results in a termination for the convenience of the government, *North Am. Rockwell Corp.*, ASBCA 14329, 72-1 BCA ¶9207; *T.M.C., Sys. & Power Corp.*, ASBCA 15211, 72-1 BCA ¶9209. The effect of such a holding is to entitle the contractor to recover the costs of winding up contract performance even though the costs are in excess of the contract cost estimate. The action required by the government to avoid termination for convenience is described in *T.M.C. Systems* at 42,730:

> Under appropriate circumstances a CPFF contract containing a Limitation of Cost clause can be permitted to expire under the terms of that clause. In order for this to occur the Government must provide a contractor with reasonably prompt notice that it intends to permit the contract to expire by its terms and provide the contractor with guidance as to the steps to be taken to close out the contract.

F. Actions Under Other Clauses

When the government, under some other clause of the contract, takes action that involves an increase in the cost of performance, it is often argued that the action constitutes a constructive approval of an overrun. Under the pre-1966 LOC and LOF clauses, these arguments were sometimes successful. However, the present clauses were drafted to overcome this result. First, the general provision in ¶(d) of the LOC clause and ¶(f) of the LOF clause requires a specific notification of overrun funding. Second, specific language concerning changes and terminations was incorporated into the clauses. This section deals with government actions under these and other clauses.

1. Changes

Until 1966, the Armed Services Board of Contract Appeals held that the Changes clause overrode the LOC clause, *Ryan Aeronautical Co.*, ASBCA 6244, 61-1 BCA ¶2911; *Douglas Aircraft Co.*, ASBCA 10495, 66-2 BCA ¶6049. Thus, when the government ordered changes that increased the cost of work called for under the contract, the contractor was entitled to recover costs incurred in excess of the contract's estimated costs and attributable to performance of the changed work. The current LOC and LOF clauses were amended to provide that a change does not entitle the contractor to additional funding unless the contracting officer expressly increases the estimated cost. Specifically, the following paragraph was incorporated into the standard LOC clause in FAR 52.232-20:

> (g) Change orders shall not be considered an authorization to exceed the estimated cost to the Government specified in the Schedule, unless they contain a statement increasing the estimated cost.

In the absence of such an express notification of an increased estimated cost, the contractor is ordinarily precluded from recovering an overrun resulting from the change order. See *Ebasco Servs., Inc. v. United States*, 37 Fed. Cl. 370 (1997); *International Tech. Corp.*, ASBCA 48759, 96-2 BCA ¶28,335; *Dynamics Research Corp.*, ASBCA 18326, 74-1 BCA ¶10,425; and *Breed Corp.*, ASBCA 14523, 72-1 BCA ¶9304.

Thus, under the current LOC/LOF clauses, a contractor must determine whether a change can be accomplished within the estimated cost or whether additional funds will be required. If additional funds will be required, notice must then be given to the contracting officer. In some cases, however, these provisions have not been strictly applied because of less than satisfactory contract administration by both the contractor and the government. Where a change was ordered with the knowledge that an overrun would result, the contractor was not required to give another notice, *Recon Sys., Inc.*, IBCA 1214-9-78, 79-2 BCA ¶14,058, *recons. denied*, 80-1 BCA ¶14,245. The board in *Recon* did not mention that the contract contained the revised clause. In ruling upon the government's motion for reconsideration, however, the board specifically rejected the contention that the new clause precluded recovery of the overrun, stating at 70,180:

> Despite the knowledge that funds were exhausted and that the work was not complete, the contracting officer did not respond to appellant's requests for funding the additional work for over 2 years. On December 2, 1977, the contracting officer's letter indicated that: "Our program personnel advised us that there are no funds available to cover the cost overrun." The project officer was first asked about the availability of funds by a letter dated November 16, 1977, from a contract specialist. The contracting officer failed to make a timely determination of the availability of funds and to advise the appellant accordingly, but rather allowed the final tasks under the contract to be sent to the contractor and the Government to accept and use the end product. The actions of the contracting officer were consistent with an intent to fund the additional work under the contract; and only after learning that funds were not available 2 years after the added work was required did the Government raise the technical defense that the LOCC did not obligate the Government to provide the additional funding. The question of whether the additional funds to complete the contract would have been made available upon timely actions of the contracting officer is now moot. Failure to act resulted in the project officer ordering the added work and the acceptance by the Government of the benefits of the added work. In these circumstances, we confirm our finding that the Government must pay for the costs of the constructive change which resulted in costs over the contract ceiling being incurred after notice that the contract funds were fully expended.

In *Magnavox Co.*, ASBCA 17455, 74-1 BCA ¶10,495, prior to and following receipt of the required 60-day notice from the contractor, the government issued a number of substantial change orders altering the cost situation so much that the contractor became unaware of when funding limits were exceeded. Despite a failure to secure prior written authorization for the overrun, as strictly required under the current LOC/LOF clauses, the contractor was allowed to recover its costs. The board found that the government's change orders, after notice, made the overrun situation unforeseeable, and, therefore, recovery was allowed on an "impossibility" theory. Similarly, in *A.T. Kearney, Inc.*, DOTCAB 1263, 83-2 BCA ¶16,835, *recons. denied*, 84-1 BCA ¶17,052, the board held that a unilaterally directed change may operate to waive the ceiling price. However, although the contract contained the revised clause, the board cited cases involving the earlier clause to support its conclusion.

The contracting officer may issue a change with new funding that may only be used to cover work called for by the change, *PB Farradyne, Inc.*, DOTBCA 4063, 00-1 BCA ¶30,683. There the board refused to permit an excess amount provided for the changed work to be used to cover an overrun where notice had not been given as required.

In *Michael Weller, Inc. v. Office of Navajo & Hopi Indian Relocation*, GSBCA 10627-NHI, 94-2 BCA ¶26,849, the board stated that this provision in the LOC clause would not apply to changes that were outside of the scope of the contract. However, the board denied the claim for overrun costs because the changes that had caused the overrun were within the scope of the contract.

2. Inspection and Correction of Defects

Under the pre-1966 LOC clause, the cost of correcting work as ordered by the contracting officer under the Inspection and Correction of Defects clause was recoverable even though the cost exceeded the contract cost estimate and the contractor had not complied with the provisions of the clause, *Telecomputing Corp.*, ASBCA 8607, 1964 BCA ¶4173, *reh'g denied*, 65-1 BCA ¶4794. Although the current LOC clause has not been changed to overcome this decision explicitly, the general language of the LOC and LOF clauses, ¶¶(d) and (f) respectively, state that the contract limitations apply except "as required by other provisions of this contract, specifically citing and stated to be an exception to this clause." Since there is no such language in the current Inspection clauses for cost-reimbursement contracts in FAR 52.246-3, -5, and -8, it is likely that the board's decision in *Telecomputing* is no longer applicable. Thus, when the contractor is ordered to correct defective work under any of these clauses, the procedures of the LOC clause should be closely followed. If, following these procedures, corrective work is not performed in accordance with the directions of the contracting officer because the contract funds have been exhausted and the government has refused to provide additional funding, these clauses provide other remedies of the government including default termination. It is questionable whether these remedies should apply in such circumstances.

3. Government-Furnished Property

A contractor is not entitled to recover costs, incurred in attempting to overcome defects in government-furnished property (GFP), that are over the cost limitation, *Booz, Allen & Hamilton, Inc.*, IBCA 1027-3-74, 76-1 BCA ¶11,787. There the board held that the GFP clause was clearly not meant to be an exception to the LOC clause, citing ¶(d) of the LOC clause, which provides that the limitations of the clause are binding "[e]xcept as required by other provisions of this contract specifically citing and stated to be an exception of this clause." The board held that the contractor failed to show a basis for holding the LOC clause inapplicable or for imposing an obligation on the government to fund costs in excess of the estimated cost. The same result was reached in *Falcon Research & Dev. Co.*, ASBCA 26322, 83-1 BCA ¶16,510.

4. Termination

Paragraphs (d)(2) and (e) of the LOC clause and ¶¶(f)(2) and (h) of the LOF clause make the cost limitation procedures applicable to costs incurred as a result of termination of the contract. Thus, termination costs in excess of the cost limitation have been denied, *F2 Assocs., Inc.*, ASBCA 52397, 01-2 BCA ¶31,530; *Imaging Science Techs. X-Ray Imaging Div., Inc.*, ASBCA 52497, 00-2 BCA ¶30,924; *Moon Eng'g Co.*, ASBCA 49210, 99-1 BCA ¶30,187. See *Textron Defense Sys.*, ASBCA 47352, 96-2 BCA ¶28,332, *aff'd*, 143 F.3d 1465 (Fed. Cir. 1998), stating that these clauses require the contractor to monitor performance so that it can stop work "with sufficient unexpended funds . . . to cover termination costs." This rule applies to termination settlement expenses as well as costs incurred in performance prior to the termination. See, however, *Breed Corp. v. United States*, 223 Ct. Cl. 702 (1980), holding that the contracting officer, with full knowledge that the contract funds had been exhausted, "waived" the benefit of the LOC clause by requesting that the contractor take specific termination actions. The court reasoned that the contractor was reasonably led to believe that the government would fund the termination costs. The boards have applied this rule to hold that when a contracting officer terminates a contract for convenience knowing that the contract limitation has been reached, such action will be construed as a waiver of the limitation with regard to termination settlement expenses, *HTC Indus., Inc.*, ASBCA 40562, 93-1 BCA ¶25,560; *TDC Mgmt. Corp.*, DOTCAB 1802, 91-2 BCA ¶23,815, *recons. denied*, 91-2 BCA ¶24,061; *A.T. Kearney, Inc.*, DOTCAB 1263, 83-2 BCA ¶16,835, *recons. denied*, 84-1 BCA ¶17,052.

5. Other Clauses

The provision in ¶(d) of the LOC clause stating that the contract limitations apply except "as required by other provisions of this contract, specifically citing and stated to be an exception to this clause," will preclude contractors from claiming overrun costs caused by other clauses calling for price adjustments. See *Moon Eng'g Co.*, ASBCA 49210, 99-1 BCA ¶30,187, denying reimbursement of overrun costs allegedly caused by the Protest After Award clause in FAR 52.233-3, and an agency Substitution of Key Personnel clause, and *Textron Defense Sys.*, ASBCA 47352, 96-2 BCA ¶28,332, *aff'd*, 143 F3d 1465 (Fed. Cir. 1998), denying reimbursement of overrun costs allegedly caused by the Stop Work Order clause in DAR 7-105.3(c) (similar to the current clause in FAR 52.242-15, Alternate I).

G. Equitable Distribution of Property

Paragraph (h) of the LOC clause and ¶(k) of the LOF clause state that "the government and the contractor shall negotiate an equitable distribution of all property produced or purchased under the contract, based upon the share of costs incurred by each." In *Breed Corp.*, ASBCA 14523, 86-3 BCA ¶19,086, the board reasoned that this provision only applies to specific "non-severable" property created "in part before and in part after the cost limit is reached." However, *Die Casters Int'l, Inc. v. United* States, 74 Fed. Cl. 174 (2006), held that the provision also applied to the property acquired on a cost-sharing contract. This provision is applicable in spite of the fact that the contractor failed to meet the clause's notice requirements, *Systems Integrated,* ASBCA 54439, 07-1 BCA ¶33,575, *aff'd,* 276 Fed. Appx. 1000 (Fed. Cir. 2008).

In such a situation, the government has the choice of not calling for delivery of the property or paying for the overrun costs incurred in creating the property if it demands delivery of the property. See *SMS Agoura Sys., Inc.*, ASBCA 51441, 99-2 BCA ¶30,524, requiring the contracting officer to negotiate to pay for an equitable share of property that could not be returned to the contractor, and *JRS Indus., Inc.*, ASBCA 32256, 86-3 BCA ¶19,222, requiring the contracting officer to either return a share of such property to the contractor or negotiate to pay for the share of the property created with overrun expenditures. When the contracting officer would not follow this direction, the board awarded the contractor the overrun costs of creating the property, *JRS Indus., Inc.*, ASBCA 33871, 87-2 BCA ¶19,796. In *Breed,* the board also held that the contractor has no right to equitable distribution of property produced before the overrun has occurred. Thus, the contractor will be entitled to no overrun funding if the government demands the delivery of such property. Conversely, if the contractor spends overrun funds creating property that is "severable," the government has no right to equitable distribution of the property and must fund the overrun if it decides to take the property, *American Mach. & Foundry Co.*, ASBCA 8862, 65-1 BCA ¶4654; *Douglas Aircraft Co.*, ASBCA 10495, 66-2 BCA ¶6049; *Frederick Burk Found. for San Francisco State College,* ASBCA 15728, 73-1 BCA ¶9959; *Flight Dynamics Res. Corp.*, ASBCA 35248, 88-3 BCA ¶20,861. The equitable distribution of property provision does not apply to services where no tangible property is delivered to the government, *Systems Eng'g Assocs. Corp.*, ASBCA 38592, 91-2 BCA ¶23,676. In *Die Casters International* the court held that the government had breached the contract by failing to negotiate an equitable distribution of the property but that the contractor had failed to prove that it was damaged when the property was turned over to a foreign government.

While it would appear that the equitable distribution of property provision provides an adequate remedy for a contractor if the government retains property with no additional funding, *Scan-Tech Sec., L.P. v. United States,* 46 Fed. Cl. 326 (2000), holds that the contractor may also have a "taking" claim if the government keeps property paid for with overrun funds.

H. Ceilings

Another method of controlling the funding of cost-reimbursement contracts is to include "ceilings" in the contract. If such ceilings are clearly written, they will require the contractor to complete the work even though the government does not fund overruns. Although ceilings are often incorporated into the contract after a number of overruns have occurred, they may also be included at the outset. Since these ceilings are adopted on an ad hoc basis, numerous problems in determining their legal effect may be encountered. One major problem is determining whether the ceiling operates to deny the contractor's right to stop work when the ceiling is reached. Uncertainty also exists concerning the interrelationship of the ceiling with other contract provisions. The two most commonly used types of ceilings are ceilings on overall cost and ceilings on overhead. Overhead ceilings are imposed either on a dollar basis or on the overhead rate. They are limitations on the allowability of cost and do not change the nature of the contractor's obligation. For cases holding that ceilings are validly used by the government, see *Ragsdale, Beals, Hooper & Siegler v. Dep't of Treasury,* GSBCA 13142-TD, 96-1 BCA ¶27,930; *Rice v. Martin Marietta Corp.*, 13 F.3d 1563 (Fed. Cir. 1993); and *CRC Sys., Inc. v. General Servs. Admin.*, GSBCA 11173, 93-2 BCA ¶25,842. The latter decision contains an extensive discussion of this issue.

The Court of Claims has stated that overall cost ceilings will be strictly construed against the government in the event of ambiguities, *George W. Sturm Assocs. v. United States,* 190 Ct. Cl. 691, 421 F.2d 723 (1970). It is thus incumbent upon the government to exercise careful draftsmanship in preparing such provisions. Failure to do so may provide an opportunity for the use of alternative methods of cost allocation to defeat the purpose of the ceiling. For example, in *Singer-General Precision, Inc. v. United States,* 192 Ct. Cl. 435, 427 F.2d 1187 (1970), a contractor was permitted, in a project definition contract, to allocate costs in excess of the ceiling to its overhead, as a bidding expense.

A precisely drafted ceiling will operate both to deprive the contractor of additional funding and require the contractor to complete performance within the stipulated amount. In *LSi Serv. Corp. v. United States,* 191 Ct. Cl. 185, 422 F.2d 1334 (1970), the court reasoned at 186:

Plaintiff entered into a written contract with the contracting officer of the Department of HEW for the purpose of providing and managing an evaluation of 1966-1967 Field Projects Under Title I of the Elementary and Secondary Education Act for the National Advisory Council for the Education of Disadvantaged Children. The period of the evaluation was from November 4, 1966, to March 20, 1967. The entire agreement was contained in a written contract headed "Cost Reimbursement Contract," which provided for an estimated cost of $57,210 and a fixed fee of $4,005. Article 22 of the contract stated that if the contractor had reason to believe that the total cost of the contract would be substantially greater or less than the estimated cost, he would submit a written revised estimate to the contracting officer. Thereupon, the contracting officer would decide whether to allow any excess costs and then notify the contractor of that decision in writing. The inclusion of such an article would normally make the agreement a cost reimbursement contract, which by its nature does not specifically limit costs. The contract in question, however, also contained the following:

ARTICLE 17. COST LIMITATION

Notwithstanding, the Terms and Conditions of Article 22 entitled "Limitation of Cost" of the General Provisions, the Contractor agrees to faithfully and diligently pursue and complete the work specified in this proposal SP 9-67-1A at a maximum total cost, including fee of $61,215.00.

* * *

The board held, and we agree, that Article 17 converted what would have been a cost-plus contract into a limited-price contract. Article 17 stated that notwithstanding the payment provisions of Article 22, the cost limit stated in Article 17 was to prevail. The board found that the contract was clearly understood to contain a fixed-price provision, that this provision did not render the agreement ambiguous, and that the contractor could not reasonably construe it differently. See *Sun Shipbuilding & Dry Dock Co. v. United States*, 183 Ct. Cl. 358, 393 F.2d 807 (1968). The board also found that even under Article 22 plaintiff could not recover, since it had not complied with the provisions of that article of the contract. Nothing has been suggested to us to show that these findings were incorrect.

A substantially similar conclusion was reached by the HUD Board of Contract Appeals in *Urban Mgmt. Consultants of San Francisco, Inc.*, HUDBCA 75-28, 76-2 BCA ¶12,000, where the parties executed the following modification of a CPFF technical assistance contract:

GOVERNMENT'S SHARE; CEILING AND PAYMENT

A. The total estimated cost and ceiling to be borne by the Government for costs incurred for the performing of this contract consisting of allowable direct and indirect cost and the fixed fee is $87,450. All additional costs required to complete the work required under the contract shall constitute the Contractor's contributed share.

In *Peterson Bldrs., Inc. v. United States*, 31 Fed. Cl. 650 (1994), the court held that the following clause, added in a modification to a CPIF contract, precluded the contractor from recovering costs above the ceiling:

The ceiling price set forth in this modification constitutes the maximum liability of the Government to pay (cost and fee) for completion of the work specified in CLINS 0001 through 0009, as modified through the date of this modification, and including the changes listed on Attachment "A" hereto. The Government shall have no obligation to pay for contract performance in excess of the ceiling price set forth above (except as set forth in this modification) unless the ceiling price is modified pursuant to other provisions of this contract providing for an equitable adjustment of the contract price.

The following shall apply if, and when, allowable costs under CLINS 0001 through 0009 equal the ceiling price:

a. Notwithstanding any other clause of this contract to the contrary, the Government will not reimburse the Contractor for allowable costs incurred and fee in excess of the ceiling price.

b. Notwithstanding General Provision I-3, "Limitation of Cost,"—the Contractor (1) shall complete all work under CLINS 0001 through 0009 even though allowable costs incurred exceed the ceiling price and (2) shall bear one hundred percent (100%) of the costs incurred to complete CLINS 0001 through 0009 in excess of the ceiling price.

See also *Aurora Optics, Inc.*, ASBCA 48766, 96-1 BCA ¶28,077, where the board found that the contractor was entitled to no additional compensation for costs incurred above a ceiling provided for in the following clause:

> The Government and the Contractor hereby agree that, notwithstanding the principles set forth in the clauses of this contract entitled "Allowable Cost and Payment," [and] "Limitation of Cost," and the provisions set forth in the clause of this contract entitled "Fixed Fee," the Government's obligation to reimburse the Contractor for allowable and allocable costs incurred in performance of this contract and to pay the fixed fee is limited to a total payment of $498,653. Any allowable and allocable costs incurred in performance of this contract which would cause the total reimbursable expenses due the Contractor under this contract to exceed $461,745 will be absorbed by the Contractor by a reduction in the fixed fee until the fixed fee is zero and the reimbursable expenses equal $498,653, and thereafter shall be treated as unreimbursable expenses.

The same result was reached in *National Civil Serv. League*, HUDBCA 76-23, 78-2 BCA ¶13,455, *recons. denied*, 79-1 BCA ¶13,563, *aff'd*, 226 Ct. Cl. 478, 643 F.2d 768 (1981), where the board stated at 66,438:

> The Board made no express finding on whether Appellant could have stopped work pursuant to the Limitation of Cost clause, as amended by the ceiling provision. Since Appellant did not stop work under the provisions of that clause, the question is moot. Our decision must be based solely on the facts as presented, and it is uncontroverted that Appellant incurred costs in excess of the ceiling. As stated in the initial decision in this appeal, the ceiling provision was clearly intended to avoid any obligation to fund an overrun, whether or not anticipated by the contractor. Modification No. 5 expressly set forth the intent of the parties that "any costs exceeding the ceiling amount are to be borne by the contractor solely." Assuming, arguendo, that Appellant could have stopped work upon reaching the ceiling amount, the parties nevertheless clearly allocated the risk of an unintentional overrun solely to Appellant. The *General Electric* decision [194 Ct. Cl. 678, 44 F.2d 420 (1971)] does not compel a contrary result, since the Court there was not considering the effect of a ceiling provision.

In *United Shoe Mach. Corp.*, ASBCA 11936, 68-2 BCA ¶7328, the board held that a ceiling on a cost-reimbursement contract is applicable to both direct and indirect costs of performance whether known or unknown to the contractor. In *Lockheed Calif. Co.*, DOTCAB 72-9, 75-1 BCA ¶11,149, a contractor performing under an incrementally funded cost-sharing-no-fee contract was denied recovery for closure costs, even though these costs were not provided for in the estimated cost and the work was ordered after the contract completion date, since the board found that the following provisions constituted a maximum obligation for allowable costs:

> The Government shall not be liable for repayment of any costs which, when added to costs already paid or payable to the Contractor, exceed the following:
>
> * * *
>
> For this Contract FA-SS-66-7, the total estimated contract cost.

In *Solar Turbines, Inc. v. United States*, 26 Cl. Ct. 1249 (1992), the parties had modified a CPAF development contract to add a ceiling amount but had provided that, if it reached the ceiling, the contractor could request a termination for convenience. The court rejected the contractor's claims for amounts spent in excess of the ceiling, holding that the government had not induced the contractor to incur the additional costs without requesting termination by misrepresenting the prospect that it would procure the product if the contractor completed the development with its own funds.

In *General Dynamics Corp. v. United States*, 229 Ct. Cl. 399, 671 F.2d 474 (1982), the parties converted a fixed-price incentive contract to a cost-reimbursement contract and included the cost-reimbursement termination clause in the contract. They also added a clause stating that the contractor was required to complete the work within a specified ceiling amount and that the contractor would bear all costs of completing performance above that amount. The government terminated the contract for default, refused to pay the contractor's costs, and asserted a right to reprocurement costs. The court held that the contractor was entitled to recover its costs up to the ceiling amount but that the government could recover from the contractor its costs of reprocurement above the ceiling amount if the default termination was deemed proper. On remand, the board held that the termination was improper, *General Dynamics Corp.*, DOTCAB 1232, 83-1 BCA ¶16,386.

II. CHANGES AND TECHNICAL DIRECTION

Cost-reimbursement contracts give agencies considerable flexibility to alter or direct the course of the work during performance of their contracts. This permits the accommodation of changing requirements as well as the ability to adopt different methods of performing the work which have been recommended by contractors as the work progresses. This flexibility is provided by two means—the use of the standard Changes—Cost-Reimbursement clause in FAR 52.243-2 and the use of an agency clause covering technical direction.

A. Entitlement to Additional Fee

Since, as discussed above, the LOC and LOF clauses control the amount of costs that the contractor may be reimbursed, the major issue that arises in the use of the changes and technical direction clauses is the amount of additional fee that the contractor is entitled to for performing any additional work that is required by orders of the government. In general, to recover additional fee, the contractor must establish that such work was not required by the original contract.

Since the statement of work in most cost-type contracts contains a relatively broad description of the work, it is frequently difficult for a contractor to establish that it is being required to perform work beyond what was originally contemplated. See, for example, *Burns & Roe, Inc.*, EBCA 102-11-79, 81-2 BCA ¶15,386, where the board denied additional fee because it concluded that the contractual document was unambiguous in requiring the contractor to perform all of the contract work at the original fee even though the effort which was originally forecast to require seven years had been stretched out to a projected 17 years. In reaching this conclusion, the board reviewed the record of negotiations and found that the government had warned the contractor that this was the intent of the contract language. In some cases, looking behind the statement of work to the parties' negotiations will yield the opposite result. For example, in *H. K. Ferguson Co.*, ASBCA 2826, 57-1 BCA ¶1293, the board found that the contractor was entitled to additional fee because the estimated cost was the best measure of the "baseline" of work originally called for under the contract. The board explained its reasoning as follows at 4027-28:

> Preliminary to consideration of increases in the amount and character of the work, it is necessary to decide what work was originally required by the contract and covered by the fixed fee. There is a close relation between the work required by the contract and the estimated cost. This is required for budgetary purposes and to comply with the legal requirement that a contract not be made without funds adequate for its fulfillment. It may be stated as a general proposition that the estimated cost is on the work required by the contract and that any work not included in the estimated cost is not included in the contract, although the accuracy of the estimated cost is not guaranteed and the "Changes" article expressly states that errors and omissions in computing the estimated cost are not a basis for adjustment of the fixed fee. To say that the scope of the contract includes a substantial amount of work that was not taken into account in determining the estimated cost is to say that the contract was entered into in violation of law.
>
> The general idea that a change must be a change in the work beyond the contemplation of the parties at the time the contract was negotiated in order to be a basis for adjustment in the fixed fee is sometimes expressed by the phrase "change in scope." However, the use of this convenient short-hand expression must not cause us to lose sight of the concept behind it. The "Changes" article does not refer to scope. What constitutes a change causing a material increase in the amount or character of work cannot be determined from the dictionary meaning of "scope."

> The fixed fee is the contractor's compensation for doing the work prescribed by the contract, that is, the work contemplated by the parties when the contract was negotiated and on which the fee was based. The amount of work cannot be increased materially without an adjustment of the fee simply because the contract description of the ten facilities is so general as to be equally descriptive of the work actually performed. A change in scope does not necessarily entail a change in verbal description.

Similar reasoning was employed by the board in *Associated Aero Science Lab., Inc.*, ASBCA 15451, 72-1 BCA ¶9293. There the parties entered into a CPAF contract that contained a detailed description of the work, together with a clause that indicated estimated levels of effort to be expended by the contractor at various contractor-owned and government-owned facilities. The board held that the government changed the work, entitling the contractor to additional fee, when it directed the contractor to perform a greater amount of work at the contractor-owned facility than had been reflected in the contract estimates. The board stated at 43,059:

> Appellant has made the point, and the parties have stipulated, that the work performed at appellant's installations during the latter part of 1966 and in 1967, necessitated employment, training, recruitment support and supervision of professional and a higher grade of technical-personnel, compared to what would have been necessary for employees who worked at the on-station locations. Since the fixed fee was negotiated based upon a pattern of work which was included in the contract by way of estimates of direct labor cost and numbers of employees at each installation, it is our opinion that the drastic shifts from on-station to contractor facility work, and the added responsibilities of supervising a different mix of employees did in fact constitute a change. For this change, appellant is entitled to an equitable adjustment in the fixed-fee.

In *Thomas O'Connor & Co.*, ASBCA 15123, 71-2 BCA ¶8926, a CPFF subcontractor sought additional fee when the government, in order to avoid payment of overtime premiums, directed the subcontractor to shorten its work week. The board found that the government's action, which extended the time of performance and increased the subcontractor's nonreimbursable fixed costs, entitled the subcontractor to recover additional fixed fee under the Changes clause. The board arrived at this conclusion based on the fact that the parties had discussed the performance period in negotiating the fixed fee and the subcontractor had used the shorter projected time of performance in computing the nonreimbursable fixed costs.

Merely adding additional funds to the contract does not entitle the contractor to additional fees where there has been no change in the "nature of the work," *Pacific Architects & Eng'rs, Inc.*, ASBCA 19636, 77-2 BCA ¶12,555. For other cases finding no entitlement to additional fee, see *PRC Info Sciences Co.*, EBCA 171-5-81, 82-2 BCA 15,866 (government speeded up early part of work); *Program Resources, Inc.*, ASBCA 21656, 78-1 BCA ¶12,867 (labor rates had increased but the government was not involved in the union actions leading to the increase); and *Raytheon Serv. Co.*, DOTCAB 1363, 84-2 BCA ¶17459 (government allowed reimbursement for additional overhead costs but the level of effort for performance was not altered). Conversely, merely expending less costs than anticipated should not entitle the government to reduce the fee. However, if the government constructively reduces the work contemplated, it would thereby become entitled to a reduction in fee, *RJO Enters., Inc.*, DOTCAB 2951, 96-2 BCA ¶28,379 (permitting litigation of this issue).

B. Technical Direction

Because the statement of work contained in most cost-reimbursement contracts sets forth only a broad description of the contract objectives, the government frequently reserves the right to direct contractors with regard to the elements of performance as the work progresses. This is accomplished through the use of Technical Direction clauses, which authorize the government to issue instructions and guidance on the detailed aspects of contract performance.

1. Nature of Technical Direction

A variety of technical direction clauses have been used by the government. The primary purpose of these clauses is to authorize a specific individual, usually designated as the Contracting Officer's Technical Representative (COTR), to direct the details of the contractor's work but not to make changes. Examples of such clauses are included in NFS 1852.242-70 and Environmental Protection Agency Acquisition Regulation (EPAR) 1552.237-71, as follows:

National Aeronautics & Space Administration

TECHNICAL DIRECTION (SEP 1993)

(a) Performance of the work under this contract is subject to the written technical direction of the Contracting Officer Technical Representative (COTR), who shall be specifically appointed by the Contracting Officer in writing in accordance with NFS FAR Supplement 18-42.270. "Technical direction" means a directive to the Contractor that approves approaches, solutions, designs, or refinements; fills in details or otherwise completes the general description of work or documentation items; shifts emphasis among work areas or tasks; or furnishes similar instruction to the Contractor. Technical direction includes requiring studies and pursuit of certain lines of inquiry regarding matters within the general tasks and requirements in Section C of this contract.

(b) The COTR does not have the authority to, and shall not, issue any instruction purporting to be technical direction that—

(1) Constitutes an assignment of additional work outside the statement of work;

(2) Constitutes a change as defined in the changes clause;

(3) Constitutes a basis for any increase or decrease in the total estimated contract cost, the fixed fee (if any), or the time required for contract performance;

(4) Changes any of the expressed terms, conditions, or specifications of the contract; or

(5) Interferes with the contractor's rights to perform the terms and conditions of the contract.

(c) All technical direction shall be issued in writing by the COTR.

(d) The Contractor shall proceed promptly with the performance of technical direction duly issued by the COTR in the manner prescribed by this clause and within the COTR's authority. If, in the Contractor's opinion, any instruction or direction by the COTR falls within any of the categories defined in paragraph (b) of this clause, the Contractor shall not proceed but shall notify the Contracting Officer in writing within 5 working days after receiving it and shall request the Contracting Officer to take action as described in this clause. Upon receiving this notification, the Contracting Officer shall either issue an appropriate contract modification within a reasonable time or advise the Contractor in writing within 30 days that the instruction or direction is—

(1) Rescinded in its entirety; or

(2) Within the scope of the contract and does not constitute a change under the Changes clause of the contract, and that the Contractor should proceed promptly with its performance.

(e) A failure of the Contractor and Contracting Officer to agree that the instruction or direction is both within the requirements of the contract and does not constitute a change under the Changes clause, or a failure to agree upon the contract action to be taken with respect to the instruction or direction, shall be subject to the Disputes clause of this contract.

(f) Any action(s) taken by the contractor in response to any direction given by any person other than the Contracting Officer or the COTR shall be at the Contractor's risk.

Environmental Protection Agency

TECHNICAL DIRECTION (AUG 2009)

(a) Definitions.

Contracting officer technical representative (COTR), means an individual appointed by the contracting officer in accordance with Agency procedures to perform specific technical and administrative functions.

Task order, as used in this clause, means work assignment, delivery order, or any other document issued by the contracting officer to order work under a service contract.

(b) The Contracting Officer's Representative(s) may provide technical direction on contract or work request performance. Technical direction includes:

(1) Instruction to the contractor that approves approaches, solutions, designs, or refinements; fills in details; completes the general description of work; shifts emphasis among work areas or tasks; and

(2) Evaluation and acceptance of reports or other deliverables.

(c) Technical direction must be within the scope of work of the contract and any task order thereunder. The Contracting Officer's Representative(s) does not have the authority to issue technical direction which —

(1) Requires additional work outside the scope of the contract or task order;

(2) Constitutes a change as defined in the "Changes" clause;

(3) Causes an increase or decrease in the estimated cost of the contract or task order;

(4) Alters the period of performance of the contract or task order; or

(5) Changes any of the other terms or conditions of the contract or task order.

(d) Technical direction will be issued in writing or confirmed in writing within five (5) days after oral issuance. The contracting officer will be copied on any technical direction issued by the Contracting Officer's Representative.

(e) If, in the contractor's opinion, any instruction or direction by the Contracting Officer's Representative(s) falls within any of the categories defined in paragraph (c) of the clause, the contractor shall not proceed but shall notify the contracting officer in writing within 3 days after receiving it and shall request that the contracting officer take appropriate action as described in this paragraph. Upon receiving this notification, the contracting officer shall:

(1) Advise the contractor in writing as soon as practicable, but no later than 30 days after receipt of the contractor's notification, that the technical direction is within the scope of the contract effort and does not constitute a change under the "Changes" clause of the contract;

(2) Advise the contractor within a reasonable time that the government will issue a written modification to the contract; or

(3) Advise the contractor that the technical direction is outside the scope of the contract and is thereby rescinded.

(f) A failure of the contractor and contracting officer to agree as to whether the technical direction is within the scope of the contract, or a failure to agree upon the contract action to be taken with respect thereto, shall be subject to the provisions of the clause entitled "Disputes" in this contract.

(g) Any action(s) taken by the contractor, in response to any direction given by any person acting on behalf of the government or any government official other than the contracting officer or the Contracting Officer's Representative, shall be at the contractor's risk.

The fundamental purpose of these clauses is to provide flexibility in the administration of cost-reimbursement contracts without having to process contractual actions through the formal contracting process. Thus, technical personnel in the agency are permitted to direct the work on a step-by-step basis as they observe the course of performance. This allows the agency to utilize the funds allocated to the contract in a manner that is most likely to meet the government's ultimate objectives and assists the contractor in identifying elements of performance which will be of greatest benefit to the agency.

2. Distinguishing Technical Direction and Changes

Because instructions and orders issued under Technical Direction clauses call upon the contractor to perform only the work originally contemplated in the statement of work, they are covered by the fee in the basic contract. It follows that such orders do not entitle the contractor to recover any additional fee. On the other hand, when the contractor is required to perform work beyond what was originally contemplated (and not covered by the original fee), the contractor is entitled to recover additional fee pursuant to the contract's Changes clause. It is because of this question of recovery of additional fee that the distinction between technical directions and changes is an important one.

Technical Direction clauses deal with this issue by stating that contract changes may not be implemented through the process of technical direction. Hence, they place the burden on the contractor to distinguish between technical direction and changes and to inform the contracting officer if it believes that any technical direction is in the nature of a change. This is explicit in ¶(e) of the EPA clause and in ¶(d) of the NASA clause. In effect, this means that a contractor that proceeds to follow the technical direction of the agency will be seen as giving up its claim that the work being done actually constitutes a change for which additional fee should be paid and may be denied the cost of an improperly issued change order. See *Winter v. Cath-dr/Balti Joint Venture*, 497 F.3d 1339 (Fed. Cir. 2007), rejecting a claim for compensation for changes ordered by a project manager on a fixed-price contract because they were not ordered by the contracting officer.

3. Limited Authority of Technical Director

Most Technical Direction clauses state that the technical director is not authorized to make changes. Such a statement gives added weight to a government contention that technical direction should not be construed to be a constructive change. See *Inez Kaiser & Assocs., Inc.*, ASBCA 22212, 88-2 BCA ¶20,732, denying a claim for additional fee because the government project officer had no authority to issue changes. This demonstrates that the initial burden is on the contractor to assert claims to the contracting officer that the technical direction order actually constitutes a contract change. See also *Optical E.T.C., Inc.*, ASBCA 53350, 04-1 BCA ¶32,608 (technical direction from COR added work causing overrun but contractor failed to give notice under LOF clause); *JJM Sys., Inc.*, ASBCA 51152, 03-1 BCA ¶32,192 (instruction from COTR added work causing overrun but contractor failed to give notice under LOF clause); *AVANTE Int'l Sys. Corp.*, ASBCA 26649, 83-1 BCA ¶16,416 (instructions from technical director caused the contractor to incur an overrun but contractor precluded from recovering the overrun since the technical director lacked authority to make changes to the work and the contractor failed to contact the contracting officer concerning these changes). But see *Franklin W. Peters & Assocs.*, IBCA 762-1-69, 71-1 BCA ¶8615, where the board held that a direction issued by the government project officer was a change because of the project officer's close relationship with the contracting officer.

In these circumstances, a contractor must exercise caution in following technical direction orders, which should be screened by business personnel so that there is complete awareness of their total impact on contract performance. Most contractors expect to alter the work under cost-reimbursement contracts to a significant extent as work progresses and are not insistent on fee adjustments for each alteration. Contractors do, however, expect to be paid an additional fee if the cumulative work significantly exceeds the amount anticipated when the contract was negotiated. It is in this area that the Technical Direction clause can create difficulties if care is not exercised during contract administration.

C. Changes

When the government requires a contractor to perform work beyond that which is originally contemplated, the contractor is entitled to an equitable adjustment in the estimated cost and fixed fee pursuant to the standard cost-reimbursement Changes clause in FAR 52.243-2. A "change" in the work can be accomplished in two ways—through formal change orders or by way of so-called "constructive changes." The basic rules regarding contract changes have been formulated in the substantial litigation involving the Changes clause in fixed-price contracts, as discussed in Chapter 4 of Cibinic, Nash & Nagle, *Administration of Government Contracts* (4th ed. 2006). These rules will be summarized in this section.

1. Formal Changes

A formal change order is one where the contracting officer issues an order specifically citing the Changes clause.

a. *Procedures*

While the Changes clause authorizes contracting officers to issue unilateral change orders, the regulations generally express a preference for bilateral changes so that the impact on cost and schedule can be determined in advance and appropriate adjustments in the estimated cost, fixed fee, and contract schedule can be negotiated before work is begun. See FAR 43.201. Such changes would be issued by bilateral amendment to the contract. If the parties cannot accurately predict the impact of the change, a unilateral change order will be used and the equitable adjustment negotiated later. Both types of actions can be carried out on Standard Form 30, set forth in FAR 53.301-30.

b. *Effect of Limitation of Cost Clause*

As previously discussed, the Changes clause does not override the current LOC clause, with the result that unilateral orders issued pursuant to the Changes clause to perform additional work generally do not entitle a contractor to recover costs in excess of the contract's estimated costs. Note, however, that while a contractor may not be entitled to recover an overrun resulting from the performance of extra work, it may nevertheless be entitled to additional fee. In *Booz, Allen & Hamilton, Inc.*, IBCA 1027-3-74, 76-1 BCA ¶11,787, the board rejected the contractor's contention that it was entitled to recover for an overrun incurred in making corrections in government furnished property (ordered pursuant to the Government Furnished Property clause) but held that the contractor was entitled to recover additional fee. The board concluded that the LOC clause had no applicability to a claim for increased fees based upon "changes to the work or work not contemplated by the contract as written." See also *Falcon Research & Dev. Co.*, ASBCA 26322, 83-1 BCA ¶16,510.

c. *Limitation on Change Order Authority*

The authority of the government to order alterations in the quality and quantity of performance pursuant to the Changes clause is limited to the extent that the clause only authorizes changes "within the general scope" of the work originally contemplated. Thus, government orders to perform work beyond the general scope of the contract (frequently referred to as "cardinal changes") are not mandatory under the Changes clause and may be treated by the contractor as a government breach of contract, *Edward R. Marden Corp. v. United States*, 194 Ct. Cl. 799, 442 F.2d 364 (1971). If the contracting officer orders the contractor to proceed with the work, however, a contractor is taking a risk not to continue working and file a claim. See *Alliant Techsystems, Inc. v. United States*, 178 F.3d 1260 (Fed. Cir. 1999), *reh'g denied*, 186 F.3d 1379 (Fed. Cir. 1999), sustaining a default termination when the contractor refused to perform work that had been ordered by the improper exercise of an option. The court held that this was a change within the general scope of the contract as had been held in prior decisions finding such orders to be constructive changes.

The boards and courts generally determine whether ordered changes are within the scope of the work by asking whether the function of the work as changed is the same as that originally called for. If the changed work performs essentially the same function as the unchanged work, it is likely that the change will be found to have been within the scope of the contract.

See *Keco Indus., Inc. v. United States*, 176 Ct. Cl. 983, 364 F.2d 838 (1966), *cert. denied*, 386 U.S. 958 (1967) (change from gas to electric refrigeration units was within the scope because the units were basically the same, with the exception of the power system), and *Wunderlich Contracting Co. v. United States*, 173 Ct. Cl. 180, 351 F.2d 956 (1965) (extensive changes to the details of a hospital requiring over 50% additional performance time were within the scope because the resulting hospital was not substantially different from that contracted for).

While the number of changes ordered is generally not controlling on the question of whether such change are outside of the scope of the contract, *Coley Properties Corp.*, PSBCA 291, 75-2 BCA ¶11,514, a large number of changes, which significantly disrupt contract performance, may give rise to such a determination, *Air-A-Plane Corp. v. United States*, 187 Ct. Cl. 269, 408 F.2d 1030 (1969).

The case with perhaps the most relevance to the question of whether changes under cost-type contracts are outside of the scope of the contract is *General Dynamics Corp. v. United States*, 218 Ct. Cl. 40, 585 F.2d 457 (1978), where a contractor building submarines for the Navy under two contracts alleged that there had been changes outside of the scope of the contract when the Navy ordered significant design-related changes following the loss of the nuclear submarine U.S.S. Thresher. The ordered changes caused an approximate $100 million increase in price on the $60 million contracts. The court found that the changes were within the scope of the contract, reasoning essentially that the contractor should have anticipated that a contract for high technology items such as nuclear submarines would encompass significant design-related changes to accommodate subsequent developments in submarine technology.

Some actions by the contracting officer are prohibited under the Changes clause. For example, increases or decreases in the quantity of major items may not be ordered under the Changes clause of the contract, *General Contracting & Constr. Co.*, 84 Ct. Cl. 570 (1937). Orders to delay contract performance are also not within the contracting officer's authority under the Changes clause, *Cosmos Eng'rs, Inc.*, IBCA 979-12-72, 73-1 BCA ¶9972. This right is provided to the contracting officer under the Suspension of Work or Stop Work Order clauses. The boards, however, have sometimes creatively categorized such delays as changes in the manner or method of performance and permitted the action under the Changes clause. See *Fred A. Arnold, Inc.*, ASBCA 18915, 75-2 BCA ¶11,496, where the board held that a delay in furnishing information, which forced the contractor to perform out of sequence, was a change in the method of performance under the Changes clause. Additionally, orders that change the terms and conditions of a contract are not within the contracting officer's authority under the Changes clause, *BMY—A Div. of Harsco Corp.*, ASBCA 36926, 91-1 BCA ¶23,565. Neither can a contracting officer decrease the contract funding when the contractor has already incurred costs and earned fees under the contract, *TEM Assocs., Inc.*, DOTCAB 2556, 93-2 BCA ¶25,759.

d. Notice Requirements

The cost-reimbursement contract Changes clause calls for the contractor to assert its right to an adjustment "within 30 days from the date of receipt of the written order." This notice requirement has been enforced only if the government can demonstrate that it has been prejudiced by the lack of notice, *Precision Standard, Inc.*, ASBCA 54027, 03-2 BCA ¶32,265; *Powers Regulator Co.*, GSBCA 4668, 80-2 BCA ¶14,463; *Chimera Corp.*, ASBCA 18690, 76-1 BCA ¶11,901, and the boards continue to apply this prejudice requirement, *Precision Standard, Inc.*, ASBCA 54027, 03-2 BCA ¶32,265; *Rockwell Int'l Corp.*, EBCA C-9509187, 02-2 BCA ¶32,018. If prejudice to the government is found, a few boards have subjected the contractor a higher burden of proof in proving the claim rather than outright rejection of the claim, *Resource Conservation Corp. v. General Servs. Admin.*, GSBCA 13399, 97-1 BCA ¶28,776; *M. M. Sundt Constr. Co.*, ASBCA 17475, 74-1 BCA ¶10,627.

2. Constructive Changes

The Changes clause has also served as a vehicle for contractor claims against the government under the so-called "constructive change" doctrine, whereby either communications or conduct of government officials, although not taking the form of a formal change order, has the effect of requiring the contractor to perform different work than that which was originally contemplated. This legal theory was developed for fixed-price contracts and provided contractors an administrative means of recovering additional compensation for such work. While the necessity for processing such claims is not as great on cost-reimbursement contracts, it is still a viable means for a contractor to maximize its fee recovery by claiming an additional fee when constructive changes occur. Claiming a constructive change for work not performed is also a means for the government to obtain a reduction in fee, *Northrop Grumman Corp. v. United States*, 41 Fed. Cl. 645 (1998) (cost-plus-incentive-fee contract). Thus, the legal theories developed on fixed-price contracts are equally applicable to cost-reimbursement contracts.

a. *Elements of Constructive Changes*

(1) More Work

In order to establish a constructive change, there must be proof that the contractor has done more work than was originally contemplated and that the extra work has increased the time or cost of performance. This aspect of a constructive change is normally addressed by close analysis of the requirements of the contract to ascertain the precise amount of work agreed to by the parties. If the contractor has merely performed this work, there will be no basis for a claim of constructive change.

(2) Government Involvement

If it can be demonstrated that more work has been done than originally contemplated, the contractor must then show that the government caused the extra work. This can be done in two ways. First, it can be demonstrated that the extra work was "ordered" by some government conduct or communication. Such conduct or communication must be done by with the knowledge of an authorized official such as a contracting officer. Second, government causation can be established by government fault, such as by the inclusion of defective specifications in the contract. In that case, the government direction on the solution to the problem must come from an authorized official. See *Winter v. Cath-dr/Balti Joint Venture*, 497 F.3d 1339 (Fed. Cir. 2007).

(3) Notice Requirements

The 30-day notice requirement in the Changes clause is not applicable to constructive changes because it calls for notice only after receipt of a "written order." However, boards of contract appeals have occasionally applied this notice requirement to constructive change claims, following the long-standing rule that failure to provide notice within 30 days after learning of the "order" giving rise to the change will preclude recovery if the government is prejudiced by the lack of notice. However, prejudice is rarely found. See, for example, *Max Blau & Sons, Inc.*, GSBCA 9827, 91-1 BCA ¶23,626, and *Watson, Rice & Co.*, HUDBCA 89-4468-C6, 90-1 BCA ¶22,499, finding no prejudice from lack of timely notice.

When the constructive change claim is based on an order or conduct of a government employee without contracting officer authority, the contracting officer should be notified so that an effort can be made to resolve the problem. While the lack of such notice will not necessarily bar the claim, it may significantly limit the contractor recovery. See, for example, *Singer Co. v. United States*, 568 F.2d 695 (Ct. Cl. 1977); *Lamar Constr. Co.*, ASBCA 39593, 92-2 BCA ¶24,813; and *Calfon Constr., Inc. v. United States*, 18 Cl. Ct. 426 (1989).

Many cost-reimbursement contracts contain other notice requirements, such as that in the Technical Direction clauses discussed above or in the Notification of Changes clause in FAR 52.243-7. In *Grumman Aerospace Corp.*, ASBCA 46834, 03-1 BCA ¶32,203, the board indicated that the notice requirements under this clause should be treated the same as that under other clauses, stating at 159,185:

> We believe it legally sound to treat the Notification of Changes written notice requirement no differently than other written notice requirements under similar equitable adjustment-type clauses in Government contracts, such as the Changes clause, Differing Site Conditions clause, and Suspension of Work clauses. Under these clauses, we have held, following *Hoel-Steffen Construction Company v. United States*, 456 F.2d 760 (Ct. Cl. 1972), that written notice requirements should not be construed hypertechnically to deny legitimate contractor claims

when the Government was otherwise aware of the operative facts. *See Central Mechanical Construction*, ASBCA Nos. 29431, et al., 85-2 BCA P 18,061 and cases cited.

In addition there are a number of special notice requirements, not specifically enumerated in the contract, which the boards and courts have applied in considering various types of constructive-change claims. The special notice requirements pertinent to each type of constructive change are discussed below. As a result, contractors should give prompt notification upon learning of circumstances that might give rise to a constructive change claim.

b. Effect of Limitation of Cost Clause

As discussed above, the current LOC clause provides that a change order does not entitle the contractor to recover costs in excess of the contract's estimated cost unless the contracting officer has expressly increased the estimated cost. This rule has also been applied to constructive changes, *TDC Mgmt. Corp.*, DOTCAB 1802, 91-2 BCA ¶23,815, *recons. denied*, 91-3 BCA ¶24,061; *Jerry Warner & Assocs.*, ASBCA 33056, 90-l BCA ¶22,392.

c. Types of Constructive Changes

The boards and courts have recognized four principle types of constructive changes.

(1) Disagreements Over Contract Requirements

Perhaps the greatest number of constructive changes involves situations where the contractor and the government disagree as to the work required by the contract. For a disagreement over contract requirements to rise to the level of a constructive change, the contractor must prove that the government has "ordered" the performance of more costly or time-consuming work than was originally contemplated and that the contractor has given proper notice that the order calls for extra work.

(A) Additional Work

If the government's interpretation of the contract is correct, ordering the contractor to follow that interpretation will not result in additional work. However, if the contractor's interpretation is correct, more work will have been ordered. Thus, this element of the constructive change will turn on determining the correct interpretation of the contract. This issue is typically resolved through the use of the normal principles of contract interpretation. The court or board reviews the contract language, the actions and communications of the parties, and the basic rules of risk allocation to determine what is required by the contract and whether either party has been at fault in not identifying the problem in time to resolve it prior to performance. See Chapter 2 of Cibinic, Nash & Nagle, *Administration of Government Contracts* (4th ed. 2006) for a detailed description of this process.

(B) Government Involvement

In this type of constructive change, the government is responsible because it has insisted that its incorrect interpretation be followed. In cost-type contracts, the order to perform extra work typically takes the form of instructions or directions issued pursuant to the Technical Direction clause. The usual Technical Direction clause attempts to prevent the charge that it constitutes a contract change and states that technical representatives are not authorized to issue changes and that directions constituting changes are to be processed under the Changes clause so that appropriate adjustments to fee, estimated costs, and contract schedule can be negotiated. The result of this language may be that a contractor will be denied the additional fee if it is ordered to do additional work pursuant to the instructions of a technical representative. See, however, *Franklin W. Peters & Assocs.*, IBCA 762-1-69, 71-1 BCA ¶8615, where the board held that a contractor was entitled to additional fee for performing extra work ordered by the project officer. The board rejected the government's contention that recovery was precluded by the Technical Direction clause, which restricted the authority of technical representatives to issue changes. The board found that the restriction was "abrogated" by language in a contract modification stating that certain aspects of the work were to be performed "as directed" and "as approved" by the project officer. It also relied upon the fact that a copy of the instruction issued by the project officer, that formed the basis for the contractor's claim, had been sent to the contracting officer.

In fixed-price contracts, constructive change orders have been found when government employees suggested that the contractor perform in a certain manner, *Lorentz Bruun Co.*, GSBCA 1023, 1964 BCA ¶4357, interpreted contract language in a way that required extra work, *Triangle Elec. Mfg. Co.*, ASBCA 15995, 74-2 BCA ¶10,783, rejected a product or method of performance, *J.B. Williams Co. v. United States*, 196 Ct. Cl. 491, 450 F.2d 1379 (1971), or observed the performance of extra work without inquiring why it was being performed, *BH Servs., Inc.*, ASBCA 39460, 93-3 BCA ¶26,082. These decisions may no longer be applicable because the Federal Circuit greatly restricted the authority of such personnel in *Winter v. Cath-dr/Balti Joint Venture*, 497 F.3d 1339 (Fed. Cir. 2007). See also *Information Sys. & Networks Corp. v. United* States, 81 Fed. Cl. 740 (2008), finding no constructive change when government technical personnel discussed the issuance of an ECP with the contractor but no ECP was formally issued. Thus, contractors should now immediately inform the contracting officer of such actions and request that they be confirmed in writing.

(C) Notice

The requirement for notice to the contracting officer was stated as a "duty to protest," i.e., to inform the contracting officer that a communication by a government employee is being treated as an order to do extra work, in *J.A. Ross & Co. v. United States*, 115 F. Supp. 187 (Ct. Cl. 1953), at 190:

> Whenever the defendant orders work done which the plaintiff thinks is in violation of the contract, or in addition to its requirements, plaintiff is required to protest against doing it, or to secure an order in writing before doing it. It is basic in all Government contracts that the plaintiff cannot do work which it is not required to do by the contract, without registering a protest against being required to do it, or securing an order for extra work, and then later make a claim against the Government for additional compensation.

As indicated above, the Technical Direction clause included in many cost-type contracts may make such notice a contractual requirement by providing that instructions issued under the clause that constitute a change must be brought to the attention of the contracting officer for processing under the Changes clause.

(2) Defective Specifications and Nondisclosure of Information

A second major type of constructive change occurs when the contractor incurs additional expense or encounters delay, as a result of attempting to perform according to defective government specifications or missing information which should have been furnished by the government.

(A) Additional Work

The additional work caused by the defective or incomplete specifications can take the form of wasted effort, delay and disruption, engineering effort to identify and solve the problem, or added costs of satisfactory work. Government liability in these cases is predicated upon breach of the government's implied warranty of specifications, *United States v. Spearin*, 248 U.S. 132 (1918), or a duty to disclose important information in its possession, which it knew was not reasonably available to the contractor, *Helene Curtis Indus., Inc. v. United States*, 312 F.2d 774 (Ct. Cl. 1963); *General Precision, Inc.*, ASBCA 12078, 70-1 BCA ¶8144. Constructive-change claims of this kind are rarely encountered in cost-type contracts since the statement of work generally contains only a broad description of the contract's objectives with little or no detail as to methods or manner of performance. See *T&G Aviation, Inc.*, ASBCA 40428, 00-2 BCA ¶31,147, where the board held that the government's right to give technical direction "is insufficient to render the [performance] specification a design type and to trigger the implied warranty."

(B) Government Involvement

The government is found liable for this type of constructive change because it has failed to fulfill its duty to provide specifications that are adequate to permit performance at the costs originally estimated, *J. W. Hurst & Son Awnings, Inc.*, ASBCA 4167, 59-1 BCA ¶2095. With constructive changes based upon defective specifications and nondisclosure, there is no requirement for a government act or communication inducing the contractor to perform extra work since the change is attributable to performance problems that the contractor encounters as a result of its contractual obligation to go forward with the work called for in the contract, *Consolidated Diesel Elec. Corp.*, ASBCA 10486, 67-2 BCA ¶6669. Thus, government liability is predicated on fault in providing the defective information or not disclosing sufficient information.

(C) Notice

The boards and courts have fashioned a prejudice-type notice rule for cases involving defective specifications. The rule precludes recovery where the contractor encounters performance problems that might have been avoided if the contractor had given prompt notice of the defect, *Kings Elec. Co. v. United States*, 341 F.2d 632 (Ct. Cl. 1965); *Dynalectron Corp. v. United States*, 518 F.2d 594 (Ct. Cl. 1975); *Flathead Contractors, LLC v. Dep't of Agriculture*, CBCA 118, 07-1 BCA ¶33,556. In *Axel Elecs., Inc.*, ASBCA 18990, 76-1 BCA ¶11,667, the board stated at 55,664:

> If the contractor knows itself to be performing work for which contemplated additional costs are going to be charged to the Government, then notice of such claim must be given to the Government in order for the contractor to recover such costs. Such rule allows the Government to protect itself and to have the choice of electing alternatives in the event the Government finds merit in the claim.

Thus, a cost-type contractor who attempts to perform according to a specification that it should recognize as defective and does so without notifying the government of the defect may not be entitled to recover additional fee or costs incurred after the notice should have been given. This same rule may preclude recovery for government failure to disclose information if a contractor who is encountering unforeseen performance difficulties continues to incur costs without promptly informing the Government of the situation.

(3) Acceleration

A third major type of constructive change recognized by the boards and courts involves constructive accelerations whereby the government requires the contractor to "speed up" its performance of the work. In almost all cases, a constructive acceleration occurs when the government orders the contractor to meet the current contract schedule in the face of excusable delays or delays resulting from changes or differing site conditions. Since such delays give the contractor an entitlement to schedule extensions in accordance with the Excusable Delays clause in FAR 52.249-14, the Changes clause in FAR 52.243-2, of the Differing Site Conditions clause in FAR 52.236-2, an order to meet the unadjusted schedule is tantamount to an order to complete the work in advance of that schedule. The five common elements of a constructive acceleration are:

(1) Existence of a given period of excusable delay;

(2) Knowledge by the government of such delay;

(3) Some statement or act by the government that can be construed as an acceleration order;

(4) Notice by the contractor that the order is a constructive change; and

(5) Incurrence of additional costs of accelerated effort.

See *Fermont Div., Dynamics Corp.*, ASBCA 15806, 75-1 BCA ¶11,139, *aff'd*, 578 F.2d 1389 (Ct. Cl. 1978).

(A) Additional Work

In order to recover for a constructive acceleration, the contractor must show that it has incurred costs in attempting to "accelerate" its performance, but recovery does not depend upon showing that the contractor has actually avoided delay, *Varo, Inc.*, ASBCA 15000, 72-2 BCA ¶9717. The added "work" in constructive accelerations is normally overtime and shift premiums, expediting costs, and loss of efficiency because of the altered manner of performing the work.

(B) Government Involvement

Government responsibility for acceleration costs occurs only when it orders the acceleration. A number of different kinds of communications by the government have been found to constitute orders to accelerate the work—a direct order to "speed up" performance to make up for delays, *Hagstrom Constr. Co.*, ASBCA 5698, 61-1 BCA ¶3090; an order to complete ahead of schedule, *Varo, Inc.*, ASBCA 15000, 72-2 BCA ¶9717; a request that the contractor complete in accordance with contract schedule, *Raymond Int'l of Del., Inc.*, ASBCA 13121, 70-1 BCA ¶8341; a threat to terminate for default, *William Lagnion*, ENGBCA 3778, 78-2 BCA ¶13,260; and a refusal to grant a time extension coupled with assessment of liquidated damages, *Keco Indus., Inc.*, ASBCA 8900, 1963 BCA ¶3891.

(C) Notice

There are essentially two types of notice that a contractor should give in order to ensure recovery for constructive acceleration of the work. First, the contractor must give notice of a delay for which it is entitled to additional time. While it sometimes has been held that the contractor must actually make a formal request for a time extension to establish a constructive acceleration, the key factor seems to be government knowledge of the facts giving rise to an excusable delay, *Corbetta Constr. Co.*, PSBCA 299, 77-2 BCA ¶12,699; *William Lagnion*, ENGBCA 3778, 78-2 BCA ¶13,260.

The contractor should also promptly notify the contracting officer that it is treating a particular act or communication as an order to accelerate performance of the work. See *Eggers & Higgins v. United States*, 185 Ct. Cl. 765, 403 F.2d 225 (1968), where the contractor was refused recovery for an alleged constructive acceleration. The court found that the government was prejudiced by the contractor's failure to give notice that it was construing the government's refusal to grant a time extension as an acceleration order.

(4) Noncooperation or Interference

Another major category of constructive change arises when the government fails to cooperate with the contractor or actively hinders, interferes with, or delays the contractor's performance.

(A) Additional Work

The added work that occurs because of this type of constructive change can be in the nature of higher costs of performing work not called for by the contract or wasted effort and other costs of disruption. Hence, this type of change can have the characteristics of either a disagreement between the parties on the proper interpretation of the contract or a defective specification situation. However, in this instance, the matter is brought to a head by faulty or unreasonable government action during the administration of the contract whereby the government is held to have breached its duty to cooperate with the contractor. For a case with particular relevance to the issue of the government's duties of cooperation and noninterference, owed to cost-type contractors, see *Ingalls Shipbuilding Div., Litton Sys., Inc.*, ASBCA 17717, 76-1 BCA ¶11,851. In this case, the board found that the government had constructively changed a fixed-price shipbuilding contract by failing to make timely delivery of essential materials. The board stated at 56,718:

> [T]he contract as executed by the parties divided the responsibility for successful performance between them. While appellant had the responsibility to deliver the three nuclear submarines by the dates spelled out in the contract, the Government undertook the responsibility to acquire the hull steel with which construction of the three submarines necessarily began. Under such circumstances, the parties should have been partners in the undertaking, working toward the common goal of having the submarines delivered by the specified dates. Instead, when the Government was unable to discharge its responsibility for delivering the hull steel in keeping with appellant's requirements, it displayed an arm's-length attitude that was unsuited for the contractual arrangement that existed between the parties.

(B) Government Involvement

Liability in these cases is based upon government breach of an implied duty of cooperation or an implied duty of noninterference, *Lewis-Nicholson, Inc. v. United States*, 213 Ct. Cl. 192, 550 F.2d 26 (1977); *CRF*, ASBCA 18748, 76-2 BCA ¶12,129. Thus, government conduct during performance requires the contractor to perform in a more costly or time-consuming manner than was originally contemplated. Common examples of government conduct that have been found to constitute breaches of the implied duties of cooperation and noninterference include: failure to prevent one contractor from interfering with performance of another contractor, *Hensel Phelps Constr. Co.*, ENGBCA 3368, 74-2 BCA ¶10,728; failure to provide assistance to the contractor, *Hardrives, Inc.*, IBCA 2319, 94-1 BCA ¶26,267; failure to provide adequate access to the work site, *Reliance Enters.*, ASBCA 20808, 76-1 BCA ¶11,831; and overzealous inspection by government personnel, *Adams Mfg. Co. v. United States*, 175 Ct. C1. 288, 358 F.2d 986 (1966).

Constructive changes of this type have also been recognized when the contracting officer is unreasonable in exercising discretion granted by the contract to approve of the method and manner of performance. To be unreasonable in exercising discretion to grant or withhold such approval the contracting officer must deny the contractor a reasonable method of performance with no commensurate benefit to the government. In *Chris Berg, Inc. & Assocs.*, ASBCA 3466, 58-1 BCA ¶1792, the board found a constructive change where the contracting officer rejected the contractor's proposed method of thawing permafrost under a performance specification requiring government approval of the procedure to be used. This result has also been reached where the government failed to approve of a product proposed under a "brand name or equal" specification, *W.G. Cornell Co. v. United States*, 179 Ct. Cl. 651, 376 F.2d 299 (1967), and where the government failed to approve a subcontractor proposed by the contractor, *Huber, Hunt & Nichols, Inc.*, VACAB 1200, 77-1 BCA ¶12,500.

(C) Notice

In most constructive-change cases involving a failure to cooperate or hindrance of performance, there is an active controversy between the government and the contractor, with the result that the contracting officer will have actual notice of the circumstances giving rise to the alleged constructive change. Nevertheless, contractors should give prompt notification to the contracting officer of any instance of noncooperation or interference by a government official that potentially has an adverse impact on the time or cost of performance. See *Raifield Indus.*, ASBCA 13418, 77-1 BCA ¶12,308, where the contractor's failure to protest lack of cooperation by government inspection personnel precluded recovery.

III. DELAYS

In fixed-price contracts the risk of delays is generally allocated between the parties, with the government bearing the full risk of delays under its control, the contractor bearing the risk of delays under its control, and both parties sharing risk with regard to delays outside the control of either party. This risk allocation is carried out through the use of two types of clauses—excusable delay provisions in the default termination clauses that give the contractor the right to a time extension for all delays beyond its control and without its fault or negligence and Suspension of Work or Government Delay of Work clauses which gives the contractor the right to a price adjustment for all delays caused by the government. See Chapter 6 of Cibinic, Nash & Nagle, *Administration of Government Contracts* (4th ed. 2006), containing complete coverage of the applicable of these clauses. While this risk-allocation scheme is not completely applicable to cost-reimbursement contracts, it is followed to a large degree.

A. Time Extensions for Excusable Delays

Almost all cost-reimbursement contracts contain a separate clause, Excusable Delays, FAR 52.249-14, dealing with the contractor's right to a time extension for such delays. The definition of excusable delays is basically the same as that used in fixed-price contracts—delays arising "out of causes beyond the control and without the fault or negligence of the contractor." It is generally held that such causes must be "extraneous" to the contractor, *Carnegie Steel Co. v. United States*, 240 U.S. 156 (1916); *Austin Co. v. United States*, 161 Ct. Cl. 76, 314 F.2d 518, *cert. denied*, 375 U.S. 830 (1963). Under this interpretation, delays caused by factors normally under the control of the contractor, i.e., manpower, financing, machines, equipment, etc., are not delays falling within this provision.

Paragraph (c) of the clause provides for a schedule extension upon the occurrence of an excusable delay. However, the government is given the alternative of terminating the contract for the convenience of the government.

A standard clause applicable to CPIF contracts prevents additional costs resulting from excusable delays from impacting the incentive fee by excluding such costs from the fee computation. The clause in FAR 52.216-10 excludes costs arising out of:

> (i) Any of the causes covered by the Excusable Delays clause to the extent that they are beyond the control and without the fault or negligence of the Contractor or any subcontractor.

When delivery incentives are included in CPIF contracts, the incentive provisions should cross-reference the Excusable Delays clause, making it clear that the delivery incentive operates only after the schedule adjustments called for by that clause.

B. Additional Compensation for Government-Caused Delays

Most cost-reimbursement contracts do not contain a clause dealing specifically with additional compensation for government-caused delays. However, FAR 42.1305(b) permits the use of the Stop-Work Order (Alternate 1) clause in FAR 52.243-15 in all cost-reimbursement contracts. This clause permits the contracting officer to unilaterally order the contractor to stop work with a resulting equitable adjustment in the cost and fee. See *Raytheon STX Corp. v. Dep't of Commerce*, GSBCA 14296-COM, 00-1 BCA ¶30,632, compensating a contractor for the additional costs of performance (but not additional fee) incurred as a result of a stop-work order issued when the government shut down for lack of appropriations. See also *Optimal Data Corp.*, IBCA 1695, 85-3 BCA ¶18,179, where the board considered a constructive delay claim under this clause but denied the claim because the contractor failed to prove that the government breached its obligations under the contract.

The result of the lack of a clause permitting compensation for government caused delays unless they are ordered by the contracting officer is that the contractor will be paid any additional costs incurred because of such delays if the LOC and LOF clauses are complied with but may not be granted any additional fee. In fixed-priced contracts, the courts have denied contractors profits on breach of contract claims resulting from government-caused delays. See *Meva Corp. v. United States*, 206 Ct. Cl. 203, 511 F.2d 548 (1975). Similarly, the Suspension of Work clause, FAR 52.212-12, and the Government Delay of Work clause, FAR 52.212-15, both provide that no profit will be paid for delays. In *Burns & Roe, Inc.*, EBCA 102-11-79, 81-2 BCA ¶15,386, a claim for additional fee based on delays in performance was denied because the CPFF contract did not include a remedial clause for delays.

IV. INSPECTION AND CORRECTION OF DEFECTS

The government's rights and the contractor's obligations with respect to the quality of work are covered by different clauses, depending upon the nature of the work. The various Inspection clauses in cost-reimbursement contracts are as follows: FAR 52.246-3, Inspection of Supplies; FAR 52.246-5, Inspection of Services; FAR 52.246-8, Inspection of Research & Development; and FAR 52.246-9, Inspection of Research & Development (Short Form).

A. Inspection

These clauses provide that at any time during the performance period all work in progress is subject "to the extent practicable" to inspection and testing by the government. To this end the contractor is required to provide reasonable facilities and assistance to government personnel, both at its plants and offices as well as those of its subcontractors. In addition, the contractor must provide and maintain its own inspection system—one that meets government approval. The government, however, must not be unreasonable in its failure to give approval to the contractor's inspection system. See *Herlo Corp.*, ASBCA 20859, 76-2 BCA ¶12,125, where in a fixed-type contract a contractor recovered for "heightened" inspection efforts caused by the government's unfounded questioning of the contractor's quality control. The clauses provide that "the Government shall perform inspections and tests in a manner that will not unduly delay the work." While the clauses do not provide for an equitable adjustment when government inspection interferes unreasonably with contractor performance, it can be argued that such conduct entitles the contractor to a fee adjustment. Some support for this position is found in *Russell R. Gannon Co. v. United States*, 417 F.2d 1356 (Ct. Cl. 1969), where the Court of Claims found that the government breached the contract when it did not make inspectors available when they were reasonably needed and, therefore, impeded the contractor's performance. The court held that the contractor could recover damages under the fixed-price contract in that case. In a cost-reimbursement contract, government interference or failure to cooperate could be considered a constructive change.

B. Correction of Defects

All of the clauses, with the exception of the R&D short form, provide for the correction of defects. The contractor's obligation to correct extends for six months following acceptance under the Supplies and long form R&D clauses. The Services clause is silent concerning any time period for correcting nonconforming services. This clause also does not refer to the "acceptance" of services. The Services clause merely states at FAR 52.246-5(d):

> If any of the services performed do not conform with contract requirements, the Government may require the Contractor to perform the services again in conformity with contract requirements, for no additional fee.

Under this clause, it is uncertain how long the contractor is obligated to reperform the services. It also appears that the government has only a reasonable time after the services are performed to order correction.

Unlike fixed-price contracts, these clauses require the contractor to correct any defects—not merely latent defects. However, under the Supplies and long form R&D clauses, the contractor's obligation to make corrections ceases six months after acceptance, while under fixed-price contracts the contractor's obligation to correct latent defects continues indefinitely, FAR 52.246-2. See *Federal Pac. Elec. Co.*, IBCA 334, 1964 BCA ¶4494.

Under these clauses, the contractor is generally entitled to recover the costs of making corrections while a fixed-price contractor bears the cost of doing corrective work. See ¶(f) of the Supplies and long form R&D clauses which provide that the cost of correcting defective work is allowable subject to the normal allowability rules. Paragraph (h) of these clauses limits the application of this rule by stating that such costs are not allowable if the defective work is due to "(1) fraud, lack of good faith, or willful misconduct on the part of the Contractor's managerial personnel or (2) the conduct of one or more of the Contractor's employees selected or retained by the Contractor after any of the Contractor's managerial personnel has reasonable grounds to believe that the employee is habitually careless or unqualified." The Services clause is not so explicit, merely requiring in ¶(d) that the contractor may be required to reperform defective services "for no additional fee." In *Morton-Thiokol, Inc.*, ASBCA 32629, 90-3 BCA ¶23,207 the contractor purchased railroad ties that did not meet contract specifications. The government refused to reimburse the contractor for the full costs of the railroad ties—reducing the cost by the projected utilization loss. The government stated that it was not required to show any degree of "negligence, much less fraud or gross misconduct, to disallow the cost of defective work." The board disagreed, holding that the costs were allowable absent a showing that the defect resulted from gross misconduct. This same reasoning has been applied when pricing of terminations under fixed price contracts is cost-based. See *Caskel Forge, Inc.*, ASBCA 7638, 1962 BCA ¶3318, involving a convenience termination claim, where the board stated at 17,108:

> Costs of producing defective work are normally reimbursable under a cost reimbursement contract, unless it is established that the defective production resulted from "the contractor's own fault or folly" or "careless conduct of the work or other disregard of his contractual duties." 21 Comp. Gen. 149, 151.

This rule has been followed in *New York Shipbuilding Co.*, ASBCA 15443, 73-1 BCA ¶9852 (reimbursement required unless defects resulted from "gross disregard of contractual obligations"); *D.E.W. & D.E. Wurzbach, (J.V.)*, ASBCA 50796, 98-1 BCA ¶29,385 (test is "gross disregard of contractual obligations"); and *Best Foam Fabricators, Inc. v. United States*, 38 Fed. Cl. 627 (1997) (reimbursement unless "gross disregard of contractual obligations" or defects are so extensive "as to render costs unreasonable"). See also *TDC Mgmt. Corp.*, DOTCAB 1802, 91-3 BCA ¶24,091, where the government sought to avoid payment of costs on the grounds that the contractor had breached a fiduciary duty. The board held that costs incurred after the breach were allowable unless the government could show that the breach damaged the government by precluding successful completion of the contract and that the contractor was no longer performing the contract work.

The Supply and long-form R&D clauses provide that if the contractor fails to correct deficiencies within a reasonable time, the government may—

(1) Contract out or otherwise correct the work and charge the contractor "any increased cost" or make an equitable reduction in the fee;

(2) In the case of articles not delivered, require such delivery or reduce the fee; or

(3) Terminate for default.

The clauses provide that orders to perform corrective work do not entitle contractors to recover additional fee. While it has been suggested that cost-type contractors are not entirely discouraged from performing defective work since they are generally able to recover the costs of doing corrective work, the need to make frequent or substantial corrections may eventually threaten the contractor's ability to recover the full fee in circumstances where the contractor exhausts the contract funds without completing the work. Counterbalancing this danger is the fact that a contractor is entitled to overhead on the direct costs of doing corrective work, and the overhead may be applied to coverage of its fixed costs. See Gilbert J. Ginsburg, "Allocation of Risk: Contractor Responsibility for Injury to Government Property and to Third Parties Under Supply and R&D Contracts," 2 Pub. Cont. L.J. 333 (1969).

The contractor is excused from correcting defects when the government refuses to fund beyond the total estimated cost under the LOC or LOF clauses. Thus, the government has the contractual right to refuse to accept defective work and to order corrective work only if it is willing to provide the money to cover the costs of doing the desired remedial work. However, the Supplies and long-form R&D clauses provide that the government may at any time "without cost to the Government" require the correction of defects attributable to fraud, lack of good faith, or willful misconduct on the part of the contractor's officers or management personnel. Similar language included in the Government Furnished Property and Ground Flight and Risk clauses was the subject of litigation in *Fairchild Hiller Corp.*, ASBCA 14387, 72-1 BCA ¶9202. In that case, the board gave a narrow construction to this language, holding that proof of negligence is not sufficient to establish willful misconduct or lack of good faith.

V. TERMINATION

There are three methods available to the contracting officer for concluding the contractor's performance before the work is completed. The first is simply to fail to provide additional funds under the LOF or LOC clause when the available funds have been expended and the work is incomplete. This technique is discussed in detail in Section I. The other two methods of concluding performance are provided for in a single Termination clause in cost-reimbursement contracts, FAR 52.249-6. This clause includes coverage of both terminations for default and terminations for the convenience of the government.

The power of the government to terminate a contract when contract completion is no longer in the government's best interest has long been recognized even in the absence of a termination clause. See *United States v. Corliss Steam-Engine Co.*, 91 U.S. 321 (1875); *Circle, Inc.*, ENGBCA 3258, 72-1 BCA ¶9451. The *Corliss* case also holds that a contracting officer is authorized to negotiate binding settlement agreements upon the termination. These two aspects of the *Corliss* decision have generally been relied upon as the authority for inclusion of convenience termination clauses in government contracts by the executive department without specific, statutory authority. See Navy Contract Law Sec. 5.5 (2d Ed. 1959), Peter L. Dounis and Frederick W. Forman, "Historical Significance of Termination of Contracts for the Convenience of the Government," 14 Fed. B.J. 191 (1954); Covington Hardee, "Termination of Military Contracts," 32 Texas L. Rev. 172 (1953).

The Termination clause at FAR 52.249-6 provides:

(a) The Government may terminate performance of work under this contract in whole or, from time to time, in part, if—

(1) The Contracting Officer determines that a termination is in the Government's interest; or

(2) The Contractor defaults in performing this contract and fails to cure the default within 10 days (unless extended by the Contracting Officer) after receiving a notice specifying the default. "Default" includes failure to make progress in the work so as to endanger performance.

In cost-reimbursement contracts, unlike fixed-price contracts, there are relatively small differences in the financial impact of default and convenience terminations. Under both types of termination actions, the cost-type contractor is entitled to recover all allowable costs incurred during performance and also receives a portion of the contract fee. In a convenience termination, the fee is measured on a percentage-of-completion basis excluding fee on subcontractor billings; in a default termination, the fee is paid only on the amount of work delivered to and accepted by the government. See *Tri-Delta Corp.*, ASBCA 17456, 75-1 BCA ¶11,160, where the board held that the contractor was entitled to recover allowable costs following a default termination but concluded that, since no deliveries had been made under the contract, the contractor was not entitled to any fee. Thus, the most important immediate effect of default termination is that the contractor does not recover fees attributable to work not accepted. See *General Dynamics Corp.*, DOTCAB 76-9A, 78-2 BCA ¶13,281, *recons. denied*, 78-2 BCA ¶13,415, *aff'd*, 671 F.2d 474 (Ct. Cl. 1982), where the board stated that the cost-reimbursement Termination clause required that "settlement of a default under a contract containing the clause be performed in the same manner and with the same consequences as when the contract is terminated for 'convenience,' subject only to the possible disallowance of unearned fee and settlement proposal preparation costs."

Another difference between default and convenience terminations under cost-reimbursement contracts is that ¶(a) of the Termination clause requires that a contractor must be given a 10-day cure notice prior to termination for default while no advance notice need be given of termination for convenience. The 10-day cure notice need not be given in the case of an anticipatory repudiation of the contract, since the repudiation effectively cancels the contract, *Beeston, Inc.*, ASBCA 38969, 91-3 BCA ¶24,241. However, omission of the cure notice will invalidate the default termination unless the repudiation is unequivocal. See *Griffin Servs., Inc.*, ASBCA 53802, 03-1 BCA ¶32,200, converting a termination for default one a cost-reimbursement contract to one for convenience when the government rescinded a cure notice and did not issue a new one prior to termination for default. See also Cibinic, Nash & Nagle, *Administration of Government Contracts* 991-92 (4th ed. 2006).

A. Convenience Termination

The Termination clause confers extremely broad convenience termination rights, permitting termination when it is in "the Government's interest." The meaning of this language is not specifically defined in either the clause or in procurement regulations. However, the courts have construed it to give the government full power to terminate with only two exceptions.

The first exception is that "[t]he termination of a contract for the convenience of the government is valid only in the absence of bad faith or a clear abuse of discretion," *National Factors, Inc. v. United States*, 492 F.2d 1383, 1387 (Ct. Cl. 1974). It has been extremely difficult to establish bad faith because of the very stringent proof requirements. See *Kalvar Corp. v. United States*, 543 F.2d 1298 (Ct. Cl. 1976), *cert. denied*, 434 U.S. 830 (1977), where the court stated at 1301-02:

> Any analysis of a question of Governmental bad faith must begin with the presumption that public officials act "conscientiously in the discharge of their duties." *Librach v. United States*, 147 Ct. Cl. 605, 612 (1959). The court has always been "loath to find to the contrary," and it requires "'well-nigh irrefragable proof' to induce the court to abandon the presumption of good faith dealing." *Knotts v. United States*, 128 Ct. Cl. 489, 492, 121 F. Supp. 630, 631 (1954).
>
> In the cases where the court has considered allegations of bad faith, the necessary "irrefragable proof" has been equated with evidence of some specific intent to injure the plaintiff. Thus, in *Gadsden v. United States*, 111 Ct. Cl. 487, 489-90, 78 F. Supp. 126, 127 (1948), the court compared bad faith to actions which are "motivated alone by malice." In *Knotts, supra*, at 128 Ct. Cl. 500, 121 F. Supp. 636, the court found bad faith in a civilian pay suit only in view of a proven "conspiracy . . . to get rid of plaintiff." Similarly, the court in *Struck Constr. Co. v. United States*, 96 Ct. Cl. 186, 222 (1942) found bad faith when confronted by a course of Governmental conduct which

was "designedly oppressive." But in *Librach, supra*, at 147 Ct. Cl. 614, the court found no bad faith because the officials involved were not "actuated by animus toward the plaintiff."

No bad faith was found in *Northrop Grumman Corp. v. United States*, 46 Fed. Cl. 622 (2000), where the government terminated a cost-reimbursement contract in order to consolidate work under a single contractor to increase the efficiency of the program. See also *Rice Sys., Inc. v. United States*, 62 Fed. Cl. 608 (2004), where the court found no bad faith in terminating an SBIR contract for convenience when the contractor could not find a substitute principle investigator with adequate credentials and could not prove to the court that the agency had rejected the proposed principle investigators based on gender or national origin discrimination.

Bad faith has been found in two cases overturning convenience terminations. In *Libertatia Assocs., Inc. v. United States*, 46 Fed. Cl. 702 (2000), the court found that both the contracting officer and the contracting officer's representative had a specific intent to injure the contractor as demonstrated by their strong personal animosity toward the company president and other employees. In *Travel Centre v. General Servs. Admin.*, GSBCA 14057, 98-1 BCA ¶29,536, *recons. denied*, 98-1 BCA ¶29,541, the board found bad faith where intentional misconduct of government employees had led the contractor performing an indefinite delivery/indefinite quantity contract to estimate its price based on quantities known to be incorrect. The board described the government actions in subsequent litigation, 99-2 BCA ¶30,521, at 150,714:

> [I]t (1) provided estimates of expected business purportedly (but not actually) based upon a survey, (2) required offerors to base their proposals on those estimates, (3) promised offerors that the winning firm would be a "preferred provider" of the procured services, and (4) knew prior to award that this promise was false because the winner would not be able to provide any services to a major part of the Government.

There are no reported decisions applying an "abuse of discretion" standard to find a termination for convenience termination improper.

The second exception to the broad power to terminate for convenience is the "changed circumstances" exception that was enunciated in *Torncello v. United States*, 681 F.2d 756 (Ct. Cl. 1982). There the court ruled that the Termination for Convenience clause cannot be used to avoid anticipated profits unless there is some change in circumstances between the time of the award of the contract and the time of terminating. The government had awarded a requirements contract to Torncello but had bought one type of work under the contract from a competing bidder at a cheaper price which it knew of at the time of awarding the original contract. The court found that no changed circumstances had occurred and denied the government the right to use the clause. This exception was construed to be very narrow in *Krygoski Constr. Co. v. United States*, 94 F.3d 1537 (Fed. Cir. 1996), *cert. denied*, 520 U.S. 1210 (1997), where the court stated that the exception applies only if the government "enters a contract with no intention of fulfilling its promises." See Cibinic, Nash & Nagle, *Administration of Government Contracts* 1079-82 (4th ed. 2006) for a discussion of the cases dealing with these exceptions.

When a contracting officer terminates a cost-reimbursement contract for convenience, knowing that the ceiling price has been reached, the government waives the contract cost ceiling regarding the tasks a contractor must perform under the termination for convenience clause. If the contracting officer intends otherwise, the termination notice must explicitly state that intention. *A.T. Kearney, Inc.*, DOTCAB 1263, 83-2 BCA ¶16,835, *recons. denied*, 84-1 BCA ¶17,052. See also *TDC Mgmt. Corp.*, DOTCAB 1802, 91-2 BCA ¶23,815, *recons. denied*, 91-3 BCA ¶24,061.

B. Default Termination

The scope of the government's right to terminate for default under cost-reimbursement contracts has not been litigated frequently. However, a default termination was sustained in *United Schools of Am., Inc.*, ASBCA 38628, 90-3 BCA ¶23,199, where the contractor had performed defective work and had given no satisfactory response to a cure notice. See also *TEM Assocs., Inc.*, DOTCAB 2556, 93-2 BCA ¶25,759, where the board accepted as valid a default termination for anticipatory repudiation where the contractor stated it would no longer perform the contract.

All default terminations under the FAR 52.249-6 clause must be preceded by a cure notice. See *Griffin Servs., Inc.*, ASBCA 53802, 03-1 BCA ¶32,200, converting a default termination to one for convenience because the agency withdrew a cure notice and did not issue another one before terminating for default.

The termination clause sets forth two situations where default termination is proper: (1) failure to complete the work according to the terms of the contract and (2) failure to make progress in the prosecution of the work. Under fixed-price contracts, where these same bases for default termination are present, the government generally bears a considerable burden in attempting to justify default termination for failure to make progress, *Lisbon Contractors, Inc. v. United States*, 828 F.2d 759 (Fed. Cir. 1987). See Cibinic, Nash & Nagle, *Administration of Government Contracts* 929-35 (4th ed. 2006).

C. Rights of the Parties Upon Termination

Once a contract is terminated, the contractor's duty to continue performance ceases. Likewise, the obligation of the government to pay for further work ceases (except for continuing costs of the contractor attributable to the terminated work). The parties' rights and obligations are governed solely by the Termination clause of the contract and the applicable regulations.

After a termination the contractor can no longer be required to correct defects in work performed prior to the termination and will recover costs attributable to such defective work unless it is established that the defects resulted from "the contractor's own fault or folly" or "careless conduct of the work or other disregard of his contractual duties," *New York Shipbuilding Co.*, ASBCA 15443, 73-1 BCA ¶9852 at 46,019 (quoting 21 Comp. Gen. 149, 151 (B-18974) (1941)).

A terminated contract may be reinstated if the government determines that the contractor can complete the work satisfactorily, FAR 49.102(d). See *Stancil-Hoffman Corp.*, Comp. Gen. Dec. B-193001.2, 80-2 CPD ¶226, finding inherent government authority to reinstate contracts terminated for either default or the convenience of the government.

D. Procedures Upon Giving and Receiving Notice of Termination

In the process of contract termination each of the contracting parties has certain responsibilities with respect to termination.

1. Government

The government initiates the termination by giving the contractor notice that the contract is terminated. The government must send written notice of termination to the contractor, specifying the type, date, and extent (partial or complete) of termination, as well as any relevant special instructions such as instructions concerning disposition of inventory and special tooling, FAR 49.102(a). It is good practice to send an email or telegraph followed by a more detailed letter. FAR 49.601-2 contains suggested forms for this notice. If the notice does not clearly specify that the termination is for default, it will be considered a termination for convenience, *Stroud Realty*, HUDBCA 75-13, 76-1 BCA ¶11,770. See also *Kisco Co. v. United States*, 610 F.2d 742 (Ct. Cl. 1979), where a default termination notice was held ineffective because it did not state that it was a final decision of the contracting officer under the Disputes clause and did not give 10 days to cure the default. Compare *Philadelphia Regent Bldrs. v. United States*, 634 F.2d 569 (Ct. Cl. 1980), where the court upheld a default termination despite several minor defects in the default notice.

FAR 49.105 states that after a termination notice is issued, the termination contracting officer shall:

(1) Direct the action required of the prime contractor;

(2) Examine the settlement proposal of the prime contractor and, when appropriate, the settlement proposals of subcontractors;

(3) Promptly negotiate settlement with the contractor and enter into a settlement agreement; and

(4) Promptly settle the contractor's settlement proposal by determination for the elements that cannot be agreed on, if unable to negotiate a complete settlement.

2. Contractor

The contractor's responsibilities after receipt of a termination notice are specified in FAR 49.104.

a. *Stop Work Immediately*

Since costs incurred after termination may be disallowed, all work on the contract should cease by the effective date of the termination. However, FAR 31.205-42(b) recognizes that certain performance costs that unavoidably continue after termination will be allowed. The test here is reasonableness under the circumstances. Of course, if the termination is partial, the contractor remains obligated to complete the unterminated portion of the contract.

b. *Give Notice to Subcontractors or Vendors and Settle Their Claims*

Upon receipt from the government of written notice of termination, the contractor should immediately send similar termination notices to all its subcontractors or vendors. Placing of further subcontracts should, of course, be discontinued. Following notice, the contractor should then attempt settlement of all subcontract and vendor claims and liabilities arising from the termination. The contractor should obtain government approval of such settlements. In the event of legal proceedings instituted by the subcontractors or vendors (who have no direct legal rights against the government), the contractor should immediately give notice thereof to the government.

The government has the right to direct the contractor to assign terminated subcontracts and purchase orders to the government. The government does not generally do so, however, preferring to have the contractor settle with the subcontractors and vendors, even in the event of litigation between the contractor and its subcontractors. In the event that subcontracts or orders are assigned to the government, the government may then settle and pay them directly, without going through the contractor.

Unless the government directs that subcontracts be assigned to it, the subcontractors have no right to direct payment from the government, 52 Comp. Gen. 377 (B-176596) (1972). GAO reached this conclusion even though the subcontractor had shipped termination inventory directly to the government at the government's request. The GAO stated that the government would be liable if it guaranteed payment to the subcontractor. Thus, a terminated subcontractor that is concerned about the solvency of its contractor should consider asking the government to guarantee payment for termination inventory as a condition to shipping it.

Potential problems with terminated subcontractors getting paid by their contractor led the Armed Services Board of Contract Appeals to hold that a contractor is not entitled to be paid by the government for its subcontractors' costs resulting from the termination unless and until it has actually paid the subcontractors, *Atlantic, Gulf & Pacific Co.*, ASBCA 13533, 72-1 BCA ¶9415, *recons. denied*, 72-2 BCA ¶9698, *aff'd*, 207 Ct. Cl. 995 (1975). This decision would seem to afford protection to subcontractors, but the subcontractor should not sit back and wait for payment. The subcontractor should keep the contracting officer informed of the fact that it has not been paid.

c. *Prepare Termination Inventory Schedules and Dispose of Termination Inventory*

Initially, the contractor should submit termination inventory schedules to the government in order to expedite prompt settlement of the contractor's claim, FAR 49.303-2 (calling for submission within 120 days after receipt of the termination notice). The standard form available for this purpose is Standard Form 1428. See FAR 53.301-1428. Guidance on filling out inventory schedules is contained in FAR 45.602-1. "Termination inventory" as defined in FAR 2.101 includes:

> [A]ny property purchased, supplied, manufactured, furnished, or otherwise acquired for the performance of a contract subsequently terminated and properly allocable to the terminated portion of the contract. It includes

Government-furnished property. It does not include any facilities, material, special test equipment, or special tooling that are subject to a separate contract or to a special contract requirement governing their use or disposition.

Termination inventory can include raw materials and work-in-process and completed supplies that do not conform to the contract specifications, provided that the percentage of nonconforming inventory is reasonable. In *Best Lumber Sales*, ASBCA 16737, 72-2 BCA ¶9661, the contractor was allowed full cost recovery when up to 15% of the termination inventory was defective.

The contractor then has certain responsibilities with respect to termination inventory. The contractor must protect and preserve the inventory complying with any government directions with respect thereto. Unused inventory must be delivered to the government to the extent the government directs it to do so. The remaining termination inventory is to be sold, as authorized and directed by the government. Any inventory remaining after the plant clearance period will either be accepted by the government or placed in storage, as agreed upon by the government and the contractor. Paragraph (e) of the Termination clause requires the contracting officer to remove the items from the contractor's location within 15 days or enter into a storage agreement.

d. *Vouchering for Costs*

The contractor is permitted to continue to submit vouchers for costs incurred up to the last day of the sixth month after termination of the contract, FAR 49.302. Although this regulation permits contractors to stop vouchering for costs at any time after termination, the better practice is to voucher for all costs as they are incurred.

e. *Submit Settlement Proposals and Effect Final Settlement*

The final procedural step is the submission of a settlement proposal. This is done using Standard Form 1437, FAR 53.301-1437, which summarizes all costs and fee previously vouchered and all additional costs and fee being claimed. In the unlikely event that all costs have been previously vouchered, the proposal will only be for the fee that is claimed to be due, FAR 49.302.

A contractor's settlement proposal must be submitted to the government within one year from the effective date of the termination, FAR 49.303-1, 49.206-1(a). In *Do-Well Mach. Shop, Inc. v. United States*, 870 F.2d 637 (Fed. Cir. 1989), the court held that the requirement that the settlement proposal be submitted no later than one year after the termination was not inconsistent with the Contract Disputes Act. Thus, the failure to file within the time limit was a valid defense that could be raised by the government. In *Dual, Inc.*, ASBCA 53827, 06-1 BCA ¶33,243, the board dismissed an appeal of a contracting officer decision to give no compensation for a termination for convenience because the contractor had forfeited its corporate charter at the time the proposal was submitted and the one year had expired before it was reinstated. The contractor did not contest the contracting officer's citation of the FAR 52.249-6 clause as the basis for the termination although it was not in the contract. In *Industrial Data Link Corp.*, ASBCA 49348, 98-1 BCA ¶29,634, *recons. denied*, 98-2 BCA ¶29,775, the government was permitted to deny all payments and recover progress payments on a fixed-price contract where the contractor did not submit the settlement proposal within one year. Contractor's should exercise extreme care in submitting these proposals within the required one-year period or obtaining a time extension. See *England v. The Swanson Group, Inc.*, 353 F.3d 1375 (Fed. Cir. 2004), holding that the board of contract appeals has no jurisdiction to hear an appeal made from a contracting officer determination if the contractor had not submitted a settlement proposal.

A contractor must settle subcontractor claims and include these amounts in its settlement proposal. In *Parsons Global Servs., Inc.*, ASBCA 58731, 11-1 BCA ¶34,632, the contractor attempted to have subcontractor claims resolved by taking them to the termination contracting officer and appealing his refusal to settle them under the Contract Disputes Act but the board denied jurisdiction on the grounds that there was no dispute concerning a routine request for payment, stating at 170,655:

> Direct settlements by the government with subcontractors are authorized by FAR 49.108 but, in fact, are discouraged by the provision. FAR 49.108-8 affords the TCO discretion to intervene but states the "general rule"

that "the prime contractor is obligated to settle" with and pay the subcontractor. There is no evidence or argument that the TCO somehow abused his discretion in denying the requests or disputed the government's eventual liability to pay properly submitted subcontract "settlement" costs. To argue that the TCO's determination was the equivalent of a "dispute," would effectively deprive the TCO of his discretionary right and be contrary to the general intent of FAR 49.108-8 to use the direct settlement option sparingly. In essence, the TCO's direction required appellant to simply settle its subcontract claims in accordance with customary and standard termination procedures. No persuasive reason has been given for appellant not doing so. To the extent that the costs claimed are cognizable under the Termination clause, appellant should include them in an appropriate amendment to its termination settlement proposal.

3. Settlement

Following submission of the settlement proposal, the contracting parties should negotiate the terms of a final settlement, and if no resolution is possible, the government must unilaterally determine the amount due to the contractor, applying standards set forth in the Termination clause.

a. Negotiated Settlement

Paragraph (g) of the Termination clause gives the contracting officer great latitude in determining the amount to be paid to the contractor for the costs incurred and the fee earned. See FAR 49.103 calling for the negotiation of a "fair and prompt" settlement. This negotiation can be greatly simplified if the contractor is able to "voucher out" the costs within the allowable six months period.

At the conclusion of negotiations, the termination contracting officer must prepare for inclusion in the termination case file and for use by reviewing authorities a settlement negotiation memorandum describing the principal elements of the settlement, FAR 49.110. The memorandum must include "explanations of matters involving differences and doubtful questions settled by agreement, and the factors considered." This information will assist reviewing authorities in understanding the basis for the settlement.

FAR 49.111 provides that each "agency shall establish procedures, when necessary, for the administrative review of proposed termination settlements." Prior to 1984, this provision required that the termination settlement be reviewed by a termination settlement board when the amount of the termination involved $50,000 or more. Settlements have been invalidated when required approvals were not obtained, *Atlantic Gulf & Pac. Co. v. United States*, 207 Ct. Cl. 995 (1975); *Bromley Contracting Co.*, DOTCAB 1284, 84-2 BCA ¶17,233.

b. Settlements by Determination

Where the parties are unable to agree upon the amount of the termination settlement, the contracting officer must make a unilateral determination of the amount to which the contractor is entitled, FAR 49.109-7. The Termination clause, FAR 52.249-6, provides the following guidance to the contracting officer in making his determination:

> (h) If the Contractor and the Contracting Officer fail to agree in whole or in part on the amount of costs and/or fee to be paid because of the termination of work, the Contracting Officer shall determine, on the basis of information available, the amount, if any, due the Contractor, and shall pay that amount, which shall include the following:
>
>> (1) All costs reimbursable under this contract, not previously paid, for the performance of this contract before the effective date of the termination, and those costs that may continue for a reasonable time with the approval of or as directed by the Contracting Officer; however, the Contractor shall discontinue those costs as rapidly as practicable.

(2) The cost of settling and paying termination settlement proposals under terminated subcontracts that are properly chargeable to the terminated portion of the contract if not included in subparagraph (h)(1) of this clause.

(3) The reasonable costs of settlement of the work terminated, including—

(i) Accounting, legal, clerical, and other expenses reasonably necessary for the preparation of termination settlement proposals and supporting data;

(ii) The termination and settlement of subcontracts (excluding the amounts of such settlements); and

(iii) Storage, transportation, and other costs incurred, reasonably necessary for the preservation, protection, or disposition of the termination inventory. If the termination is for default, no amounts for the preparation of the Contractor's termination settlement proposal may be included.

(4) A portion of the fee payable under the contract, determined as follows:

(i) If the contract is terminated for the convenience of the Government, the settlement shall include a percentage of the fee equal to the percentage of completion of work contemplated under the contract, but excluding subcontract effort included in subcontractors' termination proposals, less previous payments for fee.

(ii) If the contract is terminated for default, the total fee payable shall be such proportionate part of the fee as the total number of articles (or amount of services) delivered to and accepted by the Government is to the total number of articles (or amount of services) of a like kind required by the contract.

(5) If the settlement includes only fee, it will be determined under subparagraph (h)(4) of this clause.

Since the costs to be paid upon termination are "costs reimbursable under the contract," they are governed by the applicable Cost Principles. These cost recovery rules are treated extensively in Chapters 8-10, but there are special rules on allowability of legal fees and other professional-services costs in preparing termination claims. It should be noted that, with regard to such professional-services costs, the cost principles allow only the costs involved in preparation and presentation of the claim to the contracting officer. Thus, costs associated with an appeal contesting a termination for default, even though successful, and costs of presenting a termination claim to a board of contract appeals are unallowable, *Q. V.S., Inc.*, ASBCA 7513, 1963 BCA ¶3699. Contingent legal fees are unallowable under FAR 31.205-33(b), although retainers are allowable, *Atlantic, Gulf & Pacific Co.*, ASBCA 13533, 72-1 BCA ¶9415, *recons. denied*, 72-2 BCA ¶9698, *aff'd*, 207 Ct. Cl. 995 (1975), and fees computer at reasonable hourly rates are allowable (even if the agreement with the attorney is a contingent fee agreement), *SUFI Network Servs., Inc. v. United States*, 105 Fed. Cl. 184 (2012). In the case of default terminations, the contractor is not entitled to any costs incurred in preparation of its settlement proposal.

If there is no explicit provision in a cost sharing contract regarding the issue, the government must pay all of the contractor's costs (rather than a share of the costs) upon termination because the clause calls for the payment of "all cost reimbursable under this contract," *Jacobs Eng'g Group, Inc. v. United States*, 434 F.3d 1378 (Fed. Cir. 2006). However, the government is not required to pay a fee to the contractor in such circumstances, *Jacobs Eng'g Group, Inc. v. United States*, 75 Fed. Cl. 752 (2007).

c. Fee Recovery

In the case of convenience terminations, the contractor is entitled to a fee proportional to the percentage of work completed excluding fee on subcontractor billings. FAR 49.305-1 states that—

factors such as the extent and difficulty of the work performed by the contractor (e.g., planning, scheduling, technical study, engineering work production and supervision, placing and supervising subcontracts, and work performed by the contractor in (1) stopping performance, (2) settling terminated subcontracts, and (3) disposing of termination inventory) shall be compared with the total work required by the contract or by the terminated portion. The contractor's adjusted fee shall not include an allowance for fee for subcontract effort included in subcontractors' settlement proposals.

FAR 49.305-2 provides more detailed guidance for construction contracts. In *Lockheed Martin Corp. v. England*, 424 F.3d 1199 (Fed. Cir. 2005), the court ruled that, in accordance with the last sentence in FAR 49.305-1(a), the contractor was not entitled to a fee on subcontract work that had been completed before the termination but had not been included in a contractor' voucher before the termination and hence was "included in" the termination settlement proposal. In *UNC Nuclear Indus., Inc.*, EBCA 412-4-88, 90-1 BCA ¶22,463, the board held that the proportion of days worked was not a correct means of prorating the fee. In *Technology, Inc.*, ASBCA 14083, 71-2 BCA ¶8956, *recons. denied*, 72-1 BCA ¶9281, the board found that the best measure of the percentage of completion was the percentage of direct labor dollars expended (not total costs which included subcontracts). See also *Lockheed Martin Corp.*, ASBCA 53032, 03-2 BCA ¶32,408, rejecting the contractor's argument that it should be paid fee on subcontractor work because it had a leader-follower contract. In *System Dev. Corp.*, ASBCA 16947, 73-1 BCA ¶9788, the board held that the calculation should be based on the percentage of work completed not by paying the contract rate of fee on incurred costs. In *Textron Defense Sys.*, ASBCA 47352, 96-2 BCA ¶28,332, *aff'd*, 143 F.3d 1465 (Fed. Cir. 1998), it was held that the percentage of completion technique did not apply to award fees in a CPAF contract, but in *Northrop Grumman Corp. v. Goldin*, 136 F.3d 1479 (Fed. Cir. 1998), it was held that the contractor was entitled to a percentage of the entire award fee in a CPAF contract even though some of the fee had not been "allocated" to the pool. The government bears the burden of proof as to the appropriate fee reduction, *Emerson Elec. Co.*, ASBCA 15591, 72-1 BCA ¶9440.

When a default termination is involved, the contractor is only entitled to a portion of the fee prorated for the number of articles or services delivered and accepted by the government (or percentage of work completed in construction contracts). The principal difference between these two measurements is that, for convenience terminations, work-in-process is included, while in default terminations, it is not included, *Tri-Delta Corp.*, ASBCA 17456, 75-1 BCA ¶11,160.

E. Partial Terminations

Under the Termination clause, the government may terminate the contract "in whole, or from time to time in part." If the government terminates part of the contract, the contractor must continue to perform the unterminated portion of the work. There appear to be few practical limitations on the government's rights to terminate portions of the contract work. See *Lieb Bros., Inc.*, ASBCA 10007, 73-2 BCA ¶10,131, which sustains a partial termination that deleted the profitable part of a construction project and required performance of the balance of the work. Where there is a partial termination, the contractor recovers its costs by continuing to submit vouchers as the costs are incurred, FAR 49.304-3. A pro-rata share of the fee is recovered through the submission of a settlement proposal, FAR 49.304-2.

VI. BREACH OF CONTRACT

The government has infrequently argued that it has the right to remedies for a cost-type contractor's breach of the contract. The possible remedies are restitution of all payments on the basis of total failure of performance or damages.

The only case permitting the government to obtain restitution is *Tennessee Dep't of Employment Sec.*, LBCA 81-BCA-9, 84-1 BCA ¶16,978, where the board found that the contractor had "totally failed" to perform its contractual obligations under a cost-reimbursement contract. The contractor did not complete performance, and the work that was accomplished was so defective as to be worthless. The board sustained the government's demand for repayment of all costs reimbursed to the contractor, likening the government's claim to one of common law restitution. Unfortunately, the board discussed neither the reasonableness cost principle nor the LOC clause. It would seem that if the performance was as bad as indicated, the government would have been able to make a case that the contractor had performed the work in a faulty manner. Similarly, it might have been able to establish that the costs were unreasonable. This case appears to be the type of case envisioned by the following GAO memorandum:

LEGAL MEMORANDUM ON DUTY OF COST-TYPE CONTRACTOR TO EXERCISE "DUE CARE" IN MAKING REIMBURSABLE EXPENDITURES

(Prepared by the Office of General Counsel, General Accounting Office)

There is substantial legal support for the proposition that a contractor performing work on a cost-reimbursement basis must use the same skill and ability that it would use in performing work for a fixed price. In *Title Guarantee & Trust Co. v. Pam*, 155 N.Y.S. 337 (1915), *aff'd*, 192 App. Div. 268 (182 N.Y.S. 824), *aff'd*, 232 N.Y. 441 (134 N.E. 525), the New York Supreme Court stated:

> When a person contracts with a corporation with a reputation for the successful completion of large enterprises to do work at cost and a percentage, he has the right to expect the same skill and ability to be applied to his work that it would give where its profit was dependent upon its ability to do the work at a cost less than the contract price. . . . If the contractor fails to do this, he should only be allowed the reasonable cost and his percentage.

In the case of *Wendel v. Maybury et al.*, (La. Ct. of App., 1954), 75 So.2d 379, 383, the court stated:

> Under a cost-plus contract, the contractor is obligated to use his utmost endeavors to see that the owner gets value received.

As was stated by the court in *Shaw et al. v. Bula Cannon Shops, Inc.* (Miss. Sup. Ct., 1949) 38 So.2d 916, 918:

> The contractor does not have the right to expend any amount of money he may see fit upon the work, regardless of the propriety, necessity, or honesty of the expenditure, and then compel repayment by the other party, who has confided in his integrity, ability and industry.

Other cases supporting this proposition are *Hitt v. Smallwood* (Va. Spec. Ct. of App., 1926) 133 S.E. 503; and *Walsh Services, Inc. v. Feek* (Wash. Sup. Ct., 1954), 274 P. 2d 117.

No case has been found in the federal decisions dealing specifically with the question of responsibility of a cost-plus-a-fixed-fee contractor for negligent or improvident expenditures. However, we believe the principles enunciated in the cases mentioned above have equal applicability to federal cost-reimbursement-type contracts. The United States has the same right as a private person to expect that its cost-reimbursement contractors will perform work on behalf of the Government with the same degree of care, industry, and economy that they would exercise if they were performing the work under a fixed-price contract.

It has also been argued that a cost-reimbursement contractor is potentially liable for breach of contract damages. This possibility has been discussed in two cases where damage suits were brought by the government against a cost-type contractor, *United States v. Duggan*, 210 F.2d 926 (8th Cir. 1954), and *United States v. Bentley & Sons Co.*, 16 F.2d 895 (2d Cir. 1927). The precedential value of these decisions is rather uncertain. The *Duggan* decision, however, would seem to support the view that present cost-type agreements do not present any inherent bar to the government's entitlement to damages against a delinquent cost-type contractor. In *Duggan*, the circuit court reversed a district court order dismissing a government action for damages following an alleged breach by the contractor. The government had terminated the CPFF contract for default because the contractor failed to manufacture and deliver items according to the contract specifications. The contract contained an agreement reserving certain post-termination claims in the government's favor. The circuit court rejected the contractor's claim (and the district court's conclusion) that the government was limited to administrative adjustment of its rights under the contract and went on to conclude at 932:

> We do not find in the contract any agreement between the parties for the administrative determination of the claims of the Government against the Contractor upon the termination of the contract. Even if there had been in the contract no express reservation of claims in favor of the Government against the Contractor, we think the

Contractor would not be relieved from liability to the Government for any loss proximately resulting from the failure of the Contractor to perform its obligations under the contract or its legal obligation to reimburse the Government for moneys received by the Contractor to which it was not entitled.

Two potential limitations on the precedential value of *Duggan* as support for government breach of contract claims should be noted. First, the issue of the government's right to recover damages from a cost-type contractor was not explicitly addressed by the court. Second, the nature of the government's damages claim in *Duggan* was for reprocurement costs, now presumably unavailable following termination for default of a cost-reimbursement contract. See also *United States v. Boyd*, 378 U.S. 39 (1964), where the Supreme Court observed in dicta at 46:

Whether manufacturing products for sale to the Government or furnishing services, the cost-plus contractor has undertaken contractual obligations. If he properly performs his contract, he earns his fee; if he does not, he may lose the contract, be liable for damages and be forced to liquidate the organization which was built to perform the contract.

In Frank Reda's "Cost Contractor's Liability for Damages," 9 A.F. JAG L. Rev. 31 (1967), the author argues that a cost-type contractor might be liable for damages and summarizes his position as follows:

Cost-type agreements now in general use evidently contain no inherent bar to the Government's right to breach of contract damages. While few authorities point directly to this conclusion, no authorities point directly to the opposite conclusion. The right of an injured party to seek default damages is fundamental. It cannot be lightly dismissed lest the sanctity of costtype agreements be destroyed. It is recognized that many cost-type agreements call merely for the contractor's best efforts to meet schedule or performance goals. Failure to meet these goals under a best effort agreement would not, of course, constitute breach of contract. But where the contractor has solemnly promised to meet a stated delivery schedule or to attain a specified performance goal, he should be held to this promise.

Despite these statements, it would seem that in order to recover damages from a cost-reimbursement contractor under the present FAR requiring the clauses discussed above, the government would be required to prove that the contractor acted unreasonably in performing the contract. See *Enviroslove, LLC*, DOTBCA 4463, 06-1 BCA ¶33,241, taking jurisdiction of a government claim that the contractor breached a time-and-materials contract by failing to respond to an order to clean up hazardous waste. The contract contained Alternate V of the FAR 52.249-6 Termination clause which contains similar provisions to the cost-reimbursement provisions. In *Flight Dynamics Research Corp.*, ASBCA 35248, 88-3 BCA ¶20,861, the government was not successful in proving unreasonable conduct. There the contractor stopped work after overrunning the estimated cost of the contract. The government had another person complete the final report under the contract and sought to recover from the contractor the amount paid to this third person for completing the report. The government argued that the contractor should have reserved sufficient funds to complete the report. The board denied recovery, finding that there was no contractual requirement to reserve the funds and that the government had not established that the contractor had failed to use its best efforts to perform within the estimated cost.

VII. SUBCONTRACTING

Several standard contract provisions affect subcontracting activity under cost-reimbursement contracts.

A. Competition in Subcontracting

FAR 44.204(c) requires the use in all cost-reimbursement contracts over $150,000 of the following clause in FAR 52.244-5 requiring competition on the awarding of subcontracts:

COMPETITION IN SUBCONTRACTING (DEC 1996)

(a) The Contractor shall select subcontractors (including suppliers) on a competitive basis to the maximum practical extent consistent with the objectives and requirements of the contract.

(b) If the Contractor is an approved mentor under the Department of Defense Pilot Mentor-Protege Program (Pub. L. 101-510, section 831 as amended), the Contractor may award subcontracts under this contract on a noncompetitive basis to its proteges.

B. Subcontract Approval

Preaward notice of the awarding of certain subcontracts is required. 10 U.S.C. § 2306(e) provides:

> (1) Except as provided in paragraph (2), each cost contract and each cost-plus-a-fixed-fee contract shall provide for notice to the agency by the contractor before the making, under the prime contract, of—
>
> > (A) a cost-plus-a-fixed-fee subcontract; or
> >
> > (B) a fixed-price subcontract or purchase order involving more than the greater of (i) the simplified acquisition threshold, or (ii) 5 percent of the estimated cost of the prime contract.
>
> (2) Paragraph (1) shall not apply to a prime contract with a contractor that maintains a purchasing system approved by the contracting officer for the contract.

This statute was amended in Pub. L. No. 108-136, Nov. 24, 2003, to add ¶(2). A similar requirement is contained in 41 U.S.C. § 3905(c) with the omission of ¶(2). This requirement is implemented by FAR 44.201-2 and ¶(e) of the Subcontracts clause in FAR 52.244-2.

For many years, cost-reimbursement contractors were also required to obtain consent of the contracting officer before awarding subcontracts. However, the FAR has now been modified to remove this requirement if the contractor has an approved purchasing system—unless the contracting officer imposes special consent requirements. This policy is implemented in FAR Subpart 44.2 and is stated in the following mandatory Subcontracts clause in FAR 52.244-2:

> (c) If the Contractor does not have an approved purchasing system, consent to subcontract is required for any subcontract that—
>
> > (1) Is of the cost-reimbursement, time-and-materials, or labor-hour type; or
> >
> > (2) Is fixed-price and exceeds—
> >
> > > (i) For a contract awarded by the Department of Defense, the Coast Guard, or the National Aeronautics and Space Administration, the greater of the simplified acquisition threshold or 5 percent of the total estimated cost of the contract; or
> > >
> > > (ii) For a contract awarded by a civilian agency other than the Coast Guard and the National Aeronautics and Space Administration, either the simplified acquisition threshold or 5 percent of the total estimated cost of the contract.
>
> (d) If the Contractor has an approved purchasing system, the Contractor nevertheless shall obtain the Contracting Officer's written consent before placing the following subcontracts:
>
> ____
>
> ____
>
> ____

This clause also contained detailed guidance on the information that is required when notifying the contracting officer that subcontracts have been awarded. FAR 44.202-2 and 44.203 provide guidance to contracting officers on the factors to be considered in granting consent to a subcontract.

Consent to a subcontract confers no rights of the subcontractor against the government, *Toxco, Inc. v. Chu*, 801 F. Supp.2d 1 (D.D.C. 2011).

When subcontract approval is required the contracting officer may ratify, in writing, any subcontract. However, the contracting officer is not required to ratify even if contract performance is complete. In *McDonnell Douglas Corp.*, NASABCA 467-13, 68-2 BCA ¶7316, the board held that the government was not required to reimburse the contractor for costs attributable to subcontracts entered into without the contracting officer's approval, stating at 34,029:

> The subcontract clause is placed in CPFF contracts first to assure compliance with the statutory provision that in cases such as this the contractor gives notice prior to placing a subcontract and, second, to give the contracting officer an opportunity to exercise judgment in the selection of source and terms of the subcontract before it becomes binding. . . . While the subcontract clause gives the Contracting Officer authority to approve or disapprove a subcontract, he should not exercise it arbitrarily, but only if there are justifiable reasons. We do not believe the Contracting Officer's disapproval of the subcontract here was arbitrary but was based on good reasons. The subcontract clause also places on the Contracting Officer a duty to disapprove a subcontract if he believes it is not in the best interest of the Government.

See also *Housing Auth. of New Haven*, HUDBCA 74-3, 78-2 BCA ¶13,237, where the board, denying reimbursement for costs incurred under a disapproved subcontract, stated that "charges incurred under a subcontract which has not been consented to or ratified are not eligible for payment . . . if the Contracting Officer's refusal is not arbitrary or unreasonable." In 41 Comp. Gen. 424 (B-147220) (1961), GAO stated at 427:

> [I]t seems clear that the Contracting Officer should not approve a subcontract entered into by the prime contractor if the execution of such subcontract would be prejudicial to the interest of the Government. It is also apparent that a condition prejudicial to the Government would arise if the Contracting Officer were to approve a subcontract entered into at an unreasonably high price.

The boards have sometimes indicated that a contractor's failure to obtain subcontract approval as required by an express contract provision will not result in disallowance of costs if those costs are reasonably necessary for performance and satisfy other requirements of allowability, *Aeronca Mfg. Corp.*, ASBCA 3844, 58-1 BCA ¶1724; *Norman E. Miller & Assocs.*, WDBCA 1460, 4 CCF ¶60,465 (1948). See also *Wyman-Gordon Co.*, ASBCA 5100, 59-2 BCA ¶2344; and *Westinghouse Elec. Corp.*, ASBCA 21634, 80-2 BCA ¶14,726.

C. Contractor Purchasing System Reviews

Contractors obtain approval of their purchasing systems (to avoid the subcontract notification or consent requirements) by requesting their administrative contracting officer to perform a purchasing system review in accordance with FAR Subpart 44.3. FAR 44.302(a) calls for such reviews if the contractor's sales to the government exceed $25 million per year excluding competitively awarded firm-fixed-price and fixed-price with economic price adjustment contracts as well as contracts for commercial items. The review is a detailed analysis of the contractor's purchasing practices with special attention paid to the degree of price competition obtained. Once a purchasing system has been approved, the administrative contracting officer is required to determine every three years whether a new review is required.

D. Small Business Requirements

FAR 19.702 requires any contractor receiving a contract for more than the small purchase limitation to agree in the contract that a variety of types of small business concerns will have the maximum practicable opportunity to participate in contract performance consistent with its efficient performance." FAR 19.708(a) requires the following clause in FAR 52.219-8 to be used to place this responsibility on contractors:

UTILIZATION OF SMALL BUSINESS CONCERNS (JUL 2013)

(a) It is the policy of the United States that small business concerns, veteran-owned small business concerns, service-disabled veteran-owned small business concerns, HUBZone small business concerns, small disadvantaged business concerns, and women-owned small business concerns shall have the maximum practicable opportunity to participate in performing contracts let by any Federal agency, including contracts and subcontracts for subsystems, assemblies, components, and related services for major systems. It is further the policy of the United States that its prime contractors establish procedures to ensure the timely payment of amounts due pursuant to the terms of their subcontracts with small business concerns, veteran-owned small business concerns, service-disabled veteran-owned small business concerns, HUBZone small business concerns, small disadvantaged business concerns, and women-owned small business concerns.

(b) The Contractor hereby agrees to carry out this policy in the awarding of subcontracts to the fullest extent consistent with efficient contract performance. The Contractor further agrees to cooperate in any studies or surveys as may be conducted by the United States Small Business Administration or the awarding agency of the United States as may be necessary to determine the extent of the Contractor's compliance with this clause.

(c) *Definitions.* As used in this contract—

HUBZone small business concern means a *small business concern* that appears on the List of Qualified HUBZone Small Business Concerns maintained by the Small Business Administration.

Service-disabled veteran-owned small business concern—

(1) Means a small business concern—

(i) Not less than 51 percent of which is owned by one or more service-disabled veterans or, in the case of any publicly owned business, not less than 51 percent of the stock of which is owned by one or more service-disabled veterans; and

(ii) The management and daily business operations of which are controlled by one or more service-disabled veterans or, in the case of a veteran with permanent and severe disability, the spouse or permanent caregiver of such veteran.

(2) *Service-disabled veteran* means a veteran, as defined in 38 U.S.C. 101(2), with a disability that is service-connected, as defined in 38 U.S.C. 101(16).

Small business concern means a small business as defined pursuant to Section 3 of the Small Business Act and relevant regulations promulgated pursuant thereto.

Small disadvantaged business concern means a *small business concern* that represents, as part of its offer that—

(1)(i) It has received certification as a small disadvantaged business concern consistent with 13 CFR part 124, Subpart B;

(ii) No material change in disadvantaged ownership and control has occurred since its certification;

(iii) Where the concern is owned by one or more individuals, the net worth of each individual upon whom the certification is based does not exceed $750,000 after taking into account the applicable exclusions set forth at 13 CFR 124.104(c)(2); and

(iv) It is identified, on the date of its representation, as a certified small disadvantaged business in the Dynamic Small Business Search database maintained by the Small Business Administration; or

(2) It represents in writing that it qualifies as a small disadvantaged business (SDB) for any Federal subcontracting program, and believes in good faith that it is owned and controlled by one or more socially and economically disadvantaged individuals and meets the SDB eligibility criteria in 13 CFR 124.1002.

Veteran-owned small business concern means a small business concern—

(1) Not less than 51 percent of which is owned by one or more veterans (as defined at 38 U.S.C. 101(2)) or, in the case of any publicly owned business, not less than 51 percent of the stock of which is owned by one or more veterans; and

(2) The management and daily business operations of which are controlled by one or more veterans.

Women-owned small business concern means a small business concern—

(1) That is at least 51 percent owned by one or more women, or, in the case of any publicly owned business, at least 51 percent of the stock of which is owned by one or more women; and

(2) Whose management and daily business operations are controlled by one or more women.

(d)(1) Contractors acting in good faith may rely on written representations by their subcontractors regarding their status as a small business concern, a veteran-owned small business concern, a service-disabled veteran-owned small business concern, a HUBZone small business concern, a small disadvantaged business concern, or a women-owned small business concern.

(2) The Contractor shall confirm that a subcontractor representing itself as a HUBZone small business concern is certified by SBA as a HUBZone small business concern by accessing the System for Award Management database or by contacting the SBA. Options for contacting the SBA include—

(i) HUBZone small business database search application Web page at *http://dsbs.sba.gov/dsbs/search/dsp_searchhubzone.cfm*; or *http://www.sba.gov/hubzone*;

(ii) In writing to the Director/HUB, U.S. Small Business Administration, 409 3rd Street, SW., Washington DC 20416; or

(iii) The SBA HUBZone Help Desk at *hubzone@sba.gov*.

In addition, 15 U.S.C. § 637(d)(4) requires that larger contracts contain a requirement for a "subcontracting plan" that establishes percentage goals for the utilization of each of these types of small businesses. FAR 19.702(a) places this requirement on contracts in excess of $650,000 ($1,500,000 for construction contracts) that have "subcontracting possibilities." This requirement is implemented by the use of the Small Business Subcontracting Plan clause in FAR 52.219-9. Contractors can meet this requirement by adopting master plans for a location or division, FAR 19.704(b). Small businesses are not required to submit subcontracting plans under FAR 19.702(b). See *Chaves Painting*, Comp. Gen. Dec. B-198793, 80-2 CPD ¶97. In a negotiated procurement, failure to submit and negotiate an acceptable subcontracting plan prior to the time of award may contribute to a nonresponsibility determination, 15 U.S.C. § 637(d)(4)(C). In addition, failure to adhere to the terms of the subcontracting plan during performance is considered a material breach of contract and may serve as a basis for default termination action, 15 U.S.C. § 637(d)(8).

When a subcontracting plan is required, 15 U.S.C. § 637(d)(4)(F) requires the government to assess liquidated damages if the contractor does not make a good faith effort to comply with the plan. This requirement is implemented by including the Liquidated Damages—Subcontracting Plan clause in FAR 52.219-16 in all contracts requiring subcontracting plans. Guidance on the application of this clause is contained in FAR 19.705-7.

Contracting officers are also permitted to include the Incentive Subcontracting Program clause in FAR 52.219-10 in contracts requiring a subcontracting plan. This clause calls for the payment of an amount between one and ten percent of the subcontracting dollars above the goal in the plan as a bonus to the contractor. Minimal guidance on the use of this clause is contained in FAR 19.708(c).

E. Buy American

Contracts generally contain clauses that implement the Buy American Act (BAA), 41 U.S.C. § 8302 - 05, which expresses a preference for American-made products. See FAR Subpart 25.1. Of greatest relevance in cost-reimbursement contracting is the requirement that "end items" be manufactured in the United States. An end item is considered to have been "manufactured" in the United States if it was assembled in the United States from components that themselves were "substantially all" manufactured, mined, or produced in the United States. "Substantially all" is defined by Executive Order No. 10582, 19 Fed. Reg. 8723 (Dec. 17, 1954), as being over 50%. Thus, over 50% of the value of the components must be comprised of components manufactured in the United States. However, the parts of the components can be foreign in origin. Thus, the domestic content of the product is relatively unimportant in determining whether a product is manufactured in the United States. Rather, the determination is made through the application of very technical rules, which are not set forth in the FAR. Consequently, offerors are exposed to the possibility of losing an award if they do not understand the rules. See *Orlite Eng'g Co.*, Comp. Gen. Dec. B-229615, 88-1 CPD ¶300, where, in a fixed-price contract, the contracting officer determined that the contractor was not offering a domestic end product and, therefore, adjusted the contractor's bid by adding the prescribed 50% evaluation factor; this action displaced the contractor as the low bidder. An offeror may also be subject to criminal liability under the False Claims Act, 18 U.S.C. § 287, for mistakenly certifying that its product is of domestic origin. See *United States v. Rule Indus., Inc.*, 878 F.2d 535 (1st Cir. 1989).

The FAR does not define the term "manufacture." Generally, however, if an end product or component is composed of a group of components or parts, "manufacture" is conceived of as the process of final assembly. See *Hamilton Watch Co.*, Comp. Gen. Dec. B-179939, 74-1 CPD ¶306 (watch movement was manufactured when it was assembled); *Textron, Inc. v. Adams*, 493 F. Supp. 824 (D.D.C. 1980) (reassembly after disassembly constituted manufacture). See a contrary holding in *Ampex Corp.*, Comp. Gen. Dec. B-203021, 82-1 CPD ¶163, where GAO held that the fact that the base unit was disassembled and reassembled in the process of manufacturing did not change the fact that it was manufactured in Japan. If, however, the end product or component is an item that has gone through several processes, manufacture is usually found to have occurred if there has been a fundamental change in the item. See *Yohar Supply Co.*, Comp. Gen. Dec. B-225480, 87-1 CPD ¶152 (manufacture occurred when company stamped out components from rolled sheets of steel, bent components into shape, and smoothed them); and *Davis Walker Corp.*, Comp. Gen. Dec. B-184672, 76-2 CPD ¶182 (manufacture occurred first when steel rod was turned into bright wire and again when the bright wire was galvanized). The basic test is whether the operations performed on the foreign item create a basically new material or result in a fundamental change in the item. See *A. Hirsh, Inc.*, Comp. Gen. Dec. B-237466, 90-1CPD ¶247, ruling that domestic processing of foreign-bought horsehair—including sterilization, sorting, cutting, inspecting, blending with oil, wrapping, and trimming—was not "manufacturing," because after all the processing, the horsehair was still horsehair. See also *TRS Research*, Comp. Gen. Dec. B-285514, 2000 CPD ¶128, ruling that "refurbishing" foreign containers was not manufacturing because it did not "transform or alter the essential nature of the containers."

The Trade Agreements Act of 1979, 19 U.S.C. § 2501, *et seq.*, gives the President authority to waive the Buy American Act and this has been done by Executive Order No. 12260, 46 Fed. Reg. 1653 (Dec. 31, 1980). See FAR Subpart 25.4 for guidance on the application of this act, as well as later, narrower acts regarding treaties promoting free trade, and the procedures to be followed when such acts apply. The rules governing the preference for domestic items are covered in detail in Cibinic, Nash & Yukins, *Formation of Government Contracts* 1614-32 (4th ed. 2011).

VIII. KEY PERSONNEL CLAUSES

In some cases, particularly for research and study contracts, the government attempts to maintain control over the nature and quality of the contractor's performance by including clauses in the contract requiring the use of key individuals from the contractor's organization; the government will have relied upon the experience, skill, and expertise of these individuals in deciding to award the contract. These clauses generally require the consent of the contracting officer for the substitution of key personnel. While they contain no remedy for the failure to utilize the key personnel, they may be viewed as a technique whereby the government endeavors to ensure that it gets work of the quality and nature for which it bargained.

The key personnel clause used by the National Aeronautics & Space Administration is set forth in NFS 1852.235-71:

KEY PERSONNEL AND FACILITIES (MAR 1989)

(a) The personnel and/or facilities listed below (or specified in the contract Schedule) are considered essential to the work being performed under this contract. Before removing, replacing, or diverting any of the listed or specified personnel or facilities, the Contractor shall (1) notify the Contracting Officer reasonably in advance and (2) submit justification (including proposed substitutions) in sufficient detail to permit evaluation of the impact on this contract.

(b) The Contractor shall make no diversion without the Contracting Officer's written consent; provided, that the Contracting Officer may ratify in writing the proposed change, and that ratification shall constitute the Contracting Officer's consent required by this clause.

(c) The list of personnel and/or facilities (shown below or as specified in the contract Schedule) may, with the consent of the contracting parties, be amended from time to time during the course of the contract to add or delete personnel and/or facilities.

[List here the personnel and/or facilities considered essential, unless they are specified in the contract Schedule.]

Numerous other agencies have adopted similar clauses. See, e.g., HHSAR 352.242-70 (Department of Health & Human Services); EPAAR 1552.237-72 (Environmental Protection Agency), IAAR 1952.215-70 (Broadcasting Board of Governors), HUDAR 2452.237-70 (Department of Housing & Urban Development), EDAR 3452.243-70 (Department of Education) and AGAR 452.237-74 (Department of Agriculture).

These clauses attempt to impose a contractual duty on the contractor to use the personnel listed in the clause but recognize that future events may make this impracticable. Thus, they require that the contractor obtain the written consent of the contracting officer whenever one of the listed personnel cannot be used to perform the contract. In *Cardiometrix v. Dep't of the Treasury*, GSBCA 13462-TD, 97-1 BCA ¶28,775, and *National Medical Staffing, Inc.*, ASBCA 40391, 92-2 BCA ¶24,837, contractors were validly terminated for default when they could not provide substitute personnel of equal competence with the key personnel listed in the contract. In *Urban Inst. for Human Servs., Inc.*, ASBCA 28795, 84-2 BCA ¶17,260, the contractor was denied a higher salary paid to a substituted project director because the contracting officer had not approved the substitution. However, the government cannot unreasonably reject a qualified substitute person, *Washington Consulting Group, Inc.* HUDBCA 89-4489-EA1, 92-1 BCA ¶24,477. There are also cases on similar clauses requiring consent to changing subcontractors. These cases find it to be an abuse of discretion for the contracting officer to deny approval when the substitute subcontractor is equally competent to the subcontractor listed in the contract, *Hoel-Steffen Constr. Co. v. United States*, 684 F.2d 843 (Ct. Cl. 1982); *Liles Constr. Co. v. United States*, 455 F.2d 527 (Ct. Cl. 1972); *Richerson Constr., Inc. v. General Servs. Admin.*, GSBCA 11161, 93-1 BCA ¶25,239. It could also be a constructive change to the contract if the contracting officer demands that the contractor use more qualified personnel than those listed in the clause, *Watson, Rice & Co.*, HUDBCA 89-4468-C6, 90-1 BCA ¶22,499. In that case, however, the board found that the contracting officer's "suggestions" that different, more qualified subcontractor personnel be used did not rise to the level of an "order" for purposes of finding a constructive change.

IX. GOVERNMENT PROPERTY

Under cost-reimbursement contracts, the government generally follows the policy of acting as a "self-insurer," which relieves contractors of most of the risk of loss or damage to government property in the contractor's possession. This policy is based upon the government's desire to avoid reimbursing its contractor for the cost of commercial insurance. Paragraph

(h) of the Government Property clause, FAR 52.245-1, sets forth the limited risk of loss imposed on contractors with cost-reimbursement contracts and FAR 31.205-19(e)(2)(iv) makes the cost of broadly insuring government property an unallowable cost by stating limited circumstances when such costs are allowable.

A. Definition of Government Property

In cost-type contracts, "Government property" consists of two general categories of property: (1) items furnished to the contractor by the government for performance of the work and (2) property acquired by the contractor for performance of the work. FAR 45.101 defines these terms as follows:

> *Contractor-acquired property* means property acquired, fabricated, or otherwise provided by the contractor for performing a contract and to which the Government has title.
>
> *Government-furnished property* means property in the possession of, or directly acquired by, the Government and subsequently furnished to the contractor for performance of a contract. Government-furnished property includes, but is not limited to, spares and property furnished for repair, maintenance, overhaul, or modification. Government-furnished property also includes contractor-acquired property if the contractor-acquired property is a deliverable under a cost contract when accepted by the Government for continued use under the contract.
>
> *Government property* means all property owned by or leased to the Government. Government property includes both Government-furnished property and contractor-acquired property. Government property includes material, equipment, special tooling, special test equipment, and real property. Government property does not include intellectual property and software.

B. Management of Government Property

Part 45 of the FAR was rewritten in 2007 to allow contractors to management government property using commercial techniques. Thus, FAR 45.103(b) states that agencies "will not generally require contractors to establish property management systems that are separate from a contractor's established procedures, practices, and systems." This policy is implemented in ¶(b) of the Government Property clause, FAR 52.245-1, which contains no specific property management requirements but states that the contractor's system "shall be adequate to satisfy the requirements of this clause."

C. Title

The Government Property clause, FAR 52.245-1, which is included in cost-reimbursement contracts, governs the vesting of title to contractor-acquired property in the government. This clause provides as follows:

> (e) Title to Government property.
>
> > (1) All Government-furnished property and all property acquired by the Contractor, title to which vests in the Government under this paragraph (collectively referred to as "Government property"), is subject to the provisions of this clause. The Government shall retain title to all Government-furnished property. Title to Government property shall not be affected by its incorporation into or attachment to any property not owned by the Government, nor shall Government property become a fixture or lose its identity as personal property by being attached to any real property.
> >
> > * * *
> >
> > (3) Title under Cost-Reimbursement or Time-and-Material Contracts or Cost-Reimbursable contract line items under Fixed-Price contracts.

(i) Title to all property purchased by the Contractor for which the Contractor is entitled to be reimbursed as a direct item of cost under this contract shall pass to and vest in the Government upon the vendor's delivery of such property.

(ii) Title to all other property, the cost of which is reimbursable to the Contractor, shall pass to and vest in the Government upon—

(A) Issuance of the property for use in contract performance;

(B) Commencement of processing of the property for use in contract performance; or

(C) Reimbursement of the cost of the property by the Government, whichever occurs first.

The scope of ¶(3) of this clause is not clear. It would appear to be intended to give the government title to property that was bought by the contractor for incorporation into the work product of the contract but not immediately charged as a direct cost. However, state courts in tax litigation have interpreted it to give the government title to property acquired by the contractor and charged to indirect cost accounts. See *Northrop Grumman Corp. v. County of Los Angeles*, 134 Cal. Ct. App. 4th 424 (Ct. App. 2005); *Strayhorn v. Raytheon E-Sys., Inc.*, 101 S.W.3d 558 (Tex. App. 2003); *Hughes Aircraft Co. v. County of Orange*, 96 Cal. App. 4th 540 (Ct. App. 2002); *Motorola, Inc. v. Arizona Dep't of Revenue*, 993 P.2d 1101 (Ariz. Ct. App. 1999); *McDonnell Douglas Corp. v. Director of Revenue*, 945 S.W.2d 437 (Mo. 1997); *Aerospace Corp. v. State Bd. of Equalization*, 267 Cal. Rptr. 685 (Ct. App. 1990). The *Northrop Grumman* and *Hughes* court refused to follow *TRW Space & Defense Sector v. County of Los Angeles*, 58 Cal. Rptr. 2d 602 (Ct. App. 1996), which had reached the opposite conclusion. Compare *Raytheon Co. v. Comm'r of Revenue*, 916 N.E.2d 372 (Mass. Sup. Ct. 2009), where the court agreed that the contractor had "sold" indirect cost property to the government but held that the state tax still applied because that sale was "incidental" to its business. The ramification of these decisions is not clear but contractors should be aware that property being used in their indirect cost departments may be considered to be government property with all of the obligations that that entails.

D. Risk of Loss

Paragraph (h) of the Government Property clause, FAR 52.245-1, which is included in cost-reimbursement contracts, provides generally that "the Contractor shall not be liable for loss of Government property furnished or acquired under this contract. . . ." There are three exceptions to this rule— insured risks, willful misconduct of managerial personnel and revocation of the government assumption of risk because of inadequate property management practices.

1. Insured Risks

A contractor is liable for losses attributable to "a risk . . . covered by insurance or (for which) the Contractor is otherwise reimbursed," but only "to the extent of such insurance or reimbursement." The meaning of this last phrase was considered in *Space Sciences, Inc.*, NASABCA 566-21, 67-2 BCA ¶6708. In that case, the contractor had taken insurance at its own expense under a cost-reimbursement contract. When the government property was damaged, the government refused to reimburse the contractor for the cost of repairing the property on the grounds that it was covered by insurance. The board held that the existence of insurance precluded recovery even though the insurance premiums had not been charged as a cost of performance and the contractor was unable to collect from the insurer because the contractor did not file a timely claim. The board reasoned that since the clause in the cost-reimbursement contract precluded recovery of such costs in either of two circumstances: (1) the loss was covered by insurance or (2) the contractor was reimbursed for the loss—the fact that the contractor had not recovered from the insurance company did not entitle the contractor to recover from the government.

2. Willful Misconduct

The clause provides that the contractor is responsible for loss or damage to government property resulting from the willful misconduct or lack of good faith on the part of any of the contractor's directors, officers, managers, superintendents, or equivalent representatives who have supervision or direction of "all or substantially all" of the contractor's business or operations at any plant or location or of a separate and complete "major industrial operation." Apparently, no decided case has ever held a contractor liable under a clause of this type. In *McDonnell-Douglas Corp.*, NASABCA 865-28, 68-1 BCA ¶7021, the board held that "willful misconduct" means not merely "aggravated forms of negligence" (e.g., "gross negligence") but rather a "knowing disregard for greatly unreasonable risks." Applying this definition, the board held that the contractor was entitled to reimbursement (under very similar language in the Insurance-Liability to Third Persons clause, FAR 52.228-7) for the entire amount of a workmen's compensation award by the state. The award included a sum "in the nature of a penalty" for the contractor's "willful misconduct" in failing to take certain precautions to prevent the accident that injured the employee. Similar language included in a Ground and Flight Risk clause was analyzed in *Fairchild Hiller Corp.*, ASBCA 14387, 72-1 BCA ¶9202. The board stated at 42,698-99:

> [I]t must show that the criticized failure of appellant's managerial personnel in regard to maintenance and administration of a program for the protection and preservation of aircraft in the open, as aircraft No. 62-1831 was here, or during operation, in accordance with sound industrial practice, amounted to "willful misconduct or lack of good faith" (ASPR 10-404(a), Cl., par. (d)(i)) [now FAR 28.303].
>
> The authorities are unanimous in holding that proof of negligence does not establish willful misconduct or lack of good faith. *See Acker v. Schultz*, 74 F. Supp. 683 (S.D.N.Y. 1947); *Berry Bros. Buick, Inc. v. General Motors Corp.*, 257 F. Supp. 542 (E.D. Pa. 1966). Mere indifference to duty also is not enough. *Ibid.* What amounts to willful misconduct or lack of good faith is to be "recreant" to one's duty (*Tyler v. Grange Assurance Association*, 3 Wash. App. 167, 473 P.2d 193), to refuse deliberately to perform a plain, well-understood contractual or statutory obligation without just cause or excuse (*Brandoline v. Lindsay*, 269 Cal. App. 2d 319; *NLRB v. Knoxville Publishing Co.*, 124 F.2d 825 (6th Cir. 1942)). Willful misconduct has also been described as the conscious failure to use the necessary means to avoid peril and indifference to its consequences. *Holman v. Brady*, 241 Ala. 487, 3 So.2d 30; *Ridge v. Boulder Creek etc. School District*, 60 Cal. App. 2d 453, 140 P.2d 990; *see also Meadows v. Vaughn*, 81 Ga. App. 45, 57 S.E.2d 689; *Goepp v. American Overseas Airlines*, 281 App. Div. 105, 117 NYS 2d 276. When faced with this problem, the NASA Board has reached the same result. *McDonnell-Douglas Corporation*, No. 865-28, 68-1 BCA ¶7021. Under contracts involving a similar managerial responsibility clause our predecessor, the War Department Board of Contract Appeals, has adopted a comparable approach. *Cf.*, *Sweet Briar, Inc.*, BCA Nos. 986, 987 (1945).
>
> We thus reach the final question: did the conduct of appellant's managerial personnel evince a refusal to perform its duty, a conscious failure to use appropriate means to avoid industrial accidents and indifference to their consequences so that its performance of its job can be characterized as permeated with misconduct in safety matters and with that suggestion of duplicity or dishonesty which the law calls bad faith. *See Fenner v. American Insurance Co. of N.Y.*, 97 S.W.2d 741 (Tex. Civ. App.). We believe that on the record made here this question must clearly be answered in the negative.
>
> Appellant's general manager and his deputy might be criticized for inadequate enforcement of their own or contractually-required safety programs at the working level. But at the higher management level they had instituted a program and a safety management which was clearly adequate compliance with appellant's obligations and they had, even if often at Air Force suggestion or prodding, greatly improved the safety of appellant's facility. Nothing in the record proves that they took their responsibility for aircraft safety lightly, that they were unmindful of it, or failed to give it substantial personal attention. Conflicting considerations of scheduling and performance may have at times counterbalanced their consideration of aircraft safety. But there is no evidence that they subordinated their responsibility for safety to other goals to such an extent that one could find willful misconduct or lack of good faith in regard to safety concerns.

3. Inadequate Property Management

The third exception in the clause is if the contracting officer has revoked the government's assumption of risk because the contractor's property management practices "are inadequate and/or present an undue risk" and the contractor has "failed to take timely corrective action." Paragraph (g)(3) of the clause requires the contractor to prepare a corrective action plan when the government has made such a determination and to take corrective action. Although FAR 45.104(b) states that the contracting officer may revoke the government's assumption of risk, there is no direct statement in the clause allowing such revocation.

4. Other Government Property

Risk of loss or damage to aircraft to be delivered to or furnished by the government is normally covered by a separate contract provision known as the Ground and Flight Risk clause in cost-type contracts, DFARS 252.228-7001. Under this clause, the contractor is not liable for loss of or damage to the aircraft, above its assumption of risk, unless the damage is due to "willful misconduct or lack of good faith" on the part of the contractor's managerial personnel and provided that all members of the contractor's flight crew have been approved by the government. The clause provides that the contractor assumes the risk in the amount of $100,000 or 20% of the estimated cost of the contract, whichever is less. The contractor is entitled to be paid for an aircraft that is destroyed, including an equipment installed in it, under termination for convenience principles, *Vought Aircraft Co.*, ASBCA 47357, 00-1 BCA ¶30,721. If the government orders repair or replacement of the aircraft, the contractor is entitled to an "equitable adjustment" in the "contract price" (presumably estimated cost and fee in a cost-reimbursement contract), as well as in the delivery schedule. Thus, if the damage to the aircraft is substantial, the contractor gets additional fee for repairing it.

Similar protection is afforded the contractor with respect to government property where damage after acceptance results from defects or deficiencies in supplies delivered or services performed. There are three different clauses in this area: Limitation of Liability, FAR 52.246-23; Limitation of Liability—High-Value Items, FAR 52.246-24; and Limitation of Liability— Services, FAR 52.246-25. These clauses also contain exceptions for willful misconduct of managerial personal and insured risks. In *United States ex rel. Roby v. Boeing Co.*, 302 F.3d 637 (6th Cir. 2002), the court held that the -24 clause did not relieve the contractor from liability for damages under the Civil False Claims Act for falsely stating that the aircraft met the contract specifications.

E. Government-Furnished Property

If the government furnishes property to the contractor to enable it to perform the contract, ¶(d) of the Government Property clause, FAR 52.245-1, states that the contracting officer shall "consider" an equitable adjustment if the property is furnished late or is not suitable for its intended purpose. The clause requires timely notice of the problem and requires the contractor to follow the direction of the contracting officer in remedying property that is not suitable for its intended purpose. As discussed above, such equitable adjustments are subject to the Limitation of Cost clause. See Cibinic, Nash & Nagle, *Administration of Government Contracts* 630-41 (4th ed. 2006), for coverage of this equitable adjustment process as it applies to fixed-price contracts.

F. Protection for the Contractor

Where the contractor is relieved from liability for damage to the government's property under a CPFF contract, the contractor's fee is not affected. However, under a CPIF contract, if the contractor spends additional funds to repair or replace damaged government property, the increase in cost could cause its fee to be reduced. In order to avoid this result, the standard Incentive Fee clause in FAR 52.216-10 excludes the following costs in computing the amount of incentive fee to which the contractor is entitled:

> (v) any claim, loss, or damage resulting from a risk for which the Contractor has been relieved of liability by Government Property clause.

Thus, the contractor is given complete fee protection under CPIF contracts for any damage it causes to government property if it has been relieved of liability for damage to or loss of that property. The question has been raised whether this type of fee protection comports with the basic purpose underlying the use of incentive type contracts—to motivate the contractor to do the work in the most efficient manner by typing fee recovery to cost effectiveness. See Gilbert J. Ginsburg, "Allocation of Risk: Contractor Responsibility for Injury to Government Property and to Third Parties Under Supply and R&D Contracts," 2 Pub. Cont. L.J. 333 (1969).

X. THIRD-PARTY LIABILITY

Under cost-reimbursement contracts, a contractor is normally required to carry liability insurance in the types and amounts listed in FAR 28.307-2, as follows:

> (a) *Workers' compensation and employer's liability.* Contractors are required to comply with applicable Federal and State workers' compensation and occupational disease statutes. If occupational diseases are not compensable under those statutes, they shall be covered under the employer's liability section of the insurance policy, except when contract operations are so commingled with a contractor's commercial operations that it would not be practical to require this coverage. Employer's liability coverage of at least $100,000 shall be required, except in States with exclusive or monopolistic funds that do not permit workers' compensation to be written by private carriers. (See 28.305(c) for treatment of contracts subject to the Defense Base Act.)
>
> (b) *General liability.* (1) The contracting officer shall require bodily injury liability insurance coverage written on the comprehensive form of policy of at least $500,000 per occurrence.
>
> (2) Property damage liability insurance shall be required only in special circumstances as determined by the agency.
>
> (c) *Automobile liability.* The contracting officer shall require automobile liability insurance written on the comprehensive form of policy. The policy shall provide for bodily injury and property damage liability covering the operation of all automobiles used in connection with performing the contract. Policies covering automobiles operated in the United States shall provide coverage of at least $200,000 per person and $500,000 per occurrence for bodily injury and $20,000 per occurrence for property damage. The amount of liability coverage on other policies shall be commensurate with any legal requirements of the locality and sufficient to meet normal and customary claims.
>
> (d) *Aircraft public and passenger liability.* When aircraft are used in connection with performing the contract, the contracting officer shall require aircraft public and passenger liability insurance. Coverage shall be at least $200,000 per person and $500,000 per occurrence for bodily injury, other than passenger liability, and $200,000 per occurrence for property damage. Coverage for passenger liability bodily injury shall be at least $200,000 multiplied by the number of seats or passengers, whichever is greater.
>
> (e) *Vessel liability.* When contract performance involves use of vessels, the contracting officer shall require, as determined by the agency, vessel collision liability and protection and indemnity liability insurance.

For third-party liabilities exceeding the amount of insurance, the contractor may be reimbursed subject to the limitations in the Insurance Liability to Third Party clause, FAR 52.228-7. For costs beyond those limitations, the only recourse for the contractor is one of the indemnifications for unusually hazardous risks.

A. Insurance-Liability to Third Persons Clause

Under cost-reimbursement contracts, the government normally acts as an insurer by agreeing to assume the risk of its contractors' uninsured third-party liabilities. Such agreements are embodied in the Insurance-Liability to Third Persons clause authorized for inclusion in cost-reimbursement type contracts, FAR 52.228-7. This clause provides that contractors are entitled to recover for liabilities to third persons for death, personal injury, and loss of or damage to property (other than property owned, occupied, used, or in the care or custody of the contractor) "not compensated by insurance or otherwise, arising out of the performance of this contract."

1. Funding Aspects

Subparagraph (c)(2) of the clause states that the contractor is entitled to recover "without regard to and as an exception to the limitation of cost or the limitation of funds clause of this contract." Paragraph (d) of the clause, however, limits liability under ¶(c) to the availability of appropriated funds at the time the contingency occurs. This clause is based upon the GAO's position that government assumption of contingent and undetermined liabilities beyond the amount of funds appropriated at the time of loss would violate the Anti-Deficiency Act. See 62 Comp. Gen. 361 (1983). See also *Shell Oil Co. v. United States*, 108 Fed. Cl. 422 (2013); *E.I. DuPont de Nemours & Co. v. United States*, 365 F.3d 1367 (Fed. Cir. 2004); *Les Establissements Eiffel-Asie*, ASBCA 22596, 80-2 BCA ¶14,779; and 54 Comp. Gen. 924 (B-168106), 74-2 CPD ¶3. While liability to third parties has rarely occurred during the performance of cost-reimbursement contracts, the limitation of cost recovery to available appropriations poses a major risk to a contractor that is performing work that could result in significant personal injury or death. Such risk must be covered by other contractual provisions such as an indemnification clause.

2. Contractor Gross Negligence

The Insurance-Liability to Third Parties clause permits recovery by the contractor for uninsured third-party liability "whether or not caused by the negligence of the Contractor or of the Contractor's agents, servants, or employees." However, this clause also contains exceptions that preclude recovery for uninsured third-party liability resulting from "willful misconduct or lack of good faith" on the part of the contractor. In *McDonnell-Douglas Corp.*, NASABCA 865-28, 68-1 BCA ¶7021, a contractor performing a CPFF contract was held liable for the death of one of its employees under a California Workman's Compensation statute that permitted recovery for a fatal injury sustained as a result of an employer's "serious and willful misconduct." The contractor sought reimbursement from the government under a standard Insurance-Liability to Third Persons clause. Applying federal law to interpret the clause, the board held that the contractor was entitled to recover, reasoning that since the clause did not distinguish between varying degrees of negligence, something qualitatively different from negligence must be proved by the government in order to defeat the contractor's claim for recovery. The board concluded that a conscious, knowing disregard of a risk had to be proved. Because the government failed to prove that the contractor was guilty of anything beyond "gross negligence," the contractor was entitled to recover under the clause.

3. Fee Unaffected

In CPFF contracts, a contractor does not lose any fee if it is reimbursed for its liability to third persons. The fee in CPIF contracts is also not affected by third-person liability reimbursements. The standard Incentive Fee clause in FAR 52.216-10 provides that the following costs are to be excluded in computing the final incentive fee:

> (iv) The purchase and maintenance of additional insurance not in the target cost and required by the Contracting Officer, or claims for reimbursement for liabilities to third persons pursuant to the Insurance-Liability to Third Persons clause. FAR 52.216-10.

B. Indemnification Provisions

Several statutes authorize government indemnification of contractors for losses not covered by private insurance. Some of these statutes call for indemnification only from "unusually hazardous" risks without defining this term. These statutes permit the government to indemnify contractors for losses without limiting the amount to funds appropriated at the time the losses occurred.

1. Department of Defense

The following indemnification statute applies to DOD:

10 U.S.C. § 2354. Contracts: indemnification provisions

(a) With the approval of the Secretary of the military department concerned, any contract of a military department for research or development, or both, may provide that the United States will indemnify the contractor against either or both of the following, but only to the extent that they arise out of the direct performance of the contract and to the extent not compensated by insurance or otherwise:

(1) Claims (including reasonable expenses of litigation or settlement) by third persons, including employees of the contractor, for death, bodily injury, or loss of or damage to property, from a risk that the contract defines as unusually hazardous.

(2) Loss of or damage to property of the contractor from a risk that the contract defines as unusually hazardous.

(b) A contract, made under subsection (a), that provides for indemnification must also provide for—

(1) notice to the United States of any claim or suit against the contractor for the death, bodily injury or loss of or damage to property; and

(2) control of or assistance in the defense by the United States, at its election, of that suit or claim.

(c) No payment may be made under subsection (a) unless the Secretary of the department concerned, or an officer or official of his department designated by him, certifies that the amount is just and reasonable.

(d) Upon approval by the Secretary concerned, payments under subsection (a) may be made from—

(1) funds obligated for the performance of the contract concerned;

(2) funds available for research or development, or both, and not otherwise obligated; or

(3) funds appropriated for those payments.

Regulations governing agency procedures for inclusion of indemnity provisions pursuant to this statute are set forth at DFARS 235.070-1. The clause at DFARS 252.235-7001 provides that, with the prior written approval of the contracting officer, the contractor may include in any subcontract a provision requiring the contractor to indemnify the subcontractor for liability arising out of risks defined in the contract to be unusually hazardous. Paragraph (i) of this clause provides that:

> The Government shall indemnify the Contractor if the Contractor has an obligation to indemnify a subcontractor under any subcontract at any tier under this contract for the unusually hazardous risk identified in this contract only if—
>
> (1) The Contracting Officer gave prior written approval for the Contractor to provide in a subcontract for the Contractor to indemnify the subcontractor for unusually hazardous risks defined in this contract;
>
> (2) The Contracting Officer approved those indemnification provisions.

Paragraph (j) of this clause also authorizes the government to discharge its obligation to indemnify the contractor for liability to subcontractors by making payments "directly to subcontractors or to persons to whom the subcontractors may be liable."

2. Public Law 85-804; 50 U.S.C. §§ 1431-36

This statute has been interpreted as authorizing the DOD, NASA, and certain other agencies to indemnify contractors against unusually hazardous or nuclear risks. While the use of Pub. L. No. 85-804 is limited to activities that "facilitate the national defense," it appears that this term can be quite liberally construed. In Executive Order 10789, 23 Fed. Reg. 8897 (Nov. 14, 1958), the President authorized ten civilian agencies to use Pub. L. No. 85-804, and it has occasionally been used on civilian procurements.

Authorization for use of Pub. L. No. 85-804 for indemnification of unusually hazardous nuclear risks may be granted only by "the Secretary or Administrator of the agency concerned, the Public Printer, or the Chairman of the Board of Directors of the Tennessee Valley Authority," FAR 50.201(d). When such authorization is granted, the FAR 52.250-1 Indemnification Under Public Law 85-804 clause, with Alternate 1, is used for cost-reimbursement contracts. That alternate states that indemnification is not limited by existing appropriations, or the LOC or LOF clauses. The procedures for requesting indemnification and processing such requests are contained in FAR 50.403.

The original implementation of this statute, Executive Order No. 10789, 23 Fed. Reg. 8897 (1958), limited relief to "the amounts appropriated and the contract authorization provided therefor." Doubts raised about the propriety of using Pub. L. No. 85-804 as the basis for indemnity, because of this limitation, were removed by the issuance of Executive Order No. 11610, 36 Fed. Reg. 13755 (July 22, 1971), which provides at ¶IA that this limitation upon relief available under Pub. L. No. 85-804 "shall not apply to contractual provisions which provide that the United States will hold harmless and indemnify the contractor against any of the claims or losses." However, this same paragraph also states that this exception to the general limitation upon relief applies only to "risks that the contract defines as unusually hazardous or nuclear in nature." Executive Order No. 11610 also permits subcontractors to obtain the same indemnity protection as contractors and authorizes agency heads to require contractors to purchase and maintain all available financial protection from private sources as a condition to indemnity under Pub. L. No. 85-804.

3. 51 U.S.C. § 20138(c)

NASA has authority to indemnify "any user of a space vehicle" for liability to third parties arising out of "activities carried on in connection with the launch, operations or recovery of a space vehicle." The Act provides that indemnification under such an indemnity agreement "may be limited to claims resulting from other than the actual negligence or willful misconduct of the user." Payments pursuant to such agreements are to be made either from funds available for research and development not otherwise obligated or from funds appropriated for such payments. For a dispute on the interpretation of an indemnification clause under this statute, see *SPACEHAB, Inc.*, ASBCA 54880, 06-2 BCA ¶33,341.

4. Price-Anderson Act; 42 U.S.C. § 2210

Originally added in 1957 to the Atomic Energy Act, the Price Anderson Act provides for indemnification of government contractors for liability arising from a limited class of nuclear incidents. Enacted to "Protect the public and encourage the development of the atomic energy industry," the Act has proved necessary to secure the participation of companies facing substantial risks uninsurable through private insurance sources.

The compensation scheme under the Price-Anderson Act was summarized as follows by the Supreme Court in *Duke Power Co. v. Carolina Envtl. Study Group*, 438 U.S. 59 (1978), at 64:

> In its original form, the Act limited the aggregate liability for a single nuclear incident to $500 million plus the amount of liability insurance available on the private market—some $60 million in 1957. The nuclear industry was required to purchase the maximum available amount of privately underwritten public liability insurance, and the Act provided that if damages from a nuclear disaster exceeded the amount of that private insurance coverage, the Federal Government would indemnify the licensee and other "persons indemnified" in an amount not to exceed $500 million. Thus, the actual ceiling on liability was the amount of private insurance coverage plus the Government's indemnification obligation which totaled $560 million.
>
> Since its enactment, the Act has been twice amended, the first occasion being on the eve of its expiration in 1966. These amendments extended the basic liability limitation provisions for another 10 years and added a provision which had the effect of requiring those indemnified under the Act to waive all legal defenses in the event of a

substantial nuclear accident. This provision was based on a congressional concern that state tort law dealing with liability for nuclear incidents was generally unsettled and that some way of insuring a common standard of responsibility for all jurisdictions— strict liability—was needed. A waiver of defenses was thought to be the preferable approach since it entailed less interference with state tort law than would the enactment of a federal statute prescribing strict liability. See S. Rep. No. 1605, 89th Cong., 2d Sess. 6-10 (1966).

In 1975, Congress again extended the Act's coverage until 1987, and continued the $560 million limitation on liability. However, a new provision was added requiring, in the event of a nuclear incident, each of the 60 or more reactor owners to contribute between $2 and $5 million toward the cost of compensating victims, 42 U.S.C. § 2210(b). Since the liability ceiling remained at the same level, the effect of the "deferred premium" provision was to reduce the Federal Government's contribution to the liability pool. In its amendments to the Act in 1975, Congress also explicitly provided that "in the event of a nuclear incident involving damages in excess of [the] amount of aggregate liability, the Congress will thoroughly review the particular incident and will take whatever action is deemed necessary and appropriate to protect the public from the consequences of a disaster of such magnitude," 42 U.S.C. § 2210(e).

Implementing regulations for the Price-Anderson Act are set forth at 10 C.F.R. 140. For a detailed discussion of the mechanics of the price-Anderson Act, see "Nuclear Power and the Price-Anderson Act: Promotion Over Public Protection," 30 Stan. L. Rev. 393 (1978). The Act has been subsequently amended and extended in 1988, Pub. L. No. 100-408, Pub. L. No. 102-486, in 1998, Pub. L. No. 105-362; and in 2005, Pub. L. No. 109-58 (extending the provisions through Dec. 31, 2025).

5. Veterans Health Administration; 38 U.S.C. § 7316(e)

This section was added to title 38 by Pub. L. No. 102-40, Title IV, § 401 (a)(3), Department of Veterans Affairs Health-Care Personnel Act of 1991. With the approval of the Secretary, the government may hold harmless a contractor for negligence in the performance of medical care and treatment to veterans (including clinical studies or investigations) when the injured person does not have a remedy under the Federal Tort Claims Act, 28 U.S.C. § 1346(b).